THE OXFORD HANDBOOK OF

PHILOSOPHY OF RELIGION

THE OXFORD HANDBOOK OF

PHILOSOPHY OF RELIGION

Edited by

WILLIAM J. WAINWRIGHT

OXFORD

UNIVERSITY PRESS

2005

OXFORD
UNIVERSITY PRESS

Oxford   New York
Auckland   Bangkok   Buenos Aires   Cape Town   Chennai
Dar es Salaam   Delhi   Hong Kong   Istanbul   Karachi   Kolkata
Kuala Lumpur   Madrid   Melbourne   Mexico City   Mumbai
Nairobi   São Paulo   Shanghai   Taipei   Tokyo   Toronto

Copyright © 2005 by Oxford University Press, Inc.

Published by Oxford University Press, Inc.
198 Madison Avenue, New York, New York 10016

www.oup.com

Oxford is a registered trademark of Oxford University Press

Library of Congress Cataloging-in-Publication Data
The Oxford handbook of philosophy of religion / edited by William J. Wainwright.
p. cm.—(Oxford handbooks in philosophy)
Includes bibliographical references and index.
ISBN 0-19-513809-0
1. Religion—Philosophy.   I. Wainwright, William J.   II. Series.
BL51.O94 2004
210—dc22   2004043890

1 3 5 7 9 8 6 4 2
Printed in the United States of America
on acid-free paper

Contents

PART II APPROACHES

Contributors

WILLIAM P. ALSTON   Professor of Philosophy Emeritus, Syracuse University.

LYNNE RUDDER BAKER   Professor of Philosophy, University of Massachusetts–Amherst.

SARAH COAKLEY   Edward Mallinckrodt Professor of Divinity, Divinity School, Harvard University.

PAUL DRAPER   Professor of Philosophy, Florida International University.

C. STEPHEN EVANS   University Professor of Philosophy and Humanities, Baylor University.

RICHARD M. GALE   Professor of Philosophy Emeritus, University of Pittsburgh.

JEROME I. GELLMAN   Professor of Philosophy, Ben Gurion University of the Negev.

PAUL J. GRIFFITHS   Schmitt Professor of Catholic Studies, University of Illinois–Chicago.

WILLIAM HASKER   Professor of Philosophy Emeritus, Huntington College.

JEFFREY JORDAN   Associate Professor of Philosophy, University of Delaware.

BRIAN LEFTOW   Nolloth Professor of Philosophy of the Christian Religion, University of Oxford.

WILLIAM E. MANN   Marsh Professor of Intellectual and Moral Philosophy, University of Vermont.

GEORGE I. MAVRODES   Professor of Philosophy Emeritus, University of Michigan.

D. Z. PHILLIPS   Danforth Professor of the Philosophy of Religion, Claremont Graduate University and Rush Rhees Research Professor, University of Wales–Swansea.

ALEXANDER R. PRUSS   Assistant Professor of Philosophy, Georgetown University.

PHILIP L. QUINN   John A. O'Brien Professor of Philosophy, University of Notre Dame.

WILLIAM L. ROWE   Professor of Philosophy, Purdue University.

PETER VAN INWAGEN   John Cardinal O'Hara Professor of Philosophy, University of Notre Dame.

WILLIAM J. WAINWRIGHT   Distinguished Professor of Philosophy Emeritus, University of Wisconsin–Milwaukee.

MEROLD WESTPHAL   Distinguished Professor of Philosophy, Fordham University.

NICHOLAS WOLTERSTORFF   Noah Porter Professor of Philosophical Theology Emeritus, Yale Divinity School.

LINDA ZAGZEBSKI   Kingfisher College Chair of the Philosophy of Religion and Ethics, University of Oklahoma.

THE OXFORD HANDBOOK OF

PHILOSOPHY
OF RELIGION

INTRODUCTION

WILLIAM J. WAINWRIGHT

THE expression "philosophy of religion" did not come into general use until the nineteenth century, when it was employed to refer to the articulation and criticism of humanity's religious consciousness and its cultural expressions in thought, language, feeling, and practice. Historically, philosophical reflection on religious themes had two foci: first, God or Brahman or Nirvana or whatever else the *object* of religious thought, attitudes, feelings, and practice was believed to be, and, second, the human religious *subject*, that is, the thoughts, attitudes, feelings, and practices themselves. The first sort of philosophical reflection has had a long history. In the West, for example, discussions of the nature of God (whether he is unchanging, say, or knows the future, whether his existence can be rationally demonstrated, and the like) are incorporated in theological treatises such as Anselm's *Proslogion* and *Monologion*, Thomas Aquinas's *Summas*, Maimonides' *Guide for the Perplexed*, and al-Ghazali's *Incoherence of the Philosophers*. They also form part of influential metaphysical systems like Plato's, Plotinus's, Descartes', and Leibniz's. Hindu Vedanta and classical Buddhism included sophisticated discussions of the nature of the Brahman and of the Buddha, respectively. Many contemporary philosophers of religion continue to be engaged with these topics (see, for example, chapters 1 through 5 and 8).

The most salient feature of this sort of philosophy of religion is its attempts to establish truths about God or the Absolute on the basis of unaided reason. Aquinas is instructive. Some truths about God can be known only with the help of revelation. Examples are his triune nature and incarnation. Other truths about him, such as his existence, simplicity, wisdom, and power, are included in his revelation to us but can also be known through reason. And Aquinas proceeds to show how reason can establish them. What we would today call philosophy of religion (or natural theology) is thus an integral part of his systematic theology. Early modern philosophers like Descartes, Leibniz, and Locke are only incidentally concerned with purely theological issues, but they too insist that some important truths about God can be established by purely philosophical reflection.

The notion that we should accept *only* those religious beliefs that can be established by reason was not commonly expressed until the later part of the seventeenth century, however, and not widely embraced until adopted by the eighteenth-century Enlightenment. The consequences of the new commitment to reason alone depended on whether important religious truths could be established by natural reason. Deists believed that they could. Human reason can prove the existence of God and immortality and discover basic moral principles. Because these religious beliefs are the only ones that can be established by unaided human reason, they alone are required of everyone. They are also the only beliefs needed for religious worship and practice. Beliefs wholly or partly based on some alleged revelation, on the other hand, are needless at best and pernicious at worst. Others, such as Hume, adopted a more skeptical attitude toward reason's possibilities. In their view, reason is unable to show that "God exists" or that any other important religious claim is significantly more probable than not. The only proper attitude for a reasonable person to take, therefore, is disbelief (atheism) or unbelief (agnosticism). The result of this insistence on reason alone was thus that religion either became desiccated, reduced to a few simple beliefs distilled from the rich traditional systems that had given life to them, or ceased to be a live option.

Reaction was inevitable, and took two forms. One was a shift from theoretical to practical (moral) reason. Kant, for example, was convinced that "theoretical" or "speculative" reason could neither prove nor disprove God's existence or the immortality of the soul. Practical reason, on the other hand, provided a firm basis for a religion lying within the "boundaries of reason alone." The existence of God and an afterlife can't be established by theoretical reason. A *belief* in them, however, is a necessary presupposition of morality. Others, such as Friedrich Schleiermacher, shifted their attention from intellectual belief and moral conduct to religious feelings and experience. In their view, the latter, and not the former, are the root of humanity's religious life. Both approaches were widely influential in the nineteenth and early twentieth century. The first fell into neglect with the waning of philosophical idealism in the first half of the twentieth century, although interest in it has recently resurfaced (see chapter 14). The second has continued to be attractive to many important philosophers of religion (see chapters 6 and 10).

Philosophy of religion was comparatively neglected by academic philosophers in the first half of the twentieth century. There were several reasons for this. One was the widespread conviction that the traditional "proofs" were bankrupt. Believers and nonbelievers alike were persuaded that Hume and Kant had clearly exposed their fatal weaknesses. Another was the demise of nineteenth-century idealism. The twentieth-century heirs of the German and Anglo-American idealists (Hastings Rashdall, W. R. Sorley, A. C. Ewing, and A. E. Taylor, among others) had many interesting things to say about God, immortality, and humanity's religious life. But their views increasingly fell on deaf ears as analytic philosophy replaced idealism as the dominant approach among English-speaking academics. (The "process philosophy" of A. N. Whitehead and his followers emerged as an alternative to idealism and analytic philosophy that could accommodate religious interests. It was never more than a minority viewpoint, however, and finds itself today in much the same position that philosophical idealism was in in the early part of the twentieth century; its demise too seems immanent.) This is not to say that nothing of interest to philosophers of religion was transpiring during this period.

Five developments were especially important. The first was the impact of theologians like Karl Barth, Emil Brunner, and Paul Tillich on philosophers interested in religion. The second was the influence of religious existentialism, including both the rediscovery of Søren Kierkegaard and the work of contemporaries like Gabriel Marcel and Martin Buber. A third was the renewal of Thomism by Jacques Maritain, Etienne Gilson, and others. A fourth was the rise of religious phenomenology; Rudolf Otto and others tried to accurately describe human religious experience as it appears to those who have it. Finally, philosophers who were sympathetic to religious impulses and feelings yet deeply skeptical of religious metaphysics attempted to reconstruct religion in a way that would preserve what was thought to be valuable in it while discarding the chaff. Thus, John Dewey suggested that the proper object of faith isn't supernatural beings but "the unity of all ideal ends arousing us to desire and actions," or the "active relation" between these ideals and the "forces in nature and society that generate and support" them. In Dewey's view, "any activity pursued in behalf of an ideal end against obstacles and in spite of threats of personal loss because of a conviction of its general and enduring value is religious in quality"[1] (see chapter 9).

After a half century of comparative neglect, analytic philosophers began to take an interest in religion in the 1950s. Their attention was initially focused on questions of religious language. Were sentences like "God forgives my sins" used to express factual claims, or did they instead express the speaker's attitudes or commitments? If those who uttered them *did* express factual claims, what kind of claims were they? Could they be empirically verified or falsified, for example, and, if they could not, were they really cognitively meaningful? (For more on this debate, see chapters 9, 10, 18, and 19.)

What was unanticipated was that the young analytic philosophers of religion who were being trained during this period were to become responsible for a resurgence of philosophical theology that began in the mid-1960s and continues to dominate the field in English-speaking countries today. The revival was fueled by a comparative loss of interest in the question of religious language's cognitive meaningfulness (it being generally thought that attempts to show that religious sentences do not express true or false factual claims had been unsuccessful), and a conviction that Hume's and Kant's allegedly devastating criticisms of philosophical theology did not withstand careful scrutiny. On the positive side, developments in modal logic, probability theory, and so on offered tools for introducing a new clarity and rigor to traditional disputes.

Three features of the revival are especially noteworthy. The first was a renewed interest in the scholastics and in seventeenth- and eighteenth-century philosophical theology. There were at least two reasons for this. One was the discovery that issues central to the debates of the 1960s and 1970s had already been examined with a sophistication and depth lacking in most nineteenth- and early twentieth-century discussions of the same problems. The other was the fact that a significant number of analytic philosophers of religion were practicing Christian or Jewish theists. Figures such as Aquinas, Scotus, Maimonides, Samuel Clark, and Jonathan Edwards were attractive models for these philosophers for two reasons. There is a broad similarity between the philosophical approaches of these medieval and early modern thinkers and contemporary analytic philosophers: precise definitions, careful distinctions, and rigorous argumentation are features of both. In addition, these predecessors were self-consciously Jewish or Christian; a conviction of the truth or splendor of Judaism or Christianity pervades their work. They were thus appealing models for contemporary philosophers of religion with similar commitments.

A second feature of contemporary analytic philosophy of religion is the wide array of topics it addresses. The first fifteen years or so of the period in question were dominated by discussions of issues traditionally central to the philosophy of religion: Is the concept of God coherent? Are there good reasons for thinking that God exists? Is the existence of evil a decisive reason for denying God's existence? However, beginning in the 1980s, a number of Christian analytic philosophers turned their attention to such specifically Christian doctrines as the Trinity, the Incarnation, and the Atonement. Most of the articles and books on these topics were attempts to show that the doctrines in question were coherent or rational. But some were more interested in the bearing of theological doctrines on problems internal to the traditions that include them. Marilyn Adams, for example, has argued that Christian martyrdom and Christ's passion have important implications for Christian responses to the problem of evil, and Robert Oakes has made similar claims for the Jewish mystical doctrine of God's withdrawal (*tzimzum*). Still other analytic philosophers of religion have tried to show that theism can cast light on problems in other areas of philosophy—that it can give a better account of the logical features of natural laws, for example, or of the nature of numbers, sets, and other mathematical objects, or of the apparent objectivity of moral claims.[2] (On the last, see chapter 14.)

A third characteristic of recent philosophy of religion is its turn toward epistemology. Medieval and seventeenth-century philosophical theology exhibited a feature that has been insufficiently appreciated since the eighteenth century and is especially prominent in Augustine and Anselm: its devotional setting. Anselm's inquiry, for instance, is punctuated by prayers to arouse his emotions and stir his will. His inquiry is a divine-human collaboration in which he continually prays for assistance and offers praise and thanksgiving for the light he has received. His project as a whole is framed by a desire to "contemplate God" or "see God's face." Anselm's attempt to understand what he believes by finding reasons for it is largely a means to this end.[3] Several hundred years later, Blaise Pascal argued that although the evidence for the truth of the Christian religion is ambiguous, it is sufficient to convince those who seek God or "have the living faith in their hearts." Reflection on the work of predecessors like these suggests two things. The first is that the aim of philosophical theology is not, primarily, to convince nonbelievers of the truth of religious claims but, rather, self-understanding: to enable the believer to grasp the implications of, and reasons for, his or her religious beliefs. The project, in other words, is faith in search of understanding. The second is that a person's attitudes, feelings, emotions, and aims have an important bearing on his or her ability to discern religious truths. C. Stephen Evans, for example, has suggested that faith may be a necessary condition of appreciating certain reasons for religious belief. I have argued that a properly disposed heart may be needed to grasp the force of evidence for theistic belief.[4] Common to much recent religious epistemology is a rejection of any form of evidentialism that insists that religious beliefs are reasonably held only if they are supported by evidence that would convince *any* fair-minded, properly informed, and intelligent person regardless of the state of his or her heart (see chapters 10 and 13).

As its history indicates, the aims of philosophers of religion can be quite diverse. Arguments are sometimes employed apologetically. For example, Samuel Clarke and William Paley attempted to construct proofs that would convince any fair-minded and intelligent reader of God's existence and providential government of human affairs. These proofs had begun to lose their power to persuade educated audiences by the end of the eighteenth century, however, and so Friedrich Schleiermacher and others turned to religious feelings (a sense of absolute dependence or of the unity of all things in the infinite) to justify religion to its "cultured despisers." But although Schleiermacher thought that the heart and not the head is religion's primary source, the aim of his argument was still apologetic.

Yet philosophy of religion can have other purposes. Theistic proofs, for example, have been used to persuade nonbelievers of the truth of theism. But, as we have seen, they can also be used devotionally, and this is sometimes their primary purpose. Thus, Udayana's *Nyayakusumanjali* (which can be roughly translated as "A bouquet of arguments offered to God") has three purposes: to convince unbelievers, to strengthen the faithful, *but also to please Siva* "by presenting it as an offering at his footstool." Regardless of the success Udayana's arguments may or may not have had in achieving his first two goals, they have value as a gift offered to God; their construction and presentation is an act of worship.[5]

Philosophy of religion is sometimes part of a larger philosophical project. For example, for Hegel, religion is the self-representation of Absolute Spirit in feeling and images. As such, it is a stage in a historical process that culminates in philosophy (i.e., in *Hegel's* philosophy!). Descartes provides another example. His *Meditations* introduce ontological arguments for God's existence to help resolve skeptical doubts raised earlier in the text (see chapter 4).

Philosophy of religion can also be part of the so-called Enlightenment project. Religious beliefs, institutions, and practices are critically examined in an attempt to eliminate those that can't survive the scrutiny of impartial reason. Hume's *Dialogues* and *The Natural History of Religion* and Kant's reflections on religion and morality are examples. The "hermeneutics of suspicion" practiced by Marx, Nietzsche, and Freud is an extension of the same project. According to these thinkers, religion is an expression of "false consciousness." Its beliefs, feelings, and practices lack rational support and rest on motives that cannot be consciously acknowledged without destroying their credibility (see chapter 19).

Finally, philosophy of religion can be an attempt to make sense of, or account for, *religion*, and not a reflection on its *object* (God, Nirvana, and the like). George Santayana's interpretation of religion as a kind of poetry, a feelingful contemplation of ideal forms, is an example; Hume's *Natural History of Religion* is another. As these examples indicate, attempts of this sort are seldom neutral. Santayana, for instance, takes naturalism for granted, and Hume is independently convinced that historical religions are not only irrational but morally and socially pernicious. Wittgensteinians, on the other hand, insist that *their* attempts to make sense of religion are an exception to this rule; their project, they claim, is to simply understand religion, not judge it (see chapter 18).

Until quite recently, philosophy of religion has been somewhat myopic. Since the only religions with which Western philosophers have been intimately acquainted are Judaism and Christianity (and, to a lesser extent, Islam), it is not surprising that they have focused their attention on theism. (Discussions of mysticism have proved one noteworthy exception.) Increased knowledge of Asian and other traditions has made this attitude seem unduly parochial. There is no intrinsic reason, however, why the tools of analytic or continental philosophy can't be profitably applied to non-Western doctrines and arguments, and good work is currently being done in this vein by Stephen Phillips, Paul Williams, Steven Collins, Gerald Larson, and a number of others. Paul Griffiths, for example, has suggested that "perfect being theology" (the attempt to explore the implications of the concept of a reality greater than which none can be thought) can be deployed to explain (and criticize) the emergence of doctrines of the cosmic Buddha in the Mahayana traditions. Work of this sort is essential because a defense of one's favored religion's perspective should include reasons for preferring it to its important competitors. The Western doctrine of creation ex nihilo, for instance, should be compared with the Visistadvaitin notion that the world is best viewed as God's body.[6] Again, because the Buddhist's claim that everything is impermanent is logically incompatible with the assertion that God is eternal and unchanging, both theists and Buddhists need to attend to the views of each other. (For more on these issues, see chapters 3 and 16.)

Another weakness of contemporary philosophy of religion is that the analytic and continental traditions have developed in comparative isolation from each other. This is due to several factors. For one thing, analytic philosophers of religion are usually trained and housed in departments of philosophy, and most of the best departments in English-speaking countries are dominated by analytic philosophy. Continental philosophers of religion, on the other hand, are often (although not always) trained and housed in departments of religion or theology. Their interests, too, are different. Analytic philosophers of religion have tended to focus on God or the religious object and on the rational credentials of claims about it. Continental philosophy of religion has tended to focus on religion and the human subject; it has also been more concerned with religion's ethical implications, especially its bearing on oppression and liberation.

The isolation of the two traditions is unfortunate because each needs what the other has to offer. Analytic philosophers of religion, for instance, need to take the hermeneutics of suspicion seriously, for, as Merold Westphal has said, they have been largely blind "to the cognitive implications of finitude and sin."[7] As a result, they have usually ignored the ideological uses and abuses of theistic metaphysics and the ethical issues this raises. The critiques of Marx, Nietzsche, Freud, Jacques Derrida, and contemporary feminists can and should alert analytic philosophers of religion to these perils (see chapters 19 and 20).

Continental philosophers of religion, on the other hand, too often ignore questions of truth and rational adequacy. This is unfortunate for two closely related reasons. The first is ethical: we fail to respect the men and women whose beliefs and practices we examine if we don't treat their claims to truth and rational superiority with the same seriousness that they do. The second is this: if Christianity, say, or Buddhism *is* true, it matters infinitely. So if either is a live possibility, a deeply serious concern with its truth or falsity, its reasonableness or unreasonableness, is the only rational option. Inattention or indifference to the truth and rational credentials of the traditions one examines is a clear indication that one doesn't take them as live possibilities, and hence doesn't invest them with the same importance or seriousness that their adherents do.

There are some indications that analytic and continental philosophers of religion are beginning to learn from each other. One can only hope that this trend increases in the future.

The Oxford Handbook of Philosophy of Religion is divided into two parts. Part 1 covers the most frequently discussed problems in the field. Part 2 consists of essays assessing the advantages and disadvantages of the four currently most influential ways of doing philosophy of religion; each is by a well-known practitioner of the way he or she discusses. The essays in Part 2 are a unique feature of this volume and are important for two reasons. First, one's philosophical approach affects one's selection of problems and the way one frames them, and this, in turn, affects one's results. For example, followers of Emmanuel Levinas or feminist philosophers of religion have different takes on the problem of evil than do analytic philosophers. No picture of the philosophy of religion that ignores them can be complete. Second, although the analytic approach dominates the practice of philosophy of religion in English-speaking countries and is beginning to make significant inroads on the continent, there are other historically important and potentially illuminating ways of doing philosophy of religion. It is therefore important that a general reference work of this sort acquaint the reader with the variety of approaches to the discipline.

The twenty chapters of this volume are written by prominent experts in the field. Each chapter is expository, critical, and representative of a distinctive viewpoint. In being expository, the chapters formulate and elucidate important competing positions on their topic (e.g., religious experience or the problem of evil) or the history and nature of the philosophical approach to the philosophy of religion that they are discussing (the analytic, say, or feminist). In being critical, the chapters carefully assess the views presented on their topics or the strengths and alleged weakness of their approach to the philosophy of religion. Readers will thus see not only what the prominent views and approaches in philosophy of religion are but encounter noteworthy criticisms of them as well. In being representative of a distinctive viewpoint the chapters present their authors' own views on the topic or approach. Readers will thereby encounter not only exposition and criticism but the substantial development of a viewpoint on the subject under discussion by a well-known author in the discipline. Finally, in addition to exposition, criticism, and original philosophical development, each chapter includes topical bibliographies identifying key works in the field. It is our hope that the *Handbook*'s combination of topical and methodological comprehensiveness, criticism, and original philosophical development will provide the reader with a unique and invaluable reference work on the philosophy of religion.

NOTES

1. John Dewey, *A Common Faith* (New Haven: Yale University Press, 1934), 42, 50–51, 27.

2. See Marilyn McCord Adams, *Horrendous Evils and the Goodness of God* (Ithaca, N.Y.: Cornell University Press, 1999), and Robert Oakes, "Creation as Theodicy: A Defense of a Kabbalistic Approach to Evil," *Faith and Philosophy* 14 (1997): 510–21. For attempts to offer theistic accounts of natural laws, mathematical objects, and moral claims see, e.g., Del Ratzsch, "Nomo(theo)logical Necessity," and Christopher Menzel, "Theism, Platonism, and the Metaphysics of Mathematics," both in *Christian Theism and the Problems of Philosophy*, ed. Michael D. Beaty (Notre Dame, Ind.: University of Notre Dame Press, 1990), 184–207 and 208–29, respectively; Philip L. Quinn, *Divine Commands and Moral Requirements* (Oxford: Clarendon Press, 1978); and Robert M. Adams, *Finite and Infinite Goods* (New York: Oxford University Press, 1999).

3. See Marilyn McCord Adams, "Praying the *Proslogion*: Anselm's Theological Method," in *The Rationality of Belief and the Plurality of Faith*, ed. Thomas D. Senor (Ithaca, N.Y.: Cornell University Press, 1995), 13–39.

4. See C. Stephen Evans, *Passionate Reason: Making Sense of Kierkegaard's Philosophical Fragments* (Bloomington: Indiana University Press, 1992), and William J. Wainwright, *Reason and the Heart* (Ithaca, N.Y.: Cornell University Press, 1995).

5. John Clayton, "Piety and the Proofs," *Religious Studies* 26 (1990): 19–42.

6. It should be noted, however, that, on the Visistadvaitin view, bodies are absolutely dependent on souls although souls are not dependent on bodies. So the differences between the two views should not be exaggerated. See William J. Wainwright, *Philosophy of Religion*, 2d edition (Belmont, Calif.: Wadsworth, 1998), 192–96.

7. Merold Westphal, "Traditional Theism, the AAR and the APA," in *God, Philosophy, and Academic Culture*, ed. William J. Wainwright (Atlanta: Scholars Press, 1996), 21–27.

PART I

PROBLEMS

CHAPTER 1

....

DIVINE POWER, GOODNESS, AND KNOWLEDGE

....

WILLIAM L. ROWE

In the major religions of the West—Judaism, Christianity, and Islam—the dominant theological tradition has long held that among the attributes constituting the nature of God are to be counted his unlimited power (omnipotence), perfect goodness, and unlimited knowledge (omniscience). Within this theological tradition stands the work of many influential theologians and philosophers such as Maimonides (1135–1204), Aquinas (1225–1274), and al-Ghazali (1059–1111), who have labored to explain how we should understand these fundamental aspects of the divine nature. Our aim here is both to explain these three attributes of the divine nature and to discuss some of the difficulties philosophers and theologians have suggested arise when we endeavor to conceive of a being possessing such extraordinary attributes. Before beginning this task, however, we should note that the attributes ascribed to God in the historically dominant theological tradition within the major Western religions—including unlimited power (omnipotence), perfect goodness, and unlimited knowledge (omniscience)—are not characteristic of the entire history of thought about God in these religious traditions. Indeed, in the early religious texts that are authoritative in these traditions one can find descriptions of the divine being that do not suggest, let alone imply, that God is omnipotent, perfectly good, and omniscient. In the Old Testament of the Christian Bible, to cite just one example, God, through his prophet Samuel, orders Saul to totally exterminate a tribe of people, the Amaleks, to "kill both man and woman, infant and suckling, ox and sheep, camel and ass" (1 Samuel 15). Upon receiving his orders from on high Saul dutifully kills the Amalek men, women, children, and infants, but takes for himself and his men the best of the oxen, sheep, and lambs. On learning of this, God is angry and regrets making Saul king because, although Saul carried out his order to kill all the men, women, children, and infants, he did not follow God's order to slaughter all the livestock as well. On reading such a story one can hardly avoid the conclusion that the being giving such orders is viewed as a tribal deity rather than an omnipotent, perfectly good, omniscient being. And just as in the youthful periods of these three great religions one can find indications that God was then thought to be something less than an omnipotent, perfectly good, omniscient being, so too in the modern period one can find views of God, even among prominent theologians, that are clearly departures from the dominant conception of God in the great religions of the West. Some theologians in the modern period, for example, have conceived of God as a natural process in nature (Wieman 1958), or as a nonpersonal power of being (Tillich 1957). Nevertheless, if one considers the long history of theological thought in the West, it is clear that the dominant view of God is that he is a person who is eternal, all-powerful (omnipotent), all-knowing (omniscient), and perfectly good. Moreover, it is understandable why this should be so. For central to the idea of God is that God is worthy of unreserved praise, admiration, and worship. And when we seriously reflect on the qualities in a being that are most deserving of unreserved praise, admiration, and worship, we naturally think of qualities such as knowledge, wisdom, power, goodness, and justice. Hence, it is no accident that over time there emerged the idea of God as a being that is perfectly good, all-knowing, and all-powerful. And it is fitting that we should seek an understanding of what is meant when one thinks of God in this way.

POWER

When we consider the idea of a being possessing power, we generally think of that being as able to bring about certain things or certain states of affairs. We might ask, for example, "Does God have sufficient power to bring it about that the earth should cease to revolve around the sun?" In asking this question we assume that there is a certain state of affairs (a way things could be): *the earth's not revolving around the sun*. We know that this state of affairs isn't actual, that in fact *the earth's revolving around the sun* is the way things actually are. But we wonder whether God has sufficient power to bring it about that from now on *the earth's not revolving around the sun* is the way things are. In short, we wonder whether God can make actual (actualize) the state of affairs: *the earth's not revolving around the sun*. And one useful way of approaching the question of whether God is omnipotent, whether God possesses unlimited power, is to ask whether God can actualize states of affairs that involve massive changes from the way things are, states of affairs like *the earth's not revolving around the sun*. If God lacks the power to actualize that state of affairs, then, clearly, God is not omnipotent. For there would be a state of affairs, *the earth's not revolving around the sun*, that God is unable to make actual. One way, then, of considering the extent of God's power is to focus on various states of affairs that are not actual and ask ourselves whether God has sufficient power to make them actual, to actualize them. And if we find that there are states of affairs God cannot actualize, we then must consider whether his being unable to actualize those states of affairs shows that he is deficient in power and, therefore, not omnipotent. Before proceeding with that task, however, it will be helpful to distinguish three different types of states of affairs.

Some states of affairs are *necessary*; they are such that they simply cannot fail to be actual. Other states of affairs are *contingent*; they are such that they can be actual and they can fail to be actual. And still other states of affairs are *impossible*; they are such that they simply cannot be actual. Consider *2 + 2's being 4*, *George W. Bush's being the 54th president of the United States*, and *Smith's being exactly 20 years old and 35 years old at the same time*. The first of these is a *necessary* state of affairs; it cannot fail to be actual. The second is a *contingent* state of affairs; it is such that although it is actual, it might not have been actual at all. (*Al Gore's being the 54th President of the United States* is also a *contingent* state of affairs. It is such that although it is not actual, it could have been actual.) And our third example is an *impossible* state of affairs. It is such that it simply cannot be actual. Of it we might say: "Even God could not bring about *Smith's being exactly 20 years old and 35 years old at the same time*." For no matter how powerful a being is, no being can bring it about that an impossible state of affairs (a state of affairs that simply cannot be actual) is, nevertheless, an actual state of affairs. Having distinguished these three sorts of states of affairs, we can now see that it would be a mistake to think that for God to be omnipotent he must be able to actualize any state of affairs whatever. For, as Aquinas clearly saw, power extends only to what is possible. Whatever is impossible does not come within the scope of power because it cannot have the aspect of possibility. Thus, Aquinas says, "It is more appropriate to say that such things cannot be done, than that God cannot do them" (1945, *Summa Theologica*, I, 25, art. 3). And surely he is right about this. The fact that no one, including God, can actualize an impossible state of affairs does not detract from the power of anyone, including God.

Thus far, it looks as though we might characterize God's being omnipotent as God's having the power to actualize any state of affairs that isn't *impossible*. But consider some necessary state of affairs such as *2 + 2's being 4*. Necessary states of affairs aren't impossible. Indeed, they are actual no matter what any agent does or does not bring about. So, it makes no sense to think that some being can "bring it about" that a necessary state of affairs is *actual*. For it is possible to bring it about that a state of affairs is actual only if that state of affairs can fail to be actual. And, as we've seen, a necessary state of affairs cannot fail to be actual. Perhaps, then, we should characterize God's being omnipotent as God's having the power to actualize any state of affairs that is *contingent*—neither *impossible* nor *necessary*. But consider *George W. Bush's not being the 54th President of the United States*. This is a contingent state of affairs. For although Bush is the 54th President, it logically could have been otherwise. But is it *now* in God's power to bring it about that George W. Bush is not the 54th President of the United States? Well, if it is *now* in God's power to bring it about that George W. Bush is not the 54th President of the United States, then it is in God's power so to act that some fact wholly about the past would not have been a fact at all. And while it is true that at some time in the past God could have prevented Bush's victory, few would think that it is now, after the fact, in his power to do so. As Aristotle observed, "No one deliberates about the past but only about what is future and capable of being otherwise, while what is past is not capable of not having taken place; hence Agathon is right in saying: 'For this alone is lacking, even in God, to make undone things that have once been done'" (1941, *Nicomachean Ethics*, VII, 2. 1139).

In light of these considerations, perhaps we should say that for God to be omnipotent is for God to have the power to bring about *any* state of affairs that is contingent and not inconsistent with some fact wholly about the past. But while this seems right as far as it goes, it does not go far enough. For not only does God *now* lack the power to bring about a state of affairs (e.g., *George W. Bush's not being the 54th president of the United States*) that directly conflicts with some fact wholly about the past, but he cannot *now* actualize a state of affairs that both has already been actualized and is such that it cannot be actualized again. For some states of affairs, like *Franklin Roosevelt's being elected president of the United States in 1932*, are such that, once actualized, they can never be actualized again, whereas others, like *Franklin Roosevelt's being elected president of the United States*, are such that they can be actualized more than once. So, perhaps we should say that for God to be omnipotent is for God to have the power to bring about *any* state of affairs that is contingent, not inconsistent with some fact wholly about the past, and not already actualized and such that it can never be actualized again. This broader account accords with our sense that God cannot now actualize dated past facts such as *Franklin Roosevelt's being elected president of the United States in 1932*.

It would be a relief now to declare victory on what it is for God to be omnipotent, and move on. But there are two further issues in the account of God's absolute power that need to be considered. First, suppose we humans sometimes are free to perform some action and free not to perform it. Suppose, for example, that Jones causes his decision to change jobs while having at the time the power not to cause that decision. In short, Jones *freely* decides to change jobs. Is it in God's power to cause Jones's freely deciding to change jobs? It does not seem so. God can, of course, cause Jones to decide to change jobs. But if God does so, then Jones lacks the power not to decide to change jobs: Jones doesn't freely decide to change jobs. This means that, although omnipotent, God cannot cause Jones's *freely* deciding to change jobs, or any other free acts of beings other than himself. At best, God can arrange for Jones to be in a situation in which God knows that Jones will freely decide to change jobs. So, we have to add the free decisions of agents other than God to the list of states of affairs that God, although omnipotent, cannot directly cause to be actual.

The second issue concerns the fact that God lacks powers with respect to what actions he himself performs. That God lacks certain powers with respect to himself follows from the fact that God is *essentially* morally perfect, *essentially* all-knowing, and *essentially* eternal. Because it is an impossibility for a being whose very nature is to be eternal, morally perfect, and all-knowing to cease to exist (to not be eternal), to perform a morally wicked act (to not be morally perfect), or to believe to be true something that is false (to not be all-knowing), God's infinite power cannot be understood as implying that God can do what is morally wrong, make a mistake due to ignorance, or commit suicide. Because our powers do extend to such activities, it may appear that God's power is limited by virtue of some of his other essential attributes.

One way of understanding the issue before us is to consider the difference between

a. God's causing there to be a square circle

and

b. God's causing there to be an innocent person who suffers intensely for no good reason

Both (a) and (b) are impossible states of affairs. But (a) is impossible because what God is said to cause is itself an impossible state of affairs (something's being a square circle), whereas (b) is not impossible by virtue of what God is said to cause (someone's suffering intensely for no good reason) being impossible. There is nothing inherently impossible in some person's suffering intensely for no good reason. The impossibility of (b) is not due to the state of affairs God is there said to cause; it is due to *God's causing* that state of affairs to be actual. For intrinsically bad states of affairs that are not required by any outweighing good are simply impossible for an all-knowing, morally perfect being to bring about. And yet those very same intrinsically bad states of affairs may lie within the power of other beings to cause, beings who are not hampered by being essentially morally perfect. This means that given God's other essential attributes, there are states of affairs that we may have the power to bring about that God is unable to bring about. Before addressing this concern, however, let's complete our account of what it is for God to be omnipotent. For God to be omnipotent is for God to have the power to bring about *any* state of affairs that is contingent provided it is not inconsistent with some fact wholly about the past, not already actualized and such that it can never be actualized again, not consisting of a free action of some other agent, and not such that God's bringing it about is inconsistent with any of his essential attributes.

The question we're left with is whether God can truly be omnipotent given that there are states of affairs some of us can bring about that God (by virtue of some other essential attribute) does not have the power to bring about. This is an interesting issue. There is some intuitive pull to the idea that—putting aside an agent's free acts—an omnipotent being must be able to cause to be actual any state of affairs that any other being is able to cause to be actual. Alternatively, there is some intuitive pull to the idea that an omnipotent being need only be more powerful than any other being. And this latter idea may allow that some being can bring about a state of affairs that the omnipotent being cannot. Still, if we compare the idea of an omnipotent, *essentially* perfect being to the idea of an omnipotent being who, say, behaves in a morally good way but is not *essentially* morally perfect, we may be inclined to think that the latter being would be more powerful than the former by virtue of having the power to cause there to be an innocent person who suffers intensely for no good reason, even if, by virtue of being morally good but not *essentially* morally perfect, the being in fact always refrains from doing so. These are interesting issues that philosophers continue to discuss (for an illuminating discussion of this issue, see Morris 1987, ch. 3).

As we've seen, it is no easy matter to present a *complete account* of what it is for God to be omnipotent. Indeed, one influential philosopher (Geach 1977) has concluded that the task is impossible. Others (Flint and Freddoso 1983; Rosen-krantz and Hoffman 1980b; Wierenga 1989) have pressed on with the task and produced quite promising accounts of what it is for God to be omnipotent. In these and other discussions, one particular example has been rather widely discussed, the so-called paradox of the stone. Because God is all-powerful, it seems that he must be able to create a stone of any possible weight. The question then arises: Can God create a stone so heavy he cannot lift it? If he can, then he is not omnipotent, for he cannot lift a stone that he can create. On the other hand, if he cannot, then he is not omnipotent, for he cannot create a stone so heavy he cannot lift it. So, God is not omnipotent. Various solutions to this paradox have been offered. The solution favored here is perhaps the simplest. Given that God is omnipotent, it is impossible that there should be an object so heavy he cannot lift it. Therefore, a solution to the paradox is that God cannot create a stone so heavy he cannot lift it, for it is logically impossible for there to be a stone—or any other object, for that matter—that God is unable to lift. And, as we have seen above, it is no limitation of power to be unable to bring about something that is logically impossible. For power extends only to what is possible.

Goodness

The idea that God is perfectly good, like the idea that God is all-powerful, is connected to the view that God is a being who deserves unconditional gratitude, praise, and worship. For if a being were to fall short of perfect goodness, it would not be worthy of unreserved praise and worship. So, God is not just a good being, his goodness is unsurpassable. Moreover, according to the classical theology of the principal religions of the West, God doesn't simply happen to be perfectly good. As with his absolute power and total knowledge, it is his *nature* to be that way. God necessarily could not fail to be perfectly good. It was for this reason that we observed in the section on God's power that God does not have the power to do what would be morally wrong for him to do. For intentionally doing what is morally wrong for one to do is inconsistent with being perfectly good. It is worth noting that in saying that God is essentially good, we are doing more than saying that *necessarily* God is a perfectly good being. We are saying in addition that *the being who is God* cannot cease to be perfectly good. *Necessarily*, a bachelor is unmarried. But someone who is a bachelor can cease to be unmarried. Of course, when this happens (the bachelor marries), he no longer is a bachelor. Unlike the bachelor, however, the being who is God cannot give up being God. The bachelor next door can cease to be a bachelor. But the being who is God cannot cease to be God. Being a bachelor is not part of the nature or essence of a being who is a bachelor. But being God, and thus being perfectly good, is part of the nature or essence of the being who is God.

We've noted that an essential aspect of God's perfect goodness is his being *morally perfect*. Moral goodness is applicable only to conscious agents. Trees, flowers, and the like are not capable of moral goodness. Among conscious agents, however, there is, in addition to moral goodness, a kind of goodness we can best think of as *nonmoral goodness*. The difference between moral and nonmoral goodness in beings capable of consciousness is reflected in two statements that might be made on the occasion of someone's death: "He led a good life" and "He had a good life." The first statement concerns his moral goodness; the latter centers chiefly on nonmoral goodness such as happiness, good fortune, and so on. God's perfect goodness involves both moral goodness and nonmoral goodness. God is a morally perfect being, but it is also a part of his perfect goodness to enjoy supreme happiness. God's supreme happiness, as well as his moral perfection, constitutes an essential aspect of his goodness.

God has been held to be the source or standard of our moral duties, both negative duties (e.g., the duty not to take innocent human life) and positive duties (e.g., the duty to help others in need). Commonly, religious people believe that these duties are somehow grounded in divine commandments. A believer in Judaism, for example, may view the ten commandments as fundamental moral rules that determine at least a good part of what one is morally obligated to do or refrain from doing. Clearly, given his absolute moral perfection, what God commands us to do must be what is morally right for us to do. But are these things morally right because God commands them? That is, does the moral rightness of these things simply consist in the fact that God has commanded them? Or does God command these things to be done because they are right? If we say the second, that God commands them to be done because he sees that they are morally right, we seem to imply that morality has an existence apart from God's will or commands. But if we say the first, that what makes things right is God's willing or commanding them, we seem to imply that there would be no right or wrong if there were no commands issued by God.

While neither answer is without its problems, the dominant answer in religious thinking concerning God and morality is that what God commands is morally right independent of his commands. God's commanding us to perform certain actions does not make those actions morally right; they are morally right independent of his commands and he commands them because he sees that they are morally right. How, then, does our moral life depend on God? Well, even though morality itself need not depend on God, perhaps our *knowledge* of morality is dependent on (or at least greatly aided by) God's commands. Perhaps it is the teaching of religion that leads human beings to view certain actions as morally right and others as morally wrong. Also, the practice of morality may be aided by belief in God. For although an important part of the moral life is to do one's duty out of respect for duty itself, it would be too much to expect of ordinary humans that they would relentlessly pursue the life of moral duty even though there were no grounds for associating morality with well-being and happiness. Belief in God may aid the moral life by providing a reason for thinking that the connection between leading a good life and having a good life (now or later) is not simply accidental. Still, what of the difficulty that certain things are morally right apart from the fact that God commands us to do them? Consider God's belief that $7 + 5 = 12$. Is it true that $7 + 5 = 12$ because God believes it? Or does God believe that $7 + 5 = 12$ because it is true that $7 + 5 = 12$? If we say the latter, as it seems we should, we imply that certain mathematical statements are true independent of God's believing them. So, we already seem committed to the view that the way some things are is not ultimately a matter of God's will or commands. Perhaps the basic truths of morality have the same status as the basic truths of mathematics.

In addition to both his moral goodness and his nonmoral goodness, there is a third sort of goodness that God has been thought to possess, a goodness that, unlike the two kinds just discussed, is found throughout the entire realm of existing beings or things, a form of goodness best described as *metaphysical goodness*. This idea of goodness flourished in the writings of the neo-Platonists and profoundly influenced religious thinking in the West, chiefly through the writings of Augustine and Pseudo-Dionysius. Two related ideas make up metaphysical goodness. The first is that whatever has being is good. This idea lies behind the medieval theme that evil is simply a privation of being, an absence of good. So, nothing that exists can be fully evil, for insofar as something exists it has some degree of goodness. The second idea contained in the notion of metaphysical goodness is that the value of the created universe increases in proportion to the variety of kinds of beings God creates. For the purpose of the created world is to reflect the infinite goodness of God. And this is best reflected by God's creating a variety of kinds of creatures, rather than only one kind of creature.

The main problem connected with the classical view that God is necessarily perfectly good is the problem of determining to what extent it makes sense to praise or thank God for his good acts. As we've seen, it is very important to the theistic view of God that he deserves our unconditional gratitude and praise for his good acts. But if God's being essentially perfectly good makes it *necessary* for him to do what he sees as the best thing to be done, then it is difficult to make any sense of thanking him or praising him for doing what is best for him to do. It seems that he would not be deserving of our gratitude and praise for the simple reason that he would act of necessity and not freely. After all, being perfect, he couldn't fail to do what he sees as the best thing to be done. Of course, if God had acquired his perfections by his own free will, developing himself to be wise, powerful, and morally perfect, then we could in some derivative sense thank him for doing what he sees to be best and wisest on the whole. For he would be responsible for possessing the perfections that now make it necessary for him to do what he sees to be the best for him to do. But because God's absolute perfections are part of his nature, and not acquired by him over time as a result of his own efforts, it would appear that he is not responsible even in a derivative sense for doing what he sees to be best and wisest on the whole. In short, so the objection goes, when God does what he sees to be the best and wisest course of action he acts of necessity and not freely. That being so, it makes no sense to praise God for doing what he sees to be the best and wisest course of action.

One way of trying to make sense of praising and thanking God for doing what he sees to be the best and wisest course of action is to note that in human affairs we distinguish between acts that constitute one's moral duty and acts that are good to do but are not morally required, acts that are superogatory, beyond the call of duty. Sometimes the best act one can perform is an act that is beyond what duty demands. Such an act—*giving all one has to help others in need*, for example—is superogatory, beyond what one's moral duty requires, and failing to do it is not a failure to do what morality requires of you, whereas *giving none of what one has to help others in need* may well be a failure to fulfill one's moral duty to help those in need. If this distinction applies to God, we might see God's nature as necessitating his doing what duty demands, but not requiring him to do those acts beyond the call of duty. In which case, we can indeed praise God and thank God for his gracious acts that are beyond what moral duty requires. But we should note that a number of religious thinkers have held that this distinction does not apply to an omnipotent, essentially perfect being. As the eighteenth-century British theologian Samuel Clarke insisted, "Though God is a most perfectly free agent, he cannot but do always what is best and wisest on the whole" (1738/1978, IV, 574). In short, given his absolute perfections, God is not free to fail to do what is best and wisest on the whole. Freely doing what is beyond the call of duty is an option only for beings who are free to fail to do what they see to be the best thing for them to do.

It is important to note that the difficulty of reconciling thanking and praising God for doing what is best and wisest to be done is limited to situations in which there is a best action available for God to perform. Leibniz, the prominent eighteenth-century German philosopher, relying on the principle that God must always create what he sees to be the best, concluded that the actual world is the best of all possible worlds. If there is a best possible world, then it would appear that God had no choice other than to create it. But if there is no best world, if for every world creatable by God there is a better world God can create, then even God could not create a best world. If that were so, it might be reasonable for God to choose a good world to create, and his selection of that world rather than some better or worse world might be a free choice for which he is responsible. The inhabitants of that world might then be grateful to God for creating them, for he could have created some other world instead. Alternatively, if there are several possible worlds equally good and none better, God would be free to select one of those worlds to create and may be responsible for creating it.

The conclusion we've reached—that God's absolute goodness and moral perfection preclude his being free to create a world less than the best, provided there is a best world he can create—has seemed to many to unduly restrict God's powers with respect to creation. In a well-known article, "Must God Create the Best?" Robert M. Adams (1972) argued that even if there is a best world that God can create, he would do no wrong in creating a world less than the best provided the lives of its creatures were on the whole good. Suppose, to come to the heart of

Adams's argument, we concede this point and allow that a perfect being need not be doing something *morally wrong* in creating a world less than the best provided the world he did create was one in which its inhabitants lived good and productive lives. Still, if a perfect being had a choice between creating a world in which its creatures are happier, more understanding of others, more loving, and so on than the creatures of some other world, wouldn't such a being prefer to create the better world? Wouldn't God's choice of the inferior world indicate some defect or mistake? Adams's response to this objection is that God's choice of a less excellent world could be explained in terms of his *grace*, which is considered a virtue in Judeo-Christian ethics. It is Adams's understanding of the Judeo-Christian view of grace that lies at the core of his objection to the Liebnizian view that the most perfect being "cannot fail to act in the most perfect way, and consequently to choose the best." So, any answer to Adams's view that God need not choose to create the best world must take into account his view that the Judeo-Christian view of grace implies that God may create a world less than the best.

Adams defines the concept of grace as "a disposition to love which is not dependent on the merit of the person loved" (1972, 324). Given this definition and given two worlds, W_1 and W_2, that differ in that the persons in W_1 are happier and more disposed to behave morally than are the persons in W_2, with the result, let us suppose, that W_1 is a better world than W_2, it is clear that a gracious God would not love the persons in W_1 more than the persons in W_2. Or, at the very least, it is clear that were God to love the persons in W_1 more than the persons in W_2 it would not be because they are morally better and/or happier. As Adams remarks, "The gracious person loves without worrying about whether the person he loves is worthy of his love" (324). So, by virtue of his grace, either God would love all persons to an equal degree, or the fact that he might love one person more than another would have nothing to do with the fact that the one has a greater degree of merit or excellence than another. As Adams puts it, "The gracious person sees what is valuable in the person he loves, and does not worry about whether it is more or less valuable than what could be found in someone else he might have loved" (324). And he explains that in the Judeo-Christian tradition, grace is held to be a virtue that God has and humans ought to have.

Given that grace is as Adams has defined it and that grace is a virtue God possesses, what may we infer about the world, God creates? Can we infer with Leibniz that if there is a best world, God must create that world? It is difficult to know what to say here. All that we've learned from Adams thus far is that it would be something other than love that would motivate God to choose the best world, or any other world, for that matter. For because grace is a disposition to love without regard to merit, God will be unable to select one world over another if all he has to go on is his grace. His grace (love toward creatures independent of their degree of merit) will leave him free to create any world that has creatures able to do moral good or evil, regardless of how good or bad they may be in that world. So, if God has a reason to choose one creaturely world over another—rather than blindly picking one out of the hat, so to speak—that reason will have little or nothing to do with his grace. For given the doctrine of grace, God's love for creatures is not based on the quality (moral, religious, etc.) of the lives they lead, and it is difficult to see what else about their lives it could be based on. In fact, the implication of the Judeo-Christian doctrine of grace for God's selection of a world to create seems to be entirely negative: rather than giving a reason why he might select a particular creaturely world, or rule out other creaturely worlds, it simply tells us that if God creates a world with creatures, his love of the creatures in that world cannot be his reason for creating it. For his love for creatures is entirely independent of who they are and the kind of lives they lead. To base his love on who they are and the kind of lives they lead would be to take those persons and their lives as more deserving of his love than other persons and their lives.

What we've seen thus far is that God's grace—his love of creatures without respect to their merit—cannot provide God with a reason to create the best world, or any particular world less than the best. This means that whatever reason God has for choosing to create one creaturely world over another cannot be found in his gracious love for creatures. In what, then, given that God has a reason for creating one world over another, would that reason reside? It would reside, I suggest, in his desire to create the very best state of affairs that he can. Having such a desire does not preclude gracious love. It does not imply that God cannot or does not equally love the worst creatures along with the best creatures. Loving parents, for example, may be disposed to love fully any child that is born to them, regardless of whatever talents that child is capable of developing. But such love is consistent with a *preference* for a child who will be born without mental or physical impairment, a child who will develop his or her capacities for kindness toward others, who will develop his or her tastes for music, good literature, and so on. And in like manner, God will graciously love any creature he might choose to create, not just the best possible creatures. But that does not rule out God's having a preference for creating creatures who will strive not only to have a good life but also to lead a good life, creatures who will in their own way freely develop themselves into "children of God." Indeed, although God's gracious love extends to every possible creature, it would be odd to suggest that, therefore, he could have no preference for creating a world with such creatures over a world in which creatures use their freedom to abuse others, use their talents to turn good into evil, and devote their lives to selfish ends. Surely, God's graciously loving all possible creatures is not inconsistent with his having a preference to create a world with creatures who will use their freedom to pursue the best kind of human life. How could he not have such a preference? Furthermore, if God had no such preference, his gracious love for creatures would give him no reason to select any particular possible world for creation. For his gracious love for each and every creature fails to provide a reason to create one creature rather than another, or to create the creatures in one possible world rather than those in another. So, if God is not reduced to playing dice with respect to selecting a world to create, there must be some basis for his selection over and beyond his gracious love for all creatures regardless of merit. And that basis, given God's nature as an absolutely perfect being, would seem to be to do always what is best and wisest to be done. And surely the best and wisest for God to do is to create the best world he can. Doing so seems to be entirely consistent with God's gracious love of all creatures regardless of their merit.

Adams, however, rejects this view, a view that sees God's gracious love of creatures without respect to merit as entirely consistent with his having an all-things-considered preference to create the best world he can. After noting that divine grace is love that is not dependent on the merit of the person loved, Adams proceeds to draw the conclusion that although God would be free to create the best creatures, he cannot have as his *reason* for choosing to create them the fact that they are the best possible creatures: "God's graciousness in creating does not imply that the creatures He has chosen to create must be less excellent than the best possible. It implies, rather, that even if they are the best possible creatures, that is not the ground for His choosing them. And it implies that there is nothing in God's nature or character which would require Him to act on the principle of choosing the best possible creatures to be the object of His creative powers" (1972, 324). By my lights, God's disposition to love independent of the merits of the persons loved carries no implication as to what God's *reason* for creating a particular world may be, other than that his reason cannot be that he *loves* the beings in this world more (or less) than the beings in other worlds. And, of course, having an all-things-considered preference for creating the best world need not be rooted in a *greater love* for beings who are better than other beings. God's grace does rule out choosing to create the best world because he *loves* its inhabitants more than the inhabitants of some lesser world. But it does not rule out God's choosing to create the best world so long as he does not love its inhabitants more than he loves the inhabitants of lesser worlds. Adams must be supposing that if God's reason for creating one world rather than another is the fact that the creatures in the first world are much better than the creatures in the second world, it somehow logically follows that God must love the creatures in the first world more than he loves the creatures in the second. But there is nothing in his presentation of the view that God's love for creatures is independent of their merit that yields this result. It is doubtful, therefore, that the Judeo-Christian concept of grace rules out the view of Leibniz and Clarke that God must create the best world if there is a best world to create.

KNOWLEDGE

As we've seen, a being worthy of unconditional praise and devotion will possess certain perfections in the highest possible degree, for otherwise, one could conceive of a being more worthy of our praise and devotion. In addition to maximal power and goodness, the long tradition of classical theism has maintained that God possesses the perfection of maximal knowledge. For a being who is immensely powerful and good but somewhat lacking in knowledge would not be as deserving of our respect, reverence, and awe as a being who, in addition to being all-powerful and perfectly good, possessed *complete* knowledge of all that is possible to be known. But, as with God's possession of total power and perfect goodness, there are difficulties in understanding what it would be for a being to be omniscient, knowing all there is to be known. In addition, there is the question of whether God's knowledge of all the truths there are is compatible with other features of the theistic worldview, such as the strong emphasis on human freedom and responsibility.

What is possible to be known? The most obvious answer is propositions that are true. If a certain claim is true—whether about the past, the present, or the future—then unless it's like "No one knows anything," it seems possible that someone should know that proposition to be true. Accordingly, if God is all-knowing, we should expect God to know all the propositions that are true. So, if God exists, he now knows that two World Wars occurred in the twentieth century. And he knows that it is now the twenty-first century. Moreover, if it is true that no World Wars will occur in the twenty-second century, then God now knows that no World Wars will occur in the twenty-second century. If he did not know all these truths he would be lacking in knowledge of what is possible to be known and, therefore, would not be omniscient. Moreover, God's knowledge is generally held to be immediate or direct, not inferred from evidence that he has gathered.

In suggesting that God *now* knows truths about the future we inevitably suggest that, like us, God is a temporal being, existing in time. Of course, he is not a temporal being in the sense of having a beginning or an end in time. He is temporal in the sense of being *everlasting*, existing at every moment from a beginningless past to an unending future. While this is the dominant view of God in the modern period, it must be noted that from the time of Augustine up through the medieval period a number of important religious thinkers viewed God as outside of time and having a knowledge of events in time (past, present, and future) akin to the knowledge we have of what happens in the present. They took the view that *temporal* existence imposes limitations not appropriate with respect to God. For if we consider our lives spread over time, we cannot but note that we possess only one part of our temporal lives at a time. As Boethius (480–524) put it, "For whatever lives in time lives in the present, proceeding from past to future, and nothing is so constituted in time that it can embrace the whole span of its life at once. It has not yet arrived at tomorrow, and it has already lost yesterday; even the life of this day is lived only in each moving, passing moment" (1962, *The Consolation of Philosophy*, prose VI).

In contrast to beings in time, the medievals in question viewed God as having his infinite, endless life wholly present to himself, all at once. Thus, they held that God exists outside of time and comprehends each event in time in a way similar to our comprehension of our experiences at the moment they are happening to us. On this view of God there is no such thing, strictly speaking, as divine *fore-knowledge*, and, therefore, it may seem, no problem about how, given God's knowledge of our future acts, we can be free in the future to do something other than what God has always known we would do. For, so the argument goes, since God is not a temporal being his knowledge of events is not *temporally prior* to their occurrence.

However, a number of contemporary philosophers of religion are doubtful that it is coherent to think that God fully comprehends what is going on *now* if he exists outside of time. Moreover, it is difficult to comprehend how God can act in the world unless he exists in time. He would have to will eternally that a certain event occur at a particular time, even though when that time comes he does not at that time bring that event about—for he could at that time bring it about only if he existed at that time. So, the view that God is not in time has significant implications for how one understands God's actions and his knowledge of the events that happen in time. But we will here regard the eternalist's view as a minority report on the nature of God's knowledge, and continue to examine the problem of God's knowledge on the more generally accepted position that God is eternal in the sense of being *everlasting*, existing at every moment from a beginningless past to an unending future.

Because God's knowledge of the past, present, and future is both complete and infallible, God unerringly knew before we were born everything we will do. But how does God acquire his knowledge of future events? One way would be for God to simply ordain or predetermine the events that take place in the future. As the Westminster Confession states, "God from all eternity did . . . freely and unchangeably ordain whatsoever comes to pass." Clearly, if God has determined in advance everything that will occur in the future, then by knowing his own determining decrees he thereby knows all the events that will transpire in the future. But although such a view may express the majesty and power of God over all that he has created, it makes it difficult to understand how our future lives may in some significant ways be up to us. How can we be free in the future to do this or that if before the world began God determined everything that will come to pass? Indeed, the authors of the Westminster Confession seemed to have recognized the difficulty, for its next line reads, "Yet . . . thereby is no violence offered to the will of the creatures." But few nowadays think that it is possible for God to determine at the moment of creation all future human actions and still provide for humans to be free to act otherwise than God has ordained for them to act. If God determined before you were born that on a certain day in the future you will do X, then when that day comes it won't be in your power to refrain from doing X. For if it were, it would be in your power on that day to prevent an event (your doing X) from occurring that God long ago decreed to occur on that day. And no one seriously thinks that creatures enjoy that degree of power over God's eternal decrees. So, however it is that God knows from eternity our future free actions, actions we bring about but have the power not to bring about, it cannot be that he knows them because he has decreed from eternity that we should perform those actions. Should we then say that God's knowledge of our future actions derives from his determining decrees, but that our future actions are not performed freely? Although that position has the virtue of consistency, it deprives God's creatures of moral responsibility for their actions, since they lack the power not to perform those actions. So, however it is that God knows in advance what we will *freely* do, his knowledge cannot be based on his predetermining decrees.

It may seem that the only problem concerning divine foreknowledge and human freedom concerns the *source* of God's foreknowledge of human free acts. But there is an equally serious problem concerning whether divine foreknowledge itself—whatever its source may be—is consistent with human freedom. We can see what this problem is by considering the following argument:

1. God knew before we are born everything we will do.
2. If God knew before we are born everything we will do, it is never in our power to do otherwise.
3. If it is never in our power to do otherwise, then there is no human freedom. Therefore,
4. There is no human freedom.

If we replace "knew" in premise 2 with "decreed," there is, as we've seen, a very good reason to accept premise 2. But why should the mere fact that before you were born God knew that you would now be reading this sentence deprive you of the power not to have read it? The answer given by those who accept 2 is that to ascribe to you the power not to have read the sentence you just read is to ascribe to you a power no one can possess: the power to alter the past. For since you did read the sentence it is true that *before you were born God knew that you would read it*. But if a few moments ago it was in your power not to read it, it seems that it was then in your power to change the past, to make it the case that before you were born God did not know that you would read that sentence today. But no one has the power to change the past. And it is not acceptable to say that until you actually read the sentence in question there was no past fact to the effect that God knew before you were born that you would read that sentence at the moment you did. For that simply denies the doctrine of divine foreknowledge, that God knew in advance what you would do.

Although there is more than one response to this line of argument, the one we shall consider here is due to William of Ockham (1285–1349) and can be briefly stated. The basic point Ockham makes is to note a distinction between two sorts of facts about the past: facts that are *simply* about the past, and facts that are *not simply* about the past. To illustrate this distinction, consider two facts about the past, facts about the year 1941:

f1:   In 1941 Japan attacks Pearl Harbor.
f2:   In 1941 a war begins between Japan and the United States that lasts five years.

Relative to the year 1950, f1 and f2 are both *simply* about the past, for all the facts they state are, as it were, over and done with before 1950 occurs. Relative to 1943, however, while f1 is *simply* about the past, f2 is *not simply* about the past. Although f2 is a fact about the past relative to 1943—for f2 is in part about 1941, and 1941 lies in 1943's past—f2, unlike f1, implies a certain fact about 1944, a time future to 1943. f2 implies

f3:   In 1944 Japan and the United States are at war.

Since f2 implies f3, a fact about the future relative to 1943, relative to 1943 f2 is a fact about the past, but not simply a fact about the past. And the important point to note is that in 1943 it may have been in the power of generals and statesmen in the United States and Japan so to act that f2 would not have been a fact about the past at all. For there may well have been certain actions that were not but could have been taken by one or both of the groups in 1943, actions that, had they been taken, would have brought the war to an end in 1943. If that is so, then it was in the power of one or both of the groups in 1943 to do something such that had they done it a certain fact about 1941, f2, would not have been a fact about 1941.

It is important to note that had the generals and statesmen in 1943 exercised their power to end the war in 1943 they would *not* have changed the past relative to 1943. It is not as though prior to their action it was a fact that the war would end in 1945, and what they would have done was to put a different fact into the past than was there before they acted. Power over the past is not power to *change* a fact that the past contains. It is power to determine what possible facts that are future to the time of one's action are contained in the past, provided those future-oriented facts depend on what one does in the present. Thus, if we suppose that it was in your power a moment ago not to read the first sentence of this paragraph, a power you did not exercise, then before you were born God knew that you would read that sentence a moment ago. But, on Ockham's view, if you had exercised your freedom not to read it, what God would have known before you were born is that you would not read that sentence a moment ago. By thus distinguishing facts that, relative to a certain time, are simply about the past from facts that are not simply about the past, Ockham sought to harmonize God's temporal foreknowledge with human freedom to have acted otherwise than we in fact did act.

MAXIMAL PERFECTION

We've considered the three divine perfections that constitute the core of the classical concept of God in Western civilization. If God is, as this tradition holds, the greatest possible being, then he must possess each of these perfections in the highest possible degree. And for that to be so, these three perfections must be mutually compatible and each perfection must have a highest possible degree. We've noted that there *may* be a difficulty in establishing the compatibility of perfect goodness and omnipotence, because a being whose nature is to be perfectly good is incapable of doing evil. But so long as omnipotence is understood to require only that no other being could possibly be as powerful, the fact that God, being necessarily good, cannot do evil will not imply that he cannot be both perfectly good and omnipotent. The more significant difficulty in establishing the possibility of a being having these three perfections in the highest possible degree is that some aspects of God's goodness do not appear to possess a highest possible degree. We've noted three aspects of God's goodness: moral goodness, nonmoral goodness, and metaphysical goodness. What is unclear is whether nonmoral goodness, specifically happiness, or metaphysical goodness, is such that there is a highest possible degree of it that a being can possess. It does seem, however, that although beings differ in their degrees of moral goodness, there is an upper limit to moral goodness such that it is not possible to have a greater degree of moral goodness. Consider increasing degrees of largeness in angles. An angle of 20 degrees is larger than an angle of 15 degrees, and so on. On one standard account of what an angle is there are angles of ever increasing size that approach the limit for an angle at 360 degrees. So the largest possible angle is an angle of 360 degrees. If the degree of moral goodness that may be exhibited by conscious beings has an upper limit, then God will be a morally perfect being having the highest possible degree of moral goodness. But also consider the series of positive integers. As opposed to our series of angles, the series of positive integers does not converge on a limit. To *any* positive integer we can always add 1 and produce a still larger integer. Hence, while given our standard definition of an angle, there is such a thing as an angle than which a larger is not possible, there is no such thing as a positive integer than which a larger is not possible. And the question we face is whether the increasing degrees of happiness or increasing degrees of metaphysical goodness converge on an upper limit, or instead are such that no matter what degree of happiness or metaphysical goodness something possesses it is always possible that it (or something else, perhaps) should possess a still greater degree of happiness or metaphysical goodness. If the latter should be the case, then the theistic God, as traditionally conceived, is not a possible being. But it is fair to say that at the present time we lack demonstrative proof on either side of this issue.

WORKS CITED

Adams, Robert M. 1972. "Must God Create the Best?" *Philosophical Review* 81: 317–32.

Aquinas. 1945. *Basic Writings of Saint Thomas Aquinas,* ed. Anton Pegis, vol. 1. New York: Random House.

Aristotle. 1941. *Nicomachean Ethics,* in *The Basic Works of Aristotle,* ed. Richard McKeon. New York: Random House.

Boethius. 1962. *The Consolation of Philosophy,* prose VI, tr. Richard Green. New York: Bobbs-Merrill.

Clarke, Samuel. [1738] 1978. *Works.* In four volumes in *British Philosophers and Theologians of the 17th and 18th Centuries.* New York: Garland.

Flint, T., and A. Freddoso. 1983. "Maximal Power." In *The Existence and Nature of God,* ed. Alfred Freddoso. Notre Dame, Ind.: University of Notre Dame Press.

Geach, Peter. 1977. *Providence and Evil.* Cambridge, England: Cambridge University Press.

Morris, Thomas. 1987. *Anselmian Explorations.* Notre Dame, Ind.: University of Notre Dame Press.

Rosenkrantz, G., and J. Hoffman 1980a. "The Omnipotence Paradox, Modality, and Time." *Southern Journal of Philosophy* 18: 473–79.

———. 1980b. "What an Omnipotent Agent Can Do." *International Journal for Philosophy of Religion* 11: 1–19.

Tillich, Paul. 1957. *Dynamics of Faith.* New York: Harper & Row.

Wieman, Henry Nelson. 1958. *Man's Ultimate Commitment.* Carbondale: Southern Illinois University Press.

Wierenga, E. 1989. *The Nature of God.* Ithaca, N.Y.: Cornell University Press.

FOR FURTHER READING

Flint, Thomas P. 1998. *Divine Providence.* Ithaca, N.Y.: Cornell University Press.

Hasker, William. 1989. *God, Time, and Knowledge.* Ithaca, N.Y.: Cornell University Press.

Mann, William. 1975. "The Divine Attributes." *American Philosophical Quarterly* 12: 151–59.

Plantinga, Alvin. 1980. *Does God Have a Nature?* Milwaukee, Wisc.: Marquette University Press.

Stump, Eleonore, and Norman Kretzmann. 1981. "Eternity." *Journal of Philosophy* 78: 429–58.

———. 1988. "Being and Goodness." In *Divine and Human Action,* ed. Thomas V. Morris. Ithaca, N.Y.: Cornell University Press.

Swinburne, Richard. 1977. *The Coherence of Theism.* Oxford: Clarendon Press.

Yandell, Keith. 1988. "Divine Necessity and Divine Goodness." In *Divine and Human Action,* ed. Thomas V. Morris. Ithaca, N.Y.: Cornell University Press.

CHAPTER 2

DIVINE SOVEREIGNTY AND ASEITY

WILLIAM E. MANN

SEARCHING for a way to avoid the rude anthropomorphism of his contemporaries, the Presocratic philosopher Xenophanes said of God that "always he remains in the same state, in no way changing; nor is it fitting for him to go now here now there"; that "without effort, by the will of his mind he shakes everything"; that "he sees as a whole, he thinks as a whole, and he hears as a whole" (Barnes 1979, 1: 85, 93). Xenophanes' pronouncements are the first recorded sallies into philosophical theology. Although he may have had the first word, he did not have the last: his descendants include Plato, Philo, Augustine, Anselm, Aquinas, Spinoza, and a host of others.

Xenophanes emphasizes the differences between God and creatures. For many religious believers, however, it is the similarities that are most important. The God of Judaism, Christianity, and Islam is supposed to care for his creatures, know their innermost hopes and fears, respond to their prayers, strengthen them against adversity, share in their joy, console them in their sorrow and grief, judge their deficiencies, and forgive them their sins. These divine activities are *personal*; they could issue only from a being with beliefs and desires similar, in some respects at least, to ours. Any characterization of God that denied him these personal activities or negotiated them away in favor of some advantage to philosophical theology would be rightly regarded by believers as akin to replacing your loved ones with their cardboard cutouts. Thus, it happens that many theists become wary of theories in philosophical theology that emphasize the differences between

God and creatures. Perhaps no one really believes that God is Just Plain Folks. Even so, if the ascription of a particular attribute to God were to entail that God does not or cannot engage in the kinds of personal interactions mentioned above, then so much the worse for that ascription. To the extent to which philosophical theologians wish to emphasize that God is not an ordinary being, they are liable to bear the accusation that in making God Wholly Other, they have made God wholly disconnected.

Still, many of these same theists think they have excellent warrant for believing the following propositions about God, propositions that surely mark significant differences between God and creatures:

(A)   Everything that exists depends on God for its existence.
(B)   Every situation that is the case depends on God for its being the case.
(C)   God depends on nothing for his existence.
(D)   God depends on nothing for his being what he is.
(E)   God is perfectly free.

(A) and (B) are important components of a doctrine about God's metaphysical *sovereignty*. (C), (D), and (E) are central elements of a doctrine about God's metaphysical independence or *aseity* (from the Latin *a se*, from or by itself).

Widespread surface allegiance to (A)–(E) can mask deeper disagreements about how to interpret the theses and what they entail. Thus, consider the pair of theses (A)–(B). We can ask of (A) how we are to understand the scope of "everything." Are there features of reality that are not literally *things*, and that thus might be independent of God's sovereignty even while (A) is true? Does God himself fall within the scope of "everything," and if so, what sense can we make of the notion that God depends on himself for his existence? In similar fashion, we can ask how widely to interpret the phrase "every situation" (alternatively, "every state of affairs") in (B). Do such propositions as *2 + 2 = 4*, *If Jefferson is president, then Jefferson is president*, and *God is essentially omniscient* pick out situations that fall within the scope of (B)? If so, how should we understand (B)'s claim that even these situations depend on God for their being as they are? Or consider the proposition *Smith freely chooses to sin*: if true, it certainly picks out a situation. But how can Smith *freely* choose to sin if, as (B) maintains, that very situation depends on God for its being the case? And if it does depend on God, does that not make God an accomplice in Smith's sin?

Related questions beset the aseity assumptions, although perhaps not (C) so much as (D) and (E). How, for example, can God be essentially omniscient without depending on the possession of some sort of faculty for acquiring and retaining knowledge? At the core of theistic belief lies the tenet that God is a creator. How does this tenet comport with theses (D) and (E)? Many theists, from Plato on, have insisted that it is God's nature to be a creator. But if God must be a creator then there must be creatures, and so it would seem to follow, contrary to (D), that God depends on the existence of creatures for his being what he is. Moreover, if it is God's nature to create, it would seem to follow that God cannot refrain from creating something, and thus that God is not, as (E) maintains, perfectly free.

I shall discuss the issues raised in the previous two paragraphs. I do not, however, intend to remain above the fray. I shall argue for the tenability of a set of positions that many contemporary philosophical theologians regard as undercutting God's personal nature. As might be expected, I shall argue that that regard is unwarranted.

DIVINE SOVEREIGNTY

Parsimonious philosophers will suspect that (A) and (B) are one thesis too many. Some might contend that every situation is, after all, some kind of thing; thus, that thesis (B) collapses into a generously interpreted thesis (A). Others, on the contrary, might argue that a proper ontology would dispense with things as basic, construing them as complexes constructed out of situations, thereby relegating (A) to the status of corollary of (B). I do not propose to take a stand on the issue of thing- versus fact-ontologies. I shall treat (A) and (B) as relatively independent theses, commenting, however, on their interconnections as we proceed.

Creation

If asked to articulate the sense in which things depend on God for their existence, theists are apt to respond that God *created* things. Construed in this way, dependence as being created is a causal notion. Opinions begin to diverge as we press for details.

For all their impressive complexity, artistic creation and biological procreation simply involve, in different ways, the reworking of matter already on hand. If one thinks of God's creative role along these lines, one may arrive at a picture of creation like the one put forward by Timaeus (Plato 1997, 1234–36): the universe is the ultimate artifact, the handiwork of an enormously powerful and benevolent craftsman. If we find reason to complain about the imperfections we find in the product, the blame is to be laid on the refractory nature of the chaotic, preexisting matter with which the craftsman had to work. (Not even the most skilled violin maker can achieve much success if the only raw materials available are Styrofoam and cotton string.)

Timaeus's account models creation on a causal process with which we are familiar enough. The familiarity, however, comes at a price that many theists are unwilling to pay. Matter, on Timaeus's account, exists and has its nature in independence from the craftsman-creator. A fairly straightforward application of (A) tells against construing divine creation as a species of material rearrangement.

The doctrine of creation ex nihilo removes Timaeus's limitation. According to Augustine, for example, the universe was made out of "concreated" matter, that is, matter created simultaneously with the creation of the universe (1960, 367). A natural extension of Augustine's claim is to suppose that in creating the universe, God created the fundamental particles, stuff, or energy that makes up the universe, and that God set the laws and parameters that describe thereafter the behavior of the physical processes that occur in the universe.

Creation ex nihilo is a significant departure from Timaeus's folksy account. It is one thing to give you titanium tubing and ask you to build a bicycle. It is quite another to ask you to build a bicycle out of nothing whatsoever. But for many believers, Augustine included, the doctrine of creation ex nihilo, although true, is insufficient by itself to express the nature of God's creative activity and the dependency of creatures on God. For one thing, the doctrine gives us no reason to think that the creator still exists: sometimes artifacts outlast their artificers. For another, the doctrine by itself does nothing to validate the sentiment that God created *us*. Without such validation it is hard to see why it is appropriate for believers to respond to God as a spiritual parent. It is difficult to conjure up an attitude of filial piety toward a being whose sole contribution was to set into motion a chain of events that resulted, say, approximately 15 billion years later, in one's coming into existence. Although compatible with the doctrine of creation out of nothing, the deistic portrait of God as the cosmic artificer, whose craft is so supreme that he need not—and thus does not—subsequently attend to what he has created, is a poor resemblance to the believer's picture of God as personal.

One way of retouching the deistic portrait is to suppose that God does intervene in creation on occasion to perform miracles, not necessarily to adjust anything that has gone awry, but rather to make manifest his providential concern. Many believers, however, who may doubt ever having witnessed a miracle do not stake their claim for God's active, personal nature solely on such impressive divine sorties. For these believers miracles, almost by definition, occur in stark contrast to the way God sustains the everyday functioning of the world.

Conservation

Traditional theology has a remarkable strategy for characterizing God's sustaining function. The strategy involves two maneuvers. The first is to distinguish generation and corruption from creation and annihilation. Reserve the term "creation" for the bringing of things into existence out of nothing. Then the term for the action opposite to creation is not "destruction" or "corruption" but "annihilation," the returning of a thing to nonbeing. It is easy enough to destroy a bicycle—by hydraulic press, oxyacetylene torch, or teenage children. These are familiar types of corruption. To annihilate a bicycle, in contrast, would entail the *elimination*, not just the transformation, of a certain amount of the universe's mass/energy. Just as no natural agent can build the bicycle out of nothing, so no natural agent can annihilate it.

The second maneuver is to insist that despite the apparent inviolability of the universe's mass/energy, it has no inherent potentiality to continue to exist from one moment to the next. This claim has sometimes been put forward as a consequence of the doctrine of creation ex nihilo: anything having its origin in nonbeing will, left to its own devices, collapse back immediately into nonbeing. Alternatively, the claim has sometimes been defended by arguing that although the laws of nature along with the initial conditions of things at an instant may entail (in a suitably deterministic universe) what will occur at a future instant, since every instant of time is logically independent from every other instant, the laws and initial conditions are insufficient to guarantee that the future instant will exist. It is compatible with this claim that created things have the power to bring about changes both in themselves and among other created things. What created things cannot do, however, is continue to exist without God's ever-present conserving activity.

Proponents of the strategy maintain that God's conserving power is "equipollent" to God's creative power. What they mean by this claim, at a minimum, is that it takes as much divine activity to sustain the created world from one instant to the next as it did to create it. Divine conservation is a kind of continuous creation (see Quinn 1983 for details).

A protest to divine conservation is that whereas the deistic portrait places God too far in the background, divine conservation makes God appear too near. In Greek mythology, Atlas was required to support forever the heavens on his shoulders. Divine conservation imposes a much more monumental burden on God: not just this firmament, but all of creation; not just to keep one body from falling through space but to keep everything from lapsing into nonbeing. Moreover, divine conservation appears to exacerbate the problem of evil. For it would seem that God does not merely allow atrocities to occur; he aids and abets the perpetrators by keeping them in existence throughout the commission of their atrocities.

One might cast about for some position that falls between the aloofness of deism and the coziness of divine conservation. But it is hard to see what such a position could be, such that it would not spawn even more serious problems of its own. Will the hypothetical position maintain that only *some* things must be continually sustained by God? If so, which ones? Why are the others privileged? And would not their privileged status encroach on divine sovereignty? Or will the position claim that some creaturely functions occur independently of God's sustaining activity? At first blush, this version holds more promise. Some functions can outlast their hosts: if God were to snuff out the sun, its function of irradiating my garden would persist thereafter for approximately eight minutes. An adroit theologian might even be tempted to try to exempt sinful functions from God's support. To be sure, this version will invoke questions analogous to those listed earlier in the paragraph. But worse yet, it rests on a faulty assumption. A function may outlast some of its ancestral hosts, but no part of it can occur without being embedded in some host or other. And those hosts must be sustained in *their* existence. The last photons emitted from the sun immediately prior to its annihilation must themselves be sustained in existence if they are to irradiate my garden eight minutes hence: after-effects do not earn an exemption just in virtue of being after-effects. More generally, a function must be a function *of* some ensemble or sequence of things. If the function is spread over a period of time, the things on which the function depends must be kept in existence long enough to host the function. Sins are no exception; they must have perpetrators. Even if we suppose that a sinful act is freely committed, in some strong, indeterministic sense of freedom, that supposition does not gainsay the fact that the sinner must be kept in existence long enough to commit the sin.

It is not obvious, then, that intermediate positions are philosophically better off than divine conservation. But how bad is the case against divine conservation? Recall that two considerations were raised against it. One rested on a comparison to the plight of Atlas. Theists are entitled to regard the comparison as invidious. Atlas's chore is burdensome because it is imposed as a punishment and his strength is limited. But God is supposed by most theists to be a being of unlimited power and a being against whom no other being can prevail. Thus, it is hard to see how, for such a being, the conservation of creation could be exhausting drudgery. Conservation would be a problem if it took *all* of God's unlimited power to create and conserve something ex nihilo, or if God inflicted the burden of creation on himself as some sort of act of supreme self-flagellation. Neither hypothesis seems remotely plausible.

The second worry about divine conservation was that it appears to confer on theism a particularly nasty version of the problem of evil. Theists typically concede that God *permits* evil to occur while denying that God *commits* evil. It is possible to see too much moral difference in the distinction between doing and allowing to happen. But in this case, the strategy of downplaying the difference is a dangerous one for the theist to pursue. It might have the unhappy result of assimilating divine doing to a type of mere passive allowing. Alternatively, it might promote divine allowing up to the level of active doing, which would validate the second worry. I suggest a different strategy, one more narrowly tailored to divine conservation. The strategy is to argue that divine conservation does not *increase* the problem of evil for a theist who is willing to grant that God permits evil to occur.

Let us begin by considering this principle:

(1)   If x keeps y in existence while y does ϕ, then x is also responsible for doing ϕ.

(1) is surely false. An oxygen tank may enable an arsonist to continue breathing while setting fire to a building, but the arsonist's crime cannot be imputed to the tank. If some modification of (1) is going to be plausible, it must incorporate appropriate restrictions into x's knowledge, x's power, even the sort of responsibility ascribable to x. Skipping a few intermediary iterations, we can examine this descendant of (1):

(1')   If x knows (a) that she is keeping y in existence while y does ϕ, (b) that y's doing ϕ is morally impermissible, and (c) that she could have terminated y's existence but chose not to, then x has done something that is morally impermissible.

(I take the consequent of (1') to leave it open whether x is to be charged with doing ϕ or with some other offense, such as being an accessory during the fact.)

As a general principle, (1') is implausible. Suppose that a medical technician knowingly keeps a patient alive while the patient commits perjury. From knowing just that much about the case one has no warrant to infer that the technician has acted in a morally impermissible way. There are, of course, ways in which the technician's case is not parallel to God's—indeed, that is one of the consequences of the doctrine of divine conservation—but they do not affect a general point that emerges here. An agent's knowingly and voluntarily keeping another agent in existence while the other agent does something forbidden is just one way an agent can allow evil to occur. Some cases of allowing evil to occur are culpable, but some, like the medical technician's case, need not be. Until shown otherwise, a theist is entitled to assume that divine conservation, insofar as it allows evil to occur, is nonculpable. Nothing I have said here diminishes the seriousness of the problem of evil. But I do not think that divine conservation adds to the problem.

Space and Time

It is natural to suppose that the scope of creation includes all beings. There are two ubiquitous features about creation, however, that deserve special treatment, namely, space and time. Space and time seem not to be part of the cast of characters in the drama of creation, but rather more like the theater in which the drama unfolds. Were they then always just *there*, so to speak, waiting to receive creatures? Newton thought so: Newtonian absolute space and time exist in splendid indifference to the objects that might occupy them. Leibniz dissented from Newton's absolutist conception, maintaining that space and time are essentially relational. Instead of a Newtonian container, impervious to whatever its contents might be, think of space and time as a network constituted in its entirety by existing things and the spatial and temporal relations—relations like *above, between, to the left of, earlier than*—among the existing things. On Newton's view, God could have created the world so that it consisted solely of an infinitely extended space and time populated by nothing. On Leibniz's view, not even omnipotent God could have done that, any more than God could have created a nephew without an aunt or uncle. Relations cannot exist without their relata. Leibniz contended, in addition, that relations are "unreal," in the sense that attributions of relations holding among things reduce to or can be analyzed into properties inherent only in the things themselves. Thus, for Leibniz the existence of a spatiotemporal manifold requires that there be a plurality of things bearing spatiotemporal relations among themselves, and that the relations thereby borne are nothing over and above the properties inherent to the things (see Alexander 1956).

Theists need not choose sides on the issue of absolute versus relational space and time. It might seem initially as though Leibniz's view accommodates divine sovereignty more easily than Newton's. For on Leibniz's view, the creation of space and time is simply a by-product of the activity of creating a world of sufficient complexity to involve its creatures in spatiotemporal relations. But Newtonians can rejoin that God's sovereignty also extends to the creation of absolute space and time. Perhaps the most startling feature of the rejoinder is that, when combined with the thesis that time is infinitely extended—more precisely, the part of that thesis that maintains that time has no beginning—the rejoinder entails that God created something that has no beginning! But a similar result will follow on Leibniz's view for any Leibnizian who maintains that some created things have existed forever.

The doctrine of divine conservation may help to dispel some of the air of paradox. According to divine conservation, the only difference between creation and conservation is that "creation" applies to the divine activity that results in a thing's first coming into being and "conservation" applies to the divine activity that keeps the thing in existence once it has come into being. If some things, like Newtonian space and time, have no beginning, then they have been perpetually conserved; they just have no first coming-to-be. (Note that it would seem to be a consequence of divine conservation that if some things are beginningless and have been conserved at all times by God, then God must be infinitely old. I argue later that the inference is invalid.)

Contingent Truth

Let us say that a proposition is contingently true if it is true but might have been false. In the idiom of possible worlds, a contingently true proposition is one that is true in the actual world but false in some possible worlds. The Leibnizian imagery of God's choosing among the possible worlds extends God's creative sovereignty not only to creating and sustaining the actual world, but also to determining which world would be actual by his selecting which set of contingent propositions would become the set of contingently true propositions. Theists should have no qualms about much of this imagery. It grounds a theistic explanation for the phenomenon of "fine-tuning," that is, the observation that if the physical parameters had had virtually any other values than the ones they actually have, then a vastly different kind of universe, most likely to be inhospitable to life, would have existed. But other aspects of the Leibnizian imagery are more controversial. For centuries there has been a thriving cottage industry devoted to the problem of divine foreknowledge and future contingents: Does the set of contingent propositions selected by omniscient God include in it propositions specifying what his creatures would freely do in the future? Is it coherent to suppose both that God knowingly selected a world in which, say, the proposition *In 2020 Smith will cheat on her income taxes* is true and that Smith will cheat on her income taxes freely? If God selects a world in which that proposition is true, what role, if any, is left for Smith's selection? Compatibilists, philosophers who maintain that human freedom is compatible with determinism, will see no particular problem here: divine determination is just one kind of determination and not a kind of coercion. In contrast, libertarians, who insist that human freedom requires the absence of any kind of determination, will tend to stake out a class of propositions specifying free human decisions about which not even God knows the truth-values in advance. It is not the purpose of this essay to provide adequate treatment of the problem. It is more in this essay's ambit to ask a different question, one that concerns the very status of contingent propositions: Even if God gets to determine which contingent propositions will be true, who got to determine that the propositions were contingent?

Necessary Truth

Many philosophers have alleged that the necessary propositions stand apart from the contingent propositions. Necessarily true propositions are true and could not have been false. They are true in every possible world. Necessarily false propositions are false and could not have been true; they are false in every possible world. According to Leibniz, God surveyed all the infinitely many, infinitely diverse possible worlds in the process of selecting which world would be made actual by his creative choice. The imagery alone does not settle the issue of what God *saw* when he surveyed the possible worlds. Did God perceive that there were some propositions that just kept on coming up true in each possible world, some that always turned out false, and still others that were true in some worlds and false in others? This way of describing things suggests that God was a passive observer of the galaxy of possible worlds, able to single out one of them, to be sure, for creation, but not able to alter the modal status—contingent or necessary—of the propositions describing the worlds. Or was it rather that God's "seeing" the possible worlds was God's *determining* their structure, thereby conferring modal status on propositions?

The dichotomy of propositions, contingent versus necessary, is typically understood to be exclusive (no proposition is supposed to be both contingent and necessary) and exhaustive (no proposition is supposed to be neither). Philosophers as diverse as Descartes and Quine have, for reasons as diverse as the philosophers themselves, challenged the dichotomy. Quine regards the distinction as invidious, founded on bad metaphysics and having no more classificatory warrant than, say, the distinction between thoughts about the natural numbers and thoughts entertained on Tuesdays.

There is scholarly controversy about what Descartes' views on the subject are (see Curley 1984). There is one defensible interpretation, however, that goes like this. God's omnipotence extends even over what we call the necessary truths. God has it in his power, for example, to make the sum of 2 and 3 not equal to 5. On this interpretation, every proposition is, from the point of view of God's power, *metaphysically contingent*. Yet God also made us so that, given our cognitive constitution, it is *epistemically necessary* for us that $2 + 3 = 5$. That is, we are incapable of conceiving what it would be like for the sum of 2 and 3 not to equal 5. Inasmuch as every proposition is metaphysically contingent, God's power over what propositions would be true is not constrained in any way. The firm belief we creatures have that some truths could not have been otherwise than what they are is a consequence not of their metaphysical necessity—for there is no such thing—but rather of their epistemic necessity for us.

If Descartes' motivation is to make God master of the modal economy, then I think we must conclude that he has failed. For on the account just sketched, there remain metaphysical necessities over which God has no control. On this Cartesian account it is impossible even for omnipotent God to hold our present cognitive capacities fixed while enabling us to comprehend what it would be like for $2 + 3 \neq 5$. (An act of divine revelation could have the effect of warranting a person in believing that the sum of 2 and 3 could have been 7. But unless the revelation somehow enhances the believer's intellect, the believer is not equipped to know what it would be like for the proposition to be true.) The Cartesian account has another consequence that may be unsettling for many theists. If every proposition is metaphysically contingent, then propositions about God's nature are not exempt. To take examples, the propositions that God is omniscient, omnipotent (which, keep in mind, plays a central role in the present interpretation of Descartes' views), perfectly good, or even that God exists are at best contingently true. But, to anticipate discussion coming later in this essay, it has generally been taken to be a consequence of God's aseity that God's existence and nature are metaphysically necessary.

The Cartesian strategy of demoting all necessary truths to contingent truths thus comes with a cost. Perhaps it is a cost a theist would be willing to pay for securing an especially strong version of divine sovereignty. Perhaps not. There is another way of approaching the same issues that has its roots in the thought of Augustine. The Cartesian strategy appears to be founded on the unlimited power of God's will. What I call the Augustinian strategy takes as its point of departure the integrity of God's intellect. Plato had said that the Forms, abstract entities denoted by expressions like Justice, Beauty, and The Good (or Goodness Itself), are eternal, unchanging, perfect exemplars, which concrete things only deficiently resemble, and the objects on which objective knowledge depends. Augustine claimed to be merely following Plato's lead in locating the Forms in the mind of God (1982, 79–81). Augustine's move is an affirmation of God's sovereignty: if the Forms are God's thoughts or ideas, then their very existence depends on God's thinking them.

We can, I believe, embellish the Augustinian strategy by connecting the notion of Forms as divine thoughts to the notion of necessary truth. If they are to serve the function of grounding necessary truth, and thereby ensure the possibility of stable, objective knowledge as opposed to inconstant, wavering belief, the Forms, construed as divine ideas, must at a minimum be eternal objects of God's thinking. Particular triangles scrawled in the sand or on the blackboard come and go and may not (cannot?) have the sum of their interior angles quite equal to 180 degrees. But The Triangle Itself never ceases to exist or falls short of having its interior angles sum to 180 degrees. (Or at least this is true of The Euclidean Triangle Itself!) But it is not clear that God's eternally thinking of The Triangle is sufficient to explain why it is a necessary truth that its interior angles sum to 180 degrees. Even if we suppose that necessary truths are eternally true, it need not follow that eternal truths are necessarily true. We should not rule out of court the view that God knew "from eternity" that Adam would sin at such and such a time, yet that Adam's sinning was contingent.

The embellished Augustinian strategy proceeds by pointing out that omniscient God's "thinking" about The Triangle is actually God's having *comprehensive knowledge* of The Triangle. Such comprehensive knowledge entails knowing The Triangle's *essence*. Generalizing, we may say that each Form has an essence, a set of properties that the Form must have if it is to be the Form that it is. Many of the necessary truths, then, are propositions specifying the essential properties of the Forms. In knowing these propositions to be necessarily true, God knows, among other things, that he cannot have comprehensive knowledge of The Triangle without knowing that its interior angles necessarily sum to 180 degrees. To say God cannot comprehend The Triangle in any other way is not to point out a constraint on God's powers, but rather to say something about the rational structure of God's mind.

Let us see if we can make this notion more precise. The Augustinian strategy insists on three points. First, there are necessary truths. Second, the necessity of these truths entails that it is impossible even for God to alter them. Yet—this is the third point—these necessary truths depend on God's cognitive activity for their status. The apparent tension between the latter two claims can be alleviated by appealing to the notion of supreme rationality to explain the necessary truths rather than vice versa. The necessary truths are the deliverances of a supremely rational mind. Had this mind failed to exist, there would have been no necessary truths. Had this mind failed to have been supremely rational, there would be no explanation of necessity. Of course, the Augustinian strategy maintains that the proposition that supremely rational God exists is itself a necessary truth. What follows from this, on the Augustinian strategy, is that God is the explanation of his own existence. That consequence is an important part of a doctrine of God's aseity, to be discussed below.

Here are two final observations about the Augustinian strategy. First, although we launched it from a Platonic platform, the strategy can be redeployed without commitment to the existence of the Forms. We can, for example, replace reference to The Triangle with reference to genuine triangles. The Augustinian strategy delivers a theory about necessary truth dependent on supremely rational divine cognitive activity. Whether it is accurate to describe that activity as trafficking in Forms, ideas, or whatever is something about which we can remain agnostic. It may just be that these descriptions are human ways of gesturing to an activity that is otherwise literally incomprehensible to us. There is an additional benefit of freeing the strategy from the Forms. I said earlier that on the "Formal" version of the Augustinian strategy, *many* of the necessary truths are propositions specifying the essential properties of the Forms. It is hard to see how to extend the claim to *all* necessary truths. What about, for example, "God is omniscient"?

Many theists claim that it is a necessary truth. But on the Augustinian view itself, God is emphatically not a Form. If the Formal version does not provide a uniform account of necessary truth, if we must make exceptions to it, perhaps we should favor a version that does provide a uniform account.

Second, on the standard, modal-logical interpretation of necessity, necessary propositions are necessarily necessary and contingent propositions are necessarily contingent. That is, on the standard interpretation, every proposition has its modal status fixed necessarily. If one supposes that necessity is to be explained by supremely rational divine activity, this modal-logical result is not unwelcome.

Summing Up

We have examined conceptions of divine sovereignty that have become progressively more ambitious. We began with the thesis of creation ex nihilo, according to which matter has no independent, primordial existence. We then observed that the doctrine of divine conservation extends creatures' dependence on God over moment-to-moment continued existence. We noted briefly that on either an absolutist or relational theory of space and time, these features too can be regarded as dependent on God. We raised the issue of whether God is responsible for the truth-values of all contingent propositions. Finally, we examined two versions of the thesis that God is responsible for the modal status of all propositions. The Cartesian strategy makes all propositions contingent and subject to God's omnipotence. The Augustinian strategy preserves the distinction between contingent and necessary propositions while subsuming them all under God's rational comprehension.

My guess is that thoughtful theists will converge on the doctrines of creation and conservation and be willing to extend them to space and time. They may diverge on the issue of whether God is responsible for the truth-values of *all* propositions, primarily because different and controverted conceptions of human freedom are at stake. Finally, many of them will regard the issue of God's relation to the modal economy with some indifference, not feeling strongly partisan about the Cartesian or Augustinian strategies. On all of these topics I suspect that theists will find no threat for God's status as personal.

ASEITY

The impulse to ascribe some sort of aseity to the object of one's worship has an understandable basis. Ordinary things and people can be distressingly fragile, vulnerable, inconstant, ephemeral. There are degrees: Everest is more stable and secure than a mayfly. We know, nonetheless, that even Everest's life span is finite. We know that because we know that our planet's life span is finite. We know our planet's life span is finite because we know our sun's life span is finite. And so it goes.

Theists have insisted that a God worthy of worship be exempt from these sorts of vicissitudes. God is "from everlasting to everlasting." Nothing can prevail against him. He is supposed to be equally stable and steadfast in his resolve, not subject to growth, decay, alteration, whim, or change of plan. As Xenophanes put it, "Always he remains in the same state, in no way changing." The philosophical exploration of these sentiments yields a doctrine whose main contours are captured by theses (C)–(E).

Historical Dependency and Contemporaneous Vulnerability

Let us consider (C) and (D) in tandem. Dependency relations can be historical or contemporaneous. To take a historical example first: for species that reproduce by sexual means, an offspring organism owes its being the organism it is to its parents. "Being the organism it is" can be understood in two ways. In the first, an organism's being the *kind* of organism it is depends on the kind of organism its parents were. In the second, if identity of genotype is a necessary condition for an organism's being *this* individual rather than some other individual of the same species, then *this* individual organism owes its existence to the historical event of *that* particular sperm cell meeting *that* particular egg.

Theists will insist that there are no historical dependency relations to God's existence. Greek myth provides Zeus with an ancestry, but nothing is supposed to correspond to that with God. Nor do there appear to be any other kinds of historical relations on which God depends. But if God's existence has no pedigree, it is hard to see how what God is, or God's nature, could depend historically on anything either.

Turn now to contemporaneous dependency relations. Creatures with lungs depend presently on an atmosphere rich in oxygen for their continued existence. Because the presence of an atmosphere depends on the mass of the planet, creatures with lungs also presently depend on the Earth's continuing to have sufficient mass. Here again theists will claim that there are no conditions or states on which God depends for his continuing to exist. There is no Kryptonite that can make God vulnerable, no cosmic spinach God must consume in order to save the universe's Olive Oyls from the clutches of the universe's Blutos.

Structural and Contentful Dependency

A persistent critic might concede that there are no *vulnerability* conditions on which God is dependent but insist that God is subject nevertheless to *structural* and *contentful* dependency relations. Here is one way to understand the critic's point. Many philosophers agree, partly or fully, with Locke about the identity of persons. Hardly anyone will demur from Locke's characterization of a person as "a thinking intelligent Being, that has reason and reflection, and can consider it self as it self, the same thinking thing in different times and places" (1700/1975, 335). Locke's conception of a person attributes a partial structure to a person's mind by ascribing to it some essential capacities, such as the capacities for reason, self-awareness, and memory. Somewhat more controversial is Locke's criterion for a person's identity through time. Locke thought that a person's identity through time was a function of the person's experiential memory. Roughly, x and y are the same person at different times if and only if x remembers experiencing something that y experienced. What is experienced and hence what is remembered can vary enormously among persons without the variation compromising their status as persons. Thus, Locke's theory of personal identity provides ample room for the ascription of diverse mental content to persons. Of course, one does not need to accept Locke's theory to believe we have all sorts of diverse mental content. Persons, then, have parts or components that are structurally essential to their being persons, but they also have mental states that are accidental to their being persons.

The persistent critic's point is this. Theists insist that God is personal. In fact, for theists, God would appear to pass Locke's criteria for personhood with flying colors. If so, then God must have those capacities that are essential to persons, including the capacities for reasoning, self-awareness, remembering, and—some items not mentioned by Locke but items that theists will not want to deny— capacities for perceptual awareness and willing. Now, there is a powerful psychological theory to the effect that these capacities, or the modules that serve them, are informationally encapsulated; that is, they operate on specific domains of input and in relative isolation from each other (see Fodor 1983). It follows, says the persistent critic, that God's mind is internally structured, consisting of a suite of diverse mental faculties on which God depends essentially in order to be the being he is.

Finally, here is the persistent critic's case for God's having accidental mental states that are dependent on the way the world is. Pick any contingent fact about the created world, say, that it rained last night. An omniscient God must know this fact. Part of the content of God's mind, then, is dependent on the fact that it rained last night. The example can be generalized to every contingent fact.

Simplicity and Modularity

To examine the case of structural dependency first: if God's mind were structured by informationally encapsulated modules, then some parts of God's mental activity would be opaque to other parts. Perhaps the highest level of divine consciousness, where all the information streams converge, could take in all the modular activity. The modules themselves, however, would remain relatively blinkered. Such opacity may be part of the human condition, but many theists would resist applying to God's mental activity the imagery of corporate structure, with underlings functioning on a need-to-know basis.

Aquinas and others articulated a view that is consistent with the modularity thesis about human minds yet denies the application of the thesis to God's mind. For present purposes we can single out one element of the view. It is the claim that there is no diversity of modules or "faculties" that structures the divine mind. Consider the augmented list constructed from Locke's characterization of a person: reason, self-awareness, memory, perceptual awareness, and will. Focus initially on perceptual awareness, self-awareness, and will. In humans, perceptual awareness of the created world requires the possession of the right kinds of healthy, functioning, physical organs operating in the right sorts of physical environment. If God is a spiritual being, then however God acquires awareness of creation, it cannot be in virtue of possessing the right kinds of physical receptors functioning in an environment to which they are adapted. Suppose, instead, that God is aware of all of creation simply in virtue of having created it. God knew every detail of the world he would select and knows that he has selected it. The kind of awareness that God would thus have is immediate; in having complete cognitive access to himself, God is aware of the world. Perceptual awareness and self-awareness are two separate faculties in humans, but in God, what we call perceptual awareness is subsumed under divine self-understanding.

The next step is to connect self-understanding to the will. Nothing could be clearer than that in the case of humans, what we understand about ourselves often conflicts with what we want. An integrated personality would be one in which desires and self-knowledge are in harmony. Theists presume that such integration is enjoyed by God. The more radical step is not merely to assume that whatever God understands, God wills, and vice versa, but to claim that in God, self-understanding and will are not two distinguishable modules or faculties. God's "will" is perfectly rational and God's "understanding" is perfectly voluntary; better yet, *God* is perfectly rational and voluntary, a being whose unimaginably rich mental life is lived in complete, unfragmented transparency. Theists will no doubt continue to describe God's activity in terms of belief-desire psychology, but that vocabulary is based on, and better suited for describing, compartmentalized human minds.

I cannot explore the issues more fully here, but what we have just encountered is one aspect of a doctrine about God's *simplicity*. The core of the doctrine is the principle that inasmuch as complexity is a source of fragility and dependence, a perfect being must be perfectly noncomplex (see Aquinas 1948, 1: 14–20). The aspect of divine simplicity deployed above denies modularity to God's mind. We will never know exactly what Xenophanes meant, but this denial may be what he was struggling to express when he said of God that "he sees as a whole, he thinks as a whole, and he hears as a whole."

We deferred discussion of reason and memory. To put it in a way calculated to shock, the campaign against divine modularity denies that God has reason. Here is why. Distinguish reason from understanding, reserving the latter term for the capacity to simply grasp or "see" some truth without inferring it from other truths. You and I understand that $2 + 2 = 4$; perhaps you but certainly not I understand that $789 + 987 = 1776$. In contrast, reason is a discursive practice, passing from premises to conclusion by the canons of either deductive logic, inductive logic, or decision theory.

Because God's intuitive understanding of all things is maximal, God has no need of reason. (Of course, God's understanding of the principles of discursive reasoning is also perfect. One need not be a soccer player to know the rules of the game.)

That leaves memory. I propose to defer discussion of it a bit longer.

Simplicity and Accidental Properties

The persistent critic's second claim is that the contents of God's mind include every contingent fact, knowledge of which God must have in order to qualify as omniscient. *Knowing that it rained last night*, for example, is one of tremendously many accidental properties that God has. The persistent critic's claim is that God's mind is both complex in virtue of hosting an (infinite?) number of accidental properties and dependent on the world as source of those properties.

We have already caught a glimpse of how one might respond to the dependency claim if one espouses a doctrine of divine simplicity. Knowledge of the world is part of God's self-awareness, and God's self-awareness and will are not two separate things. The critic's dependency claim appears to rest on the assumption that as things are for us, so they are for God. We are *consumers* of knowledge about the world, standing as recipients on many causal chains, beginning with situations in the world and ending with states of our minds. God, in contrast, is a *producer* of knowledge. The ordinary causal flow from thing known to knower is reversed in God's case. If God's understanding the fact that it rained last night is God's will that it rained last night, then the divine noetic/volitional activity is the cause of the fact; the fact is not the cause of the activity (see Mann 1985).

Even if we accept all this, the critic may persist, will it not be true that to be omniscient, God's mind must be characterized by a host of accidental properties? Only if we accept the inference from "God knows the contingent fact that *p*" to "God exemplifies the accidental property of *knowing that p*." The inference is easy enough to resist. At the same time, it is easy to see the attractiveness of the related inference from "Jones knows that *p*" to "Jones exemplifies the accidental property of *knowing that p*." As the etymology suggests, an accidental property is a property that a thing acquires per accidens, a modification of the thing brought about by the workings of some other thing. Jones knows that it rained last night because he saw it raining, or saw that the streets were wet this morning, or read about it in the newspaper. In each case Jones's knowledge is caused, directly or indirectly, by the fact. Given this account of accidental propertihood in terms of causal dependency, we have seen reason to think that God has no accidental properties. To put it in other terms, the doctrine of God's simplicity, together with a causal conception of an accidental property, entails that God has no such properties.

Simplicity and Eternality

Now to take up the case of memory. Never lacking in persistence, our critic bids us consider the following dilemma. "Even the supercharged sort of self-awareness that God is supposed to enjoy—no self-deception, complete transparency of self to self—is, strictly speaking, a second-order monitoring capacity of God's *present* mental states. That is, by means of self-awareness God can perceive only what is occurring in his mind now. Surely a being could have self-awareness and yet lack memory. Memory is not so much a monitoring capacity as a storage-and-retrieval capacity. Thus, if God has memory in addition to self-awareness, then the thesis that God's mind is nonmodular is false. But if God lacks memory, then the only knowledge God can have of the past is by way of retrodictive inference from present states of the world, or of God's mind, to past states. You may suppose, if you like, that God has time-indexed representations of all past events presently open to his omnicompetent gaze, much as a person might have an album of dated photographs open on a coffee table. To suppose this, however, is to concede that a memoryless God's knowledge of the past is inferential, *from* the representations *to* the past events as the best explanation for the existence and content of the representations. Retrodiction, however, is a kind of discursive reasoning that is incompatible with God's alleged simplicity. Thus, if God lacks memory, then either God is not omniscient or God is not simple."

Let us approach this issue by first recalling the motivation behind the ascription of simplicity to God. God must be noncomplex, having no components or parts, because if God had parts then God would be dependent on those parts.

Begin by taking the notion of part in its most familiar sense. Theists believe that God has no physical or material parts. Because the physical is bound so tightly with space, theists are disinclined to attribute spatial dimensions to God. At the same time, it is important to theists to be able to say that God is *at* or present to various regions of space, indeed, all of them. As Xenophanes put it, it is "not fitting" for God "to go now here now there"; not fitting, because God already *is* here *and* there. Theists have insisted, moreover, that however this notion of divine spatial presence is to be understood—here we might expect the thesis of divine conservation to elucidate the notion—it does not entail that only a part of God is in one place and another part in another. It is, rather, that God is present as a whole, in his entirety, at every spatial region (see Augustine 1960, 85).

Can a parallel case be made for God's relation to time? To be parallel, the case would have to exhibit two features. Just as God is everywhere, so God is *everywhen*, that is, there is no instant of time at which God is absent. If time is infinitely extended, having no beginning or end, then God has a beginningless and endless life. But suppose that time is not infinitely extended. Suppose, as some theories in physical cosmology maintain, that there was a first moment of time, or that there will be a last moment. Are we then to conclude that God's life is finitely circumscribed?

A theist who holds a reasonably strong version of God's sovereignty will remind us that time, as a feature of creation, depends for its existence on God, not vice versa. For such a theist it should not be the case that questions about the character of God's life depend for their answers on the nature of time, any more than they depend for their answers on the nature of space. That God is everywhen is the first of the two features necessary to construct an account of time parallel to the theist's account of space. The second is that God in his entirety is present at every instant of time. It is not the case that one temporal part or stage of God is present at one moment of time and another at another. Ordinary creatures live their lives successively, one moment at a time, passing from past to present to future. God, in contrast, lives his life comprehensively, taking in all of a creation that may be infinitely extended in time in one simultaneous act of comprehension. Taken together, the two features, everywhenness plus comprehensiveness, yield a doctrine about God's *eternality*, or mode of existence in eternity, defined by Bo-ethius as "the complete possession all at once of illimitable life" (1973, 422; see Stump and Kretzmann 1981, 431).

The doctrine of God's eternality comports nicely with the doctrine of God's simplicity. Simplicity rules out temporal parts or stages. Eternality emphasizes that "*x* has no temporal parts or stages" does not entail "*x* exists for only an instant." A theist, armed with the doctrine of God's eternality, now can reply to the persistent critic's dilemma concerning God's memory. Memory is a faculty only of time-bound creatures. The theist can cheerfully agree that God has no memory because nothing that has happened is past to God. All is present—literally *pres-*

ent—before God, with no confusion, even so, about what events in creation are temporally earlier than, later than, or simultaneous with other events. And the doctrine of God's eternality comports well with scripture: God is not merely everlasting, but from everlasting to everlasting.

Divine Freedom

The final thesis of our quintet, (E), claims that God is perfectly free. At a minimum, we would expect a perfectly free being to be utterly unconstrained. Nothing should be able to defeat or thwart such a being's activities or plans. When we reflect on this point, we may come to think that the threat to God's freedom comes not from without but from within. No creature or ensemble of creatures can prevail over God, as Zeus prevailed over Kronos. But might there not be features about God's own nature that place constraints on what God can do? I shall not attempt to canvass all the different forms this question might take. I propose instead to look at one salient case, hoping that its discussion provides insights about how to respond to related cases.

What latitude of choice did God have in creating? We can divide this question into two: Could God have refrained from creating at all? and Given that God decided to create something, must God create the best world that he can? There are four possible combinations of answers to these questions. (1) Yes, God could have refrained altogether from creating, but yes, if God has decided to create, then God must create the best possible world he can. (2) Yes, God could have refrained from creating and no, if God has decided to create something, he need not create the best world he can. (3) No, God could not have refrained from creating, and yes, God must create the best possible world he can. (4) No, God could not have refrained from creating, but no, God need not create the best world that he can. Although I do not document it here, I believe that each position has had its advocates, and that the advocates have not taken their respective positions to pose any problem for God's freedom. For present purposes, let us focus on position (3), as it appears to be the one whose acceptance would delimit God's freedom more than the others.

How can position (3) be reconciled with maximal divine freedom? Consider the first half of (3). There are clearly cases in which we say that a particular person could not have refrained from performing some action. Jill had to participate in the bank robbery because her family was being held hostage. Gil had to shoplift because he is a kleptomaniac. Jill's case is an example of external compulsion: some agency other than Jill compels her to do what she would not otherwise do.

The source of Gil's compulsive behavior is within Gil. What makes Gil's behavior a case of kleptomania is that Gil has a desire to steal that, at the moment of theft, overrides Gil's other desires, notably Gil's second-order desire not to have a desire to steal. In the conflict between first-order desire and second-order desire, the first-order desire triumphs. It is useful to contrast Gil's situation with Will's, who is, let us say, a *kleptophiliac*. Will has a desire to steal but, unlike Gil, Will has a second-order desire to maintain and nourish his first-order desire to steal. Gil would like to disown his first-order desire, while Will cheerfully endorses his. Setting aside further fictional elaboration about how Will came to acquire the desires he has, we can say that Will's thievery is more lamentable yet freer than Gil's. In particular, those theists who want to blame much of the world's evil on human misuse of freedom will deny the claim that because Will's thievery is wrong, it must be unfree.

If God is omnipotent, he cannot be subject to external compulsion. Thus, God's choosing to create cannot be like Jill's "choosing" to participate in a bank robbery. But perhaps there is something in the structure of God's desires that makes him a compulsive creator? If God's creative activity were to be labeled compulsive, there would have to be a conflict between a first-order desire to create and a second-order desire not to have that first-order desire, and the first-order desire would have to drive God's behavior. God would have to be in relevant respects like Gil, not Will.

Theists are entirely within their rights to suppose that no such conflict characterizes the divine mind, for a conflict of desires betokens an imperfectly integrated personality. But in arguing for the lack of compulsion in God, have theists left room for one of (3)'s distinctive claims, that God could not have refrained from creating? A defender of (3) must suppose that the uncoerced desire to create flows from God's self-transparent, self-ordered, and self-endorsed nature. That nature includes—or *is*—perfect goodness. A defender of (3) is likely to follow the steps first taken by Plato, maintaining that a good being must want to share its goodness with others. But others have to exist in order to share in this goodness. Thus, a perfectly good being must have the desire to create (see Plato 1997, 1236). The desire is an entailment of God's nature; the desire along with the nature are freely embraced by their possessor.

The other part of position (3) maintains that if God creates, then God must create the best world he can. This part of (3) presupposes that there is a best world God can create. One might suppose, given God's omnipotence, that the best world God can create is in fact the best of all possible worlds. It would take us too far afield to probe these suppositions. The question more directly before position (3) is this: Can God be free if God must choose the best?

In response, an advocate of (3) can develop the following line. Suppose that Antonio has the skill and resources to make violins of unsurpassable sonority and beauty. Suppose that the investment of time, energy, and resources is the same whether Antonio makes a superb or a mediocre violin. Suppose further that Antonio is under no special obligation to anyone concerning what sort of violin he will make, and that Antonio bears no malice toward the potential owner of the violin he will make. Suppose even further that there is no greater good that could have been realized had Antonio refrained from violin making. Suppose finally that Antonio knows all this. In the teeth of all these suppositions, Antonio nevertheless produces a mediocre violin. How do we explain Antonio's performance?

Antonio displays weakness of will, or knowing the good but failing to do it. Plato found such cases so unintelligible that he declared them impossible: any agent who fails to do the good must be lacking a relevant item of knowledge. We may not be persuaded by Plato's thesis as a piece of human psychology. It seems more attractive, however, as a thesis of divine psychology. For how could omnipotent God lack the willpower to do what omniscient, perfectly good God sees is the best thing to do? So if God creates, he not only will but must create the best, as the second half of (3) maintains. Any being who could create a suboptimal world would not be essentially omniscient, omnipotent, and perfectly good God. To finish the story, a defender of (3) can remind us that the necessity involved here has its source entirely in God's own uncompelled, unconflicted nature.

Recall that our strategy was to show that an advocate of (3) can plausibly advance an argument for God's maximal freedom, not because of some belief that (3) is the most acceptable position, but because (3) is the position that raises most pointedly questions about God's freedom. I am inclined to doubt, for example, that there is a best possible world or a best creatable world. Perhaps for any world God can create, there is a better world God can create, ad infinitum. If this is so, it need not be a source of limitation or frustration for God. If possible worlds just are the infinite possibilities that God entertains, then to complain that God cannot find a best among them would be finding fault with unlimited vision or imagination.

Summing Up

Most theists will agree that God depends historically and contemporaneously on nothing. There are more ambitious versions of God's aseity. One of them maintains that God's mind is not modular: what we call God's understanding and God's will, for example, are not two things in God but the same thing described vagariously by finite minds that *are* modular. Another holds that given an independently attractive conception of an accidental property, God does not have and thus does not depend on any accidental properties. Yet another claims that God's life does not depend on the occupancy of space or the passage of time. Finally, we have looked at an argument to the effect that God can be maximally free even if he must create and must create the best.

Reasonable theists can wrangle philosophically about some of these dimensions of aseity. Some of those quarrels will, I suspect, begin with the question, Do we really need to think that God is independent in *that* respect? Is it really important, for example, to think that God has no accidental properties? Here I will end with an observation and a wager. Importance is relative to a purpose. It may be important to one's philosophy, but it is not likely to be important to one's salvation that one have the right view about accidental properties. And I wager that whatever flaws there may be with some of these dimensions of aseity, they cannot be faulted for depicting God as less than fully personal.

NOTE

Earlier versions of this paper benefited from comments from Hugh McCann and William J. Wainwright.

WORKS CITED

Alexander, H. G., ed. 1956. *The Leibniz-Clarke Correspondence.* Manchester, England: Manchester University Press.

Aquinas, Thomas. 1948. *Summa Theologica.* 5 vols. Westminster, Md.: Christian Classics.

Augustine. 1960. *The Confessions of St. Augustine.* Garden City, N.Y.: Image Books.

———. 1982. *Eighty-Three Different Questions.* Vol. 70 of *The Fathers of the Church.* Washington, D.C.: Catholic University of America Press.

Barnes, Jonathan. 1979. *The Presocratic Philosophers.* 2 vols. London: Routledge & Kegan Paul.

Boethius. 1973. *Tractates, De Consolatione Philosophiae.* Cambridge, Mass.: Harvard University Press.

Curley, Edwin M. 1984. "Descartes on the Creation of the Eternal Truths." *Philosophical Review* 93: 569–97.

Fodor, Jerry A. 1983. *The Modularity of Mind.* Cambridge, Mass.: MIT Press.

Locke, John. [1700] 1975. *An Essay Concerning Human Understanding.* Oxford: Clarendon Press.

Mann, William E. 1985. "Epistemology Supernaturalized." *Faith and Philosophy* 2: 436–56.

Plato. 1997. *Complete Works.* Indianapolis: Hackett.

Quinn, Philip L. 1983. "Divine Conservation, Continuous Creation, and Human Action." In *The Existence and Nature of God,* ed. Alfred J. Freddoso, 55–79. Notre Dame, Ind.: University of Notre Dame Press.

Stump, Eleonore, and Norman Kretzmann. 1981. "Eternity." *Journal of Philosophy* 78: 429–58.

FOR FURTHER READING

Helm, Paul. 1988. *Eternal God.* Oxford: Clarendon Press.

Leftow, Brian. 1991. *Time and Eternity.* Ithaca, N.Y.: Cornell University Press.

Mann, William E. 1982. "Divine Simplicity." *Religious Studies* 18: 451–71.

———. 1997. "Necessity." In *A Companion to Philosophy of Religion,* ed. Philip L. Quinn and Charles Taliaferro, 264–70. Oxford: Blackwell.

CHAPTER 3

NONTHEISTIC CONCEPTIONS OF THE DIVINE

PAUL J. GRIFFITHS

THAT there are nontheistic conceptions of the divine is at first sight a puzzling idea. To call something "divine" is, after all, just to call it God, or at least to place it in close proximity to God; the etymology of the word (Latin *divus/deus*; Sanskrit *deva*) shows this connection, too. And "nontheistic" is derived from the Greek *theos*, which is just the word ordinarily translated into Latin as *deus*, both of which, in English, become "God." In the Nicene Creed, for example, recited in Christian churches all over the world every week, the English phrase "We [or 'I'; the Greek and Latin versions differ on this] believe in one God" renders the Greek *pisteuomen eis hena theon* and the Latin *credo in unum deum*. To speak of non-theistic conceptions of the divine is therefore a bit like speaking of nonpolitical understandings of the state: if not quite an oxymoron, at least a close approach to one.

Perhaps, however, we need not be hamstrung by etymology. In thinking about what a nontheistic conception of the divine might be, we can begin by stipulating that a theistic conception of the divine will be any understanding that takes God to be a person whose names include a good number of the following: creator, redeemer, sanctifier, lover, knower, holy one, powerful one, eternal one. Most such understandings will be Jewish, Christian, or Islamic; they will have been developed within the vast complex of thought and practice that takes itself to be identifying and thinking about the God who called Abraham to leave the land of his fathers for the promised land. But not all will. Some Indian thinkers named God in some or all of these ways (Ramanuja, who flourished in the early twelfth century, provides a classical example) and did so without knowledge of anything Jewish, Christian, or Islamic. For the most part, though, if we define theistic conceptions of the divine in this way they will be broadly Abrahamic.

On this understanding of theism, a conception of the divine is nontheistic precisely to the extent that it departs from this tradition of naming the divine. Such departure might be explicit and self-conscious; this would be so when a thinker reacts against theistic naming and tries to do better by replacing it with something different. But it might also occur as part of a tradition to which theistic naming is largely or entirely unknown. This way of approaching the question does not yield a set of necessary and sufficient conditions for the discrimination of theistic from nontheistic conceptions of the divine, but it does provide a point of entry and a rough-and-ready means for such discrimination, and this will suffice for the purposes of this chapter.

Nontheistic conceptions of the divine could be classified and discussed in many ways. One approach would be to construct a typology of possible nontheistic understandings, but this would be tedious and not terribly useful. A second approach—the one followed here—would collect some representative instances of nontheistic understandings of the divine and would comment on the concepts and argumentative strategies that inform them. Because most theistic understandings of the divine will be related in one way or another to Judaism, Christianity, or Islam, it will be easiest and most useful for purposes of contrast to take the examples from traditions of thought and practice largely or completely uninfluenced by the concepts familiar to these Abrahamic religions. This is what I shall do. The Sanskrit religious and philosophical literature of India provides a vast and rich set of resources for studying conceptions of and arguments about the divine that are historically independent (for the most part) of those to be found in the Greek, Arabic, and Latin literature of the Mediterranean world. Naturally, no systematic survey of the understandings of the divine to be found in the Indian literature will be offered, and nothing at all will be said about the literature of China, Korea, Japan, and so forth. My goal is only to offer some examples that will illustrate the range of Indian thought about the divine (about what is taken to be maximally and finally significant) and to indicate the problems and trajectories of thought they suggest for philosophers of religion.

It is important to note that philosophy of religion as understood in this volume is a largely Christian enterprise. Its problems, concepts, and methods are products of peculiarly Christian commitments and a specifically Christian history, and its agenda is driven by these commitments and this history even when those doing work in the field are not themselves Christian or are opposed to Christianity. This goes far to explain why resources that pose the question of how to understand what is maximally and finally significant from outside the Christian tradition have yet to find a significant place in philosophy of religion. Such resources are increasingly being made available in English (I mention some of them in the bibliography attached to this chapter), and there are some signs that these resources are beginning to be paid more attention by philosophers of religion; it is to be expected that this will increasingly be so as the discipline matures. The Christian nature of philosophy of religion explains, too, the approach of this chapter (and of the volume): Christian concepts and methods provide the norm against which alien concepts and methods are measured. This could be different: if Buddhist or Vedantin concepts and methods were the yardstick, and Christian ones measured by them, we would have essays on such topics as non-Buddhist conceptions of the divine and on the relation between compassion and emptiness. This is only to note what is inevitable: that the philosophy of religion is shaped by its history and should make no pretense at transcending or escaping it.

THE DIVINE TEXT

Some Indian thinkers, especially those connected with what has come to be called the Mimamsa school (the term means, literally, intense thought or investigation), took the Veda, a Sanskrit text, to be maximally, finally, and unsurpassably significant—to be, that is, divine. This, at first blush, is clearly a nontheistic conception of the divine, and one that cries out for elucidation.

More precisely and fully: some Indian thinkers came to understand a particular set of Sanskrit vocables as eternal and authorless and as a sustaining feature of the universe, a feature without which an ordered universe could not continue to exist and without which coherent human thought could not occur. These vocables, moreover, contain a set of injunctions to action—typically, but not only, to sacrificial action—whose proper performance is essential to the maintenance of the order of the universe. Finally, the vocables in question are not written objects, not graphs on paper or palm leaf. They are, rather, vibrations in the air; their written representations are helps to the memory, aids to the possibility of vocalization, but are not themselves the sacred sounds.

Such a view raises a number of questions. Among the more important (and certainly the more widely discussed by the adherents and opponents of this view in India) of these are the following. First, there is the question of the extent and accessibility of the text in question: What are its boundaries and how may it be heard, chanted, or, less desirably, read? Second, there is the question of interpretation of the Sanskrit sentences that make up the text: if these sentences command actions on whose proper performance the order of the universe depends, it will be important to know what those commands are, which means that it will be important to be able to interpret the sentences that contain them. Third, there is the very idea of an eternal and authorless text in what appears to be a natural language: Does such an idea make sense, and if it does, what kind of sense does it make? Fourth, even if the idea does make some sense, is there any reason to think it true?

The Veda's proper boundary is a matter of debate among those who take it to be eternal and uncreated. A minimalist understanding claims that the term "Veda" denotes only the collections of hymns and songs called *Rgveda*. This corpus runs to a thousand pages in printed editions and consists mostly of hymns of praise to various gods and other nonhuman beings. But some think that the Veda also includes other material, including further collections of hymns, magical spells, (prose) instruction as to the proper performance and meaning of certain ritual actions, meditations on such things as the nature of the person, the events that befall us after death, and even discussions of such technical matters as grammar and etymology. Defining the Veda's limits is typically a polemical matter; including some matter excluded by others is usually itself an element in an argument about orthodoxy, orthopraxy, or both. But however the boundaries are drawn, defenders of the Veda's eternity and authorlessness think of it as a collection of chants rather than as a written text, and therefore take access to it to be had by ear rather than by eye. This is why the Veda is called *sruti*, "that which is heard." The syllables in which it consists are memorized by certain members of the priestly (Brahminical) classes, and in order that they may be preserved without variation (as, for the most part, they seem to have been for considerably more than two thousand years), a complex system of checks and balances is built into the system of memorization. It is still possible to hear groups of small boys (always boys: memorizing the Veda is a male prerogative) in India being drilled in these methods of memorization and recitation.

Taking a text's vocables to be an eternal and authorless part of the order of things, and thinking also that the act of chanting them, as well as the performance of what they instruct, contributes to and is perhaps a necessary condition for the continuation of that order raises and presses the question of interpretation. Coming to understand what the words and sentences of such a text mean will be among the most important of tasks, and one to which a great deal of energy will naturally be devoted by those who hold the view. This was indeed the case among Mimamsakas (adherents of the Mimamsa) in India. They developed, it is not too much to say, an entire theory of language, meaning, and interpretation under the conceptual pressure of having to account for—and to provide an account of—the language of the Veda. It is not quite that a decision about the Veda's eternality and authorlessness came first and was then followed by a theory of language and meaning, as dough rises after yeast has been added. It is rather that as each of the two central Mimamsa ideas—the eternality and intrinsic authoritativeness of sound (*sabdanityatva, sabdapramanya*), on the one hand, and the authorlessness (*apauruseyatva*) of the Veda, on the other—gained precision and complexity, it demanded a corresponding development in the other so that each influenced the other by way of a feedback loop, or (to borrow a Christian metaphor) a circumincession. The result was a metaphysic and a semantics of great complexity of which only the barest sketch can be offered here. Concepts in the religious register often have this kind of fruitful focusing effect on thought: just as the idea of God has focused the conceptual attention of Christians on topics as diverse as the logic of possibility and necessity and the nature of free will, so the idea of the Veda concentrated the attention of Indian thinkers on language, meaning, and the art of interpretation.

The term "sound" (*sabda*) denotes, to a first approximation, meaning-bearing utterance. This is, for Kumarila, the greatest systematizer of Mimamsa thought (he probably flourished in the seventh century), intrinsically authoritative, which is to say naturally productive of knowledge on the part of those who hear and understand it. Meaning-bearing utterance, testimony as we might call it, stands in no need of appeal to any other belief-forming practice in order to have its own reliability justified or demonstrated. In this it is like sensory perception or reasoning: these, too, are understood to be practices whose reliability as producers of true beliefs in those who use them stands in no need of justification by appeal to practices outside themselves. Mimamsakas, like many other Indian thinkers who devoted themselves to this topic (an essentially epistemological one), were concerned about the paradoxes of infinite regress which they thought would rapidly and inevitably follow if intrinsic reliability or authoritativeness were not permitted to some belief-forming practices.

There are, no doubt, some difficulties here, but among them is not the obvious objection that this position means that sabda is always and necessarily productive of true beliefs in those who hear it. This is not so, of course, and the Mimamsakas acknowledged and thematized the fact by analyzing the faults to which testimony may be subject. These are many, but they are all related in one way or another to the use of testimony by fallible (usually human) agents. We may lie, misunderstand, be inattentive, and so forth, and when any of these lapses occurs, testimony fails, which is to say that meaning-bearing utterance does not produce true beliefs. The important point for considering the sabda in which the Veda consists, of course, is that its sounds have no human (or any other) agent involved in their creation, and as a result are necessarily free from all the errors to which testimony can be subject. The argument is simple: if testimony fails, this is only because of a failure in the agent; if there is no agential failure, then there is no testimonial failure. One important result of denying that the Veda is authored, then, is that it is thereby insulated from the possibility of failing as testimony. It becomes supremely and completely reliable—indeed, error-free—just because of its apauruseyatva, its property of not having been authored or in any other way produced by an agent. The Veda may, of course, fail to communicate truth or to command and bring about what ought to be done by being misunderstood. But this is an imperfection only in those who hear or read it, not an imperfection in the Veda itself.

This view of the Veda's infallibility and inerrancy may helpfully be contrasted with views about textual infallibility held by Jews (about the Tanakh), Christians (about the Bible), and Muslims (about the Quran). Christian views are the furthest from the Mimamsa on this matter. Even the strongest Christian views about the inerrancy of the biblical text do not attribute this inerrancy to any particular set of syllables (or vocables) in a natural language. Rather, they attribute it to what the text says, to its semantic content. This is because Christians have always encouraged translation of the text, and have then treated the translated text as of equal authority with that from which the translation was made. It follows from this that the authority of the text does not reside in any particular set of Hebrew or Greek syllables, but rather in what these syllables are taken to mean. The authority of the Bible, too, is founded on the fact that it is the word of God, which means that it has an agent as its author, something that, from the Mimamsa point of view, introduces the possibility of error. Jewish views of the authority of the Hebrew text of the Tanakh are closer to Mimamsa views of the text of the Veda, because for most Orthodox Jews (and for most of the rabbinic interpreters of that text), translations of the Hebrew do not have its authority: what counts precisely is the syllables of the Hebrew. This is also the case for Islamic views of the Arabic text of the Quran. But in both these cases, the text has no significance independent of its author, who is God. The closest approach among the Abrahamic religions to a Mimamsa view of textual authority is probably to be found among Kabbalists, for some of whom the very Hebrew syllables of the Tanakh are part of the order of the universe, and may even be thought to be so independent of the fact that God spoke them.

Mimamsa thinkers were aware that some in India wished to ground the authority of the Veda on its authorship by an omniscient being, which would be to make the Veda God's work, and thus to approach Jewish and Christian views. But they consistently and argumentatively rejected any such view. For them, the idea of an omniscient agent was incoherent, and in the arguments back and forth about this (mostly between them and the Buddhists, some of whom thought of the Buddha as omniscient), most of the difficulties familiar in Christian discussions about the matter were raised. Mimamsakas did not think that any agent could have knowledge of the future, for example, and that even if, per impossibile, there were an omniscient agent, it would be impossible for a nonomniscient agent to know this fact. Objections were raised, that is, to both the possibility of omniscience and to its knowability even if it were possible. More fundamentally, of course, Mimamsakas objected to the thought that the Veda might have an author because they took this to mean that it might be erroneous in some way—recall the link between testimony's errors and authorship—and also because they took the idea of authorship, whether by an omniscient or a nonomniscient agent, to imply that there was a time when the authored text did not yet exist. Such a claim about the Veda would call into question its beginningless (and endless) world-sustaining and world-creating functions. To say of a text that it is the word of God, then, is to say something much less significant than to say that it is eternal and authorless.

The divinity of the Veda is stated for Mimamsakas by way of the twin claims of its eternality and its authorlessness. These claims are intended to make the text of the Veda foundational for all attempts to arrive at truth, and thereby to give the task of interpreting that text unrestricted epistemic primacy. One interesting concomitant of this view is the idea that the word-meaning relation is nonconventional and nonhistorical. The relation between the Sanskrit word *loka* ("world"), for instance, and that to which it refers is itself a structural and necessary feature of the universe, a feature that could not have been otherwise. The vibrations produced when the two vocables that make up loka are uttered are related causally to the very existence of a world at least by being a sine qua non for such existence. Without the Sanskrit loka, no universe. I suspect that for most readers of this essay, this is a deeply counterintuitive view; it was not widely accepted in India, either, but for most contemporary speakers of English it probably seems obviously false. Surely, we may say, the fact that the word loka means "world" is entirely contingent? Surely the kind of relation that loka bears to the world is the same kind of relation that "world" bears to the world (or that "monde" does)? And surely, in each case the relation is entirely conventional, the result of a historical story that could have been different?

An important question for those who want to think about and defend the idea of an eternal, authorless text whose vocables order the universe is: What if these vocables are not sounded? Does the universe's order depend on their vibration, and does this in turn mean that someone, somewhere, must always be chanting the text or in some other way causing it to be sounded if the universe is not to relapse into chaos? Some Mimamsakas held a view of this kind, and something like it informs the great importance given the training of skilled reciters of the Veda. But such a view clearly had—and was perceived in India to have—some significant problems. It is always possible that the seers who were the first to chant the Veda (though not, of course, its authors) might have no descendants, or that for other reasons Vedic chant might altogether cease.

So much, then, in brief for the idea of the Veda's divinity. Does it make sense? I think it does: it is not obviously incoherent, and while it raises some difficult questions for its defenders, the tradition is very much aware of these questions and objections and has devoted significant energy to the attempt to meet them.

Judging its success at this is a large topic, but it seems reasonable to say that Mimamsakas aren't obviously offending against any epistemic duties by continuing to believe and defend the views sketched here.

A distinct question is whether anyone who doesn't already think that the Veda is eternal and authorless should be persuaded by anything the Mimamsakas say about this to come to assent to these claims. The answer to this is no. I, for example, think that the Veda is neither eternal nor authorless; that the vocables of Sanskrit are not necessary features of the universe; and that there are no non-contingent relations between the words of natural languages and nonlinguistic items—which is to say that I take all languages to be conventional. But I do not think it obvious that these things are so, which is also to say that the Mimamsa view of the Veda's divinity merits attention, and is not easy decisively to refute. This is an ordinary feature of religious views (and indeed of most complex philosophical views), and it is one that Mimamsakas would, I think, be quite happy to have pointed out. Their central concern when arguing about their deeply textual understanding of divinity was not to convince others of its truth but rather to explicate it and to defend it against objections.

Among the advantages of considering the Mimamsa's deeply serious attempt to construe the divine textually is that it calls into question the natural tendency of philosophers of religion to think that when we speak of the divine—that which is maximally and finally significant, that-than-which-a-greater-cannot-be-thought, as Anselm of Canterbury put it in Europe at the end of the eleventh century—we must be speaking of God. In suggesting that, and how, we might think of a text as that-than-which-a-greater-cannot-be-thought, the Mimamsakas do us the favor of suggesting some trajectories of thought in the philosophy of religion that do not belong to the discipline's traditional topics.

The most direct conceptual descendant in India of Mimamsa views about the Veda's eternality and authorlessness was that of Advaita Vedanta ("nondual culmination of the Veda"), perhaps the best-known outside India among Indian philosophical schools. It, too, has a nontheistic understanding of the divine, and although the substance of this understanding is very different from that of the Mimamsa, the lineage is clear enough. Those who think of the Veda as divine are called followers of the *purvamimamsa*, the "prior Mimamsa"; those who think of the divine as nondual are called followers of the *uttaramimamsa*, the "subsequent Mimamsa." There are also connections between the grammar of the thought of the two schools. As followers of the prior Mimamsa began to speculate in an abstract fashion about the nature of the sound, the sabda, that constitutes the text of the Veda, one of the names they gave it was Brahman; further argument about the nature of this Brahman was one of the routes into an analysis of the divine as strictly nondual (*advaita*), a set of speculations that provides my second example of an Indian nontheistic conception of the divine.

THE NONDUAL DIVINE

Sankara, with whom nondualism (*advaita*) is most closely associated, flourished most probably in the eighth century. He, like the followers of the prior Mimamsa, thought that philosophical thinking about what is maximally important should begin with sustained exegetical attention to the text of the Veda, most especially to that of the Upanisads, a set of speculative works in verse and prose whose composition may have begun as early as 1000 BCE, and which are taken by some to be part of the Veda. The *Brhadaranyaka Upanisad*, among the earliest of these works, begins with the pregnant line, "Dawn is the head of the sacrificial horse," a line that shows in summary form the interest of the Upanisads in connecting speculation about the nature and significance of the sacrifice with speculation about the nature of the cosmos. This connection is also one of the threads that connects the prior to the subsequent Mimamsa.

But Sankara did not share with his Mimamsaka forebears the view that the Veda is eternal and uncreated, free from authorship by gods or humans. He thought, rather, that sound exegesis and good philosophy established beyond doubt that Brahman, the really and finally real, is "one only, without a second" (*ekam eva advitiyam*, as the Upanisadic text has it). His considerable body of work was devoted to analysis of what this means and to meeting objections to it, as was that of his numerous followers and commentators.

The central doctrine of the nondualists is simple: that there is just one thing, variously called Brahman, Atman (Self; the upper-case "S" represents the metaphysical significance of the term), and (sometimes) *isvara* ("the lord"); and that this Atman-Brahman is uncompounded, which is to say that no predicates of a substantive sort can rightly be attached to it. Brahman has no temporal properties (the property "being eternal" is predicated of it, but is understood to mean the denial of all properties that predicate change), no spatial properties, and no properties that indicate internal complexity or division. This is a strictly metaphysical claim, a claim about the way things necessarily are. It has a number of epistemological and psychological correlates, of which the most important for Sankara is the claim that all cognition of diversity, whether of material objects ("this is a house, that is a pot"), or of concepts ("this is an idea of blue, that is an idea of red"), is erroneous. Such cognition is subject to ignorance (*avidya*) or illusion (*maya*), and because a very high proportion of cognition is of one of these two kinds, it follows that an equally high proportion of all human cognition is in error and needs to be corrected. It is a central goal of nondualist thinkers to provide a set of arguments and meditational practices that will bring such error to an end.

One such set of concepts is to be found in a dialogue between teacher and student given by Sankara in a work called *Upadesasahasri* (A thousand teachings). This dialogue shows with great clarity that one of the chief intuitions governing Sankara's nondualism is the idea that ignorance, which is understood most fundamentally to be error, the possession of mistaken concepts about multiplicity, is the direct cause of continued bondage in the beginningless process of rebirth and redeath that is called *samsara*. Sankara thinks that this point can be established exegetically. After quoting a string of Vedic passages, he says, "These *sruti* passages [texts from the Veda, broadly understood] indeed reveal that samsara results from the understanding that Atman is different from Brahman" (Mayeda 1979, 219, modified). If you think that you are genuinely different from the single, eternal, partless, simple Brahman, you will be denying the equation between Atman and Brahman, and as a result enmeshing yourself ever more firmly in the suffering produced by its seeming to you that you are—and always have been—subject to rebirth and redeath.

The student, not surprisingly, is puzzled by this. It doesn't seem to him that he is eternal, changeless, partless, and so forth:

> Your holiness, when the body is burned or cut, I (Atman) evidently perceive pain and I evidently experience suffering from hunger and so forth. But in all the *Srutis* and *Smrtis* [texts derived from the Veda but not strictly part of it], the highest Atman is said to be "free from evil, ageless, deathless, sorrowless, hungerless, thirstless" . . . [and so the Atman is] free from all the attributes of samsara. But I (Atman) am different in essence from it, and bound up with many attributes of samsara. How then can I realize that the highest Atman is my Atman, and that I, a transmigrator, am the highest Atman?—It is as if I were to hold that fire is cold. (Mayeda 1979, 221, modified)

This is a question about how what seems obviously false (that the Self has no changing properties) can be understood, known to be true, and asserted without contradiction. Sankara's response is that the changing properties in question aren't in fact to be predicated of the Self. Rather, their locus is the discriminating intellect (*buddhi*): it is this that takes itself to hunger, thirst, be born, and so forth, and it does so because of ignorance. Ignorance acts as a kind of prism through which the Self (which is really single and partless) appears manifold and complex. Or, to alter the simile:

> From the standpoint of the highest truth, the Self is one alone and only appears as many through the vision affected by ignorance. It is just as when the moon appears manifold to sight affected by the disease of the eye called *timira*. (225, modified)

Timira is probably a form of cataract; it is in any case a defect of the eye that produces double vision. It represents ignorance, which is a defect of the mind that produces multiple vision, the ordinary perception of difference. The question about how to understand and know to be true assertions such as *the Self does not change* or *the Self is identical with Brahman* is then simply answered: remove ignorance, and you'll no longer perceive the Self in any other way. The removal of ignorance permits the truth simply to shine forth, to be "self-established," as Sankara likes to put it. And the truth that Atman is Brahman is both true and salvific, for coming to know that it is true and to see the world in accordance with its truth is precisely to be liberated from samsara, from the suffering of rebirth and redeath.

Liberation (*moksa*), on this understanding, is not acquired but acknowledged. This is because it is not a condition that is caused to come to be; it is, rather, a condition that has always and changelessly been, and since anything that enters into causal relations must, for Sankara and his school, thereby be considered subject to change and dependence on something other than itself, it follows that Atman-Brahman cannot be produced. It might seem that it would follow that nothing can be done to bring about liberation from samsara. But this is not so, says Sankara, and to illustrate what he means he often turns to the example of the rope and the snake. If you think a coiled rope on the path in front of you is a snake, you are subject to error. What removes this condition is just and only its complementary cognition *this is not a snake*, which is entailed by the judgment *this is a rope*. For Sankara, knowing is not an act with conditions; if it were, it would be subject to cause and thus changeable. Instead, he thinks of knowing as a condition with content that is always and changelessly what it is. Removing the error *this is a snake* is an act, and is therefore subject to cause, but because the error was an unreality to begin with (an instance of maya, illusion), what the act produces is the removal of an absence. There is no causal relation between this and the realization of the truth.

Sankara and his school use a technical term to describe and define the act of making a false judgment. It is "superimposition" (*adhyasa*), and Sankara devotes a great deal of attention to its analysis because it is the hinge concept of his entire system and labels his central conceptual difficulty. If, as he does, you want to claim that all judgments that predicate properties of something are erroneous because the only thing there is cannot, because of its simplicity, have properties predicated of it at all, you will then have to explain just what a predicative judgment is and in what its error consists, and (still more difficult) how such judgments can come to be made at all if monism is true.

Sankara's ordinary definition of superimposition is: "The apparent presentation of the attributes of one thing in another thing" (Thibaut 1962, 1: 5). It is an act of judgment of the form *S is p*, and Sankara's favorite examples are the rope-snake, already mentioned; the judgment that a tree trunk seen from a distance is a man walking; and the judgment that the shiny inner surface of an oyster shell is really silver. In all these cases, an object is presented to the senses (a coil of rope, a tree trunk, an opened oyster shell), and a property is "superimposed" on it that it does not in fact possess (snakehood, personhood, silverness; Sanskrit delights in abstract nouns and forms them much more easily than does English). This model is then applied to all predicative judgments. But a difficulty for the radical monist is produced by the fact that a superimposing judgment requires a real object or locus on which or toward which the judgment predicates a property that is in fact absent there. The only candidate for such an object or locus is the Atman-Brahman, for this is the only thing there is. The predicative judgments *that thing coiled on the path in front of me is a snake* and *that thing coiled on the path in front of me is a rope* are alike in being, finally, judgments whose object is Atman-Brahman, and that (falsely) superimpose properties on the Atman-Brahman that it does not possess. The judgments are dissimilar, of course, in that one makes a conventionally true claim and the other a conventionally false claim. But the central difficulty for Sankara and his followers is to explain how it is that the nondual Atman-Brahman can be the locus or object of ignorance (all super-imposition is ignorance), for that is what the theory seems to require.

Sankara, it must be said, does not so much solve this difficulty as label it with some precision. He agrees that all judgments, even those about such matters as how life is to be lived, which sacrificial actions are to be performed, and what is one's own personal history, are instances of ignorance, deploying superimposition. He agrees, too, that there is no beginning to the process whereby such judgments are made, and that the relation between the simple, uncompounded Atman-Brahman and the endless play of erroneous judgments is one that cannot finally be understood but merely described:

> And so, the producer of the notion of the "I" . . . is superimposed upon the inner Atman, which, in reality, is the witness of all modifications . . . in this way there continues this beginningless and endless superimposition; it appears in the form of wrong conception, and is the cause of individual selves appearing as agents and enjoyers of their actions and the results of their actions, and is observed by everyone. (Thibaut 1962, 1: 9, modified)

The eternal and changeless Atman-Brahman is a "witness" to change, and change is superimposed upon it by the "individual selves," which are themselves nothing other than it. There is no genuine causal relation between witness and what is witnessed; there is only eternal parallelism or juxtaposition between the two. The imagery used by Sankara identifies the difficulty without solving it.

The same question arises again when Sankara treats the question of how the multiplicity of the material world is related to the unity of Brahman. This changes the sphere of discourse from the psychological or conceptual (What is the relation between my changing self and the changeless Self that I really am?) to the material or cosmological (What is the relation between Atman-Brahman and the multitude of material objects?), but remains essentially the same question. Sankara's view here is that although there is a sense in which such things as houses and pots must be effects (*karya*) of Brahman, this can only properly be said if it is emphasized that the effect is already present in the cause and is a kind of illusory transformation of it. This is the best way of putting matters for Sankara because it guards against the two main errors that concern him: first, the error of affirming that Brahman produces something other than itself, which would have to be said if the effect were not already present in the cause; second, the mistake of saying that the alterations or modifications apparently undergone by Brahman in producing the manifold world are anything other than apparent. If they were real rather than apparent, then, even if the effects were not other than Brahman, they would still have to be understood to produce real change in Brahman, which would contradict the view that Brahman does not change.

Sankara's picture of the world-Brahman relation, then, is that Brahman is both efficient cause (*nimitta*) and material cause (*pradhana*) of the world. This is sometimes put by saying that Brahman has a power (*sakti*) called "illusion" (maya), and that it is this that acts as the material cause of the world. Putting matters this way stresses that the world in all its variety must also be illusory, as the effects of a material cause must always share in the nature of its cause. But because illusion is itself not separate from or ontologically other than Brahman, to say that illusion (or ignorance) is the material cause of the world is just to say the same of Brahman.

For Sankara, then, the world of trees and houses and pots and persons is nothing but a set of illusory modifications of Atman-Brahman. The point of saying so, however, is not to utter a truth about the nature of Atman-Brahman. It is, rather, to make certain errors cease to function, to remove ignorance. The point of identifying the single, changeless Atman-Brahman in the way that advocates of the divine as nondual typically do, then, is not accurately to describe Atman-Brahman, but rather to bring to an end a set of peculiarly painful mistakes. This is philosophy as medicine, perhaps, philosophy as that which can, by verbal and meditational therapy, remove the pain in an amputated limb, a nonexistent locus for pain. The following passage is suggestive of what Sankara means:

> A man who wishes to attain this view of the highest truth should abandon the
> fivefold form of desire . . . which results from the misconception that such
> things as caste and stage of life belong to the Atman. And as this conception is
> contradictory to the right conception, the reasoning for negating the view that
> Atman is different from Brahman is possible. For when the conception that the
> Atman is not subject to samsara has been brought into being by scripture and
> reasoning, no contradictory conception persists. For a conception that fire is
> cold, or that the body is not subject to old age and death, does not exist.
> (Mayeda 1979, 226–27, modified)

Instances of error (of ignorance/illusion) are here likened to incoherent judgments such as *fire is cold*, and are said, straightforwardly, not to exist. They are removed just by coming to see them for what they are, which is, roughly, empty forms of words. Their removal, then, may be brought about by argument or some other kind of practice. But the point of such argument or practice is not to establish, or get taken as true, the contradictories of the incoherent judgments in question. It is, rather, just to remove them. To apply the analogy, the point of Sankara's Advaita Vedanta is not to establish itself as true, but rather to prevent its competitors from continuing as live options ("no contradictory conception persists"), and so to bring to an end the suffering that inevitably accompanies any realistically pluralist view.

Sankara's Advaita is not, then, only or even principally a nontheistic conception of the divine (though it is—or includes—such understandings). It is, instead, a theory and practice of salvation, to which the identification of the divine as nondual is instrumental. As with the prior Mimamsa's identification of the divine as a text, Sankara's position is unlikely to carry much conviction to those who do not already hold it. Following the arguments and tactics of Sankara and his epigones may nonetheless offer important and useful clarifications of Western attempts to argue for nonduality (Plotinus and Spinoza offer the most eloquent examples); it may also provoke further thought about why Christian, Jewish, and Islamic thinkers have been so concerned, unlike Sankara, to reject the idea that everything other than God is unreal.

The Divine as Buddha

Buddhism began in India in the fourth or fifth century before Christ. Although most of the details of its beginning are obscure, there is little doubt that the teachings of a man later to be called Gautama Sakyamuni and to be given the honorific title Buddha (awakened one) were among the factors of greatest importance. Unlike the Mimamsa and the Vedanta, Buddhism did not recognize the authority of the Veda, and did not develop its thought by interpreting Vedic texts. Instead—to make a long and complicated story much too short—Buddhist philosophy in India developed in large part by considering what it might mean to think of Gautama Sakyamuni, the Buddha, as of maximal and final significance, which is to say, as divine.

The legend of the Buddha, which had taken firm shape by the second century BCE, unambiguously presents him as a human being, even if a rather unusual one. He is born to a human mother, though in miraculous fashion; he grows to maturity in wealthy surroundings and is educated in a manner appropriate to his class; he renounces his life of luxury (and, in some versions, his wife and son) when the facts of human suffering become unbearably weighty to him; he spends years seeking the roots of suffering and its cure, and eventually finds them; when he does, he is awakened (becomes Buddha) to the truth, and this fact is marked by cosmic appreciation, including recognition and praise from the Vedic gods (this is one of the threads in the fabric of Buddhism that led Helmuth von Glasenapp, 1971, to aptly characterize Buddhism as a transpolytheistic religion rather than simply an atheistic one). After his awakening, Buddha begins to teach the truths he had discovered (this is his dharma, or doctrine), and in so doing to found a monastic order (the sangha) to preserve and transmit the doctrine. Eventually, at an advanced age, he dies. Buddhist speculation about the divine then focuses primarily on his person and secondarily on his teaching and the community he founded.

Much intellectual energy was devoted by Buddhists to antitheistic argument. This is not to say that Indian Buddhists rejected the existence of deities such as Indra, Brahma, and Visnu. It is rather to say that they rejected the idea that there is or could be an eternal, omniscient, omnipotent creator of all that is, and so also argued against the idea that any member of the Indian pantheon could be such a god. In arguing against the coherence of the idea of such a god, Buddhists were arguing with the many Indian thinkers who strongly affirmed it. This debate, which had a thousand-year history in India and which developed to a high pitch of scholastic precision and subtlety, is best thought of as an episode in the history of argument about a god very much like the God of Abraham. As such, it falls outside the scope of this essay, although its particulars should be of considerable interest to philosophers working in the Jewish or Christian or Islamic traditions, as it provides a splendid example of antitheistic argument developed independently of those traditions. (Some references to works on theistic and antitheistic argument in India are given in the bibliography.)

Buddhists, then, reject (the Indian version of) the God of Abraham. But in thinking about what it might mean to understand the Buddha as maximally great, they approached in some ways interestingly closely the Abrahamic idea. Buddha's divinity is certainly closer to the Abrahamic divine than is either the textual divine of the Mimamsakas or the nondual divine of the Advaita Vedantins, and this is mostly because Buddhist philosophers began their speculations about the maximally and finally significant by thinking about a person, as also did the theorists of the Abrahamic religions.

Speculation about the Buddha had its roots in devotional practice. From as far back as our texts go, Buddhists gave homage and praise to Buddha, naming him "fully and completely awakened," "accomplished in knowledge and virtuous conduct," "knower of worlds," and "teacher of gods and humans." These titles were analyzed and commented on by Buddhist thinkers much as were the honorifics given to Jesus in the New Testament by Christians; as such analysis and commentary developed, it is easy to see a movement toward attributing significance to Buddha that goes far beyond what can be borne by any particular human person. For one thing, the gods of whom Buddha is said to be the teacher are extraordinarily long-lived (though not, in the Buddhist view, either eternal or everlasting), and if Buddha is always to be their teacher his teaching activity cannot be limited to the life span of a particular individual in India 2,400 years or so ago. For another, Buddhist cosmology is remarkably generous in scope, both temporal and spatial (more so even than that of modern science), and if Buddha is really to be a knower of all worlds and a teacher of their inhabitants, his knowledge cannot, it seems, be limited and constrained as that of human individuals ordinarily is. These and similar considerations led to the development of concepts that made it possible to think of Gautama Sakyamuni as a token of a type rather than as a unique particular. Sakyamuni *the* Buddha became Sakyamuni *a* Buddha (the tradition attributes this view to Sakyamuni himself, and it certainly goes back as far as we can trace Buddhist ideas), and the question then became how best to think about the class-category "Buddha" of which Sakyamuni is a member.

The principal categories used for this purpose were those of the three bodies. Buddha, it came to be said, had three bodies, where the term "body" means something like mode of being or (as we shall see) mode of appearing.

The first of these bodies is the body of magical transformation (*nirmana-kaya*). There are many of these; Sakyamuni is an instance. Each body of magical transformation is born to a particular woman at a particular time and place, and each has a career whose outlines are like those of Sakyamuni's: he discovers the answer to the problem of suffering, teaches this answer as an awakened one, founds a community of disciples, and so on. Each body of magical transformation appears to have imperfections: each must learn what all humans must learn (language, good social habits, and so forth), and must do so by being taught. Each appears to need food and sleep and to suffer death. But Buddha cannot really have properties such as these, argued Buddhists; if it did, it would not be maximally significant and, ex definitio, not Buddha. And so these properties must be of a special kind. They must be apparent, properties that Buddha seems to have but does not really possess. Further, these must be apparent properties that are caused to come into being by the needs of living beings other than Buddha. This idea springs from the claim that Buddha is maximally salvifically efficacious with respect to the liberation of non-Buddhas from suffering, and so any apparent properties Buddha has must serve that end and must therefore be caused by the needs of those beings who are not yet liberated. Buddha in its various bodies of magical transformation appears to teach and walk and sleep and eat, then, in very much the same way that the moon appears to me to be a disc about the size of a half-dollar; or, to use a favorite Buddhist image, Buddha is a wish-fulfilling gem, a *cintamani*. Such a gem has as a property intrinsic or proper to it only that it grants to all who come into contact with it what they most desire. It has as emergent and apparent properties the granting of particular wishes. Just so for the bodies of magical transformation.

The second kind of body is of a logically similar sort. It is called the body of communal enjoyment (*sambhoga-kaya*), and of it too there are many tokens differentiated one from another by the possession of different emergently apparent properties. As with the bodies of magical transformation, there is a fundamental narrative that applies to each body of communal enjoyment. It is Buddha in residence in a gorgeously ornamented heavenly realm, Buddha present as a magnificently beautiful body around which advanced practitioners—bodhisattvas—can gather and listen to teaching and offer praise. The various heavenly realms in which bodies of communal enjoyment reside and teach are caused to come into being by the needs of bodhisattvas: these beings have progressed beyond the point at which they can benefit from interacting with a body of magical transformation like Gautama Sakyamuni, and their needs are met by the heavenly Buddhas of communal enjoyment.

There is yet a third body, the "real body" (*dharma-kaya*), which is what Buddha is in itself. This body is single or unique, unlike the bodies of magical transformation and communal enjoyment. The real body, as its name suggests, has no emergent or apparent properties. It has only essential properties, each of which is therefore eternal (beginningless, endless, changeless), like the real body itself. In analyzing the real body, the classical texts of the Indian Buddhist tradition tend to speak first of its knowledge or awareness, and then of its more properly metaphysical properties. The upshot of these analyses is that the real body's awareness is said to be universal (all that can be known is known to it), error-free, and without change: it knows what it knows effortlessly and spontaneously, just as a mirror reflects what is before it. The real body has nonpropositional omniscience, changeless knowledge-by-acquaintance of everything knowable. But this is not all. The real body is also eternally and changelessly free from any kind of suffering or imperfection; it is, as the texts usually say, eternally and naturally pure, not produced by causes, and not capable of being other than it is. It is also maximally efficacious in liberating other beings from suffering, and it does this by appearing to them as a body of magical transformation or a body of communal enjoyment. But even these appearances, these comings-to-be of emergently apparent properties, do not occur as a result of any particular volitions or intentions that Buddha has. They are, rather, like the moon's reflection in a pool of water: as the pool's surface changes (ruffled by the wind, shrunk by the hot sun), so the reflected image appears to change, but not because of any decision taken by the moon. An exhaustive account, then, of causes producing the emergence of a particular body of magical transformation or communal enjoyment can be given by describing the needs of particular living beings at a particular time.

A more abstract restatement of this picture would look like this:

(1)   Buddha is maximally salvifically efficacious,

which is axiomatic: this is just what it means to be Buddha. (1) is coupled with

(2)   Buddha is single,

which is to say that all plurality and multiplicity in Buddha is apparent, constituted exhaustively by emergently apparent properties such as *seems to be instructing me in the dharma now*. And then, because of the strong intuition that accurate awareness is a good thing, and the judgment that Buddha must have all good things, there is:

(3)   Buddha is omniscient,

which, when understood as briefly discussed above, is taken to mean:

(4)   Buddha has no beliefs.

(4) is required because of the usual understanding of what it is to have a belief (that is, to have a propositional attitude); believers are related to the states of affairs about which they have beliefs indirectly through their beliefs, and this is not something properly said of Buddha. Buddha has all the states of affairs known to it (and that is all the states of affairs that can be known) directly present to its awareness. (3) is also understood to require:

(5)   Buddha has no nonveridical awareness,

because all the factors that might cause nonveridical awareness (greed, hatred, ignorance, and so on) are by definition lacking in Buddha. (3) also suggests:

(6)   Buddha's awareness requires no volition, effort, or attentiveness,

for possessing properties of this sort was taken to entail imperfection. If Buddha needs to try to attain some previously unattained goal, or to make an effort to come to know something previously unknown, this would mean that the goods Buddha has to try to obtain are not among its essential properties. Buddha would then be able to be Buddha without possessing some goods, and this calls (1) into question, as well as sitting uneasily with the judgment that Buddha must be maximally great. Attributing effort and so on to Buddha also sits uneasily with

(7)   Buddha has no temporal properties.

This too is partly axiomatic: subjection to time and change would make Buddha less than maximally salvifically efficacious, just as knowing states of affairs temporally, as they come into being and pass away, would be less perfect than knowing them eternally. But (7) must be held together with:

(8)   Buddha seems to non-Buddhas to have temporal properties

in the various senses already discussed.

(1)–(8) raise a number of difficulties much discussed by Buddhist thinkers. Among them is the question of whether Buddhas can, on the model of Buddha-hood explored here, remember the past. It seems not, for on most accounts of memory, some causal relation to a past event or events seems required, and this may be ruled out by (6) and (7). This was of concern to Buddhists because on other grounds they wanted to say that Buddhas can remember their previous lives, and it is hard to see how such memory, even if it is restricted to bodies of magical transformation, can be categorized as an emergently apparent property, as it would seemingly have to be. Another difficulty was found in the tendency of this way of thinking to lead to something like Sankara's nondualism, a conclusion that Buddhist thinkers wanted on many grounds to avoid.

But it is beyond the scope of this essay to look more closely at these Buddhist discussions. They are, for the most part, discussions about whether the views of Buddhahood that had developed by the fifth century CE or so in India required the abandonment or modification of other items of Buddhist doctrine. They are not—again, for the most part—based on worries about whether the set of propositions (1)–(8) is internally consistent. It seemed so to Buddhist theorists, and it seems probably so to me.

WORKS CITED

Bilimoria, Purusottama. 1988. *Sabdapramana: Word and Knowledge.* Dordrecht: Kluwer.

Clooney, Francis X. 1990. *Thinking Ritually: Rediscovering the Purvamimamsa of Jaimini.* Vienna: Indological Institute of the University of Vienna.

———. 1993. *Theology after Vedanta: An Experiment in Comparative Theology.* Albany: State University of New York Press.

Coward, Harold G., and K. Kunjunni Raja, eds. 1990. *The Philosophy of the Grammarians.* Vol. 5 of *Encyclopedia of Indian Philosophies.* Delhi: Banarsidass.

Deutsch, Eliot. 1969. *Advaita Vedanta: A Philosophical Reconstruction.* Honolulu: University of Hawaii Press.

D'Sa, Francis X. 1980. *Sabdapramanyam in Sabara and Kumarila: Towards a Study of the Mimamsa Experience of Language.* Vienna: Indological Institute of the University of Vienna.

Ganeri, Jonardon. 2001. *Philosophy in Classical India.* New York: Routledge.

Glasenapp, Helmuth von. 1971. *Buddhism: A Non-Theistic Religion.* New York: Braziller.

Griffiths, Paul J. 1994. *On Being Buddha: The Classical Doctrine of Buddhahood.* Albany: State University of New York Press.

————. 1999. "What do Buddhists Expect from Anti-Theistic Argument?" *Faith and Philosophy* 16: 506–22.

Griffiths, Paul J., Noriaki Hakamaya, John P. Keenan, and Paul L. Swanson, eds. and trans. 1989. *The Realm of Awakening: A Translation and Study of Chapter Ten of Asanga's Mahayanasangraha.* New York: Oxford University Press.

Hayes, Richard P. 1988. "Principled Atheism in the Buddhist Scholastic Tradition." *Journal of Indian Philosophy* 16: 5–28.

Jackson, Roger R. 1986. "Dharmakirti's Refutation of Theism." *Philosophy East and West* 36: 315–348.

Jha, Ganganatha, trans. 1986. *The Tattvasangraha of Shantaraksita.* 2 vols. Delhi: Banarsidass.

Loy, David. 1999. *Nonduality: A Study in Comparative Philosophy.* Amherst, N.Y.: Humanity Books.

Makransky, John J. 1997. *Buddhahood Embodied: Sources of Controversy in India and Tibet.* Albany: State University of New York Press.

Matilal, Bimal Krishna. 1985. *Logic, Language and Reality: An Introduction to Indian Philosophical Studies.* Delhi: Banarsidass.

————, ed. 1994. *Knowing from Words.* Dordrecht: Reidel.

Mayeda Sengaku, trans. 1979. *A Thousand Teachings: The Upadesasahasri of Sankara.* Tokyo: University of Tokyo Press.

Mohanty, J. N. 2000. *Classical Indian Philosophy.* Oxford: Rowman and Littlefield.

Patil, Parimal. 2001. "Naming, Necessity and Isvara." Ph.D. dissertation, University of Chicago.

Phillips, Stephen H. 1995. *Classical Indian Metaphysics: Refutations of Realism and the Emergence of "New Logic."* La Salle, Ill.: Open Court.

Potter, Karl H., ed. 1981. *Advaita Vedanta up to Samkara and His Pupils.* Vol. 3 of *Encyclopedia of India Philosophies.* Delhi: Banarsidass.

————, ed. 1999. *Buddhist Philosophy from 100–350 A.D.* Vol. 8 of *Encyclopedia of India Philosophies.* Delhi: Banarsidass.

Potter, Karl H., et al., eds. 1996. *Abhidharma Buddhism to 150 A.D.* Vol. 7 of *Encyclopedia of India Philosophies.* Delhi: Banarsidass.

Sandal, Mohan Lal, trans. 1980. *Mimamsa Sutras of Jaimini.* 2 vols. Delhi: Banarsidass.

Thibaut, George, trans. 1962. *The Vedanta Sutras of Badarayana, with the Commentary by Sankara.* 2 vols. New York: Dover.

Williams, Paul. 1989. *Mahayana Buddhism: The Doctrinal Foundations.* London: Routledge.

FOR FURTHER READING

Good general works on the style and substance of Indian philosophicoreligious thought include Matilal (1985), Mohanty (2000), Ganeri (2001), and Phillips (1995). In addition, there is the *Encyclopedia of Indian Philosophies*, whose general editor is Karl H. Potter, and which now numbers eight volumes. These volumes provide descriptive and analytical material on the various Indian schools, together with summaries of the content and arguments of the main texts. The volumes edited by Potter (1981), Coward and Raja (1990), Potter et al. (1996), and Potter (1999) have proved useful in the preparation of this essay.

Useful secondary sources on the matters discussed under "The Divine Text" include Bilimoria (1988), D'Sa (1980), Clooney (1990), and Matilal (1994). Jha (1986) provides a translation of a Buddhist doxographical work that contains extensive (and accurate) exposition and critical analysis of Mimamsa ideas. Sandal (1980) gives a translation (not always either reliable or comprehensible) of the foundational work of the prior Mimamsa.

For the matters discussed under "The Nondual Divine" Thibaut (1962) and Mayeda (1979) provide English translations of two of Sankara's main works. Useful secondary sources include Deutsch (1969) and Clooney (1993). The most systematic treatment of the philosophical idea of nonduality is to be found in Loy (1999); this treats materials from many cultures and traditions.

For further exploration of the matters discussed under "The Divine as Buddha": Williams (1989) is a philosophically useful treatment of Buddhist thought in general. Hayes (1988), Jackson (1986), Griffiths (1999), and Patil (2001) discuss Buddhist antitheistic argumentation. The most comprehensive treatments of Buddhist theories about the nature of the Buddha are Griffiths (1994) and Makransky (1997). Translations of Buddhist texts treating this topic may be found in Griffiths et al. (1989) and also in Jha (1986).

CHAPTER 4

THE ONTOLOGICAL ARGUMENT

BRIAN LEFTOW

THE term "ontological argument" was Kant's name for one member of a family of arguments that began with Anselm of Canterbury. These arguments all try to prove God's existence a priori, via reasoning about the entailments of a particular description of God. The description almost always involves God's greatness or perfection. Where it does not, the argument has a premise justified by God's greatness or perfection.[1] So these arguments might better be called arguments from perfection.

I deal with the main arguments from perfection and criticisms thereof in historical order.

ANSELM: PROSLOGION 2

Anselm gave the first argument from perfection in his *Proslogion* (1078). The key passage (in ch. 2) is this:

> We believe [God] to be something than which nothing greater can be thought
> ... The Fool ... when he hears ... "something than which nothing greater can

be thought," understands what he hears, and what he understands is in his intellect. (But) it cannot exist in the intellect alone. For if it exists only in the intellect, it can be thought to exist also in reality, which is greater. If therefore it . . . exists only in the intellect, this same thing than which a greater cannot be thought, is a thing than which a greater can be thought. But this surely cannot be. So something than which no greater can be thought . . . exists . . . both in the intellect and in reality. (Charlesworth 1965, 116, my translation)

I first explicate Anselm's key phrase "something than which no greater can be thought" (henceforth "a G"). I then take up his reasoning, then the question of whether its premises are true.

"A G" is an indefinite description. Its form lets many things satisfy it (as with "something brown and red" and "something canine"). What the Fool understands is this description. A natural thought would be that what is "in his intellect," if not just a token string of words, is the property the description expresses, *being a G*. But as the argument proceeds, it supposes that the Fool "has in mind" some particular thing that has the property, an "it" that cannot exist in the mind alone. Anselm seems to suppose, in short, that by understanding the description *a G*, one comes into some sort of direct cognitive relation with something that is a G: one *thinks of* or *refers to* a particular G. For Anselm, then, being such that no greater can be thought means being such that no one nondivine can refer to a greater possible object, under any description.[2] A G is a greatest possible being to which we can refer. If there is hierarchy of greatness with a topmost level to which we can refer, then, "a G" automatically picks out only something(s) on the topmost level. If we can refer to an unending progression of ever greater possible beings, "a G" does not refer.

"A G" has a modal element: it speaks of items to which we *can* refer. To make sense of this "can," I now introduce a bit of technical terminology that will be repeatedly useful. The sentence "Possibly there are ostriches" asserts that in at least one history the universe could have, ostriches would exist. In fact, one such history has taken place. "Possibly Churchill runs a three-minute mile" asserts that in at least one history the universe could have, Churchill pulls off this surprising feat. Churchill has not yet done this, and barring reincarnation or resurrection, he will not. So it appears that actual history is not any of those in which Churchill does this: no such history has taken place. But still, it's in some sense *possible* that he do so. Every sentence instancing the form *possibly P* asserts the existence of at least one history the universe could have in which P. Every sentence instancing the form *necessarily P* asserts that there is no history the universe could have in which ¬P. The sentence "necessarily 2+2=4" asserts that there is no history the universe could have in which this is false; that is that in every possible history, 2+2=4. Every sentence using "can," of course, is equivalent to one using "possibly" (e.g., "There can be ostriches").

Philosophers call histories the universe could have *possible worlds*. So we can now explicate Anselm this way: something x *is* a G only if no nondivine being in any possible world can refer to any being greater than x actually is. Now surely, for every possible being, possibly someone or other nondivine refers to it. If that's so, then possibly something is greater than x only if possibly someone refers to that greater thing. If so, we can simplify our account of *a G*, for being a G is equivalent to being something than which there can be no greater. From now on, let's take Anselm to be talking of this property.

In *Proslogion* 5, Anselm reasons that unless it is to be less than we can think it to be, a G must be "whatever it is better to be than not to be" (Charlesworth 1965, 120), that is, have every attribute F such that having F is better than lacking F. Now if something had every such attribute, it would be a G (a G being one thing it is better to be than not to be). So if something is not a G, it lacks some F a G has, such that having this F is better than lacking F. Thus, *Proslogion* 5 implies that a G is greater than any possible non-G in at least one respect. Further, there is no respect in which a non-G surpasses a G: if a non-G has some attribute it is better to have than to lack, any G has this too, and only such attributes are respects in which something might surpass a G.[3] So overall, any G is greater than any non-G. As it's obvious that nothing in the material world is a G, we can infer that a G must at least be greater than any actual material object—including the universe. Here is a particularly impressive attribute: being greater than every other possible being in some respect and equaled by no other possible being in any respect. Such a G would be a most perfect possible being. Anselm would almost certainly hold that a G must be a most perfect possible being: if a G were not so, we could apparently think of a greater, namely one that was so. But his argument doesn't make use of this description.

Talk of Gs naturally raises questions like What is greatness? or Greater in what way? Anselm doesn't answer. But he clearly means greatness or being greater to be or involve some sort of value-property the God of Western theism has supremely. So Findlay's (1955) suggestion that we take these in terms of worthiness of worship can't be too far off the mark: let's say that greatness is either desert of worship or some combination of attributes on which this supervenes.[4] As it turns out, we needn't be more specific than this.

In *Proslogion* 4, Anselm asserts that

Df. God = *that* than which no greater can be thought,

the definite description implying that there is just one G. Anselm nowhere argues that there is just one. And this is not obvious. Something without a greater might nonetheless have an equal. If Anselm cannot rule it out that there could be two or more equal Gs, he faces a problem. For his argument will apply to as many possible Gs as there are, prima facie, and so if it works will prove that there are

many Gs. If there are, the definite description "*that* than which no greater ..."
will not refer—in which case, Anselm's argument will prove that God does *not*
exist, given (Df). Why just one possible G? One can only speculate:

i. Anselm argues that being a G entails being intrinsically simple, that is, not
having distinct purely intrinsic attributes (*Proslogion* 12; see *Monologion* 16–17).
Suppose that this is so. For any x, being x is intrinsic to x: it is a matter settled
entirely within x's boundaries, so to speak. Being simple is also intrinsic. So for
any x, if x is simple, being simple and being x must be the same attribute. But
then any simple being will be identical to x. So there can be at most one simple
being. So if being a G entails being simple, there can be at most one G—and if
attribute-identities are necessary, at most one possible G. Thus, there is at least a
good argument from premises Anselm clearly accepted to back his belief that at
most one possible being is a G.

ii. As the doctrine of divine simplicity is controversial, perhaps a better answer lies with what Anselm means by "greatness." It's axiomatic in Western theism
that whatever precisely worship *is*, at most one thing deserves it, and this thing
coexists with no rivals for worship (see, e.g., Isaiah 40:25, 44:6–7, 46:5, 9). Anselm
argues that any G must as such exist necessarily and necessarily be a G. If he's
right, and it's also the case that maximal greatness in a possible world W excludes
having a rival in W, then in no possible world does a G coexist with another G,
and there is at most one possible G.

I now turn to Anselm's reasoning.

The Reasoning

On one reading, Anselm's premises are

1.   Someone thinks of a possible object which is a G, and
2.   If any possible G is thought of but not actual, it could have been greater
     than it actually is.

The reductio runs this way. By definition, if a possible object g is a G, no possible
object in any possible state is greater than g actually is: g is in a state than which
there is no greater. Let g be the G someone thinks of. Then, as a G, g is in a state
than which there is no greater. Per (2), if g is not actual, g could have been greater
than g actually is. So if g is not actual, g is not in a state than which there is no
greater. So if g is not actual, g both is and is not in such a state. So g is actual.
So a G exists.

The argument is valid. So let us ask if its premises are true.

Ontological Commitments?

(1) is not innocent. It asserts a relation between a thinker and a possible object that is actually a G, and so brings an object into our ontology. Anselm needs it to do so if (1) is to give him a G to which to apply (2). But then if he is not blatantly to beg the question of God's existence, Anselm must also assume that this possible object is there, and is a G, even if it does not exist. And odds are that Anselm did believe in nonexistent objects.[5] But this puts an unflattering gloss on his argument. For then it seems to amount to: grant that something actually is in a state with no greater. This thing either does or doesn't exist. But how could something that didn't so much as exist be as great as all that? And of course, if that's what the argument amounts to, it's hard to see why one should grant that something actually is in such a state. The step from this admission to the conclusion seems vanishingly small.

But Anselm's argument doesn't require his ontology. One could instead read (1) in light of non-Anselmian semantic assumptions. Suppose that one denied nonexistent objects, but held that one can use satisfiable descriptions as if they refer, whether or not they do, and can properly use claims like (2) to reason about satisfiers of descriptions, whether or not the descriptions are satisfied. This would amount to running Anselm's argument within a "free" logic. Such logics carry no ontological commitments. Taken in light of these new assumptions, (1) asserts only that someone tokens an indefinite description that is possibly satisfied. (1), then, turns out no more or less problematic than the claim that

1a.   Possibly something is a G.

(2) assigns a degree of greatness to an object even if it does not actually exist; like (1), it must allow for nonexistent objects with greatness if it is not to beg the question. Even if the degree were automatically zero, this would still entail that nonexistents have properties. So we must replace (2) with a premise assigning greatness to nonexistents only in worlds in which they exist. The most straightforward replacement is probably

2a.   If possibly something is a G, but actually nothing is a G, then in any possible world W in which something is a G, that G could be greater than it is in W.

If possibly something is a G, there *is* a world W in which something is a G. So (2a) immediately yields

2b.   If possibly something is a G, but actually nothing is a G, then in some possible world W, something is a G but could be greater than it is in W.

Free logics let one use names or descriptions that do not refer as if they refer. So they reject the logical rules of universal instantiation (from "for all x, Φx," infer Φs for any singular term s) and existential generalization (from any statement Fs, infer that there is something which is F; Lambert 1983, 106–7). Thus, to show that Anselm's argument can go free-logical, one must state his reductio without using these rules. So here it is: given (1a) and (2b), if nothing is a G, then in some possible world W, something is a G but could be greater than it is in W. But it cannot be the case that in some world, a G could be greater than it is in that world: being a G is being in a state with no greater in any world. So it is not the case that nothing is a G. As far as I can see, then, given a free logic, Anselm's reductio goes through.

The Premises

If an argument is valid and its premises are true, its conclusion is true. I will not try to settle whether (1a) is true. But there is a case for (2a). For a G could be greater than it is in W just in case G lacks in W some great-making property compatible with the rest of its attributes in W. If no G exists, any G in any W lacks the property of existing in @, the actual world. But

3. For a G, for any W, existing in @ is great-making in W.

And if it is possible that a G exists, then for some G in some W, existing in @ is compatible with the rest of its attributes.

The controversial premise here is of course (3). There are two cases to consider here: W = @ and W ≠ @. For the first, I support (3) in two ways. One appeals to a general claim,

4. For any F and x, if x would be F were it to exist, then for x, existing in @ is F-making.

Suppose that Leftow would be human were he to exist. Then whoever gives Leftow existence ipso facto makes him be human. So for Leftow, existence is human-making: it makes him actually what he would be were he actual, and so human. But the properties a G would have if actual include being great. So for a G, existing in @ is great-making. Oppy (1995) suggests that (3) must rest on or be supplanted by some more general principle connecting greatness and existence, which atheists and agnostics would be reasonable to reject: "After all, there seems to be no good reason to suppose that existence in reality is a great-making property solely in the case of a [G]" (10, cf. 11).[6] But the only general principle needed is (4). (4) does not connect existence with greatness any more than with any other property, and I cannot see that atheists or agnostics have any particular reason to object to it.

The second line of argument begins that surely

5. Nothing that doesn't exist ought to be worshipped.

For worship is a kind of talking to, and it makes no sense to talk to something that isn't there. Atheists and agnostics will of course insist on (5). If (5) is true, then any G would be more deserving of worship if actual than if merely possible. For a merely possible G does not deserve worship at all, and an actual G does deserve worship. If greatness is worthiness of worship or whatever property(-ies) would subvene it, this implies that any G would be greater if actual than if merely possible, and *because* it is actual, not merely possible. So a G's being actual surely moves it at least a bit in the direction of maximal greatness. In fact, it moves it all the way, if (as it were) the G is all set to be great save for the little detail of actually existing. But then existing in @ is great-making for Gs.

Suppose, on the other hand, that W ≠ @. We then must ask why existing in some other world contributes to a G's greatness in W. One sort of reply appeals to arguments that necessary existence is great-making: if it is, then a fortiori existing in another world is. Now the claim that being a G entails existing necessarily leads to its own sort of argument from perfection. But it does so only given certain principles of modal logic. *Pros.* 2 does not commit itself to any such principles. So this sort of support would not make *Pros.* 2 depend on modal perfection-arguments. It would at most show that *Pros.* 2 has one root these other arguments do.

Another sort of response begins with two premises: that worship consists largely of giving thanks and praise, and that @, as it happens, contains concrete things whose maker might in some circumstance deserve thanks and praise for them, and for whose existence a G would account if it existed. A being that can have no greater is one than which none can be more worship-worthy. So it must deserve the greatest thanks and praise compatible with its nature. Those who worship, thank and praise God for their existence and for items in the world around them if they seem good. So if a G is to deserve maximal thanks and praise, it must be such as to deserve thanks and praise for whatever should inspire these in worlds it graces. All things in any way good in these worlds thus must owe it their very being; its contribution must suffice for their existence. The more complete this dependence, the greater the thanks and praise deserved. So another axis along which to magnify the thanks/praise a G is owed is depth of dependence: the deeper it is, the greater the thanks/praise deserved. One way dependence can be deeper is this: an item depending on the G could depend on it so thoroughly that it could not exist without the G's causal support. So via "perfect being" reasoning, we can conclude that whatever in any way ought to inspire thanks and praise and coexists with a G depends so completely on it for existence that it could not exist without the G.

Turning now to our G in W, @, again, contains many things warranting thanks and praise. Either some of these also exist in W, or none do. Suppose that some do. Then if the G does not exist in @, some things in W could have existed without depending on a G's contribution to their existence. But we've just ruled this out. And so if a G exists in W but not in @, nothing warranting thanks and praise in @ exists in W. If a G exists in W but not in @, nothing in @ could have depended on that G. For if it did, in any world, it would there depend on that G so completely that it could not exist without the G in any world—including @. So if the G does not exist in @, everything in @ is such that that G does not possibly account for its existence. If so, the G of W is not omnipotent: there are perfectly possible contingent beings for whose existence it cannot account. Surely omnipotence is great-making and exemplifiable; surely nothing can be a G without it. So existence in @ follows from a clearly great-making property. This may well make existing in @ great-making. In any case, on the present argument, nothing that does not exist in @ can be a G in any world. And so any G in any world, including W, exists in @.

I submit, then, that the amended, free-logical version of *Proslogion* 2's argument is valid, and one of its two premises has strong support.

PROSLOGION 3

In *Proslogion* 3, Anselm reasons that

> something can be thought to be, which cannot be thought not to be. This is greater than what can be thought not to be. Whence if that than which no greater can be thought, can be thought not to be, it . . . is not that than which no greater can be thought . . . So truly does something than which no greater can be thought exist, therefore, that it cannot be thought not to exist. (Charlesworth 1965, 118)

Some claim that here Anselm gives a second argument for God's existence. They do so by reading Anselm this way:

6. Possibly something is a G, and
7. Being a G entails existing necessarily. So
8. Possibly a G exists necessarily. So
9. A G exists necessarily. So
10. A G exists.

I doubt on exegetical grounds that Anselm actually means to give this argument. But as *Proslogion* 3 has led some to this argument, we can discuss it here.

(6)–(10) is a valid argument in the S5 system of modal logic. Systems of modal logic—the logic of inferences involving "possibly" and "necessarily"—differ in the claims they make about the relations between possible worlds. The distinctive feature of the S5 system of modal logic is that in it, every world is possible relative to every other world: no matter which world were actual, the same set of worlds would be possible. To see how (6)–(10) works in such a set of worlds, let the boxes below represent all the worlds that are possible:

Let existing in at least one box represent being possible, and existing in all the boxes represent existing necessarily. (6) asserts that possibly a G exists. To represent this, we enter a G in one box:

Now (8) asserts not just that it's possible that a G exist, but that it's possible that a G exist *necessarily*. What this means, in terms of our boxes, is that a G is in one box, and in that box, it's true of the G that it exists in *all* the boxes (more precisely, all the boxes possible relative to it, which in S5 *are* all the boxes). So if (8) is true, G is in W1, and in W1 it's true that if G is in W1, it is also in W2–4, so that we have

W1	W2
G	G
G	G
W3	W4

Thus, given an S5 system of relations among the boxes, (8) does entail (9): G exists necessarily (in all boxes). Now if W1–4 are *all* the worlds there are, then one of them will turn out to be actual. G is in all of them, so no matter which one is actual, G will be actual with it. So (9) entails (10). In S5, this modal argument from perfection is valid.

ANSELM'S REAL ARGUMENT

While Anselm probably did not intend (6)–(10), he *did* develop the first modal argument from perfection, in a slightly later work, the *Reply to Gaunilo*:

> Whatever can be thought and does not exist, if it existed, would be able . . . not to exist. (But) something than which no greater can be thought . . . if it existed, would not be able . . . not to exist—for which reason if it can be thought, it cannot not exist. (Charlesworth 1965, 60)

Anselm's reasoning is this:

11. If it can be thought that a G exists and no G exists, any G would exist contingently if it did exist.
12. It is not possible that a G exist contingently. So
13. It is not the case that it can be thought that a G exists and no G exists.

So

14. If it can be thought that a G exists, some G exists.
15. It can be thought that a G exists.
16. Some G exists.

There are strong a priori arguments for (12). We can recast (11) as

17. If it is possible that a G exists and no G exists, any G would exist contingently if it did exist.

and alter the rest of the argument accordingly. The advantage of doing so is that (17) comes out true within the Brouwer system of modal logic, a weaker system S5 includes. The Brouwer system is weaker than S5 because it makes a weaker claim about possible worlds: rather than assert that every world is possible relative to every other, it asserts that relative possibility is symmetric: that if A is possible relative to B, B is possible relative to A. To see that (17) is true in Brouwer, suppose that these boxes represent all the possible worlds there are:

Let's say that W1 is actual, and relative to W1, W2 is possible. Our G, God, exists only in W2. So actually, God does not exist. But W2 is possible. So it's possible that God exist. Now suppose that W2 had been actual instead of W1. In that case, God would have been actual. But if relative possibility is symmetric, then because W2 is possible relative to W1, had W2 been actual, W1 would have been possible. So had W2 been actual, a world would have been possible in which God did not exist. So had W2 been actual, God would have existed contingently: which is to say that if our G possibly exists and does not, it would exist contingently if it did exist, assuming what the Brouwer system says about relations among possible worlds.

It's also worth noting that (6) and (12) suffice on their own to prove God's existence if the correct system of modal logic for metaphysical possibility includes Brouwer. To see this, suppose that these boxes represent all the possible worlds there are:

W3	W4
	God

If W4 is actual, of course, God exists. Suppose instead that W3 is actual. Then if possibly God exists, God exists in at least one box possible relative to W3, and so God exists in W4. Per (12), God exists necessarily in W4. So if W4 were actual, God would exist necessarily, that is, in every world possible relative to W4. Per Brouwer, if W4 is possible relative to W3, W3 is also possible relative to W4. So God is necessary in W4 only if God also exists in W3. So if W3 is actual, God actually exists. So whether W3 or W4 is actual, God exists, and so given (6), (12), and Brouwer, God exists.

Modulo the change from (11) to (17), then, we can credit Anselm with the first valid modal argument from perfection.

Modal arguments from perfection face two difficulties. One lies in showing that the modal systems they invoke really are the correct logics for real metaphysical possibility. The other is epistemological. Consider Plantinga's (1974a) attribute of no-maximality, or being such that one does not coexist with a G. If this attribute is possibly exemplified, then given (12) and S5, being a G is not. A modal argument gives one reason to become a theist only if its proponent offers one not just the argument but some reason to believe the claim that being a G is possibly exemplified rather than the claim that no-maximality is. Many claim that modal arguments from perfection "beg the question" by asserting that being a G rather than no-maximality is possibly exemplified. They do not. Every argument asserts rather than justifies its own premises. If we need reason to believe in being a G rather than no-maximality, this shows not that a modal argument begs the question, but merely that another argument is needed, on behalf of one of its premises.

GAUNILO AND PARODY

Shortly after Anselm published the *Proslogion*, Gaunilo of Marmoutiers replied with a parody of the *Proslogion* 2 argument:

> (An) island more excellent than all other lands truly exists somewhere in reality (if it exists) in your mind. For it is more excellent to exist not only in the mind but also in reality. So it must necessarily exist. For if it did not, any other land existing in reality would be more excellent. And so the island you conceived to be more excellent will not be more excellent. (Charlesworth 1965, 164)

This parody isn't quite right, but we can construct the right sort on Gaunilo's behalf: let's take him to have meant that if we replace "a G" with "an island than which no greater can be thought," the resulting argument works as well as Anselm's. There is no such island. So (says Gaunilo) we know the argument isn't sound, even if we can't pinpoint its flaw.

Unfortunately for Gaunilo, some sorts of parody are easily dismissed. There is no greatest possible island, for there can always be another island better at least for containing more of what makes any other island good (Plantinga 1974b, 91–92).[7] Oppy suggests that perhaps "the greatest possible island will have an infinite surface area and . . . supply of banana trees (etc.) . . . Given (this) it will not be the case that it could have a greater supply of these things" (1995, 165). Not so: for every order of infinity, there is a higher order. Oppy also suggests that traditional theists must concede the possibility of a greatest island, for their heaven is in effect an island than which no greater is possible, whose greatness lies inter alia in conferring "eternal life and infinite attributes on its inhabitants" (165). But on traditional theist belief, not heaven but God confers eternal life, and heaven is not surrounded by water. A physical heaven might be more like a new universe. But traditional theists don't hold that heaven is a best possible physical universe, only that being in heaven is the best possible state for us—and that it is so because heaven affords each of us our closest contact with God. Further, if greatness is (roughly) worship-worthiness, it's not true that a greatest possible island would be still greater if it existed. Nonexistent islands don't deserve worship, but neither do real ones, however lovely. Here, however, Oppy has a countersuggestion. Perhaps, he wonders, a greatest possible island would have "Godlike powers of providing for its inhabitants," in which case, theists can rule out a greatest possible island only if they can rule out the possibility of "limited—localized—pantheism" (166). Oppy might have made this particularly pointed by asking Christians whether God could incarnate Himself in an island. But a divine island is great qua divine, not qua island. Despite Oppy, it remains the case that islands *as such* don't deserve worship. So Oppy has left the realm of Gaunilo's original parody, and moved into talk of what I call almost-Gods.

Deity is a kind. Most kinds can have more than one member: there are many cows. If *deity* is a kind, perhaps it can have many members, or could have had a different one. If it can or could have, parallel arguments from perfection will work for all possible Gods, yielding more Gods than monotheists want. So Anselm needs to show that

NO. There cannot in one possible world be two instances of *deity*.

One good argument for (NO) stems from a claim argued earlier, that a G must account for the existence of all good things with which it coexists. Gs are good things. So were there two Gs at once, each would have to account for the other's existence. Because —— *accounts for* ——'s *existence* is a transitive relation, this would entail that each accounts for its own existence. But this is impossible. Again, we saw earlier that a G's contribution must be both sufficient and necessary for the existence of all good things with which it coexists. If so, there cannot be two Gs at once. For suppose that A and B each suffice on their own for C's existence. Then without B's contribution, C could still exist, if A were still making its contribution. But then it's false that B's contribution is necessary for C's existence.

(NO) is true, and so multiple-G parodies are ruled out. So let's consider parodies via almost-Gods, deities whose only greater is God. Let's call one such being Zod, and say that Zod is just like God save for a slight difference in perfection we cannot conceive. Zod is to us indiscernible from God. But Zod cannot coexist with God. For God is uncreatable and has made everything other than Himself, and Zod would duplicate Him in these respects. And so we cannot accept arguments for both Zod and God. But we might read "a G" as "an almost-God than whom no greater can be thought"—describing a being whose only greater is God, who is not an almost-God. If Anselm can't explain why we should accept (1) and (2) on his reading of them but not on a parody-reading, we ought not assent to them on either reading. Further, if God is a necessary being, so is Zod. So given a modal logic including Brouwer, it's not the case both that Zod and that God possibly exist.[8] But if we can't tell Zod from God, how could we have reason to think one but not the other possible? Thus, parody yields reason to be agnostic about such claims as that being a G is possibly exemplified.

Almost-Gods threaten to multiply: perhaps for any particular degree of likeness to God, an almost-God like Him to that degree would be more worship-worthy if it existed than if it were merely possible. Whether it would, though, depends on what worship is. At least within Western monotheism, whose concept of worship Anselm presumably had in mind, worship is or includes praise without qualification or limit. What deserves only qualified or limited praise thus does not deserve worship. And anything that can have a superior can deserve only qualified or limited praise. It is great—but there can be a greater, and so its praise ought to be qualified accordingly. "O god, you are great—but there can be greater": this does not sound like worship. If it isn't, and yet someone surpassable can deserve no more, nobody surpassable can deserve worship. Nothing can unless it has no possible greater simpliciter. And now here's the rub: an almost-God has no possible greater simpliciter only if it isn't possible that there be an Anselmian G. For as we've seen, a G is greater overall than any other possible being. If a G is possible, then, no almost-God can deserve worship, and so none can be more worship-worthy if actual. And so if a G is possible, one can dismiss this sort of parody—any reason to think a G possible gives one reason simply to ignore it. Perhaps, then, one can so tweak Anselm's property of greatness as to make parody difficult.

Here an objection arises. Polytheists worshipped; what they felt, did, and said is enough like what monotheists feel, do, and say to deserve the label. Some worshipped gods other gods outranked. So one can worship something surpassed. And so there is room for worship of almost-Gods. The tweaking move is at best trivial and at worst question-begging, for it so defines worship that only God can deserve it.

This objection is confused on at least two levels. For one thing, even if polytheists did worship, nothing follows about what deserved their worship: that something *is* worshipped implies nothing about whether it *ought* to be. And no polytheist god could deserve what monotheists call worship. In worship, monotheists give all their religious thanks and praise to God. So deserving worship in the Western-monotheist sense includes deserving all of one's religious thanks and praise. No polytheist god deserves all religious thanks and praise, for none is responsible for all of our blessings. So either polytheists misdirected monotheist worship at their gods or, more charitably, what polytheists did "in church" does not count as worship *in the sense discussed above*. Further, worship for Western monotheists includes the giving of thanks and praise without limit or qualification. Polytheists, just as such, cannot consistently do this for any single god. They must limit and qualify their praise for any god in light of what they must say to other gods: they should not praise Zeus for blessings Hera gave or praise Hera to a degree only Zeus deserves. In worship, monotheists give God all their religious loyalty. Polytheists, as such, cannot give all their religious loyalty in any act of worship. Polytheists' religious loyalties compete: time spent in Venus's temple is not spent in Mars's. Monotheists have only one temple to attend. If polytheists worship, then, their worship differs from monotheists'. There is a *kind* of worship only monotheists can give, for there are attitudes one can have only to a sole object of worship.

Next epicycle: perhaps one can define the almost-greatness of almost-Gods in terms of deserving almost-worship (or almost-sole-worship, etc.), and say that almost-Gods would be almost-greater if actual. What then? Well, the problem for a *Pros.* 2 parody comes in applying the parallel to (2a). There is no maximal degree of deserving almost-worship (as vs. worship). There is no state than which there is no almost-greater. So for every state an almost-God might be in, there is an almost-greater state something could be in, and so the parody-argument will fail. I now argue the no-maximal-degree claim.

God deserves worship. Maximal likeness to God would be duplication, and so would yield something deserving worship, not almost-worship. If likeness to God is graded on a dense or continuous scale, then there is no maximum likeness to God *short* of duplication: for every nonduplicate of God, something can be more like God than it is. If God deserves worship, becoming more like God is coming closer to deserving worship. So plausibly, becoming more like God is also coming closer to deserving almost-worship, or (once over the threshold for this) deserving ever more almost-worship. If likeness to God has no maximum short of deserving worship (by duplication), there is no maximum state of *almost* deserving worship (almost duplicating God). This doesn't entail that there's no maximum state of deserving almost-worship, but it surely suggests it.

Still, it's not implausible that in some cases likeness to God *is* a granular matter, that is, comes in discrete degrees, with a maximum just shy of duplication. For we can describe such a scale: just like God save for knowing four public truths God knows, or three, or two . . . On such scales, if there are maximal states, they are along the lines of being just like God save for not knowing one public truth an omniscient being would know, or being unable to do one task omnipotence could accomplish, or being able to commit one sin. I doubt that beings like this really are possible—what could keep someone who has all eternity to figure things out, is omnipotent, and knows all the other public truths from learning the last? Be that as it may, someone with just one of these defects would be more like God than someone with all three. But which defect leaves one closest to God? Would someone not quite omnipotent be more like God than someone not quite omniscient? Someone is most like a perfect being if he or she is unlike it only in the least important ("perfecting") respect, and so this amounts to the question Which is least important: omniscience, omnipotence, or moral perfection? Given the shakiness of all intuitions here, the best reply may be that each one-defect being is more like God in his or her nondefective respects than anything defective in these respects is, but there's no answer to the question Which is most like God overall? This sparks a suggestion: perhaps each one-defect being is in a state with no greater short of being God, and so is maximally Godlike short of duplication. But this suggestion is correct only if there are no relevant gradations within each one-defect state, and that's questionable.

Consider possible beings just one truth short of public-truth omniscience. Some don't know this truth, some that. Which truth they don't know can affect their Godlikeness. Some truths are more important than others. So the lack of some truths is more important than the lack of others: it seems less important that God know the weight of a particular gnat in early Mesopotamia than that God know that floods kill. It's more Godlike ("perfecting") to get important things right. So beings are less Godlike the more important the truths they lack. Again, lacking some truths entails greater cognitive defect than lacking others: not knowing about the gnat is minor, while not knowing that modus ponens is valid is major. But it would take some doing to show that there are least important truths or lacks or defects. If some truths or lacks are more important than others, none are least important, and a being is the more Godlike in knowledge the less important the truth it lacks (or the less important the lack of this truth, or the defect it entails), then not all not-quite-omniscient beings are equally Godlike and there probably is no such thing as a most-Godlike not-quite-omniscient being. Like comments apply to lacks of power and abilities to sin.

The more like God in greatness-relevant ways, the closer to deserving worship. So if there is no greatest nonduplicative likeness to God, for every possible being deserving almost-worship, there is a state something can be in that would put it closer to deserving worship, and so make it deserve more or greater almost-worship. If possibly God exists, then, there is no state than which there is no greater for almost-Gods. Of course, if God is impossible, then again no possible being can duplicate Him, and the points just made about greater likeness to God remain, for they did not turn on the claim that God possibly exists. Possible items can be graded for likeness with impossible ones; the more nearly circular a thing, the more it is like a circular square.

So the last-epicycle parodic argument doesn't go through. On the other hand, almost-Gods make harder the epistemic problem modal arguments face: it's hard to see how to back belief that possibly God exists over belief that possibly Zod exists. And with the modal arguments there in the background, one wonders how well one can argue for (1a). For (it seems) any reason to accept (1a) would have also to be a reason to favor God over Zod. But in fact, the dialectical situation is this. To take a modal argument as reason to believe in God, one must have reason to believe that God rather than Zod is possible. For modal arguments from perfection will work as well for Zod as for God. But to take the *Pros.* 2 argument as a reason, one need only have reason to believe that God is possible, rather than more reason to believe this than to believe that Zod is.

Considering parodies for the modal argument shows that the existence of God (or Zod) would have modal consequences. If God exists, then given Brouwer, it is not so much as possible that Zod does: it's necessarily false that Zod exists. So the existence of God would have consequences for modal truths not involving the concept of God: God would have a modal footprint. And Anselm in fact held that what necessary truths there are depends on God (*Cur Deus Homo* II, 17).

DESCARTES

The Fifth of Descartes' *Meditations on First Philosophy* ([1641] 1993) offers the last fully original argument from perfection. It begins from a general attempt to show that some conceptual truths are not *just* conceptual truths, but rather reveal facts about natures independent of the mind:

> I find within me . . . ideas of certain things that, even if perhaps they do not exist anywhere outside me, still cannot be said to be nothing. And although . . . I think them at will, nevertheless they are not something I have fabricated; rather they have their own true and immutable natures. For example, when I imagine a triangle, even if perhaps no such figure exists outside my thought anywhere in the world and never has, the triangle still has a certain determinate nature, essence or form which is unchangeable and eternal, which I did not fabricate, and which does not depend on my mind. This is evident from the fact that various properties can be demonstrated regarding this triangle (which) I . . . clearly acknowledge, whether I want to or not. For this reason they were not fabricated by me . . . All these properties are patently true . . . and thus they are something and not nothing. (42–43)

Descartes then suggests that the nature of God is akin to the nature of a triangle in being something mind-independent which the mind grasps:

> The idea of God, that is . . . of a supremely perfect being, is one I discover to be no less within me than the idea of any figure . . . that it belongs to God's nature that he always exists . . . I understand no less clearly and distinctly than . . . when I demonstrate in regard to some figure . . . that something . . . belongs to the nature of that figure . . . Thus . . . the existence of God ought to have for me at least the . . . certainty that truths of mathematics (have). (43–44)

This promises a quasi-mathematical demonstration. Descartes' attempt to keep the promise runs this way:

> Existence can no more be separated from the essence of God than the fact that its three angles equal two right angles can be separated from the essence of a triangle . . . it is . . . a contradiction to think of God (that is, a supremely perfect being) lacking existence (that is, lacking a perfection) . . . it is . . . necessary for me to suppose God exists, once I have made the supposition that he has all perfections (since existence is one of the perfections) . . . Not that my thought brings this about or imposes any necessity on anything, but rather the necessity of the thing itself . . . forces me to think this. (44)

Descartes then adds further reasons to believe that his idea of God is "an image of a true and immutable nature" (45). The broad outline of Descartes' argument, then, is this: he grasps what he claims are mind-independent truths about the kind of thing God would be if there were one. And uniquely, in the case of God, the mind-independent truths about the kind require that the kind has an instance. To try to show why, Descartes tries to show that "God does not exist" entails a contradiction.

It is surprisingly hard to say exactly what this last phase of Descartes' argument is up to. I offer three readings of it, one of which subdivides.

Meditation V: One Reading

On one reading, Descartes' premises are that

18. If God does not exist, a being with all perfections lacks a perfection, and
19. *A being with all perfections lacks a perfection* entails a contradiction.

If both are true, Descartes may think, then if God does not exist, a contradiction is true. But (18) is ambiguous, between

18a. If God does not exist, then if anything has all perfections, it lacks a perfection, and
18b. If God does not exist, there is something with all perfections which lacks a perfection. (Van Inwagen 1993, 80–81)

To get a valid argument with (18a), we must read (19) as

19a. *If anything has all perfections, it lacks a perfection* entails a contradiction.

But (19a) is false. That conditional does not by itself entail a contradiction. It entails only that nothing has all perfections, which is what one would expect if a perfect being does not exist. So if the argument including (18a) is valid, it is unsound.

For Descartes, God is the sole possible being with all perfections, and so (18b) amounts to

20. If God does not exist, God exists and lacks a perfection.

(20) is false unless God actually does exist necessarily, in which case "God does not exist" is impossible and so implies anything. But then why should an atheist or agnostic accept (20)? It is on its face quite unintuitive. On another reading, (18b) asserts that if God does not exist, He "is" there, in some sense of "is" compatible with nonexistence, and has contradictory properties. This reading clearly commits us to a Meinongian ontology of nonexistent impossible objects,

for it asserts that if God does not exist, He is one. On such views, "there is" in "there is something with all perfections which lacks a perfection" does not express existence. It is instead a "wide" quantifier ranging over existent and nonexistent objects. To get a valid argument with (18b), we must read (19) as

19b.   *There is something with all perfections which lacks a perfection* entails a contradiction.

But with the quantifier read "widely," (19b) is false. On a Meinongian ontology, it is no contradiction for there to "be" contradictory nonexistent objects. Such objects are perfectly normal features of reality. What would be contradictory would be for one of them to *exist*. So the (18)–(19) argument is unsound on two readings, and on a third has a counterintuitive premise supporting which would require another, independent argument for God's (necessary) existence. Let's therefore consider a different analysis.

Meditation V: Second Try

Med. V speaks of what we do and must suppose, that is, of what our idea of God includes. Descartes later offered a "synthetic" presentation of material from his *Meditations,* and as an argument to what he seems to claim is to the same effect as *Meditation V* gave:

> To say that something is contained in the nature or concept of anything is the same as to say that it is true of that thing. But necessary existence is contained in the concept of God. Hence it is true to affirm that necessary existence exists in Him, or God Himself exists. (HR II 57)

Here the argument is in terms of concepts. There is also a reference to necessary existence, which suggests a modal argument. But by "necessary existence" Descartes means only actual existence the nature of the thing guarantees: that "actual existence is necessarily . . . linked to God's other attributes" (HR II 20). So Descartes may here suggest that the *Med.* V argument is really this:

21.   For all x, if being F is part of the concept of x, then Fx.
22.   It is part of the concept of God that if God's nature is what it is, God exists. So
23.   If God's nature is what it is, God exists.
24.   God's nature is what it is. So
25.   God exists.

The problem here is that (21) is false. It's part of the concept of Santa that he has a beard, but it's false that Santa has a beard, for it's false that anything really both is Santa and is bearded. "Santa is bearded" doesn't say anything true. It is just the right thing to say if you're telling Santa stories.

But perhaps (21) is dispensable. All Descartes really needs is

21a.   For all x, if being F is part of the concept of God, then Fgod.

One can read Descartes' *Meditation* III argument about the concept of God as an attempt to warrant (21a). It is, in effect, an argument that the concept of God has contents such that nobody has this concept unless it has an instance—that the causal story behind anyone's having that concept must include a God. If recent externalists are right, there are many such concepts, for example, *water*. And if the concept of a sort of item is externally determined in the right way, then something like (21a) will hold for it. Suppose that an appropriate externalist story about natural kind concepts is correct, and that water is a natural kind. Then because the concept of water is determined by the real external nature of water, if being H_2O is part of that concept, it follows that water is H_2O. It's not clear a priori why *God* or *perfect being* could not be an externally determined concept. And that Descartes was in general the patron saint of anti-externalism hardly precludes his claiming that there is one exception to it, which the argument from perfection reveals. On the other hand, any argument that externalism holds for the concept of God is ipso facto one that God really exists. If to back a premise in an argument for God, one needs a second, discrete argument for God, then the first argument cannot be stronger than the second and is not independent of it. So if it took such an argument to back (21a), an argument resting on (21a) would be useless.

Meditation V: Third Try

Our third reading of *Meditation* V begins by noting again its talk of God's essence and what it includes. Descartes later claimed that the *Meditation* V argument is:

> That which we clearly and distinctly understand to belong to the true and im-
> mutable nature of anything, its essence, can be truly affirmed of that thing . . .
> to exist belongs to [God]'s true and immutable nature; therefore . . . He exists.
> (HR II 19)

In accord with this, we might render the *Med.* V argument as

26.   If the "true and immutable nature" of x includes being F, then Fx.
27.   The "true and immutable nature" of God includes existence. So
28.   God exists.

To respect Descartes' claim that this somehow encapsulates *Med.* V, we might expand the argument by deriving (27) from

29. The "true and immutable nature" of God includes having all perfections, and
30. Existence is a perfection.

Perhaps Descartes did not see (21)–(25) and (26)–(30) as distinct. He distinguishes ideas that grasp "true and immutable natures" from ideas that are just "fictitious ... due to a mental synthesis" (HR II 20). If an idea does not have its content simply due to a mental operation, it grasps a mind-independent truth. That is, it has its content by grasping something that is somehow also extramentally the case. Descartes' thought, then, seems to be that some ideas grasp "natures" that have some status beyond them, the idea of God being one; for these ideas, the "nature" is just the idea's content, and so we can switch indifferently between nature-talk and talk of concepts (ideas' contents).

Descartes' talk of "true and immutable natures" has two functions in (26)–(30). One is trying to lend credibility to (29). If it's part of a thing's nature that it is F, says Descartes, we did not simply dream this up, and so we can trust our impression that such a thing would be F. But apart from this, it also sets up the claim that (27) and (29) concern some entity or truth independent of the mind. If there really is some entity or truth that logically requires that God exist, then there would be a contradiction in objective reality (not just in our ideas about it) if God did not.

Like (21), (26) is dubious but dispensable. All Descartes needs is (27), which we can recast as

27a. There is a "true and immutable nature" P which includes all perfections and is (uniquely) such that if it exists, it has an instance,

whence he can reason that

31. P exists. (27a, simplification)
32. If P exists, it has an instance. (27a, simplification)
33. P has an instance. (31, 32, MP)

Traits of our idea of God are supposed to assure us that it captures a "true and immutable nature." Why is (27a)'s second conjunct supposed to be true? One story Descartes tells is the (18)–(19) argument. But in at least one place, he tells another story about why existence is uniquely inseparable from the divine essence:

> It is not true that essence and existence can be thought the one apart from the other in God . . . because God *is* His existence. (HR II 228)

That God = God's existence explains the inseparability of God's essence and God's existence only if God = God's essence—a standard part of the doctrine of divine simplicity Descartes inherited from his Jesuit education. So what Descartes is really saying here is that the divine essence = the divine existence. The reason (27a) is true, then, could be that if there is a divine nature, it is identical with the existence of God. If this is so, then if there is in extramental reality such a nature, there is also such an existence—and so God exists. Perhaps Descartes' doctrine of divine simplicity, asserted in *Meditation* III, can help his argument in *Meditation* V.

DESCARTES: OBJECTIONS AND REPLIES

Publication of the *Meditations* led to a series of exchanges between Descartes and prominent intellectuals. The best criticisms of Descartes' argument from perfection came from Pierre Gassendi and Johannes Caterus. Caterus wrote:

> Though it be conceded that an entity of the highest perfection implies existence by its very name, yet it does not follow that that very existence is anything actual in the real world, but merely that the concept of existence is insepatably united with the concept of highest being. (The) complex "existing lion" includes both lion and . . . existence, and includes them essentially, for if you take away either it will not be the same complex . . . does not its existence flow from the essence of this composite "existent lion"? Yet (this) does not constrain either part of the complex to exist . . . Therefore, also, even though . . . a being of supreme perfection includes existence in the concept of its essence, yet it does not follow that its existence is anything actual. (HR II, 7–8)

One can put Caterus's thought this way: from premises about the content of a concept, only conclusions about the content of a concept can validly follow.

Descartes' reply in a nutshell is that his premises deal in "what belongs to the true and immutable essence of a thing," not "what is attributed to it merely by a fiction of the intellect" (HR II 19)—that is, are not merely about concepts' contents, but about extramental facts. His criterion for this seems to be that elements of a "merely fictitious" nature can rightly be separated conceptually: *winged horse* is "fictitious" because we can rightly conceive of horses without wings (HR II 20). On the other hand, if elements FG belong together as part of a "true and immutable nature," we cannot rightly conceive them apart: being F entails being G, or conversely (HR II 21). Thus, Descartes goes on to try to show that existence really does belong to God's "true and immutable nature" without merely reiterating his *Med.* V argument, by arguing that the nature of God's power itself entails His existence (HR II 21). But if one *must* show that some divine attribute entails God's existence to show that existence is of God's nature, Descartes has a problem. For if the *Med.* V argument really does include a premise about God's true, immutable nature including existence, it is then an argument for God the defense of whose premises requires another, independent argument for God's existence. If it is, it is dialectically useless. For if one can demonstrate God's existence a priori in another way, the *Med.* V argument is unneeded: it can't yield any further, independent warrant for belief in God. If one can't, it has an indefensible premise.

Gassendi wrote:

> Existence is a perfection neither in God nor in anything else; it is rather that in the absence of which there is no perfection . . . that which does not exist has neither perfection nor imperfection, and that which exists (has) its existence . . . as that by means of which the thing itself equally with its perfections is in existence . . . nor if the thing lacks existence is it said to be imperfect, (but rather) to be nothing. (HR II 186)

Descartes' reply is that possible existence is a perfection in the case of a triangle, making "the idea of a triangle superior to the ideas of chimeras," and similarly necessary existence is a perfection in God's case, making the idea of God superior to other ideas (HR II 228–29). This does not immediately address Gassendi's point about mere existence; perhaps Descartes means to add that any property a perfection entails is itself a perfection. This claim would not be implausible, as we see below in discussing Gödel.

Gassendi's second major argument was this:

> Although you say that existence quite as much as other perfections is included in the idea of a being of the highest perfection, you (just) affirm what has to be proved, and assume your conclusion as a premise. For I might also . . . say that in the idea of a perfect Pegasus (is) contained not only the perfection of having wings but also that of existing. For just as God is thought to be perfect in every kind of perfection, so is Pegasus thought to be perfect in its own kind. (HR II 187)

Descartes offers no reply to the parody. Perhaps he would treat "existing Pegasus" as he did Caterus's "existing lion": the "complex" captures no "true, immutable nature"—since it's not the case that the attribute of being Pegasus is such that necessarily, if it exists, it has an instance—and so here we do not escape the conceptual order. The Pegasus argument from perfection, Descartes might say, falls to the Caterus objection. But *if* Descartes cannot support his claim that God's nature includes existence without independent a priori proof that God exists, Gassendi is right that it begs the question.

LEIBNIZ

Leibniz worked intensely on arguments from perfection in the 1670s. He held that Descartes' argument was valid but incomplete, needing the addition of a proof that it is at least possible that God exists. His own preferred argument was modal:

> If a being from whose essence existence follows is possible . . . it exists . . . God is a being from whose essence existence follows . . . Therefore if God is possible, He exists. (Adams 1994, 137, n.9)

"A being from whose essence existence follows" is just a necessary being. So Leibniz's argument is really that

> If possibly a necessary being exists, it exists.
> God is by nature a necessary being. So
> If possibly God exists, God exists.

The first premise is just an instance of the characteristic axiom of the Brouwer system of modal logic; the argument is sound in Brouwer. The conclusion leaves Leibniz's case for God incomplete, needing, as Leibniz said of Descartes, a proof that possibly God exists. Leibniz tries to provide one.

Leibniz's possibility-argument (Plantinga 1965, 54–56) treats God as the being whose nature is a conjunction of all and only perfections, perfections being properties that are "simple," "positive," and "absolute." Simple properties do not consist of other properties. They are primitive. Positive properties are those whose natures do not include the negation of other properties. If the property F is a constituent of the property $\neg$F, every simple property is positive. Positive properties needn't be simple, though. F • G is a positive property if F and G are positive. A property is absolute if and only if its nature involves no limitations of any sort. Leibniz's argument, then, is in essence this: it's possible that God exist just in case all properties in the nature He'd have if actual are compatible. But if properties are simple, they cannot be incompatible because properties of which they consist are incompatible. If properties are positive, their natures do not include the negations of other properties. That is, for all FG, if F and G are positive, F's nature is not and does not include not having G, and G's is not and does not include not having F. But properties F and G are incompatible, thinks Leibniz, only if F includes $\neg$G, G includes $\neg$F, some property F includes includes $\neg$G, or some property G includes includes $\neg$F. Thus, if any absolute properties are simple and positive, they are compatible.

Leibniz's argument raises a number of questions: Are there simple, absolute, positive qualities? Do they include necessary existence? Do they include colors, and do colors pose a problem for the argument? Can the argument be parodied? And what about the gap between consistency and metaphysical possibility?

Simple, Positive Properties

Leibniz wanted this to come out a proof that *God* possibly exists, and so presumably took perfections to include such properties as omnipotence, omniscience, and perfect benevolence. These involve no limits of quantity or degree. Presumably they need not be instanced by an imperfect subject—they are compatible with "infinity" and "perfection." So their natures involve no limitations in *that* respect. It is a limitation to be something with knowledge and will only if there is something better to be, and this is not at all clear. But these are not obviously unanalyzable; plausible accounts of each abound. Leibniz's likely reply would be to say that perfect power, knowledge, and goodness *are* primitive properties— that although we offer accounts of them in terms of (say) generic power, knowledge, and goodness, in metaphysical fact power (for instance) in general consists in a likeness to the perfect exemplar of power, which thus figures as a primitive constituent in the general, shareable attribute of power. This amounts to applying a resemblance-nominalist account of attributes to the divine case, letting God serve as the paradigm instance: and Leibniz was indeed a nominalist, and speaks of created attributes as imperfect imitations of divine attributes in his *Monadology* (#48). If the standard divine attributes come out primitive, then they are also positive, and we've already seen that they're "absolute." Perhaps Leibniz can claim that necessary existence is the paradigm of which nonnecessary existence is an imperfect imitation. This claim is at least standard in theological tradition; one finds it, for example, in Anselm.

Colors

Colors are a problem for Leibniz. Phenomenal redness and greenness seem unanalyzable. They are also positive qualities of experience. They also seem absolute. For what limits are involved in seeming red? Not materiality: a discarnate soul could hallucinate in color, and plausibly in a hallucination *something* appears red. But no spot in any visual field can have both properties: they are incompatible. Now here Leibniz could perhaps reply that just for this reason, colors are not positive in *his* sense. Each is, after all, a determinate of a determinable, phenomenal color. And the nature of determinables may come to Leibniz's aid. For a plausible view of determinables would see them as simply disjunctions of their determinates, such that each n-tuple of the properties of which a determinable consists is internally inconsistent—in which case, each determinate implies the negation of each other determinate. If this is correct, the phenomenal colors are not Leibniz-positive. Each's nature in some manner contains the negation of the rest: certainly it entails these. So perhaps Leibniz's cause is not utterly hopeless here.

Parody and Possibility

Leibniz's argument does seem vulnerable to parody (Adams 1994, 150–51). Nothing he says indicates that his simple perfections entail one another. And it's hard to see how he could allow this. If omniscience did entail omnipotence, say, it would not be in virtue of "containing" the negation of nonomnipotence (since it doesn't contain the negation of any property). If the perfections do not entail each other, it seems possible to conjoin all save omniscience with almost-omniscience. For as none contain the negation of any other property, none contain the negation of almost-omniscience. But then the other perfections are consistent with almost-omniscience—or at least Leibniz's argument gives us as much reason to think this as to think that the perfections are all consistent. And so the argument gives us as much reason to grant the possibility of a necessarily existing almost-omniscient almost-God as we do the existence of God. But they can't both be possible. Just because we do see that it is vulnerable to parody, it's clear that Leibniz has a problem with the gap between consistency and real metaphysical possibility. The concepts of God and almost-God are equally consistent, on his showing. But it cannot be that both are possible, for at most one of these beings really exists. So we can't take Leibniz to have shown that it is possible that God or an absolutely perfect being exists.

KANT

Kant's *Critique of Pure Reason* ([1781] 1956) is often treated as the death knell of arguments from perfection. Kant claimed against Descartes that " 'being' is . . . not . . . a predicate . . . which could be added to the concept of a thing . . . It is merely the positing of a thing" (A598/B626). This denies (30), at least if we assume that every perfection is expressed by a "predicate," something that describes or characterizes an object. On this assumption, it is very nearly one of Gassendi's moves. Kant also argued this way:

34. All necessary truths are really conditional in form ("The absolute necessity of the judgment is only a conditioned necessity of . . . the predicate in the judgment" [A703–4/B621–22]).
35. Any conditional expansion of a purported necessary existential truth would be analytic as well as existential.
36. There are no analytic existential propositions (A708/B626).[9]
37. So no necessary proposition asserts the existence of anything.

(36) and (37) follow Hume. But Kant's way of supporting them is, for better or worse, his own. If (36) or (37) is true, then Descartes' argument cannot be sound, *if* its contention is in effect that "God exists" is analytic. If an argument is unsound, it either has a false premise or makes an invalid inference, and one who asserts that an argument is unsound must back the claim by showing one or the other. Kant's denial of (30) does this.

Kant supports (34) with only an example, that "necessarily a triangle has three sides" is really "necessarily, for all x, if x is a triangle, x has three sides" (A704/B622). His case for (35) is left implicit. In parallel to the triangle example, "necessarily, God exists" would on Kant's account really assert "necessarily, for all x, if x is a God, x exists." This is an "identical proposition" (A704/B622), since "x *is* a God" includes the note that x exists, at least on the plausible assumption that only existing things have any attributes at all. If this is an "identical proposition," it is also an analytic proposition, because its consequent merely makes explicit something its antecedent clearly includes. So if Kant's conditional account of necessity-claims is correct, then any necessary existential proposition is analytic. Kant's denial that existence is a "predicate"—by which he means something that describes or characterizes an object—helps back (36). Analytic propositions unfold the contents of a concept of some item. Concepts characterize their objects, that is, ascribe to them conjunctions of characterizing properties. So analytic propositions can only ascribe characterizing properties. So if existence is not a characterizing property, there can be no analytic existentials.

How much did Kant actually achieve? As to the claim that existence is not a predicate, Anselm's backing for (2), as explained above, does not involve any particular doctrine about the logical status of existence, nor even the claim that existence has some general great-making or perfective aspect. The point about existence doesn't even really cut against Descartes. One version of his argument uses the premise that existence is a perfection, but the having of a perfection could be expressed other than by what Kant would call a "real predicate." Another version claims that necessary existence is a perfection—but to claim that necessary existence is a *property* is not to claim that any existential proposition is necessary. Propositions predicating such a property need not be quantified at all. In any case, the claims that existence is not a predicate or a characterizing predicate are quite likely false. We can well understand a woman who concedes that her husband, Harvey, is not as brave as Batman or as brilliant as Lex Luthor, then adds "But at least Harvey exists!" This claim predicates existence of Harvey, telling us something substantive about him that "enlarges our concept" of Harvey, namely, that he is not a fictional character.

As to Kant's other line of attack, mathematics features numerous apparent necessary and nonconditional existential truths, for example, that there is a prime number between one and ten. (Kant's friends might dig their heels in and insist that this is really something like a claim that if anything is a series of natural numbers, it includes . . . But this would pretty plainly be stretching things.) Note that worries about the ontological status of numbers aren't really to the point here: the *truths* involved are of this form, whatever precisely it is that *makes* them true, and even if one assigns some unusual interpretation to the existential quantifier in mathematical contexts. So Kant's (34) seems frail indeed, and without it, (35) is at best irrelevant. If the logicists are right, these necessary truths are all analytic. If they are not, these are synthetic propositions which (*pace* Kant) do not concern how things must appear to us. Either way, Kant's theory of necessity is in serious trouble.

Gödel

Kant actually said little that earlier writers had not already said, and Kant's objections (I've claimed) were duds. But they were not thought so, and so arguments from perfection found few friends for the next two centuries. In 1970, mathematician Kurt Gödel developed an argument related to Leibniz's. The reasoning keys on a concept of a "positive" property that Gödel did not explain well. C. Anthony Anderson suggests that we take being positive as being "necessary for and compatible with perfection," or such that "its absence in an entity entails that the entity is imperfect and its presence does not entail (this)" (1990, 297). The two descriptions are equivalent. If a property is necessary for perfection, its absence in A entails that A is imperfect, and conversely. If a property is compatible with perfection, its presence in A does not entail that A is imperfect, and conversely. Gödel's proof (as Anderson emends it) makes these assumptions:

Definition 1.   X is divine if and only if x has as essential properties all and only positive properties.

Definition 2.   A is an essence of x if and only if for every property B, x has B necessarily just in case x's having A entails x's having B.

Definition 3.   X necessarily exists if and only if every essence of x is necessarily exemplified.
Axiom 1.   If a property is positive, its negation is not positive.
Axiom 2.   Any property a positive property entails is positive.
Axiom 3.   The property of being divine is positive.
Axiom 4.   If a property is positive, it is necessarily positive.
Axiom 5.   Necessary existence is positive.

Since being perfect is necessary for and compatible with perfection, on Anderson's reading, Definition 1 yields the claim that anything divine is by nature a perfect being. Again, on D. 1, a divine being has essentially every property necessary for perfection. Presumably having every property necessary for perfection suffices for perfection. (If it did not, something more would be necessary to attain perfection.) So D. 1 licenses the use of "perfect being theology" to fill out the concept of a divine being. If entailment is strict implication, Definition 2 encapsulates one standard account of what an essence is. Given D. 2, Definition 3 follows at once.

I now present the argument. Axiom 3 has it that the property of being divine is positive. D. 1 has it that every positive property is essential to a divine being. So being divine is essential to a divine being. D. 2 entails that any being has each of its essential properties in every world in which it exists, for if x has B necessarily, x's having A entails x's having B only if x has A necessarily. So per D. 2, any divine being is necessarily divine—divine in all possible worlds in which it exists. Per D. 1 and A. 5, any divine being is essentially a necessary existent. So any divine being is by nature divine and necessary in every possible world.

Axioms 1 and 2 jointly entail that any positive property is consistent. For a property is inconsistent just in case it entails its own negation. Per Axiom 1, if a property is positive, its negation is not positive. But per Axiom 2, if a property is positive, it entails only positive properties. So no positive property entails its own negation.

If every positive property is consistent, and *being divine* is positive, *being divine* is consistent. It is necessarily so per A. 4. We can confirm this another way: being divine is having all and only positive properties essentially. But if positive properties entail only positive properties (A. 2), and no negation of any positive property is positive (A. 1), no positive property entails the negation of any positive property. But then the set of all positive properties is consistent; none of its members entails the negation of any of its members.[10] Suppose now that if being divine is consistent, it is instanced in some possible world. Then given what we've argued so far, there is in some possible world a necessarily existent necessarily divine being: that is, it is possibly necessary that "a divine being exists" is true. Given this and the Brouwer axiom, it follows that a divine being exists.

Gödel's argument faces two basic questions. One is whether there is a contentful, theologically appropriate gloss of "positive" on which the axioms are true. The other is whether there is a sort of possibility such that (a) a concept's being syntactically consistent entails that it is possible in that sense that it be instanced, and (b) the Brouwer axiom is true for that sort of possibility and necessity.

The answer to the first question is yes. Talk of God as a perfect being is certainly appropriate theologically, and perfect being theology has been the main tool to give content to the concept of God philosophically almost as long as there has been philosophical theology. And on Anderson's gloss, the axioms come out true.

Anderson's gloss validates Axiom 1. Suppose that a property F is positive. Then by Anderson's gloss, if A lacks F, A is imperfect. If A has not-F, A lacks F. So if A has not-F, A is imperfect, and so not-F is not compatible with perfection, and so not positive. Anderson's gloss validates Axiom 2. On Anderson's gloss, if a property is not positive, either it is not necessary for or it is not compatible with perfection. If having a property F entails having some property that is not compatible with perfection, having F is not compatible with perfection—and so any property that entails something for this reason nonpositive is itself nonpositive. If a property entails a property not necessary for perfection, it entails a property a divine being can lack. Any property a divine being can lack is not part of its essence. A divine being's essence includes or entails whatever properties it has necessarily (D. 2); so any property a divine being can lack is contingent. But only properties had contingently entail the having of contingent properties. So any property that entails a property not necessary for perfection is itself contingent and not part of a divine being's essence. But a divine being's essence includes all positive properties (D. 1). So any property entailing a property that is not positive in this second way is itself not positive. Axiom 3 seems patent, for given D. 1, being divine amounts to a conjunction of all positive properties, and it's hard to see how such a conjunction could fail to be positive. As to Axiom 4, on Anderson's gloss, a property's being positive consists in two facts about property-entailment. It's plausible that properties entail what they do necessarily. As to Axiom 5, necessary existence is certainly compatible with perfection, and perfect being reasoning suggests that it is necessary for it.

There remains the modal question, of whether a concept of possibility and necessity such that being syntactically consistent (entailing no explicit contradiction) entails being in this way possible also conforms to the Brouwer axiom. Syntactic consistency amounts to "logical possibility," in one sense of the term. But not all that is possible in this narrow logical sense is really or metaphysically possible: there is no formal, explicit contradiction in the claim that something is red and green all over at once, and yet this claim is not metaphysically possible. So there is a gap between what Gödel establishes and its being metaphysically possible that a divine being exist. *And* it's a substantive question whether the Brouwer axiom governs real metaphysical possibility. We can describe coherently a set of possible worlds in which the Brouwer axiom doesn't hold, and in which, while it's possibly necessary that God exists, God does not exist. We need only two worlds to do so, in fact:

W1	W2
God exists	God does not exist

Suppose that W2 is actual, and W1 is possible relative to W2 but not vice versa. Then were W2 actual, W1 would be possible. As we're supposing that there are only these two worlds, a God who exists in W1 exists in every world possible relative to W1, if W2 is not possible relative to W1. So in W1, God exists necessarily (and W2 is impossible). Thus, since W1 is possible relative to W2, in this setup, God is possibly necessary and yet does not exist.

Gödel's argument (as emended) shows us that the concepts of a perfect being and of divinity are consistent, given a reasonable concept of perfection. But the gap between consistency and metaphysical possibility and the need to establish that the logic of metaphysical possibility includes the Brouwer axiom stand between it and the Holy Grail of proving God's existence. As well, as a modal argument, Gödel's faces the epistemic problems we've observed: the portion of the argument that contends that possibly a divine being exists may admit of significant parody. On the other hand, consistency is evidence for possibility, though defeasibly so, and if I've assessed *Proslogion* 2 correctly, that argument is promising and does not require us to deal with the epistemic problems the modal argument faces. There is (I think) little good to be said for Descartes' argument. But the *Pros.* 2 argument appears to survive objections; to accept its premise (1a) we needn't have more reason to believe in God's possibility than in Zod's; and we do have evidence that possibly God exists. So while there is of course much more to be said here, perhaps Anselm's argument has a future.

NOTES

1. Leibniz's argument, for instance, reasons simply from the claim that God is a necessary being (see below). But the latter rests on the claims that necessary existence is a perfection and that God is a perfect being.

2. Nobody nondivine is clumsy but necessary. *Proslogion* 15 asserts that God is

greater than can be thought, using the same language involved in *a G*. Anselm could not mean to say that God is too great to be thought of or described *simpliciter*, since he surely thinks that God thinks of Himself. So he must mean *a G* in terms of thinkers other than God. But Anselm wouldn't want to read *a G* simply in terms of what *we* can describe or refer to, for he believes in angels, and surely he'd hold that God is too great for angels as well as humans to describe adequately. Still, since "nobody nondivine" *is* clumsy, I henceforth replace it with "we."

3. If it is better to lack than to have F—that is, if F is an imperfection—then it is better to have than to lack ¬F, and so a G has ¬F. So a G has no imperfections. So nothing could surpass a G by surpassing one of its imperfections. If an attribute is neither a perfection nor an imperfection—neither raises nor lowers greatness—it's hard to see how it could be a respect in which one being could surpass another. For if being F makes A greater than G, presumably being F raises A's greatness past B's.

4. Oppy (1995) suggests that we need reason to think that a G, if actual, would be "a being of religious significance" since there may well be numbers too great (large) for us to "form a positive conception of" (16). Agreed. The only nonlogical vocabulary in "a G" is "thought of" and "greater." Since no religious significance attaches to the first, the second must provide some. The Findlay suggestion in effect stipulates that it does. And why not?

5. Anselm's argument requires that understanding "the G" puts one in cognitive relation to an entity, the G, which then "exists *in intellectu*." On this general approach, understanding "Santa Claus" puts one in cognitive relation with Santa Claus. Santa Claus then is the object of one's thought. But Santa Claus does not exist.

6. But see also p. 68, where Oppy (1995) seems to waver.

7. Can there also always be another being a bit better than any being we pick (Oppy 1995, 19)? We have the concept of God, which has a number of notes and is supposed in virtue of them to be a concept of the greatest possible being. And we find this connection intuitive: it's pretty hard to think of something *better* than being necessary, omnipotent, omniscient, morally perfect, and so on. So if one can show it possible that God exist, one can answer the question no. Those who offer arguments from perfection must show that this is possible anyway. So "Is it the case that for any possible being, there is always a greater?" adds nothing to their argumentative task. Moreover, —— *is a greatest possible island* wears its unsatisfiability on its sleeve. —— *is a greatest possible being* does not, if only because we're less clear on what makes beings as such "great," or what greatness is in beings. Further, on the reading of greatness I've suggested, it turns out trivially true that God is the greatest being possible, if God possibly exists.

8. To see the need for Brouwer, suppose (contra Brouwer) that relative possibility is *not* symmetric. Then there could be worlds like these:

W1	W2	W3
God		Zod

For simplicity, suppose that W1–3 are all the worlds there are, that only adjacent boxes bear links of direct relative possibility, and that W2 is actual. Say that W1 and W3 are possible relative to W2, but not vice versa. Then both God and Zod exist necessarily (each exists in the only world possible relative to the world in which it exists). And they do not possibly coexist. But both possibly exist, as W1 and W3 are both possible relative to the actual world.

9. Kant also believed in synthetic necessities. (He discussed these under the rubric of "synthetic a priori" truths. But he also held that whatever is knowable a priori is necessarily true.) But these, he held, all concern how things must appear to our senses, and God, he held, cannot appear to our senses.

10. Which probably entails that not every prima facie member of the set is actually a member. Being omniscient seems to many a prima facie perfection/positive property. So does being atemporal. Nobody is omniscient who does not know what time it is now. But many think that no atemporal being can know this (e.g., Kretzmann 1966). One conclusion from this might be that there are at least two incompatible sets of perfections, differing at least in that one includes atemporality but not omniscience and the other includes omniscience but not atemporality. But if we accept the Gödel/Anderson reasoning, no genuine perfections are incompatible. So on their account, what follows is instead that at most one of atemporality and omniscience is actually a perfection.

WORKS CITED

Adams, Robert M. 1994. *Leibniz.* New York: Oxford University Press.

Anderson, C. Anthony. 1990. "Some Emendations of Gödel's Ontological Proof." *Faith and Philosophy* 7: 292–303.

Anselm. *Proslogion* [1087] 1965. Trans. M. J. Charlesworth. Notre Dame, Ind.: University of Notre Dame Press.

Charlesworth, M. J. 1965. *St. Anselm's Proslogion with a Reply on Behalf of the Fool by Gaunilo and the Author's Reply to Gaunilo.* Trans. M. J. Charlesworth. Oxford: Clarendon Press.

Descartes, René. [1641] 1993. *Meditations on First Philosophy.* Trans. Donald A. Cress. Indianapolis, Ind.: Hackett.

Findlay, J. N. 1955. "Can God's Existence Be Disproved?" In *New Essays in Philosophical Theology,* ed. Antony Flew and Alasdair MacIntyre, 47–55. New York: Macmillan.

Haldane, Elizabeth, and G. Ross. 1931. *The Philosophical Works of Descartes,* vol. 2. New York: Cambridge University Press. (Cited as HR II)

Kant, Immanuel. [1781] 1956. *Critique of Pure Reason.* Trans. Norman Kemp Smith. London: Macmillan.

Kretzmann, Norman. 1966. "Omniscience and Immutability." *Journal of Philosophy* 63: 409–21.

Lambert, Karel. 1983. *Meinong and the Principle of Independence.* New York: Cambridge University Press.

Oppy, Graham. 1995. *Ontological Arguments and Belief in God.* New York: Cambridge University Press.

Plantinga, Alvin, ed. 1965. *The Ontological Argument.* Garden City, N.Y.: Doubleday.
Van Inwagen, Peter. 1993. *Metaphysics.* Boulder, Colo.: Westview Press.

FOR FURTHER READING

Adams, Robert. 1971. "The Logical Structure of Anselm's Arguments." *Philosophical Review* 80: 647–84.

Alston, William. 1960. "The Ontological Argument Revisited." *Philosophical Review* 69: 452–74.

Barnes, Jonathan. 1972. *The Ontological Argument.* New York: St. Martin's Press.

Chandler, Hugh. 1993. "Some Ontological Arguments." *Faith and Philosophy* 10: 18–32.

Clarke, Bowman, 1971. "Modal Disproofs and Proofs for God." *Southern Journal of Philosophy* 9: 247–58.

Coburn, Robert. 1963. "Professor Malcolm on God." *Australasian Journal of Philosophy* 41: 143–62.

Davis, Steven. 1976. "Does the Ontological Argument Beg the Question?" *International Journal for Philosophy of Religion* 7: 433–42.

Devine, Philip. 1975. "Does St. Anselm Beg the Question?" *Philosophy* 50: 271–81.

Dore, Clement. 1984. *Theism.* Dordrecht: D. Reidel.

———. 1984. "The Possibility of God." *Faith and Philosophy* 1: 303–15.

Forgie, William, 1972. "Frege's Objection to the Ontological Argument." *Nous* 6: 251–65.

———. 1976. "Is the Cartesian Ontological Argument Defensible?" *New Scholasticism* 50: 108–21.

———. 1990. "The Caterus Objection." *International Journal for Philosophy of Religion* 28: 81–104.

———. 1991. "The Modal Ontological Argument and the Necessary A Posteriori." *International Journal for Philosophy of Religion* 29: 129–41.

Gale, Richard, 1986. "A Priori Arguments from God's Abstractness." *Nous* 20: 531–43.

———. 1988. "Freedom vs. Unsurpassable Greatness." *International Journal for Philosophy of Religion* 23: 65–75.

———. 1991. *On the Nature and Existence of God.* Cambridge, England: Cambridge University Press.

Gotterbarn, Dale. 1976. "Leibniz' Completion of Descartes' Proof." *Studia Leibnitiana* 8: 105–12.

Grim, Patrick. 1979. "Plantinga's God." *Sophia* 18: 35–42.

———. 1979. "Plantinga's God and Other Monstrosities." *Religious Studies* 15: 91–97.

———. 1981. "Plantinga, Hartshorne and the Ontological Argument." *Sophia* 20: 12–16.

———. 1982. "In Behalf of 'In Behalf of the Fool.' " *International Journal for Philosophy of Religion* 13: 33–42.

Hartshorne, Charles. 1962. *The Logic of Perfection.* LaSalle, Ill.: Open Court Press.

———. 1965. *Anselm's Discovery.* LaSalle, Ill.: Open Court Press.

Hazen, Alan. 1998. "On Gödel's Ontological Proof." *Australasian Journal of Philosophy* 76: 361–77.

Hopkins, Jasper. 1972. *A Companion to the Study of St. Anselm.* Minneapolis: University of Minnesota Press.

————. 1976. "Anselm's Debate with Gaunilo." In *Analecta Anselmiana V,* ed. H. Kohlenberger, 25–53. Frankfurt: Minerva GmbH.

Kane, Robert. 1990. "The Modal Ontological Argument." *Mind* 93: 336–50.

Kenny, Anthony. 1968. "Descartes' Ontological Argument." In *Fact and Existence,* ed. Joseph Margolis, 18–36. New York: Oxford University Press.

Leftow, Brian. 1988. "Anselmian Polytheism." *International Journal for Philosophy of Religion* 23: 77–104.

————. 1990. "Individual and Attribute in the Ontological Argument." *Faith and Philosophy* 7: 235–42.

Lewis, David. 1970. "Anselm and Actuality." *Nous* 4: 175–88.

Mackie, John. 1982. *The Miracle of Theism.* New York: Oxford University Press.

Malcolm, Norman. 1960. "Anselm's Ontological Arguments." *Philosophical Review* 69: 41–62.

Mann, William. 1976. "The Perfect Island." *Mind* 85: 417–21.

————. 1991. "Definite Descriptions and the Ontological Argument." In *Philosophical Applications of Free Logic,* ed. Karel Lambert. New York: Oxford University Press.

Mason, P. 1978. "The Devil and St. Anselm." *International Journal for Philosophy of Religion* 9: 1–15.

Oppenheimer, Paul, and Edward Zalta. 1991. "On the Logic of the Ontological Argument." In *Philosophical Perspectives V,* ed. James Tomberlin, 509–29. Atascadero, Calif.: Ridgeview Press.

Plantinga, Alvin. 1967. *God and Other Minds.* Ithaca, N.Y.: Cornell University Press.

————. 1986. "Is Theism Really a Miracle?" *Faith and Philosophy* 3: 109–34.

Rowe, William. 1976. "The Ontological Argument and Question-Begging." *International Journal for Philosophy of Religion* 7: 425–32.

Shaffer, Jerome. 1962. "Existence, Predication and the Ontological Argument." *Mind* 71: 307–25.

Sobel, Jordan. 1987. "Gödel's Ontological Proof." In *On Being and Saying,* ed. Judith Thomson, 241–261. Cambridge, Mass.: MIT Press.

Stone, Jim. 1989. "Anselm's Proof." *Philosophical Studies* 57: 79–94.

Tooley, Michael. 1981. "Plantinga's Defense of the Ontological Argument." *Mind* 90: 422–27.

Van Inwagen, Peter. 1977. "Ontological Arguments." *Nous* 11: 375–95.

Wainwright, William. 1978. "Unihorses and the Ontological Argument." *Sophia* 17: 27–32.

CHAPTER 5

COSMOLOGICAL AND DESIGN ARGUMENTS

ALEXANDER R. PRUSS AND
RICHARD M. GALE

INTRODUCTION

UNLIKE the ontological argument, which appeals only to highly sophisticated philosophers who delight in highly abstract deductive reasoning, cosmological and design arguments figure prominently in the argumentative support that everyday working theists give for their faith. The reason for this broad pastoral appeal is that these arguments begin with commonplace facts about the world and then, by appeal to principles that look plausible, establish the existence of a being who, while not shown to have all of God's essential properties, properties that God must have to exist, is at least a close cousin of the God of traditional Western theism. Our plan is to begin with a preliminary botanization of these arguments, indicating their similarities and differences, and then discuss each of them separately, giving prominence to the many different forms they take.

PRELIMINARY BOTANIZATION

Each of the two arguments begins with a contingent existential fact. A contingent fact is a true proposition that has the possibility of being true and the possibility of being false, in which possibility is understood in the broadly logical or conceptual sense. By extension, a contingent being is one who has both the possibility of existing and the possibility of not existing, with a necessary being not having the possibility of not existing. The arguments differ with respect to the type of existential fact that they select. For design arguments it will be a fact that reports some natural object or process that displays design, purpose, function, order, and the like. It might be the fact that there is life, self-replicating organisms, consciousness, conscience, law-like regularity and simplicity, natural beauty, and apparent religious miracles. In contrast, a cosmological argument's existential fact does not have any of these sorts of valuable features. It might be the fact that there exists a total aggregate of contingent beings (the universe), or maybe that there exists at least one contingent being, or that one object depends on another for its existence.

The two types of argument also differ in the way they go from their initial contingent existential fact to the existence of a supernatural God-like being who is the cause of this fact. A cosmological argument, typically, demands a cause of this fact in the name of the principle of sufficient reason (hereafter PSR), which is suitably tailored so that every fact of this kind actually has an explanation. This is followed by an explanatory argument to show that the only possible explanation for this fact is in terms of the intentional actions of a God-like being. Thus, a cosmological argument standardly has the following three components:

1. A contingent value-neutral existential fact
2. A version of PSR that requires that every fact of this kind has an explanation
3. An explanatory argument to show that the only possible explanation of this fact is in terms of the intentional actions of a supernatural, God-like being

In contrast, the typical design argument does not demand an explanation for the initial contingent existential fact on the basis of some version of the PSR but instead employs principles of inductive reasoning to infer that it is highly probable that this fact is caused by a supernatural, God-like being. These principles might involve principles of analogical reasoning or abductive inference (inference to the best explanation). Thus, the typical design argument has the following three components:

1'. A contingent valuable existential fact
2'. Some principle of inductive reasoning

3'. An explanatory argument to show that the probable explanation of this fact is in terms of the intentional actions of a supernatural, God-like being

It is important to stress that these components comprise only the typical design argument, for there are versions of the design argument that do not employ 2' and 3'. Some design arguments do not induce but instead deduce from the fact reporting some occurrence of natural design that there is a supernatural designer-creator of this occurrence, it supposedly being an analytic truth that something displaying design or purpose must have a designer or purposer. This does not make for an effective argument, as its opponents will be within their rights to charge its existential fact component with begging the question. There are Thomistic-type design arguments that also attempt to deduce the theistic conclusion from the initial existential fact but do not appeal to this trivializing analytic truth but instead some high-level metaphysical principle requiring that there be as much reality in the cause as in the effect.

COSMOLOGICAL ARGUMENTS

With these preliminaries out of the way, we can begin our survey of the different types of cosmological arguments. In the thirteenth century, Saint Thomas Aquinas presented Five Ways of proving the existence of God, the first three of which are versions of the cosmological argument (Aquinas 1969, part 1, question 2, article 2). The First Way begins with the contingent fact that one object is moved by another, the Second that one thing depends for its existence on the causal efficacy of a contemporaneous being, and the Third that there exists a contingent being. These are commonplace observational facts that only a complete skeptic about our senses would want to challenge. The explanatory arguments in the First and Second Ways are based on the impossibility of there being, respectively, an infinite regress of objects simultaneously being moved by other objects or objects depending for their existence on the simultaneous causal efficacy of another being. These regresses, therefore, must terminate with a being who is capable respectively of moving another object without itself being moved by another or causing the existence of something without itself being caused to exist. Thomas then identifies this first mover or cause with God on the basis of our common ways of speaking about God—"and this is what everyone understands by God"—thereby papering over a serious gap problem, since the Five Ways do not establish that this being has all of the essential divine attributes. Thomas does give arguments to close the gap (questions 3–11), but limitations of space preclude our discussing them here.

The intuition underlying Thomas's rejection of the possibility of an actual infinity of simultaneous movers or causers is far from obvious, especially because, according to most commentators, he did not think it impossible to have an actual past infinite regress of nonsimultaneous causes, as, for example, an actual infinite regress of past begetters. We will make an attempt to draw out his intuition in a way that gives some plausibility to it. The causal relation in a series of simultaneous causes or movers involves transitivity in that if X simultaneously moves (causes) Y and Y simultaneously moves (causes) Z, then X moves (causes) Z. Nonsimultaneous causation is not transitive, since, even though you were begot by your parents and they in turn were begot by their parents, you were not begot by the latter.

One reason that might be given for the impossibility of an actual infinite regress of simultaneous causes or movers is that if there were such a regress, there would be no member of the regress that could be held to be morally responsible, a fit subject of either praise or blame, for the initial event or object in the regress. But this can't be the right reason, because not all causal explanations are forensic in the sense of giving an individual who is to be praised or blamed for the effect. Maybe Thomas's underlying intuition can be fleshed out by considering these two examples. In one, a group of boys attempts to get into the movies free by having each boy point to the boy behind him as he enters the theater and when the ticket taker stops the last boy in the group for the tickets he claims not to know who these other boys are. (Richard Gale did it but Alexander Pruss did not, as he grew up in communist Poland.) The last boy has to pay for himself, but all the others get in free. Now suppose that the regress of boys pointing behind themselves to another boy is infinite. Plainly, the theater owner would not be happy with this arrangement, as he would never get paid, just as you would never succeed in cashing a check if it were covered by a bank account that in turn was covered by another and so on ad infinitum. A system of credit, like a succession of boys entering a theater, must terminate with some actual cash. A second example involves a train of cars that simultaneously push each other, such that the first car is simultaneously moved by a second, and the second by a third, and so on ad infinitum. If the regress of movers were infinite, there would be no explanation of where the oomph, the energy, the power to move, comes from.

There is an implicit appeal to a version of the PSR to the effect that something cannot come out of nothing. This can be made clearer by considering a circle of causes. Thomas ruled this to be impossible for the same intuitive reason that he proscribed an infinite regress of simultaneous movers or causes. Imagine that you meet someone who looks like you would look in ten years. She claims to be your future self and to have traveled ten years backward in time to give you instructions on how to build a time machine. Subsequently, you build one and then travel ten years backward in time so as to inform your past self about how to build a time machine. The intuitive grounds for Thomas's rejection of the possibility of this closed causal loop is that it violates the PSR, for there is no answer to the question of from whence came the knowledge of how to build a time machine. Similarly, there is no answer to the question of from whence came the power to move an object or causally sustain its existence in the case of an infinite regress of simultaneous movers or causers.

The Third Way begins with the unexceptionable contingent existential fact that there now exists at least one contingent being. Can some version of the PSR be employed so as to deduce that there exists a necessary being that causes the existence of this contingent being? A contingent being has the possibility of not being, and thus, given an infinite number of times, either through an infinitely extended past or a past time interval that is comprised of an infinity of moments of time, this possibility will be realized at some past time. Each moment is like a roll of the dice, an opportunity for this possibility to be realized. The PSR tells us that something cannot come out of nothing, so there has to be a cause of this being's coming into existence at this past time. Therefore, something had to cause this being to come into being out of nothing. But why couldn't this cause be itself a contingent being and it, in turn, be caused to begin to exist by an even earlier contingent being, and so on ad infinitum? Thomas's answer as to why this regress of contingent beings is impossible seems to commit an egregious quantificational blunder. For he says that if there were to exist only contingent beings, then, since for each of them there is a past time at which it doesn't exist, there is a past time at which each one of them does not exist. And, if there ever were nothing, then, given the PSR, nothing would subsequently exist, which contradicts the patent existential fact that there now exists at least one contingent being. This argument seems to commit the same howler as is committed by inferring from the fact that for every woman there is a man that there is a man who is for every woman (talk about polygamy!). In logical terms, that fallacy is $(x)(\exists y)xRy \supset (\exists y)(x)xRy$. But it is hard to believe that a great philosopher committed so obvious a blunder. With a little charity and imagination something interesting can be made out of the Third Way, but we shall not attempt to do so here.[1]

The Kalam cosmological argument of the medieval Islamic philosophers, which has been defended in recent times by William Lane Craig (1979), also invokes the impossibility of infinite regress but in a different way than Thomas did in his first two Ways. It selects as its contingent existential fact that there now exists a universe—an aggregate comprised of all contingent beings. It then argues that the universe must have begun to exist, for otherwise there would be an actual infinite series of past events or time, which is conceptually absurd. Because something cannot come out of nothing, there had to be a cause for the universe coming into being at some time a finite number of years ago. And this cause is identified with God, which again occasions the gap problem. Notice that the version of the PSR that is appealed to is a restricted and thus less vulnerable version of the PSR; for whereas the unrestricted version requires explanation for every thing that exists or fails to exist, the restricted version requires an explanation only for a being's coming into existence.

Just why is it impossible for there to be an actual infinity of past events or times? The answer is not obvious. Thomas, for one, did not think it to be impossible. Two kinds of arguments have been given. First, there are descendants of Zeno's arguments. It is not possible actually to go through an infinite series of events, for before going through the last event of the series, one would already have to have gone through an infinite series, and before the second last event, one would already have to have traversed an infinite series, and so on: the task could never have got started. But if there was an actual infinity of past events, then our world has traversed an infinite set of events, which is impossible. This argument depends on an anthropocentric notion of "going through" a set. The universe does not go through a set of events in the sense of planning which to go through first in order to get through the second, and so on.

The other kind of argument given by Kalam arguers is that the very concept of infinity is incoherent. Imagine Hilbert's hotel, where there are infinitely many rooms, numbered 1, 2, 3, and so on, and where even if all rooms are occupied, space can always be found for a new visitor by shifting the occupant of room 1 to room 2, moving room 2's occupant to room 3, and so on. The slogan outside the hotel would say: "Always full, always room for more," and the Kalam arguer takes this to be incoherent. Or consider an infinite series of events, again numbered 1, 2, 3, and so on. Then, the subseries consisting of the even-numbered events should have fewer events in it. But in fact it does not, as can be seen by writing the two series one on top of the other:

$$1 \quad 2 \quad 3 \quad 4 \quad 5 \quad 6 \quad 7 \ldots$$
$$2 \quad 4 \quad 6 \quad 8 \quad 10 \quad 12 \quad 14 \ldots$$

and noting that each member of the top series corresponds precisely to each member of the bottom series. Hence, the series of even-numbered events is both smaller and not smaller than the upper series. These arguments against an actual infinity, however, are all based on a confusion between two notions of "bigger than." One notion is numerical: a set is bigger than another if it has a greater number of members. The other notion is in terms of part-to-whole relations: a whole is bigger than any proper part. When dealing with finite quantities, anything that is bigger in the part-to-whole sense is also bigger in the numerical sense. But this is not so in the case of infinite quantities. Although in the part-to-whole sense there are more people in the hotel after a new guest arrives and there are more members of the original series of events, in the numerical sense there are not. Indeed, mathematicians take the failure of the part-to-whole sense of "bigger than" to imply the numerical sense to be the defining feature of infinity.

Alternately, the Kalam arguer may make use of modern scientific theories, such as that of the Big Bang. However, in those cases, the argument is still subject to the possibility that the theories will turn out to be false, or that it will turn out that there is a prior *physical* cause of some sort to the Big Bang.

Probably the most powerful of the traditional cosmological arguments, as it involves the least amount of conceptual baggage and controversial assumptions, is the one given by Newton's follower Samuel Clarke (1705) at the beginning of the eighteenth century. Like the Kalam argument, it begins with the contingent existential fact that there now exists an aggregate of all the contingent beings there are, but unlike this argument, it does not have to invoke any controversial claims about the impossibility of infinite aggregates. It demands an explanation for the existence of this universe on the basis of a more general version of the PSR than the one employed in the Kalam argument, namely, that there is an explanation for the existence of every contingent being, even if it always existed. For explanatory purposes, the universe itself counts as a contingent being, since it is an aggregate of all the contingent beings there are. It therefore must have a causal explainer. This cause cannot be a contingent being. For if a contingent were to be the cause, it would have to be a cause of every one of the aggregate's constituents. But since every contingent being is included in this aggregate, it would have to be a cause of itself, which is impossible. The cause, therefore, must be some individual outside the aggregate; and, since an impossible individual cannot cause anything, it must be a necessary being that serves as the causal explainer of the aggregate. This holds whether the aggregate contains a finite or an infinite number of contingent beings. Even if there were to be, as is possible for Clarke, an infinite past succession of contingent beings, each causing the existence of its immediate successor, there still would need to be a cause of the entire infinite succession.

It is at this point that David Hume (1980), writing about half a century after Clarke, raised what is considered by many to be a decisive objection to Clarke's argument. He claimed that for any aggregate, whether finite or infinite, if there is for each of its constituents an explanation, there thereby is an explanation for the entire aggregate. Thus, if there were to be an infinite past succession of contingent beings, each of which causally explains the existence of its immediate successor, there would be an explanation for the entire infinite aggregate, and thus no need to go outside it and invoke a necessary being as its cause. Hume's claim that explanation is in general agglomerative can be shown to be false (see Gale 1991; Pruss 1998). For it is possible for there to be a separate explanation for the existence of each constituent in an aggregate, say each part of an automobile, without there thereby being an explanation of the entire aggregate, the automobile. The explanation for the latter would be above and beyond these several separate explanations for the existence of its constituent parts, as, for example, one that invokes the assembling activity in a Detroit factory.

William Rowe (1975) has given a variant version of Clarke's argument. He chooses as his initial contingent existential fact that there exists at least one contingent being. This is the plaintive cry that one might hear in a coffeehouse, "Why is there something rather than nothing?", to which, according to Sidney Morgenbesser, God's response is, "Look, you guys, suppose I created nothing, you still wouldn't be happy." The point of Morgenbesser's witticism is that even if there were to be nothing, that is, no contingent beings, the PSR still would require that there be an explanation for this big negative fact. The PSR is an equal-opportunity explainer, not giving a privileged status to positive reality. We ask "Why is there something rather than nothing?" simply because there happens to be something rather than nothing. The PSR requires there be an explanation for the contingent fact that there exists at least one contingent being. It cannot be given in terms of the causal efficacy of another contingent being, since this would result in a vicious circularity. Thus, it must be in terms of the causal efficacy of a necessary being.

This completes our brief survey of traditional cosmological arguments. It is now time to critically evaluate them. It was seen that each faced an unresolved gap problem consisting in its failure to show that the first cause, unmoved mover, or necessary being has all of the essential divine attributes. The most serious form the gap problem takes concerns the moral qualities of this being. Here the problem of evil has been appealed to by the likes of Hume to argue that probably it is not an all-good but rather a morally indifferent being. This, no doubt, is the point of a bumper sticker that reads, "God does exist. He just doesn't want to get involved." To counter the challenge of evil, it is necessary to construct theodicies for the known evils and give convincing design arguments, which is the topic of the next section.

The most vulnerable premise in these arguments is its PSR, whether in its universal or restricted form. It is imposing on the nontheist opponent of these arguments to ask him or her to grant that every true contingent proposition (or some restricted set of them) actually has an explanation, for this, in effect, is to grant that the universe is rational through and through. And this occupies almost as high an echelon in one's wish book as does the existence of God. Hume argued that we can conceive of an uncaused event, and, since whatever is conceivable is possible in reality, PSR is false. Bruce Reichenbach (1972) charges that Hume confuses epistemic with ontological conditions. To be sure, there is a distinction between what is conceivable and what could exist, the former concerning the epistemic and the latter the ontological order. Nevertheless, Reichenbach's rebuttal is far too facile, for it fails to face the fact that our only access to the ontological order is through the epistemic order. The only way that we humans can go about determining what has the possibility of existing is by appeal to what we can conceive to be possible. Such modal intuitions concerning what is possible are fallible; they are only prima facie acceptable, because they are subject to defeat by subsequent ratiocination. They are discussion beginners, not discussion enders. In philosophy we must go with what we ultimately can make intelligible to ourselves at the end of the day, after we have made our best philosophical efforts. What can the defender of the PSR say to get us to give up our prima facie Humean modal intuition? Plainly, the onus is on her, since it is she who uses the PSR as a premise in her cosmological argument.

Some cosmological arguers claim that PSR is self-evident, in the way the law of excluded middle (that for every proposition, p, p-or-not-p) might be, and accuse those who reject it with having a bias against theism. However, claims of self-evidence are of little use to those who are not party to them, just as that the law of excluded middle appears self-evident to us is of no help to those intuitionist mathematicians who do not see it this way. Claims of self-evidence simply end discussions, and accusations of bias are a two-edged sword.

Another way of supporting PSR is to show that it is pragmatically rational for an inquirer to believe it, since by believing that everything has an explanation the believer becomes a more ardent and dedicated inquirer and thus is more apt to find explanations than if she did not believe this. This pragmatic sense of rational concerns the benefits that accrue to the believer of the PSR proposition, as contrasted with the epistemic sense of rational that concerns reasons directed toward supporting the truth of the proposition believed. Because cosmological arguments attempt to establish the epistemic rationality of believing that God exists, they cannot employ a premise that concerns only the pragmatic rationality of believing some proposition, such as the PSR, for this would commit the fallacy of equivocation, since "rational" would be used in both the pragmatic and the epistemic sense. In essence, it would be arguing that it is epistemically rational to believe a proposition p because it is pragmatically rational to believe some proposition q, from which p follows or which is needed for the deduction of p.

A more reasonable argument for the PSR is an inductive one based on our numerous and ever increasing successes in explaining contingently true propositions. The problem with such an inductive argument is that there is a significant difference between the contingent events and objects within the universe that form its inductive sample and the universe as a whole. Thus, it is risky to infer that what holds for the former also holds for the latter.

Recently, we have concocted a new version of Clarke's cosmological argument that manages to make do with a very weak version of the PSR that requires only that for every contingently true proposition it is possible that it have an explanation, thereby making it more difficult for the argument's nontheist opponent to reject the PSR premise. Thus, it is not required that the proposition reporting the existence of the universe comprised of all the contingent beings there are actually have an explanation, only that it is possible that it does.

Once our opponent has granted the following weak version of the PSR

W-PSR. For every contingently true proposition, p, there is a possible world w that contains the propositions p, q, and that q explains p.

we are able to deduce from it the strong version of the PSR, namely,

S-PSR. For every contingently true proposition, p, there is a proposition q and that q explains p.

in which a possible world is a maximal, compossible conjunction of abstract propositions. It is maximal because for every proposition, p, either p is one of its conjuncts or not-p is; and it is compossible in that all of its conjuncts could be true together. This deduction, which is due to Pruss, goes as follows:

1. For every contingently true proposition, p, there is a possible world w that contains the propositions p, q, and that q explains p. W-PSR.
2. p is contingently true and there is no explanation of p. Assumption for indirect proof.
3. There is a possible world w that contains the propositions (p and there is no explanation of p), q and that q explains (p and there is no explanation of p). From 1 and 2.
4. In w, q explains p. True because explanation distributes over a conjunction.
5. In w, proposition p both does and does not have an explanation. From 3 and 4.
6. It is not the case that p is contingently true and there is no explanation of p. From 2–5 by indirect proof.
7. It is not the case for any proposition p that p is contingently true and there is no explanation of p. From 6.

Once we have established by this deduction that there actually is an explanation for the existence of the universe, we show by a series of deductions, which cannot be gone into here, that it is in terms of the free intentional actions of a very intelligent and powerful necessarily existent supernatural being. It must be a necessary being because the universe contains all the contingent beings there are. Because this necessarily existent being freely creates the universe, our argument escapes Schopenhauer's objection to the cosmological argument as being like a taxicab that we hire and then dismiss when we have reached our destination. For the cosmological arguer begins by demanding, on the basis of the PSR, an explanation for a certain contingent existential fact, but when she arrives at our desired destination, God, she dismisses the PSR because she does not require an explanation for the fact that God exists and causes the existence of this fact.

Because our explainer is a necessary being, it is a self-explaining being in the sense that there is a successful ontological argument for its existence, even if we aren't smart enough to give it. And, because it *freely* causes the existence of the universe, the act of creation is a self-explaining action for a libertarian theory of freedom, which is the theory favored by the theist.

Once our opponent realizes that W-PSR logically entails S-PSR, she might no longer grant us W-PSR, charging it with begging the question. Whether an argument begs the question is relative to the epistemic circumstances of its opponent before the argument is given, not after it has been given. But this response would not silence Graham Oppy, for he claims that "once you understand W-PSR *properly*, you can see that it entails S-PSR; and S-PSR is something which nontheists have good reason to refuse to accept . . . Those nontheists who were 'willing to grant W-PSR' before they heard the argument which Gale and Pruss give should then say that they didn't *fully* understand what it was to which they were giving assent" (2000, 349). Herein Oppy is demanding that *proper* or *full* understanding be closed under deduction. This demand is contrived and has the unwanted consequence that every valid deductive argument, when its premises are *fully* understood, can rightly be charged with begging the question.

Although Oppy's demand is unacceptably strong, it still is true that to have an adequate understanding of a proposition one must know some of its entailment relationships. One would not understand, for example, the proposition that this is a material object unless one were prepared to deduce from it that this occupies space. (Please, no Castenada-type counterexamples of the "I went to kiss Mary but her lips were not extended" sort!) But, plainly, one can understand that this is a material object without being aware of the very complex propositions that it entails within mereological theory.

We are not able to give a precise criterion for distinguishing between those entailment relations that are constitutive of understanding a given proposition and those that are not, since the concept of understanding is a pragmatic one and thus context-sensitive. But this does not mean that we cannot identify clear-cut cases of someone understanding a proposition and those in which she does not. And certainly one can understand a proposition that uses a modal concept without knowing every theorem of modal logic, just as one can understand a proposition employing geometrical concepts without knowing every theorem of geometry.

The most challenging objection to our argument has been given by Kevin Davey and Rob Clifton (2001). Their strategy is to find a proposition that is strongly incompatible with W-PSR, in that if either is true in any possible world the other is true in none, and which is at least as plausible a candidate for being logically possible as is W-PSR. Their candidate for such a proposition is that there is a contingent proposition that lacks an explanation in the actual world, say that there are cats, or the universe for that matter. This modal intuition seems at first blush to have as much prima facie plausibility as does our modal intuition that every contingent proposition possibly has an explanation. But it turns out that these plausible modal intuitions are strongly incompatible. For W-PSR entails S-PSR and thus that in no possible world is there an unexplained contingent proposition. But the Davey-Clifton intuition entails that there is just such a world.

The strategy that we adopt for breaking this tie in modal intuitions is to show that one of the two rival modal intuitions coheres better with other of our background modal intuitions. To begin with, our belief in W-PSR coheres better with our proclivity to seek an explanation for any contingently true proposition. That we seek such an explanation shows that we do accept W-PSR, for we would not seek an explanation if we did not believe that it is at least logically possible that there is one. Second, we know what it is like to verify that a given proposition has an explanation, namely, by discovering an explanation for it, but we do not know what it is like to verify that a given contingently and verifiably true proposition does not have an explanation. Furthermore, since we know what it is like to verify that a proposition has an explanation, we know what it is like to verify that it possibly has an explanation, given that actuality entails possibility. We do not, however, know what it is like to verify that a proposition does not possibly have an explanation: there are just too many possible worlds for that to be accomplished. It is beside the point to respond that we know how to falsify the proposition that some proposition does not have an explanation but not the proposition that it has an explanation, since a proposition's truth-conditions are directly tied to its conditions of verification, not those for its falsification. These two considerations lend credence to the claim that, in the epistemic order, W-PSR is more deeply entrenched than is the Davey-Clifton claim that it is possible that a given contingent proposition has no explanation. From this conclusion it is reasonable to infer that, in the logical or conceptual order, W-PSR is a better candidate than is the Davey-Clifton proposition for being possible.

TELEOLOGICAL ARGUMENTS

The teleological argument for the existence of God, or at least for a designer of the universe, has never received a more rhetorically powerful formulation than in William Paley's (1802) analogy of the watch. We find a watch lying on a heath. We examine it. We see that its parts fit and work together in an intricate manner, and infer that the watch was designed by an intelligent agent. The inference could be made even if we had never seen a watch before. Similarly, when we look at biological mechanisms, we descry a similar complexity and we should likewise infer that the biological mechanisms were designed, but by a proportionately more intelligent being.

The argument does not tell us much about the designer, but we can at least infer that the ultimate designer is at least in part immaterial. For if the designer were a physical being, he too would have intricately put together parts, since any completely material intelligent being will have to be constituted out of a number of carefully interrelated parts, and the argument from design could be repeated. But a regress could be argued to be vicious here for reasons similar to those in the cosmological argument: if there was just an infinite regress, the complexity of design would never get explained. Moreover, we have empirical reasons against accepting an infinite regress of physical beings as designers, namely, the empirical evidence that our universe has finite age.

We see here the ingredients of any argument from design. A design argument, like a cosmological argument, begins with a contingent existential fact, but, unlike a cosmological argument, one that has a valuable status, such as that there exists natural beauty, widespread lawlike regularity, and the like. It must be stressed that the fact about design is a morally desirable one. Otherwise, nothing could be inferred about the goodness, as contrasted with the intelligence and power, of the person who brings about the fact. Moreover, if the design explanation is to be satisfactory, the existential fact should be one that an intelligent person would not be too unlikely to desire: if we have a group of stones strewn about apparently at random, we would not expect that an intelligent person desired *precisely* that combination.

To avoid the charge of begging the question, the premise in a design argument that reports the existence of some natural object or process that displays design or purpose must not be taken in such a way that it immediately entails that there exists a designer or purposer, for that would bring on a justified charge of begging the question from the opponent of the argument. Rather, it must be taken to mean that there exists a natural object or process that has an *apparent* design, purpose, or function, leaving it an open question as to what sort of a cause, if any, there is of this apparent design. It is then inferred that the item was in fact designed by an intelligent agent. To be God, the designer would have to be among other things all-good. The moral qualities of the designer would have to be inferred from known facts about the world. Many items showing apparent design have been adduced, including biological mechanisms, the apparent fine-tuning of the constants in the laws of nature, the regularity of the laws of nature, altruism, consciousness, the existence of various natural kinds of animals, the purposefulness of things in nature, and even miracles—this last, special case being discussed in another chapter in this book. The inference in the argument is typically nondeductive: the argument may involve analogy to artifacts of human design, as in

Paley's case, or an inductive appeal to data that things showing a certain kind of complexity are in fact designed by intelligent agents, or inference to best explanation, or some other way of recognizing the marks of intelligent design.

In his *Dialogues Concerning Natural Religion*, David Hume (1980) considers a teleological argument in which it is inferred that the universe as a whole resembles human artifice, and therefore also has an intelligent designer, though a proportionately greater one. Hume objects that there is a serious disanalogy between the whole universe and human artifice. Any disanalogy weakens an analogical argument. But to do serious damage, the disanalogy needs to show a difference in those respects of the supposedly analogous cases that are essential to the argument. What is essential to the teleological argument, its defender will insist, is that both watches and the universe, or some subset of it such as a biological organism, show a marvelously complex interrelation of parts, and Hume does not attack the similarity in this respect.

However, Hume insists that what is essential to inferring the designer of things like watches and houses is that we have *seen* things of this sort with this kind of complexity and on this scale made by human beings, whereas we could not have seen universes being designed since by definition the universe is unique. If we had not seen mechanisms made by humans, we would not infer that the watch found on the heath is designed. But surely, even if one found some mysterious complex interrelated mechanisms, ones with the complexity of a watch, on a different planet, where one *knew* that they were not designed by humans, one would infer the existence of an intelligence behind them. Thus, the inference of design does not depend on its being human designers that are inferred. Rather, the inductive data of seeing humans construct artifacts open our eyes to seeing how intelligence in general functions and what products rational agency produces. And, in any case, Hume's reply fails if the form of the argument from design is not analogical but, say, that of an inference to the best explanation.

However, the most powerful blow against Paley's argument was not struck by Hume but by Charles Darwin, who argued that the mechanisms that impressed Paley so much probably were generated by the natural process of organisms mutating and only the fitter ones surviving to reproduce. Nondeductive teleological arguments can be challenged in various ways. One of the ways is to show the existence of a satisfactory explanation of the items in question by a nondesigned natural process, since that would challenge the claim that the theistic explanation is the only or the best one available. It might well be that *both* a theistic and a naturalistic explanation are true, but in the presence of a naturalistic one, the theistic one may not be needed or may not be the best one. Of course, for the naturalistic explanation to be satisfactory, the naturalistic process cannot be an *improbable* one. It will not do to explain the existence of a watch by saying that the molecules making it up randomly came together under the influence of quantum randomness, because this process would be ridiculously improbable. However, the Darwinian claim is that mutation plus natural selection makes the existence of complex biological mechanisms probable.

The Darwinian account does not deal a deathblow to Paley-type arguments. First of all, evolution does nothing to explain why there were living organisms on earth in the first place. Evolution only functions when a self-reproducing entity is on the scene: it cannot explain the coming-to-be of such entities. And prima facie we would expect that any self-reproducing organism would have a certain minimal complexity. The simplest independent living organism we know of is the *Mycoplasma genitalium*, whose genetic code comprises 517 genes, with the DNA consisting of about 193,000 codons, each of which can code for one of twenty amino acids. Experiments suggest that only about 265 to 350 of the genes are needed for life (Hutcheson et al. 1996). But even the 265 shortest genes would have a total length of 4,239 codons.[2] Because each codon codes for one of twenty amino acids, this gives us $20^{4239} \approx 10^{5515}$ possible DNA sequences of this length,[3] and the chance that a random DNA sequence of the appropriate length would be equivalent to the particular sequence of one *Mycoplasma genitalium* organism is thus less than one in 10^{5515}.

We can call an event whose probability is less than 10^{100} "astronomically improbable," since it would not be likely to have been generated in the 12 to 18 billion years our universe has been around, even if each of the molecules in the universe, there being no more than about 10^{80} of them, tried to randomly produce the event a hundred times a second. In practice, other DNA sequences could produce an organism with the same functional properties; there are many other organisms than this *Mycoplasma* that would be sufficient to start life; and there are scenarios for the start of life that do not involve a full-blown independent DNA-based organism coming about at random (see, e.g., Gesteland, Cech, and Atkins 2000). Thus, the actual probability is higher than one in 10^{5515}. However, the number gives one some idea of how difficult the life-production task is. We still do not have a reasonably probable scientific explanation for the origin of life, and so the possibility that a Paley-type argument will succeed is still open.

Second, in a surprising development, there are scientists and mathematicians, most notably Michael Behe (1996) and William Dembski (1999a, 1999b), who question whether Darwinian evolution can account for all biological mechanisms. Thus, Behe argues that whatever the plausibility of Darwinism for explaining macroscopic features of organisms, on the microscopic level we find biochemical complexity of such a degree that it could not be expected to come about through natural selection. The problem is that there are *irreducible complexities*: systems that only benefit the organism once *all* the parts are properly installed. A system having irreducible complexity cannot be expected to evolve gradually step by step through natural selection. Behe has argued that the cilia of bacteria, our immune system, and the blood-clotting system exhibit irreducible complexity. Findings like this have been challenged and evolutionary mechanisms for at least some of these systems have been proposed. At the moment, this dispute is not resolvable and we must await future scientific breakthroughs. There is, however, at least some chance that the Paley argument in almost its classical form may yet come back.

Instead of focusing on biological detail, many modern teleological arguers prefer to point to the apparent fact that the laws of nature, and the various constants in them, are precisely such as to allow for life (see, e.g., Leslie 1988). For instance, the universal law of gravitation states that the force between two masses is equal to G times the product of the masses divided by the square of the distance, where G is the gravitational constant equal approximately to 6.672×10^{-11} in the metric system. But although this constant could, prima facie, have any other real number as its value, only a narrow range of values of that constant would allow for, say, the formation of apparent prerequisites for life, such as stars. Likewise, it is claimed that were the laws of nature themselves somewhat different, life could not form.

Of course, it could be that the progress of science will unify all the laws of nature in a way that exactly predicts the values of the constants, and in a way that will make it seem "natural" that the laws and constants are as they are. However, this has not been done yet, and we can only go by what we have right now. It is claimed that, right now, our only good putative explanation of the laws and constants is design.

Gilbert Fulmer (2001) has replied that the discussions of the fine-tuning of the constants in the laws of nature all presuppose that we are working in a range of values similar to those that actually obtain, or at least that we are working with laws of nature generally like ours. But how do we know that once we look at the totality of all possible laws of nature and constants therein, we might not find that the majority of these are compatible with life, albeit perhaps life of a significantly different sort than we find here? In reply to this kind of an argument, Leslie (1988) has used the analogy of a wasp on a wall. Imagine we see that a wasp on a wall was hit by a dart. Around the wasp, there is a large clear area with no wasps. We are justified in inferring that someone *aimed* the dart at the wasp even if there are lots of wasps further away on the wall. To infer design, one does not need the paucity of fine-tuned universes simpliciter, but simply in our local area. Besides, we do have good reason to think that if we look at all possible universes, it is not the case that the majority of them can support life.

Finally, the many universes anthropic principle (MUAP) can be brought in. This principle states that there exist infinitely many universes, either sequentially or simultaneously, and thus it is not improbable that some of them would contain observers, while evidently we can observe only a universe that can contain observers. The MUAP claims in general that we have no right to be surprised to observe a feature of the universe necessary for the production of intelligent life, since it is likely that at least one of the infinitely many universes would contain that feature, and we cannot observe any other. Thus, perhaps, there are infinitely many universes, in which case we would expect that at least one would exhibit the kind of fine-tuning that makes life possible, and obviously we couldn't observe any other.

There are two forms the MUAP takes. First, it might be that, necessarily, all logically possible universes concretely exist, as in David Lewis's (1986) extreme modal realism. Unfortunately, Lewis's theory runs into a multitude of paradoxes. To give just the simplest, note that Lewis's theory undercuts inductive reasoning. Suppose God phoned you and, after having assured you with sufficiently impressive miracles that he is God, told you that he created at least as many universes with the same past as yours in which gravity fails to hold tomorrow as ones in which gravity continues tomorrow, but neglected to tell you which kind of universe he put you in. By standard canons of reasoning, you would be rationally required to assign at least as great epistemic probability to the claim that the law of gravitation will not hold tomorrow as to the claim that it will. Therefore, your inductive inference that tomorrow gravity will hold as it has always held would be undercut. But Lewis's theory is just like this call from God: Lewis tells us that all logically possible universes exist, and certainly then there will be at least as many worlds that have the same past as this world in which gravity will fail to hold tomorrow as ones where gravity will continue as before. Thus, Lewis's theory gives data undercutting induction, and hence we should reject Lewis's theory.

Alternatively, it could be that all or infinitely many universes exist satisfying the same *basic* laws of nature, albeit with different constants in them. It does not matter here whether these universes exist simultaneously or sequentially. This version of MUAP, however, fails to block the question of why *these* basic laws of nature hold rather than others. It might, after all, be that the vast majority of possible sets of laws of nature could not support intelligent enmattered life because the vast majority would involve massive irregularity. For instance, intuitively, there are a lot more possible laws of gravitation that involve many discontinuities and irregularities in the formula for the force as a function of the distance than there are highly regular laws, and it might be that life could exist only in what is intuitively only a small fraction of the universes governed by such irregular laws, though making these intuitions more precise would be a nontrivial task.

It is worth noting parenthetically that a multiple-universe theory has also been used to neutralize the argument against theism from evil. Donald Turner (2003) proposes that a perfectly good God would create all universes that are sufficiently good, that is, which it is better to create than not to. As long as our universe is above that cut-off line, God was justified in creating it, even though superior universes abound, for to create our universe and the superior ones is better than just creating the superior ones. Thus, multiple universes can just as much be used in defense of theism as in defense of atheism.

Another kind of teleological argument, which has been promoted by Richard Swinburne (1968), is based on the fact that the universe displays widespread lawlike regularity and simplicity. It is argued that there are only two possible explanations for a fact: either a scientific explanation in terms of boundary conditions and laws of nature, or a personalistic explanation in terms of the intentional activity of an agent. Now, because a scientific explanation explains facts by invoking laws of nature, it cannot explain why there *are* laws of nature on the pain of circularity. Thus, if there is an explanation, it must be one that is given in terms of the intentional activity of a designer.

Several replies are available. The first is simply to deny the call for explanation here. The basic laws of nature are rock-bottom, and they have no explanation. This approach is particularly attractive if one is willing to bite the bullet and accept the implausible claim that the laws of nature that in fact actually hold are logically necessary. Once one admits, however, that the laws are contingent, one faces the following difficulty, at least if one has the Humean intuition that all possible states of the universe are prima facie equally likely to happen temporally after any one given state[4]: prima facie, it is vastly improbable that things should behave in a regular way. Unfortunately, it is very difficult, if not impossible, to assign precise probabilities to such things as universes. Hence, this argument may necessarily have to be run on an intuitive level, though aided by simpler cases. As a toy model, imagine a discrete Humean universe containing only one particle of a fixed type and whose only degrees of freedom are in the spatial position, and whose space-time has a temporal series consisting of a hundred instants of time, and the spatial structure of a 10-by-10 grid. There are 10^{200} such universes. A minimal constraint on regularity is that the particle doesn't fly around to noncontiguous grid locations, but in each time step is either where it was previously or at one of the up to eight neighboring grid locations. There are fewer than 100×9^{99} universes satisfying this constraint. Thus, the probability that a randomly chosen toy model universe will satisfy the minimal regularity constraint is less than the astronomically small value of 10^{-100}. Moreover, as the grid becomes finer and finer and the time-series becomes closer and closer to being continuous, this probability decreases exponentially.

Thus, a fortiori, the initial probability of a regular universe with continuous space and time is exceedingly small on Humean assumptions, and indeed probably zero. On the design hypothesis, on the other hand, a regular universe has a probability that is not astronomically low. For an intelligent agent has good reason to produce order, order being objectively valuable and necessary for the existence of forms of life capable of intentional action, and the probability of an agent doing what she has good reason to do is not astronomically low. After all, prima facie, an agent is not any less likely to be good than she is to be evil or to be neutral, and so one might assign a probability of $\frac{1}{3}$ that the agent will be good, and then at the least some probability like 0.000001 (which, though small, is not astronomically so) that if she is good, she will produce a universe exhibiting order. This would yield a probability like at least 0.00000033 that an intelligent designer of the universe would produce a universe exhibiting order, which is so much higher than the astronomically small probability on Humean design-free intuitions that it significantly increases the ratio of the probability of the design hypothesis to the Humean hypothesis.

An alternative reply to the Swinburne argument is to invoke MUAP. Recall that MUAP posits infinitely many universes but notes that there is a selection effect: we can observe only a universe that has observers in it. Now, a universe that for the most part displays causal regularity is a necessary prerequisite for there to exist finite knowers and agents, since empirical knowledge depends on identifying persisting objects. If so, then we have no right to be surprised at the order in the universe given a many-universes theory.

Swinburne (1968) attacks the MUAP reply to his argument by noting that it is at most order in the past, and even then only in our local neighborhood, that is required for knowers and observers. Thus, even if there are many universes and we preselect for those that contain observers, nonetheless on Humean grounds we should still find future order, and order outside our local neighborhood, to be quite improbable. To see this more clearly, suppose in our toy model above we preselect first for those universes where the minimal condition for regularity is satisfied for the first fifty time steps. Nonetheless, only fewer than one in 10^{50} of these universes continues being regular for the next fifty steps. Indeed, on a Humean MUAP account, we would expect future disorder to be highly probable, and hence as order continues to be observed, the Humean MUAP reply becomes more and more disconfirmed. Likewise, order outside our galaxy disconfirms the Humean MUAP reply.

Observe that in a number of the nondeductive teleological arguments, issues of probability theory require further investigation. We intuitively feel that it is highly improbable prima facie that there be a nondesigned universe that exhibits regular lawlikeness. But making this intuition precise is a nightmare. There are infinitely many possible universes that exhibit lawlike regularity and infinitely many that do not. The infinite numbers here may even be beyond cardinality (for instance, it has been shown that the collection of all possible worlds is not a set and hence lacks cardinality; see Pruss 2001). Perhaps the argument can be made only on an intuitive level, on the same intuitive level at which we say that it is highly unlikely that a given integer about which nothing more is known is in fact prime even though the cardinality of the set of prime numbers is the same as that of the integers.

Likewise, the thorny issue of how initially plausible the hypothesis of the existence of a designer is to someone needs to be discussed. If one thinks that the existence of a designer has astronomically small epistemic probability, then one will not be impressed by arguments showing that some form of complexity has a similarly small probability of arising by chance. However, few reasonable people think that the existence of God has a probability as low as 10^{-100}.

The above arguments were all nondeductive. However, John Haldane (Smart and Haldane 2003) has given a deductive Thomistic teleological argument. In the history of our universe, we see that on at least several occasions, a qualitatively new thing such as life or mind has developed, and a qualitatively new thing by definition could not have arisen gradually. Moreover, if a cause is to explain the coming into existence of such a positive quality as life or mind, it must itself either formally or eminently have that quality, to use Descartes' terminology, where to have F "formally" is just to be F and where to have F "eminently" is to have this quality as an idea in one's mind in the sense of its being an intentional accusative of one of its thoughts. (Saint Thomas already used this principle in his argument that the first cause of all contingent beings must be at least as perfect as the sum total of all the perfections of creatures: see Aquinas 1969, part 1, question 4, article 2.) Thus, randomness will not explain the coming into existence of qualitatively new things, such as life or mind. Nor will one explain the existence of life or mind by positing an infinite series of living or mindful things, each descended from the next, since it will still not be explained where the positive quality came from in the first place.

Therefore, one must either come to a necessary being that has life or mind, and whose having of life or mind is a consequence of its essence, or to a person who has life eminently and mind both eminently and formally (it being impossible to have any quality eminently without formally having mind). In either case, we can conclude the existence of an intelligent first cause for the existence of mind. The Paley-type arguments merely gave us a God of the gaps: should science discover new naturalistic explanations of things, these arguments would fall through. But like Swinburne's lawlikeness argument, Haldane's argument gives principled reasons for the claim that an intelligent being is needed for the explanation of the phenomenon in question. Therefore, Haldane does not need to worry as each new issue of *Nature* comes out that a naturalistic challenger to his argument will be found. The argument as stated above is abductive: a theistic-type explanation is the only one possible, and hence true. To make it into a fully deductive argument, one needs to add the principle of sufficient reason as an explicit premise. For then, there is an explanation, and hence the only possible explanation must be the explanation. And of course, the Achilles heel of this Thomistic argument is the controversial metaphysics of qualitative difference behind it.

Finally, note that teleological arguments face the same kind of gap problem as infect cosmological ones. Just as there is a gap between being a first cause and being God, there is a gap between being a very powerful and intelligent designer and being God. The most serious part of the gap concerns the goodness of the designer, due to the fact that there is a lot of apparently unjustified evil, where an evil is unjustified if it would preclude the existence of God because no morally exonerating excuse would exist for permitting it. To close the gap, the teleological arguer, like the cosmological arguer, must find a way of neutralizing the problem of evil, either through constructing a theodicy that gives God a justification for permitting these evils or by showing that a theodicy is not needed. Thus, we see the need to do the philosophy of religion in a global manner.

NOTES

We would like to thank Roland Hirsch, George Hunter, and David Keller for helpful discussion of and comments on biological matters. We are most grateful to William Wainwright for a number of very helpful editorial and substantial comments.

1. We leave it as an exercise to the reader to see that Aquinas's argument could be made valid if he were to stop allowing for the possibility of an infinite number of past contingent beings and assume instead that there have been only finitely many such beings.

2. Based on data in the online gene database for the *Mycoplasma genitalium* available at www.tigr.org.

3. With two sequences counted as equivalent if they code for the same amino acids.

4. Hume (1993, section IV, part I) asked rhetorically if when we consider a priori what will happen to a stone left without support in the air there is "any thing we discover in this situation, which can beget the idea of a downward, rather than upward, or any other motion, in the stone or metal." Hume thinks the answer is negative, because he sees no prima facie reason to think any one state is more likely to come after a given initial state than any other state is.

WORKS CITED

Aquinas, Thomas. 1969. *Summa Theologiae: Volume 1: The Existence of God: Part One: Questions 1–13.* Garden City, N.Y.: Image Books.

Behe, Michael J. 1996. *Darwin's Black Box.* New York: Simon and Schuster.

Clarke, Samuel. 1705. "An Improved Version of the Argument." In Brody (1992): 138.

Craig, William L. 1979. *The Kalam Cosmological Argument.* London: Macmillan.

———. 1980. *The Cosmological Argument from Plato to Leibniz.* New York: Barnes & Noble.

Davey, Kevin, and Robert Clifton. 2001. "Insufficient Reason in the 'New Cosmological Argument.'" *Religious Studies* 37: 485–90.

Dembski, William A. 1999a. *The Design Inference: Eliminating Chance through Small Probabilities.* Cambridge, England: Cambridge University Press.

———. 1999b. *Intelligent Design: The Bridge between Science and Theology.* Downers Grove, Ill.: InterVarsity.

Fullmer, Gilbert. 2001. "A Fatal Logical Flaw in Anthropic Principle Design Arguments." *International Journal for Philosophy of Religion* 49: 101–10.

Gale, Richard M., 1991. *On the Nature and Existence of God.* London: Cambridge University Press.

Gesteland, R. F., T. R. Cech, and J. F. Atkins. 2000. *The RNA World.* Cold Spring Harbor, N.Y.: Cold Spring Harbor Laboratory Press.

Hume, David. 1980. *Dialogues Concerning Natural Religion.* Indianapolis: Hackett.

———. 1993. *An Enquiry Concerning Human Understanding.* Indianapolis: Hackett.

Hutcheson, C. A., et al. 1996. "Global Transposon Mutagenesis and a Minimal Mycoplasma Genome." *Science* 286: 2165–69.

Leslie, John. 1988. "The Prerequisites for Life in Our Universe." In *Proceedings of the [1987] Cracow Conference,* ed. G. V. Coyne, S. J., M. Heller, and J. Zycinski. Vatican City: Specola Vaticana. Reprinted in Gale and Pruss (2003).

Lewis, David. 1986. *On the Plurality of Worlds.* Oxford: Basil Blackwell.

Oppy, Graham. 2000. "On 'A New Cosmological Argument.' " *Religious Studies* 36: 345–53.

Paley, William. 1802. "The Analogy of the Watch." In Brody (1992): 158–69.

Pruss, Alexander R. 1998. "The Hume-Edwards Principle and the Cosmological Argument." *International Journal for Philosophy of Religion* 43: 149–65.

———. 2001. "The Cardinality Objection to David Lewis's Modal Realism." *Philosophical Studies* 104: 167–76.

Reichenbach, Bruce. 1972. *The Cosmological Argument.* Springfield, Ill.: Charles Thomas.

Rowe, William L. 1975. *The Cosmological Argument.* Princeton: Princeton University Press.

Smart, J. J. C., and J. J. Haldane. 2003. *Atheism and Theism.* 2nd edition, part II. Malden, Mass.: Blackwell.

Swinburne, Richard G. 1968. "The Argument from Design." *Philosophy* 43. Reprinted in Brody (1992): 189–201.

Turner, Donald A. "The Many-Universes Solution to the Problem of Evil." In Gale and Pruss (2003).

FOR FURTHER READING

Brody, Baruch A., ed. 1992. *Readings in the Philosophy of Religion: An Analytic Approach.* 2nd edition. Englewood Cliffs, N.J.: Prentice Hall.

Dawkins, Richard. 1988. *The Blind Watchmaker.* London: Penguin Books.

Gale, Richard M., and Alexander R. Pruss, eds. 2003. *The Existence of God.* Aldershot, England: Ashgate.

Grünbaum, Adolf. 1998. "A New Critique of Theological Interpretations of Physical Cosmology." *Philo* 1: 15–34. Reprinted in Gale and Pruss (2003).

McPherson, Thomas. 1972. *The Argument from Design.* London: Macmillan.

CHAPTER 6

MYSTICISM AND RELIGIOUS EXPERIENCE

JEROME I. GELLMAN

IN modern usage, "mysticism" refers to mystical experience and to practices, discourse, institutions, and traditions associated therewith. The term "mystical experience" enjoys a great variety of meanings, retaining some of that variety among philosophers. There is no choice but to stipulate meaning for the purposes of this essay. A wide definition of "mystical experience" will be more in the spirit of how it figures in general culture, and a narrow definition will echo a meaning common among philosophers.

1. MYSTICAL EXPERIENCE

1.1 The Wide Sense of "Mystical Experience"

In the wide sense, let us say that a "mystical experience" is:

A (purportedly:) *super* sense-perceptual *or sub* sense-perceptual experience granting acquaintance of realities or states of affairs that are of a kind not accessible by way of sense perception, somatosensory modalities, or standard introspection.

(1) A *super* sense-perceptual experience includes perception-like content of a kind not appropriate to sense perception, somatosensory modalities (including the means for sensing pain and body temperature, and internally sensing body, limb, organ, and visceral positions and states), or standard introspection. Some mystics have referred to a "spiritual" sense or senses, corresponding to the perceptual senses, appropriate to a nonphysical realm. A super sense-perceptual mode of experience may accompany sense perception (see "extrovertive" experience, section 3.1). For example, a person can have a super sense-perceptual experience while watching a setting sun. The inclusion of the supersensory mode is what makes the experience mystical.

(2) A *sub* sense-perceptual experience is either devoid of phenomenological content altogether, or nearly so (see "pure conscious events," sections 5 and 6), or consists of phenomenological content appropriate to sense perception, but lacking in the conceptualization typical of attentive sense perception (see below on "unconstructed experiences").

(3) "Realities" includes beings, such as God, as well as abstract "objects," such as the Absolute. "Acquaintance" of realities means the subject is aware of the presence of (one or more) realities.

(4) "States of affairs" includes, for example, the impermanence of all reality and that God is the ground of the self. "Acquaintance" of states of affairs can come in two forms. In one, a subject is aware of the presence of (one or more) realities on which (one or more) states of affairs supervene. An example would be an awareness of God (a reality) affording an awareness of one's utter dependence on God (a state of affairs). In its second form, "acquaintance" of states of affairs involves an insight directly, without supervening on acquaintance of any reality. An example would be coming to "see" the impermanence of all that exists following an experience that eliminates all phenomenological content.

(5) Mystical experience is alleged to be "noetic," involving knowledge of what a subject apprehends (James 1958).

(6) Parasensual experiences such as religious visions and auditions fail to make an experience mystical. The definition also excludes anomalous experiences such as out-of-body experiences, telepathy, precognition, and clairvoyance. All of these are acquaintance with objects or qualities *of a kind* accessible to the senses or to ordinary introspection, such as human thoughts and future physical events. (A degree of vagueness enters the definition of mystical experience here because of what is to count as a "kind" of thing accessible to nonmystical experience.)

In the wide sense, mystical experiences occur within the religious traditions of Judaism, Christianity, Islam, Indian religions, Buddhism, and primal religions. In most of these traditions, the experiences are allegedly of a supersensory reality, such as God, Brahman, or, as in some Buddhist traditions, Nirvana (Takeuchi 1983, 8–9). Many Buddhist traditions, however, make no claim for an experience of a supersensory reality. Some cultivate instead an experience of "unconstructed awareness," involving an awareness of the world on a relatively or absolutely nonconceptual level (Griffiths 1993). The unconstructed experience is thought to grant insight, such as into the impermanent nature of all things. Some Buddhists describe an experience of *tathata* or the "thisness" of reality, accessible only by the absence of ordinary sense-perceptual cognition. These Buddhist experiences are sub sense-perceptual, and mystical, since thisness is claimed to be inaccessible to ordinary sense perception. Some Zen experiences, however, would not count as mystical by our definition, involving acquaintance with neither a reality nor a state of affairs (Suzuki 1970).

1.2 The Narrow Sense of "Mystical Experience"

In the narrow sense, "mystical experience" refers to a subclass of mystical experience in the wide sense. Specifically, it refers to:

> A (purportedly:) super sense-perceptual or sub sense-perceptual *unitive* experience granting acquaintance of realities or states of affairs that are of a kind not accessible by way of sense-perception, somatosensory modalities, or standard introspection.

A *unitive* experience involves a phenomenological de-emphasis, blurring, or eradication of multiplicity. Examples are experiences of the oneness of nature, "union" with God (see section 3.2.1), the Hindu experience that Atman is Brahman (that the self/soul is identical with the eternal, absolute being), the Buddhist unconstructed experience, and "monistic" experiences, devoid of all multiplicity. (On "unitive" experiences, see Smart 1958, 1978; Wainwright 1981, ch. 1.) Excluded from the narrow definition, though present in the wide one, are, for example, a dualistic experience of God, a Jewish kabbalistic experience of a single supernal *sefirah*, and shamanistic experiences of spirits. These are not mystical in the narrow sense, because not unitive experiences.

Hereafter, "mystical experience" will be used in the narrow, more philosophical sense of these terms. Accordingly, *mysticism* pertains to practices, discourse, institutions, and traditions associated with unitive experiences only.

2. Religious Experience

"Religious experience" too can be given a wide and a narrow definition. In its wide sense, "religious experience" would refer to any experience appropriate to a religious context or that has a "religious" flavor. This would include much of mystical experience, religious visions and auditions, nonmystical Zen experiences, and various religious feelings, such as religious awe and sublimity. Also included is what Friedrich Schleiermacher (1963) identified as the fundamental religious experience: the feeling of "absolute dependence."

In the narrow sense, "religious experience" would take in all of these save mystical experiences. Thus, "religious" and "mystical" become exclusive categories, even when the mysticism belongs to a religious tradition. In what follows, "religious experience" will appear in the narrow sense.

2.1 Numinous Experience

We can call *numinous* (from *numen*, meaning divine or spirit) experience the category of religious experience left over when you subtract mystical experience in the narrow sense from mystical experience in the wide sense. That is, a numinous religious experience would be a *nonunitive* experience (purportedly) granting acquaintance of realities or states of affairs that are of a kind not accessible by way of sense perception, somatosensory modalities, or standard introspection. Your garden-variety sense of God's presence would count as a numinous experience. Numinous experiences contrast with religious experiences that involve, for example, feelings but no acquaintance with nonsensory realities or states of affairs.

Rudolf Otto (1957, section 15) reserved the term "numinous experience" for experiences allegedly of a reality perceived of as "wholly other" than the subject, producing a reaction of dread and fascination before an incomprehensible mystery. In the sense used here, Otto's numinous experience is but one kind of our "numinous" experience.

Typically, mystical traditions establish disciplines of contemplation, meditation, and other techniques intended to transform a mystic's egocentric self-enclosure. This is deemed crucial for inducing mystical consciousness, and is often a distinguishing mark of what precedes mystical, rather than religious, experience. Not all such practices and disciplines, however, hope for unitive experiences. For example, Native American practices involve lengthy preparation for experiencing sacred realities solely in what we are here calling "numinous" experiences (Brown 1991, 111–12).

3. CATEGORIES OF MYSTICAL EXPERIENCES

Mystical and religious experiences can be classified in various ways, in addition to the built-in difference between mystical super sense-perceptual and sub sense-perceptual experiences. This section notes two common distinctions.

3.1 Extrovertive and Introvertive

When an experience includes sense-perceptual content, we may say it is an *extrovertive* experience. There are mystical extrovertive experiences, as in a consciousness of the unity of all of nature, as well as numinous extrovertive experiences, as when experiencing God's presence when gazing at a snowflake. When wholly nonsensory, we may say an experience is *introvertive*. An experience of nothingness or emptiness, in some mystical traditions, and an experience of God resulting from a disengagement from sense experience would be examples of introvertive experiences (see sections 5 and 6).

3.2 Theistic and Nontheistic

A favorite distinction of Western philosophers is between theistic experiences, which are purportedly of God, and nontheistic ones. Nontheistic experiences can be of an ultimate reality other than God or of no reality at all. Numinous theistic experiences are dualistic, where God and the subject remain clearly distinct, while theistic mysticism pertains to either *union* or *identity* with God.

3.2.1 *Union with God*

Philosophers have identified a mystical experience of "union" with God, where this signifies a rich family of experiences rather than a single experience. "Union" involves a falling away of the separation between a person and God, short of identity. Christian mystics have variously described union with the Divine. This includes Bernard of Clairvaux's unification by "mutuality of love," Henry Suso's likening himself in union to a drop of water falling into wine, taking on the taste and color of the wine (1953, 185), and Jan van Ruysbroeck's description of "iron within the fire and the fire within the iron" (see Pike 1992, ch. 2). Nelson Pike has identified three stages in the union experience: quiet, full union, and rapture (ch. 1).

3.2.2 *Identity with God*

Mystics sometimes speak as though they have a consciousness of being identical with God. Examples are the Islamic Sufi mystic Husayn Hallaj proclaiming "I am God" (see Schimmel 1975, ch. 2) and the Jewish Hasidic master Rabbi Shneur Zalman of Liady, who wrote of a person as a drop of water in the ocean of the Infinite with an illusory sense of individual "dropness." The (heretical) Christian mystic Meister Eckhart made what looked very much like identity declarations (see McGinn 2001; Smith 1997). It is an open question, however, when such declarations are to be taken as identity assertions, with pantheistic or acosmic intentions, and when they are perhaps variations on descriptions of union-type experiences.

4. INEFFABILITY AND PARADOXALITY

4.1 Ineffability

William James affirmed that a mark of mystical experiences was their "ineffability," wherein "the subject of it immediately says it defies expression, that no adequate report of its contents can be given in words" (1958, 292–93). Following James, mystical experience is often associated with "ineffability," that is, "indescribability." Unfortunately, there is some confusion about whether the experience, the object of the experience, or both are supposed to be ineffable. Ineffability has been challenged on logical grounds, in that one could not refer to something ineffable, and that there is a logical contradiction in applying the concept "ineffable" to something to which none of our concepts are supposed to apply (Plantinga 1980, 23–25; Yandell 1975). Richard Gale (1960) and Ninian Smart (1958, 69) each argue that "ineffability" is (merely) an honorific title marking the value and intensity of the experience for the mystic. Wayne Proudfoot (1985) argues that mystics could not know that what they experienced could not be expressed in any possible language, because they do not know every possible language. He concludes that the ineffability claim only *prescribes* that no language system shall be applicable to it. The word "ineffable" thus serves to create and maintain a sense of mystery (125–27). However, because mystics could not know that a mystical object was indescribable in any possible language, it does not follow they would not, in their enthusiasm, make a claim beyond their knowledge. In any case, mystics might reasonably believe that because languages known to them cannot describe what they experienced, in all likelihood no other human language could describe it either.

William Alston maintains that the philosophical emphasis on ineffability is out of all proportion to what mystics have made of it (1991, 32). There exists a strand of so-called apophatic mysticism in which God is said to be unknown. However, even apophatic mystics have had much to say about their experiences and about God. Alston offers that "indescribability" refers to the difficulty of describing in literal terms, rather than by metaphor, analogy, and symbols. This is not a peculiar mark of mysticism, however, since quite common in science, philosophy, and religion.

Philosophers who have stressed ineffability as a mark of the mystical may be attempting to mark mysticism as "irrational," thus excluding it from more sensible human pursuits. Grace Jantzen has advanced a critique of the emphasis on ineffability as an attempt to remove mystical experiences from the realm of rational discourse, placing them instead into the realm of the emotions (1995, 344). Others have staunchly defended the "rationality" of mysticism against charges of irrationalism (Staal 1975).

4.2 Paradoxicality

Scholars of mysticism sometimes stress the "paradoxical" nature of mystical experiences. As with ineffability, it is not always clear whether the experience, the mystical object, or both are supposed to be paradoxical. We can discern four relevant senses of "paradoxical." (1) According to its etymology, "paradoxical" refers to what is surprising or "contrary to expectation." (2) Language can be intentionally "paradoxical" in using a logically improper form of words to convey what is not intended to be logically absurd. This may be for rhetorical effect or because of difficulty in conveying a thought without resort to linguistic tricks. (3) As in philosophy, a "paradox" can involve an unexpected logical contradiction, as in the "Liar Paradox." (4) Walter Stace sees paradoxality as a universal feature of mystical experiences, equating "paradoxality" with an *intended* logical contradiction (1961, 212; see section 5 on Stace).

Insofar as mystical experience is out of the ordinary, and the unitive quality strange (for ordinary folk, at least), reports of them may very well be surprising or contrary to expectation. Hence, they may be paradoxical in sense (1). Reports of mystical experiences may be paradoxical also in sense (2), because at times mystical language does assume logically offensive forms, when actual absurdity may not be intended. However, paradox in this sense occurs less frequently in firsthand reports of mystical experiences and more in second-order mystical systems of thought (Moore 1973; Staal 1975).

There is no good reason, however, why mystical experiences or their objects should be paradoxical in either senses (3) or (4). In general, there is no good reason for thinking that reports of mystical experience should imply logical absurdity. The attempt to designate mystical experiences as paradoxical in these senses may be but another try at painting mysticism into an irrational corner. We may be too eager to take logically deviant language at its most literal. For example, Zen Buddhism speaks of reaching a state of mind beyond both thought and "no-thought." However, rather than referring to a middle state, neither thought nor no-thought, often the intention is to point to a state of mind in which striving is absent and labeling of mental activities ceases. The mind of "no effort" strives neither for thought nor for no-thought. No logical absurdity infects this description. Frits Staal (1975) has argued that paradoxical mystical language has been used systematically to make logically respectable claims. While mystics use much literal language in describing experiences (Alston 1992, 80–102), the literality need not extend to paradox in senses (3) or (4).

5. PERENNIALISM

Various philosophers, sometimes dubbed "perennialists," have attempted to identify common mystical experiences across cultures and traditions.

Walter Stace's (1960, 1961) perennialist position has generated much discussion. Stace proposes two mystical experiences found "in all cultures, religions, periods, and social conditions." Stace identifies a universal extrovertive experience that "looks outward through the senses" to apprehend the One or the Oneness of all in or through the multiplicity of the world, apprehending the "One" as an inner life or consciousness of the world. The Oneness is experienced as a sacred objective reality, in a feeling of "bliss" and "joy." Stace's universal extrovertive experience (or the experienced reality, it is not always clear which) is paradoxical, and possibly ineffable (1961, 79).

Second, Stace identifies a universal, "monistic," introvertive experience that "looks inward into the mind," to achieve "pure consciousness," that is, an experience phenomenologically not *of* anything (1961, 86). Stace calls this a "unitary consciousness." Some have called this a "pure conscious event" or PCE (Forman 1993b, 1999; see section 6). A PCE consists of an "emptying out" by a subject of all experiential content and phenomenological qualities, including concepts, thoughts, sense perception, and sensuous images. The subject allegedly remains with "pure" wakeful consciousness. Like his extrovertive experience, Stace's universal introvertive experience involves a blissful sense of sacred objectivity, and is paradoxical and possibly ineffable. Stace considers the universal introvertive experience to be a ripening of mystical awareness beyond the halfway house of the universal extrovertive consciousness.

Stace assimilates theistic mystical experiences to his universal introvertive experience by distinguishing between *experience* and *interpretation*. The introvertive experience, he says, is the same across cultures. Only interpretations differ. Theistic mystics are pressured by their surroundings, says Stace, to put a theistic interpretation on their introvertive experiences. Ninian Smart (1965) also maintained the universality of the monistic experience, arguing that abstract descriptions of theistic mystical experiences reflected an interpretive overlay on an experiential base common to both theistic and nontheistic experiences.

Stace has been strongly criticized for simplifying or distorting mystical reports (for a summary, see Moore 1973). For example, Pike (1992, ch. 5) criticizes the Stace-Smart position because in Christian mysticism union with God is divided into discernable phases, which find no basis in Christian theology. These phases, therefore, plausibly reflect experience and not forced interpretation.

In contrast to Stace, R. C. Zaehner (1961) identified three types of mystical consciousness: (1) a "panenhenic" extrovertive experience, an experience of oneness of nature, one's self included; (2) a "monistic" experience of an undifferentiated unity transcending space and time; and (3) theistic experience where there is a duality between subject and the object of the experience. Zaehner thought that theistic experience was an advance over the monistic, since the latter expressed a self-centered interest of the mystic to be included in the ultimate.

William Wainwright (1981, ch. 1) has described three modes of mystical extrovertive experience: (1) a sense of the unity of nature; (2) a sense of nature as a living presence; and (3) the sense that everything transpiring in nature is in an eternal present. Wainwright recognizes the Buddhist unconstructed experience as a fourth mode of extrovertive experience. Wainwright, like Zaehner, distinguishes two mystical introvertive experiences, one of pure empty consciousness, and theistic experience marked by an awareness of an object in "mutual love."

6. PURE CONSCIOUS EVENTS

6.1 The Defenders of Pure Conscious Events

Much philosophical discussion has taken place over whether PCEs ever occur, and if they do, whether they are significant in mysticism. Defenders of PCEs depend on alleged references to pure consciousness in the mystical literature. One striking example is the Buddhist philosopher Paramaartha, who stated explicitly that all of our cognitions were "conditioned" by our concepts save for the non-sensory "unconditioned" Buddhist experience of emptiness (Forman 1989). Another example cited is from the writings of the Christian mystic Meister Eckhart that describe a "forgetting" that abandons concepts and sense experience to sink into a mystical "oblivion" (Forman 1993a). In addition, Robert Forman (1993b) has testified to a PCE he himself endured, describing it as an empty consciousness from which one "need not awake."

6.2 Criticism of the Defense of Pure Conscious Events

(1) Reports of PCEs in the literature may not be decisive. We should suspect *idealization* in at least some instances. Idealization occurs when an ideal goal is falsely presented as achieved. Whether or not pure consciousness ever occurs, we should suspect it might be presented as though it did. (2) The PCE defenders exaggerate the centrality of complete emptying out in mysticism. It is questionable if it is central in the mainstream of Christian mysticism, for example, where typically the mystic forgets all else to better contemplate God. Typical is the Christian mystic Jan Ruysbroeck, who wrote that emptying oneself is but a prelude to the mystical life of contemplating God through an act of divine grace (Zaehner 1961, 170–71). Likewise, the "shedding of corporeality" in early Hasidism was meant only to enable the mystic to contemplate the unified supernal structure of the divine sefirot. And the Zen master Dogen wrote about "wrongly thinking that the nature of things will appear when the whole world we perceive is obliterated" (1986, 39). (3) Accordingly, reports of emptying out and forgetting may refer only to an emptying of ordinary experiential content, making room for an extraordinary content. This accords well with the conception of *ayin* (nothingness) in Jewish mysticism, which is positively saturated with divine reality (Matt 1997). Some have claimed that even for Meister Eckhart emptying out is having one's mind on no object other than God, rather than an absolute emptiness of content (Matt 1997). (4) Perennialists may be exaggerating the wakefulness of some emptying out. The Islamic Sufi *fana* experience ("passing away") is sometimes described as an unconscious state, and the Sufi might become purely unconscious on finding God in *wajd* (Schimmel 1975, 178–79). Therefore, an emptying out might sometimes simply be pure *un*consciousness. (5) Even if a subject honestly reports on a PCE, there may have been conceptual events the subject either repressed or experienced in a nebulous way (Wainwright 1981, 117–19).

7. CONSTRUCTIVISM

Constructivism underscores the conceptual "construction" of mystical experience. Let us call "weak constructivism" the view that there is no mystical experience without concepts, concepts being what "construct" an experience. Let us call "hard constructivism" the view that a mystic's specific cultural background massively constructs—determines, shapes, or influences—the nature of mystical experiences (see Hollenback 1996; Jones 1909, introduction; Katz 1978). Hard constructivism entails the denial of perennialism on the assumption that mystical traditions are widely divergent (see section 7.3). Weak constructivism is strictly consistent with perennialism, however, since consistent with there being some transcultural mystical experience involving concepts. Both strong and weak constructivist arguments have been mobilized against the existence of PCEs.

7.1 Weak Constructivist Arguments against PCE Defenders

Here is a sampling of weak constructivist arguments against PCE defenders. (1) PCEs are impossible because of the "kind of beings" that we are (Katz 1978, 59). It is a fact about humans that we can experience only with the aid of memory, language, expectations, and conceptualizations. Therefore, we cannot have a "pure" awareness, empty of all content. (2) PCEs cannot be "experiences" (Proudfoot 1985, ch. 4; Bagger 1999, ch. 4). We must distinguish, the claim goes, between an "event" and an "experience." That X "has an experience" E entails that X conceptualizes E. Hence, even if pure conscious *events* happen to occur, they do not count as "experiences" until the subject conceptualizes them. At that moment, they cease to be "pure consciousness." (3) A survey of mystical literature shows that typical mystical experiences are conceptual in nature and not empty of concepts. (4) An epistemological objection: subjects could not know they had endured a PCE. They could not know this during a PCE, because it is supposed to be empty of all conceptual content (Bagger 1999, 102–3). A subject could not know this by remembering the PCE, since there is supposed to be nothing to observe, and hence nothing to remember. Neither could a subject surmise that a PCE had transpired by remembering a "before" and an "after," with an unaccounted for middle. This would fail to distinguish a PCE from plain *un*consciousness. Indeed, it seems to matter little whether a subject who emerges with mystical insights underwent a PCE or was simply unconscious. (5) A second epistemological objection: suppose a PCE has occurred and that a subject knows that, somehow. Still, there is a problem of the relationship of a PCE to the subsequent claims to knowledge, such as when Eckhart purportedly grounds knowledge of the soul and

God as one, in a PCE (see Forman 1993a). If, in a PCE, subjects were empty of all experiential content, they could not claim to have had acquaintance *of* anything (Bagger 1999, 102–3).

7.2 Criticism of Weak Constructivism

Several objections can be raised against the weak constructivist position. (1) The argument from the kind of beings we are against the possibility of a PCE is not convincing. While our cultural sets shape our ordinary experience, this argument gives no good reason why we could not enjoy experiences on a preconceptual level of awareness, especially through a regimen of training. Steven Katz, the author of this argument, notes our "most brutish, infantile, and sensate levels" of experience when we were infants (1988, 755). It's hard to see why in principle we could not retrieve an unconceptualized level of experience. (2) It makes little difference whether a PCE is an "experience" or only an "event." A PCE occurs within a wider experience of the subject, including the subject's coming out of the PCE and assigning it meaning. Let this wider experience be the "experience" under discussion. (3) The textual evidence that objectors cite against PCEs often seems consistent with the view that PCEs exist and that different traditions place different interpretations on them (Pike 1992, supplemental study 2). (4) Neuropsychological studies of mystical experience point to the possibility of events of pure consciousness. A theory by Eugene d'Aquili and Andrew Newberg (1993, 1999) claims to account for PCEs by reference to occurrences in the brain that cut off ordinary brain activity from consciousness. This theory, if upheld, would provide physiological support for episodes of pure consciousness (for more on this theory, see section 13.1). (5) There need be no problem about mystics knowing they had PCEs. If we accept a reliabilist account of knowledge, a belief is knowledge if produced by a reliable cognitive mechanism (perhaps with some further conditions). "Awakening" from (what is in fact) a PCE, if it produces the belief that one has "awakened" from a PCE, could be a reliable cognitive mechanism sufficient for knowing one had had a PCE. If we stick to an evidentialist conception of knowledge, mystics could have evidence they had endured a PCE, though not at the precise time of its occurrence. Here's how: (a) By hypothesis, a PCE is an event of conscious awareness. (b) A conscious event can have elements one does not note at the time, but recalls afterward. This is especially possible when the recall immediately follows the event. (c) Therefore, it should be possible for a mystic who endures a PCE to recall immediately afterward the very awareness that was present in the PCE, even though that awareness was not an object of consciousness at the time of the PCE. The mystic, recalling the PCE awareness, could note that the awareness had been of a "pure" type. Because the recall takes place in conjunction with the PCE, the entire complex becomes enfolded into one recognizable "experience" of the mystic. (6) Defenders of PCEs can champion their epistemological significance, although PCEs are not *of* anything. Recall that the noetic quality of a mystical experience can come from an acquaintance of states of affairs involving an insight directly, without supervening on acquaintance of any reality (see section 1.1, clause [4]). In addition, an experience is mystical as long as it grants such an acquaintance. The insight need not be exactly simultaneous with what makes the experience mystical. Hence, a person could undergo a PCE, which then granted acquaintance of states of affairs by a direct insight. The PCE plus the insight would constitute a complex mystical experience that afforded awareness of a state of affairs not otherwise accessible.

7.3 Strong Constructivism against Perennialism

Strong constructivism's main argument against perennialism in general (not just against PCEs) may be presented as follows (Katz 1978):

> Premise (A): The conceptual scheme a mystic possesses massively determines, shapes, or influences the nature of the mystical experience.
>
> Premise (B): Mystics of different mystical traditions possess pervasively different conceptual schemes.
>
> Conclusion: Therefore, there cannot be a common experience across cultural traditions. That is, perennialism is false.

The strong constructivist denies the distinction between experience and interpretation, since our conceptual apparatus shapes our very experience. If successful, the argument would show that there were no common numinous experiences across religious traditions either.

7.4 Criticism of Strong Constructivism

This section summarizes objections against strong constructivism that are not objections to weak constructivism as well. (1) It seems quite possible for subjects in the first instance to apply "thin" descriptions to experiences, involving only a small part of their conceptual schemes. Only on second thought, perhaps, will they elaborate on their experience in terms of the richness of their home culture. This would be like a physician with a headache, who experiences the pain in the

first instance just like ordinary folk and only subsequently applies medical terminology to the headache (King 1988). If so, there is a possibility of common
first-instance mystical experiences across cultures, contrary to Premise (A). (2)
Premise (A) is thrown into further doubt by expressions of surprise by mystics-
in-training about what they experience (Gellman 1997, 145–46; Barnard 1997, 127–
130), as well by heretical types of experience occurring with mystics acculturated
in orthodox teachings, such as Meister Eckhart and Jacob Boehme (see Stoeber
1992, 112–113). These illustrate the possibility of getting out from under one's mystical background to have new experiences. Likewise, strong constructivism's inherently conservative take on mysticism will struggle to explain transformations
within mystical traditions, and cannot easily account for innovative geniuses
within mystical traditions. (3) Two people walk together down the street and see
an approaching dog. One experiences the dog as "Jones's favorite black terrier
that came in second in last year's competition," while the other experiences it as
"a stray mutt that the dogcatchers should take away." There is an interesting sense
in which they are having the same experience: seeing that black dog at that place,
at that time. Because of conceptual differences in experiencing, however, the constructivist would insist that there was no worthwhile sense in which both dog-
sighters had the *same* experience. Similarly, there exists an interesting commonality of theistic experiences across mystical traditions, despite conceptual disparity.
The conceptual differences are not sufficient to deny this important commonality
(Wainwright 1981, 25). (4) Specific cultural conditioning does not influence everyone to the same degree and in the same way. Individuals have rich and varied
personal histories that influence their experiential lives in widely differing ways.
A "fat people must drive fat cows" approach to mysticism fails to mirror the
complex human phenomenon of acculturation. (5) Mystical traditions characteristically involve disciplines aimed at loosening the hold of one's conceptual scheme
on subsequent experience. Techniques practiced for years promote a pronounced
inhibition of ordinary cognitive processes, sometimes called "deautomization"
(Deikman 1980). This plausibly restricts the influence of one's cultural background
on one's mystical experiences, in turn making possible identical experiences across
mystical traditions. (6) The strong constructivist overemphasizes the influence of
premystical religious teaching on the mystic's experience. Mystical experiences can
circle around and reinvent meaning for the doctrines. An example is the Jewish
Kabbalistic transformation of the notion of *mitzvah* ("commandment") to that
of "joining" or "connection" with God. (7) Strong constructivism fails to account
well for widely differing mystical understandings of the same religious text. For
example, the Hindu text *The Brahma Sutra* is monistic for Shankara (788–820),
a "qualified dualism" for Ramanuja (ca. 1055–1137), and yet again a strict dualism
for Madhva (1199–1278) (see Radhakrishnan 1968, introduction). Likewise, the
teaching of emptiness in the Buddhist text *The Prajñaparamita Heart Sutra* re-

ceives quite disparate unpacking in different streams of Buddhism. It's plausible to conclude that distinct experiences were responsible, at least in part, for these differences.

On the one hand, talk about mystical experiences "the same" across all mystical traditions should be taken with a tablespoon of salt, if scholars claim to have discovered them solely from isolated descriptions of experiences. It is difficult to assess the nature of an experience without attending to how it "radiates" out into the structure of the local mystical theory and life of which it is a part (see Idel 1997). Nevertheless, it does seem possible to generalize about experiences "similar enough" to be philosophically interesting.

8. On the Possibility of Experiencing a Mystical Reality

In a position related to constructivism, William Forgie (1984, 1994) has argued that there could not be an experience "of God," if we understand experience "of X" to mean that it is phenomenologically given that the experience is of X. Forgie argues that phenomenological content can consist of general features only, and not features specifically identifying God as the object of experience. He compares this to your seeing one of two identical twins. Which one of the two you are perceiving cannot be a phenomenological given. Likewise, perhaps you can have an experience consisting of various phenomenological qualities, but that you experience *God* in particular cannot be a phenomenological datum. Subjects must surmise that they experience God. Forgie's type of argument applies as well to objects of mystical and religious experiences other than God. Nelson Pike argues, against Forgie, that the individuation of an object can be a component of the phenomenological content of an experience, drawing on examples from sense perception (1992, ch. 7).

Forgie assumes that the phenomenological content of a theistic experience must be confined to data akin to the "sense data" of sensory experience, somehow analogous to colors, shapes, movement, sounds, tastes, and the like. Individuation is absent from phenomenological content of that sort. Pike, for his part, teases out alleged phenomenological content for individuating God from analogies to ordinary sense perception. Both philosophers restrict experiences of God to phenomenal content somehow analogous to sense perception. This might be a mistake. Consider, for example, that God could appear to a person mystically, and at the same time transmit, telepathy-like, the thought that this is God appearing.

Imagine further that this thought had the flavor of being conveyed to one from the outside, rather than as originating in the subject. The thought that "This is God appearing" would be part of the phenomenological content of the subject's present (complex) experience (though not part of the mystical mode of the experience as defined in section 1.1), and yet not the product of an interpretation by the subject. Indeed, reports of experiences of God sometimes describe what seems to come with the thought included that "This is God." Whatever the epistemological merits of such an experience might be, it would be quite natural to say that its phenomenology includes the datum that it is an experience "of God," in particular.

9. Epistemology: The Doxastic Practice Approach and the Argument from Perception

There are two distinct epistemological questions to be asked about religious and mystical experience. The first is whether a situated person is warranted in thinking that his or her experiences (or perhaps those of one's religious affiliates) are veridical or have evidential value. The second is whether "we" who in our wisdom examine the phenomenon of such experiences "from afar" are warranted in thinking them veridical or endowed with evidential value. These questions, though related, can be answered independently of one another.

The major philosophical defense of the right of a person to accept his or her religious experience as valid (whether or not "we" are entitled to see validity in the phenomenon of religious experience) may be called the "doxastic practice approach." The major defense of the evidential value of at least some religious experiences, from a general vantage point, may be called the "argument from perception."

9.1 The Doxastic Practice Approach

William Alston (1991) has defended beliefs a person forms based on mystical and religious experience, Alston defines a "doxastic practice" as consisting of socially established ways of forming and epistemically evaluating beliefs with a certain kind of content from various inputs, such as cognitive and perceptual (100). The practice of forming physical-object beliefs derived from sense perception is an example of one "doxastic practice," and the practice of drawing deductive conclusions from premises is another. Alston argues that the justification of every doxastic practice is "epistemically circular"; that is, its reliability cannot be established in an independent way. This includes the "sense-perception practice." However, we cannot avoid engaging in doxastic practices. Therefore, Alston contends, it is rational to continue to engage in them providing there is no good reason to think they are *un*reliable. Now, there exist doxastic practices consisting of forming beliefs grounded on religious and mystical experiences such as "God is now appearing to me." Such, for example, is the "Christian doxastic practice." It follows that it is rational for a person to take the belief outputs of such a practice as true unless the practice is shown to be unreliable.

9.2 The Argument from Perception

Various philosophers have defended the evidential value, to one degree or another, of some religious and mystical experiences, principally with regard to experiences of God (Baillie 1939; Broad 1953; Davis 1989; Gellman 1997, 2001; Swinburne 1991, 1996; Wainwright 1981; Yandell 1993). These philosophers have stressed the "perceptual" nature of experiences of God, hence the name given here, the "argument from perception." We can summarize the approach as follows:

(1) Experiences of God have a subject-object structure, with a phenomenological content allegedly representing the object of the experience. Also, subjects are moved to make truth claims based on such experiences. Furthermore, as with sense perception, there are mystical procedures for getting into position for a mystical experience of God (Underhill 1945, 90–94), and others can take up a suitable mystical path to try to check on the subject's claims (Bergson 1935, 210). In all these ways, experiences of God are like sense perception.

(2) Perception-like experiences count as (at least some) evidence in favor of their own validity. That a person *seems* to experience some object is some reason to think he or she really does have experiential contact with it (Swinburne 1991, 254). So, experiences of God count as (at least some) evidence in favor of their own validity.

(3) Agreement between the perceptions of people in different places, times, and traditions enhances the evidence in favor of their validity (Broad 1953). Hence, agreement about experiences of God in diverse circumstances enhances the evidence in their favor.

(4) Further enhancement of the validity of a religious or mystical experience can come from appropriate consequences in the life of the person who had the experience, such as increased saintliness (Wainwright 1981, 83–88).

(5) (1)–(4) yield *initial* evidence in favor of the validity of (some) experiences of God.

Whether any experiences of God are veridical in the final reckoning will depend on the strength of the initial evidential case, on other favorable evidence, and on the power of counterconsiderations against validity. Defenders of the argument from perception differ over the strength of the initial evidential case and have defended the staying power of the argument from perception against counterevidence to varying degrees.

10. An Epistemological Critique: Disanalogies to Sense Experience

Several philosophers have argued against either the doxastic practice approach or the analogy to sense perception, or both (Bagger 1999; Fales 1996a, 1996b, 2001; Gale 1994, 1995; C. Martin 1955; M. Martin 1990; Proudfoot 1985; Rowe 1982). Here the focus will be on objections related specifically to religious and mystical experience, rather than to general epistemological complaints, beginning with alleged disanalogies to sense experience.

Although Alston defends the perceptual character of mystical experiences of God for his doxastic practice approach, there need be no restriction to the perceptual on the inputs of a doxastic practice. Hence, disanalogy between experiences of God and sense perception would not be harmful to this approach (Alston 1994). Relevant disanalogy would negatively affect the argument from perception.

10.1. Lack of Checkability

The analogy to sense perception allegedly breaks down over the lack of appropriate cross-checking procedures for experiences of God. With sense perception, we can cross-check by employing inductive methods to determine causally relevant antecedent conditions; can "triangulate" an event by correlating it with other effects of the same purported cause; and can discover causal mechanisms connecting a cause to its effects. These are not available for checking on mystical experiences of God. Evan Fales argues that "cross-checkability" is an integral part of any successful perceptual epistemic practice. Therefore, the perceptual epistemic practice in which mystical experiences of God are embedded is severely defective (Fales 2001). Others conclude that claims to have experienced God are "very close" to subjective claims like "I seem to see a piece of paper" rather than to objective claims like "I see a piece of paper" (C. Martin 1955).

William Rowe observes that God may choose to be revealed to one person and not to another. Therefore, unlike with sense perception, the failure of others to have an experience of God under conditions similar to those in which one person did does not impugn the validity of the experience. Therefore, we have no way of determining when an experience of God is delusory. If so, neither can we credit an experience as authentic (Rowe 1982).

10.2 God's Lack of Space-Time Coordinates

Some philosophers have argued that there could never be evidence for thinking a person had perceived God (Gale 1994, 1995; see Byrne 2001). For there to be evidence that a person experienced an object O, and did not have just an "O-ish impression," it would have to be possible for there to be evidence that O was the common object of different perceptions (not necessarily simultaneous with one another). This, in turn, would be possible only if it were possible to distinguish perceptions of O, specifically, from possible perceptions of other objects that might be perceptually similar to O. This latter requirement is possible only if O exists in both space and time. Space-time coordinates make it possible to distinguish O from objects of similar appearance existing in other space-time coordinates. God, however, does not exist in both space and time. Therefore, there could never be evidence that a person had experienced God.

11. EVALUATION OF THE
DISANALOGY ARGUMENTS

The disanalogists take the evidential credentials of sense perception as paradigmatic for epistemology. They equate confirming and disconfirming evidence with evidence strongly analogous to the kind available for sensory perception. However, the evidential requirement should be "confirming empirical evidence," *be it what it may*. If God-sightings have confirming evidence, even if somewhat different from the kind available for sense perception, they will then be evidentially strengthened. If God-sightings do not have much confirming empirical evidence, be it what it may, they will remain unjustified for that reason, and not because they lack cross-checks appropriate to sense perception.

Perhaps the disanalogy proponents believe that justification of physical object claims should be our evidential standard because only where cross-checks of the physical object kind are available do we get sufficient justification. However, our ordinary physical object beliefs are far oversupported by confirming evidence. We have extremely luxurious constellations of confirming networks there. Hence, it does not follow that were mystical claims justified to a lesser degree than that, or not by similar procedures, they would be *un*justified.

A problem with the argument from God's lack of dimensionality is that the practice of identifying physical objects proceeds by way of an interplay between qualitative features and relative positions to determine both location and identity. The judgments we make reflect a holistic practice of making identifications of place and identity together. There is no obvious reason why the identification of God cannot take place within its own holistic practice, with its own criteria of identification, not beholden to the holistic practice involved in identifying physical objects (see Gellman 2001, ch. 3, for a sketch of such a holistic practice). We should be suspicious of taking the practice of identifying physical objects as paradigmatic for all epistemology.

12. AN EPISTEMOLOGICAL CRITIQUE: RELIGIOUS DIVERSITY

If the doxastic practice approach or argument from perception works for theistic experiences, they should work for nontheistic experiences as well. In the history of religions, we find innumerable gods, with different characteristics. Shall we say they all exist? Can belief in all of them be rational (Hick 1989, 234–35)? In addition, there are experiences of nonpersonal ultimate realities, such as the Nirguna Brahman of Indian religions. Nirguna Brahman cannot be an ultimate reality if God is (234–35). The argument from perception cannot work for both, so works for neither. Furthermore, different theistic faiths claim experience of the one and only God, ostensibly justifying beliefs that are in contradiction with one another (Flew 1966, 126). If the argument from perception leads to such contradictory results, it cannot provide evidence that experiences of God are valid.

Straight away, we can discount experiences of polytheistic gods because of their being embedded in bizarre, fantastic settings and because of the relative paucity of reports of actual experiences of such beings. Regarding clashing experiences within theistic settings, Richard Swinburne has proposed an ascent to generality as a harmonizing mechanism. Swinburne believes that conflicting descriptions of objects of religious experience pose a challenge only to detailed claims, not to general claims of having experienced a supernal being (1991, 266).

John Hick (1989, ch. 14) has proposed a "pluralistic hypothesis" to deal with the problem of religious diversity. According to the pluralistic hypothesis, the great world faiths embody different perceptions and conceptions of one reality that Hick christens "the Real." The Real itself is never experienced directly, but has "masks" or "faces" that are experienced, depending on how a particular culture or religion thinks of the Real. The Real itself is, therefore, neither personal nor impersonal, these categories being imposed on the Real by different cultural contexts. Hence, the typical experiences of the major faiths are to be taken as validly of the Real, through mediation by the local face of the Real.

Hick has been criticized for infidelity to the world's religious traditions. However, we should understand Hick to be providing a theory *about* religions rather than an exposition religions themselves would endorse (for criticism of Hick, see D'Costa 1987). Some propose harmonizing some conflicting experiences by reference to God's "inexhaustible fullness" (Gellman 1997, ch. 4). In at least some mystical experiences of God, a subject experiences what is presented as proceeding from an intimation of infinite plenitude. Given this feature, a claim to experience a personal ultimate, for example, can be squared with an experience of an impersonal ultimate: one "object," identified as God or Nirguna Brahman, can be experienced in its personal attributes or in its impersonal attributes, from out of its inexhaustible plenitude.

Whether any of these particular solutions succeed, the experiential data are too many for us to simply scrap on the grounds of contradictory claims. We should endeavor to retain as much of the conflicting data as possible by seeking some means of conciliation.

13 · AN EPISTEMOLOGICAL CRITIQUE: NATURALISTIC EXPLANATIONS

Bertrand Russell once quipped, "We can make no distinction between the man who eats little and sees heaven and the man who drinks much and sees snakes. Each is in an abnormal physical condition, and therefore has abnormal perceptions" (1935, 188). C. D. Broad wrote, to the contrary, "One *might need to be* slightly 'cracked' in order to have some peep-holes into the super-sensible world" (1939, 164). Thus is the issue engaged whether we can explain away religious and mystical experiences by reference to naturalistic causes.

Wainwright (1981, ch. 2) has argued that a naturalistic explanation is compatible with the validity of an experience since God could bring about an experience through a naturalistic medium. However, we should take into account that there might be naturalistic explanations that would make it implausible that God would appear by just *those* ways (this is elaborated in section 13.2).

Various psychological naturalistic explanations of religious and mystical experience have been offered, including pathological conditions, such as hypersuggestibility, severe deprivation, severe sexual frustration, intense fear of death, infantile regression, pronounced maladjustment, and mental illness, as well as nonpathological conditions, including the inordinate influence of a religious psychological "set" (Davis 1989, ch. 8; Wulff 2000). In addition, some have advanced a sociological explanation for some mysticism, in terms of the sociopolitical power available to an accomplished mystic (Fales 1996a, 1996b).

Naturalistic proposals of these kinds exaggerate the scope and influence of the cited factors, sometimes choosing to highlight the bizarre and eye-catching at the expense of the more common occurrences. Also, some of the proposals, at least, are perfectly compatible with the validity of experiences of God. For example, a person's having a religious psychological set can just as well be a condition for enjoying and being capable of recognizing an experience of God as it can be a cause of delusion.

13.1 Neuropsychological Explanations

Neuropsychological research has been conducted to look for unique brain processes involved in religious and mystical experiences, resulting in a number of competing theories (Wulff 2000). The "explaining away" enters when one claims that "It's all in the head." The most comprehensive current theory, that of d'Aquili and Newberg (1993, 1999), proposes the prefrontal area of the brain as the locus of special brain activity during mystical episodes. Through "deafferentiation," or cutting off of neural input to that area of the brain, they claim, an event of pure consciousness occurs. The patterns set up in the brain create an overwhelming experience of "absolute unitary being." If reinforcement of a certain hypothalamic discharge then occurs, this will prolong the feeling of elation and will be interpreted as an experience of God. Otherwise, there will arise a deep peacefulness due to the dominance of specified hypothalamic structures. This gets interpreted as an experience of an impersonal, absolute ground of being. The theory associates numinous experiences with variations in deafferentiation in various structures of the nervous system, and lesser religious experiences with mild to moderate stimulation of circuits in the lateral hypothalamus. The latter generate religious awe: a complex of fear and exaltation (d'Aquili and Newberg 1993, 195). The brain functions in related ways in aesthetic experience as well (d'Aquili and Newberg 2000).

The authors themselves do not say their theory shows there to be nothing objective to mystical or religious experience. However, they do recommend explaining away objective differences between, for example, theistic and nontheistic experiences. And their theory could be utilized in an "It's all in the head" strategy.

Batson, Schoenrade, and Ventis (1993) maintain (comparing religious experiences to creative problem solving) that a person who has a religious experience faces an existential crisis and attempts to solve it within fixed cognitive structures, which are embedded in the brain's left hemisphere. This yields no solution. The person may then undergo a transforming religious experience, in which the brain temporarily switches from left-hemisphere to right-hemisphere dominance, from verbal/conceptual thinking to nonverbal insight "beyond" the person's dominant conceptual structure. The switch then reverberates back to restructure the left-hemisphere conceptual network, now made apt for dealing with the existential crisis. The right-hemisphere switch can account for the sense of "ineffability," since the right hemisphere is not analytic or verbal (Fenwick 1996). Because the shift involves "transcending" the cognitive, it may explain the conviction of having contact with a "transcendent realm." If offered as a naturalistic "explaining away," this theory would imply that what a person thinks is an experience of God, say, is really an experience of temporary right-hemisphere dominance. The theory has the drawback, however, of applying only to conversion experiences and not to other religious and mystical episodes.

Other theories that have attracted attention include one focusing on anomalous features of the temporal lobes of the brain, the locus for epileptic conditions (Persinger 1987). One study even claims to have discovered a correlation between temporal lobe epilepsy and sudden conversion experiences (Dewhurst and Beard 1970). James Austin (1998), a neurologist and himself a Zen practitioner, has developed a theory of brain transformations for prolonged Zen meditative practice. The theory is based on gradual, complex changes in the brain, leading to a blocking of our higher associative processes. Austin believes that the Zen *kensho* experience, according to him an experience of reality "as it is in itself," is an experience with (relatively) shut-down neural activity.

13.2 Evaluation of Neuropsychological Explanations

It would seem that a neuropsychological theory could do no more than relate what happens in the brain when a mystical or religious experience occurs. It could not tell us that the ultimate cause for a theory's favored brain events was altogether internal to the organism. On the other hand, such a theory could help rule out cases of suspected deception and block the identification of mystical experiences with mere emotion. True, there may not be out-of-brain "God receptors" in the body, analogous to those for sensory perception, which might reinforce a suspicion that it's all in the head. However, out-of-brain receptors are neither to be expected nor required with nonphysical stimuli, as in mystical experiences. God, for example, does not exist at a physical distance from the brain. Furthermore, God could act directly on the brain to bring about the relevant processes for a subject to perceive God.

On the other hand, a neuropsychological theory would put pressure on claims to veridical experiences if it could point to brain processes implausibly grounding a veridical experience. The implausibility would flow from a being of God's nature wanting to make itself known by just *that* way. Suppose, for (an outlandish) example, researchers convinced us that all and only experiencers of God had a brain defect caused only by a certain type of blow to the shoulder to people with a genetic propensity to psoriasis, and that the area of the defect was activated in the experiences. This might not *prove* that experiences of God were delusory, but would raise serious doubts. It is too early in the research, however, to say that implausible brain conditions have been found for experiences of God.

14. THE SUPERIORITY OF NATURALISTIC EXPLANATION

Some philosophers have argued that because the "modern inquirer" assumes everything ultimately explicable in naturalistic terms, in principle we should reject any supernatural explanation of mystical and religious experience (Bagger 1999). Invoking God to explain mystical experiences is like invoking miracles to explain natural phenomena. We should match our elimination of miracles from our explanatory vocabulary by an elimination of a supernatural explanation of mystical experiences of God. Hence, we do not have to wait until we discover a live alternative explanation to the theistic explanation of mystical experiences of God. We should resist a theistic explanation in the name of our epistemic standards. Hence, we should reject both the doxastic practice approach and the argument from perception.

This argument ignores the efforts of theistic philosophers to square special divine activity with a modern scientific understanding of the world (Swinburne 1989). Whether they have succeeded is a question beyond the scope of the present essay, however. A defender of the doxastic practice approach or the argument from perception might point out that contemporary canons of explanation were formed not so much in full awareness of the rich historical phenomenon of mystical experiences of God, but in willful ignorance of it. The nontheistic models of good explanation were born in sin, ignoring what many would consider a good, supernatural explanation for these experiences. Of course, a person for whom supernatural explanation is not a live option would have reason to reject the argument from perception and refuse to engage in a doxastic practice of identifying valid God-experiences. However, most defenders of the argument from perception advance it at best as a defensible line of reasoning, rather than as a proof of valid experiences of God that should convince anyone, and the doxastic practice approach is not meant to convince everybody to participate in a theistic doxastic practice.

15. MYSTICISM, RELIGIOUS EXPERIENCE, AND GENDER

Feminist philosophers have criticized the androcentric bias in mysticism and its philosophical treatment. There are three main objections. (1) Contemporary male philosophers treat mysticism as most centrally a matter of the private psychological episodes of a solitary person. Philosophers believe these private experiences reveal the meaning and value of mysticism (Jantzen 1994, 1995). Instead, philosophers should be studying the sociopolitical ramifications of mysticism, including its patriarchal failings. (2) Scholars of mysticism have systematically ignored or marginalized much of women's mysticism. Closer attention to women would reveal the androcentric bias in male mysticism (Jantzen 1995). (3) The traditional male construction of God has determined the way male philosophers think of theistic experience. Thus, theistic experience is conditioned from the outset by patriarchal conceptualizations and values, and by sex-role differentiation in the practice of religion (Raphael 1994). Typically, the view states, men understand theistic experience as a human subject encountering a being wholly distinct, distant, and overpowering. A paradigm of this approach is Rudolf Otto's "numinous experience" of a "wholly other" reality, unfathomable and overpowering, engendering a sense of dreaded fascination. The mystic is "submerged and overwhelmed" by his own nothingness (Otto 1957). Otto claims that this is *the* foundational experience of religion. This approach, it is claimed, is mediated by the androcentrism of Otto's worldview, entrapped in issues of domination, atomicity, and submission. Feminist thinkers tend to deny the dichotomy between the holy and the creaturely that makes Otto's analysis possible (see Daly 1973; Goldenberg 1979). Feminist theologians stress the immanent nature of the object of theistic experience and bring to prominence women's experience of the holy in their fleshly embodiment, denigrated by androcentric attitudes.

The feminist critique poses a welcome corrective to undoubted androcentric biases in mysticism and mystical studies. Regarding (1), although studying the sociopolitical ramifications of mysticism is certainly a mandatory undertaking and should contribute to future social justice, it is not necessarily the task of philosophers, and certainly not all philosophers. A division of labor should free philosophers to examine the important phenomenological and epistemological aspects of mysticism for their own sake, always in awareness of possible androcentric prejudices. Objection (2) has begun to bring about a welcome change with scholarship dedicated to women's mysticism and its significance (Brunn and Epiney-Burgard 1989; Beer 1992; Borchert 1994). Regarding (3), we must distinguish between Otto's androcentric claim that his type of numinous experience constitutes religious experience at its most profound and the rich variegation of religious and mystical experience of men throughout history. This includes men's experiences of God's immanent closeness as well as mystical union with God, quite opposite, by feminist lights, to Otto's numinous experience. The study of gender in religious experience and mysticism has barely begun and promises new insights into and revisions of our understanding of these human phenomena.

WORKS CITED

Alston, William P. 1991. *Perceiving God: The Epistemology of Religious Experience.* Ithaca, N.Y.: Cornell University Press.

———. 1992. "Literal and Nonliteral in Reports of Mystical Experience." In *Mysticism and Language,* ed. Steven T. Katz, 80–102. New York: Oxford University Press.

———. 1994. "Reply to Commentators." *Philosophy and Phenomenological Research,* 54: 891–899.

Austin, James H. 1998. *Zen and the Brain: Toward an Understanding of Meditation and Consciousness.* Cambridge, Mass.: MIT Press.

Bagger, Matthew C. 1999. *Religious Experience, Justification, and History.* Cambridge, England: Cambridge University Press.

Baillie, John. 1939. *Our Knowledge of God.* Oxford: Oxford University Press.

Barnard, G. William. 1997. *Exploring Unseen Worlds: William James and the Philosophy of Mysticism.* Albany: State University of New York Press.

Batson, C. Daniel, Patricia Schoenrade, and W. Larry Ventis. 1993. *Religion and the Individual. A Social-psychological Perspective.* Oxford: Oxford University Press.

Beer, Frances, 1992. *Women and Mystical Experience in the Middle Ages.* Woodbridge, Suffolk: Boydell Press.

Bergson, Henri. 1935. *The Two Sources of Morality and Religion.* Trans. R. A. Audra and C. Berenton. London: Macmillan.

Borchert, Bruno. 1994. *Mysticism: Its History and Challenge.* York Beach, M.: Samuel Weiser.

Broad, C. D. 1939. "Arguments for the existence of God, II." *Journal of Theological Studies* 40: 156–67.

———. 1953. *Religion, Philosophy, and Psychical Research.* London: Routledge and Kegan Paul.

Brown, Joseph Epes. 1991. *The Spiritual Legacy of the American Indians.* New York: Crossroad Publishing.

Brunn, Emilie Zum, and Georgette Epiney-Burgard. 1989. *Women Mystics in Medieval Europe.* Trans. Sheila Hughes. New York: Paragon House.

Byrne, Peter. 2001. "Perceiving God and Realism." *Philo* 3: 74–88.

Daly, Mary. 1973. *Beyond God the Father, toward a Philosophy of Women's Liberation.* Boston: Beacon Press.

d'Aquili, Eugene, and Andrew Newberg. 1993. "Religious and Mystical States: A Neuropsychological Model." *Zygon* 28: 177–200.

———. 1999. *The Mystical Mind: Probing the Biology of Religious Experience.* Minneapolis: Fortress Press.

———. 2000. "The Neuropsychology of Aesthetic, Spiritual, and Mystic States." *Zygon* 35: 39–51.

Davis, Carolyn Franks. 1989. *The Evidential Force of Religious Experience.* Oxford: Clarendon Press.

D'Costa, Gavin. 1987. *John Hick's Theology of Religions: A Critical Evaluation.* Lanham, Md.: University Press of America.

Deikman, Arthur. 1980. "Deautomatization and the Mystic Experience." In *Understanding Mysticism,* ed. Richard Woods, O.P., 240–69. Garden City, N.Y.: Doubleday.

Dewhurst, K., and A. W. Beard. 1970. "Sudden Religious Conversions in Temporal Lobe Epilepsy." *British Journal of Psychiatry* 117: 497–507.

Dogen. 1986. *Shobogenzo: Zen Essays by Dogen.* Trans. Thomas Cleary. Honolulu: University of Hawaii Press.

Fales, Evan. 1996a. "Scientific Explanations of Mystical Experiences, Part I: The Case of St. Teresa." *Religious Studies* 32: 143–163.

———. 1996b. "Scientific Explanations of Mystical Experiences." *Religious Studies* 32: 297–313.

———. 2001. "Do Mystics See God?" In *Contemporary Debates in the Philosophy of Religion,* ed. Michael L. Peterson. Oxford: Blackwell.

Fenwick, P. 1996. "The Neurophysiology of Religious Experiences." In *Psychiatry and Religion: Context, Consensus, and Controversies,* ed. Dinesh Bhugra, 167–77. London: Routledge.

Flew, Antony. 1966. *God and Philosophy.* London: Hutchinson.

Forgie, William. 1984. "Theistic Experience and the Doctrine of Unanimity." *International Journal of the Philosophy of Religion* 15: 13–30.

———. 1994. "Pike's *Mystic Union* and the Possibility of Theistic Experience." *Religious Studies* 30: 231–42.

Forman, Robert K. C. 1989. "Paramaartha and Modern Constructivists on Mysticism:

Epistemological Monomorphism versus Duomorphism." *Philosophy East and West* 39: 393–18.

———. 1993a. "Eckhart, Gezucken, and the Ground of the Soul." In *The Problem of Pure Consciousness, Mysticism and Philosophy*, ed. Robert Forman, 121–59. New York and London: Oxford University Press.

———. 1993b. Introduction to *The Problem of Pure Consciousness, Mysticism and Philosophy*, ed. Robert Forman, 3–49. New York: Oxford University Press.

———. 1999. *Mysticism, Mind, Consciousness*. Albany: State University of New York Press.

Gale, Richard M. 1960. "Mysticism and Philosophy." *Journal of Philosophy* 57: 471–81.

———. 1994. "Why Alston's Mystical Doxastic Practice is Subjective." *Philosophy and Phenomenological Research* 54: 869–75.

———. 1995. *On the Nature and Existence of God*. Cambridge, England: Cambridge University Press.

Gellman, Jerome. 1997. *Experience of God and the Rationality of Theistic Belief*. Ithaca, N.Y.: Cornell University Press.

———. 2001. *Mystical Experience of God: A Philosophical Enquiry*. London: Ashgate Publishers.

Goldenberg, Naomi. 1979. *The Changing of the Gods*. Boston: Beacon Press.

Griffiths, Paul J. 1993. "Pure Consciousness and Indian Buddhism." In *The Problem of Pure Consciousness, Mysticism and Philosophy*, ed. Robert Forman, 121–59. New York: Oxford University Press.

Hick, John. 1989. *An Interpretation of Religion: Human Responses to the Transcendent*. London: Macmillan.

Hollenback, Jess Byron. 1996. *Mysticism: Experience, Response, and Empowerment*. University Park: Pennsylvania State University Press.

Idel, Moshe. 1997. " '*Unio mystica*' as a Criterion: 'Hegelian' Phenomenologies of Jewish Mysticism." In *Doors of Understanding: Conversations in Global Spirituality in Honor of Ewert Cousins*, ed. Steven Chase, 303–33. Quincy, Ill.: Franciscan Press.

James, William. 1958. *The Varieties of Religious Experience*. New York: Mentor Books.

Jantzen, Grace M. 1994. "Feminists, Philosophers, and Mystics." *Hypatia* 9: 186–206.

———. 1995. *Power, Gender, and Christian Mysticism*. Cambridge, England: Cambridge University Press.

Jones, Rufus M. 1909. *Studies in Mystical Religion*. London: Macmillan.

Katz, Steven T. 1978. "Language, Epistemology, and Mysticism." In *Mysticism and Philosophical Analysis*, ed. Steven T. Katz, 22–74. New York: Oxford University Press.

———. 1988. "Responses and Rejoinders." *Journal of the American Academy of Religion* 56: 751–57.

King, Sallie B. 1988. "Two Epistemological Models for the Interpretation of Mysticism." *Journal of the American Academy of Religion* 56: 257–79.

Martin, C. B. 1955. "A Religious Way of Knowing." In *New Essays in Philosophical Theology*, ed. Antony Flew and Alasdair Macintyre, 76–95. London: SCM Press.

Martin, Michael. 1990. *Atheism: A Philosophical Justification*. Philadelphia: Temple University Press.

Matt, Daniel C. 1997. "Varieties of Mystical Nothingness: Jewish, Christian, and Buddhist." In *Wisdom and Logos: Studies in Jewish Thought in honor of David Winston*, ed. David T. Runia and Gregory E. Sterling. *The Studia Philonica Annual, Studies in Hellenistic Judaism* 9: 316–31. Atlanta: Scholars Press.

McGinn, Bernard. 2001. *The Mystical Thought of Meister Eckhart: The Man from Whom God Hid Nothing.* New York: Crossroad Publishing.

Moore, Peter. 1973. "Recent Studies of Mysticism: A Critical Survey." *Religion* 3, 146–56.

Otto, Rudolf. 1957. *The Idea of the Holy.* 2nd edition. Oxford: Oxford University Press.

Persinger, Michael A. 1987. *Neuropsychological Bases of God Beliefs.* New York: Praeger.

Pike, Nelson. 1992. *Mystic Union: An Essay in the Phenomenology of Mysticism.* Ithaca, N.Y.: Cornell University Press.

Plantinga, Alvin. 1980. *Does God Have a Nature?* Milwaukee: Marquette University Press.

Proudfoot, Wayne. 1985. *Religious Experience.* Berkeley: University of California Press.

Radhakrishnan, S., trans. 1968. *The Brahma Sutra: The Philosophy of Spiritual Life.* With introduction and notes. New York: Greenwood Press.

Raphael, Melissa. 1994. "Feminism, Constructivism, and Numinous Experience." *Religious Studies* 30: 511–26.

Rowe, William. 1982. "Religious Experience and the Principle of Credulity." *International Journal for Philosophy of Religion* 13: 85–92.

Russell, Bertrand. 1935. *Religion and Science.* Oxford: Oxford University Press.

Schimmel, Annemarie. 1975. *Mystical Dimensions of Islam.* Chapel Hill: University of North Carolina Press.

Schleiermacher, Friedrich. 1963. *The Christian Faith.* English translation of the second German edition. Ed. H. R. Mackintosh and J. S. Stewart. New York: Harper & Row.

Smart, Ninian. 1958. *Reasons and Faiths.* London: Routledge and Kegan Paul.

———. 1965. "Interpretation and Mystical Experience." *Religious Studies* 1: 75–87.

———. 1978. "Understanding Religious Experience." In *Mysticism and Philosophical Analysis,* ed. Steven T. Katz, 10–21. New York: Oxford University Press.

Smith, Huston. 1997. " 'Come higher my friend': The Intellective Mysticism of Meister Eckhart." In *Doors of Understanding: Conversations in Global Spirituality in Honor of Ewert Cousins,* ed. Steven Chase, 201–17. Quincy, Ill.: Franciscan Press.

Staal, Frits. 1975. *Exploring Mysticism.* London: Penguin.

Stace, Walter T. 1960. *The Teachings of the Mystics.* New York: New American Library.

———. 1961. *Mysticism and Philosophy.* London: Macmillan.

Stoeber, Michael. 1992. "Constructivist Epistemologies of Mysticism: A Critique and a Revision." *Religious Studies* 28: 107–16.

Suso, Henry. 1953. *Little Book of Eternal Wisdom and Little Book of Truth.* Trans. J. M. Clark. London: Faber and Faber.

Suzuki, Shunryu. 1970. *Zen Mind, Beginner's Mind.* ed. Trudy Dixon. New York: Weatherhill.

Swinburne, Richard, ed. 1989. *Miracles.* New York: Macmillan.

———. 1991. *The Existence of God.* Revised edition. Oxford: Clarendon Press.

———. 1996. *Is There a God?* Oxford: Oxford University Press.

Takeuchi, Yoshinori. 1983. *The Heart of Buddhism.* Trans. James W. Heisig. New York: Crossroad.

Underhill, Evelyn. 1945. *Mysticism: A Study in the Nature and Development of Man's Spiritual Consciousness.* London: Methuen.

Wainwright, William J. 1981. *Mysticism: A Study of Its Nature, Cognitive Value, and Moral Implications.* Madison: University of Wisconsin Press.

Wulff, David M. 2000. "Mystical Experience." In *Varieties of Anomalous Experience: Examining the Scientific Evidence,* ed. Etzel Cardena, Steven Jay Lynn, and Stanley Krippner, 397–440. Washington, D.C.: American Psychological Association.

Yandell, Keith. 1975. "Some Varieties of Ineffability." *International Journal for Philosophy of Religion* 6: 167–79.

———. 1993. *The Epistemology of Religious Experience.* New York: Cambridge University Press.

Zaehner, R. C. 1961. *Mysticism, Sacred and Profane.* New York: Oxford University Press.

CHAPTER 7

PASCAL'S WAGERS AND JAMES'S WILL TO BELIEVE

JEFFREY JORDAN

DURING the summer of 1955 John von Neumann, the mathematical genius and pioneer of Game Theory, was diagnosed with an advanced and incurable cancer. When the disease confined him to bed, von Neumann converted to Christianity. As might be expected of the inventor of the minimax principle, von Neumann was reported to have said, perhaps jovially, that Pascal had a point: if there is a chance that God exists and that damnation is the lot of the nonbeliever, then it is logical at the end to believe (Macrae 1992, 379).

Pascal's point was his famous wager. Pascal's wager is a pragmatic argument in support of theistic belief. *Theism* is the proposition that *God exists*. *God* we will understand as a title for the individual who is omnipotent, omniscient, and morally perfect. A *theist* is anyone who believes that God exists. Pragmatic arguments employ prudential reasons on behalf of their conclusions. A prudential reason for a proposition is a reason to think that believing that proposition would be beneficial. Pascal (1623–1662), a French mathematician and philosopher, is famous, in part, for his contention that, if the evidence is inconclusive, one can properly consult prudence: "Your reason suffers no more violence in choosing one rather than the other . . . but what about your happiness? Let us weigh the gain and the loss involved by wagering that God exists" (1995, 153).[1] According to Pascal, theistic belief, because of its prudential benefits, defeats its doxastic rivals of disbelief and suspended belief. Other theistic arguments, such as the ontological proof, say, or the cosmological argument seek to provide epistemic reasons in support of theism. An epistemic reason for a proposition is a reason to think that that proposition is true or likely.

Pascal's wager was a revolutionary apologetic device. It is not an argument for the claim that God exists. That sort of argument appeals to evidence, whether empirical or conceptual. The wager is an argument that *belief* in God is pragmatically rational, that inculcating a belief in God is the action dictated by prudence. To say that an action is pragmatically rational implies that it is in one's best interests to do that action. Rationality and truth can diverge, of course. But in the absence of conclusive evidence of truth, Pascal contends, rationality should be our guide. Pascal's pragmatic turn, though foreshadowed in earlier writers, was an attempt to argue that theistic belief was the only proper attitude to adopt when faced with the question of the existence of God. Because reason cannot determine the answer, it must yield the field to prudence, which, if the wager succeeds, wins the day for theism. Impressively enough, even though the evidence should be inconclusive regarding theism, one would be positively irrational not to believe if the wager succeeds. The wager is designed not to show that theistic belief is rationally permissible but to show that unbelief is rationally impermissible.

The wager presupposes a distinction between (A) a proposition being rational to believe, and (B) inducing a belief in that proposition being the rational thing to do. Although a particular proposition may lack sufficient evidential warrant, it could be that forming a belief in the proposition may be the rational thing, all things considered, to do. So, if there is a greater benefit associated with inducing theistic belief than with any of its competitors, then inducing a belief that God exists is the rational thing to do.

Like the ontological proof and the cosmological argument, the wager is protean. Pascal himself formulated several versions of it. Since Ian Hacking's (1972) seminal article on the wager, three versions have been recognized within the concise paragraphs of the *Pensées*. In this chapter I suggest there's a fourth version as well, a version that in many respects anticipates the argument of William James (1956) in his 1896 essay "The Will to Believe." This fourth wager argument, I contend, differs from the better-known three in that it has as a premise the proposition that theistic belief is more rewarding than nonbelief in this life, independent of whether God exists or not. As we will see, a variant of this fourth wager is the strongest of Pascal's wagers.

THE LOGIC OF PASCAL'S WAGERS

As already mentioned, Pascal's wager comes in at least four formulations. There are also versions of the wager that are not found in Pascal's *Pensées*. For instance, it is commonly thought that the prospect of hell, or an infinite disutility, is employed in the wager. It is not. Still, one could easily construct a Pascal-style wager argument employing the prospect of hell as a possible outcome. One finds that dismal prospect, for instance, employed in the *Port-Royal Logic* presentation of the wager. Despite the infelicities associated with the title *Pascal's wager*, we will continue to use it for any of the family of Pascalian wagers that has as its conclusion the proposition that one should believe in God, whether found in the *Pensées* or not.

Every member of the family of Pascalian wagers shares at least three constitutive features. The first is that Pascalian wagers constitute a distinct class among pragmatic arguments. As mentioned above, pragmatic arguments have premises that are prudentially directed rather than truth-directed. But Pascalian wagers are not just pragmatic arguments. They are pragmatic arguments that have the structure of gambles, a decision made in the midst of evidentiary uncertainty. Pascal assumed that a person, just by virtue of being in the world, is in a betting situation such that one must bet one's life on whether there is or is not a God. This may be a world in which God exists or this may be a world in which God does not exist. The upshot of wager-style arguments is simply that if one bets on God and believes, then there are two possible outcomes. Either God exists and one enjoys an eternity of bliss, or God does not exist and one loses very little. On the other hand, if one bets against God and wins, one gains very little. But if one loses that bet, the consequences may be horrendous. Because the first alternative has an outcome that overwhelms any possible gain attached to nonbelief, the choice is clear to Pascal. Even if reason does not provide an answer, prudence does; one should try to believe. There is everything to gain and little, if anything, to lose.

This leads to the second constitutive feature: a Pascalian wager is a decision situation in which the possible gain or benefit associated with one of the alternatives *swamps* all the others. With Pascal's wager, the possible gain of theism is supposed to be infinitely greater than that of nonbelief. Because an infinite gain minus any finite loss is still infinite, the possible gain attached to theistic belief appears nonpareil. Pascalian wagers can come in topics that are not religious, however, so it is best to understand the swamping property as a gain that is vastly greater than any of its rivals, even if it is not an infinite gain. Typically, the gain is so great as to render the probability assignments, even if they are known, nearly irrelevant.

The third feature has to do with the object of the gamble. The object must be something that is of extreme importance. Belief in God is not the only relevant object. For instance, one might employ a Pascalian argument to contend that the catastrophic consequences that may flow from global warming make conservation measures compelling, even if the risk of catastrophe is less likely than not. Or one can imagine a Pascalian wager, call it the "patient's wager," in which a person diagnosed with a terminal disease, having exhausted the available conventional therapies, deliberates whether to invest any effort in alternative, unconventional therapies as a long-shot desperate last hope. This sort of Pascalian wager, like a desperate "Hail Mary" pass on the last play of a football game, is a "go-for-broke-since-there's-nothing-to lose" wager. Pascalian wagers deal with subjects that are of great concern. As long as one's argument is pragmatic, has the structure of a gamble, exhibits the swamping property, and has to do with something of an ultimate concern, one is using an argument form due to Pascal.

THE APOLOGETIC ROLE OF THE WAGERS

While we cannot know the role in his projected apologetic work Pascal intended for his wagers, there are hints. Two important hints come early, in fragment 680. First is the sentence "Let us now speak according to natural lights" (Pascal 1995, 153). The second is the use of the indefinite article. "If there is a God, he is infinitely beyond our comprehension" (153). These sentences suggest that Pascal intended the wagers as arguments for the rationality of theistic belief, and not as arguments for the rationality of Christian belief. It is likely that Pascal had in mind a two-step apologetic strategy. The first step would consist of the four wagers, an ecumenical argument in support of theism generally, with the second step consisting of arguments for Christianity in particular.

As an ecumenical argument in support of theism, the wagers were designed to show that theistic belief is rational. Appeals to fulfilled prophecy and to miracles were Pascal's favored arguments by which his reader was to be led to Christianity. Many of the *Pensées* fragments consist of arguments that either Christianity is the true religion, or that it is superior to Judaism and Islam in significant respects (see passages 235–76, for instance). If this speculation is sound, then Pascal's apology was very much in line with the standard seventeenth- and eighteenth-century apologetic strategy: argue first that there is a god, and then identify which god it is that exists. This is the strategy adopted by Robert Boyle (1627–1691) and by Bishop John Tillotson (1630–1694), for instance, and by those, like William Paley (1734–1805), who employed the design argument to argue for a divine designer, and then used the argument from miracles to identify that designer.

A FAMILY OF WAGERS

About a third of the way into *Pensées* 680 a dialogue commences. Along with most commentators, I assume that Pascal formulates the wager arguments in response to questions and comments from the unnamed interlocutor.

Prior to presenting his wager arguments Pascal sets the stage with certain observations. The first is that neither the nature nor the existence of God admits of rational proof: "Reason cannot decide anything . . . Reason cannot make you choose one way or the other, reason cannot make you defend either of two choices" (1995, 153). This should not be taken as asserting that evidence and argument are irrelevant to philosophical theology. Pascal did not think that. While certain kinds of arguments and evidence are irrelevant, other kinds *are* relevant. Furthermore, Pascal clearly thought that his wager arguments were not only relevant but also rationally compelling. Second, wagering about the existence of God is unavoidable: "You have to wager" (154). Wagering is a forced decision: to refuse to wager is tantamount to wagering against. A forced decision between alternatives occurs whenever deciding nothing is equivalent to one of the alternatives. We can understand wagering on God as taking steps to inculcate theistic belief. Pascal was not, and no Pascalian need be, a doxastic voluntarist. A Pascalian wager does not assume that belief is under our direct control. What is necessary is that we can bring about belief in a roundabout, indirect way. For those making a pro-wager Pascal suggests a regimen of imitating the faithful by "taking holy water, having masses said" (156). Wagering against, then, is failing to take steps to bring about theistic belief. It is not anachronistic to note the Jamesian similarities here: wagering about God arises because argument and evidence and reason are inconclusive. Moreover, wagering is forced, and, clearly, the matter is momentous and involves, for most of Pascal's readers, living options.

Be that as it may, Hacking (1972) identifies three versions within the *Pensées* fragments. The first, which Hacking dubs the "argument from dominance," is conveyed within the admonition to "weigh up the gain and the loss by calling that heads that God exists . . . If you win, you win everything; if you lose, you lose nothing. Wager that he exists then, without hesitating" (Pascal 1995, 154).

Rational optimization requires adopting a particular alternative among several mutually exclusive and jointly exhaustive options, whenever doing so may render one better off than not doing so, and in no case could doing so render one worse off. According to Pascal theistic belief dominates.[2] Consider:

	God exists	~ (God exists)[3]
Believe[4]	F1	F2
~ (Believe)	F3	F4

In this matrix there are two states of the world (possible ways that the world might be), one in which God exists and one in which God does not exist; and two acts (choices available to the agent), whether to bring about belief or not. Given that the outcomes associated with the acts have the relations F1 $>>$ F3, and F2 is at least as good as F4, belief weakly dominates not believing.[5] Because nowhere in passage 680 does Pascal suggest that nonbelief results in hell, or in an infinite disutility, if God exists, no great disvalue has been assigned to F3. The argument from dominance proceeds as follows:

1. For any person S, if one of the alternatives, α, available to S has an outcome better than the outcomes of the other available alternatives, and never an outcome worse than the others, S should choose α. And,
2. Believing in God is better than not believing if God exists, and is no worse if God does not exist.[6]
   Therefore,
C. One should believe in God.

This first wager is an example of a decision under uncertainty. Whenever one deliberates with knowledge of the outcomes but no knowledge of the probabilities associated with those outcomes, one faces a decision under uncertainty. On the other hand, if one deliberates armed with knowledge of both the outcomes and the probabilities associated with those outcomes, one faces a decision under risk.

Typically, decisions under risk require an "objective evidential basis for estimating probabilities, for example, relative frequencies, or actuarial tables, or the relative strengths of the various propensities of things (states of affairs) that affect the outcome" (Rawls 2001, 106). With decisions under uncertainty no such basis is available. Given Pascal's claim that "if there is a god, he is infinitely incomprehensible to us . . . we are incapable, therefore, of knowing either what He is or if

He is" (1995, 153), it is not surprising that his first version of the wager is a decision under uncertainty.

The conclusion—that one should believe that God exists—is an "ought of rationality." Pascal probably did not intend, nor need a Pascalian for that matter, to limit the imperative force of (C) to pragmatic rationality only. The idea of (C) is that belief in God is not merely pragmatically rational but rational all things considered. Let's distinguish between something being rationally compelling and something being plausible. An argument is rationally compelling if, on grasping the argument, one would be irrational in failing to accept its conclusion. A rationally compelling argument is one that it is rational all things considered to accept. On the other hand, an argument is plausible if, on grasping the argument, one would be reasonable or rational in accepting its conclusion, but one would not be irrational in failing to accept it. Pascal believed that his wager made theistic belief rationally compelling.

The transition to the second version of the wager is precipitated by the interlocutor's objection to the assumption that theistic wagering does not render one worse off if God does not exist. In response, Pascal introduces probability assignments to the discussion, and, more important, the idea of an infinite utility:

> Since there is an equal chance of gain and loss, if you won only two lives instead of one, you could still put on a bet. But if there were three lives to win, you would have to play . . . and you would be unwise . . . not to chance your life to win three in a game where there is an equal chance of losing and winning. (1995, 154)

While probability plays no part in the first argument, it has a prominent role in the second version of the wager, which Hacking calls the "argument from expectation." The argument from expectation is built on the concept of maximizing expected utility. Perhaps employing a nascent principle of indifference, it assumes that the probability that God exists is one-half. It also assumes that the outcome of right belief if God exists is of infinite utility.[7]

One calculates the expected utility of an act φ by multiplying the benefits and probabilities of each outcome associated with φ, subtracting any respective costs, and then summing the totals from each associated outcome. So, the expected utility of believing in God, given an infinite utility and 0.5 probabilities, is:

$$(\infty \times \tfrac{1}{2}) + (F_2 \times \tfrac{1}{2}) = \infty.$$

With the assumption of an infinite utility theistic belief easily outdistances not believing, no matter what finite value is found in F_2, F_3, or F_4:

	God exists ½	~(God exists) ½	
Believe	0.5, ∞	0.5, F2	EU = ∞
~ (Believe)	0.5, F3	0.5, F4	EU = finite value

Put schematically:

3. For any person S, and alternatives, α and β, available to S, if α carries a greater expected utility than does β, S should choose α. And,
4. Given that the existence of God is as likely as not, the expected utility of believing in God infinitely exceeds that of not believing. Therefore,
C. One should believe in God.

Hacking asserts that the assumption of equal chance is "monstrous." Perhaps it is. The beautiful thing about infinite utility, though, is that infinity multiplied by any finite value is still infinite. The assumption that the existence of God is just as likely as not is needlessly extravagant, for, as long as the existence of God is judged to be greater than zero, believing will always carry an expected utility greater than that carried by nonbelief. And this is true no matter the value or disvalue associated with the outcomes F2, F3, and F4. This observation underlies the third version of the wager, which Hacking titles the "argument from dominating expectation." In this version, p represents an indeterminate positive probability greater than zero and less than one-half:

	God exists p	~ (God exists) 1 − p	
Believe	p, ∞	1 − p, F2	EU = ∞
~ (Believe)	p, F3	1 − p, F4	EU = finite value

No matter how unlikely it is that God exists, as long as there is some positive nonzero probability that he does, believing is one's best bet:

5. For any person S, and alternatives, α and β, available to S, if the expected utility of α exceeds that of β, S should choose α. And,
6. Believing in God carries more expected utility than does not believing, given that the existence of God has a positive, nonzero probability. Therefore,
C. One should believe in God.

Because of its ingenious employment of infinite utility, the third version has become what most philosophers think of as Pascal's wager. We will refer to it as the *canonical version.*

The fourth version of the wager is found in the concluding remarks that Pascal makes to his interlocutor in *Pensées* 680:

> But what harm will come to you from taking this course? You will be faithful, honest, humble, grateful, doing good, a sincere and true friend. It is, of course, true; you will not take part in corrupt pleasure, in glory, in the pleasures of high living. But will you not have others?
> I tell you that you will win thereby in this life. (1995, 156)

The fourth version brings us full circle, away from arguments under risk and back to an argument under uncertainty. This version remedies the defect that precluded the first argument from strict dominance.

	God exists	~ (God exists)
Believe	∞	F2
~ (Believe)	F3	F4

Like its predecessors, the fourth version implies that the benefits of belief vastly exceed those of nonbelief if God exists; but, unlike the others, the fourth implies that F2 > F4. No matter what, belief is one's best bet. Belief strictly dominates nonbelief. Let's call this version of the wager the "argument from strict dominance":

7. For any person S, if among the alternatives available to S, the outcomes of one alternative, α, are better than those of the other available alternatives, S should choose α. And,
8. Believing in God is better than not believing, whether God exists or not. Therefore,
C. One should believe in God.

Premise (8) is true only if one gains simply by believing. Pascal apparently thought that this was obvious. Sincere theistic belief results, he thought, in virtuous living, and virtuous living is more rewarding than vicious living. The response of Pascal's interlocutor, we might plausibly imagine, would be that Pascal has made an illicit assumption: Why think that virtuous living requires theism? And even if virtuous living requires theism, why think that being morally better is tantamount to being better off all things considered? Now whether virtue is its own reward only in a theistic context or not, the relevant point is whether theistic belief provides more benefit than not believing, even if God does not exist. If it does, then this is an important point when considering the many-gods objection.

THE MANY-GODS OBJECTION

Like the canonical version, the fourth version seems vulnerable to what's known as the many-gods objection. Notice that in all four arguments the wager consists of a 2 x 2 matrix: there are two acts available to the agent, with only two possible states of the world. From Pascal's day to this, critics have been quick to point out that Pascal's partitioning of the possible states of the world overlooks the obvious: What if some deity other than God exists? Perhaps there's a deity that harbors animus toward theism, such that he or she rewards nonbelief (Martin 1990, 232–34). In effect, the many-gods objection asserts that Pascal's 2 x 2 matrix is flawed because the states it employs are not jointly exhaustive of the possibilities. Let's expand the Pascalian matrix:

	G	N	D
Believe in G	F_1 ∞	F_2	F_3
Believe in Neither	F_4	F_5	F_6 ∞
Believe in D	F_7	F_8	F_9 ∞

With D representing the existence of a nonstandard deity, a "deviant" deity, and N representing the world with no deity of any sort (call this state "naturalism"), theistic belief no longer strictly dominates.[8] With infinite utility residing in columns G and D, and with the values of F_3, F_4, and F_7 presumably the same, even weak dominance seems lost to theism, since there's no state in which theism is better than its competitors. Just as the many-gods objection is thought by many to be the bane of the third version, one might think it is fatal to the fourth version of the wager as well.

Still, all is not lost for the Pascalian as long as there's good reason in support of (8). With (8) in hand, the Pascalian could salvage from the ruins of the fourth version a wager that circumvents the many-gods objection. Given that the lower two cells of the D column are the same as the upper cell of the G column, and that $F_3 = F_4 = F_7$, the Pascalian can employ the N column as a principled way to adjudicate between believing theistically or not. That is, whether one believes theistically, or believes in a deviant deity, or refrains from believing in any deity at all, one is exposed to the same kind of risk (F3 or F4 or F7). The worst outcomes of theistic belief, of deviant belief, and of naturalistic belief are on a par. Moreover, whether one believes theistically, or believes in a deviant deity, or refrains from believing in any deity at all, one enjoys eligibility for the same kind of reward ($\infty = \infty = \infty$). The best outcomes, that is, of theistic belief, of deviant belief, and of naturalistic belief are on a par. Given (8), however, we would have good reason to believe that F2 > F5. In addition, we have no evidence to think there's any deviant analogue of (8). We have no reason, that is, to think that belief in a deviant deity correlates with the kind of positive benefits associated with theistic belief. But this absence of evidence to think that belief in a deviant deity is associated with positive benefit, conjoined with the obvious opportunity costs arising from such a belief, is itself reason to think that F2 > F8. Indeed, no matter how we might expand the matrix to accommodate the exotica of possible divinity, we would have reason to believe that F2 exceeds any this-world outcome associated with the exotica.[9] So, given that F2 > F5 and that F2 > F8, even if the 2 x 2 matrix is abandoned in favor of an expanded one, a Pascalian beachhead is established:

9. For any person S making a forced decision under uncertainty, if one of the alternatives, α, available to S has an outcome as good as the best outcomes of the other available alternatives, β and γ, and never an outcome worse than the worst outcomes of β and γ, and, excluding the best outcomes and worse outcomes, has only outcomes better than the outcomes of β and γ, S should choose α. And,

10. Theistic belief has an outcome better than the other available alternatives if naturalism obtains. Therefore,

C. One should believe in God.

Premise (9) is a cousin of the weak dominance principle. If there's at least one state in which a particular alternative has an outcome better than that of the others and, moreover, that alternative has no outcome worse than the worst outcomes of the other alternatives, then that alternative weakly dominates.

This version of the wager, I contend, is the strongest member of the Pascalian family. It is valid and is not obviously unsound: one can reasonably accept both premises. With this wager in hand, we might do no better than to invoke James: "Pascal's argument, instead of being powerless, then seems a regular clincher, and is the last stroke needed to make our faith . . . complete" (1956, 11).

THE WILL TO BELIEVE

The argument presented by William James (1842–1910) in his 1896 essay "The Will to Believe" is too often interpreted as just a version of Pascal's wager.[10] It is more than that. Unlike the wager, the focus of James's argument extends far beyond the issue of the rationality of theistic belief to include various philosophical issues (for instance, whether to embrace determinism or indeterminism), and even matters of practical life. James's argument, in its attack on what we might call the agnostic imperative (suspend belief whenever the evidence is insufficient), makes the general epistemological point that "a rule of thinking which would absolutely prevent me from acknowledging certain kinds of truth if those kinds of truth were really there, would be an irrational rule" (1956, 28). If James is correct, then the agnostic imperative, which we might understand more fully as for all persons S and propositions p, it is permissible for S to believe that p only if S has evidence that p is more likely than not, is false.

The foil of James's essay, and a prominent early proponent of what we're calling the agnostic imperative, is W. K. Clifford (1845–1879). Clifford argued:

> If I let myself believe anything on insufficient evidence, there may be no great harm done by the mere belief; it may be true after all, or I may never have occasion to exhibit it in outward acts. But I cannot help doing this great wrong towards Man, that I make myself credulous. The danger to society is not merely that it should believe wrong things, though that is great enough; but that it should become credulous, and lose the habit of testing things and inquiring into them; for then it must sink back into savagery. (1879, 185–186)

Clifford famously presented the agnostic imperative as a rule of morality: "It is wrong always, everywhere, and for any one, to believe anything upon insufficient evidence" (1879, 186). If Clifford's rule of morality is correct, then anyone who believes a proposition that he or she does not take to be more likely than not is, thereby, immoral.

James's primary concern in the "Will to Believe" essay is to argue that Clifford's rule is irrational. James contends that Clifford's rule is but one intellectual strategy open to us. A proponent of Clifford's rule advises, in effect, that one should avoid error at all costs, and thereby risk the loss of certain truths. But another strategy open to us is to seek truth by any means available, even at the risk of error. James champions the latter via the main argument of the "Will to Believe" essay:

11.   Two alternative intellectual strategies are available:

   • Strategy A: Risk a loss of truth and a loss of a vital good for the certainty of avoiding error.
   • Strategy B: Risk error for a chance at truth and a vital good.

12. Clifford's rule embodies Strategy A. But,
13. Strategy B is preferable to Strategy A because Strategy A would deny us access to certain possible kinds of truth. And,
14. Any intellectual strategy that denies access to possible truths is an inadequate strategy. Therefore,
15. Clifford's rule is unacceptable.

James asserts that "there are . . . cases where a fact cannot come at all unless a preliminary faith exists in its coming" (1956, 25). Among other examples he provides of this particular kind of truth is that of social cooperation:

> A social organism of any sort whatever, large or small, is what it is because each member proceeds to his own duty with a trust that the other members will simultaneously do theirs. Wherever a desired result is achieved by the co-operation of many independent persons, its existence as a fact is a pure consequence of the precursive faith in one another of those immediately concerned. (24)

And if James is right that there is a kind of proposition that has as a truth-maker its being believed, what we might call "dependent truths," then proposition (13) looks well supported.

Of course, accepting proposition (15), and advancing an alternative strategy of seeking truth via any available means, even at the risk of error, does not entail that anything goes. An important part of James's essay restricts what legitimately might be believed in the absence of adequate evidence.

To facilitate matters, I paraphrase eight definitions made by James:

- *Hypothesis*: Something that may be believed.
- *Option*: A decision between two hypotheses.
- *Living option*: A decision between two live hypotheses.
- *Live hypothesis*: Something that is a real candidate for belief. A hypothesis is live for a person just in case that person lacks compelling evidence disconfirming that hypothesis, and the hypothesis has an intuitive appeal for that person.
- *Momentous option*: The option may never again present itself, or the decision cannot be easily reversed, or something of importance hangs on the choice. It is not a trivial matter.
- *Forced option*: The decision cannot be avoided, the consequences of refusing to decide are the same as actually deciding for one of the alternative hypotheses.
- *Genuine option*: One that's living, momentous, and forced.
- *Intellectually open*: Neither the evidence nor arguments conclusively decide the issue.

James's contention is that any hypothesis, that's part of a genuine option and that's intellectually open may be believed, even in the absence of sufficient evidence. No rule of morality or rationality is violated if one accepts a hypothesis that's genuine and open.

The relevance of all of this to theistic belief, according to James, is that:

> Religion says essentially two things . . . the best things are the more eternal things, the overlapping things, the things in the universe that throw the last stone, so to speak, and say the final word . . . The second affirmation of religion is that we are better off even now if we believe [religion's] first affirmation to be true . . . The more perfect and more eternal aspect of the universe is represented in our religions as having personal form. The universe is no longer a mere *It* to us, but a *Thou* . . . We feel, too, as if the appeal of religion to us were made to our own active good-will, as if evidence might be forever withheld from us unless we met the hypothesis half-way. (1956, 25–27)

According to James, just as one is not likely to make friends if one is aloof, one is not likely to become acquainted with the deity, if there is such, if one seeks that acquaintance only after sufficient evidence has been obtained. There are possible truths belief in which is a necessary condition of obtaining evidence for them. Let's call the class of propositions whose evidence is restricted to those who first believe "restricted propositions." Dependent propositions and restricted propositions are James's counterexamples to Clifford's rule. They are two examples of the kinds of truths that Clifford's rule would keep one from acknowledging.

One might object that James has at best shown only that theistic belief is momentous if God exists. If God does not exist, and, as a consequence, the vital good of eternal life does not obtain, then no vital good is at stake. To answer this objection a Jamesian might focus on what James calls the second affirmation of religion—we are better off even now if we believe—and take that affirmation to include positive benefits that are available, via pro-belief, even if God does not exist. In the context of the Western religious tradition, the second affirmation is expressed, in part, by propositions (8) and (10).

Given that theism is intellectually open and that it's part of a genuine option, and given that there are vital goods attached to theistic belief, James says, the hope that it is true is a sufficient reason to believe.

A common complaint about James's argument is that it presupposes doxastic voluntarism. Doxastic voluntarism is the thesis that persons can acquire beliefs at will, that persons have direct control over their beliefs. Perhaps the most prominent objection along these lines is due to Bernard Williams (1972), who argues, in effect, that it's not possible to both believe that p and to know that p is false. But if doxastic voluntarism were true, that would be possible. Williams's argument may present a problem for doxastic voluntarism, but it does not present one for James. For one thing, James's proposal is operative only when the evidence is inconclusive, and is not operative in the face of conclusive adverse evidence. James does not countenance believing when the evidence is clear that the hypothesis is less likely than not. For another thing, James's talk of believing this or that hypothesis can be replaced with talk of accepting this or that hypothesis. And whether belief is under our control or not, acceptance surely is.

Another objection commonly leveled against James's argument is that "it constitutes an unrestricted license for wishful thinking ... if our aim is to believe what is true, and not necessarily what we like, James's universal permissiveness will not help us" (Hick 1990, 60). That is, *hoping* that a proposition is true is no reason to think that it *is*. This objection is false and unfair. As we have noted, James does not hold that the falsity of Clifford's rule implies that anything goes. Restricting the relevant permissibility class to propositions that are intellectually open and part of a genuine option provides ample protection against wishful thinking. Moreover, why think that believing what's true and believing what we like are necessarily mutually exclusive? Some philosophers have suggested that James thought that passional reasoning was, under certain circumstances, a reliable means of acquiring true beliefs.[11] If certain uses of the passions are a reliable means of acquiring true belief, then the wishful thinking charge is irrelevant.

A more interesting objection contends that James's argument fails "to show that one can have a sufficient moral reason for self-inducing an epistemically unsupported belief" (Gale 1991, 383). This objection contends that there is a weighty moral duty to proportion one's beliefs to the evidence, and that this duty flows from moral personhood: to be a morally responsible person requires that one have good reasons for each of one's beliefs. But to believe an epistemically unsupported proposition is to violate this duty and is thus, in effect, a denial of one's own personhood.[12] Or think of it another way: as intellectual beings, we have the dual goal of maximizing our stock of true beliefs and minimizing our stock of false ones. Clifford's rule derives its moral validity, one might contend, from that intellectual goal. And from Clifford's rule flows our duty to believe only those propositions that enjoy adequate evidential support. James's argument would, if operative, thwart our intellectual goal by permitting us to violate Clifford's rule.

Can a morally responsible person ever have a moral duty to believe a proposition that lacks adequate evidence, a duty that outweighs the alleged Cliffordian duty of believing only those propositions that enjoy adequate support? It seems so. To see this, we must indulge in a bit of science fiction, and employ what we might call the "ET argument." Suppose Clifford is abducted by very powerful and very smart extraterrestrials that demonstrate their intent and power to destroy the Earth. Moreover, these fiendish ETs offer but one chance of salvation for humankind: that Clifford acquire and maintain the belief that the solar system is geocentric and not heliocentric. Clifford adroitly points out that he cannot just will this belief. The ETs, devilish in their anticipation and in their technology, provide him with a supply of one-a-day doxastic-producing pills, such that simply swallowing a pill produces the requisite belief for twenty-four hours. I submit that Clifford would do no wrong by swallowing the pills and, hence, bringing about and maintaining belief in a proposition that's much less likely than not. Indeed, Clifford would be wrong *not* to swallow the pills. Moreover, because one is never irrational in doing one's moral duty, not only would Clifford not be immoral, he would not even be irrational in bringing about and maintaining belief in a geocentric solar system. Given the distinction between (A) a proposition being rational to believe, and (B) inducing a belief in that proposition being the rational action to do, it may be that a particular proposition lacks sufficient evidential warrant, but that forming a belief in that proposition is the rational action to perform.

One might claim that the ET argument fails because it is valid only if a proposition like the following is true:

J.   If S is morally justified in doing things that will predictably result in her doing x, then S is morally justified in doing x.[13]

But one might argue that (J) is false. For instance, one might allege that the following is a counterexample to (J):

> Suppose an evil and powerful tyrant offers me the following choice: die now, or submit to an irreversible and irresistible hypnotic suggestion which will cause me to kill myself five years from now. I have no other option. Surely I am practically [and morally] justified in submitting to hypnosis in these cir-cumstances. But it would be bizarre to maintain that five years from now, I am practically [and morally] justified in killing myself. (Mills 1998, 34–35)

But this is no counterexample to proposition (J). Proposition (J) is specifically about actions. Irreversible and irresistible events that happen to one are clearly not actions of that person. In the alleged counterexample, one's killing oneself is not an action, it is a foreseeable and unavoidable effect of gaining an additional five years of life. Of course, the failure of this attack on proposition (J) does not entail that (J) is true, but given its intuitive appeal there's reason to accept it.

PRAGMATIC ARGUMENTS
AND BELIEF IN GOD

Perhaps one further characteristic shared by Pascal's wager and James's argument should be mentioned: these are arguments that many people, such as von Neumann, actually employ. There are people who are persuaded by them. I doubt that the same is true of, say, the ontological argument. A close examination of the wager and the will-to-believe argument is important, then, not only for their inherent philosophical interest, but also to determine whether these arguments merit the trust that people actually accord them.

NOTES

1. In the Levi translation the relevant passage is 680; in the Lafuma edition the passage is 343. All *Pensées* citations are to the Levi edition.

2. As described, the first version of the wager is an argument from *weak* dominance.

3. The matrix employed to represent Pascal's wager consists of three important components: states of the world (ways the world could be), acts (actions open to decision), and outcomes (anticipated effects of each act if a particular state occurs):

States

Acts   Outcomes

Depending on the number of Acts and States (2 x 2, or 2 x 3, or 3 x 3 . . .) the Outcomes will be arranged in cells, which are numbered sequentially from the upper left-hand cell across. For example:

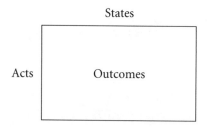

States

	F1	F2
Acts		
	F3	F4

4. While it may be better to understand the acts as bringing about belief, and remaining within nonbelief, for convenience, I will formulate the acts as simply *Believe* and ~ (*Believe*).

5. The expression $X >> Y$ should be understood as X *greatly exceeds Y*.

6. Clearly enough, the acts in this case have no propensity to bring about the states.

7. While objective probabilities are standardly used in calculating expected utility, subjective (or epistemic, or personalist) probabilities can be employed as well. The wager can accommodate either objective probability assignments or subjective ones.

8. By "nonstandard deity" I mean the gerrymandered fictions of philosophers. See, for instance, Saka (2001, 321–41).

9. Even though it is possible to imagine any number of deviant gods, any extension beyond a 3 x 3 matrix is logically redundant given that F2 exceeds the "this world" outcomes of the deviant deities, and given that the best cases and worse cases are on a par.

10. For additional detail on James, consult Bird (1986, 161–81).

11. See Wainwright (1995, 84–107).

12. I do not suggest that this brief argument is an adequate summary of Gale's detailed objection to James.

13. Proposition (J) is modeled on a proposition discussed by Mills (1998, 34–35).

WORKS CITED

Bird, Graham. 1986. *William James*. London. Routledge and Kegan Paul.

Clifford, W. K. 1879. *Lectures and Essays*. Vol. 2. London: Macmillan.

Gale, Richard. 1991. *On the Nature and Existence of God*. Cambridge, England: Cambridge University Press.

Hacking, Ian. 1972. "The Logic of Pascal's Wager." *American Philosophical Quarterly* 9: 186–92.

Hick, John. 1990. *Philosophy of Religion*. 4th ed. Englewood Cliffs, N.J.: Prentice Hall.

James, William. 1956. "The Will to Believe." In *The Will to Believe and Other Essays in Popular Philosophy*. New York: Dover.

Macrae, Norman. 1992. *John von Neumann*. New York: Pantheon.

Martin, Michael. 1990. *Atheism: A Philosophical Justification*. Philadelphia: Temple University Press.

Mills, Eugene. 1998. "The Unity of Justification." *Philosophy and Phenomenological Research* 58: 27–50.

Pascal, Blaise. 1995. *Pensées*. Trans, Honor Levi. Oxford: Oxford University Press.

Rawls, John. 2001. *Justice As Fairness: A Restatement*. Ed. E. Kelly. Cambridge, Mass.: Belknap Press.

Saka, Paul. 2001. "Pascal's Wager and the Many-gods Objection." *Religious Studies* 37: 321–41

Wainwright, William. 1995. *Reason and the Heart: A Prolegomenon to a Critique of Passional Reason*. Ithaca, N.Y.: Cornell University Press.

Williams, Bernard. 1972. "Deciding to Believe." In *Problems of the Self: Philosophical Papers 1956–1972*, 136–51. Cambridge, England: Cambridge University Press.

FOR FURTHER READING

Armour, Leslie. 1993. *"Infini Rien": Pascal's Wager and the Human Paradox.* Carbondale: Southern Illinois University Press.

Brown, Geoffrey. 1984. "A Defence of Pascal's Wager." *Religious Studies* 20: 465–79.

Cargile, James. 1966. "Pascal's Wager." *Philosophy* 41: 250–57.

Duff, Antony. 1986. "Pascal's Wager and Infinite Utilities."*Analysis* 42: 107–9.

Feldman, Richard. 2000. "The Ethics of Belief." *Philosophy and Phenomenological Research* 60: 667–95.

Foley, Richard. 1994. "Pragmatic Reasons for Belief." In Jordan 1994a.

Fouke, Daniel, C. 1989. "Argument in Pascal's *Pensées.*" *History of Philosophy Quarterly* 6: 57–68.

Hájek, Alan. 2000. "Objecting Vaguely to Pascal's Wager." *Philosophical Studies* 98: 1–16.

Jackman, Henry. 1999. "Prudential Arguments, Naturalized Epistemology, and the Will to Believe." *Transactions of the Charles S. Peirce Society* 35: 1–37.

Jordan, Jeffrey. 1991. "Duff and the Wager." *Analysis* 51: 174–76.

———. 1993. "Pascal's Wager and the Problem of Infinite Utilities." *Faith and Philosophy* 10: 49–59.

———, ed. 1994a. *Gambling on God: Essays on Pascal's Wager.* Littlefield, Md.: Rowman & Littlefield.

———. 1994b. "The St. Petersburg Paradox and Pascal's Wager." *Philosophia* 23: 226–240.

———. 1996. "Pragmatic Arguments and Belief." *American Philosophical Quarterly* 33: 409–20.

———. 1998. "Pascal's Wager Revisited." *Religious Studies* 34: 419–31.

McClennen, Edward. 1994. "Pascal's Wager and Finite Decision Theory." In Jordan 1994a.

Meiland, Jack. 1980. "What Ought We to Believe? Or the Ethics of Belief Revisited." *American Philosophical Quarterly* 17: 15–24.

Morris, Thomas. 1994. "Wagering and the Evidence." In Jordan 1994a.

Quinn, Philip. 1994. "Moral Objections to Pascalian Wagering." In Jordan 1994a.

Rescher, Nicholas. 1985. *Pascal's Wager: A Study of Practical Reasoning in Philosophical Theology.* Notre Dame, Ind.: University of Notre Dame Press.

Ryan, Jack. 1945. "The Argument of the Wager in Pascal and Others." *New Scholasticism* 19: 233–50.

Schlesinger, George. 1994. "A Central Theistic Argument." In Jordan 1994a.

Sorensen, Roy. 1994. "Infinite Decision Theory." In Jordan 1994a.

Wernham, James. 1987. *James's Will-to-believe Doctrine: A Heretical View.* Montreal: McGill-Queen's University Press.

CHAPTER 8

THE PROBLEM
OF EVIL

PETER VAN INWAGEN

1. INTRODUCTORY REMARKS:
THE PROBLEM OF EVIL AND THE
ARGUMENT FROM EVIL

THERE are many ways to understand the phrase "the problem of evil." In this chapter, I understand this phrase as a label for a certain purely intellectual problem—as opposed to an emotional, spiritual, pastoral, or theological problem (and as opposed to a good many other possible categories of problem as well). The fact that there is much evil in the world (that is to say, the fact that many bad things happen) can be the basis for an argument for the nonexistence of God (that is, of an omnipotent and morally perfect God. But I take these qualifications to be redundant: I take the phrases "a less than omnipotent God" and "a God who sometimes does wrong" to be self-contradictory, like "a round square" or "a perfectly transparent object that casts a shadow.") Here is a simple formulation of this argument:

> If God existed, he would be all-powerful and morally perfect. An all-powerful and morally perfect being would not allow evil to exist. But we observe evil. Hence, God does not exist.

Let us call this argument "the argument from evil"—glossing over the fact that there are many arguments for the nonexistence of God that could be described as arguments from evil. The intellectual problem I call the problem of evil can be framed as a series of closely related questions addressed to theists: How would you respond to the argument from evil? Why hasn't it converted you to atheism (for surely you've long known about it)? Is your only response the response of faith—something like, "Evil is a mystery. We must simply trust God and believe that there is some good reason for the evils of the world"? Or can you *reply* to the argument? Can you explain how, in your view, the argument can be anything less than an unanswerable demonstration of the truth of atheism?

These questions present theists with a purely intellectual challenge. I believe this intellectual challenge can be met. I believe it can be met by critical examination of the argument. I believe critical examination of the argument shows that it is indeed something less than an unanswerable demonstration of the truth of atheism. I attempt just such a critical examination in this chapter. In this chapter, we shall *examine* this argument, hold it up to critical scrutiny.

2. THE "MORAL INSENSITIVITY" CHARGE

Before we examine the argument from evil, however, we must consider the charge that to examine it, to treat it as if it was, as it were, just another philosophical argument whose virtues and defects could be weighed by impartial reason, is a sign of moral insensitivity—or downright wickedness. One might suppose that no argument was exempt from critical examination. But it is frequently asserted, and with considerable vehemence, that it is *extremely* wicked to examine the argument from evil with a critical eye. Here, for example, is a famous passage from John Stuart Mill's *Three Essays on Religion*:

> We now pass to the moral attributes of the Deity . . . This question bears a very different aspect to us from what it bears to those teachers of Natural Theology who are encumbered with the necessity of admitting the omnipotence of the Creator. We have not to attempt the impossible problem of reconciling infinite benevolence and justice with infinite power in the Creator of a world such as this. The attempt to do so not only involves absolute contradiction in an intellectual point of view but exhibits to excess the revolting spectacle of a jesuitical defense of moral enormities. (1875, 183)

I cannot resist quoting, in connection with this passage from Mill, a poem that occurs in Kingsley Amis's (1966) novel *The Anti-death League* (it is the work of one of the characters).[1] This poem puts a little flesh on the bones of Mill's abstract Victorian prose. It contains several specific allusions to just those arguments Mill describes as jesuitical defenses of moral enormities. Its literary effect depends essentially on putting these arguments, or allusions to them, into the mouth of God.

To a Baby Born without Limbs

This is just to show you who's boss around here.
It'll keep you on your toes, so to speak.
Make you put your best foot forward, so to speak,
And give you something to turn your hand to, so to speak.
You can face up to it like a man,
Or snivel and blubber like a baby.
That's up to you. Nothing to do with Me.
If you take it in the right spirit,
You can have a bloody marvelous life,
With the great rewards courage brings,
And the beauty of accepting your LOT.
And think how much good it'll do your Mum and Dad,
And your Grans and Gramps and the rest of the shower,
To be stopped being complacent.
Make sure they baptize you, though,
In case some murdering bastard
Decides to put you away quick,
Which would send you straight to LIMB-O, *ha ha ha.*
But just a word in your ear, if you've got one.
Mind you, DO *take this in the right spirit,*
And keep a civil tongue in your head about Me.
Because if you DON'T,
I've got plenty of other stuff up My sleeve,
Such as leukemia and polio
(Which, incidentally, you're welcome to any time,
Whatever spirit you take this in).
I've given you one love-pat, right?
You don't want another.
So watch it, Jack.

I am afraid I must accuse Mill (and the many other authors who have expressed similar sentiments) of intellectual dishonesty.

Philosophy is *hard*. Thinking clearly for an extended period is hard. It is easier to pour scorn on those who disagree with you than actually to address their arguments. And of all the kinds of scorn that can be poured on someone's views, moral scorn is the safest and most pleasant (most pleasant to the one doing the pouring). It is the safest kind because, if you want to pour moral scorn on someone's views, you can pretty much take it for granted that most people will regard what you have said as unanswerable; you can take it as *certain* that everyone who is predisposed to agree with you will believe you have made an unanswerable point. You can pretty much take it for granted that your audience will dismiss any attempt your opponent in debate makes at an answer as a "rationalization"—that great contribution of modern depth psychology to intellectual complacency and laziness. Moral scorn is the most *pleasant* kind of scorn to deploy against those who disagree with you because a display of self-righteousness—moral posturing— is a pleasant action whatever the circumstances, and it's nice to have an excuse for it. No one can tell me Mill wasn't enjoying himself when he wrote the words "exhibits to excess the revolting spectacle of a jesuitical defense of moral enormities." (Perhaps he was enjoying himself so much that his attention was diverted from the question, What would it be to exhibit a revolting spectacle in moderation?)

To people who employ the argument from evil and attempt to deflect critical examination of this argument by that sort of moral posturing, I can only say, Come off it. These people are, in point of principle, in exactly the same position as those defenders of law and order who, if you express a suspicion that a man accused of abducting and molesting a child has been framed by the police, tell you with evident disgust that molesting a child is a monstrous crime and that you're defending a child molester.

3. GOD'S OMNIPOTENCE, HIS MORAL PERFECTION, AND HIS KNOWLEDGE OF EVIL

Having defended the moral propriety of critically examining the argument from evil, I will now do just that. The argument presupposes, and rightly, that two features God is supposed to have are "nonnegotiable": that he is omnipotent and morally perfect. That he is omnipotent means that he can do *anything*—provided his doing it doesn't involve an intrinsic impossibility. (Thus, even an omnipotent being can't draw a round square. And God, although he is omnipotent, is unable to lie, for *his* lying is as much an intrinsic impossibility as a round square.) To say that God is morally perfect is to say that he never does anything morally wrong—that he could not possibly do anything morally wrong. If omnipotence and moral perfection are nonnegotiable components of the idea of God, this fact has the following two logical consequences. (1) If the universe was made by an intelligent being, and if that being is less than omnipotent (and if there's no other being who *is* omnipotent), the atheists are right: God does not exist. (2) If the universe was made by an omnipotent being, and if that being has done even one morally wrong thing (and if there isn't another omnipotent being, one who never does anything morally wrong), the atheists are right: God does not exist. If, therefore, the Creator of the universe lacked either omnipotence or moral perfection, and if he claimed to be God, he would be either an impostor (if he claimed to be omnipotent and morally perfect) or confused (if he admitted that he was less than omnipotent or less than morally perfect and still claimed to be God).

One premise of the simple version of the argument set out above—that an all-powerful and morally perfect being would not allow evil to exist—might well be false if the all-powerful and wholly good being were ignorant, and not culpably ignorant, of the existence of evil. But this is not a difficulty for the proponent of the simple argument, for God, if he exists, is omniscient. The proponent of the simple argument could, in fact, defend his premise by an appeal to far weaker theses about the extent of God's knowledge than "God is omniscient." If the simple argument presents an effective prima facie case for the conclusion that there is no omnipotent and morally perfect being who is omnisicent, it presents an equally effective prima facie case for the conclusion that there is no omnipotent and morally perfect being who has even as much knowledge of what goes on in the world as we human beings have. The full panoply of omniscience, so to speak, does not really enter into the initial stages of a presentation and discussion of an argument from evil. Omniscience, omniscience in the full sense of the word, will become important only when we come to examine responses to the argument from evil that involve free will (see Section 9).

How shall we organize our critical examination of the argument from evil? I propose that we imagine in some detail a debate about the existence of God, and that we try to determine how effective a debating point the reality of evil would be for the party to the debate who was trying to show that there was no God.

4. A Description of an Ideal Debate about the Existence of God

Let us imagine that we are about to watch part of a debate between an atheist ("Atheist") and a theist ("Theist") about whether there is a God. This debate is being carried on before an audience of agnostics. As we enter the debating hall (the debate has evidently been going on for some time), Atheist has the floor. She is trying to convince the agnostics to abandon their agnosticism and become atheists like herself. Theist is not, not in this part of the debate anyway, trying to convert the agnostics to theism. At present, he is trying to convince the agnostics of only one thing: that Atheist's arguments should not convert them to atheism. (By an odd coincidence, we have arrived just at the moment at which Atheist is beginning to set out the argument from evil.) I mean these fictional characters to be ideal types, ideal representatives of the categories "atheist," "theist," and "agnostic": they are all highly intelligent, rational, and factually well informed; they are indefatigable speakers and listeners, and their attention never wanders from the point at issue. The agnostics, in particular, are moved by a passionate desire for truth. They want to get the question of the existence of God *settled*, and they don't at all care *which way* it gets settled. Their only desire is—if this should be possible—to leave the hall with a *correct belief* about the existence of God, a belief they have *good reason* to regard as correct. (They recognize, however, that this may very well not be possible, in which case they intend to remain agnostics.) Our two debaters, be it noted, are not interested in changing *each other's* beliefs. Each is interested in the effects his or her arguments will have on the beliefs of the agnostics and not at all in the effects those arguments will have on the beliefs of the other debater. One important consequence of this is that neither debater will bother to consider the question, Will my opponent accept this premise? Each will consider only the question, Will the agnostics accept this premise?

Can Atheist use the argument from evil to convert these ideal "theologically neutral" agnostics to atheism—in the face of Theist's best efforts to block her attempt to convince them of the truth of atheism? Our examination of the argument from evil will be presented as an attempt to answer this question.

5. Atheist's Initial Statement of the Argument from Evil; Theist Begins His Reply by Making a Point about Reasons

Atheist, as I have said, is beginning to present the argument from evil to the audience of agnostics. Here is her initial formulation of the argument:

Since God is morally perfect, he must desire that no evil exist—the nonexistence of evil must be what he *wants*. And an omnipotent being can achieve or bring about whatever he wants—or at least whatever he wants that is intrinsically possible, and the nonexistence of evil is obviously intrinsically possible. So if there were an omnipotent, morally perfect being who knew about these evils—well, they wouldn't have arisen in the first place, for he'd have prevented their occurrence. Or if, for some reason, he didn't do that, he'd certainly remove them the instant they began to exist. But we observe evils, and very long-lasting ones. So we must conclude that God does not exist.

What shall Theist say in reply? I think he should begin with an obvious point about the relations between what one wants, what one can do, and what one will, in the event, do:

> I grant that, in some sense of the word, the nonexistence of evil must be what a perfectly good being *wants*. But we often don't bring about states of affairs we can bring about and want to bring about. Suppose, for example, that Alice's mother is dying in great pain and that Alice yearns desperately for her mother to die—today and not next week or next month. And suppose it would be easy for Alice to arrange this—she is perhaps a doctor or a nurse and has easy access to pharmacological resources that would enable her to achieve this end. Does it follow that she will act on this ability she has? It does not, for Alice might have *reasons* for not doing what she can do. (She might, for example, think it would be morally wrong to poison her mother; or she might fear being prosecuted for murder.) The conclusion that evil does not exist does not, therefore, follow *logically* from the premises that the nonexistence of evil is what God wants and that he is able to bring about the object of his desire—since, for all logic can tell us, God might have reasons for allowing evil to exist that, in his mind, outweigh the desirability of the nonexistence of evil.

But Theist must say a great deal more than this, for, if we gave her her head, Atheist could make a pretty good prima facie case for two conclusions: that a morally perfect creator would take pains to prevent the suffering of his creatures, and that the suffering of creatures could not be a necessary means to any end for an omnipotent being. Theist must, therefore, say something about God's reasons for allowing evil, something to make it plausible to believe there might be such reasons. Before I allow him to do this, however, I will introduce some terminology that will help us to understand the general strategy I am going to have him follow in his discussion of God's reasons for allowing evil to exist.

6. A DISTINCTION: "THEODICY" AND "DEFENSE"

Suppose that I believe in God and that I think I know what God's reasons for allowing evil to exist are and that I tell them to you. Then I have presented you with what is called a theodicy, from the Greek words for "God" and "justice." Thus, Milton, in *Paradise Lost*, tells us that the purpose of the poem is to "justify the ways of God to men"—"justify" meaning "exhibit as just." (Here I use "theodicy" in Alvin Plantinga's sense. Other writers have used the word in other senses.) If I could present a theodicy, and if the audience to whom I presented it found it convincing, I'd have an effective reply to the argument from evil, at least as regards that particular audience. But suppose that, although I believe in God, I *don't* claim to know what God's reasons for allowing evil are. Is there any way for someone in my position to reply to the argument from evil? There is. Consider this analogy.

Your friend Clarissa, a single mother, left her two very young children alone in her flat for several hours very late last night. Your Aunt Harriet, a maiden lady of strong moral principles, learns of this and declares that Clarissa is unfit to raise children. You spring to your friend's defense: "Now, Aunt Harriet, don't go jumping to conclusions. There's probably a perfectly good explanation. Maybe Billy or Annie took ill, and she decided to go over to St Luke's for help. You know she hasn't got a phone or a car and no one in that neighborhood of hers would come to the door at two o'clock in the morning." If you tell your Aunt Harriet a story like this, you don't claim to know what Clarissa's reasons for leaving her children alone really were. And you're not claiming to have said anything that shows that Clarissa really is a good mother. You're claiming only to show that the fact Aunt Harriet has adduced doesn't prove Clarissa isn't a good mother; what you're trying to establish is that for all you or Aunt Harriet know, she had some good reason for what she did. And you're not trying to establish only that there is some remote possibility that she had a good reason. No lawyer would try to raise doubts in the minds of the members of a jury by pointing out to them that for all they knew his client had an identical twin, of whom all record had been lost, and who was the person who had actually committed the crime his client was charged with. That may be a possibility—I suppose it *is* a possibility—but it is too remote a possibility to raise real doubts in anyone's mind. What you're trying to convince Aunt Harriet of is that there is, as we say, *a very real possibility* that Clarissa had a good reason for leaving her children alone, and your attempt to convince her of this consists in your presenting her with an example of what such a reason *might* be.

Critical responses to the argument from evil—at least responses by philosophers—usually take just this form. A philosopher who responds to the argument from evil typically does so by telling a story, a story in which God allows evil to exist. This story will, of course, represent God as having reasons for allowing the existence of evil, reasons that, if the rest of the story were true, would be good ones. Such a story philosophers call a *defense*. A defense and a theodicy will not necessarily differ in content. A's defense may, indeed, be verbally identical with B's theodicy. The difference between a theodicy and a defense is simply that a theodicy is put forward as true, while nothing more is claimed for a defense than that it represents a real possibility—or a real possibility given that God exists. If I offer a story about God and evil as a defense, I hope for the following reaction from my audience: "Given that God exists, the rest of the story might well be true. I can't see any reason to rule it out." The logical point of this should be clear. If the audience of agnostics reacts to a story about God and evil in this way, then, assuming Atheist's argument is valid, they must reach the conclusion Theist wants them to reach: that, for all they know, one of Atheist's premises is false. And if they reach that conclusion, they will, for the moment, remain agnostics.

Some people, if they are familiar with the usual conduct of debates about the argument from evil, may be puzzled by my bringing the notion "a very real possibility" into my fictional debate at this early point. It has become something of a custom for critics of the argument from evil first to discuss the so-called logical problem of evil, the problem of finding a defense that contains no internal logical contradiction; when the critics have dealt with this problem to their own satisfaction, as they always do, they go on to discuss the so-called evidential (or probabilistic) problem of evil, the problem of finding a defense that (among certain other desirable features) represents, in my phrase, a real possibility. A counsel for the defense who followed a parallel strategy in a court of law would first try to convince the jury that his client's innocence was logically consistent with the evidence by telling a story involving twins separated at birth, operatic coincidences, and mental telepathy; only after he had convinced the jury by this method that his client's innocence was logically consistent with the evidence would he go on to try to raise *real* doubts in the jurors' minds about his client's guilt.

I find this division of the problem artificial and unhelpful and will not allow it to dictate the form of my discussion of the argument from evil. I am, as it were, jumping right into the evidential problem (so-called; I won't use the term) without any consideration of the logical problem. Or none as such, none under the *rubric* "the logical problem of evil." Those who know the history of the discussions of the argument from evil in the 1950s and 1960s will see that many of the points I make, or have my creatures Atheist and Theist make, were first made in discussions of the logical problem.

All right. Theist's response will take the form of an attempt to present one or more defenses, and his hope will be that the response of the audience of agnostics to this defense, or these defenses, will be, "Given that God exists, the rest of the story might well be true. I can't see any reason to rule it out." What form could a plausible defense take?

One point is clear: a defense cannot simply take the form of a story about how God brings some great good out of the evils of the world, a good that outweighs those evils. At the very least, a defense will have to include the proposition that God was *unable* to bring about the greater good without allowing the evils we observe (or some other evils as bad or worse). And to find a story that can plausibly be said to have this feature is no trivial undertaking. The reason for this lies in God's omnipotence. A human being can often be excused for allowing, or even causing, a certain evil if that evil was a necessary means, or an unavoidable consequence thereof, to some good that outweighed it—or if it was a necessary means to the prevention of some greater evil. The eighteenth-century surgeon who operated without anesthetic caused unimaginable pain to his patients, but we do not condemn him because (at least if he knew what he was about) the pain was an unavoidable consequence of the means necessary to a good that outweighed it: saving the patient's life, for example. But we should condemn a present-day surgeon who had anesthetics available and who nevertheless operated without using them—even if his operation saved the patient's life and thus resulted in a good that outweighed the horrible pain the patient suffered.

7. THEIST'S REPLY CONTINUES; THE INITIAL STATEMENT OF THE FREE-WILL DEFENSE

There seems to me to be only one defense that has any hope of succeeding, and that is the so-called free-will defense.[2] I am going to imagine Theist putting forward a very simple form of this defense; I will go on to ask what Atheist might say in response:

> God made the world and it was very good. An indispensable part of its goodness was the existence of rational beings: self-aware beings capable of abstract thought and love and having the power of free choice between contemplated alternative courses of action. This last feature of rational beings, free choice or free will, is a good. But even an omnipotent being is unable to control the exercise of free choice, for a choice that was controlled would ipso facto not be free. In other words, if I have a free choice between x and y, even God cannot ensure that I choose x. To ask God to give me a free choice between x and y

and to see to it that I choose x instead of y is to ask God to bring about the intrinsically impossible; it is like asking him to create a round square or a material body with no shape. Having this power of free choice, some or all human beings misused it and produced a certain amount of evil. But free will is a sufficiently great good that its existence outweighs the evils that have resulted and will result from its abuse; and God foresaw this.

Theist's presentation of the free-will defense immediately suggests several objections. Here are two that would immediately occur to most people:

> How could anyone possibly believe that the evils of this world are outweighed by the good inherent in our having free will? Perhaps free will is a good and would outweigh, in Theist's words, "a certain amount of evil," but it seems impossible to believe that it can outweigh the amount of physical suffering (to say nothing of other sorts of evil) that actually exists.

> Not all evils are the result of human free will. Consider, for example, the Lisbon earthquake or the almost inconceivable misery and loss of life produced by the hurricane that ravaged Honduras in 1997. Such events are not the result of any act of human will, free or unfree.

In my view, the simple form of the free-will defense I have put into Theist's mouth is unable to deal with either of these objections. The simple form of the free-will defense can deal with at best the existence of *some* evil—as opposed to the vast amount of evil we actually observe—and the evil with which it can deal is only the evil that results from the acts of human beings. I believe, however, that more sophisticated forms of the free-will defense do have interesting things to say about the vast amount of evil in the world and about the suffering caused by earthquakes and hurricanes and other natural phenomena. Before I discuss these "more sophisticated" forms of the free-will defense, however, I want to examine two objections that have been brought against the free-will defense that are so fundamental that, if they were valid, they would refute any elaboration of the defense, however sophisticated. These objections have to do with free will. I am not going to include them in my dialogue between Atheist and Theist, for the simple reason that, in my view, anyway, they have not got very much force, and I do not want to be accused of fictional character assassination; my Atheist has more interesting arguments at her disposal. But I cannot ignore these arguments: the first has been historically important and the second turns on a point that is likely to occur to most readers.

8. An Objection to the Free-will Defense: God *Can* Control the Exercise of Free Choice

The first of the two arguments is essentially this: the free-will defense fails because free will and determinism are compatible; God could, therefore, create a world whose inhabitants are free to do evil but do only good.

This might seem a surprising argument. Why should anyone believe that free will and determinism were compatible?

Well, many very able philosophers *have* believed this, and for reasons unrelated to theological questions. Philosophers of the stature of Thomas Hobbes, David Hume, and John Stuart Mill have held that free will and determinism are perfectly compatible: that there could be a world in which the past determined a unique future and whose inhabitants were nonetheless free agents. Philosophers who accept this thesis are called "compatibilists." It is not hard to see that *if* the compatibilists are right about the nature of free will, the free-will defense fails. If free will and determinism are compatible, an omnipotent being *can*, contrary to a central thesis of the free-will defense, create a person who has a free choice between x and y and ensure that that person choose x rather than y.

Those philosophers who accept the compatibility of free will and determinism defend their thesis as follows: being free is being free to do what one wants to do. Prisoners in a jail, for example, are unfree because they want to leave and can't. The man who desperately wants to stop smoking but can't is unfree for the same reason—even though the barrier that stands between him and a life without nicotine is psychological, and not a physical thing like a wall or a door. The very words "free will" testify to the rightness of this analysis, for one's will is simply what one wants, and a free will is just exactly an unimpeded will. Given this account of free will, a Creator who wants to give me a free choice between x and y has only to arrange matters in such a way that the following two "if" statements are both true: *if* I were to want x, I'd be able to achieve that desire, and *if* I were to want y, I'd be able to achieve *that* desire. And a Creator who wants to ensure that I choose x rather than y has only to implant in me a fairly robust desire for x and see to it that I have no desire at all for y. And these two things are obviously compatible. Suppose, for example, that there was a Creator who had placed a woman in a garden and had commanded her not to eat of the fruit of a certain tree. Could he so arrange matters that she have a free choice between eating of the fruit of that tree and not eating of it—and also *ensure* that she not eat of it? Certainly. To provide her with a free choice between the two alternatives, he need only see to it that two things are true: first, that if she wanted to eat of the fruit of that tree, no barrier (such as an unclimbable fence or paralysis of the limbs or a neurotic fear of trees) would stand in the way of her acting on that desire, and, second, that if she wanted *not* to eat of the fruit, nothing would force her to act contrary to *that* desire. And to ensure that she not eat of the fruit, he need only see to it that not eating of the fruit be what she desires (and that she have no other desire in conflict with this desire). An omnipotent and omniscient being could therefore bring it about that every creature with free will always freely did what was right.

Having thus shown a proposition central to the free-will defense to be false, the critic can make the consequences of its falsity explicit in a few words. If a morally perfect being could bring it about that every creature with free will always freely did what was right, there would of necessity be no creaturely abuse of free will, and evil could not possibly have entered the world through the creaturely abuse of free will. The so-called free-will defense is thus not a defense at all, for it is an impossible story.

We have before us, then, an argument for the conclusion that the story called the free-will defense is an impossible story. But how plausible is the account of free will on which the argument rests? Not very, I think. It certainly yields some odd conclusions. Consider the lower social orders in *Brave New World*, the "deltas" and "epsilons." These unfortunate people have their deepest desires chosen for them by others, by the "alphas" who make up the highest social stratum. What the deltas and epsilons primarily desire is to do what the alphas tell them. This is their primary desire because it has been implanted in them by prenatal and postnatal conditioning. (If Huxley were writing today, he might have added genetic engineering to the alphas' list of resources for determining the desires of their slaves.) It would be hard to think of beings who better fitted the description "lacks free will" than the deltas and epsilons of *Brave New World*. And yet, if the compatibilists' account of free will is right, the deltas and epsilons are exemplars of beings with free will. Each of them is always doing exactly what he wants, after all, and who among *us* is in that fortunate position? What he wants is to do as he is told by those appointed over him, of course, but the compatibilists' account of free will says nothing about the *content* of a free agent's desires: it requires only that there be no barrier to acting on them. The compatibilists' account of free will is, therefore, if not evidently false, at least highly implausible—for it has the highly implausible consequence that the deltas and epsilons are free agents. And an opponent of the free-will defense cannot show that that story fails to represent a "real possibility" by deducing its falsity from a highly implausible theory.

9. A Second Objection to the Free-will Defense: Free Will Is Incompatible with God's Omniscience

I turn now to the second argument for the conclusion that any form of the free-will defense must fail: the free-will defense, of course, entails that human beings have free will; but the existence of a being who knows the future is incompatible with free will, and an omniscient being knows the future, and omniscience belongs to the concept of God; hence, the so-called free-will defense is not a possible story—and is therefore not a defense at all.

Most theists, I think, would reply to this argument by trying to show that divine omniscience and human free will were compatible, for that is what most theists believe. But I find the arguments, which I will not discuss, for the incompatibility of omniscience and freedom, if not indisputably correct, at least pretty convincing, and I will therefore not reply in that way. (And I think that the attempt of Augustine and Boethius and Aquinas to solve the problem by contending that God is outside time—that he is not merely everlasting but altogether nontemporal—is a failure. I don't mean to say that I reject the proposition that God is outside time; I mean that I think his being outside time doesn't solve the problem.) I will instead reply to the argument by engaging in some permissible tinkering with the concept of omniscience. At any rate, I believe it to be permissible for reasons I shall try to make clear.

In what follows, I am going to suppose that God is everlasting but temporal, that he is not "outside time." I make this assumption because I do not know how to write coherently and in detail about a nontemporal being's knowledge of (what is to us) the future. Now consider these two propositions:

X will freely do A at t.
Y, a being whose beliefs cannot be mistaken, believes now that X will do A at t.

These two propositions are consistent with each other or they are not. If they are consistent, there is no problem of omniscience and freedom. Suppose, then, that they are inconsistent, and suppose free will is possible. (If free will isn't possible, the free-will defense is self-contradictory for that reason alone.) Then it is impossible for a being whose beliefs cannot be mistaken to have beliefs about what anyone will freely do in the future. Hence, if free will exists it is impossible for any being to be omniscient. Now, if the existence of free will implies that there cannot be an omniscient being, it might seem, by that very fact, to imply that there cannot be an omnipotent being. For if it is intrinsically impossible for any being now to know what someone will freely do tomorrow or next year, it is intrinsically impossible for any being now to *find out* what someone will freely do tomorrow or next year; and a being who can do anything can find out anything. But this inference is invalid, for an omnipotent being is, as it were, excused from the requirement that it be able to do the intrinsically impossible. This suggests a solution to the problem of free will and divine omniscience: why should we not qualify the concept of omniscience in a way similar to the way the concept of omnipotence is qualified? Why not say that even an omniscient being is unable to know certain things—those such that its knowing them would be an intrinsically impossible state of affairs. Or we might say this: an omnipotent being is also omniscient if it knows everything it is able to know. If we say, first, that the omnipotent God is omniscient in the sense that he knows everything that, in his omnipotence, he is able to know, and, second, that he does not know what the future free acts of any agent will be, we do not contradict ourselves—owing to the fact that (now) finding out what the future free acts of an agent will be is an intrinsically impossible action.

I must admit that this solution to the problem of free will and divine foreknowledge raises a further problem for theists: Are not most theists committed (for example, in virtue of the stories told about God's actions in the Bible) to the proposition that God at least sometimes foreknows the free actions of creatures? This is a very important question. In my view, the answer is no, at least as regards the Bible. But a discussion of this important question is not possible within the scope of this chapter.

10. Atheist Contends That the Free-will Defense Cannot Account for the Amount and the Kinds of Evil We Observe

I conclude that neither an appeal to the supposed compatibility of free will and determinism nor an appeal to the supposed incompatibility of free will and omniscience can undermine the free-will defense.

Let us return to Atheist, who, as I said, has better arguments at her disposal than those considered in sections 8 and 9. What shall she say in response to the free-will defense? What she should do, I think, is to concede a certain limited power to the free-will defense and to go on to maintain that this power is *essen-*

tially limited. Her best course is to concede that the free-will defense shows there might be, for all anyone can say, a certain amount of evil, a certain amount of pain and suffering, in a world created by an all-powerful and morally perfect being, and to conduct her argument in terms of the amounts and the kinds of evil that we actually observe. Her best course is to argue for the conclusion that neither the simple version of the free-will defense I have had Theist present nor any elaboration of it can constitute a plausible account of the evil, the bad things, that actually exist. I have mentioned two points about the evil we observe in the world that would probably occur to most people immediately upon hearing Theist's initial statement of the free-will defense: that the amount of suffering (and other evils) is enormous and must outweigh whatever goodness is inherent in the reality of free will; that some evils are not caused by human beings and cannot therefore be ascribed to the creaturely abuse of free will. I will now ascribe to Atheist a rather lengthy speech that takes up these two points—and a third, perhaps less obvious.

> I will concede that the free-will defense shows that the mere existence of *some evil or other* cannot be used to prove the nonexistence of God. If we lived in a world in which everyone, or most people, suffered in certain relatively minor ways, and if each instance of suffering could be traced to the wrong or foolish acts of human beings, you would be making a good point when you tell these estimable agnostics that, for all they know, these wrong or foolish acts are free acts, that even an omnipotent being cannot determine the outcome of a free choice, and that the existence of free choice is a good thing, sufficiently good to outweigh the bad consequences of its occasional abuse. But the evil we actually observe in the world is not at all like that. First, the sheer *amount* of evil in the world is overwhelming. The existence of free will may be worth some evil, but it certainly isn't worth the amount we actually observe. Second, there are lots of evils that can't be traced to the human will, free or unfree. Earthquakes and tornados and genetic defects and . . . well, one hardly knows where to stop. These two points are familiar ones in discussions of the argument from evil. I want also to make a third point, which, although fairly well-known, is not quite so familiar as these. Let us consider certain particular very bad events—"horrors" I will call them. Here are some examples of what I call horrors: a school bus full of children is crushed by a landslide; a good woman's life is gradually destroyed by the progress of Huntington's Chorea; a baby is born without limbs. Some horrors are consequences of human choices and some are not (consider, for example, William Rowe's [1979] case of a fawn that dies in agony in a forest fire before there were any human beings). But whether a particular horror is connected with human choices or not, it is evident that God could have prevented the horror without sacrificing any great good or allowing some even greater horror.
>
> Now a moment ago I mentioned the enormous amount of evil in the world, and it is certainly true that there is in some sense an enormous *amount* of evil in the world. But the word "amount" at least suggests that evil is quantifiable, like distance or weight. That may be false or unintelligible, but if it is

true, even in a rough-and-ready sort of way, it shows that horrors raise a problem for the theist that is distinct from the problem raised by the enormous amount of evil. If evil can be, even roughly, quantified, as talk about amounts seems to imply, it might be that there was *more* evil in a world in which there were thousands of millions of relatively minor episodes of suffering (broken ribs, for example) than in a world in which there were a few horrors. But an omnipotent and omniscient creator could be called to moral account for creating a world in which there was even *one* horror. And the reason is obvious: that horror could have been "left out" of creation without the sacrifice of any great good or the permission of some even greater horror. And leaving it out is exactly what a morally perfect being would do; such good things as might depend causally on the horror could, given the being's omnipotence and omniscience, be secured by (if the word is not morally offensive in this context) more "economical" means. Thus, the sheer *amount* of evil (which might be distributed in a fairly uniform way) is not the only fact about evil Theist needs to take into account. He must also take into account what we might call (again with some risk of using morally offensive language) *high local concentrations* of evil—that is, horrors. And it is hard to see how the free-will defense, however elaborated, could provide any resources for dealing with horrors.

I will, finally, call your attention to the fact that the case of "Rowe's fawn," which I briefly described a moment ago, is a particularly difficult case for Theist. True, however sentimental we may be about animals, we must admit that the death of a fawn in a forest fire is not much of a horror compared with, say, a living child's being thrown into a furnace as a sacrifice to Baal. The *degree* of horror involved in the event is not what creates the special difficulty for theists in this case. What creates the difficulty is rather the complete causal isolation of the fawn's sufferings from the existence and activities of human beings. No appeal to considerations in any way involving human free will can possibly be relevant to the problem with which this case confronts Theist, the difficulty of explaining why an omnipotent and morally perfect being would allow such a thing to happen.

11. THEIST ELABORATES THE FREE-WILL DEFENSE: EVIL RESULTS FROM A PRIMORDIAL ESTRANGEMENT OF HUMANITY FROM GOD

This is Atheist's response to the free-will defense. How is Theist to reply? If I were he (and in some sense I am), I would reply as follows.

The free-will defense, in the simple form in which I've stated it, suggests—though it does not entail—that God created human beings with free will, and then just left them to their own devices. It suggests that the evils of the world are the more or less unrelated consequences of uncounted millions of largely unrelated abuses of free will by human beings. Let me propose a sort of plot to be added to the bare and abstract story called the free-will defense. Consider the story of creation and rebellion and the expulsion from paradise we find in the first three chapters of Genesis. Could this story be true—I mean literally true, true in every detail? Well, no. It contradicts what science has discovered about human evolution and the history of the physical universe. And that is hardly surprising, for it long antedates these discoveries. The story is a reworking—with much original material—by a Hebrew author or authors of elements found in many ancient Middle Eastern mythologies. Like Virgil's *Aeneid*, it is a literary refashioning of materials that were originally mythical and legendary, and it retains a strong flavor of myth. It is possible, nevertheless, that the first three chapters of Genesis are a mythicoliterary representation of actual events of human prehistory. The following is consistent with what we know of human prehistory. Our current knowledge of human evolution, in fact, presents us with no particular reason to believe this story is false:

> For millions of years, perhaps for thousands of millions of years, God guided the course of evolution so as eventually to produce certain very clever primates, the immediate predecessors of *Homo sapiens*. At some time in the past few hundred thousand years, the whole population of our prehuman ancestors formed a small breeding community—a few thousand or a few hundred or even a few score. That is to say, there was a time when every ancestor of modern human beings who was then alive was a member of this tiny, geographically tightly knit group of primates. In the fullness of time, God took the members of this breeding group and miraculously raised them to rationality. That is, he gave them the gifts of language, abstract thought, and disinterested love—and, of course, the gift of free will. Perhaps we cannot understand *all* his reasons for giving human beings free will, but here is one very important one we *can* understand: He gave them the gift of free will because free will is necessary for love. Love, and not only erotic love, implies free will. The essential connection between love and free will is beautifully illustrated in Ruth's declaration to her mother-in-law, Naomi:

> And Ruth said, Entreat me not to leave thee, or to return from following after thee: for whither thou goest, I will go; and where thou lodgest, I will lodge: thy people shall be my people and thy God my God: where thou diest, will I die, and there will I be buried; the Lord do so to me, and more also, if aught but death part thee and me. (Ruth 1: 16, 17)

It is also illustrated by the vow Mr. van Inwagen, the author of my fictional being, made when he was married:

> I, Peter, take thee, Elisabeth, to my wedded wife, to have and to hold from this day forward, for better for worse, for richer for poorer, in

sickness and in health, to love and to cherish, till death us do part, according to God's holy ordinance; and thereto I plight thee my troth.

God not only raised these primates to rationality—not only made of them what we call human beings—but also took them into a kind of mystical union with himself, the sort of union Christians hope for in Heaven and call the Beatific Vision. Being in union with God, these new human beings, these primates who had become human beings at a certain point in their lives, lived together in the harmony of perfect love and also possessed what theologians used to call preternatural powers—something like what people who believe in them today call paranormal abilities. Because they lived in the harmony of perfect love, none of them did any harm to the others. Because of their preternatural powers, they were able somehow to protect themselves from wild beasts (which they were able to tame with a look), from disease (which they were able to cure with a touch), and from random, destructive natural events (like earthquakes), which they knew about in advance and were able to avoid. There was thus no evil in their world. And it was God's intention that they should never become decrepit with age or die, as their primate forbears had. But, somehow, in some way that must be mysterious to us, they were not content with this paradisal state. They abused the gift of free will and separated themselves from their union with God.

The result was horrific: not only did they no longer enjoy the Beatific Vision, but they now faced destruction by the random forces of nature, and became subject once more to old age and natural death. Nevertheless, they were too proud to end their rebellion. As the generations passed, they drifted further and further from God—into the worship of invented gods (a worship that sometimes involved human sacrifice), inter-tribal warfare (complete with the gleeful torture of prisoners of war), private murder, slavery, and rape. On one level, they realized, or some of them realized, that something was horribly wrong, but they were unable to do anything about it. After they had separated themselves from God, they were, as an engineer might say, "not operating under design conditions." A certain frame of mind became dominant among them, a frame of mind latent in the genes they had inherited from a million or more generations of ancestors. I mean the frame of mind that places one's own desires and perceived welfare above everything else, and that accords to the welfare of one's relatives and the other members of one's tribe a subordinate privileged status, and assigns no status at all to the welfare of anyone else. And this frame of mind was now married to rationality, to the power of abstract thought; the progeny of this marriage were continuing resentment against those whose actions interfere with the fulfillment of one's desires, hatreds cherished in the heart, and the desire for revenge. The inherited genes that produced these baleful effects had been harmless as long as human beings had still had constantly before their minds a representation of perfect love in the Beatific Vision. In the state of separation from God, and conjoined with rationality, they formed the genetic substrate of what is called original or birth sin: an inborn tendency to do evil against which all human efforts are vain. We, or most of us, have some sort of perception of the distinction between good and evil, but, however we struggle, in the end we give in and do evil. In all cultures there are moral codes (more similar than some would have us believe), and the members of every tribe and nation stand condemned not only by alien moral codes but by their own. The only human beings who consistently do right in their own eyes, whose consciences are always clear, are those who, like the Nazis, have given themselves over entirely to evil, those who say, in some twisted and self-deceptive way what Milton has his Satan say explicitly and clearly: "Evil, be thou my Good."

When human beings had become like this, God looked out over a ruined world. It would have been just for him to leave human beings in the ruin they had made of themselves and their world. But God is more than a God of justice. He is, indeed, more than a God of mercy—a God who was merely merciful might simply have brought the story of humanity to an end at that point, like a man who shoots a horse with a broken leg. But God, as I have said, is more than a God of mercy: he is a God of love. He therefore neither left humanity to its own devices nor mercifully destroyed it. Rather, he set in motion a rescue operation. He put into operation a plan designed to restore separated humanity to union with himself. This defense will not specify the nature of this plan of atonement. The three Abrahamic religions, Judaism, Christianity, and Islam, tell three different stories about the nature of this plan, and I do not propose to favor one of them over another in telling a story that, after all, I do not maintain is true. This much must be said, however: the plan has the following feature, and any plan with the object of restoring separated humanity to union with God would have to have this feature: its object is to bring it about that human beings once more love God. And, since love essentially involves free will, love is not something that can be imposed from the outside, by an act of sheer power. Human beings must choose freely to be reunited with God and to love him, and this is something they are unable to do of their own efforts. They must therefore cooperate with God. As is the case with many rescue operations, the rescuer and those whom he is rescuing must cooperate. For human beings to cooperate with God in this rescue operation, they must know that they need to be rescued. They must know what it means to be separated from him. And what it means to be separated from God is to live in a world of horrors. If God simply "canceled" all the horrors of this world by an endless series of miracles, he would thereby frustrate his own plan of reconciliation. If he did that, we should be content with our lot and should see no reason to cooperate with him. Here is an analogy. Suppose Dorothy suffers from angina, and that what she needs to do is to stop smoking and lose weight. Suppose her doctor knows of a drug that will stop the pain but will do nothing to cure the condition. Should the doctor prescribe the drug for her, in the full knowledge that if the pain is alleviated, there is no chance she will stop smoking and lose weight? Well, perhaps the answer is yes, if that's what Dorothy insists on. The doctor is Dorothy's fellow adult and fellow citizen, after all. Perhaps it would be insufferably paternalistic to refuse to alleviate Dorothy's pain in order to provide her with a motivation to do what is to her own advantage. If one were of an especially libertarian cast of mind, one might even say that someone who did that was "playing God." It is far from clear, however, whether there is anything wrong with *God's* behaving as if he were God. It is at least very plausible to suppose that it is morally permissible for God to allow human beings to suffer if the result of suppressing the suffering would be to deprive them of a very great good, one that far outweighed the suffering. But God does shield us from *much* evil, from a great proportion of the sufferings that would have resulted from our rebellion if he did nothing. If he did not shield us from much evil, all human history would be at least this bad: every human society would be on the moral level of Nazi Germany—or worse, if there is a "worse." But, however much evil God shields us from, he must leave a vast amount of evil "in place" if he is not to deceive us about what separation from him means—and, in so deceiving us, to remove our only motivation for cooperating with him in the working out of his plan for divine-human reconciliation. The amount he has left us with is so vast and so horrible that we cannot really comprehend it, especially if we are middle-class Europeans or Americans. Nevertheless, it could have been much worse. The inhabitants of a world in which human beings had separated themselves from God and he had then simply left them to their own devices would regard our world as a comparative paradise. All this evil, however, will come to an end. There will come a time after which, for all eternity, there will be no more unmerited suffering. Every evil done by the wicked to the innocent will have been avenged, and every tear will have been wiped away. If there is still suffering, it will be merited: the suffering of those who refuse to cooperate with God in his great rescue operation and are allowed by him to exist forever in a state of elected ruin—those who, in a word, are in Hell.

One aspect of this story needs to be brought out more clearly than it has been. If the story is true, much of the evil in the world is due to chance. There is generally no explanation of why *this* evil happened to *that* person. What there is is an explanation of why evils happen to people without any reason. And the explanation is: that is part of what our being separated from God means: it means our being the playthings of chance. It means not only living in a world in which innocent children die horribly, it means living in a world in which each innocent child who dies horribly dies horribly for no reason at all. It means living in a world in which the wicked, through sheer luck, often prosper. Anyone who does not want to live in such a world, a world in which we are the playthings of chance, had better accept God's offer of a way out of that world.

I will call this story the *expanded* free-will defense. I mean it to include the "simple" free-will defense as a part. Thus, it is a feature of the expanded free-will defense that even an omnipotent being, having raised our remote ancestors to rationality and having given them the gift of free will, which included a free choice between remaining united with him in bonds of love and turning away from him to follow the devices and desires of their own hearts, was not able to *ensure* that they have done the former—although we may be confident he did everything omnipotence could do to raise the probability of their doing the former. But, before there were human beings, God knew that, however much evil might result from the elected separation from himself, and consequent self-ruin, of his human creatures—if it should occur—the gift of free will would be, so to speak, worth it. For the existence of an eternity of love depends on this gift, and that eternity outweighs the horrors of the very long but, in the most literal sense, temporary period of divine-human estrangement.

Here, then, is a defense, the expanded free-will defense. I contend that the expanded free-will defense is a possible story (internally consistent, at least as far as we can see); that, given that there is a God, the rest of the story might well be true; that it includes evil in the amount and of the kinds we find in the actual world, including what is sometimes called natural evil, such as the suffering caused by the Lisbon earthquake. (Natural evil, according to the expanded free-will defense, is a special case of the evil that results from the abuse of free will; the fact that human beings are subject to destruction by earthquakes is a consequence of a primordial abuse of free will.) I concede that it does not help us with cases like "Rowe's fawn"—cases of suffering that occurred before there were human beings or that are for some other reason causally unconnected with human choice. But I claim to have presented a defense that accounts for all actual *human* suffering.

That was a long speech on the part of Theist. I now return to speaking in propria persona. I have had Theist tell a story, a story he calls the expanded free-will defense. You may want to ask whether *I* believe this story I have put into the mouth of my creature. Well, I believe parts of it and I don't disbelieve any of it. (Even those parts I believe do not, for the most part, belong to my faith; they are merely some of my religious opinions.) I am not at all sure about "preternatural powers," for example, or about the proposition that God shields us from much of the evil that would have been a "natural" consequence of our estrangement from him. But what *I* believe and don't believe is not really much to the point. The story I have told is, I remind you, only supposed to be a defense. Theist does not put forward the expanded free-will defense as a theodicy, as a statement of the real truth of the matter concerning the coexistence of God and evil. Nor would I, if I told it in circumstances like Theist's. Theist contends only, *I* contend only, that the story is—given that God exists—true for all anyone knows. And I certainly don't see any very compelling reason to reject any of it. In particular, I don't see any reason to reject the thesis that God raised a small population of our ancestors to rationality by a specific action on, say, June 13, 116,027 BC, or on some such particular date. It is not a discovery of evolutionary biology that there are no miraculous events in our evolutionary history. It *could* not be, any more than it could be a discovery of meteorology that the weather at Dunkirk during those fateful days in 1940 was not due to a specific and local divine action. It *could*, of course, be a discovery of evolutionary biology that the genesis of rationality was not a sudden, local event. But no such discovery has been made. If someone, for some reason, put forward the theory that extraterrestrial beings visited the earth, and by some prodigy of genetic engineering, raised some population of our primate ancestors to rationality in a single generation (something like this happened in the movie *2001: A Space Odyssey*), this theory could not be refuted by any facts known to physical anthropology.

12. ATHEIST TURNS TO THE CONSIDERATION OF A *PARTICULAR* HORRIBLE EVIL

How might Atheist respond to the expanded free-will defense, given that this defense is, as I argued, consistent with what science has discovered about human prehistory? If I were in her position, I would respond to Theist in some such words as these:

> You, Theist, may have told a story that accounts for the enormous amount of evil in the world, and for the fact that much evil is not caused by human beings. But I don't think you appreciate the force of the argument from horrors (so to call it), and I think I can make the agnostics, at any rate, see this. Let me state the argument from horrors a little more systematically; let me lay out its premises explicitly, and you can tell me which of its premises you deny.
>
> There are many horrors, vastly many, from which no discernible good results—and certainly no good, discernible or not, that an omnipotent being couldn't have got without the horror; in fact, without any suffering at all. Here is a true story. A man came upon a young woman in an isolated place. He overpowered her, chopped off her arms at the elbows with an axe, raped her, and left her to die. Somehow she managed to drag herself on the stumps of her arms to the side of a road, where she was discovered. She lived, but she experienced indescribable suffering, and although she is alive, she must live the rest of her life without arms and with the memory of what she had been forced to endure. No discernible good came of this, and it is wholly unreasonable to believe that any good could have come of it that an omnipotent being couldn't have achieved without employing the raped and mutilated woman's horrible suffering as a means to it. And even if this is wrong and some good came into being with which the woman's suffering was so intimately connected that even an omnipotent being couldn't have got the good without the suffering, it wouldn't follow that that good outweighed the suffering. (It would certainly have to be a very great good to do that.)
>
> I will now draw on these reflections to construct a version of the argument from evil, a version that, unlike the version I presented earlier, refers not

to all the evils of the world, but just to this one event. (The argument is modeled on the central argument of William Rowe's "The Problem of Evil and Some Varieties of Atheism" [1979].) I will refer to the events in the story I have told collectively as "the Mutilation." I argue:

(1) If the Mutilation had not occurred, if it had been, so to speak, simply *left out* of the world, the world would be no worse than it is. (It would seem, in fact, that the world would be significantly *better* if the Mutilation had been left out of it, but my argument doesn't require that premise.)
(2) The Mutilation in fact occurred and was a horror.
(3) If a morally perfect creator could have left a certain horror out of the world he created, and if the world he created would have been no worse if that horror had been left out of it than it would have been if it had included that horror, then the morally perfect creator would have left the horror out of the world he created—or at any rate, he would have left it out if he had been able to.
(4) If an omnipotent being created the world, he was able to leave the Mutilation out of the world (and was able to do so in a way that would have left the world otherwise much as it is).

There is, therefore, no omnipotent and morally perfect creator.

You, Theist, must deny at least one of the four premises of this argument; or at any rate, you must show that serious doubts can be raised about at least one of them. But which?

So speaks Atheist. How might Theist reply? Atheist has said that her argument was modeled on an argument of William Rowe's. If Theist models his reply on the replies made by most of the theists who have written on Rowe's argument, he will attack the first premise (see, for example, Wykstra 1996). He will try to show that, for all anyone knows, the world (considered under the aspect of eternity) is a better place for containing the Mutilation. He will try to show that for all anyone knows, God has brought, or will at some future time bring, some great good out of the Mutilation, a good that outweighs it, or else has employed the Mutilation as a means to preventing some even greater evil; and he will argue that, for all anyone knows, the great good achieved or the great evil prevented could not have been, respectively, achieved or prevented, even by an omnipotent being, otherwise than by some means that essentially involved the Mutilation (or something else as bad or worse).

13. THEIST DISCUSSES THE RELATION OF THE EXPANDED FREE-WILL DEFENSE TO THE QUESTION WHETHER AN OMNIPOTENT AND MORALLY PERFECT BEING WOULD ELIMINATE EVERY PARTICULAR HORROR FROM THE WORLD

I am not going to have Theist reply to Atheist's argument in this way. I find (1) fairly plausible, even if I am not as sure as Atheist is (or as sure as most atheists who have discussed the issue seem to be) that (1) is true. I am going to represent Theist as employing another line of attack on Atheist's response to his expanded free-will defense. I am going to represent him as denying premise (3), or, more precisely, as trying to show that the expanded free-will defense casts considerable doubt on premise (3). And here is his reply:

Why should we accept premise (3) of Atheist's argument? I have had a look at Rowe's defense of the corresponding premise of his argument, the entirety of which I will quote: "[This premise] seems to express a belief that accords with our basic moral principles, principles shared both by theists and non-theists." (1979, 337)

But what are these "basic moral principles, shared both by theists and non-theists"? Rowe does not say, but I believe there is really just one moral principle it would be plausible to appeal to in defense of premise (3). It might be stated like this.

If one is in a position to prevent some evil, one should not allow that evil to occur—not unless allowing it to occur would result in some good that would outweigh it or preventing it would result in some other evil at least as bad.

Is this principle true?

I think not. (I can, in fact, think of several obvious objections to it. But most of these objections would apply only to the case of human agents, and I shall therefore not mention them.) Consider this example. Suppose you are an official who has the power to release anyone from prison at any time. Blodgett has been sentenced to ten years in prison for felonious assault. His sentence is nearing its end, and he petitions you to release him from prison a day early. Should you? Well, the principle says so. A day spent in prison is an evil—if you don't think so, I invite you to spend a day in prison. Let's suppose that the only good that results from putting criminals in prison is the deterrence of crime. (This assumption is made to simplify the argument. That it is false introduces no real defect into the argument.) Obviously, nine years, 364 days spent in prison is not going to have a significantly different power to deter felonious assault from ten years spent in prison. So: no good will be secured by visiting on Blodgett that last day in prison, and that last day spent in prison is an evil. The principle tells you, the official, to let him out a day early. This much, I think, is enough to show that the principle is wrong, for you have no such obligation. But the principle is in more trouble than this simple criticism suggests.

It would seem that if a threatened punishment of n days in prison has a certain power to deter felonious assault, a threatened punishment of $n - 1$ days spent in prison will have a power to deter felonious assault that is not significantly less. Consider the power to deter felonious assault that belongs to a threatened punishment of 1,023 days in prison. Consider the power to deter felonious assault that belongs to a threatened punishment of 1,022 days in prison. There is, surely, no significant difference. Consider the power to deter felonious assault that belongs to a threatened punishment of 98 days in prison. Consider the power to deter felonious assault that belongs to a threatened punishment of 97 days in prison. There is, surely, no significant difference. Consider the power to deter felonious assault that belongs to a threatened punishment of one day in prison. Consider the power to deter felonious assault that belongs to a threatened punishment of no time in prison at all. There is, surely, no significant difference. (In this last case, of course, this is because the threat of one day in prison would have essentially *no* power to deter felonious assault.)

A moment's reflection shows that if this is true, as it seems to be, then the moral principle entails that Blodgett ought to spend no time in prison at all. For suppose Blodgett had lodged his appeal to have his sentence reduced by a day not shortly before he was to be released but before he had entered prison at all. He lodges this appeal with you, the official who accepts the moral principle. For the reason I have set out, you must grant his appeal. Now suppose that when it has been granted, clever Blodgett lodges a second appeal: that his sentence be reduced to ten years minus two days. This second appeal you will also be obliged to grant, for there is no difference between ten years less a day and ten years less two days as regards the power to deter felonious assault. I am sure you can see where this is going. Provided only that Blodgett has the time and the energy to lodge 3,648 successive appeals for a one-day reduction of his sentence, he will escape prison altogether.

This result is, I take it, a reductio ad absurdum of the moral principle. As the practical wisdom has it (and this is no compromise between practical considerations and strict morality; it *is* strict morality), You have to draw a line somewhere. And this means an *arbitrary* line. The principle fails precisely *because* it forbids the drawing of morally arbitrary lines. There is nothing wrong, or nothing that can be determined a priori to be wrong, with a legislature's setting ten years in prison as the minimum punishment for felonious assault— and this despite the fact that ten years in prison, considered as a *precise span of days*, is an arbitrary punishment.

The moral principle is therefore false—or possesses whatever defect is the analogue in the realm of moral principles of falsity in the realm of factual statements. What are the consequences of its falsity, of its failure to be an acceptable moral principle, for the "argument from horrors"? Let us return to the expanded free-will defense. This story accounts for the existence of horrors— that is, that there are horrors is a part of the story. The story explains why there are such things as horrors (at least, it explains why there are postlapsarian horrors) although it says nothing about any particular horror. And to explain why there are horrors is not to meet the argument from horrors.

A general account of the existence of horrors does not constitute a reply to the argument from horrors because it does not tell us which premise of the argument to deny. Let us examine this point in detail. According to the expanded free-will defense, God prevents the occurrence of many of the horrors that would naturally have resulted from our separation from him. But he cannot, so to speak, prevent all of them, for that would frustrate his plan for reuniting human beings with himself. And if he prevents only some horrors, how shall he decide which ones to prevent? Where shall he draw the line—the line between threatened horrors that are prevented and threatened horrors that are allowed to occur? I suggest that wherever he draws the line, it will be an arbitrary line. That this must be so is easily seen by thinking about the Mutilation. If God had added that particular horror to his list of horrors to be prevented, and that one alone, the world, considered as a whole, would not have been a significantly less horrible place, and the general realization of human beings that they live in a world of horrors would not have been significantly different from what it is. The existence of that general realization is just the factor in his plan for humanity that (according to the expanded free-will defense) provides his general reason for allowing horrors to occur. Therefore, preventing the Mutilation would in no way have interfered with his plan for the restoration of our species. If the expanded free-will defense is a true story, God has made a choice about where to draw the line, the line between the actual horrors of history, the horrors that are *real*, and the horrors that are mere averted possibilities, might-have-beens. The Mutilation falls on the "actual horrors of history" side of the line. And this fact shows that the line is an arbitrary one, for if he had drawn it so as to exclude the Mutilation from reality (and left it otherwise the same) he would have lost no good thereby and he would have allowed no greater evil. He had no reason for drawing the line where he did. But then what justifies him in drawing the line where he did? What justifies him in including the Mutilation in reality when he could have excluded it without losing any good thereby? Has the victim of the Mutilation not got a moral case against him? He could have saved her and he did not, and he does not even *claim* to have achieved some good by not saving her. It would seem that God is in the dock, in C. S. Lewis's words; if he is, then I, Theist, am playing the part of his barrister, and you, the Agnostics, are the jury. I offer the following obvious consideration in defense of my client: there was no nonarbitrary line to be drawn. Wherever God drew the line, there would have been countless horrors left in the world—his plan requires the actual existence of countless horrors—and the victim or victims of any of those horrors could bring the same charge against him that we have imagined the victim of the Mutilation bringing against him.

But I see Atheist stirring in protest; she is planning to tell you that, given the terms of the expanded free-will defense, God should have allowed the *minimum* number of horrors consistent with his project of reconciliation, and that it is obvious he has not done this. She is going to tell you that there *is* a nonarbitrary line for God to draw, and that it is the line that has the minimum number of horrors on the "actuality" side. But there is no such line to be drawn. There is no minimum number of horrors consistent with God's plan of reconciliation, for the prevention of any one particular horror could not possibly have any effect on God's plan. For any n, if the existence of n horrors is consistent with God's plan, the existence of $n-1$ horrors will be equally consistent with God's plan. To ask what the minimum number of horrors consistent with God's plan is is like asking, What is the minimum number of raindrops that could have fallen on England in the nineteenth century that is consistent with England's having been a fertile country in the nineteenth century? Here is a simple analogy of proportion: a given evil is to the openness of human beings to the idea that human life is horrible and that no human efforts will ever alter this fact as a given raindrop is to the fertility of England.

And this is why God did not prevent the Mutilation—insofar as there is a "why." He had to draw an arbitrary line and he drew it. And that's all there is to be said. This, of course, is cold comfort to the victim. Or, since we are merely telling a story, it would be better to say: if this story were true and known to be true, knowing its truth would be cold comfort to the victim. But the purpose of the story is not to comfort anyone. It is not to give an example of a possible story that would comfort anyone if it were true and that person knew it to be true. If a child dies on the operating table in what was supposed to be a routine operation and a board of medical inquiry finds that the death was due to some factor the surgeon could not have anticipated and that the surgeon was not at fault, that finding will be of no comfort to the child's parents. But it is not the purpose of a board of medical inquiry to comfort anyone; the purpose of a board of medical inquiry is, by examining the facts of the matter, to determine whether anyone was at fault. And it is not my purpose in offering a defense to provide even hypothetical comfort to anyone. It is to determine whether the existence of horrors entails that God is at fault—or, rather, since by definition God is never at fault, to determine whether the existence of horrors entails that an omnipotent creator would be at fault.

It is perhaps important to point out that we might easily find ourselves in a moral situation like God's moral situation according to the expanded free-will defense, a situation in which we must draw an arbitrary line and allow some bad thing to happen when we could have prevented it, and in which, moreover, no good whatever comes of our allowing it to happen. In fact, we do find ourselves in this situation. In a welfare state, for example, we use taxation to divert money from its primary economic role in order to spend it to prevent or alleviate various social evils. And how much money, what proportion of the gross national product, shall we—that is, the state—divert for this purpose? Well, not none of it and not all of it (enforcing a tax rate of 100 percent on all earned income and all profits would be the same as not having a money economy at all). And where we draw the line is an arbitrary matter. However much we spend on social services, we shall always be able to find some person or family who would be saved from misery if the state spent (in the right way) a mere $1,000 more than it in fact plans to spend. And the state can *always* find another $1,000, and can find it without damaging the economy or doing any other sort of harm.

14. Concluding Remarks: Evaluating Theist's Response to the Argument from Evil

So Theist replies to Atheist's argument from horrors. But we may note that Theist has failed to respond to an important point Atheist has made. As he himself conceded, his reply takes account only of *postlapsarian* horrors. There is still to be considered the matter of prelapsarian horrors, horrors such as Rowe's poor fawn. There were certainly sentient animals long before there were sapient animals, and the paleontological record shows that for much of the long prehuman past, sentient creatures died agonizing deaths in natural disasters. Obviously, the free-will defense cannot be expanded in such a way as to account for these agonizing deaths, for only sapient creatures have free will, and these deaths cannot therefore have resulted from the abuse of free will—unless, as C. S. Lewis has suggested, prehuman animal suffering is ascribed to a corruption of nature by fallen angels (1940, 122–24). Interesting as this suggestion is, I do not propose to endorse it, even as a defense. I confess myself unable to treat this difficult problem adequately within the scope of this chapter. I should have to devote a whole essay to the problem of prelapsarian horrors to say anything of value about it. I must simply declare this topic outside the scope of this chapter. I refer the reader to my essay "The Problem of Evil, the Problem of Air, and the Problem of Silence," (van Inwagen 1991), which contains a defense—not a version of the free-will defense—that purports to account for the sufferings of prehuman animals. I will remark that this defense shares one important feature of the expanded free-will defense. This defense, too, requires God to draw an arbitrary line; it allows God to eliminate much animal suffering that would otherwise have occurred in the course of nature, but it requires him, as it were, to *stop* eliminating it at some point, even though no good is gained by his stopping at whatever point he does stop at. I would thus say that God could have eliminated the suffering of Rowe's fawn at no cost and did not, and that this fact does not count against his moral perfection—just as the fact that he could have eliminated the Mutilation at no cost and did not does not count against his moral perfection. But the nature of the goods involved in this other defense is a subject I cannot discuss here.

Let me put this question to the readers of this chapter: Has Theist successfully replied to the argument from horrors *insofar as those horrors are events that involve human beings*? Well, much depends on what further things Atheist might have to say. Perhaps Atheist has a dialectically effective rejoinder to Theist's reply to the argument from horrors. But one must make an end somewhere. The trouble with real philosophical debates is that they almost never come to a neat and satisfactory conclusion. Philosophy is argument without end. I do think this much: if Atheist has nothing more to say, the Agnostics should render a verdict of "not proven" as regards premise (3) of the argument from horrors and the moral principle on which it is based, namely, that, if it is within one's power to prevent some evil, one should not allow that evil to occur unless allowing it to occur would result in some good that would outweigh it or preventing it would result in some other evil at least as bad.

Let me put a similar question before the readers of this chapter as regards the extended free-will defense and the problem of the vast amount of evil (including the vast amounts of natural evil): Does Theist's presentation of the extended free-will defense constitute a successful reply to Atheist's contention that an omnipotent and morally perfect God would not allow the existence of a world that contains evil in the amount and of the kinds we observe in the world around us *insofar as this contention involves only evils that befall human beings*? Again, much depends on what further things Atheist might have to say. My own opinion is this: if Atheist has nothing further to say, an audience of agnostics of the sort I have imagined should concede that *for all anyone knows*, a world created by an omnipotent and morally perfect God might contain human suffering in the amount and of the kinds we observe.[3]

NOTES

1. In the novel, there are several minor illiteracies in the poem (e.g., "whose" for "who's" in the first stanza). (The fictional author of the poem, a well-educated man, was trying to hide the fact of his authorship.) I have corrected these, despite the judgment of Martin Amis that the illiteracies are an intended part of the literary effect of the poem (intended, that is, by its real author, Kingsley Amis, not by its fictional author).

2. Almost all theists who reply to the argument from evil employ some form of the free-will defense. The free-will defense I am going to have Theist employ derives, at a great historical remove, from Saint Augustine. A useful selection of Augustine's writings on free will and the origin of evil (from *The City of God* and the *Enchiridion*) can be found in Melden (1955, 164–77).

For a *very* different approach to the problem of evil (to the purely intellectual problem considered in this chapter *and* to many other problems connected with trust in God and the very worst evils present in his creation), see Marilyn McCord Adams, *Hor-*

rendous Evils and the Goodness of God (1999). I find this book unpersuasive (as regards its general tendency and main theses; I think Adams is certainly right about many relatively minor but not unimportant points), but endlessly fascinating. I hope that my friend Marilyn, if she reads the sentence to which this note is appended, will take special notice of the words "seems to me," and will accept my assurance that their presence in that sentence is not a mere literary reflex.

For another important but *very* different discussion of the problem of evil, see Eleonore Stump's Stob Lectures, *Faith and the Problem of Evil* (1999).

Many recent versions of the free-will defense (including the version developed in the seminal work of Alvin Plantinga) can be found in Pike (1964), Adams and Adams (1990), and Peterson (1992), collections that contain excellent and representative selections from the important philosophical work on the argument from evil that had been published as of their copyright dates.

Three important book-length treatments of the problem of evil, all in the Augustinian (or "free will") tradition, are Lewis (1940), Geach (1977), and Swinburne (1998).

3. For another version of Theist's argument (in which something like the story here called the expanded free will defense is presented not as a defense but as a theodicy—a "theodicy" in a weaker sense than the word is given in this chapter), see van Inwagen (1988).

A longer version of the debate between Atheist and Theist concerning the "argument from horrors" is contained in van Inwagen (2000).

WORKS CITED

Adams, Marilyn McCord. 1999. *Horrendous Evils and the Goodness of God.* Ithaca, N.Y.: Cornell University Press.

Adams, Marilyn McCord, and Robert Merrihew Adams, eds. 1990. *The Problem of Evil.* Oxford: Oxford University Press.

Amis, Kingsley. 1966. *The Anti-death League.* London: Victor Gollancz.

Geach, P. T. 1997. *Providence and Evil.* Cambridge, England: Cambridge University Press.

Howard-Snyder, Daniel, ed. 1996. *The Evidential Argument from Evil.* Bloomington: Indiana University Press.

Lewis, C. S. 1940. *The Problem of Pain.* London: Macmillan.

Melden, A. I., ed. 1955. *Ethical Theories.* 2nd edition. Englewood Cliffs, N.J.: Prentice-Hall.

Mill, John Stuart. 1875. *Three Essays on Religion.* London: Longmans, Green.

Peterson, Michael L., ed. 1992. *The Problem of Evil.* Notre Dame, Ind.: University of Notre Dame Press.

Pike, Nelson, ed. 1964. *God and Evil.* Englewood Cliffs, N.J.: Prentice-Hall.

Rowe, William L. 1979. "The Problem of Evil and Some Varieties of Atheism." *American Philosophical Quarterly* 16: 335–41. Reprinted in Adams and Adams, 1990.

Stump, Eleonore. 1999. *Faith and the Problem of Evil.* Grand Rapids, Mich.: Stob Lectures Endowment.

Swinburne, Richard. 1998. *Providence and the Problem of Evil*. Oxford: Oxford University Press.

Van Inwagen, Peter. 1988. "The Magnitude, Duration, and Distribution of Evil: A Theodicy." *Philosophical Topics* 16: 161–87. Reprinted in van Inwagen 1995; in Eleonore Stump and Michael Murray, eds., *The Big Questions: Philosophy of Religion* (Oxford: Blackwell, 1999); in Joel Feinberg and Russ Shafer-Landau, eds., *Reason and Responsibility*, 11th edition (Belmont, Calif.: Wadsworth/Thompson, 2002); and in William Lane Craig, ed., *Philosophy of Religion: A Contemporary Reader*, forthcoming from Edinburgh University Press.

———. 1991. "The Problem of Evil, the Problem of Air, and the Problem of Silence." *Philosophical Perspectives, Vol. 5, Philosophy of Religion*: 135–65. Reprinted in Howard-Snyder 1996, and in van Inwagen 1995.

———. 1995. *God, Knowledge, and Mystery: Essays in Philosophical Theology*. Ithaca, N.Y.: Cornell University Press.

———. 2000. "The Argument from Particular Horrendous Evils." *Proceedings of the American Catholic Philosophical Association* (annual supplement to the *American Catholic Philosophical Quarterly*) 74: 65–80.

Wykstra, Stephen John. 1996. "Rowe's Noseeum Arguments from Evil." In Howard-Snyder 1996, 126–50.

CHAPTER 9

RELIGIOUS LANGUAGE

WILLIAM P. ALSTON

1. INTRODUCTION

THE first order of business is the disavowal of the title. To speak of religious "language" is, at best, misleading. There is no language that is used only for religious purposes. "Do you speak English, French, or religious?" What this jibe reflects is that in the proper sense of "language," in which it is what is studied by linguists, a language contains resources for anything that its users have occasion for talking about. The term "religious language" is a special case of the bad habit of philosophers to speak of a special language for each terminology or broad subject matter (the "language of physics," the "language of ethics," etc.). This evinces neglect of the crucial distinction between language and speech. The former is an abstract system that is employed primarily for communication, and the latter is that employment. What is erroneously called religious language is the use of language (any language) in connection with the practice of religion—in prayer, worship, praise, thanksgiving, confession, ritual, preaching, instruction, exhortation, theological reflection, and so on. Despite what I have just said, I will continue to go along with the term religious language, and not only in the title. It is too well entrenched in the literature to be wholly ignored.

The laundry list just given indicates the tremendous range of religious uses of language. Another way of bringing this out is to consider the diversity to be found in religious writings. Sacred books contain cosmological speculations, fictional narratives, historical records, predictions, commandments, reflections on human life, moral insights, theological pronouncements, and legal codes. In devotional literature we find biographical reminiscences, theologizing, rules of spiritual life, suggestions for spiritual development, and descriptions of religious experience.

All of these present interesting topics for study. But philosophers have been narrowly selective in their approach to the field. Dominated for the most part by epistemological and metaphysical concerns, they have concentrated on what look to be factual statements about God or other objects of religious worship. They have been preoccupied with two questions. (1) Are such apparent statements the genuine article? Can they be construed as making genuine truth claims or are they to be understood in some other way? (2) If they are what they seem to be, just what claims are they making? This second concern plunges them into the most fundamental issues in the philosophy of language. Take the putative statement, "God made the heavens and the earth." If this is a genuine truth claim, it raises two basic questions. (1) Just who (or what) are we referring to by "God," and how, if at all, is this reference secured? This is an instance of the general problem of understanding singular reference. (2) How are we to understand the predicate "made the heavens and the earth"? More generally, what sorts of predicates, if any, can be intelligibly, and possibly truly, applied to God? We may call this the "problem of theological predication." The organization of this chapter reflects these dominant philosophical concerns.

Many philosophers and theologians have protested against the concentration of philosophers on religious statements to the neglect of other religious uses of language. Their complaint can be briefly summed up as follows. The heart of religion is found in talk *to* God in prayer, worship, and liturgy. Talk *about* God is a secondary phenomenon that gets its religious significance by its dependence on the former. I find this criticism to be valid if, but only if, the study of religious statements is divorced from its connection with more basic aspects of the religious life, as too often it is in philosophical treatments. But it need not be so. The valid concerns of philosophers with statements about God can be pursued while recognizing their connections with the rest of religion.

Instead of speaking of *predicates* of religious statements, we could speak of religious *concepts*. Because predicates express concepts, problems about the meaning of the former are translatable into problems about the content of the latter. Instead of asking how predicates applied to God are to be understood, we could just as well ask about the content of concepts applied to God. And because genuine statements express beliefs, instead of asking whether our efforts at religious statements make claims to objective truth, we could ask whether alleged beliefs about God are capable of objective truth value. Because of the "linguistic turn" that has been so prominent in twentieth-century philosophy, the linguistic style of formulation has been much more prominent. But the fact that speech gets its meaning by virtue of the thoughts it expresses is a reason to think that the formulation in terms of thought is more fundamental. I will be moving freely from one of these formulations to the other, except in those cases, like the question of whether certain statements about God should be understood literally or figuratively, that require a linguistic formulation.

One other preliminary point. I said that the central concern of philosophers with religious language had to do with statements about God *or other objects of religious worship.* That second disjunct was added because to give a truly comprehensive treatment of religious statements, we must range over religions that recognize an ultimate reality that is not thought of as personal in the way God is in "theistic" religions like Judaism, Christianity, and Islam. But I cannot aspire here to so complete a coverage. Because the philosophical problems and positions with which I will be dealing have their home in a theistic, primarily Judeo-Christian, religious setting, I will limit myself to statements about God. There is enough variety in the way God is construed in theistic religions to keep us occupied.

2. Can There Be Statements about God with Truth Values?

From my preliminary statement of problems, I begin with the one an affirmative answer to which is required for the other problems to arise, namely, whether what appear to be statements about God that have an objective truth value really have that status or are something quite different—expressions of emotion or attitude, commitment to a policy of action or a lifestyle, ways of evoking "disclosures" by the use of symbols, or whatever. In the 1950s and 1960s many philosophers embraced "verificationism," the view that an attempted factual assertion can have an objective truth value only if it is, in principle, subject to empirical verification or falsification. In that period a number of philosophers of religion applied this principle to alleged statements about God and took them to fail the test. Verificationism was made prominent in the early twentieth century by a group known as the Vienna Circle, prominent members of which included Rudolf Carnap, Moritz Schlick, and Otto Neurath. The view was originally developed in the philosophy of science, but severe difficulties led to its progressive abandonment in the field of its birth. Though news of its demise took a while to reach metaphysics, philosophy of religion, ethics, and other outlying territories, it is no longer a major concern in those areas either. But because there is still a small but determined rear guard of the movement in philosophy of religion, I will briefly review the main difficulties with verificationism. Before doing that, I will point out that its application to talk about God is by no means as straightforward as is often supposed. It depends on how we think of God and his relation to the world whether empirical confirmation and disconfirmation of statements about God are possible. But limitations of space prevent my going into that here.[1]

The most serious defect in verificationism is this. Any statement that is not, like "The liquid is cloudy," formulated in observational terms, and hence that is not directly tested by observation, can receive confirmation or disconfirmation from the results of observation only if it is conjoined with "bridge principles" that are partly in observational and partly in nonobservational terms, and hence make it possible for the results of observation to have a logical bearing on "theoretical" principles. Thus, laws of thermodynamics, when conjoined with principles that spell out how to measure the temperature of a substance, can be tested by such measures. The reason this consideration is fatal to verificationism as a criterion of genuine factuality is that no one has been able to put restrictions on bridge principles that will let in nonobservational statements the verificationists want to treat as verifiable and exclude those they do not. Here is a simple example of the latter. We can take any nonobservational statement, for example, "God is perfectly good," and make it subject to empirical test by conjoining it with a hypothetical statement like "If God is perfectly good, then it will rain tomorrow here." This conjunction implies "It will rain tomorrow here," and this makes an observation of the weather have a bearing on the justification of the theological statement. No doubt, it would be absurd to accept this bridge principle. But bridge principles in science often have no antecedent plausibility. And despite the expenditure of a lot of effort, no one has been able to come up with a plausible criterion of acceptability for bridge principles that will let in accepted scientific examples and keep out theological and metaphysical examples.

Here is another indication of what is wrong with verificationism. In the history of science, hypotheses, for example, the atomic hypothesis concerning the constitution of matter, were originally put forward without anyone as yet having any idea as to how they could be empirically tested. Eventually the atomic hypothesis was brought into effective connection with empirical tests. But unless the hypothesis was understandable as a factual claim at the earlier stages, those developments would have been impossible.

If one is convinced, despite the criticisms just mounted, that no utterances about God, as construed in developed theistic religion, are factually meaningful, how will one construe them? There are a number of alternatives. The simplest one is to avoid the necessity of any reconception by ignoring them altogether or, in Hume's memorable phrase, consigning them to the flames. But if one is sufficiently motivated to retain God-talk, there are a number of ways to do so while avoiding any reference to a transcendent deity. These can be divided into two main groups. One seeks to preserve the statemental character by giving a purely natural-world meaning to God-talk. The other chooses to interpret putatively statemental talk about God as expressive of feelings, attitudes, commitments, and the like.

Here are two examples of the first alternative. The American theologian Henry Nelson Wieman defines "God" in naturalistic terms as "that interaction between individuals, groups, and ages which generates and promotes the greatest possible mutuality of good" (Wieman, McIntosh, and Otto 1932, 13). This preserves the beneficence of God, but the personal being is completely lost. In defense of his suggestion, Wieman has this to say: "Can men pray to an interaction? Yes, that is what they always pray to, under any concept of God. Can men love an interaction? Yes, that is what they always love. When I love Mr. Jones, it is not Mr. Jones in the abstract, but the fellowship of Mr. Jones. Fellowship is a kind of interaction" (ibid., 17). Mr. Jones would no doubt be disappointed to learn that what was loved was not himself but rather fellowship with him.

Another naturalistic reinterpretation of theistic talk is found in the English biologist Julian Huxley's book *Religion without Revelation* (1957). He identifies God the Father with the forces of nonhuman nature (the "creator"), God the Holy Spirit as the ideals for which men are striving (at their best), and God the Son as human nature itself, which is, more or less, utilizing the forces of nature in the pursuit of those ideals. Thus, he gives us a naturalistic Trinity. He even includes the unity of the three persons in one God under the guise of the essential unity of all these aspects of nature.

The second group is extremely varied. The early twentieth-century Spanish-American philosopher George Santayana took religious doctrines as primarily symbolic of value commitments and attitudes. In *Reason in Religion* (1905) he distinguished two components of a religious doctrine, or "myth," as he preferred to say. There is (1) an evaluation of some sort, which is (2) expressed in the form of a picture or story. For example, the Christian "myth" of God's incarnation in Jesus Christ and his sacrificial and unmerited death on the cross to atone for the sins of men can be regarded as a symbol of the moral value of self-sacrifice. That moral conviction can be expressed much more forcefully and effectively by that story than by just saying "Self-sacrifice is a noble thing." Santayana also considers religious myths to have the function of guiding our lives in certain directions. This directive function is emphasized in Braithwaite (1955). He takes religious statements "as being primarily declarations of adherence to a policy of action, declarations of commitment to a way of life" (80). We also find such an approach in the American theologian Gordon Kaufman. He says that the question of the existence of God is a question of the viability and appropriateness of an orientation, a true or valid understanding of human existence (1993, 35–46).

It is clear that much speech about God does have these expressive and directive functions, and if we have discarded the truth claims that are ordinarily taken to undergird those functions, the latter will be all that is left. But we will be forced into these reconstruals by the verifiability criterion only if more traditionally construed statements about God are not empirically confirmable, and only if empirical confirmability is a necessary condition of factual meaningfulness. Because I have presented reason for rejecting the latter, the argument from verificationism against the possibility of factual truth claims about God can be ignored, and we can proceed to consider problems that arise with respect to such truth claims.

3. AUTONOMY OF RELIGIOUS LANGUAGE?

The next problem on the agenda is whether, as suggested by Wittgenstein and others, religious "language" is so completely distinct from other uses of language as to constitute a separate "language game," with its own battery of concepts, criteria of intelligibility, criteria of truth, and so on. The most powerful of the current voices that sound this note is D. Z. Phillips (1970, 1976). In a long series of books he repeatedly insists that religious beliefs are held subject only to criteria that are internal to religious discourse. He takes this to imply not only that the traditional arguments for the existence of God have no bearing on the acceptability of religious beliefs, but that with respect to religions like Judaism, Christianity, and Islam that rest on claims about historical events, ordinary historical research has no bearing on their acceptability. This seems strongly counterintuitive. How could reasons for and against the existence of God be irrelevant to the epistemic status of beliefs that presuppose that existence? And if Christianity is based, at least partly, on certain beliefs about the life, ministry, teaching, actions, death, and resurrection of Jesus of Nazareth, how could historical research into this be irrelevant to the status of those religious commitments, even though it cannot settle the questions decisively? Consider the price Phillips is willing to pay for this freedom from vulnerability to "outside" considerations. He holds that there are different concepts of truth, existence, and reality for different language games. In believing that it is true that Jesus was raised from the dead on the third day, we are not using the same concept of truth we use when wondering whether it is true that in 1200 BC the inhabitants of Crete spoke a form of Greek. And in believing that God really exists, we are not using the same notions of reality and existence that we use in asserting that King Arthur really existed and denying that there really are any unicorns.

This is a high price indeed for being able to insulate religious discourse from contact with its surroundings. It certainly doesn't feel as if we mean something different by "true," "real," and "exist" in religious and nonreligious contexts. As for "true," Phillips's position could be defended by an epistemic conception of truth according to which the truth of a belief amounts to some sort of favorable epistemic status for the belief, together with the claim that epistemic criteria for religious beliefs are different from criteria for other beliefs. But to restrict ourselves to the first of these claims, it comes into direct conflict with the obvious point that it is a necessary and sufficient condition of its being *true* that Jesus arose from the dead that Jesus did arise from the dead; our epistemic situation with respect to the belief has nothing to do with the matter.

Although Phillips often shies away from the suggestion, it may be that what is most fundamentally behind the above views is a certain nonstatemental way of understanding the content of religious beliefs. He more than once talks as if he thinks that in affirming such beliefs we do not mean to be asserting anything about a reality that transcends the natural world, but rather expressing attitudes toward the world of nature and human life. Believing in God is variously said to be seeing a meaning in one's life (Phillips 1970, 8), seeing the possibility of eternal love (21, 29), looking on one's life and regulating it in a certain way (157). Again, "The religious pictures give one a language in which it is possible to think about human life in a certain way . . . When these thoughts are found in worship, the praising and the glorifying does not refer to some object called God . . . we see that the religious expressions of praise, glory, etc. are not referring expressions. These activities are expressive in character, and what they express is called the worship of God" (Phillips 1976, 149–50).

To be sure, believing in God could essentially involve all that and also be a belief about a transcendent (and immanent) ultimate reality. But the above passages clearly show that Phillips thinks the aspects specified are all there is to it.

4. Meaning and Religious Practice

Another possible reason for Phillips's Wittgensteinian position on the sui generis character of religious belief, thought, and discourse is a conviction that its constituent terms and concepts are intelligible only from within religious practice. To fully understand "grace" or "love" ("agape") or "spiritual" or "glory" as they are used in Christian discourse one must be sufficiently involved in the Christian form of life, in prayer and worship and in viewing the world and one's life in certain ways. I have put a consideration of this idea into a separate section to emphasize that it need not be associated with the "different criteria of acceptability" and "different concepts of 'truth' and 'existence'" that Phillips accepts. The possibility of this independence rests on two considerations. First, the "meaning depends on practice" position need not hold that this is the only source of meaning, or the entire source of meaning, for religious terms. As I just formulated it, the claim is only that to *fully* understand these terms, involvement in Christian practice is needed. That leaves room for a partial understanding by outsiders and hence susceptibility to evaluation by epistemic criteria that hold both inside and outside. Second, terms that depend on the form of life for part of their meaning by no means exhaust the religious lexicon. It is rife with terms used exactly as they are in other contexts. Consider the Nicene Creed. It contains such phrases as "he was *crucified* under Pontius Pilate; he *suffered death* and was *buried*" and such words and shorter phrases as "*man*," "apostolic *church*," "*all* that is," and "for *us*." In petitionary prayer we ask for healing of sick bodies, strength, courage, and acceptance of what we cannot change. It strains credulity to suppose that such terms and phrases are used in special religious senses that differ from the senses in which they are used elsewhere. For both of these reasons, the acceptance of a partial dependence of some constituents of religious discourse on religious practice for their meaning is compatible with a denial of Phillips's contentions discussed in the previous section.

So what are we to say about the "dependence on practice" thesis? I find it very plausible. It is dubious that talk of divine grace, or divine glory, or agape will be as fully as possible understood by those who have not experienced such things in their lives, who have not gained some sense of what it is like to have been a recipient of grace or agape, to have found themselves bestowing agape on others, to have experienced the glory of God in nature, contemplation, or worship. These terms can be given theological definitions: thus, "grace" can be defined as "a freely bestowed gift by God that goes beyond the creation and preservation of the recipient." But if that's the whole story, they will lack the dimensions of meaning that enable them and the realities they denote to play a significant role in the life of the believer. But both because other aspects of their meaning can be common to believer and unbeliever, and because of the other terms of religious discourse that can be wholly shared across the divide, this point about the derivation of meaning from active involvement in the form of life does not support the radical form of autonomy for religious discourse espoused by the likes of Phillips.

5. REFERENCE TO GOD

The foregoing had the function of clearing the ground for the discussion of reference to God and the status of predicates (concepts) applied to God that will constitutes the bulk of this chapter.

First, the question of reference to God. How are we to pick out God as what we are thinking or talking about? By virtue of what is the statement (thought) directed to God rather than to something (someone) else or to nothing? I address these questions against the background of the main alternatives for understanding singular reference in general.

Perhaps the most natural answer to the question "By virtue of what do we refer to a particular individual?" is the descriptive one. One refers to Hillary Clinton by having in mind a uniquely exemplified description, for example, "the junior senator from New York" or "Bill Clinton's wife." Note that both of these descriptions themselves contain attempted singular references: New York, Bill Clinton, and the present time. (Prior to Hillary's election, the junior senator from New York was Charles Schumer.) And these descriptions are typical in that respect. It is rare to find purely qualitative properties that are uniquely exemplified, like "the first human being to run a four-minute mile." The dependence of most such descriptions on other singular references has the consequence that although descriptivist reference is not uncommon, it can hardly be supposed to constitute a way in which reference could be instituted from scratch. This is hardly a problem for reference to God, however, for this is one case in which we can find a proliferation of descriptions that do not contain other singular references and that uniquely apply to God if to anything: "the omniscient knower," "the omnipotent agent," "the source of all being for everything other than itself," "the necessarily existent being," and so on.

The idea that reference always, or even usually, depends on such descriptions, has been effectively criticized by Kripke, Donnellan, and others. Kripke (1972) points out that there are cases of successful reference to X in which the subject, S, does not have, and does not suppose herself to have, any description that uniquely applies to X. Thus, he suggests that many people use "Aristotle" to refer to the famous philosopher with that name without being able to specify any identifying description other than "a famous philosopher" or "an ancient Greek philosopher." He also argues that even where S has a description that he takes to fix the reference to X and succeeds in referring to X, it isn't always by virtue of that description. These cases are divided into (1) those in which nothing uniquely satisfies the description and (2) those in which it is something other than X that uniquely satisfies it. Kripke illustrates (1) with Jonah, on the assumption that none of the putatively uniquely identifying descriptions from the story succeeds in identifying the prophet about whom the legend grew up or anyone else. He illustrates (2) with a story about someone who succeeds in referring to the mathematical logician Gödel, where all he knows about Gödel is that he proved the incompleteness of arithmetic. But suppose that it was someone other than Gödel who did that. Kripke maintains that the speaker can still be referring to Gödel even though the only uniquely satisfied description he has available is satisfied by someone else.

Kripke's suggestion for an effective nondescriptivist way of securing reference runs as follows. First there is an initial "baptism." There the practice of using that name to refer to that entity is established by intending to do so, fixing the nominatum in mind by virtue of a perceptual presentation of it. People who subsequently use the name (or other referring expression) to pick out the same entity do so by acquiring the practice from someone further up the chain of transmission, intending to use it to refer to the same entity as one's donor does. Thus it is that one can succeed in referring to a particular Greek philosopher with "Aristotle" without having in mind any description that uniquely picks out that philosopher. Though this mode of reference is commonly termed a *causal* theory, on the grounds that the speaker achieves unique reference to O by way of a (direct or indirect) causal relation to O, I refer to it here as a *direct* theory of reference.

Before continuing with a discussion of how all this applies to reference to God, let me set aside a possible confusion. In considering how reference to God is possible, I do not intend to be establishing the existence of God. Of course, if God does not exist, I cannot succeed in referring to him, there being no such him to refer to. But the discussion of referring to God, as a topic in the religious use of language, is limited to considering how one could succeed in referring to God if God exists, and if there is more than one way, what implications the differences between them have for religious thought and discourse.

Of the two modes of reference I have distinguished, it is obvious that the descriptive approach plays an important part in reference to God. It would be very unusual for one who takes oneself to be referring to God not to have any idea of what God is like. And, as noted above, purely qualitative uniquely identifying descriptions (if they are exemplified at all) are much more plentiful for God than for other objects of attempted reference. And, of course, reference to God could be a purely descriptive affair. If one believes that there is an omniscient, omnipotent, perfectly good personal source of being for everything else that is— however one came by this belief, whether by philosophical argument, growing up surrounded by people who seemed to take it for granted, being initiated into the worship of and prayer to such a being, or whatever—then one could take such descriptions as picking out what one is talking about when uttering sentences with "God" as subject, even if the reference had no other source.

But it is very common for direct reference to come into the picture as well. One reason for this is that people normally pick up the linguistic practice of referring to God, as well as other religious practices, from those who introduce them to these practices. Hence, it is normal for religious believers to stand at the end of a chain of transmission of a religious referring practice, a chain of the sort envisaged by Kripke. Typically we learn to refer to God in praying to God, directing praise, thanksgiving, confession to God, entering into alleged interaction with God in sacraments and ritual, and so on. We learn to refer to God as the being with whom we and our guides are in contact in all this. Thus, even if, as is normally the case, we also learn identifying descriptions of God in the course of this training in the practice, those descriptions do not constitute our only means of picking out God. We also think of God as the one referred to in such practices by all our predecessors in the religious tradition in question.

At this point I need to sharpen up the distinction between direct and descriptive reference. I have been taking the former from Kripke's conception of an "initial baptism" followed by a chain of transmission. But, although I presented the initial baptism as involving a direct perceptual identification of the object, Kripke himself correctly points out that the "baptizer" might pick out the object descriptively as well. This indicates that the taxonomy needs to be more complex. We need to distinguish direct reference into primary and derived. The former involves zeroing in on the referent as a current object of experience. The latter involves standing at the end of a chain of transmission that originated in an experientially based identification of an object. Should we make the same distinction for descriptive reference? We could distinguish between making a descriptive reference from scratch, wholly on one's own resources, and doing so by deriving the descriptions from others. But here the distinction is less important, for once one derives identifying descriptions from others and so long as one remembers them, one is able to cut oneself loose from the source and use them just as one would if one had thought them up oneself. There is no important difference between the use of identifying descriptions by their original inventor, and their use by one who has learned them from others. But reference by perceptual encounters with an object cannot be transmitted to others in such a way as to make them usable in the same way as by the original perceiver. If a person picks up the practice of referring to God from someone who connected the term with an object of experience, and the former lacks a firsthand experience of God himself, then it is only by virtue of the source of the transmission of the referring practice that his reference to God can be called direct.

Things are this complicated even for "pure" cases, but they get more complicated with mixed cases, which are much more numerous in real life. Kripkean chains often involve multiple lines of transmission with different origins, and some of the latter may involve direct and some descriptive reference. Moreover, a person's reference to God that starts as purely derivative from a chain may later be mixed with experiential encounters with God. And this in turn may be mixed with novel identifying descriptions. But sufficient unto the day is the complication thereof. I will restrict my sights to relatively pure cases.

It will not have escaped the reader's notice that in the foregoing I have been assuming that there is such a phenomenon as perception or "experiential encounter" with God.[2] I have treated this matter in detail in Alston (1991) and do not have space here even to stick my toe in the water. Suffice it to say that there have been innumerable records of such experiences and no doubt many more unrecorded ones. For some documentation, see, in addition to the above, James (1902) and Beardsworth (1977). Lest one think that we are beyond all that now in this "enlightened" age, several recent sociological surveys show that well over half of Americans believe themselves to have had at some time an experience of God. One should also distinguish between direct and indirect experience of God, the latter coming through experience of something in nature or elsewhere in the natural world. Either kind could stand at the origin of a practice of referring to God. It is also relevant to note the plausibility of supposing that (putative) experiential encounters with God are prominent in the originating events of a religious tradition, as the Bible and other sacred texts make clear.

What important difference, if any, does it make whether a referring practice is primarily direct or descriptive? Here are two. (1) It makes a difference as to what is and is not negotiable. If reference is primarily fixed by descriptions, then the attributes there specified define what it is to be God. And so, if an alleged referent turns out not to have such an attribute, that shows that it was not God to which we were referring. It's the attributes that call the shots. Whereas if it is experiential encounter that primarily fixes the reference, the order of priority is reversed. If what one was experiencing turns out not to have some features one believes God to have, there is at least the option of denying these features to be necessary for divinity. If descriptive reference is basic, we set the requirements for being God; if a referent doesn't live up to them, it isn't God. If experiential reference is basic, then what is thus experienced is God whether he lives up to some favored description or not (so long as we continue to fix the reference by experience[s]). (2) Experientially based reference makes possible a wider commonality between religions. Even if different world religions have radically different views on the nature of Ultimate Reality, they could all be worshipping the same Reality. This would just be a particular example of the general truth that people can disagree, even radically, about the nature of something, even though they are all aware of, and referring to, the same something.

One final note on referring to God. Consider a person or group whose reference to God is both descriptively and experientially based. Which of these is more fundamental? We can explore this by considering (actual or possible) situations in which the two bases give conflicting results. Say that, although one initially takes the being encountered in prayer, worship, and so on to conform to the account of divine nature in classical Christian theology, one comes to doubt that the being so encountered is like that in some important respects. (Process theology is in this situation, denying that the God encountered in the Christian religious practice is omnipotent, the source of all being for everything else, and timeless; see Hartshorne 1941; Griffin 2001). Which will give way? Which takes priority in such conflicts? I can't see that there is a resolution to this problem that fits every such case. It all depends on how deeply rooted each of the contenders is in the person or group in question, and on how unambiguous each of them is on the issues. Because religious experience is notoriously subject to a variety of interpretations, while theological systems are more clear-cut, this tends to favor the priority of the descriptive. But the first factor, degree of rootedness, can go either way. I have given much more extensive treatment of the issues aired in the prior two paragraphs in "Referring to God" in Alston (1989).

6. Differences in Predicates Applied to God and to Creatures

Having examined the subject term of statements about God, we can now turn to the predicates. How are they to be understood? Remember that we are discussing this question in the light of the rejection of the thesis that there are no genuine religious truth claims. Hence, we take for granted that what look like statements about God do have a truth value and go on from there to raise questions about the predicates involved.

The first question is this: Why is there a problem? Predicates applied to God— "makes . . . ," "knows . . . ," "loves . . . ," "forgives . . . ," "speaks . . ."—are all very familiar. Why should there be a problem about our understanding of them?

To see why there is a problem here we need to realize that the above terms are typical of those applied to God in that they are borrowed from elsewhere. We learn what it is to make or know something, to love or forgive someone, to speak to someone from our experience of and interaction with other people. We then understand God's making, knowing, or forgiving, if we do and to the extent we do, by some sort of extension of our understanding of these terms in their human application to their use in application to God. And so the basic problem is: What kind of extension?

Is it necessary that we borrow terms learned in another sphere of discourse for talk of God, or could it be otherwise? Could we establish theological predicates from scratch on their home ground, just as we do with terms for speaking of human beings? No, the existing order is our only alternative, and for the following reason. We have the kind of cognitive access to human beings that undergirds a common vocabulary for speaking of each other, but we lack that support for speaking of God. A parent can tell by observation when the child is perceiving another person talking or making something, and this makes it possible to introduce the child to the established meanings of "speak" and "make" in their human application. But we can't do anything analogous vis-à-vis God. Even if the child can be aware of God's speaking to her or forgiving her or comforting her, the parent can't tell when the child is aware of this unless the child informs the parent of it. And that presupposes that the child has already learned how to apply these terms to God. Thus, there is no possibility of building up a theological vocabulary from scratch. To be sure, once we have a stock of divine predicates that have been derived from their human originals, special theological terms, like "grace" or "omnipotence" or "indwelling" can be introduced on their basis, perhaps with the help of the learner's participation in religious practice. But there is no possibility of cutting loose completely from the human prototypes and doing the whole thing on its own. So we are stuck with the problem of how we can derive terms suitable for theological use from terms originally applied to human beings.

The simplest way is to make no change at all. Apply the terms to God in just the same sense as that in which we apply them to human beings. When terms are used in the same sense in two or more applications, we speak of applying them *univocally*. Note that this option does not require us to make the absurd assumption that God is just like a human being in all respects. Why shouldn't we use "know" or "power" or "good" with exactly the same meaning in human and divine applications, while fully recognizing that God has infinitely more knowledge and power and goodness than any human being? But there are strong reasons for denying complete univocity across human and divine discourse, given plausible ways of assigning meanings to the relevant terms in their human applications.

Let me make explicit some constraints that govern this discussion. First, the senses of terms applied to God must be construed in such a way that it is at least possible that they are *true* of God. It is, no doubt, psychologically possible for someone to apply terms to God in exactly the sense in which they are true of human beings. But if that makes it impossible for the resulting statements to be true, that does not give us what we are after. Second, our decision as to whether a term in a given sense could be true of God depends on what God is like, and there are, notoriously, many theological disagreements about this. In the ensuing discussion I presuppose a position on the divine nature that is widely shared in classical Christian theology.

The most obvious reasons for lack of complete univocity concern the fact that we are embodied and God is not. This prevents action terms like "speak" from being univocally applied. To say that I *spoke* to you has as part of its meaning that I made sounds by the use of my vocal organs. But because God has no vocal organs, that cannot be part of what it means for God to speak to someone. In saying I parted the waters, part of what that means is that I moved parts of my body, for example, arms, in certain ways that resulted in waters being parted. But, again, because God has no arms or other bodily parts, that cannot be even part of what is meant by "God parted the waters." To be sure, it is not always clear exactly what belongs to the *meaning* of a term, as contrasted with what we unhesitatingly believe about its denotation. Far from it. And it could be reasonably denied that movement of bodily parts is involved in the *meaning* of "He spoke" or "He parted the waters" where we refer to a human agent. Although it is indubitable that bodily movement is required for human overt action, that may not be any part of what is *meant* in asserting it. But it is at least plausible that this is part of the meaning.

There are many other reasons for denying complete univocity. Thus, if part of what is meant by Jones *knowing* that Smith is discouraged is that Jones has a *belief* that Smith is discouraged that meets certain further epistemic conditions, and if, as I argued in Alston (1989, ch. 9), God has no beliefs, it follows that "know" is not univocally applied. But this conclusion depends not only on a controversial thesis about God's cognition, but also on a controversial thesis about human knowledge. For a final example, consider the even more controversial position that God is timeless, that he does not live through a succession of moments but exists "all at once" in an eternal now. We, by contrast, are very much immersed in time. What it means for us to have and carry out plans, purposes, and intentions, and what it is for us to perform acts of forgiveness, judgment, and bringing things into existence essentially involves moving through a temporal series of stages. Hence, if God is atemporal, talk of God's purposes, intentions, and activities cannot be univocal with talk of human purposes, intentions, and activities.

7. Partial Overlap in Meaning

Thus, there will be some differences in the meaning of at least many predicates in their human and divine applications. But what differences, and what implications does this have for our ability to speak meaningfully and appropriately of God? In the rest of this chapter I consider several kinds of difference in the order of their radicality, what can be said for and against them, and their implications.

The smallest significant step beyond univocity would involve some tinkering with the human senses so as to meet points of the sort just made. First, think of divine immateriality. If we subtract bodily movement from human action concepts, is there anything left? Of course there is. My parting the waters is not just a matter of my moving my arms and hands in a certain way. There is also my *willing* to do so for the sake of the waters being parted, as well as the actual resultant parting. (If you prefer not to speak of willing, you could substitute an intention or choice.) In the human case, the bodily movement functions as a bridge or conduit between the willing and the external result, enabling the willing to issue in that result. But God's lack of a body does not prevent his willing a certain external result to bring about that result and thereby doing so, just by willing it. Quite the contrary. After all, God is omnipotent. He doesn't need any bodily operation to bring about the willed result. Thus, by starting with the human action concept and weeding out the bodily intermediary, we wind up with a concept that, while retaining the most crucial part of the human concept, could be true of an immaterial deity.

We may take this example as a model for transforming predicates applied to us into predicates suitable for divine application. What this gives us is partial univocity, an alternative pervasively ignored in the millennia-old discussion of this problem. Most thinkers concerned with the issue, seeing that complete univocity will not work, have tended to jump immediately to some of the more radical solutions discussed below. But partial univocity is a serious option, one that deserves much more exploration. For another example, consider what is necessary to modify concepts of human temporal operations to make them applicable to an atemporal deity. The trick here is to replace temporal relations with relations of priority-posteriority, and of dependence of one aspect on another, that do not require temporality for their realization. Consider carrying out an intention, something that involves temporal sequence in the human case. How could it be construed for an atemporal deity? Let's say that one of God's purposes is to bring Robinson to realize that he can be what God intended him to be only if he renounces sacrificing everything else to making as much money as possible. For this illustration it doesn't matter just what means God uses to bring this about; they would all involve some influences on Robinson's thoughts, beliefs, attitudes, and feelings. Let's say God's purpose is not to bring this about in a flash, but to cause a continual process in Robinson's mind that will eventually lead to the intended result. This intended effect is a temporal process. But must God be involved in a temporal process in order to bring this about? Not necessarily. There could be relations of dependence of one aspect of God's willing on another in God's single eternal now that are, so to say, functionally equivalent to temporal relations of cause and effect. God wills that certain temporal psychological processes take place in Robinson by virtue of his willing that these processes eventuate in a certain result, and as a result of all this divine willing that result does eventuate. All this without God himself having to live through successive divine stages. We have partial univocity of human and divine carrying out of purposes, a univocity with respect to the dependence of certain aspects on others, along with a difference between temporality and atemporality.

For a more extended example, consider the concepts of psychological states that figure in the motivation of intentional actions. In Alston (1989, chs. 3 and 4), I developed the idea that functional concepts of psychological states can be univocally applied to God and to us. For a proper exposition of this, I refer you to the book just mentioned. But the general idea is that a functional concept is in terms of the function of its object, not in terms of its structure or intrinsic character. Thus, a loudspeaker is anything with the function of converting electronic signals into sound; this is compatible with a great variety of composition and design, as any audio buff can testify. So if we conceive a desire, an intention, a belief, or a bit of knowledge in terms of its function in the motivation of action, then that concept can apply to items that are radically different in their composition and structure, even as radically as the divine psyche differs from the human psyche.

8. Literal and Metaphorical Speech about God

Thus, partial univocity constitutes one way of walking a tightrope between crude anthropomorphism (total univocity) and total mystery, abandoning any attempt to make intelligible and appropriate truth claims about God. But there are non-negligible reasons for thinking that it leans too far off the tightrope toward anthropomorphism and does not take adequate account of divine mystery, the respects in which God is radically other than human beings and other creatures. Again, our judgment on this will depend on our view of the divine nature, and that in turn will depend on our attitudes toward the most important sources of the view of radical otherness. Here I mention only two such sources and the way they make things difficult for my partial univocity position.

First, consider the person who is, perhaps, the greatest thinker in the Christian tradition, Saint Thomas Aquinas. For a variety of reasons, both philosophical and theological, he held that God is absolutely *simple*. He meant this in the most absolute sense possible. There are no real distinctions in God between different attributes, faculties, and actions. There is no real distinction between God and his nature or his nature and his existence. Aquinas is by no means the only classical Christian theologian to regard God as absolutely simple, but he gives a particularly uncompromising and trenchant expression of the doctrine (*Summa Theologiae*, 1964, pt. I, q. 3). It is not difficult to see how the doctrine is incompatible with partial univocity. Even if the latter can accommodate divine immateriality and atemporality, the terms it deems univocal across human and divine applications are such that in predicating them of God one is committing oneself to real distinctions between God himself and the property denoted by the predicate. In fact, one cannot use propositional forms of human discourse (the only forms available to us) without expressing such distinctions. The only way a form of speech could be perfectly appropriate to divine simplicity would be to say everything about God all at once with no division of any kind between aspects of this speech, something that is far beyond human powers. It is no wonder that Aquinas says in *Summa Contra Gentiles*. "As to the mode of signification, every name is defective" (1955, pt. I, ch. 30).

The other main source of an emphasis on divine otherness is extreme mystical experience as the main clue to the divine nature. This is experience in which all distinctions, even the distinction between subject and object, are blotted out in an absolutely undifferentiated unity. If one's take on God stems primarily from such an experience, one comes, by a different route, to a view of God strikingly similar to Aquinas's doctrine of simplicity. God is construed as so void of distinctions that none of our concepts (each of which represents certain features rather than others) can be true of him. Mystics are naturally drawn to the via negativa. Thus, Pseudo-Dionysius Areopagite, the sixth-century mystic who is the major fountainhead of medieval mystical theology, writes, "It [the Divine] is not soul, not intellect . . . not greatness, not smallness . . . not moved, not at rest . . . not powerful, not power . . . not living, not life . . . not one, not unity, not divinity, not goodness . . . not something among what is not, not something among what is" (1980, 221–22). One can hardly get more negative than that! This approach too is incompatible with partial univocity.

If even partial univocity will not do, what alternatives are open? An obvious one is metaphor. It is as obvious as anything can be that much talk of God uses terms metaphorically. "His *hands* prepared the dry land." "The Lord is my *rock* and my *fortress*." "The Lord is my *shepherd*." No one wishes to maintain that God literally has hands, herds sheep, or is a rock or a fortress. In saying things like this we are using what is literally denoted by these terms as an imaginative, vivid way of bringing out certain features of God. God is like a shepherd in caring for the well-being of his creatures. He is like a rock in being constant and unchangeable in his basic purposes. In creating he does the sort of thing human agents do with their hands. These points about God can be brought out forcefully by expressing them metaphorically.

But is metaphor used in religion only for a rhetorically more effective way of saying what could have been said literally? Or is (all or some) metaphorical speech about God ineliminable, irreplaceable by literal speech? I will not try to decide this question here (for a discussion, see Alston 1989, ch. 1). Instead, I will consider an even more radical position, that all (intelligible) talk of God is metaphorical (McFague 1982). This implies that there is no literal speech about God, though it is not equivalent to that, since metaphor is not the only alternative to the literal.

Before continuing the discussion of this issue it will be useful to examine the concepts of metaphorical and literal speech, especially since these notions are roughed up quite a bit by philosophers and others.

When I make a literal use of a predicate, I make the claim that the property signified by that predicate in the language (or one of such properties) is possessed by what is referred to by the subject of the statement. If I am using "player" literally, in one of its senses, in saying "He's one of the players," I claim, let's say, that he is one of the actors. But what are we doing if we use the term meta-phorically, as Shakespeare has Macbeth do when he says "Life's a poor player that struts and frets his hour upon the stage and then is heard no more"? It's clear that life is not really an actor. Macbeth is "presenting" his hearers with the sort of thing of which the term is literally true; call that an *exemplar*. And he suggests that the exemplar can usefully be taken as a model of life, that considering such a person will reveal certain important features of life. Metaphorical speech varies along a continuum from just throwing the exemplar up for grabs and leaving the hearer to make of it what she will, and making a fairly definite statement with it. The Macbeth quotation approximates the first extreme of the continuum, while Churchill's famous statement "Russia has dropped an iron curtain across the continent" approximates the second. A serious claim that all talk of God is meta-phorical would imply that much of it is making fairly determinate truth claims.

Literal speech is often confused with clearly distinct matters, for example *factual* claims and *precise* speech. As for the former, we can use terms just as literally in requests, questions, and expressions of attitudes as in factual state-ments. As for the latter, I can use words literally and be speaking vaguely or otherwise indeterminately. The standard meaning of many terms, for example "bald," is vague. If I say "Jones is bald," I will be speaking with less than complete precision as to just how much hair he has. A confusion typical of discussion of religious language is between literality and univocity. That they are distinct is shown just by the fact that "univocal" is a relational predicate, having to do with at least two different uses of a term, while "literal" can be applied to a single use. A specially important difference for this discussion is that when, as I suggested earlier, we alter human predicates to make them suitable for divine application, the result of this transformation can be used literally even though not univocally with their human use.

Metaphoricism does promise a way of walking a fine line between univocity and a purely negative theology. On the one hand, as just seen, it provides a way of making truth claims, albeit less than ideally determinate ones. On the other hand, it stops short of applying any of our concepts straightforwardly to God, instead exhibiting their literal denotations as models for thinking about God's nature, attitudes, or actions. Metaphorical statements suggest, hint at, what God is like without presuming to say it explicitly.

But in opposition to taking metaphor to be the whole story, it certainly seems that much talk of God is not metaphorical at all and seems, for all the world, to be literal. First, some trivial examples. Negative statements are clearly literal. There is no trace of metaphor in saying "God is *im*material, *a*temporal, *not* restricted to one spatial location, *not* dependent on anything else for his existence." But, of course, the main issue concerns positive attributions. And many of those also do not look metaphorical in the least. Consider "God *comforts* us and *strengthens* us in adversity, *forgives* the sins of the truly repentant, *communicates* to us how we should live." If these are not literal applications of the concepts these terms express in the language, then we must seek some alternative to straight literality other than metaphor. The main case for taking them to be literal is that, for the most part, the attributions have to do with results of divine action in the world, rather than seeking to give details about the divine agency itself. Thus, "God comforted me in my distress" reports an effect on my state of mind of something God did without seeking to go into more detail as to just what it was that God did to bring this about. What seems to be literal speech about God is not restricted to statements that fit this model; I mention them only as a particularly plausible case of literality. My suggestion in section 7 that we can make literal application of functional psychological concepts to God represents a bolder claim for the possibility of literal speech about God. But even if that goes beyond the bounds of possibility, there are less controversial cases, like the above.

9. Analogical Speech about God

If metaphor doesn't cover the whole field and partial univocity is rejected for unduly neglecting divine otherness, the only feasible alternative is to find some further way in which talk of God can use terms literally. But remembering that the only terms we have are taken from talk of creatures, or derivative therefrom, and if even partial univocity is ruled out, what possibility is left to apply terms literally to God? A new alternative emerges once we realize that we can use creaturely terms in their literal senses to speak of God, while respecting divine otherness, provided we recognize that these terms cannot be strictly true of God as they stand. But if they are flatly false of God, that will be no help unless we are to fall back into irreducible metaphor. Hence, the present approach will have to be that the literal meaning of the terms bear some analogy to what is true of God, but that we are unable to say explicitly just what the respect(s) of analogy are, for if we could, we would be back in partial univocity. This position goes under the name of an *analogical* use of terms.[3] I will give brief presentations of several versions of the view.

Historically the analogical position is most prominently associated with Saint Thomas Aquinas. Here is a brief sketch of his treatment (for more details, see Alston 1993). It is fundamental to Aquinas's theology that "All the perfections of all things are in God" (1964, pt. I, q. 4, art. 2), and hence that when we deal with what he calls "pure perfection terms," those that signify properties that have no limitation to creatures, like goodness, power, and life (and unlike bodily strength and temporal everlastingness), the properties in question, if abstractly enough conceived, are common to God and creatures. But still the terms are not completely univocal, nor can they be analyzed into a part that is and a part that is not, just because of the point that the "mode" in which the perfections are realized are radically different in an absolutely simple being like God and composite beings like us. Hence, the upshot is that in saying things like "God knows everything knowable," we can be saying something true because of the likeness between divine and human knowledge, but we cannot make fully explicit what this likeness amounts to because of the residual inadequacy of all terms used in discursive speech to represent how it is with an absolutely simple being. That doesn't mean that the (pure perfection) terms are not used literally, used to attribute the property their meaning in the language fits them to express. It is, rather, that none of them succeed in making fully explicit just what we are saying about God.

Thus, Aquinas leaves loose ends dangling in talk about God. He thinks this is inevitable because of divine simplicity. But there are other versions of the analogy view that do not accept the divine simplicity doctrine. Here are two examples.

First is the view that talk about God involves the use of "models," an idea fully developed in Barbour (1974). A model in science, such as the familiar billiard-ball model of a gas, is "an imagined mechanism or process, postulated by *analogy* with familiar mechanisms or processes and used to construct a *theory* to correlate a set of *observations*" (30). It is not a "literal picture" of reality, but it can used to suggest a variety of features of the reality under investigation. Religious models have a similar structure and status. They are based on analogies; they too are not literal pictures of reality, though they can serve to suggest and point to important features of God (50). They also serve to express attitudes and direct action. But unlike the situation in science, where once a theory has been suggested by a model, it can eventually be developed so that the model that gave birth to it can be left behind (though still useful for an imaginative grasp), in religion models are the closest we can come to a cognition of God. Barbour does not make fully explicit why he thinks that we cannot adequately grasp truths about God directly. But he seems to think that God is so radically different from any creature that no creaturely terms portray God as he is in himself. Even the most conceptually elaborated theology is dealing with a model by which we can get enough of a grasp of God and of divine-human relations to inform our religious thoughts, feelings, attitudes, and practices. We can never zero in on just where these models fall short of an adequate grasp of God himself.

My final example of these "analogy without a completely explicit specification of the limits thereof" views is taken from two essays by I. M. Crombie (1955, 1957). Crombie too feels that even our best efforts fall short of portraying God and his activities just as they are. He, like Barbour, is not very specific as to what he thinks keeps us from going further, but again there is the general sense that God is too infinite, too radically different from creatures, to allow terms taken from talk of creatures, however modified, to be true of him as he is.

Going back to reference for the moment (Crombie is one of the very few who realize that the subject and predicate of statements about God present different problems), Crombie makes the interesting suggestion that reference to God is achieved by directing one's attention out of the natural world "in a certain direction." The direction is given by, for example, reflecting on the contingency of the world and looking toward a contrasting necessary being (something Crombie thinks one cannot properly conceive), or by reflecting on our imperfections and thinking of an absolutely perfect being that would be wholly without such flaws.

To return to our present concern with predicates, Crombie holds that "when we speak about God, the words we use are intended in their ordinary sense (for we cannot make a transfer, failing familiarity with both ends of it), although we do not suppose that in their ordinary interpretation they can be strictly true of him. We do not even know how much of them applies" (1955, 122). The beginning of this quote implies a literal, indeed univocal use of the predicates, and the end of it rules out analyzing that literal meaning into a part that strictly applies to God and a part that does not. And so, like Aquinas and Barbour, Crombie leaves us wondering how we can suppose we are saying anything reasonably determinate about God. His originality consists in the answer he gives to this challenge: "The things we say about God are said on the authority of the words and acts of Christ, who spoke in human language, using parable; and so we too speak of God in parable—authoritative parable, authorized parable; knowing that the truth is not literally that which our parables represent . . . trusting, because we trust the source of the parables, that in believing them and interpreting them in the light of each other, we shall not be misled, that we shall have such knowledge as we need to possess for the foundation of the religious life" (122–23). This is an extended use of "parable," in which anything we say of God, even something so simple as "God wants us to have loving communion with him," counts as a parable. Though the words do not strictly apply, we have the authority of Christ (God incarnate) for taking them to be close enough to the strict truth about God to be an adequate guide to our relations with God and with our fellows. Note that this resolution of the problem holds, at best, only for those who accept the authority of Christ; it is an account of the meaning the statements have for those within the Christian community. As such, it is of narrower application than the views of Aquinas and Barbour on this topic. But within those limits it is worthy of careful consideration.

10. MY VIEW OF TALK ABOUT GOD

The essay up to this point, and that is almost all of it, is focused on an exposition and critical discussion of various views on the topics with which it deals. Though I have, from time to him, dropped some hints as to where I stand on these issues, it may not be amiss, in conclusion, to put together a brief statement of my take on the field. First of all, as made explicit in section 2, although there is much nonstatemental speech in the practice of religion—petition, confession, thanksgiving, expressions of feelings and attitudes—there are also *statements* about God that can be assigned (at least approximate) objective truth values. And the statements have a foundational role in the religious life, since they make explicit the rationale for petitionary prayer, confession, thanksgiving, worship, and so on. Second, to refer back to section 8, in opposition to pan-metaphoricism, I hold that many statements about God use (at least some of) their terms literally rather than metaphorically or in any other figurative way. Third, I believe that in some of these cases these terms, all of which are taken from our talk of creatures or derived from terms that are, are used in just the same sense as that in which they are used of creatures. This is fully the case only with very abstract terms like "exists," "powerful," and "not dependent on anything." But with more concrete terms, like action terms, and conative terms, like "intends to bring about his kingdom on earth," we are not left with a supposition of a divine-human analogy that we cannot make fully explicit, as the thinkers discussed in the previous section suppose. On the contrary, as I illustrated in section 7, such terms can be analyzed into an abstract component that can be applied univocally and that goes some way toward specifying the relevant analogy, and a more concrete part that is not strictly appropriate to God. This partial univocity gives us a secure foundation for the less determinate and explicit portions of our talk of God.

I want to be careful not to claim too much for this partial univocity position. Even where we can find an abstract univocal core, as in my suggestion of a functional account of psychological predicates, that falls far short of saying as much as we would like to be able to say about divine knowledge, intentions, desires, tendencies, and so on. What is left over is left to the realm of the inexplicit "pointing in a certain direction," to use Crombie's way of putting it, or to metaphorical, symbolic, model-dependent speech. It is no accident that Jesus, when asked by his disciples how to pray, did not begin his answer: "Say 'Thou who are the source of the being of everything other than himself, in something like the way in which a human father is the source of the being of his offspring . . .'" Instead, he unselfconsciously made a metaphorical use of the term "father." That is itself a "parable" of our need to go beyond partial univocity in religious discourse, even if that is as viable as I take it to be.

NOTES

1. For a thorough discussion of this, see Heimbeck (1969).

2. Just as all this discussion of reference is conducted without assuming that God exists, so the discussion of experience of God does not assume that what seems like that to the subject is veridical percepton, only that it is, phenomenologically, a case of perception, what seems to the subject like perception.

3. Of course, the partial univocity position itself implies an analogy between divine and human properties, but I reserve the term "analogical" here for a view that denies the possibility of an explicit literal formulation of the points of analogy.

WORKS CITED

Alston, William P. 1989. *Divine Nature and Human Language.* Ithaca, N.Y.: Cornell University Press.

———. 1991. *Perceiving God.* Ithaca, N.Y.: Cornell University Press.

———. 1993. "Aquinas on Theological Predication: A Look Backward and a Look Forward." In *Reasoned Faith,* ed. Eleonore Stump, 145–78. Ithaca, N.Y.: Cornell University Press.

Aquinas, Saint Thomas. 1955. *Summa contra gentiles.* Trans. A. C. Pegis. Garden City, N.Y.: Doubleday.

———. 1964. *Summa theologiae.* Trans. Herbert McCabe. London: Eyre & Spottswoode.

Barbour, Ian G. 1974. *Myths, Models, and Paradigms.* New York: Harper & Row.

Beardsworth, Timothy. 1977. *A Sense of Presence.* Oxford: Oxford Religious Experience Research Unit.

Braithwaite, R. B. 1955. *An Empiricist's View of the Nature of Religious Belief.* Cambridge, England: Cambridge University Press.

Crombie, I. M. 1955. "Arising from the University Discussion." In *New Essays in Philosophical Theology,* ed. Antony Flew and Alasdair MacIntyre, 109–30. London: SCM Press.

———. 1957. "The Possibility of Theological Statements." In *Faith and Logic,* ed. Basil Mitchell, 31–83. London: Allen & Unwin.

Davidson, Donald, and Gilbert Harman, eds. 1972. *Semantics of Natural Language.* Dordrecht, Holland: D. Reidel.

Pseudo-Dionysius Areopagite. 1980. *The Divine Names and Mystical Theology.* Trans. John D. Jones. Milwaukee: Marquette University Press.

Griffin, David Ray. 2001. *Reenchantment without Supernaturalism: A Process Philosophy of Religion.* Ithaca, N.Y.: Cornell University Press.

Hartshorne, Charles. 1941. *Man's Vision of God and the Logic of Theism.* New York: Harper & Row.

Heimbeck, Raeburne S. 1969. *Theology and Meaning.* Stanford: Stanford University Press.

Huxley, Julian. 1957. *Religion Without Revelation.* New York: New American Library.

James, William. 1902. *The Varieties of Religious Experience.* New York: Modern Library.

Kaufman, Gordon. 1993. *In Face of Mystery: A Constructive Theology.* Cambridge, Mass.: Harvard University Press.

Kripke, Saul. 1972. "Naming and Necessity." In *Semantics of Natural Language,* ed. Donald Davidson and Gilbert Harman. Dordrecht: D. Reidel.

McFague, Sallie. 1982. *Metaphorical Theology.* Philadelphia: Fortress Press.

Phillips, D. Z. 1970. *Faith and Philosophical Enquiry.* London: Routledge & Kegan Paul.

———. 1976. *Religion without Explanation.* Oxford: Basil Blackwell.

Santayana, George. 1905. *Reason in Religion.* New York: Charles Scribner's Sons.

Wieman, Henry Nelson, D. C. MacIntosh, and Rudolph Otto. 1932. *Is There a God?* Chicago: Willett, Clark.

FOR FURTHER READING

Bevan, Edwin. 1957. *Symbolism and Belief.* Boston: Beacon Press.

Ferré, Frederick. 1962. *Language, Logic, and God.* London: Eyre & Spottswoode.

Flew, Antony, and Alasdair MacIntyre, eds. 1955. *New Essays in Philosophical Theology.* London: SCM Press.

Mitchell, Basil, ed. 1957. *Faith and Logic.* London: Allen & Unwin.

Mondin, Battista. 1968. *The Principle of Analogy in Protestant and Catholic Theology.* The Hague: Martinus Nijhoff.

Ramsey, Ian T. 1957. *Religious Language: An Empirical Placing of Theological Phrases.* London: SCM Press.

———. 1964. *Models and Mystery.* Oxford: Oxford University Press.

Rowe, William L. 1968. *Religious Symbols and God.* Chicago: University of Chicago Press.

Soskice, Janet Martin. 1985. *Metaphor and Religious Language.* Oxford: Clarendon Press.

Tillich, Paul. 1955. "Theology and Symbolism." In *Religious Symbolism,* ed. F. Ernest Johnson. New York: Harper & Bros.

CHAPTER 10

RELIGIOUS EPISTEMOLOGY

NICHOLAS WOLTERSTORFF

THE TASK OF EPISTEMOLOGY

RELIGIONS are highly complex components of our human existence. What is it, within such a complex, that belongs to the subject matter of the epistemologist?

Adherence to a religion and participation therein typically incorporate such actions as worship, prayer, meditation, self-discipline, commemorating certain persons and events, treating certain writings as canonical, allowing one's beliefs and actions to be formed by one's own and others' interpretation of those writings, acting in certain characteristic ways in society, and associating with one's fellow adherents for all the above activities. Typically they also incorporate a variety of propositional attitudes: hoping that certain events will take place, trusting that certain events will take place, regretting that certain events did take place, believing that certain things are true about God, about the cosmos, about the natural world, about human beings—their misery and glory, their history, their institutions. Wittgenstein's phrase "form of life" is appropriate: adherence to and participation in a religion is a form of life.

What evokes adherence to and participation in a religion is typically also complex: being reared within the religion often plays a role, as do reasoning, interpretation of the canonical scriptures of the religion, and experience—sometimes experience whose content is uncanny, sometimes experience whose content is ordinary things uncannily experienced.

So once again, our question: What is it, within that complex that is a religion, that belongs to the subject matter of the epistemologist? And let me make explicit what we all know to be the case: religion always comes in the form of religions, in the plural; there is no such thing as religion as such, only this religion, that religion, and so forth.

Well, the epistemologist will be interested in those experiences. If the experience is of something uncanny (as I called it), he'll want to figure out whether its content is simply an inner state of oneself or something external to the self that transcends the ordinary—God, perhaps, or the Real, the One, the sacred, whatever. If it's of the ordinary uncannily experienced, he'll try to understand what it is to experience the starry heavens above as a manifestation of God's creative handiwork, to experience a child's sing-song as God speaking to one, and so forth.

In addition, the epistemologist will be interested in those propositional attitudes—those hopings, those trustings, those regrettings, those believings. He'll be interested in what it is that accounts for the emergence of these attitudes; for example, are religious beliefs all formed by inference from other beliefs or are some formed by belief-forming processes more fundamental than that of inference? Above all, he'll be interested in the conditions under which one and another truth-relevant merit is present in, or absent from, those propositional attitudes. Hopes, regrets, beliefs, and so forth are rational, warranted, justified, entitled, reliably formed, certain, and the like; here I'm using a sprinkling of merit-denoting words from the epistemologist's lexicon. The epistemologist wants to illuminate the conditions for the presence and absence of such merits.

Let me bring to the surface some assumptions in what I have just said. I assume, in the first place, that propositional attitudes do have merits and defects; that seems just obvious. I assume, in the second place, that whereas some of these have something to do with truth, others do not. One good thing about beliefs is that they are components in desirable emotions; some beliefs, for example, make one happy. But making one happy has nothing to do with truth; false beliefs are just as good at making one happy as true ones. By contrast, the merit in a belief of being reliably formed, to take just one example, obviously does have something to do with truth. Third, I assume that beliefs are not unique in possessing truth-relevant merits but that other propositional attitudes possess such merits as well; just as a belief may be rational or not, so also a hope may be rational or not. And last, I assume that there's not just one truth-relevant merit that we find in beliefs and other propositional attitudes but a plurality of such. The point of this last remark is that, until rather recently, epistemology in the twentieth-century analytic tradition was almost always conducted under the assumption that there's just one truth-relevant merit, sometimes called "justification," sometimes called "rationality." The literature was then filled with competing theories of justification or rationality. The assumption seems to me decisively false. Here is perhaps the clearest example. It's one thing for a person to hold a belief that he's not entitled to hold, one that he ought not to hold; it's quite another thing for a person to hold a belief that's not been reliably formed. Yet both entitlement and reliable formation are truth-relevant merits in beliefs.

I said that it belongs to the work of the epistemologist to illuminate the conditions under which truth-relevant merits are present in propositional attitudes generally. As a matter of fact, however, epistemologists have concentrated almost entirely on beliefs; discussions of the epistemology of hope, for example, are rare indeed. So also when it comes to the epistemology of religion; prominent though hope, trust, regret, and so forth are within religions, the epistemology of religion has focused almost entirely on religious beliefs. I speculate that the reason for this is that epistemology has been in the clutches of the preoccupation of philosophers with knowledge—and because knowledge, in the twentieth-century analytic tradition, has been understood as a species of belief. In contrast to the expansive account that I have just given of the subject matter of epistemology, many writers would have led off by saying that epistemology is *theory of knowledge*. They would have had etymology on their side; *episteme* in Greek means *knowledge*, and *logos* means *theory*, hence, theory of knowledge. My response is that if one actually looks at how epistemology has developed, one sees that it long ago outstripped the etymology of its name. Though John Locke, for example, was concerned to articulate an account of knowledge, he was at least as concerned, if not more, to articulate an account of what I am calling "entitlement."

I regard it as regrettable that epistemology has concentrated almost entirely on belief and knowledge, to the neglect of other propositional attitudes—particularly regrettable in the case of the epistemology of religion. But since here is not the place to set about correcting that defect, I too will focus on beliefs in what follows. And since another chapter in this book is devoted to "Mysticism and Religious Experience," I will say very little about what it is that evokes religious belief.

DEVELOPMENTS IN TWENTIETH-CENTURY RELIGIOUS EPISTEMOLOGY

One important development in twentieth-century religious epistemology has been the greatly increased sophistication of arguments for both "natural" and "revealed" religion, to use the somewhat misleading terminology of the Enlightenment. Preeminent has been the work of Richard Swinburne (1979, 1981, 1992, 1996). I myself judge that the development that will prove of greatest and most enduring historical significance, however, is the attack that has been launched on the claims made concerning religion by Enlightenment evidentialism and positivist verificationism. Accordingly, let me focus my discussion on that development.

A central thesis of the Enlightenment was that religious belief, if it's to be entitled, must be rationally grounded in the deliverances of reason and experience; the corresponding thesis of the positivists was that religious discourse, if it's to be used to make assertions, must be empirically verifiable. Both theses have become untenable. In the writings of epistemologists one often finds "rational" used as a synonym of "entitled." Using it thus, we can put the conclusion that has emerged like this: religious belief does not have to be rationally grounded to be rational, nor does religious language have to be empirically verifiable to be assertorically meaningful.

The best-known and most influential movement arguing for the latter conclusion has been Wittgensteinian philosophy of religion; the best-known and most influential arguing for the former has been so-called Reformed epistemology. Accordingly, it's to these two movements that I will devote the bulk of my attention, considering them in the order mentioned. That done, I will conclude by exploring the fascinating convergence between these two movements, on the one hand, and the attitude toward religion expressed by Heidegger in some of his writings.

These three bodies of thought emerge from very different philosophical ancestries and get articulated in very different philosophical styles. Their polemical partners are different: for Wittgenstein, it's logical positivism; for Reformed epistemology, it's Enlightenment evidentialism; for Heidegger, it's ontotheology. The understandings they propose as an alternative to those they attack are likewise different. What makes it nonetheless worth considering all three together is a fascinating convergence around (at least) two fundamental points.

Even casual inspection makes plain that few if any religious beliefs are rationally grounded in the deliverances of reason and experience. The thought of the Wittgensteinians, of the Reformed epistemologists, and of Heidegger, converges around the conviction that many of the religious beliefs of many people are nonetheless OK; the believer is entitled to his or her beliefs even though they're not rationally grounded. There is in that way an affirmation by all three of the worth of the religion of ordinary people—an affirmation of the worth of the everyday in the face of contrary claims for the indispensability of theory.

I should perhaps add, lest there be any misunderstanding, that none of these three lines of thought holds that "anything goes" in religious belief; they agree that some of the religious beliefs that people hold are ones they're not entitled to. The Reformed epistemologists have been more emphatic on this point than the others, but there's no disagreement. The problem with Enlightenment eviden-

tialism, so say the Reformed epistemologists, is not its contention that some religious beliefs are entitled and some not, but that it operates with a mistaken
criterion for entitlement.

Second, all three developments contest the standard picture of religious beliefs
as add-on explanations: explanations that the religious person adds on to the
beliefs she shares with her nonreligious fellows. An alternative that emerged in
the three developments I will be discussing—prominent in the Wittgensteinians,
part of the ever-present theoretical background in Heidegger—is that religious
beliefs are *interpretive* in character, and that in good measure the reality and
experience that they interpret are not transcendent reality and mystical experience
but ordinary reality and ordinary experience: beauty, morality, cruelty, love, birth,
death, authority, origins. The difference between the religious and the nonreligious
person remains even when we set off to the side mystical experiences and con-
victions purely about the transcendent. In good measure the interpretations that
constitute the religious person's belief-structure are not interpretations of other
things but alternative interpretations of the same things.

In this respect, all three movements are inheritors of the understanding of
religion developed by Schleiermacher in his *Speeches on Religion to Its Cultured
Despisers* (1988). The "essence" of religion, for Schleiermacher, consisted in a certain mode of *interpretation-as*, specifically, in the interpretation of ordinary, finite,
contingent reality as the manifestation of something of an entirely different order:
the infinite, the whole, whatever. Schleiermacher says, in one passage, that "to
accept everything individual as a part of the whole and everything limited as a
[presentation] of the infinite is religion" (105).[1] Accordingly, "to a pious mind
religion makes everything holy and valuable, even unholiness and commonness
itself" (113).

ENLIGHTENMENT EVIDENTIALISM

As will be clear from what I have said, all three of the movements I am considering
have been polemical in their orientation. That is to say, they have placed themselves in opposition to earlier views, both mounting arguments against those views
and developing alternatives. It's my judgment that one does not fully understand
the significance of the moves made unless one understands the polemical partner.
Accordingly, it's with a brief sketch of the polemical partners of Reformed epistemology and of Wittgensteinianism that I will begin; I'll save a sketch of Heidegger's polemical partner for when we get to him.

In the Enlightenment of the late seventeenth and eighteenth centuries there emerged the idea of a religion rationally grounded in the deliverances of reason and experience. The high medievals, such as Anselm and Aquinas, had the idea of a rationally grounded theology; it would not be a mistake to see the Enlightenment idea as a descendent of that medieval idea. But it's a descendent, not the same idea. For theology was understood by the medieval thinkers as a *scientia*, a science, a *Wissenschaft*, whereas the great Enlightenment figures who talked about religion and articulated the idea of a rationally grounded religion most definitely did not have the Wissenschaft of theology in mind. The best indicator of that is this: whereas most people in Locke's day (and ours) were not theologians, Locke thought that everybody in his society ought to take seriously, in the way we'll shortly be getting to, the idea of a rationally grounded religion. Immanuel Kant was considerably less clear than Locke on who was to take seriously the idea of a rationally grounded religion; it appears to me that it was not the citizenry in general but the intellectuals of society that he had in mind. That's just a small group within Locke's citizenry. Even so, the difference from the medieval idea of a rationally grounded theology is clear: theologians constituted only a small proportion of the intellectuals in Kant's society; they constitute an even smaller proportion in ours.

Given that Locke was also considerably more clear than Kant on what should be done with the idea of a rationally grounded religion, not just on who should be doing it, let me concentrate on presenting his line of thought. An additional reason for concentrating on Locke is that his thought became far more influential than Kant's in the English-speaking world.

The topic of chapter 17 of book 4 of John Locke's *Essay Concerning Human Understanding* (1975) is "Of Reason"; the topic of the following chapter is "Of Faith and Reason, and their Distinct Provinces." With his eye on the topic of the upcoming chapter, Locke, in concluding chapter 17, observes that there is a "use of the word *reason*, wherein it is *opposed to faith*." Common though he judged that use of "reason" to be in his day, Locke thinks it's incorrect; and in any case, it's not, he says, how he will be using the word. He then concludes the chapter with this rousing passage in which he sums up one of the principal themes in what has preceded and introduces us to the main theme in what will follow:

> I think it may not be amiss to take notice, that however *faith* be opposed to reason, *faith* is nothing but a firm assent of the mind: which if it be regulated, as is our duty, cannot be afforded to any thing, but upon good reason; and so cannot be opposite to it. He that believes, without having any reason for believing, may be in love with his own fancies; but neither seeks truth as he ought, nor pays the obedience due to his maker, who would have him use those discerning faculties he has given him, to keep him out of mistake and error. He that does not this to the best of his power, however he sometimes lights on truth, is in the right but by chance; and I know not whether the

luckiness of the accident will excuse the irregularity of his proceeding. This at least is certain, that he must be accountable for whatever mistakes he runs into: whereas he that makes use of the light and faculties God has given him, and seeks sincerely to discover truth, by those helps and abilities he has, may have this satisfaction in doing his duty as a rational creature, that though he should miss truth, he will not miss the reward of it. For he governs his assent right, and places it as he should, who in any case or matter whatsoever, believes or disbelieves, according as reason directs him. (IV, xvii, 24)

Note in the first place that the doxastic merit (*doxa* = belief, in Greek) on which Locke has his eye here is what I called entitlement. Like a drum roll, the theme of obligation is struck over and over again in the passage. What Locke has already argued is that we are under obligation to our Maker to govern our belief-forming faculties, to the end of arriving at truth and avoiding mistake and error. What he now insists on is that this also holds when it comes to faith, that is, to beliefs comprised within what the seventeenth- and eighteenth-century writers called "revealed religion." We're not exempt in religion from the obligation to govern our assent right. In particular, we must have "reason for believing," says Locke; we must believe or disbelieve "as reason directs" us.

The passage reads as if Locke thinks we should, in general, so discipline ourselves that we don't believe anything at all except for good reason: "He that believes," says Locke, "without having any reason for believing, may be in love with his own fancies; but [does not seek] truth as he ought." But earlier chapters from book 4 of the *Essay* make clear that that was not his view.

Some beliefs are evoked in us not by reasoning but by our "perception" of the corresponding facts—"perception" being Locke's metaphor for the activity in question. I don't believe the proposition that $1 + 1 = 2$ on the basis of some reason for it; what could such a reason possibly be? My belief is evoked in me by my rational intuition, as I'll call it, of the fact that $1 + 1 = 2$. So, too, I don't believe that I'm dizzy (when I am) on the basis of some reason for it; again, what could such a reason possibly be? My belief is evoked in me by my experience, more specifically, by my introspective experience, of the fact that I am dizzy. Reason and introspective experience are, for Locke, modes of direct cognitive access to certain of the facts of reality; they are what Locke calls, in the passage I quoted, "discerning faculties." At the same time, they are faculties of belief formation: one's rational intuition or introspective experience of some fact typically evokes in one a belief whose propositional content corresponds to those facts. They have these two sides to themselves: modes of direct cognitive access and faculties of belief formation.

Whether it was Locke's view that perception—using "perception" in the ordinary sense of the word now, not in Locke's metaphorical sense—is also a distinct mode of experiential cognitive access to certain facts, specifically, to facts of external reality, and a faculty of corresponding belief formation, is not entirely clear. I think the textual evidence tilts toward the conclusion that it is not, but that perception, on his view, consists in introspective awareness of certain facts of inner experience plus inferences from beliefs about those facts—these beliefs evoked in one by the awareness—to facts about external reality. For our purposes here, we can leave this question open, whether sensory perception is a distinct mode of experiential access to certain facts of reality, specifically, facts of external reality, and simply say that it was Locke's view that reason and experience both give us direct cognitive access to certain of the facts of reality and, when working properly, evoke in us beliefs whose propositional content corresponds to those facts: I rationally intuit that $1 + 1 = 2$, and that evokes in me the corresponding belief that $1 + 1 = 2$; I introspectively experience that I am feeling dizzy, and that evokes in me the corresponding belief that I am feeling dizzy; and so forth. Reason and experience evoke in us what we in the twentieth century have called "immediate" or "basic" beliefs—in contrast to *mediate* beliefs, which are those formed in us on the basis of other beliefs.

It is crucial to realize that "reason" is being used ambiguously in the above discussion: as the name for the faculty of rational intuition, whereby we come to believe necessary truths immediately, and as the name for the faculty of reasoning from premises to conclusions, whereby we come to believe certain propositions mediately.

The points just made will prove useful later in our discussion; the immediate occasion for making them, however, was to clarify what it was that Locke wanted to say about believing for reasons. It sounded as if it was his view that we ought never to believe anything but for good reasons. That was not his view. We're all entitled to believe immediately that $1 + 1 = 2$; likewise, we're all entitled to believe immediately that we're dizzy (when we are). About religious faith it definitely was his view, however, that it "cannot be afforded to any thing, but upon good reason." I have already mentioned that the word "faith," in Locke's traditional terminology, was used to stand for assent to propositions of revealed religion. Locke's view as to the relevance of reasoning was the same, however, for natural religion as for revealed religion: a person ought not to believe propositions of natural religion except for good reasons.

Why so? If it's not true for beliefs in general that they must be formed (and held) for good reason, why is that the case for religious beliefs? Why isn't it permissible to hold at least some of these immediately?

Two considerations came together to drive Locke to his conclusion. In the first place, neither reason nor experience gives us direct cognitive access to the facts corresponding to our religious beliefs. Take the most fundamental of all beliefs in any theistic religion, namely, that God exists. This is neither a necessary fact, self-evident to us, to which rational intuition gives us access, nor, Locke claims, is it a fact to which introspective or perceptual experience gives us access. That is one consideration.

We can get at the other consideration by asking why it's not acceptable to believe that God exists by accepting what others tell one, or because one finds the conviction just welling up within one. Both positions had their devotees in Locke's day, the former, in the person of defenders of tradition, the latter, in the person of the so-called enthusiasts. Well, says Locke, religion is a matter of maximal concernment, "concernment" being his word. For everyone of us, there's nothing more important than getting our religious beliefs right; our salvation depends on it. And if it's of maximal importance to us that we get it right, then we have to do our best by way of the use and governance of our belief-forming faculties—"to the best of [our] power," as Locke puts it in the passage quoted. And doing our best will consist of rationally grounding our religious beliefs in the deliverances of reason and experience. For it is reason and experience, introspective and perhaps perceptual—in contrast to tradition and beliefs that just well up in us—that give us direct cognitive access to certain of the facts of reality. Starting from the deliverances of reason and experience, we do the best job we can of drawing inferences.

And so it is that we get the conclusion: it's obligatory on all who hold religious beliefs that those be rationally grounded in the deliverances of reason and experience. It should be clear from the preceding that Locke was of the view that it's no more acceptable for the nonreligious than for the religious person to rest content with such nonreligious beliefs as are planted in him by tradition or just well up, he knows not how. When it comes to religion, we are all, religious and nonreligious alike, to believe or disbelieve "according as reason directs" us.

POSITIVIST VERIFICATIONISM

For the sake of convenience, let me give the title "evidentialism" to the classic Enlightenment position concerning religious belief that I have just explicated, namely, that the intellectuals among us, and perhaps the nonintellectuals as well, are entitled to their religious beliefs only if those are rationally grounded in the deliverances of reason or experience. Evidentialism is a term that's come to be commonly used in recent years for the position in question. Though Enlightenment evidentialism was certainly in the background of Wittgenstein's remarks on religion, his immediate polemical partner was the logical positivism of the first half of the twentieth century. Logical positivism is rightly seen as a child of the

Enlightenment; the status given by Enlightenment evidentialism to rational grounding in the deliverances of reason and experience has its counterpart in the positivist thesis that a condition of a sentence having meaning is that it be either analytic or empirically verifiable. Nonetheless, the child has its own distinct features.

What animated the thought of the logical positivists was the deep conviction that insofar as knowledge is concerned, science is the road ahead for humanity. Logical positivism was thus a species of scientism. For most of us today that gives it a strange musty smell. Too much has happened between then and now for us to find science a plausible object of veneration.

Anyone who holds the view that when it comes to knowledge, science is the road ahead for humanity, and who wants to get beyond the stage of preachment, is immediately confronted with the question: How is science to be differentiated from the mass of other ways that people employ in their attempt to gain knowledge? How is it to be *demarcated*, to use a term that the positivists themselves used?

It was in its answer to this question that positivism marked a distinctly new development in Western thought. Let's turn to language, they said, and let's distinguish between *meaningful* and *meaningless* discourse. What demarcates science from all other discourse is that scientific discourse is meaningful, whereas all other is meaningless. The positivists took to calling all discourse other than scientific discourse "metaphysics." It was, need I say, a pejorative term in their hands. The fatal flaw in metaphysics, said the positivists, is not, as previous writers had contended, something epistemological; the problem is not that metaphysics lacks good grounds for the truth claims it makes. The fatal flaw is linguistic: the metaphysician isn't saying anything meaningful. Of course, he thinks he is, or he wouldn't speak and write at such length. But in fact, there's no meaning to what he says. And since his talk is without meaning, the questions of whether there are good grounds for believing what he says, whether there *could be* good grounds, and so forth, cannot even arise.

The question that now cries out for answer is obvious: What's the test for whether a piece of discourse is or is not meaningful? As their answer, the positivists proposed their now famous criterion for meaning: a sentence is meaningful if and only if it's either analytically true or false, or empirically verifiable.

The positivists, criterion in hand, energetically set about trying to clarify the distinction they were employing between analytic and synthetic sentences, trying to develop an account of the nature of analytic truth and falsehood, and trying to refine and articulate the concept of *verifiability* so that all sentences of reputable natural science, and no sentences of "metaphysics," satisfied the concept. Even by their own lights, they failed in all three endeavors; it was especially their inability to devise a criterion of verifiability satisfactory for the purpose of demarcation that proved a bitter pill to swallow. One does still notice positivist yearnings in certain philosophers, but as a doctrine affirmed up front, logical positivism has disappeared among philosophers. Its disappearance is one of the most dramatic examples of the disappearance of an *ism* in the entire history of philosophy. It was in its heyday, however, when Wittgenstein was doing his work.

WITTGENSTEINIANISM

I think the best way to understand Wittgenstein's philosophy of religion generally, and his epistemology of religious belief in particular, is to see him as exploiting a qualification that the logical positivists early on attached to their criterion of meaning. Shortly after they had propounded their starkly elegant criterion—a sentence is meaningful if and only if it's either analytically true or false, or empirically verifiable—the positivists found themselves forced to qualify it. The qualification was there already in A. J. Ayer's youthfully exuberant *Language, Truth, and Logic.* When it's said of a person that what he said or wrote lacks meaning, the clear implication is that he should retract his words and try again—unless, perchance, he is entertaining children with jabberwocky. But whereas it was noted soon after the positivists first issued their criterion that moral judgments do not satisfy it, the positivists were not so revolutionary as to recommend that we stop making moral judgments. Instead, they said that the criterion should be understood as a criterion for just one kind of meaning.

It proved unexpectedly difficult to say what kind that was. Rather than cataloguing the suggestions, let me just mention the one that eventually pretty much won the day: the criterion of meaning is to be understood as a criterion for whether one has said something true or false. Since to say something true or false is make an assertion, we can say that the criterion was to be understood as a criterion for *assertoric* meaning. Sentences not satisfying the criterion, such as sentences expressing moral judgments, may have a positive role in human life; of many of them it may be appropriate to say that they are meaningful. But the acceptance of the positivist criterion of assertoric meaning imposes on one's analysis of that meaning the restriction that such sentences cannot be analyzed as being used to make assertions.

In his *Belief, Change, and Forms of Life* of 1986, D. Z. Phillips, today the most prominent Wittgensteinian philosopher of religion, remarked:

> If we look back to the 1950's, we find, in the literature, a certain kind of disagreement between philosophical believers and philosophical unbelievers which still persists today. The unbelievers suggested that the problematic core of religious beliefs was to be found, not in their falsity, but in their meaninglessness.

The believers, on the other hand, argued that the beliefs were meaningful. By and large, however, the believers and the unbelievers agreed on the criteria of meaningfulness which had to be satisfied. (80)

Phillips then goes on to remark:

Under Wittgenstein's influence, some philosophers have suggested that these disputes are an irrelevance, since they never raise the question of whether the criteria of meaningfulness should have been agreed on in the first place. What has happened, it is suggested, is that criteria of meaning appropriate to certain aspects of human life and activity are made synonymous with meaning as such. One obvious example in our culture has been the tendency to elevate scientific criteria and procedures in such a way. What we ought to do by contrast, it was said, is to enquire into the meanings which religious beliefs have in the forms of life of which they are a part. Instead of constructing theories of meaning which determine what is to count as meaning, we should look at the use concepts actually have. This was the force of Wittgenstein's command, "Don't think. Look!" (80)

The history here is a bit shaky. The "unbelievers" to whom Phillips is alluding in the first passage are logical positivists. But as I indicated above, the positivists conceded, rather early, that their criterion was not a criterion for *all* modes of meaning. To affirm that there are types of meaning not captured by the positivist criterion, and to inquire into some of those alternative modes, is so far not to repudiate positivism. Admittedly, the inquiry by the positivists into alternative modes of meaning was desultory. It was desultory, however, not because they pulled the boner of equating scientific meaning with meaning as such, but because of their veneration of science; they weren't interested in other modes of discourse.

An important issue of interpretation posed by Wittgenstein's own relatively brief remarks on religion is whether his interpretation of religious discourse presupposed the unacceptability of the positivist criterion of assertoric meaning. That Wittgenstein did in fact regard the criterion as unacceptable is decisively clear from other writings of his. What's also decisively clear is that in his remarks on religion he did not head-on challenge the criterion. The contested issue then is this: Does his analysis of religious discourse tacitly assume the unacceptability of the criterion? Or was he instead exploiting the opening that the positivists themselves had offered when they conceded that there are other modes of meaning than assertoric meaning?

The issue pivots, naturally, on whether Wittgenstein thought that in using primary religious language the religious person is making assertions. I myself think the evidence tilts toward the conclusion that he did not think that; accordingly, that's the interpretation I will develop. That's also the interpretation most Wittgensteinians adopt, so far as I can tell—though showing this to their satisfaction would get us into complicated issues and take a long time. It's my further impression that most Wittgensteinian philosophers of religion are of the view that religious language is not used to make reference to God or anything else "transcendent"—not even *theistic* religious language. The Psalmist's exclamation "Bless the Lord O my soul," while not an assertion, nonetheless gives the appearance of being used to refer to God; most of the Wittgensteinians regard that appearance as misleading.[2] For my purposes in this essay, of showing the convergence among Wittgensteinianism, Reformed epistemology, and Heidegger, it doesn't make much difference which interpretation we adopt.

In what he himself says about religious language, Wittgenstein does not employ his concept of a *language game*. I think his followers are right, though, in interpreting him as holding that the language of religion, as it occurs among us, can be thought of as constituting a distinct language game—or better, given the diversity of human religions, as a number of distinct language games. To understand the force of this claim, we must be aware that a language game, as Wittgenstein thinks of it, does not consist of a fragment of language but of a way of using a fragment of language. A given fragment of language can be employed in distinct language games; when it is, it will typically function quite differently in those distinct games. Our goal here is to understand how religious language works *when functioning religiously*, that is, how it works when it's being employed in a *religious* language game. To do so, we must understand how religious language games function in those *forms of life* (or aspects of forms of life) that are humanity's religions. A religious language game makes possible a religious form of life; it both shapes and gives expression to it.

The most prominent function of religious language, in the thought of the Wittgensteinians, is the *expressive* function. Religious language games are expressive of a certain deep way of interpreting and valuing one's experience. They are "in no sense . . . based on hypotheses or opinions. They are not founded on anything, but express values concerning what is deep and important for the people concerned—birth, death, hunting, cultivation of the crops, personal relations, etc." (Phillips 1976, 36). The contrast with the Enlightenment picture of religion as add-on explanations could not be more clear! Here's how Wittgenstein puts the point in one place:

> Christianity is not a doctrine, not, I mean, a theory about what has happened and will happen to the human soul, but a description of something that actually takes place in human life. For "consciousness of sin" is a real event and so are despair and salvation through faith. Those who speak of such things (Bunyan for instance) are simply describing what has happened to them, whatever gloss anyone may want to put on it. (1980, 28e)

And here is D. Z. Phillips:

> Religious beliefs or practices are . . . expressions of what went deep in people's lives. That man's misfortunes are said by him to be due to his dishonouring the ghosts of slain warriors is itself the form that depth takes here; it is an

expression of what the dead mean to him and to the people amongst whom he lives. That a man says that God cares for him in all things is the expression of the terms in which he meets and makes sense of the contingencies of life. Of course, there is nothing inherently deep in the form of words in which a magical or religious utterance is expressed. The depth comes from the lives of the people in which such utterances play a part. The same words in the mouth of another person or in a different context might simply be trivial. (1976, 114–15)

To speak of language as functioning *expressively* in religious language games is to invite the thought that *first* the religious person arrives at the valuational interpretation, and then, *in order to express* that, utters the words. That in turn invites the thought that the same valuational interpretation might in principle have been expressed in other words. The truth is that it is by the totality of one's religious practices that one valuationally interprets one's experiences in a religious way, and one's participation in the relevant religious language game is to be counted *among* those practices; it's a *component* of them, albeit, then, an *expressive* component. The person who exclaims with the Psalmist (103:1), "Bless the Lord, O my soul, and all that is within me, bless God's holy name," is not thereby just *expressing* her religious way of valuationally interpreting experience; she is thereby *actually interpreting and valuing experience* in a religious way. Perhaps, says another prominent Wittgensteinian, Rush Rhees, "we could put the matter by asking whether the connexion between religious language and religious life is an external or an internal one. And if it is put like that, I would say that it is an internal one. And to your question of whether it 'makes sense to say that a person's life might be different *in that sort of way*' without using any of the language of religion, I would on the whole say, 'No, it does not make sense' . . . Reverence and devotion and exaltation . . . would not be what they are without the language of them" (1969, 120–21, 125).

To the suggestion that religious language games are expressions and enactments of value-laden interpretations of what we experience, Wittgenstein added another suggestion—though to this other he gave less prominence. Religious language games also function *regulatively*. They provide us, for example, with pictures whereby we orient our lives. For me, says Wittgenstein, to believe in the Resurrection would be for "a certain picture [to] play the role of constantly admonishing me" (1966, 56). In another passage he says, "It strikes me that a religious belief could only be something like a passionate commitment to a system of reference. Hence, although it's *belief*, it's really a way of living, or a way of assessing life. It's passionately seizing hold of *this* interpretation. Instruction in a religious faith, therefore, would have to take the form of a portrayal, a description, of that frame of reference, while at the same time being an appeal to conscience" (1980, 64e).

It's important to add that a religious language game is the game of a community with a tradition. One *learns* to use language thus; one learns what is right to say and what is wrong to say, thereby learning the "grammar" of that language thus used. In learning to use it thus, one learns that peculiar mode of valuatively interpreting one's experience and of regulating one's life that it is the function of religious language to be expressive of. In learning the language, the person learns to interpret experience and orient life in the religious way.

What is that way? Wittgenstein assumes that most of us already know; we don't await his telling us. Accordingly, he doesn't say much on the matter, apart from emphasizing the characteristic unshakeability and comprehensiveness of religious belief. Speaking of a man who believes in the Last Judgment, Wittgenstein says that "he has what you might call an unshakeable belief. It will show, not by reasoning or by appeal to ordinary grounds for belief, but rather by regulating for in all his life. This is a very much stronger fact—foregoing pleasures, always appealing to this picture. This in one sense must be called the firmest of all beliefs, because the man risks things on account of it which he would not do on things which are by far better established for him. Although he distinguishes between things well-established and not well-established" (1966, 54).

As already noted, it follows from the above points that religious beliefs are not explanations or hypotheses, nor are religious rituals attempts at causal efficacy. A typical charge against religious beliefs is that they are poor explanations and ill-grounded hypotheses, and against religious rituals that they are patently ineffective. That is what Wittgenstein, in his remarks on Frazer's *The Golden Bough*, took Frazer to be saying. Such charges represent a gross misunderstanding of religion. "Frazer is much more savage than most of his savages," says Wittgenstein, "for these savages will not be so far from any understanding of spiritual matters as an Englishman of the twentieth century. His explanations of the primitive observances are much cruder than the sense of the observances themselves" (1971, 34).

What accounts for Wittgenstein's fury? It arises, I suggest, from his life-long sense that religion goes deep in human life, coupled with his conviction that to construe religious beliefs as explanations, and religious rituals as the technology of magic, is to treat religion as something utterly trivial and misguided: the explanations turn out to be oddball and the rituals, stupid. The whole approach must be brushed aside. The rituals

> can be seen as a form of language, a symbolism in their own right; a language and a symbolism which are expressive in character . . . When the adoption of a baby is marked by the woman pulling the child from beneath her clothes, then, to use Wittgenstein's words, "it is crazy to think there is an *error* in this and that she believes she has borne the child." The ritualistic gesture expresses her attitude to the adopted child; she will be as close to it as if she had given birth to it. (Phillips 1976, 35)

A religion such as Christianity is not *based*, more or less securely, on claims about historical facts. Instead, it offers us a (historical) narrative and says: now believe! But not, believe this narrative with the belief appropriate to a historical narrative, rather: believe through thick and thin, which you can do only as the result of a life. *Here you have a narrative, don't take the same attitude to it as you take to other historical narratives!* Make a *quite different* place in your life for it. There is nothing *paradoxical* about that! . . . Queer as it sounds: The historical accounts in the Gospels might, historically speaking, be demonstrably false and yet belief would lose nothing by this; *not*, however, because it concerns "universal truths of reason"! Rather, because historical proof (the historical proof-game) is irrelevant to belief. (Wittgenstein 1980, 32e)

It also follows from the above that the demand of the Enlightenment evidentialists, that the religious person base his beliefs on evidence, displays a deep misunderstanding of the nature of religious belief. Suppose that a person who interprets and values food as a gift utters some such words as "Thank you, God, for this food" as a way of expressing that. In speaking thus, she is not asserting something for which she ought to have evidence, as she is not asserting something. As Wittgenstein puts it:

> The point is that if there were evidence, this would in fact destroy the whole business . . . Suppose, for instance, we knew people who foresaw the future; made forecasts for years and years ahead; and they described some sort of a Judgement Day. Queerly enough, even if there were such a thing, and even if it were more convincing than I have described, belief in this happening wouldn't be at all a religious belief . . .
>
> Here we have people who treat this evidence in a different way. They base things on evidence which taken in one way would seem exceedingly flimsy. They base enormous things on this evidence. Am I to say they are unreasonable? I wouldn't call them unreasonable.
>
> I would say, they are certainly not *reasonable*, that's obvious.
>
> "Unreasonable" implies, with everyone, rebuke.
>
> I want to say: they don't treat this as a matter of reasonability.
>
> Anyone who reads the Epistles will find it said: not only that it is not reasonable, but that it is folly.
>
> Not only is it not reasonable, but it doesn't pretend to be . . .
>
> Why shouldn't one form of life culminate in an utterance of belief in a Last Judgement? But I couldn't either say "Yes" or "No" to the statement that there will be such a thing. Nor "Perhaps," nor "I'm not sure."
>
> It is a statement which may not allow of any such answer. (1966, 56–58)

One might reply by remarking that in this passage Wittgenstein himself suggests that in religious language games there is talk of "evidence" and of the offering of reasons. How, then, can he say that it is in principle mistaken for the philosopher to insist on evidence? The answer of the Wittgensteinian is that the mistake of the philosopher was to require of the believer what *he, the philosopher*, has in mind by evidence—namely, evidence for propositions believed or asserted. It would have been quite another matter if he had been talking about *evidence* and *reasons* as those are understood *within* religious language games. There, "reasons look entirely different from normal reasons" (Wittgenstein 1966, 56).

And if the philosopher does understand "evidence" and "reasons" as does the religious person, then what has to be noted is that it is entirely out of place for the philosopher to present himself in the role of critic bringing to the ignorant a message concerning the importance of reasons and evidence. Religious believers already offer reasons for and against their speaking as they do. They are far from being of the view that "anything goes" in religion. The history of eucharistic controversy within Christianity makes that abundantly and painfully clear. Nobody, though, would regard a chemical analysis of the eucharistic host as relevant to the controversy—though if some scientist claimed that he had discovered some chemical process whereby he could change ordinary bread into muscle and ordinary wine into blood, that would have to be taken seriously by the Christian. Characteristic of the Wittgensteinians is their insistence that different language games each have their own distinct "grammar" for *evidence, truth, fact, justification*, and the like. As Phillips remarks, for "religious beliefs, the grammar of 'belief' and 'truth' is not the same as in the case of empirical propositions or the prediction of future events" (1976, 143).

But suppose the objector moves up a level. Suppose it be granted that within religious language games, reasons are offered for and against what is said; and suppose it also be granted that, since language used religiously is not functioning assertorically, one cannot ask for evidence for the truth of what was asserted. Still, don't the participants in a religious form of life have to *justify their participation*? And don't the practitioners of a religious language game have to *justify their practice*?

Fundamental in the thought of the Wittgensteinian philosophers of religion is their insistence that these questions be answered with a no. As Norman Malcolm puts it:

> One of the primary pathologies of philosophy is the feeling that we must *justify* our language-games. We want to establish them as well-grounded, but we should consider here Wittgenstein's remark that a language-game "is not based on grounds. It is there—like our life."
>
> *Within* a language-game there is justification and lack of justification, evidence and proof, mistakes and groundless opinions, good and bad reasoning, correct measurements and incorrect ones. One cannot properly apply these terms to a language-game itself. It may, however, be said to be "groundless," not in the sense of a groundless opinion, but in the sense that we accept it, we live it. We can say, "This is what we do. This is how we are." . . .
>
> Religion is a form of life; it is language embedded in action—what Wittgenstein calls a "language-game." Science is another. Neither stands in need of justification, the one no more than the other. (1977, 152, 154)

It is these claims that constitute the so-called fideism of Wittgensteinian philosophy of religion. Wittgensteinians are fideists concerning religious language games in exactly the same way that they are fideists concerning scientific language games and concerning our material-object language game. In no case, so it is said, is one called on to justify one's participation in the game. Though Malcolm, like other Wittgensteinians, is not fully explicit on the matter, one surmises that his reason for thinking one *needn't* justify one's participation in one or another of these language games is that one *couldn't*.

REFORMED EPISTEMOLOGY

By the time Reformed epistemology appeared on the scene, in the early 1980s, logical positivism was dead and buried. What remained very much alive was the evidentialism that emerged in the Enlightenment: the claim, in Locke's version of it, that for religious beliefs to be rational (entitled) they have to be rationally grounded in the deliverances of reason and experience.

Confronted with such a claim, the religious believer has two options. She can accept the validity of the claim and set out to provide the requisite grounding for her religious beliefs if they don't already have it; or she can challenge the claim. If she goes with the first option and succeeds in providing the grounding, she can continue to believe what she did, though now she'll be doing it on this new basis. If she fails, she must give up her beliefs. Or she may partially succeed and partially fail. In that case, she must revise her belief system downward, as it were, until she believes only as much as she has succeeded in grounding. Rather than engaging in the grounding endeavor, the Reformed epistemologists chose the second of the two main options: they challenged the religious epistemology of the Enlightenment on its central claim.

How did they conduct the challenge? They began by noting that a great many religious beliefs are not in fact rationally grounded in the deliverances of reason and experience. A good many of them are not rationally grounded in anything at all; they were neither formed, nor are they maintained, on the basis of other beliefs. As such, they are what Alvin Plantinga, one of the initiators of Reformed epistemology, has called "basic beliefs." One might also call them "immediate beliefs," on the ground that they are not formed by the "mediation" of inference.

Some beliefs are formed by believing what others tell one. Some are evoked by mystical experience. Others are formed by reading and interpreting scripture. Yet others are evoked by a person's experience of one or another aspect of the world or human existence. Here, for example, is what Plantinga says in one passage:

> Upon having done what I knew is cheap, or wrong, or wicked I may feel guilty in God's sight and form the belief *God disapproves of what I've done.* Upon confession and repentance, I may feel forgiven, forming the belief *God forgives me for what I've done.* A person in grave danger may turn to God, asking for his protection and help; and of course he or she then forms the belief that God is indeed able to hear and help if he sees fit. When life is sweet and satisfying, a spontaneous sense of gratitude may well up within the soul; someone in this condition may thank and praise the Lord for his goodness, and will of course form the accompanying belief that indeed the Lord is to be thanked and praised. ([1981] 1998, 477)

Earlier I made the point that one thing that unites all three lines of thought I am considering in this essay is their rejection of the traditional picture of religious beliefs as add-on explanations. The point is particularly clear in this passage from Plantinga. It's the experience of wrongdoing, remorse, danger, and delight that immediately evokes the belief—and the experience of flowers and mountains, of stars and the moral law. And though not all of Plantinga's examples can be felicitously construed as examples of a religious *interpretation* of experience, some are certainly of that sort: I interpret my feeling forgiven as a sign or manifestation of God's forgiving me; I interpret this "sweet and satisfying" portion of my life as a sign or manifestation of God's goodness.

As mentioned earlier, the Reformed epistemologist makes a considerable point of saying that not all religious beliefs are entitled—or warranted, or reliably formed, or whatever be the doxastic merit in view. Not only are some of the mediate ones not entitled; some of the immediate ones also are not. Some basic beliefs are not *proper.* What initially grabbed the attention of the Reformed epistemologist, however, was the Enlightenment claim that *none* of the immediate ones is entitled. Why, he asks, would anyone suppose that that was true? Or to put it from the other side: Why would anyone suppose that religious beliefs, to be truth-relevantly meritorious, must always be based on other beliefs that are not religious in character?

Vast numbers of religious beliefs are not held on the basis of other beliefs. None of these, so it's claimed, is OK as it is. To be acceptable, something has to be done to them; they have to be provided with rational bases. Theorists will, of course, play an indispensable role in the construction of such bases. So what we have, in the line of thought we're considering, is a massive critique of the practices of the everyday in favor of the practices that are the province of the theorist. Why accept this critique? Why suppose that it is on target?

We know, from our discussion earlier in this essay, the answer that John Locke gave to this question. When dealing with religion, we're obligated to do the human best in governing and regulating belief formation and maintenance. With respect to immediate beliefs, the best are those evoked by experience or rational intuition whose propositional content corresponds to the fact that's experienced or intuited. Now add to this Locke's assumption that God can neither be experienced by introspection or perception, nor be rationally intuited. It just follows that immediate religious beliefs are unacceptable. The acceptable ones, if there are such, will be found among those that are based on acceptable nonreligious immediate beliefs.

This being the reason offered for the supposed necessity of rational grounding, the Reformed epistemologist proceeds to scrutinize this Enlightenment epistemology, this version of "classical foundationalism," as it's customarily called. What he has to say on this score has by now become so well-known that there's no point in dwelling on it. Let me just observe that the attack has concentrated on three points of vulnerability.

For one thing, versions of classical foundationalism, Locke's included, always prove to give the wrong results. For example, sometimes it will be a matter of maximal concernment to form correct beliefs about the future. Hume showed decisively, however, that inductively formed beliefs about the future are neither direct deliverances of experience and reason nor capable of being rationally grounded in such deliverances. Accordingly, doing the best in one's formation of such beliefs cannot take the form of conforming to Locke's proposal.

Second, classical foundationalism proves to have an odd referential incoherence about it. Consider the proffered criterion for entitled belief. If the criterion is correct, then it seems clear that no one is entitled to hold it. Nobody would be entitled to hold it immediately; the criterion is not a self-evident necessary fact that we can rationally intuit, nor, obviously, is it a fact of our inner life or the external world. And nobody has yet stepped forth with an argument that successfully bases the criterion on properly held immediate beliefs about necessary facts, the inner life, or the external world. That leaves open the possibility that, on a *correct* account of entitlement, some person somewhere is entitled to hold the criterion. And that may just possibly be true. But then notice this oddity: he would be entitled to hold it only because it's false; if it were correct, he would not be entitled to hold it.

Third, in his book *Perceiving God*, William P. Alston (1991) attacks the assumption that God cannot be an object of perception. Mystical experience has standardly been assumed to be a purely subjective phenomenon; the question traditionally raised has been whether, from this subjective experience, we can make well-grounded inferences to the existence, character, and action of God. Alston challenges the assumption. In the context of a carefully articulated general theory of perception that he calls "the theory of appearing," he argues for understanding mystical experience as God appearing to the person in such a way that the person *perceives* God.

It's worth adding that though the Reformed epistemologists have themselves not objected much to the understanding of reason and experience that underlies Enlightenment evidentialism—reason and experience give us direct cognitive access to certain facts and evoke in us beliefs whose propositional content corresponds to those facts—a good many other philosophers have mounted vigorous objections to this understanding.[3]

To attack Locke's classic Enlightenment reason for holding that religious beliefs, to be doxastically meritorious, have to be rationally grounded, is of course not to show that there is nowhere a good and sufficient reason for this view. Even less is it to show that the view is false; people hold good views for bad reasons all the time. But in the years that have elapsed since Reformed epistemology came on the scene, no one has stepped forward to offer good reasons for evidentialism concerning religious beliefs. Surely we are by now entitled to assume that the thesis is mistaken: it's not true that religious beliefs in general have to be rationally grounded in the deliverances of reason and experience to be doxastically meritorious. Some do, some don't.

Let me put the point more precisely. Assume that *entitlement* is the doxastic merit one has in view. An entitled belief is one that one is permitted to hold; conversely, a belief that one ought not to hold is one that one is not entitled to hold. It's important, then, to recognize that *entitlement to believe* is very much a situated phenomenon. For almost any proposition that one person is entitled to believe in his situation, there will be another person in another situation who is not entitled to believe that proposition. To the question, Is one entitled to believe P? the answer must almost always be, It all depends. Is one entitled to believe that Santa Claus comes around every Christmas? It all depends. There are surely some children somewhere who are entitled to believe that; I and those who read this essay are surely *not* entitled to believe it.

The Reformed epistemologist would make it easy for himself if it were his claim that somewhere there's someone with an immediate religious belief that's doxastically meritorious. That's not his claim. His claim is the much stronger one; that in the belief systems of people such as the author and readers of this essay, intellectuals in modern Western society, one finds immediately held religious beliefs that are doxastically meritorious—entitled, warranted, or whatever.

Reformed epistemology, as I have presented it thus far, is a polemic. Positive claims have of course been made, some explicitly, some implicitly; no polemic can be entirely negative. In the face of an influential critique of the everyday, the Reformed epistemologist has affirmed, for example, the worth of our everyday practices for the formation of religious beliefs. Nonetheless, Reformed epistemology began with the negative polemic that I have described. In the last decade or so of the twentieth century, Reformed epistemologists have gone well beyond the polemic with which the movement began to offer what one might think of as an *account of* the worth of our everyday practices for the formation of religious beliefs. In *Perceiving God,* Alston has offered an account of the rationality of those religious beliefs that are about mystical experience and are evoked thereby. In his trilogy on warrant (1993a, 1993b, 2000), Alvin Plantinga first articulated a general theory of warranted belief, and then, within that context, offered an account of the warrant of religious beliefs; at the foundation of his account is the anthropological claim, admittedly controversial, that human beings are naturally disposed to form immediate beliefs about God. Religion does not originate as a system of explanation in competition with, or as a supplement to, science.

HEIDEGGER

I count myself among Reformed epistemologists. As such, I have my disagreements with Wittgensteinian philosophy of religion, particularly with its (apparent) assumption that religious language is both nonassertoric and, with respect to God, nonreferential. I hold that much of it is used to refer to God and to make predications about God. On this occasion, though, I have set these disagreements off to the side so as to highlight the innovation in religious epistemology that together these movements represent. That innovation, I have suggested, is especially to be located in these two themes: religious beliefs are not for the most part arrived at as explanations of one thing and another; and the religious beliefs of ordinary people are for the most part OK as they are. In conclusion, let me briefly call attention to the affinity of these movements, with respect to these two themes, to some of Heidegger's central claims concerning religion.[4]

Heidegger's corpus is vast, and the passages relevant to our topic, numerous. Here I will attend to just three central texts. Two of them originated as lectures: "Phenomenology and Theology" (1976) and "The Onto-Theo-Logical Constitution of Metaphysics" (1969). The third originated as a letter-essay: "Letter on Humanism" (1977). The discussion would naturally be enriched by bringing other Heideggerian texts into the picture, but it would not, so I judge, be altered in any fundamental way.

The role occupied for Wittgensteinian philosophy of religion by logical positivism, and for Reformed epistemology by Enlightenment evidentialism, is occupied for Heidegger by metaphysics, understood as what he calls "ontotheology." (The term was borrowed from Kant's *Critique of Pure Reason,* A632=B660.) That is to say: ontotheology is Heidegger's polemical partner. One cannot understand his thought on religion—or indeed, on anything else—without understanding what he has in mind by ontotheology, and why he is so relentlessly on the attack against it.

Begin with the question that Heidegger raises in "The Onto-Theo-Logical Constitution of Metaphysics": "How does the deity enter into philosophy?" (1969, 55). When it enters, it does so, says Heidegger, on philosophy's terms: "The deity can come into philosophy only insofar as philosophy, of its own accord and by its own nature, requires and determines that and how the deity enters into it" (56). Specifically, the deity enters philosophy on the terms and requirements of ontotheology; for ontotheology is metaphysics, and metaphysics is at the core of traditional philosophy.

And what is *ontotheology*? Starting with beings, the metaphysician raises the question of Being. The question bifurcates. The metaphysician asks, for one thing, What is Being as such, so as to account for the fact that all these different beings are *beings*? Second, he asks What is Being as such, so as to account for *there being* all these beings? The first question is the ontological question; the second, the theological question. Each asks for an account, for a *logos*; both are "logics." What unites them is that each, in its own way, is inquiring into the grounding of beings in Being. Hence: onto-theo-logic. Here's how Heidegger puts it in one passage:

> Metaphysics thinks of the Being of beings both in the ground-giving unity of what is most general, what is indifferently valid everywhere [ontology], and also in the unity of the all that accounts for the ground, that is, of the All Highest [theology]. The Being of beings is thus thought of in advance as the grounding ground. Therefore all metaphysics is at bottom, and from the ground up, what grounds, what gives account of the ground. (1969, 58)

Once again, then: How does the deity enter philosophy? The deity enters philosophy "as the first cause, the *causa prima* that corresponds to the reason-giving path back to the *ultima ratio*, the final accounting." It enters "as *causa sui*. This is the metaphysical concept of God" (60). Causa sui "is the right name for the god of philosophy" (72).

What then follows, in Heidegger's text, are these provocative words:

> Man can neither pray nor sacrifice to this god. Before the *causa sui*, man can neither fall to his knees in awe nor can he play music and dance before this god. The god-less thinking which must abandon the god of philosophy, god as *causa sui*, is thus perhaps closer to the divine God. Here this means only: god-less thinking is more open to Him than onto-theo-logic would like to admit. (1969, 72)

We have to hear that last sentence as meaning: thinking that isn't engaged in the project of trying to explain is perhaps more open to the divine God than is such thinking.

In his "Letter on Humanism," Heidegger in effect removes the "perhaps" from this passage. He's been rehearsing his contention in earlier writings that being-in-the-world is "the basic trait of the *humanitas* of *homo humanus*" (1977, 228). He observes that some of his readers have interpreted this as an affirmation of atheism; there is only *Dasein* (man) and the material world. He then refers to a passage in an earlier article of his that "no one bothers to notice" (229). The passage is this:

> Through the ontological interpretation of Dasein as being-in-the-world no decision, whether positive or negative, is made concerning a possible being toward God. It is, however, the case that through an illumination of transcendence we first achieve an *adequate concept of Dasein*, with respect to which it can now be asked how the relationship of Dasein to God is ontologically ordered. (229–30)

"Transcendence," in this passage, refers of course to *Being*—in contrast to beings. Having cited the passage, Heidegger then goes on to say this: "If we think about this remark too quickly, as is usually the case, we will declare that such a philosophy [i.e., his philosophy] does not decide either for or against the existence of God. It remains stalled in indifference. Thus it is unconcerned with the religious question. Such indifferentism ultimately falls prey to nihilism" (230).

Heidegger then proceeds to insist, in words that ooze annoyance with his misinterpreters, that though his philosophy does not settle the issue of theism one way or the other, it does put us in a position where we can rightly consider the issue. It is thus not indifferent to the issue, let alone offering the atheistic answer:

> Thinking that proceeds from the question concerning the truth of Being questions more primordially than metaphysics can. Only from the truth of Being can the essence of the holy be thought. Only from the essence of the holy is the essence of divinity to be thought. Only in the light of the essence of divinity can it be thought or said what the word "God" is to signify. Or should we not first be able to hear and understand all these words carefully if we are to be permitted as men, that is, as eksistent creatures, to experience a relation of God to man? How can man at the present stage of world history ask at all seriously and rigorously whether the god nears or withdraws, when he has above all neglected to think into the dimension in which alone that question can be asked? But this is the dimension of the holy . . . Perhaps what is distinctive about this world-epoch consists in the closure of the dimension of the hale [*des Heilen*]. Perhaps that is the sole malignancy [*Unheil*]. (1977, 230)

It would take us much too far afield to consider here what is that manner of thinking that Heidegger urges as the alternative to ontotheology, or even to explore why he thinks the ontotheological mode of thinking is so deleterious. Let us ask, instead, what we are to make of the words, "Or should we not first be able to hear and understand all these words carefully if we are to be permitted as men . . . to experience a relation of God to man." It's not entirely clear what we are to make of them. I think it's not implausible, however, to hear them as an allusion to Heidegger's thought in his lecture "Phenomenology and Theology."

Christian theology, says Heidegger—and now he most emphatically does not mean ontotheology—Christian theology "is a knowledge of that which initially makes possible something like Christianity as an event in world history" (1976, 9). And what does make something like Christianity possible as an event in world history? Faith, says Heidegger. Faith makes it possible. He goes on to explain that Christian faith does not arise from Dasein, nor "spontaneously through Dasein." Rather, faith arises "from that which is revealed in and with this mode of existence, from what is believed. For the 'Christian' faith, that which is primarily revealed to faith, and only to it, and which, as revelation, first gives rise to faith, is Christ, the crucified God . . . The crucifixion . . . and all that belongs to it is an historical event . . . One 'knows' about this fact only *by believing*" (9).

Christian theology, then, is "the science of faith," thus understood. It is "the science of faith insofar as it not only makes faith its object and is motivated by faith, but because this objectification of faith itself properly has no other purpose than to help cultivate faithfulness itself" (12).

The difference between theology, thus understood, and ontotheology is too obvious to need comment. Christian theology does not arrive at God by pressing the quest for explanation to its ultimate consequence; it arrives at God by attending to faith in the crucified God. Faith is not the property of the intelligentsia; it inhabits all those to whom God is revealed in Christ. As such, it's OK as it is. It can use the ministrations of Christian theology. But it doesn't need to be rationally grounded to make it acceptable.

NOTES

1. Where I have "presentation" in brackets in my quotation of the passage, the translator has "representation." The German is *darstellung*. There seems to me no doubt that darstellung here means *presentation,* not *re*-presentation.

2. The clear exception to the analysis of religious language generally as nonreferential, including theistically religious language, was O. K. Bouwsma (1984); Bouwsma held that the word "God" is typically used to refer to God. Whether he was also of the view that some primary religious language is assertoric in function is less clear. What he constantly emphasized was the nonassertoric function of religious language; the religious person addresses God in prayer, issues encouragement and warnings to his fellows, and so on.

3. In the analytic tradition, the most influential article mounting objections to this understanding is Wilfrid Sellars, "Empiricism and the Philosophy of Mind" (1963).

4. It was reading the opening chapter in Merold Westphal's recently published *Overcoming Onto-Theology* (2001) that first brought this affinity to mind.

WORKS CITED

Alston, William P. 1991. *Perceiving God.* Ithaca, N.Y.: Cornell University Press.

Bouwsma, O. K. 1984. *Without Proof or Evidence.* Lincoln: University of Nebraska Press.

Heidegger, Martin. 1969. "The Onto-Theo-Logical Constitution of Metaphysics." In *Identity and Difference,* trans. Joan Stambaugh. New York: Harper & Row.

———. 1976. "Phenomenology and Theology." In *The Piety of Thinking,* trans. James G. Hart and John C. Maraldo. Bloomington: Indiana University Press.

———. 1977. "Letter on Humanism." trans. Frank A. Capuzzi and J. Glenn Gray. In *Basic Writings,* ed. David Farrell Krell. New York: Harper & Row.

Locke, John. 1975. *An Essay Concerning Human Understanding.* Ed. Peter H. Nidditch. Oxford: Oxford University Press.

Malcolm, Norman. 1977. "The Groundlessness of Belief." In *Reason and Religion,* ed. Stuart C. Brown. Ithaca, N.Y.: Cornell University Press.

Phillips, D. Z. 1976. *Religion without Explanation.* Oxford: Basil Blackwell.

———. 1986. *Belief, Change, and Forms of Life.* Atlantic Highlands, N.J.: Humanities Press International.

Plantinga, Alvin. 1981. "Is Belief in God Properly Basic?" *Nous* 15: 41–51. Reprinted in *Philosophy of Religion: Selected Readings,* ed., William. L. Rowe and William. J. Wainwright. 3rd edition. New York: Oxford University Press, 1998.

———. 1993a. *Warrant: The Current Debate.* Oxford: Oxford University Press.

———. 1993b. *Warrant and Proper Function.* Oxford: Oxford University Press.

———. 2000. *Warranted Christian Belief.* Oxford: Oxford University Press.

Rhees, Rush. 1969. *Without Answers.* London: Routledge & Kegan Paul.

Schleiermacher, Friedrich. 1988. *On Religion: To Its Cultured Despisers.* Trans. Richard Crouter. Cambridge, England: Cambridge University Press.

Sellars, Wilfrid. 1963. "Empiricism and the Philosophy of Mind." In *Science, Perception, and Reality.* New York: Humanities Press.

Swinburne, Richard. 1979. *The Existence of God.* Oxford: Oxford University Press.

———. 1981. *Faith and Reason.* Oxford: Oxford University Press.

———. 1992. *Revelation: From Metaphor to Analogy.* Oxford: Oxford University Press.

———. 1996. *Is There a God?* Oxford: Oxford University Press.

Westphal, Merold. 2001. *Overcoming Onto-Theology.* New York: Fordham University Press.

Wittgenstein, Ludwig. 1966. *Lectures and Conversations on Aesthetics, Psychology and Religious Belief.* Ed. Cyril Barrett. Berkeley: University of California Press.

———. 1971. "Remarks on Frazer's 'Golden Bough.' " Trans. A. C. Miles and Rush Rhees. *Human World* 3: 28–41.

———. 1980. *Culture and Value.* Trans Peter Winch. Ed. G. H. von Wright. Chicago: University of Chicago Press.

FOR FURTHER READING

Clark, Kelly. 1990. *Return to Reason.* Grand Rapids, Mich.: Eerdmans.

Plantinga, Alvin. 1983. "Reason and Belief in God." In *Faith and Rationality,* ed. Alvin Plantinga and Nicholas Wolterstorff. Notre Dame, Ind.: University of Notre Dame Press.

Wolterstorff, Nicholas. 1983. "Can Belief in God Be Rational If It Has No Foundations?" In *Faith and Rationality,* ed. Alvin Plantinga and Nicholas Wolterstorff. Notre Dame, Ind.: University of Notre Dame Press.

———. 1995. *Divine Discourse.* Cambridge, England: Cambridge University Press.

———. 1996. *John Locke and the Ethics of Belief.* Cambridge, England: Cambridge University Press.

CHAPTER 11

....

GOD, SCIENCE, AND NATURALISM

....

PAUL DRAPER

The history of Science is not a mere record of isolated discoveries; it is
a narrative of the conflict of two contending powers, the expansive
force of the human intellect on one side, and the compression arising
from traditionary faith and human interests on the other.

—John William Draper, 1875

Scientific truth and the truth of faith do not belong to the same
dimension of meaning . . . [Thus,] science which remains science cannot
conflict with faith which remains faith.

—Paul Tillich, 1957

Science can purify religion from error and superstition; religion can
purify science from idolatry and false absolutes. Each can draw the
other into a wider world, a world in which both can flourish.

  For the truth of the matter is that the Church and the scientific
community will inevitably interact; their options do not include
isolation.

—Pope John Paul II, 1988

SCIENCE AND THEOLOGY

Warfare

How is science related to theology or, more broadly, to religion? According to one view, religion has made war on science by trying to stop or limit or control scientific progress. Further, this war is inevitable, both because the questions addressed by science and religion overlap and because scientific and religious modes of thought stand in fundamental opposition to each other. Scientists are disinterested investigators who make objective and demonstrable claims based on known facts, theologians are biased apologists who make subjective and speculative claims based on unsupported opinion. This portrayal of the relationship between science and theology reached the height of its popularity at the end of the nineteenth and the beginning of the twentieth century, in part because of two very influential books: John William Draper's *History of the Conflict between Religion and Science* (1875) and Andrew Dickson White's *History of the Warfare of Science with Theology in Christendom* (1896).

The antireligious nature of this "warfare view" is quite striking. It is hard to find anyone who holds a parallel position that is equally antiscientific. Indeed, even contemporary defenders of "creation science," who oppose much of evolutionary biology, do so not because it is science, but because it is, in their opinion, based on unscientific and unsupported antireligious assumptions such as metaphysical naturalism and thus should be rejected because it is *bad* science. Of course, not all defenders of the warfare view are opposed to all religious belief. White, for example, believed that "Religion, as seen in the recognition of 'a Power in the Universe, not ourselves, which makes for righteousness' . . . will steadily grow stronger and stronger" (1896, 1: xii). For him, the warfare is, as the title of his book suggests, between science and (traditional dogmatic) theology, not between science and religion generally (Drees 1996, 68).

The warfare view is seriously flawed, both philosophically and historically. To begin with, its characterizations of science and theology are philosophically naïve. All sorts of biases influence scientific research; scientific inferences are obviously not demonstrative; and what scientists take to be the "facts" often depends in part on the theories they hold. And while much of theology (like a significant portion of science) is highly speculative, it hardly follows that theology is completely "subjective" or based only on unsupported opinion. Indeed, it is not even clear that the methods used in theology could not in crucial respects approximate those used in science (see, for example, Schlesinger 1977; Murphy 1990). The warfare view has also been criticized for ignoring the contribution of Christianity to the rise of modern science[1] and for distorting cases of alleged conflict. The first of these two historical criticisms is itself open to challenge, but the second is supported by a great deal of evidence. For example, by portraying the Galileo affair as a conflict between scientifically established truth and religious irrationality instead of (more accurately) as a conflict between two different views about the authority of science and theology, proponents of the warfare view ignore both the fact that Galileo's arguments in favor of the Copernican theory contained serious flaws and that there was disagreement both outside and inside the Catholic Church about which theory is correct (Harris 1992, 19–20; Drees 1996, 55–63).

Another example of such distortion concerns the celebrated confrontation between Samuel Wilberforce and Thomas Henry Huxley concerning Darwin's theory. The exchange occurred in 1860 at the annual meeting of the British Society for the Advancement of Science. In the discussion following the reading of a paper by, ironically, John William Draper, Wilberforce is said to have made a joke about Huxley's descent from apes. Huxley allegedly responded that he would prefer an ape for a grandfather over a man who would introduce ridicule into a grave scientific discussion. It is remarkable that so much emphasis is placed on this trivial exchange, while the bulk of Wilberforce's half-hour-long response to Draper's paper—the part that was actually recorded—is typically ignored. No doubt it is ignored because Wilberforce, who, in addition to being a serious scientist, was bishop of Oxford, is portrayed by proponents of the warfare view (e.g., White 1896, 1: 70–71) as the representative of "religion," clinging to a biblical doctrine proven false by science. But nothing could be further from the truth. In fact, Wilberforce explicitly asserted that one's scientific positions should be based on empirical evidence, not scripture. And the bulk of what he said in the discussion following Draper's paper consisted of serious scientific objections to Darwin's theory, objections that can now be answered, but which at the time cast serious doubt on the theory's viability. In fact, Darwin himself immediately began experimental work in an effort to answer those objections. Furthermore, not only is the Wilberforce legend historically inaccurate, but the broader characterization of the Victorian dispute over Darwin's theory as a battle between scientific truth and theological error is at best highly misleading, inasmuch as the evidence for Darwin's theory at that time was far from overwhelming, his most serious opponents were part of the scientific establishment of his day, and many of his defenders were clergy (Midgley 1985, 10–12).

Isolation

A second position, extremely popular among theologians and scientists for much of the twentieth century, conceives of the proper (if not actual) relationship of science to religion as one of isolation. According to this view, science and religion

GOD, SCIENCE, AND NATURALISM   275

never conflict *so long as each is properly conducted* (Midgley 1985, 13). Of course,
any conception of science and religion that effectively makes conflict impossible
will in all likelihood preclude fruitful interaction as well, hence the appropriateness
of the term "isolation" as a name for this view.

Arguments in support of this view are diverse, but they all involve an attempt
to carve out separate domains for science and religion within which each has
authority. For example, according to the well-known geneticist Theodosius Dobzhansky, "Science and religion deal with different aspects of existence. If one dares
to overschematize for the sake of clarity, one may say that these are the aspect of
fact and the aspect of meaning" (1971, 96). Of course, this raises the question of
the meaning of "meaning." Mary Midgley, interpreting Dobzhansky, associates it
with the way facts connect to form "world pictures" (1985, 13–14). Stephen Jay
Gould, an advocate of the isolation view, narrows Dobzhansky's "aspect of fact"
to facts about "the empirical constitution of the universe" and includes "ethical
values" in the domain of religion (2001, 500). Others who would want to explicitly
allow for theological *facts* recognize the expertise of scientists on factual questions
concerning the natural world while deferring to theologians on factual questions
concerning God or the supernatural. None of these suggestions, however, successfully drives an absolute wedge between science and theology. World pictures
will inevitably influence what one takes the facts to be. Values, even if they cannot
simply be "read off" nature, nevertheless depend on natural facts. And by definition a supernatural and theistic God can and does affect nature.

This is not to say that no conception of religion or science effectively isolates
the two activities. For example, if Paul Tillich is right that God is not a supreme
being or any other kind of being (and so is not limited by the condition of
existence!) but rather is being-itself, then he may also be right that science can
neither confirm nor disconfirm "the truth of faith" because "scientific truth and
the truth of faith do not belong to the same dimension of meaning" (1957, 81).
But others will insist that Tillich distorts religion or that he takes the idea of God's
transcendence to an absurd extreme. Another way to isolate both science and
religion is to defend an extreme antirealist position about science. Most scientists
and many others will, however, reject such a portrayal of science, and most religious believers will see a wolf in sheep's clothing if such a portrayal implies an
equally extreme antirealist position about theology. (For another conception of
religion that could be used to support isolationism, see "Wittgensteinianism:
Logic, Reality, and God" in this volume.)

Symbiosis

An increasingly popular position in recent years is the view that mutually beneficial interaction between science and religion is possible. Attempts have been

made to establish a dialogue between science and theology, or, more ambitiously, to integrate the two (Barbour 1990, 16–30). Such attempts include (a) new strategies in natural theology, such as design arguments based on anthropic coincidences; (b) theologies of nature, which reinterpret traditional theological doctrines making use of the latest information about nature provided by science (e.g., Polkinghorne 1989; Peacocke 1993); (c) process theology, which attempts a synthesis of science and religion by reinterpreting both in terms of a broad metaphysical system (e.g., Hartshorne 1967); and (d) naturalistic religion, which attempts to find a place for religion within a naturalistic metaphysics based on science (e.g., Drees 1996).

Conflict

Though such efforts are worthwhile, they are often accompanied by an almost naïve optimism. Talk of consonance is commonplace, of conflict (except to dismiss it) quite rare. It seems that, in (correctly) rejecting the warfare view, many contemporary writers on science and religion assume that real conflict is impossible or at least that it never occurs. There is a tendency to equate "conflict" with "logical incompatibility" and for that reason not to take it seriously. (It is no accident, for example, that the only views Ian Barbour [1990, 4–10] classifies under "conflict" are scientific materialism and biblical literalism.) But logical incompatibility is not the only nor is it the most likely form that conflict can take. The results of science might provide evidence against a theological claim even if they are compatible with it. Similarly, no one would want to restrict the use of science in natural theology to cases in which science *entails* the truth of some religious doctrine. The results of science might provide evidence for a theological claim even if they are compatible with its falsity. The key point here is that, once one gives up the safety of total isolation, one cannot assume that all interaction will be harmonious. Accordingly, one should not hide the very real possibility of conflict by arbitrarily excluding it from one's classification schemes or by including it but then interpreting it so narrowly that almost no one will believe it occurs.

Chapter 5 in this volume on cosmological and design arguments addresses some of the areas in which science is believed to support theistic religions. This chapter investigates areas of potential conflict. The goal is to show that science and metaphysical naturalism, though not inseparable, may be sufficiently close to cause trouble in the marriage of theistic supernaturalism to science, and such trouble may support a decision to divorce even if it does not logically require it. One should be warned, however, that the road to accomplishing this goal is long and winding. To complete the journey, the traveler must confront a number of very thorny issues in science and religion, issues like the problem of divine action and the foundations of methodological naturalism. To avoid getting lost on the way, some preliminary remarks about terminology are needed.

TERMINOLOGY

Let us call the domain of the natural sciences—a domain that includes stars and planets, living beings and nonliving objects, stable entities—and ephemeral events, physical objects and embodied mental and cultural entities—the natural world.

—Willem B. Drees, 1996

Nature and the Supernatural

We can define the supernatural in terms of the natural as follows:

x is supernatural =df. x is not a part of nature and x can affect nature.[2]

This definition is adequate, however, only if a tolerably clear definition of "nature" can be provided. It is not easy to find such a definition. "Nature" or "the natural world" is sometimes defined circularly as "the domain of the natural sciences." But while the circularity of this definition can be eliminated by replacing "natural sciences" with something like "biology, chemistry, and physics," the definition remains obscure, in part because it is far from clear what exactly the domains of those sciences are. Indeed, some entities, like conscious states and political systems, are thought by many to be a part of nature though not the proper object of study of any of the natural sciences.

Let us start by assuming that many of the entities currently studied by physicists and chemists are real, and let us call these entities "physical" entities. Notice that this is a very narrow, technical sense of "physical," one that separates the physical from the biological, the mental, the political, the social, the religious, the economic, and so on. If we assume that whatever else nature includes, it includes atoms, molecules, gravitational fields, and any other entities that are physical in this narrow sense, then the problem of how to define "nature" boils down to the problem of how an entity that is not physical must be related to physical entities in order to count as natural. Perhaps this problem can be solved by noting that many of the nonphysical entities that we would want to count as natural (e.g., bacteria) are causally reducible to physical entities in the sense that their causal powers are *entirely* explainable in terms of the causal powers of those entities. This suggests that an entity can be classified as natural just in case it is a physical entity or is causally reducible to physical entities.

Philosophers like Nancey Murphy (1998, 128–31), however, will regard this as overly restrictive on the grounds that some entities are part of nature by virtue of being ontologically reducible to physical entities even though they are not causally reducible to those entities. To say that a complex system is ontologically reducible to lower-level entities is to say that it is nothing but a collection of those entities organized in a certain way. No new "metaphysical ingredients" such as a substantial soul or an élan vital need to be added to the lower-level entities to produce the higher-level entity. To accept ontological reductionism without also accepting causal reductionism is, not surprisingly, highly controversial. For it commits one to believing in "downward" or "top-down" or "whole-part" causation, where these terms are taken to imply that the system or "whole" has, because of the way its parts are organized, causal powers that cannot be explained by the causal interactions of its parts with each other or with the environment. And not everyone will accept that the organization of a system's parts can do that much metaphysical work (e.g., Searle 1992, 111–12).

Suppose, however, there is such a thing as top-down causation. Perhaps, then, we should classify as natural any entity that is physical or is ontologically reducible to physical entities. Unfortunately, not everyone will accept this definition either, because, just as ontological reducibility may not entail causal reducibility, causal reducibility may not entail ontological reducibility. Thus, there may be entities (e.g., conscious states, perhaps) that are natural by virtue of being causally reducible to the entities studied by the physical sciences even though they are not composed of those entities. Again, it is far from clear that there really are such entities, but, like the issue of top-down causation, this is not an issue that can be resolved here. Thus, to remain neutral on these issues, we can define "nature" or "the natural world" as follows:

> Nature =df. the spatiotemporal universe of physical entities together with any entities that are ontologically or causally reducible to those entities.

Of course, not everyone (e.g., epiphenomenalists) will agree with this definition either, but even if it needs refinement,[3] it does suffice to sharpen the distinction between the natural and the supernatural, and thus should be adequate for the purposes of this chapter.

Notice that, on this definition, Cartesian minds would be not only nonnatural since they are neither ontologically nor causally reducible to anything physical, but also supernatural since they can by definition affect nature. This implication is not, however, a defect in the definition. Rather, it simply highlights the truly radical nature of Cartesian dualism and its deep connection to a whole host of venerable if no longer tenable ideas, such as the idea that we human beings have a "rational nature" distinct from our "animal nature" and that this rational nature separates us (and our "artificial" contrivances) from the natural world of "beasts" and bee hives and even our own bodies. Notice also that various evolutionary philosophies, by appealing to entities like an élan vital or psychic energy, which seem to be neither causally nor ontologically reducible to the entities studied by the physical sciences, count as supernaturalistic for that reason, even though the supernatural here in some sense emerges from the natural. (For a brief discussion of some of these evolutionary philosophies, see McMullin 1985, 38–43.) Finally, notice that this definition assumes there is only one spatiotemporal universe. If there is more than one, then, although one could define the natural world as the entire collection of such universes, it would be better to adopt the position that there is more than one natural world. In this way, metaphysical claims about nature or *the* natural world could be restated as claims about *our* natural world and so would have a better chance of being justified.

Varieties of Naturalism

If to be natural is to be a part of nature as defined above, then what is naturalism? Here, of course, there is more than one answer because one can be naturalistic methodologically or metaphysically or epistemologically. It is often claimed by those who embrace both science as currently practiced and some form of supernaturalistic religion that science is naturalistic methodologically but not metaphysically. "Methodological naturalism" is defined as follows:

> Methodological naturalism =df. Scientists should not appeal to supernatural entities when they explain natural phenomena.

Notice that one can be a methodological naturalist on this definition even if one believes that it is permissible for scientific explanations to refer to nonnatural entities. One advantage of this is that some of the abstract entities (e.g., numbers) to which scientific explanations routinely appeal may very well be nonnatural.

"Metaphysical naturalism" is defined as follows:

> Metaphysical naturalism =df. Supernatural entities do not exist.

Notice that, on this definition, one can be a metaphysical naturalist without rejecting the reality of nonnatural entities. This is important, because, while our knowledge of nature may provide reason to believe that nothing is supernatural, it provides little basis for the further conclusion that nature is all there is. Notice also that one can be a metaphysical naturalist without being a materialist or even a physicalist about the natural world. (This is not to deny, however, that physicalism is very likely given metaphysical naturalism.) Finally, notice that metaphysical naturalists can accept the position of philosophers like Thomas Nagel (1986, 25–27) and John Searle (1992, ch. 5) that consciousness is irreducibly subjective, even if, contrary to what Searle (116–24) contends, this forces them to reject the position that a unified scientific understanding of nature is possible.

Both metaphysical and methodological naturalism must be distinguished from the various theses to which philosophers sometimes apply the label "epistemological naturalism" or, more pejoratively, "scientism," such as the view that all knowledge is scientific knowledge; the view that, although nonscientific knowledge is possible, it has a lower epistemic status than scientific knowledge; and the view that knowledge is attainable only by methods that at least approximate those used in the (physical) sciences.

GOD'S ACTION IN THE WORLD

The way of understanding miracle that appeals to breaks in the natural order and to supernatural interventions belongs to the mythological outlook and cannot commend itself in a post-mythological climate of thought.

—John Macquarrie, 1977

Theism versus Deism

Both theism and deism, as traditionally understood, posit the existence of a supernatural God. But while they agree that God is the creator of nature, they differ concerning the degree to which God is active in nature:

Theistic supernaturalism (theism) =df. There exists a supernatural person who (timelessly or temporally) creates and sustains the natural world, acts in it, and is omnipotent, omniscient, and morally perfect.

Deistic supernaturalism (deism) =df. There exists a supernatural person who created the natural world but does not act in it.

To claim that God acts "in the natural world" is to claim that, *in addition to creating and/or sustaining the natural world*, God intentionally brings about particular natural effects involving her creatures or other parts of nature (Alston 1985, 197). For example, God is traditionally thought to provide for her creatures and, in the case of human beings, to speak to them, forgive them, punish them, guide them, and answer their prayers.

Divine acts could be either direct or indirect. A direct divine act is one in which God acts "outside of the ordinary course of nature" in the sense that he brings about a certain effect without using natural causes to do so. An indirect divine act is one in which God uses natural causes to bring about an effect. Of course, there cannot be indirect acts without direct ones. But God might limit her direct action to an initial creative act, in which case all of her acts *in the natural world* would be indirect. Thus, four sorts of personal creators are conceivable: (1) ones that do not act in the natural world, either directly or indirectly; (2) ones that act indirectly in the world but not directly; (3) ones that act directly in the world but not indirectly; and (4) ones that act both directly and indirectly in the world.

Of these four possibilities, the second and fourth seem to be the most plausible. For to believe in the third sort of creator requires one either to reject the reality of natural causes or to somehow make sense of the idea of a God who creates natural causes but never uses them to bring about any effect. And concerning the first possibility, it would be quite a challenge for a being who creates the world never to act in it at all. For if even a single effect of that being's initial creative act is intended by that being (and occurs in the circumstances and for the reasons envisioned by that being), then that being has acted indirectly in the world by virtue of intentionally bringing about that effect. Thus, a thoroughly deistic creator would have to be so limited in knowledge or goodness or rationality (or else the universe he creates would have to be so thoroughly indeterministic) that every single consequence of his act of creation would be either unforeseen or foreseen but unintended.

It is often claimed that deism fits better with a scientific view of the world than theism because it does not require God to act in the world. This position is defended on the grounds that, in order to act in the world, God would have to violate the laws of nature. Thus, because the natural sciences have established that the nomic regularities we call the laws of nature operate, not just here and now, but everywhere and always, it follows that the claim that God acts in the world, though not absolutely ruled out by science since it is possible that violations of laws of nature occur undetected by science, is nevertheless strongly disconfirmed. The next two sections show that this argument is based on at least two highly questionable assumptions. The first is that, in order to act in the world, God would have to do so directly. And the second is that, in order to act directly in the world, God would have to violate the laws of nature.

Indirect Divine Acts

It is widely believed (e.g. Polkinghorne 1989, 1–2; Clayton 1997, 206) that the mechanical world of pre–twentieth-century science is not an appropriate world for a theistic God to create, not just because it excludes the possibility of free will, but also because divine action in such a world would be impossible or at least implausible. William Alston (1985, 200–201) argues, however, that exactly the opposite is true. Everything in a mechanical world that results from God's initial creative act would be an indirect act of God in the world, so long as God intends to bring about all that he brings about, which is at least possible assuming that God is omniscient and that a mechanical world is completely deterministic. For example, if God creates a deterministic universe, intending that this initial creative act result in a thirsty rabbit finding water 12 billion years later, then it is correct to say that God quenches that rabbit's thirst (even though it is also correct to say that the water quenches that rabbit's thirst). The difficult question, then, is not how a theistic God could act in a mechanical world, but how a deistic God could fail to do so.

Of course, we may not live in a completely deterministic world. But surely it is sufficiently deterministic to allow for a great deal of indirect divine action, even if some events in the world, such as human choices that are free in the libertarian sense, are not acts of God. Thus, when a theist claims, for example, that God provides for his creatures or even speaks to, guides, or punishes them, this need not imply that God acts directly in nature. Therefore, divine action in the world does not entail the violation of laws of nature.

Direct Divine Acts

One might object, however, that a God who acts indirectly but who, with the exception of an initial act of creation, never acts directly is a quasi-deistic God, not the God of any robust theistic religion. For the God of Judaism, Christianity, and Islam is a God of miracles and answered prayer, of special rather than merely general providence and revelation, and divine activity of this sort is possible only if God bypasses the natural order and brings about an effect simply by willing that it be so. Thus, it is this sort of direct divine activity that involves the violation of laws of nature and so brings theistic religions into conflict with a scientific understanding of the world. But even if direct divine action is essential to theistic religions (which is by no means obvious), the assumption that it would *violate* established laws of nature—that its occurrence would entail that a nomic regularity established by science does not actually hold—has been challenged. Some of the most popular of these challenges appeal to quantum mechanics (e.g., Pollard 1958) or chaos theory (e.g., Polkinghorne 1989, 26–35) or both (e.g., Murphy 1995) in an attempt to find room for a law-abiding God to be actively and directly involved in the world.

A much more fundamental challenge, however, a challenge that, if successful, makes such attempts to exploit the "openness" of post–nineteenth-century science unnecessary, is made by C. S. Lewis (1947) and more recently by Alston (1985, 209–10). Alston presents the challenge as follows. He points out that whether God's direct action in the world is a violation of the laws of nature depends on the form those laws take. If those laws specify *unqualified* sufficient conditions, then direct divine action will involve a violation. If, on the other hand, they specify only what will (or must) occur in the absence of relevant conditions not specified in the law, then direct divine action will not involve a violation. Laws that specify what will happen in a closed system are not violated if the system turns out not to be closed. Alston's next premise is that, in fact, we never are justified in accepting laws of the first sort. He concludes that the only laws supported by science are of the second sort and hence that direct divine acts need not violate any laws of nature supported by science.

Divine Action and Methodological Naturalism

Even if Alston is correct, however, that does not settle the question of whether or not a belief in divine action conflicts with a belief in methodological naturalism. Indeed, it would seem that a scientist who believes in direct divine action in the world must also believe that some natural phenomena cannot be correctly explained without appealing to supernatural entities. And even a scientist who believes that God's actions in the world are all indirect must believe that a correct *ultimate* explanation of natural phenomena is impossible without appeal to supernatural entities. So there would seem to be considerable tension between a belief in divine action and a belief in methodological naturalism, even if there is no tension between divine action and the laws of nature.

Let us first examine the apparent tension between methodological naturalism and the belief that God acts directly in creating the natural world, but never acts directly in that world. A belief that God is the ultimate cause of the universe will come into conflict with methodological naturalism only when scientists begin to offer ultimate naturalistic explanations of nature as a whole. But despite the pretensions of some theoretical physicists, this is hardly imminent. Still, the belief in a divine creator, even one who never acts directly in the world, is not scientifically neutral (Plantinga 1991, 82–84). On the assumption that God is the ultimate cause of nature, some scientific explanations that would be plausible on metaphysical naturalism are implausible and some that would be implausible are plausible. For example, no one who believes that God exists and is objectively morally perfect will accept attempts by sociobiologists like E. O. Wilson (1998, ch. 11) to provide reductive naturalistic explanations of religion or morality. Nor will the typical theist be sympathetic to theories in neuroscience that deny the existence of a single subject of consciousness in order to account for the bizarre results of various experiments on people with severed corpora callosa. Or consider the reaction of scientists to models of the big bang theory according to which the universe is both temporally finite and bounded. Scientists who are metaphysical naturalists have worked very hard to find alternatives, in some cases clinging to a particular alternative like steady state theory far longer than was warranted by the evidence.

A more interesting though imaginary example concerns origin of life research. Suppose a scientist were able to create conditions in the laboratory that result in the formation of a living cell, but while it is physically possible for these conditions to occur naturally, it is so unlikely that most scientists deny that the process in question produced the first life on earth. A theist, however, might reject the probability judgment in question on the grounds that even a God who never acts directly in the world could have performed a direct act of creation that ensured from the outset that the conditions in question would occur on earth at the right time. Thus, scientists who believe in God may quite understandably accept the explanation in question, while those who are metaphysical naturalists may quite understandably reject it.

Do these examples prove that methodological naturalism is incompatible with belief in a God who creates nature but acts only indirectly in it? That depends on how, exactly, one interprets methodological naturalism. For the appeal to supernatural entities (or to metaphysical naturalism) occurs in these examples, not in the scientific explanations themselves, but rather in their evaluation or in a meta-explanation of why a certain scientific explanation is or is not considered plausible. Thus, as long as methodological naturalism is interpreted narrowly, we need not conclude that indirect divine action conflicts with methodological naturalism.

But what about direct divine action in the world? If such action is theologically necessary, then must we conclude that a commitment to theism precludes a commitment to methodological naturalism, even interpreted narrowly? The answer to this question depends on how frequently God is thought to act directly in nature. We saw earlier that most (indeed, maybe even all) of the ways God is thought to act in the world can be accounted for by indirect divine action. Thus, a belief in the very rare occurrence of direct divine acts (e.g., for the purposes of authenticating a divine messenger) would not commit a scientist to looking for supernaturalistic explanations of natural events like the origin of life, especially if Alston is right that direct divine action in nature need not violate any laws of nature supported by science.

Many theists will want to conclude, then, that there is no real conflict between methodological naturalism and theistic religions, including those religions whose doctrines imply (a limited amount of) direct divine activity in nature. Some philosophers and theologians, however, want to go beyond this conclusion. They hold that theistic supernaturalism actually provides strong positive support for methodological naturalism. On this view, theistic science and naturalistic science are methodologically equivalent. An examination of some of the arguments offered for this position is undertaken next.

GOD'S POWER, WISDOM, AND GOODNESS

> Sir Isaac Newton, and his followers, also have a very odd opinion concerning the work of God. According to their doctrine, God Almighty wants to wind up his watch from time to time: otherwise it would cease to move. He had not, it seems, sufficient foresight to make it a perpetual motion. Nay, the machine of God's making, is so imperfect, according to these gentlemen; that he is obliged to clean it now and then by an extraordinary concourse and even to mend it, as a clockmaker mends his work; who must consequently be so much the more unskilled a workman, as he is more often obliged to mend his work and set it right. According to my opinion, the same force and vigor remains always in the world, and only passes from one part of matter to another, agreeably to the laws of nature, and the beautiful pre-established order. And I hold, that when God works miracles, he does not do it in order to supply the wants of nature, but those of grace. Whoever thinks otherwise must needs have a very mean notion of the wisdom and power of God.
>
> —Leibniz, 1715, in Leibniz and Clarke 1956

Divine Competence

In the fourth section of Leibniz's first letter to Samuel Clarke, Leibniz responds to Newton's view that God occasionally acts directly in nature to keep the planets in their proper orbits. He dismisses this view because it implies, he thinks, that God is an incompetent creator—certainly not the omnipotent and omniscient creator of traditional theism. If Leibniz is right about this, then it seems to follow that a theistic God would produce a world in which the workings of nature can be explained naturalistically and hence that theism provides a justification for methodological naturalism (at least within the natural sciences). Remarkably, variations of this argument remain very popular today. It is, however, based on two questionable assumptions. The first is that an omnipotent and omniscient God could accomplish her purposes without acting directly in nature. The second is that a perfectly good God would prefer to accomplish her purposes without acting directly in nature.

Like the view that God could accomplish his purposes without allowing evil in the world, the first assumption—that God could accomplish his purposes without acting directly in nature—does not follow deductively from the view that God is omnipotent and omniscient. For not even an omnipotent being can do what is logically impossible and not even an omniscient being can know what it is logically impossible to know. Thus, for example, it might be the case both that God has good reason to create an indeterministic world and that God necessarily lacks knowledge of conditionals like "If this indeterministic universe were to be created, then these undetermined events would occur." If so, then God might very well need to engage in the sort of divine tinkering that Leibniz found so unimaginable.

Leibniz's second assumption—that a perfectly good God would prefer not to act in the world if at all possible—is even less compelling than the first. Leibniz's (frequently echoed) analogy to human clockmakers is particularly weak. A clockmaker's skill may be judged by how often his clocks need repair because it can be assumed that the clockmaker does not want to spend valuable time and effort repairing his clocks. But an omnipotent and omniscient clockmaker has no such concerns. Such a being would not be forced to forgo some other valuable project in order to act directly in nature (Alston 1985, 219, n. 14). One might object that God would prefer to create a "maintenance-free" universe simply because a universe in which God must act directly to achieve his goals is to that extent flawed or at least less perfect, no matter how well it serves God's purposes. But this objection takes the popular Enlightenment comparison of nature to a machine way too seriously. Surely the value of a theistic universe will not depend on its mechanical elegance. And even if one takes such categories of value seriously, they do not properly apply here because (unlike some of its parts) the evolving universe described by contemporary science is nothing like a machine.

Divine Faithfulness

Can Leibniz's argument be repaired? Is there any good reason to believe that a theistic God would prefer not to act directly in nature? Several philosophers and theologians appeal to God's "faithfulness" (or "reliability" or "consistency"; e.g., Polkinghorne 1989, 6; Peacocke 1993, 142) in an effort to establish that God would never "intervene" in nature. They claim that a morally perfect and hence faithful God would not establish laws of nature and then turn around and break (or suspend) them. But it is hard to see why intervention of the sort in question strikes so many thinkers as abhorrent. After all, the laws of nature do not tell us how anything or anyone *ought* to behave.

Perhaps the following argument is intended. Because of the nomic regularities in nature, human beings form reasonable expectations about the future. Thus, for those of us who believe in a God who has the power to violate those regularities, forming those expectations amounts to trusting God not to exercise that power. Hence, if God does violate them, he also violates our trust. Therefore, because the God of theism is morally perfect, it follows that the God of theism would not violate the laws of nature. This argument is far from persuasive. God's acting in an unexpected way would hardly constitute a violation of our trust in her in the absence of any implicit or explicit agreement on her part to behave in a completely predictable way. Of course, if God acted directly in nature so frequently that what is probable by our inductive standards usually turned out to be false, then, assuming that God is responsible to some extent for those standards, he could justly be accused of a reprehensible sort of unreliability. But that would require far more direct divine activity than is theologically necessary. Further, one would hope that God would faithfully and consistently pursue the good of her creatures, even if this involves the occasional direct act in nature and even if this involves making the world slightly less predictable. Therefore, it is hard to see what reason there is to believe that God's acting directly and providentially in nature does anything but faithfully fulfill a promise to do what is best for his creatures. Of course, we know that God does not in fact intervene to prevent horrific evils like the Nazi Holocaust. But that would be relevant only if we knew that, if God would intervene in any case, then she would intervene in those cases. And surely that is not something human beings can know.

Divine Generosity

Howard Van Till (1999) defends something like Leibniz's position by appealing to God's generosity instead of to her faithfulness. The central idea here is that creation is a gift from God, an act of generosity. In creating, God gives the universe and its contents being, a being partly defined by capabilities to act in various ways. These capabilities include formational ones; abilities to actualize various physical structures like molecules, stars, galaxies, and life forms (to mention a few). The greater the number of capabilities God bestows on the universe and its contents, the more generous his gift is. Thus, any direct divine act in the formational history of the universe (e.g., directly bringing into existence the first living organism on earth) would imply a less capable creation and hence less generosity on God's part. Therefore, because God is morally perfect, one would expect that she never acts directly in the formational history of the universe, that all of the causes in that history (except, of course, the ultimate cause) are natural ones, and hence that methodological naturalism, at least in the scientific investigation of that history, is justified (170–71).

But God cannot be generous to the universe unless God can benefit the universe. Thus, Van Till's argument presupposes that possessing formational capabilities actually benefits the universe. The universe, however, is not conscious. Thus (*pace* deep ecologists), the claim that it can literally be benefited (or harmed) is highly dubious at best. And even if nonconscious things can be benefited, the specific claim that possessing fully robust formational capabilities benefits the universe more than being directly cared for by God is entirely unsupported. So this attempt to provide a theological reason for denying direct divine action in the formational history of the universe is at best incomplete.[4]

THE NATURE OF SCIENCE

> Miracles lie outside of science, which by definition deals only with the natural, the repeatable, that which is governed by law.
>
> —Michael Ruse, 1982

> But, of course, methodological naturalism does not restrict our study of nature; it just lays down which sort of study qualifies as scientific. If someone wants to pursue another approach to nature—and there are many others—the methodological naturalist has no reason to object. Scientists have to proceed in this way; the methodology of natural science gives no purchase on the claim that a particular event or type of event is to be explained by invoking God's creative action directly.
>
> —Ernan McMullin, 1991

Defining "Science"

According to Michael Ruse (1982, 322), science by definition deals only with the natural, which implies that no explanation that makes reference to the supernatural is scientific. But even if Ruse is right about this, it does not follow that methodological naturalism is true. For the issue here is not a verbal one: the issue is not how the word "science" is properly used (Plantinga 1997, 146). Rather, the issue is whether or not people who investigate the causes of natural events should look only for naturalistic causes or also for supernaturalistic ones. Whether one interprets this issue as the question of whether scientists should broaden their *scientific* investigations or as the question of whether scientists should broaden their investigations beyond the boundaries of science will depend, of course, on the definition of "science." But the answer to the question will not depend on that definition. Notice, however, that attempts to demarcate science from other human activities or scientific explanation from other sorts of explanation need not involve any appeal to the definition of "science." So a consideration of such attempts must come next.

Demarcationist Dreams

Attempts to solve the "demarcation problem" and to use the solution to defend methodological naturalism frequently focus on method. Science is said to differ from other human activities because it employs a certain method, a method that is superior to the methods of other disciplines and that accounts for the great success of science. Further, this method cannot be applied to supernatural entities. Why not? Because supernatural entities are unobservable or because claims about them cannot be falsified or because supernaturalistic hypotheses cannot be tested by experiment—the exact reason given depends on how scientific method is characterized. A more direct demarcationist approach to justifying methodological naturalism focuses on scientific explanation rather than on science in general. All scientific explanations, it is claimed, explain natural events in terms of natural laws, and by definition supernatural entities are not governed by those laws. Thus, scientific explanations cannot properly make reference to supernatural entities (see, e.g., Pennock 1999, 195).

Demarcationist proposals have not fared well under close scrutiny (see Meyer 1994; Lauden 1996; Quinn 1996), which is not surprising since science is a human invention whose goals are determined by its participants and whose methods must ultimately be justified by reference to those goals, methods being, after all, means of achieving one's goals (O'Connor 1997, 25). Further, because science has more than one goal, it would be surprising if it had only a single method. Consider, for example, the distinction between nomological or inductive science and historical science. The main goal of the former is to determine how nature normally operates or functions: to discover, classify, or explain unchanging laws or properties of nature. The main goals of the latter are to reconstruct sequences of historical events and to explain particular features of nature by reference to the past (Meyer 1994, 89–90; Sober 2000, 14–18).[5] Not surprisingly, the methods used to achieve the goals of nomological science can be very different from those used to achieve the goals of historical science. On the one hand, scientists engaged in nomological science formulate laws, models, and other interesting if-then generalizations, often testing them by experiment and prediction, and making inductive generalizations based on observable data. In historical science, on the other hand, not all causal explanations fit the covering law model (Meyer 1994, 78), and many hypotheses about the past cannot be falsified and cannot be tested by prediction or experiment. Instead, they are judged on the basis of their simplicity, their fit with general background knowledge about the world, and their ability to explain specific known facts. What all this shows is that methodological naturalism cannot be adequately defended by describing something called *the* scientific method and then arguing that it cannot be applied to the supernatural. For more likely than not, the method described will be characteristic of nomological science, while appeals to the supernatural would naturally be used to answer historical questions.

More generally, it is unlikely that the demarcation problem has a solution, in which case demarcationist justifications of methodological naturalism are doomed to failure. This does not, however, entail that no justification of methodological naturalism can be based on the goals of science. For, as Robert C. O'Connor (1997, 25) has pointed out, the claim that science is a human invention does not imply that its goals are arbitrary or purely conventional. Certain goals of science are (at least on a realist construal of science) both enduring and of great importance (and justified retrospectively by the fact that they have to some extent been achieved). Understanding nature, for instance, is such a goal. Because these goals are shared by other disciplines, they cannot be used to demarcate science from all other human activities. But if restricting one's explanations to the natural helps scientists to achieve those goals, then that provides at least a prima facie justification for such a restriction.

THE GOALS OF SCIENCE

Methodological Naturalism is not so much irreligious as irrational. Hyperbole aside, strict naturalism functions . . . to close off legitimate lines of inquiry and avenues of potential explanation.

—Stephen Meyer, 1994

Permitting direct reference to divine agency in natural science severely undermines the overall quest for truth. Thus, if there is a distinctively

"Christian way of doing science," it does not come by repudiating MN [methodological naturalism].

—Robert C. O'Connor, 1997

Truth

One goal of science is to understand nature, that is, to find true explanations of natural phenomena. At first glance, this seems to provide the opponents of methodological naturalism with their strongest argument. For if a scientist takes theistic supernaturalism seriously rather than simply assuming the truth of metaphysical naturalism, then why should that scientist look only for naturalistic explanations of natural phenomena? Why not look for true explanations, whatever those might be? If God has acted directly in nature to produce, for example, the first life on earth, then to commit science to methodological naturalism is to preclude the possibility of scientists finding the truth. Moreover, scientists often appeal to factors outside of a system to account for properties of the system that they have good reason to believe cannot be explained on the assumption that the system is closed. Yet, according to methodological naturalism, such an appeal is prohibited if the system in question is nature as a whole. And it is hard to see what could justify treating this system differently other than an assumption that metaphysical naturalism is true—that there is nothing outside of nature that can affect it.

Despite the apparent strength of considerations like these, some philosophers have argued for the opposite position. For example, O'Connor (1997, 26–27) claims that methodological naturalism promotes the quest for truth for two reasons. First, by making appeals to the supernatural off-limits, it forces scientists to persist in their search for naturalistic explanations, even when the prospects for such explanations seem very dim. And such persistence has in the past borne fruit. In short, methodological naturalism is valuable because it promotes the goal of understanding reality *as far as possible in natural terms.* Second, methodological naturalism enables theologians and others offering nonnatural accounts of natural phenomena to be sure that any such account is forced to face its strongest competitor. Underlying these two reasons is the idea that a division of labor between science and theology is desirable. Both disciplines attempt to understand natural events, but science seeks natural explanations, while theology pursues supernatural explanations. In this way, our chances of discovering the truth are, according to O'Connor, maximized. A third reason for believing that methodological naturalism promotes the goal of understanding nature is offered by Alvin Plantinga (1997, 150–52), an opponent of methodological naturalism. Following Duhem, he suggests that science makes progress because of its universality—because scientists manage to cooperate. But such universality is possible only if scientists avoid employing or presupposing in their theories metaphysical claims that are not shared by other scientists.

None of these three reasons is conclusive. To begin with, surely the most they show is that appeals to the supernatural should be a last resort, or that some science but not necessarily all science should be constrained by methodological naturalism (Plantinga 1997, 152). Either way, sufficient cooperation among scientists would take place and sufficient effort would be made to find naturalistic explanations. Thus, the worry that, without an absolute prohibition on appeals to the supernatural in scientific explanations, proponents of supernaturalistic explanations would not confront their strongest competitors is unrealistic. It is also unrealistic to claim, as O'Connor does (compare McMullin 1991, 57–58), that there is nothing wrong with restricting science to the natural because others can pursue supernaturalist theories. Such a division of labor lowers the chances of anyone having the interdisciplinary expertise that would be necessary to pursue certain lines of inquiry. For example, it is unlikely that theologians without extensive training in science would be able to assess the promise of any serious supernaturalistic explanation of the origin of life. For presumably, such an explanation would be a great deal more complicated than "God made it so," and evaluating any such explanation, no matter how simple, will require the ability to evaluate the best competing naturalistic explanations.

Justification

Perhaps the most powerful argument for methodological naturalism based on the goals of science proceeds as follows. One of the central goals of all scientists is to justify their claims in such a way that most reasonable persons with sufficient expertise will accept them. But it is impossible to justify beliefs about supernatural entities in this way: no public evidence can establish their (probable) truth or falsity. Thus, even though supernaturalistic explanations might be true (and might even be justified for particular individuals), scientists should not give them, for there is nothing scientists could do to prove to other members of the scientific community that one such explanation should be accepted and another rejected.

Clearly, the key premise of this argument is that the intersubjective justification of a belief about supernatural entities is impossible. At least two reasons might be offered in support of this premise. The first is that such a belief cannot be tested by evidence; that is, it can neither be confirmed nor be disconfirmed either by new information or by what we already know (cf. Pennock 1998, 206; Sober 2000, 46–57). Let us call this the "testability problem." Notice that a very broad sense of the verb "to test" is intended here. It includes, of course, testing by experiment, but it also includes the sort of testing a historian might do: carefully comparing the ability of some hypothesis to explain various known facts to the ability of serious alternative hypotheses to explain those facts. A second reason for doubting that supernaturalistic hypotheses can be intersubjectively justified is that their probability prior to testing cannot be assessed. In other words, it is impossible to determine their (initial) degree of plausibility or implausibility, and so impossible to make a rational decision about which of them to test and impossible to determine the significance of any testing that is done. Let us call this the "plausibility problem." To refute this new argument for methodological naturalism, both the testability problem and the plausibility problem must be solved.

Of course, some scientists deny that plausibility judgments play any role in science. But philosophers have shown that scientists presuppose such judgments all the time. Indeed, even the claim that a fact is strong evidence for a hypothesis in the sense that it significantly raises the ratio of the probability of its truth to the probability of its falsehood presupposes a number of plausibility judgments. For a fact can significantly raise this ratio only if it is antecedently more probable given that theory than it is given its denial, and any precise assessment of a fact's antecedent probability given the denial of a theory is impossible unless one can assess the relative plausibility of various alternatives to that theory.[6] Furthermore, methods like statistical significance testing, which are actually employed by scientists and which ignore prior probabilities (and thus allegedly make science more "objective"), have been shown to be flawed for that very reason (e.g., Edwards, Lindman, and Savage 1963).

One response to the plausibility problem grants that plausibility judgments about supernaturalistic hypotheses are subjective, but denies that plausibility judgments about naturalistic hypotheses are any less subjective. The claim here is that, in science and in every other discipline, we just find ourselves taking certain hypotheses seriously and disregarding others. And so we test some hypotheses and not others. This is our only way of coming to any conclusions at all, since there are always infinitely many alternative hypotheses that can explain any given set of facts. Of course, if this is the correct response to the plausibility problem, then the correct conclusion to draw is that science cannot objectively justify any of its theories (which in turn suggests that truth is not an appropriate goal of science and that scientific realism should be rejected).

A different approach to the plausibility problem claims that plausibility judgments about both supernaturalistic and naturalistic hypotheses are objective, grounded in both cases on objective judgments of simplicity or content or scope. According to this view, the tendency of contemporary analytic philosophers of religion to focus on theism as opposed to other supernaturalistic hypotheses could be justified if theism and metaphysical naturalism are both plausible and so worthy of being tested, while nontheistic supernaturalistic hypotheses are not. To defend the antecedent of this conditional is not easy, but perhaps it is not impossible. One might start with the admittedly controversial conviction that idealism and (hard) materialism are false. Reality has (at least) two fundamentally different parts: the (ontoiogically) objective (often called the "physical") and the (ontologically) subjective (often called the "mental"). If this is right, then it would seem very likely that either the subjective world ultimately explains the objective or vice versa: one world is very probably a product of the other. Further, prior to testing these two options, there is no reason to prefer one of them to the other. They are precisely parallel, equal in content and simplicity, and thus equally probable initially. Therefore, prior to testing, each has a probability of close to 0.5.[7]

What does this tell us about the prior probabilities of metaphysical naturalism and theism? First, on the assumption that the objective world provides an ultimate explanation of the subjective, the prior probability of metaphysical naturalism is high. For the view that the subjective world is ultimately a product of the objective makes supernaturalism very unlikely. Second, on the assumption that the subjective world provides an ultimate explanation of the objective, the prior probability of theism is not very low. For antirealist views, according to which human minds create the objective world, are very implausible. And, as Swinburne (1979, ch. 5) has argued, atheistic or deistic or quasi-theistic hypotheses entailing the existence of supernatural minds are much less simple than theism and for that reason much less probable intrinsically. To suppose that a person who provides the ultimate explanation of all there is has unlimited power and knowledge is simpler and hence intrinsically more probable than to suppose that such a being can create some things but not others or has knowledge of some facts but not others. And a being of unlimited power and knowledge is likely to be morally perfect as well because such a being is unlikely to be influenced by nonrational desires and hence is likely to do whatever she knows to be best overall, that is, morally best. It follows, then, both that theism and metaphysical naturalism are much more plausible than any alternative hypothesis and that neither is overwhelmingly more plausible than the other. Prior to testing, each has a probability of less than 0.5, but neither has a probability that is negligibly low. Therefore, if they can be tested, then they ought to be.

Obviously, this argument contains many highly questionable premises and inferences. But assume for the sake of argument that plausibility judgments are objective and that they can be made in the case of supernaturalistic hypotheses. There remains the issue of whether supernaturalistic hypotheses can be tested. This testability problem could be solved if one could show that certain facts have a higher or lower antecedent probability given theism than they do given the denial of theism (or given some serious hypothesis like metaphysical naturalism that entails the denial of theism). For that would mean that our knowledge of those facts raises or lowers the (epistemic) probability of theism (or raises or lowers the ratio of the probability of theism to the probability of one of its serious alternatives). But what would make a fact antecedently more or less likely on theism? Are we really in a position to judge how likely it is that God would want some fact to obtain? The simplest response to these questions is to point out that moral perfection is built into the theistic hypothesis. Because we are not entirely in the dark about the preferences of such a being (at least, other considerations held equal), some facts about nature are more probable on theism than on, for example, metaphysical naturalism, and others are less probable on theism than on metaphysical naturalism. (This is why various facts about the suffering in the world present an evidential problem for theists.) Furthermore, building moral perfection into the theistic hypothesis does not make that hypothesis ad hoc if, as was suggested above, God's moral perfection is made likely by other attributes that are plausibly attributed to a personal ground of being.

The Presumption of Naturalism

> Perhaps more than anything else, the discussion between theology and science today is concerned with the presumption of naturalism; where it is not, it perhaps ought to be. By the presumption of naturalism I mean the assumption, for any event in the natural world, that its cause is a natural one rather than a supernatural one.
>
> —Philip Clayton, 1997

Prescientific Naturalism

If (as will henceforth be assumed) the testability and plausibility problems can be solved and, more generally, there are no good arguments for methodological naturalism based either on the nature of God or on the nature or methods or goals of science, then many conservative Christian thinkers (e.g., Johnson 1995) will conclude that the commitment of contemporary science to methodological naturalism has no justification—that it reflects an unsupported metaphysical bias against supernaturalistic religions. But while scientists no doubt have all sorts of biases, including religious and metaphysical ones, we shall see in the remainder of this chapter that, instead of some antireligious bias leading scientists to accept metaphysical naturalism, which in turn grounds their acceptance of methodological naturalism, it may be that metaphysical naturalism and at least a modest methodological naturalism are supported by the same evidence.

Let us approach the question of the nature of this evidence indirectly, by examining the position, common among conservative Christian thinkers, that a commitment to methodological naturalism is a recent addition to scientific practice, becoming dominant only after metaphysical naturalism became popular among scientists. This position is at best misleading because the tendency to favor naturalistic explanations emerged gradually over a long period of time. As Philip Clayton (1997, 172) points out, the presumption that natural events have natural causes existed long before the rise of modern science. Indeed, even in the Bible, explanations appealing to God, even if they are not the last resort, are often not the first (e.g., 1 Samuel 3).

Because it is unlikely that the authors of the Bible are guilty of some anti-religious metaphysical bias or that they believe that a faithful or generous God would never act directly in the world, what is the source of this prescientific presumption in favor of naturalistic explanations? No doubt it is a simple induction from past experiences. In very many cases, a little investigation reveals natural causes for natural events, even unusual ones. Thus, it follows inductively that, prior to investigation, the probability that the immediate cause of any given natural event is itself natural is high. We did not need science to teach us this.[8]

The Success of Science

Science, however, has added greatly to the strength of this presumption of naturalism (Clayton 1997, 172–74). In many cases in which no naturalistic explanation seemed particularly promising, sufficient effort in searching for one turned out to bear fruit. This is presumably why even William Dembski (1994, 132), a leading critic of methodological naturalism, claims that one should appeal to the supernatural only when one has good reason to believe that what he calls one's "empirical resources" are exhausted. Thus, although Dembski attacks the view that naturalistic explanations are *better* than nonnaturalistic ones, he does not deny that, prior to investigation or even after considerable investigation, they remain *more likely* to be true. On this point almost everyone will agree. For example, what philosopher or scientist, no matter how deeply religious, believed or even took seriously the sincere claim of some members of the Cuban community in Miami that God miraculously prevented Elian Gonzalez from getting a sunburn while at sea (rather than that his fellow survivors lied when they claimed he had been in the water for three days after his boat sank)? It is beyond dispute that, at a minimum, *almost* all natural events have other natural events as their immediate causes.

CONCLUSIONS

> For centuries the writ of empiricism has been spreading into the ancient domain of transcendentalist belief, slowly at the start but quickening in the scientific age. The spirits our ancestors knew intimately first fled the rocks and trees, then the distant mountains. Now they are in the stars, where their final extinction is possible.
>
> —Edward O. Wilson, 1998

A Modest Methodological Naturalism

A strong presumption of naturalism based on everyday experience and the success of naturalistic science justifies a modest methodological naturalism: the reason scientists should not look for supernatural causes is that natural causes are much more likely to be found. A methodological naturalism justified in this way is "modest" because it implies that scientists should look *first* for naturalistic explanations, and (depending on how strong the presumption of naturalism is) maybe second, third, and fourth too, but it does not absolutely rule out appeals to the supernatural. It allows that, in cases like Cleanthes' example of the voice from the clouds in part 3 of Hume's *Dialogues Concerning Natural Religion*, an absolute prohibition on appeals to the supernatural would arbitrarily block a possible path to truth. We can state this more modest methodological naturalism as follows: scientific explanations may appeal to the supernatural only as a last resort. Both Meyer (1994, 97) and Dembski (1994, 132), two leading opponents of methodological naturalism understood as an absolute prohibition, seem to agree with this principle, which does not depend on any metaphysical or antireligious bias.

It should be emphasized, however, that even this modest form of methodological naturalism does not sanction a god-of-the-gaps theology. It does not imply that an appeal to the supernatural is justified simply because scientists fail after much effort to find a naturalistic explanation for some phenomenon. Very strong reasons to believe there is no *hidden* naturalistic explanation would be required as well. In other words, the search for natural causes should continue until the best explanation of the failure to find one is that there is none. And if the presumption of naturalism is very strong, then that may not yet have occurred in any current area of scientific research, which means that this modest methodological naturalism may have at the present time the same practical implications as an absolute prohibition on appeals to the supernatural in science.

One might object that this form of methodological naturalism is only falsely modest. A situation in which the best explanation of our failure to find a naturalistic explanation is that there is none is, one might claim, inconceivable. Dembski (1994, 122–29), however, provides a convincing counterexample to this claim (more convincing than Cleanthes' example of the voice from the clouds). He asks us to suppose that astronomers discover a pulsar billions of light years from earth, the pulses of which signal English messages in Morse code. Further, these messages invite us to ask it questions, including problems that can be shown mathematically to require for their solution far more computational resources than are, according to our best estimates, available in the universe. We then receive verifiable answers to these questions in ten minutes. Would astronomers in these circumstances remain methodological naturalists? Would they conclude that either reverse causality or messages traveling at superluminal speeds account for the pulsar's ability to answer our questions in ten minutes despite being billions of light years away? And that our estimates of either the age of the universe or of the smallest physically meaningful unit of time or of the number of elementary particles in the universe are wildly off the mark and hence we are mistaken in thinking that the universe lacks the computational resources for solving the problems we pose to the pulsar? Not likely. The vast majority of open-minded astronomers would admit that we have good reason in these circumstances to believe that no empirical resources within nature can account for the events in question and that an appeal to a supernatural intelligence will be a part of the best explanation of these events.

But even if Dembski's pulsar example proves that supernaturalistic explanations could possibly be permitted by our modest methodological naturalism, there remains the question of whether any such explanations actually are permitted. Dembski (1994, 131–32) defends an affirmative answer to this question. He maintains that attempts to explain the cosmos and living systems naturalistically face huge obstacles and that an appeal to supernatural intelligence to account for these phenomena is justified. Of course, he admits that these phenomena are not close to as impressive as his imaginary pulsar. But he believes the evidence for a supernatural intelligence in the pulsar case is far greater than what would be needed to justify positing such an intelligence (129). Many who would agree with Dembski's analysis of the pulsar example will disagree with him about his real-life examples. The source of this disagreement may be a disagreement about the viability of naturalistic explanations of, for example, the origin of life. Or, more interesting, it may be a disagreement about how strong the presumption of naturalism is and hence how soon one should begin considering supernaturalistic explanations in a given case. Either way, many will hold that, as things stand now, there is every reason to believe that what some call "theistic science" is not at this point in time warranted. Even our modest methodological naturalism prohibits it.

Metaphysical Naturalism

We have seen that the success of science in providing naturalistic explanations of natural phenomena strengthens the presumption of naturalism and so helps to support a modest methodological naturalism. More important, though, it strongly supports metaphysical naturalism over both supernaturalism in general and theism in particular. To see why, recall that the attempts discussed earlier to provide a theological justification for methodological naturalism fail. It is at this point in the argument that the true significance of that failure is revealed. For if we lack any antecedent reason to believe that God would not want to act directly in nature, then we lack any antecedent reason on theism to expect science to be as successful in its quest for naturalistic explanations as it has been. By contrast, we have a very strong antecedent reason to expect such success on metaphysical naturalism, because there is strong antecedent reason to believe that most natural events have causes, and metaphysical naturalism *entails* that such causes must be natural ones. To put the point crudely, metaphysical naturalism "predicts" that science will succeed in discovering natural causes for natural phenomena, while supernaturalism and theism, though certainly consistent with such success, do not predict it. To put the point more precisely, such success is antecedently much more probable given metaphysical naturalism than it is given supernaturalism or given theism. Therefore, it strongly supports metaphysical naturalism over both supernaturalism and theism: it significantly raises the ratio of the probability of metaphysical naturalism to the probability of each of these other hypotheses. This argument represents an often ignored version of the problem of divine hiddenness. The problem here is not the problem of why, if God exists, she would allow reasonable nonbelief (Schellenberg 1993), but rather, the more fundamental problem of why, if God or other supernatural beings exist, science can completely ignore them and still explain so much.

One might object that, on naturalism, one would not expect natural phenomena to have explanations of any sort, while on theism, one would expect explanations of some sort, naturalistic or supernaturalistic, and so the fact that explanations of any kind are available is evidence favoring theism over naturalism. But even if this argument is sound (which is hardly a given) and so relevant to one's final assessment of the relative probabilities of theism and naturalism, it is beside the point here. Here we are interested in the evidential significance of the success of science, *given that there are explanations of one sort or another for natural phenomena*. If the scarcity of brute facts in nature can somehow be shown to support theism over naturalism, so be it. But given that scarcity—given that natural phenomena typically do have explanations—the fact that so much in nature is known to have a naturalistic explanation (and no part of nature that could have a naturalistic explanation is known not to have one) strongly supports metaphysical naturalism over theism. After all, things could have turned out differently. It might have turned out, for example, that macroevolution never occurs and hence that living organisms are not related by descent, in which case a naturalistic explanation of the living world would have been all but impossible. If things had turned out this way (and we knew it), then that would support theism over metaphysical naturalism. But then our knowledge that things did not turn out this way must support metaphysical naturalism over theism.[9]

One might object that some natural phenomena now present intractable problems for a thoroughly naturalistic science (e.g., Craig and Moreland 2000). If this is right, then, according to our modest methodological naturalism, the time has come to consider supernaturalistic explanations. But surely this is premature. It remains to be seen whether or not science will be able to provide convincing and correct naturalistic explanations of phenomena like consciousness, free will, and religion itself. Yet it is equally premature to accept current naturalistic explanations of such phenomena. As scientists continue to investigate and better understand such phenomena, the evidence against theism and other forms of supernaturalism may eventually become overwhelming. But while we have traveled a considerable distance toward that destination, it is still a significant way off, and only time will tell if it will ever be reached.

NOTES

1. The view that Christianity is at least partly responsible for the rise of modern science in Europe was briefly defended by Whitehead (1925, ch. 1). Since then, numerous authors have either defended or attacked this position. For a brief critical discussion of this literature, see Drees (1996, 77–86).

2. "=df." is short for "means by definition."

3. One limitation of this definition is that it assumes that the current word of the physical sciences on which lower-level entities exist is the last. History has shown that this is a very dangerous assumption. For example, when physics was forced to accommodate electromagnetic phenomena, it could not do so with the repertoire of entities that made up Newton's universe. Thus, radically new entities were posited, specifically electromagnetic fields, which could not be given a mechanical explanation (Nagel 1986, 52–53). Similarly, there may be one or more revolutions yet in store for physics, in which case new sorts of entities may be discovered that, because of their nomological and historical connections to atoms, fields, and so on, we will want to call physical and natural. (Notice that if physicists were to begin appealing to God in their theories, there would be no temptation to call God a physical entity because God would not be subject to laws relating him to atoms, fields, and the like, nor would he share any common origin with such entities.) If such revolutions will indeed occur, then our definition of nature in reality only captures nature *as currently understood*.

4. In the absence of philosophical argument, one can always appeal (illegitimately) to authority. And so the position that methodological naturalism can be supported the-

ologically is often defended by appealing to Saint Augustine's position on creation, which includes the view that all life forms were present in the world from the beginning, not as fully formed plants or animals, but as potencies or seed-principles that would in due time be actualized as fully formed organisms. This suggests that Augustine favors the view that God would not act directly in nature to bring forth life. But it is far from clear that Augustine regarded direct acts in the world as in any way contrary to God's nature. As Ernan McMullin (1985, 11–16) points out, the main reason why Augustine appealed to seed-principles was exegetical, not philosophical. He wanted to reconcile the claim in Genesis that God created all things together with the view, also authorized by Genesis, that natural kinds appeared gradually over time. Thus, there is no good reason to believe that Augustine was opposed philosophically to the idea of a "special creation." In fact, Augustine even allowed for the possibility that, in addition to the direct divine act that created the seed-principles, additional direct acts by God were required to actualize these potencies! Thus, were it not for his exegetical worries, Augustine might very well have favored a robust doctrine of special creationism. He almost certainly did not hold that anything about God's nature rules it out.

5. Of course, those engaged in nomological science may try to discover facts about particular objects as a means to the end of discovering laws. And historical scientists may try to discover laws as a means to the end of discovering facts about particular objects. But such overlap will not invariably occur.

6. The "antecedent" probability of a fact that is known to obtain on the basis of observation or testimony is the probability that it obtains, independent of that observation or testimony. Often, the probability of some fact given the denial of a theory is equated with its probability, given some specific alternative to that theory. But this assumes that all other alternatives are so implausible that they can be ignored.

7. One might object that the argument here relies on the notorious "principle of indifference." For a defense of that principle properly understood, see Schlesinger (1991, ch. 9).

8. Of course, the existence of a natural cause for some event is, strictly speaking, compatible, not just with an ultimate divine cause, but also with some simultaneous direct divine cause. But this would be to multiply causes far beyond what is necessary or warranted by the evidence.

9. Some fact F supports (in the sense intended here) theism (T) over metaphysical naturalism (N) if and only if $Pr(F/T) > Pr(F/N)$. But $Pr(\sim F/T) = 1 - Pr(F/T)$ and $Pr(\sim F/N) = 1 - Pr(F/N)$. Thus, $Pr(F/T) > Pr(F/N)$ if and only if $Pr(\sim F/N) > Pr(\sim F/T)$. Therefore, F supports theism over metaphysical naturalism if and only if the fact that F does not obtain supports metaphysical naturalism over theism.

WORKS CITED

Alston, William P. 1985. "God's Action in the World." In *Evolution and Creation*, ed. Ernan McMullin, 197–220. Notre Dame, Ind.: University of Notre Dame Press.

Barbour, Ian. 1990. *Religion in an Age of Science*. New York: HarperCollins.

Clayton, Philip. 1997. *God and Contemporary Science*. Grand Rapids, Mich.: Eerdmans.

Craig, William Lane, and J. P. Moreland, eds. 2000. *Naturalism: A Critical Analysis.* London: Routledge.

Dembski, William A. 1994. "On the Very Possibility of Intelligent Design." In *The Creation Hypothesis,* ed. J. P. Moreland, 113–38. Downers Grove, Ill.: InterVarsity Press.

Dobzhansky, Theodosius. 1971. *The Biology of Ultimate Concern.* London: Fontana.

Draper, John William. 1875. *History of the Conflict between Religion and Science.* New York: D. Appleton.

Drees, Willem B. 1996. *Religion, Science and Naturalism.* Cambridge, England: Cambridge University Press.

Edwards, Ward, Harold Lindman, and Leonard J. Savage. 1963. "Bayesian Statistical Inference for Psychological Research." *Psychological Review* 70.3 (May): 193–242.

Gould, Stephen Jay. 2001. "Two Separate Domains." In *Philosophy of Religion: Selected Readings,* 2nd edition, ed. Michael Peterson, William Hasker, Bruce Reichenbach, and David Basinger, 499–509. New York: Oxford University Press.

Harris, James F. 1992. *Against Relativism: A Philosophical Defense of Method.* LaSalle, Ill.: Open Court.

Hartshorne, Charles. 1967. *A Natural Theology for Our Time.* La Salle, Ill.: Open Court.

John Paul II. 1988. "Message to the Reverend George V. Coyne, S. J." In *Physics, Philosophy, and Theology: A Common Quest for Understanding,* ed. Robert J. Russell, William R. Stoeger, S. J., and George V. Coyne, S. J., M1–M14. Notre Dame, Ind.: University of Notre Dame Press, 1988.

Johnson, Phillip E. 1995. *Reason in the Balance: The Case against Naturalism in Science, Law, and Education.* Downer's Grove, Ill.: InterVarsity Press.

Lauden, Larry. 1996. "The Demise of the Demarcation Problem." In *But Is It Science? The Philosophical Question in the Creation/Evolution Controversy,* ed. Michael Ruse, 337–350. Amherst, N.Y.: Prometheus Books. Reprinted from *Physics, Philosophy, and Psychoanalysis,* ed. R. S. Cohen and Larry Lauden, 111–27. Dordrecht, Holland: D. Reidel, 1983.

Leibniz, Gottfried Wilhelm, and Samuel Clarke. 1956. *The Leibniz-Clarke Correspondence,* ed. H. G. Alexander. Manchester, England: Manchester University Press.

Lewis, C. S. 1947. *Miracles: A Preliminary Study.* New York: Macmillan.

Macquarrie, John. 1977. *Principles of Christian Theology,* 2nd edition. New York: Charles Scribner's Sons.

McMullin, Ernan. 1985. "Introduction: Evolution and Creation." In *Evolution and Creation,* ed. Ernan McMullin, 1–56. Notre Dame, Ind.: University of Notre Dame Press.

———. 1991. "Plantinga's Defense of Special Creation." *Christian Scholar's Review* 21.1 (Sept.): 55–79.

Meyer, Stephen C. 1994. "The Methodological Equivalence of Design and Descent." In *The Creation Hypothesis,* ed. J. P. Moreland, 67–112. Downers Grove, Ill.: InterVarsity Press.

Midgley, Mary. 1985. *Evolution as a Religion: Strange Hopes and Stranger Fears.* London: Methuen.

Murphy, Nancey. 1990. *Theology in the Age of Scientific Reasoning.* Ithaca, N.Y.: Cornell University Press.

———. 1995. "Divine Action in the Natural Order: Buridan's Ass and Schrodinger's Cat." In *Chaos and Complexity: Scientific Perspectives on Divine Action,* ed. Robert J.

Russell, Nancey Murphy, and Arthur Peacocke, 325–57. Vatican City State: Vatican Observatory Publications.

———. 1998. "Nonreductive Physicalism: Philosophical Issues." In *Whatever Happened to the Soul? Sceintific and Theological Portraits of Human Nature,* ed. Warren S. Brown, Nancey Murphy, and H. Newton Malony, 127–48. Minneapolis: Fortress Press.

Nagel, Thomas. 1986. *The View from Nowhere.* New York: Oxford University Press.

O'Connor, Robert C. 1997. "Science on Trial: Exploring the Rationality of Methodological Naturalism." *Perspectives on Science and Christian Faith* 49 (Mar.): 15–30.

Peacocke, Arthur. 1993. *Theology for a Scientific Age: Being and Becoming—Natural, Divine, and Human,* enlarged edition. Minneapolis: Fortress Press.

Pennock, Robert T. 1998. "The Prospects for a 'Theistic Science.'" *Perspectives on Science and Christian Faith* 50 (Sept.): 205–9.

———. 1999. *Tower of Babel: The Evidence against the New Creationism.* Cambridge, Mass.: MIT Press.

Plantinga, Alvin. 1991. "Evolution, Neutrality, and Antecedent Probability: A Reply to McMullin and Van Till." *Christian Scholar's Review* 21.1 (Sept.): 80–109.

———. 1997. "Methodological Naturalism?" *Perspectives on Science and Christian Faith* 49 (Sept.): 143–54.

Polkinghorne, John. 1989. *Science and Providence: God's Interaction with the World.* Boston: Shambhala Publications.

Pollard, W. G. 1958. *Chance and Providence: God's Action in a World Governed by Scientific Law.* New York: Scribner.

Quinn, Philip L. 1996. "The Philosopher of Science as Expert Witness." In *But Is It Science? The Philosophical Question in the Creation/Evolution Controversy,* ed. Michael Ruse, 367–85. Amherst, N.Y.: Prometheus Books. Reprinted from *Science and Reality: Recent Work in the Philosophy of Science,* ed. James T. Cushing, C. F. Delaney, and Gary M. Gutting, 32–53. Notre Dame, Ind.: University of Notre Dame Press, 1984.

Ruse, Michael. 1982. *Darwinism Defended: A Guide to the Evolution Controversies.* Reading, Mass.: Addison-Wesley.

Schellenberg, J. L. 1993. *Divine Hiddenness and Human Reason.* Ithaca, N.Y.: Cornell University Press.

Schlesinger, George N. 1977. *Religion and Scientific Method.* Dordrecht: D. Reidel.

———. 1991. *The Sweep of Probability.* Notre Dame, Ind.: University of Notre Dame Press.

Searle, John R. 1992. *The Rediscovery of the Mind.* Cambridge, Mass.: MIT Press.

Sober, Elliott. 2000. *Philosophy of Biology,* 2nd edition. Boulder, Colo.: Westview Press.

Swinburne, Richard. 1979. *The Existence of God.* Oxford: Clarendon Press.

Tillich, Paul. 1957. *Dynamics of Faith.* New York: Harper & Row.

Van Till, Howard J. 1999. "The Fully Gifted Creation." In *Three Views on Creation and Evolution,* ed. J. P. Moreland and John Mark Reynolds, 161–218. Grand Rapids, Mich.: Zondervan Publishing House.

White, Andrew Dickson. 1896. *A History of the Warfare of Science with Theology in Christendom.* 2 vols. New York: D. Appleton.

Whitehead, Alfred North. 1925. *Science and the Modern World.* New York: Macmillan.

Wilson, Edward O. 1998. *Consilience: The Unity of Knowledge.* Thorndike, Me.: Thorndike Press.

CHAPTER 12

....

MIRACLES

....

GEORGE I. MAVRODES

THE idea of the miraculous, and reports of miracles, are prominent elements in some religions. Christianity is one of those religions. In this chapter I discuss this idea primarily in the context of Christianity, though much of what I have to say will also apply to its occurrence in the other theistic religions.

From the very beginning, the accounts of the life of Jesus seem to include miraculous elements. In the four Gospels that are now part of the New Testament, Jesus is reported as having done many strange and amazing things. Most of these involve the healing of various diseases and disabilities, many of them apparently of long standing. There are also other incidents, such as walking on the water, calming a storm, and changing water into wine at a wedding feast, that do not involve healings. There is at least one striking case of a resurrection attributed to Jesus, the raising of Lazarus (John, ch. 11). And finally there is the miracle that, for many Christians anyway, overshadows all of these others in importance. That is the resurrection of Jesus himself several days after his death by crucifixion.

As we might imagine, the strange things that Jesus did often resulted in awe and amazement among those who saw them. They contributed greatly to Jesus' reputation, and they drew large crowds to him wherever he went throughout Galilee and Judea. No doubt they had a significant effect on the way his preaching was received, and on people's reaction to him personally, both before and after his death.

The idea of the miraculous, of course, was not invented by Jesus nor by the writers of the Gospels. The Judaic tradition within which Jesus began and carried out his ministry already included the idea of the miraculous. The Hebrew scriptures (now often called the Old Testament by Christians) include many such accounts of strange things being done by prophets of past time.

We should beware, however, of hastily assuming that all these strange things that Jesus did can properly be lumped together into any single convenient and useful category, such as that of miracles. After all, there is probably no one who thinks that everything that Jesus did was a miracle. And it is possible that even some of the strange things were not miracles. Of course, that raises the question of just what a miracle is, or what it is supposed to be. And that might lead to some understanding of the ways an event, even if surprising, might fail to be a miracle. That is one of the topics I discuss below.

THE CONCEPT OF MIRACLE

What is a miracle? The most significant and influential attempt in Western philosophy to define the idea of the miraculous is probably that of David Hume. This is found in his essay "Of Miracles," which constitutes section X of *An Enquiry Concerning Human Understanding* (1777), first published in 1748. Indeed, this whole essay is probably the most provocative and influential philosophical discussion of miracles in the history of Western philosophy. It touches on most of the philosophically significant questions related to this topic. I will not discuss Hume's essay systematically, but I will refer to it from time to time as a convenient way of introducing the questions that I will discuss.

Hume's definition is found in a footnote in part I of the essay. There Hume says, "A miracle may be accurately defined, a transgression of a law of nature by a particular volition of the deity, or by the interposition of some invisible agent" (1777, 115). This definition seems to me to be basically correct, in the sense that it captures and expresses what most Christians seem to have meant when they have talked about miracles. It fits well with the Christian worldview, the general sort of picture of the world that goes with the Christian faith.[1]

The definition has two parts. The first part is Hume's attempt to put into a more precise language the idea that the miracle is an event that would not have happened in the ordinary course of affairs. It happens in the world of nature, but the actions, forces, and so on, of the world of nature, acting alone, would not have brought it about. The miracle goes beyond nature in some way. Perhaps it is even something that goes contrary to the ordinary course of nature. Hume's way of putting that is that the miracle is a transgression of a law of nature.

The second part of Hume's definition ascribes this transgression to an agent of a certain sort, "the deity," or some other "invisible agent." I suppose that Hume here intends to import into his definition the idea of God that was common among Christians and with which he was familiar. And Hume himself uses the term "volition," which suggests that the sort of agent he has in mind is an intentional actor, someone who has a will. In Christianity, God is construed as a person or something like a person. That is, God is thought of as an agent who has knowledge, will, intention, and desire, as well as a capacity for action. And God is characteristically thought of as omnipotent, and as the creator of the world, thus being distinct from the world. So it is natural, within that context, to suppose that God is capable of acting in the natural world, of producing effects there. Thus, the second part of Hume's definition fits well with the way Christians (and other theists) are likely to think of miracles.

Almost all of the subsequent philosophical discussion of miracles has focused on the first element in Hume's definition, that of the relation of the allegedly miraculous event to the laws of nature. This is, of course, a crucial element. Antony Flew, a twentieth-century philosopher who was himself no friend of miracles or of Christianity, has put this point by saying, "The occurrence of a genuine miracle is, by definition, naturally impossible" (Habermas and Flew 1987, 6). This is, in fact, a useful way of putting the point, though it may initially seem paradoxical. Flew goes on to say, in the course of a debate with a theist about miracles, "The main point I want you to grasp is that all of us here have a vested interest in the idea of a strong natural order. This ought to be taken as agreed because it's only if there is that strong natural order that there is anything significant about the Resurrection" (35).

Two quick points about Flew's observation. First, it is important to take seriously the occurrence of the words "natural" and "naturally" in Flew's statements. Miracles are *naturally* impossible, but it does not follow that they are *logically* impossible. (It is pretty clear that Hume did not think that they were logically impossible. Flew does not think so either.) And from the fact that miracles are naturally impossible it does not follow that miracles do not occur. What does follow is that genuine miracles do not occur in the natural course of events in the world. But if there should be a supernatural incursion, some particular action or volition by God, then the result of that incursion might well be something that could not have occurred naturally. It would be actual, even though it was *naturally* impossible. And that is just the sort of thing that is envisioned in the first part of Hume's definition of a miracle. The actual occurrence of something that is naturally impossible could well be described as a transgression or violation of the order and course of nature.

Second, Flew refers to "a strong natural order." I think that Flew here means to claim that the natural order must be something more than merely a universal regularity in the phenomena of the world. The natural order is, of course, related somehow to pervasive regularities in the world. I will say something more about that relation later. But to make sense of the Humean idea we must suppose that there is something more to the order of nature than mere regularity, or even universal regularity. There must be something deeply embedded in the structure of the world that accounts for the regularity of the phenomena. That deeply embedded element is, I think, what corresponds to Flew's adjective, "strong." And that strong element would consist, I suppose, of a structure of causal relations, and perhaps some other relations, which bind the phenomena into pervasive patterns of regularity, imposing on the phenomena some sort of "natural" necessity.

If we accept this definition of a miracle, then we can see that there are at least three ways in which an *alleged* miracle might fail to be a *genuine* miracle. First, the alleged event may not have happened at all (as it was described). In the case of an alleged resurrection, for example, the person involved may not really have been dead at all,[2] or the person may not have really been alive afterward. Second, the alleged event may have happened as described, but it may not have been a violation of a law of nature. In the case of an alleged miraculous healing, for example, the disability may have been psychosomatic, and the subsequent recovery (even if it was rather sudden) may have been well within a natural course of events. Third, the alleged event may have been real and may have been a violation of a law of nature, but it may not have been caused by God, and perhaps not even by some other invisible or supernatural agent.

Critical discussions of miracles have focused almost entirely on the first two of these ways in which alleged miracles might fail, but there has been little discussion of the third. That third possibility, however, suggests some interesting questions. One of these is the question of whether there are, or may be, some other invisible or supernatural intentional agents in addition to God (as Hume's definition, of course, allows). In some sense, anyway, this is a question about the possibility of polytheism. Historically, Western philosophy of religion has dealt extensively with monotheism and atheism, but it has largely ignored polytheism. Of course, the major religions with which most Western philosophers have been well acquainted—Christianity, Judaism, and Islam—are officially monotheistic. They are "one-God" religions. And, I think, there are important senses in which they really are monotheistic. But many Christians also believe that reality includes the existence of some other invisible and intentional agents in addition to God. They believe, that is, in the existence of angels and devils at least. Angels and devils, if they exist, certainly would seem to fit Hume's reference to "some other invisible agent." And on some definitions for the word "god" angels and devils would count as gods (with a small "g"). If there are such beings, then, there might be a miracle whose agent is a god but not God, at least not the God acknowledged and worshipped by Christians.[3]

A somewhat different question in this area is whether there could be an event that was both a consequence of a law of nature and also a violation of a law of nature. Such an event would be, in a sense, a part of the natural order, because it would be the result of a law of nature operating in a natural context. There would be no special supernatural interference or volition involved. But the event would also be a violation of a different law of nature, one that also applied to that same natural context. In other words, this would be a case in which there was some conflict or inconsistency in the laws of nature: conformity with one law would involve the violation of another law. Such a conflict might go unnoticed for a long time because the sort of context in which the conflict occurred was rare. I do not know of any good reason for thinking that such a conflict is impossible. But I will say no more about it here.

There might also be some question about whether the idea of a violation of a law of nature is logically coherent.[4] This question is sometimes raised by calling attention to the fact that a law of nature is often expressed by, or is at least thought to entail, some universal proposition about the way things happen in the world. For example, it might be thought that there is a law of nature to the effect that all crows are black. Or (perhaps better) there are some fundamental laws of nature that entail or require that all crows be black. And it might be thought that there is a law of nature to the effect that anyone who dies remains dead thereafter, or that the proposition that all of the dead remain dead is a consequence of some more fundamental laws of nature. The logical form of these propositions (e.g., "All crows are black") is that of a universal generalization that we can state as

All A's are B's.

It seems easy to give sense to the notion of a violation of a proposition of that kind. A counterexample would be such a violation. So, for example, the actual existence of a white crow would be a counterexample to the universal proposition that all crows are black. The logical form of the corresponding proposition, asserting the existence of a crow that is not black, would be

There is an A that is not B.

So the white crow, incompatible with the generalization, would count as a violation of the corresponding "law." In the same way, a genuine resurrection from the dead would be a counterexample to the generalization that states that all of the dead remain dead, and so would be a violation of a law of nature.

These examples provide a plausible sense for a violation. Unfortunately, however, they also entail that the corresponding universal generalizations are false. If there is a white crow, for example, then it is false that all crows are black. And it would seem that a false generalization could not constitute a *genuine* law of nature. A genuine law of nature must, somehow or other, be *true*. Nor could a genuine law of nature entail a false generalization. Of course, something that was mistakenly believed to be a law of nature might entail a falsehood. But that fact itself would show it not to be a genuine law of nature. If laws of nature are construed in this way, then it seems that no law of nature can "survive" an exception. And so it is sometimes suggested that the Humean concept of a miracle is logically incoherent. The idea of a *genuine* law of nature is incompatible with the idea of a violation or exception. If that is so, then miracles (according to this definition, of course) are logically impossible after all.

What is needed for a coherent concept of miracle along these lines, then, is some notion of a genuine law of nature that allows for the law to survive in the face of some exceptions. The law need not be able to survive an unlimited number of exceptions, but it must be able to survive some. There are perhaps several ways of doing this. Here is one such way.

Let us say that a law of nature is constituted by a structural fact or set of facts in the natural world, something in the natural order that generates a uniformity in the phenomena of that world. So, for example, the uniform blackness of crows is presumably due to some genetic facts. These genetic facts, then, would constitute, or would be part of, a law of nature. But there would also be a universal generalization that would "correspond to," or would be "associated with," that law of nature. The universal generalization would not be constitutive of the law, and it would not be entailed by the law. The generalization, however, would be a true description of the world *if nothing outside of the natural order interfered with the operation of the corresponding law of nature.* That is, if nothing outside of the natural order interfered with the expression of the genetic facts, then the generalization that all crows are black would in fact be a true description of the world. But the law of nature does not guarantee that there is nothing outside of the natural order, and therefore it does not guarantee that there will never be anything that interferes with the operation of the law. Consequently, the law of nature does not entail the truth of the corresponding universal generalization.

This corresponding generalization is the place where a violation of a law of nature will become evident or noticeable. That is, the occurrence of a white crow would be a counterexample to the generalization. It would make the generalization false. However, because the generalization did not constitute the law, and because the law did not entail the generalization, the counterexample would not falsify the law. The exception would not impugn the genuineness of the law. And so the law could remain as a genuine law of nature in the face of the counterexample. The law and the counterexample could coexist in reality.

It is an interesting, and perhaps significant, fact that there is a structural parallel here with the logic of statute laws. It is, of course, often said that laws of nature are quite different from the laws in legal codes. Nevertheless, for hundreds of years it has seemed natural to use the same term "law" to refer both to the laws of nature and to the laws in legal codes. Laws in the legal sense are also associated with uniformities. The legal codes are commands that are intended to influence human behavior and to impose on it certain patterns of uniformity.

Indeed, laws in the legal sense are often expressed by means of universal generalizations about behavior: "All taxpayers shall file a return on or before 15 April." These generalizations are, of course, always (or almost always) false. Not all taxpayers do in fact file returns on or before the fifteenth of April. This fact, which falsifies the universal generalization, signifies the violation of the law. But the law is not invalidated by the violation (at least, if there are not too many violations). And so both the law and the violation belong to the reality of the social order. This structural similarity may in fact be what lies behind the convergence of terminology at this point.[5]

The Point of Miracles

What might be the point of a miracle? This question arises in connection with Hume's curiously modest statement about the conclusion of his line of argument. Near the end of his essay he says, "We may establish it as a maxim, that no human testimony can have such force as to prove a miracle, and make it a just foundation for any such system of religion." He then immediately goes on to say, "I beg the limitations here made may be remarked, when I say, that a miracle can never be proved, so as to be the foundation of a system of religion" (1777, 127).

Hume construes his own conclusion as limited in two respects. First, he says explicitly that his argument is limited to a conclusion about the insufficiency of human testimony with regard to miracles. It is therefore not about the possibility or the actuality of miracles. Second, this insufficiency bears only on whether the miracle is to be made "the just foundation" for a religion.

Perhaps Hume thought that the only way a miracle might be significant for a religion would be that of providing a just foundation for that religion. But there are at least two importantly different senses in which a miracle might be a foundation of a religion. First, there is a broadly epistemic sense, which turns our attention to the way a miracle might have a bearing on belief—inducing a belief perhaps, or providing some justification for it. The miracle might attract attention to the religion, and it might get someone to accept that religion by providing some evidence, or at least what might seem to be evidence, in support of that religion. Somewhat more strongly, the miracle might supply *sufficient* evidence to justify a person in accepting the religion. (This stronger sense might correspond to Hume's use of the word "just" in stating his conclusion.) I will say that a miracle that performs this sort of belief-related function, in either the stronger or the weaker way, is an "epistemic foundation" for the corresponding religion.[6]

It seems clear, and perhaps uncontroversial, that miracles may well have an epistemic effect and thus may constitute epistemic foundations, at least in the weak sense. At least, they may often have such an effect if they are rather striking. The Gospels repeatedly report that the strange things that Jesus did resulted in large numbers of people believing in him. After describing the resurrection of Lazarus, for example, the Gospel of John adds, "Many of the Jews therefore, who had come with Mary and had seen what Jesus did, believed in him" (11:45). And this is an oft-repeated theme throughout the Gospels. It should be added, however, that miracles are not universally effective in this way, at least in the case of Jesus. A little later, the Gospel of John observes that, "although he had performed so many signs in their presence, they did not believe in him" (12:37). And that theme is also echoed elsewhere in the Gospels.

A recent writer on miracles begins his discussion of Hume's essay by saying, "What does Hume mean by 'popular religions'? I think he means simply any religion—any theological world view—which is evidentially based chiefly or solely on the alleged occurrence of miracles: such religions as the Christianity of most Christians who have lived and (as I would say, though this is rather more controversial) the Judaism of most Jews who have lived" (Johnson 1999, 1). This view strikes me as rather unrealistic. Intellectual biographies are highly individualistic. Even people who share a large set of beliefs about certain topics—about a theological worldview, about the Christian faith, and so on—may arrange these beliefs in quite different orders with respect to the way some are taken to be evidence for others. The Gospels certainly represent some people as coming to believe in Jesus because of the miracles that they saw. For those people, the view expressed in the quotation above may well represent their intellectual biography. They saw the miracles, and took the miracles to be evidence, and on the basis of that evidence they came to believe something special about Jesus.

There are other people, however, who believe in Jesus and also believe that Jesus did miracles, but who do not believe in Jesus because they believe in the miracles. Their belief in the miracles does not occupy a privileged position in their intellectual life. It is not prior to their other religious beliefs—temporally, logically, or in any other way. They accept the miracles, some of them anyway, because they are prominent elements in the accounts of Jesus' life, and they seem to make sense in that context. And that acceptance is part of their acceptance of the whole Christian view of the context of human life, of human history, of human destiny, and so on. They may or may not have some "rationale" for accepting that whole ball of wax, but if they do, then it does not focus in any special way on miracles. It seems to me that many contemporary Christians fall into this category. It seems to me that I do myself.

Could there be a miracle that had a point other than, or in addition to, an epistemic point? Yes, or so it surely seems to me. After all, most of the miracles attributed to Jesus had some effect in addition to whatever epistemic significance they may have had. Someone was healed, wedding guests got some good wine to drink, and so on. And most of us can readily agree that many of the additional effects attributed to these miracles are good things. It would seem that these good effects might well be at least part of the intention associated with the miraculous acts. They might be, partly or wholly, the purpose for which the miraculous act was done.

Could there be a miracle that was a foundation of a religion in virtue of some nonepistemic purpose or point, rather than in virtue of its epistemic point? It would seem so. The Apostle Paul writes, "If Christ has not been raised, your faith is futile and you are still in your sins" (I Corinthians 15:17). This appears to claim that the resurrection of Jesus is an essential part of the divine project of redeeming the world from sin. It suggests that if Jesus were not in fact raised from the dead, then that whole project would be a dismal failure: we would still be in our sins. Thus, the resurrection of Jesus is construed here as being essential, foundational, to the project with which the Christian religion is concerned. This is the second way a miracle might be the foundation of a religion. I will say that a miracle that plays this role in a religion is an "effective foundation" of that religion.

To be an effective foundation of a religion the miracle must actually happen, but it need not be believed or known. There is no need for it to be "established" by testimony or in any other way. Consequently, it seems unlikely that Hume was thinking of this way of being a foundation when he formulated the second restriction of his conclusion. Perhaps, indeed, Hume thought that the only religious function of miracles was that of providing epistemic foundations. Or maybe the epistemic significance of miracles was the only feature that interested him. But so far as I can see, there is no need for us to follow him in this. And, of course, a miracle might be both an epistemic foundation and an effective foundation of a religion.

MIRACLES, PROBABILITY, AND TESTIMONY

Could human testimony provide one with a good reason for believing that a miracle had occurred? If a miracle were to serve an epistemic function, perhaps even being an epistemic foundation of a religion, it might be necessary for the miracle itself to have some positive epistemic status. It would need to be recognized as a miracle, believed, known to have occurred, or something of the sort. (At the very end of this chapter I suggest a possible exception to this generalization.) Hume speaks of giving a miracle an epistemic status of this sort as "establishing" a miracle, and his essay deals only with the power of human testimony to establish a miracle. But that might not be the only way a miracle might be established. At least one other way comes immediately to mind. A person might personally witness a miracle, and thus come to believe, or know, that the miracle had occurred. As we have noted, the Gospels report that many people were witnesses of many of Jesus' miracles (the healings, the resurrection of Lazarus, etc.), and in some of these people the miracles generated a belief in Jesus. These miracles were, in part at least, the foundation of faith in those people. But it would seem that these people did not need to rely on testimony to believe in the reality of the miracles. They saw them for themselves, or so, at least, it seemed to them.

Furthermore, unless there were people of this sort—witnesses, or at least professed witnesses—there would be no testimony about miracles. For one who testifies to an event must claim to have witnessed, or somehow experienced, the event. And so it would seem that testimony could not be the primary and fundamental way in which a miracle could acquire a positive epistemic status.

Hume, living long after Jesus, might have thought that none of his contemporaries could have any basis for believing in the reality of a miracle other than testimonial evidence. He puts into the mouth of a hypothetical "judicious reader" the observation that "such prodigious events never happen in our days." And he says that "if any civilized people have ever given admission to any of them, that people will be found to have received them from ignorant and barbarous ancestors" (1777, 119, 120). If these strictures were true, then no contemporary of Hume could be a firsthand witness of a miracle, and presumably none of us now could be in that position either. So perhaps we would be left with nothing other than testimonial evidence.

Some Christians agree with Hume that there are no modern miracles. But not all hold that position, and so these others would not consider themselves restricted to testimonial evidence. In a curious passage near the end of the essay, Hume himself says that there were some remarkable miracle reports coming out of Paris in his own time: "The curing of the sick, giving hearing to the deaf, and sight to the blind, were everywhere talked of . . . [M]any of the miracles were immediately proved upon the spot, before judges of unquestioned integrity, attested by witnesses of credit and distinction, in a learned age, and on the most eminent theatre that is now in the world" (1777, 124). So we might be allowed to take Hume's earlier comments about the ignorant and barbarous origin of all miracle stories with a grain of salt.

However that may be, many of us will think that, at least for alleged miracles that are remote in time, such as those of Jesus, testimonial accounts will often be important elements in establishing the reality of the miracle.

Hume apparently thought that human testimony could not perform that role. But this is not because Hume had a general skepticism about testimony, for he says, "There is no species of reasoning more common, more useful, and even necessary to human life, than that which is derived from the testimony of men, and the reports of eye-witnesses and spectators" (1777, 111).

Despite this high opinion of the value of testimony in reasoning about most affairs, however, Hume clearly thinks that it fails utterly with respect to miracles. Why is that? Well, his argument appeals essentially to a comparison of probabilities:

> A miracle is a violation of the laws of nature; and as a firm and unalterable experience has established these laws, the proof against a miracle, from the very nature of the fact, is as entire as any argument from experience can possibly be imagined . . . It is no miracle that a man, seemingly in good health, should die on a sudden: because such a kind of death, though more unusual than any other, has yet been frequently observed to happen. But it is a miracle, that a dead man should come to life; because that has never been observed in any age or country. There must, therefore, be a uniform experience against every miraculous event, otherwise the event would not merit that appellation . . .
>
> The plain consequence is (and it is a general maxim worthy of our attention), "that no testimony is sufficient to establish a miracle, unless the testimony be of such a kind that its falsehood would be more miraculous, than the fact, which it endeavors to establish . . ." When anyone tells me, that he saw a dead man restored to life I immediately consider with myself, whether it be more probable, that this person should either deceive or be deceived, or that the fact, which he relates, should really have happened. I weigh the one miracle against the other; and according to the superiority, which I discover, I pronounce my decision, and always reject the greater miracle. (1777, 114–16)

In this text Hume uses an unfortunate terminology. Sometimes he uses the word "miracle" and its cognates without any comparative adjectives. I understand him to be using the word there to designate an event that satisfies his definition. But in other places he uses comparative expressions such as "greater miracle" and "more miraculous." I don't see any way of making sense of the argument here without understanding these comparative expressions to be simply stylistic substitutions for the terms "probable" and "improbable." A "greater miracle" would be, then, an event that had a lower probability.

Initially at least, Hume's procedure seems to have some plausibility. Faced with competing and incompatible hypotheses, it seems plausible to accept the candidate that has a higher probability of being true (if one is going to accept either of the candidates at all). And it seems implausible to accept the one that has the lower probability, at least after one has decided that it does have the lower probability.

It is important, however, to be clear about just what the candidates are, and about just what the item is to which one is assigning a probability. For example, is the birth of quintuplets (in humans) probable or improbable? Well, quintuplets are very rare. So the probability that a randomly selected childbirth—say, the first delivery in San Francisco in 2007—will be the birth of quintuplets is very low. On the other hand, the probability that there have been some quintuplet births in the history of the world is very, very high. (And that, course, is because there are well-attested accounts of such births.) The probability that there will be at least one quintuplet birth in the United States within the next ten years is not quite that high, but it certainly is not low. So here we have three different propositions about quintuplet births, and it seems that they have three quite different probabilities. And all of these probabilities are based on experience.

Armed with this warning, we can consider the Lottery Surprise.

An organization that sponsors a very large prize lottery in the United States recently informed potential entrants that the chance of winning the grand prize was approximately one in 100 million. I suppose that this is based on an estimate of the number of entries that will be received, or something like that. So if I were to submit an entry for this lottery the probability of my winning the grand prize would be approximately 0.00000001. That is, of course, a very low probability, and I would be very surprised if I won. Assuming that the lottery is fairly drawn, every other entrant would have that same probability of winning. Suppose now that the drawing has actually been held, and that we read a short news story about it. The newspaper reports that a certain man, Henry Plushbottom of Topeka, Kansas, is the winner of the grand prize. The antecedent probability—antecedent, that is, to the news story—of Henry's being the winner is fantastically low. But what is now the consequent probability—consequent to the news story—that Henry really is the winner?

My own inclination is to say that the news story makes the probability that Henry really is the winner quite high. Of course, the account in the newspaper does not make it absolutely certain that Henry won. I know that there are mistakes in newspapers, that reporters sometimes get the facts wrong, they sometimes lie, and so on. (The *New York Times* regularly publishes a list of corrections, with a rate of about one correction for every fifty news items. And there must be other errors that go uncorrected.) But unless I have some special reason for doubt in this particular case, I would surely take the appearance of a newspaper story of this sort to raise the probability of Henry having been the winner to well above 0.5. And I think that most people would have a similar response. If we decide that this response is not rational, not epistemically proper in some way, then we will have to give up almost all uses of testimony. For in most cases, the events to which eyewitnesses testify have an extremely low antecedent probability.

If my response is rational, however, then it seems to be the case that a single testimony, a testimony given in many cases by someone whom we do not know at all, is sufficient to produce an enormous change in probability. Something whose initial probability is so small as to be almost unimaginable is converted by a single testimony into something that is substantially more probable than not. I call this the Lottery Surprise. How could a single testimony have such an enormous effect on probability? And how does this fact bear on our assessment of the probability of miracles when there is some testimony at hand?

I think that there is an answer to these questions, and that answer has a bearing on the general question of the relation of testimony to probability. The very low initial probability of Henry's being the winner is generated by thinking of Henry simply as being one of the 100 million entrants and as having the same chance of winning as any other entrant. Of course, if there were to be 70 or 80 million grand prize winners drawn, then Henry would have quite a good chance. His winning would be fairly probable. As it is, however, grand prize winners are very rare in this lottery—only one in 100 million. So Henry's winning is very improbable. But it could happen. After all, someone will win, and it could be Henry.

What about the antecedent probability of this testimony? Not the probability that the testimony is true, but the probability that this testimony would actually be given regardless of whether it is true or false. For it is the fact that this testimony is actually given that constitutes the evidence in this case. And remember that this testimony does not merely say that someone (unspecified) has won the lottery. It names a particular person.

The antecedent probability of just that testimony being given is very low. And that judgment is borne out by experience. For example, in my whole life (so far as I know) I have never been named in a news story as being a big lottery winner. I cannot recall any of my friends or acquaintances being identified in this way. Nor can I recall any of my friends or acquaintances recalling any of *their* friends or acquaintances being identified in that way. And so on.

It is crucial to understanding the Lottery Surprise that we be clear about the items to which we are assigning probabilities. The general proposition that there are mistakes in newspapers has a probability so close to 1.0 as to be morally certain. And the probability that the New York Times will have some mistake tomorrow is very high. (After all, that newspaper regularly publishes about five or ten corrections of stories in the previous edition.) But the probability that the Times will name me tomorrow as a big lottery winner is vanishingly low. That particular mistake is so rare that it has not happened even one single time in the past seventy-five years, and probably it will never happen.

The news story about a lottery winner, therefore, involves two items, and each of them has a very low antecedent probability. It was antecedently improbable that Henry would win, for he was only one entrant among 100 million. It was also antecedently improbable that he would be named in the story as the winner, for his was only one name among 100 million different names that could have appeared in that story. After all, if the reporter was going to make a mistake about who won, there are at least 100 million different ways he could make it. (He might even name someone who had not entered the lottery at all.)

The fact is that the news story involves two events, each of which, taken separately, is immensely improbable. In fact, they have the very same immense improbability. But taken together they support each other in such a way as to generate a substantial positive probability. If Henry is actually the winner, then it is probable that he will be named as such in the story, and if he is not the real winner, then it is fantastically improbable that he would be the one mistakenly identified in the paper. Therefore, his being identified as the winner makes it probable that he is really the winner.

Of course, these probabilities might not be the last word. If we had some positive reason to think that Henry was not the winner, then that might override the force of the testimony, and leave us doubting Henry's claim to fame. Or we might have additional reasons to believe that Henry was the winner, thus further strengthening his case. But what the Lottery Surprise shows is that there is nothing incredible, or even unusual, in the power of a single testimony to reverse an enormous initial improbability.

Perhaps, then, we should consider whether we have any positive reason for thinking that miracles in general, or any particular alleged miracle, are improbable. Of course, almost every aficionado of miracles will hold that they are improbable in the same sense in which quintuplets are improbable. That is, miracles are supposed to be rare, and so it is improbable that a randomly selected event will turn out to be a miracle. But that is just the kind of case to which the Lottery Surprise applies, the kind of case in which a single testimony can effect a startling reversal of probabilities. Is there any other way in which miracles are improbable?

Well, let us try a particular case. More than once Hume mentions "a dead man restored to life" as a clear example of a miracle. Probably he picked this example because of the prominence in the Christian faith of the claim that Jesus Christ was resurrected a few days after his death. So let us take that claim to be the one for which we want to make a probability assignment.

(J) Jesus of Nazareth was restored to life within a week or less of his death.

And now, what is the probability of (J)?

No doubt, different people will give different answers to that question. I already believe that this event actually did happen, and so I am inclined to say that the probability of (J) is very high. Some other people may be strongly convinced that this event never happened, and so they may well say that the probability of (J) is very low. Still other people might be puzzled and not have a ready answer at hand.

Probably these differences reflect differences in the background information, or supposed information, that we bring to the question. And of course, people differ widely in that respect. Is there any way we can go beyond or beneath these differences and identify some more fundamental basis on which to make a probability assessment? What is the really basic sort of information for such a case? Well, Hume sometimes suggests that probability assignments should in some way be based on experience. That is not an entirely unattractive suggestion. Let us try it.

It seems clear that Hume thought that the probability of (J) was very low, to say the least. So we can ask whether there is some experience that Hume had that would justify the assignment of a low probability to that proposition. But we need not make this a purely historical question. For we can also ask whether we have some experience that would justify a low assignment of probability to it.

It is easy to imagine that some people might indeed have some experience that would be relevant to a probability assignment for (J). Some contemporaries of Jesus, living in the same place, and so on, might have seen Jesus alive a few days after the crucifixion (or at least someone who looked just like Jesus and who acted just like Jesus). Such people would have a good reason, based on their experience, for assigning a high probability to (J). Or, if we prefer, we can imagine some contemporaries who saw the corpse of Jesus (or at least of someone who looked just like Jesus) decaying in the tomb two weeks after the crucifixion. If there were people who had that experience, then they would have good reason for assigning a very low probability to (J).

Hume, of course, could not have had either of these experiences. After all, he lived seventeen hundred years after Jesus, and over a thousand miles away. Whatever it was that happened to Jesus, resurrection or not, it seems unlikely that Hume could have observed it. The same thing is true about us: we also live too late and too far away. There may have been some people who were in the right place and time to observe something that was directly relevant to the probability of (J). But we are not such people and Hume was not either.

Perhaps, however, there are experiences that could have an *indirect* bearing on the probability of (J), experiences that Hume might have or that we might have. These experiences would have a direct bearing on the probability of some other proposition that had a special relation to (J). Hume indeed says some things that suggest that he is thinking of some such proposition. He says, "It is a miracle that a dead man should come to life; because that has never been observed in any age or country. There must, therefore, be a uniform experience against every miraculous event." And towards the end of the essay Hume refers to "the absolute impossibility" of miraculous events. Hume, therefore, seems to believe the following proposition:

(N) No one has ever risen from the dead.

This proposition is not directly about Jesus, nor about any other particular person. Unlike (J), it does not name anyone. It is a generalization. However, this proposition is related to (J) in an important way. If (N) is true, then (J) is false.

That is, if no one has ever risen from the dead, then Jesus did not rise from the dead. And it also seems plausible to think that if (N) is probable, then it is also probable that (J) is false. (N), therefore, seems to put a probability cap on (J). If the probability of (N) is above 0.5, then the probability of (J) must be lower than 0.5. So, if Hume assigns a high probability to (N) we can expect him to assign a low probability to (J). I suspect that this is, in fact, what Hume did.

If Hume had some experience that directly supported a high probability for (N), then he would have had an experience that indirectly supported a low probability for (J). But is there in fact some experience that Hume could have had, or some experience that we have had, that would be a good basis for assigning a high probability to (N)? It seems to me that there is no such experience.

Of course, Hume may have had a negative experience about resurrections, an experience that might be reported in this way:

(E) Hume never observed any resurrection from the dead, he never met anyone who had been restored to life after dying, etc.

I have no reason to doubt (E), and I have no inclination to doubt it. I think it is very likely that Hume never came across a genuine resurrection in his whole life. And the same is true of me. I also have never observed a resurrection. But although (E) is true, and the corresponding proposition about me is also true, these propositions have no real relevance with respect to the probability of (N). It is not the negative nature of propositions such as (E) that makes them irrelevant. It is, rather, the fact that Hume's sample and my sample are far too small relative to the scope of (N). (N) is a general proposition whose scope includes millions upon millions of particular cases, all the human deaths that belong to the history of the world. Hume, we might suppose, had some direct experience of a few human deaths and of what happened soon thereafter. Perhaps a dozen or so family members and friends. But even fifty or one hundred would be far too small to have a significant bearing on the probability of (N).

Of course, Hume's negative experience is just what we should expect if (N) is true. If there simply are no resurrections, then Hume would not run into one. But Hume's negative experience is also just what we would expect if there are real resurrections but they are quite rare. If there are, say, only half a dozen genuine resurrections among the many millions of deaths there have been in human history, then it is extremely unlikely that Hume's tiny sample would have caught one of them. So that sample is entirely unreliable in distinguishing between a world in which there are no resurrections—that is, the world as described by (N)—and a world in which there are only a few resurrections. But that distinction is crucial to this case. For there is probably no aficionado of resurrections, or of miracles in general, who thinks that they are as thick in the world as fleas on a stray dog.

In the light of this observation, one might think of strengthening the case by expanding the sample. Hume might add to his own experience the experience of his friends, and beyond that the experience of many other people in the world. And indeed, Hume seems to take just this tack. He says that a miracle "has never been observed in any age or country," and he adds that "there must, therefore, be a uniform experience against every miraculous event." And so Hume seems to appeal to something like the following proposition:

(W) No resurrection has ever been observed by anyone in the whole history of the world.

Now (W), if it were true, would indeed lend some strong support to (N). Perhaps it would not be entirely conclusive, but one would think that if there were even as many as half a dozen genuine resurrections in the history of the world, then it is likely that at least one or two of them would have been noticed by somebody. But is (W) in fact true? Of course, if (N) is true, then (W) is also true. But here we are trying to go in the other direction, using (W) as a reason for thinking that (N) is true. And if we do not begin with the assumption that (N) is true, then what reason might we have for thinking that (W) is true?

Hume claims that there is a uniform experience against resurrections, and against miracles in general. But the fact is that there is not a uniform testimony against these things. For better or worse, the testimonial picture is mixed. There are many people who, speaking about their own experience, can sincerely say that they have never observed a resurrection. And there are apparently a few people who say that they have observed a resurrection. Among these are people who said that they had seen Jesus alive a few days after his death, that they talked with him, had breakfast with him, and so on. This sort of mix in the testimonial picture—a lot of testimonies that reflect the pervasive uniformity of the world, and a few that report strange and anomalous events—is just what we should expect if miracles are indeed real but rare.

It seems to me, therefore, that there is no good reason, or at least no experience-based reason, to think that the probability of (N) is high. And so we cannot properly use (N) to justify assigning a low probability to (J). But where does that leave us with respect to the probability of (J)?

We can construe the probability of Jesus' resurrection as being very low in the same way as we construe the probability of Henry's winning the grand prize as being very low. If we take Jesus to be just a randomly selected person among the many millions of human beings who have lived in the world, and if we assume that resurrections are at best very rare in the world, then the antecedent probability of Jesus' being resurrected is very low. But this is just the sort of case to which the Lottery Surprise applies. That is, it is just the sort of case in which a single testimony generates an enormous change in the subsequent probability.

At the very end of his essay Hume throws out an intriguing suggestion:

> So that, upon the whole, we may conclude, that the Christian religion not only was at first attended with miracles, but even at this day cannot be believed by any reasonable person without one. Mere reason is insufficient to convince us of its veracity: and whoever is moved by faith to assent to it, is conscious of a continued miracle in his own person, which subverts all the principles of his understanding, and gives him a determination to believe what is most contrary to custom and experience. (1777, 131)

This statement may be merely ironic and sarcastic, a final poke at the credulity and gullibility of Christians. I think that is the way most commentators have interpreted it. But even jokes and sarcasm can include an element of truth. And maybe there is more truth in Hume's statement here than he realized. Taken at face value, the statement suggests another way in which a miracle might have an epistemic effect. Rather than hearing testimony about miracles or even witnessing a miracle themselves, believers might be the subjects of a miracle. The principal effect of this miracle, perhaps it's only effect, would be that of producing an epistemic change in the subject. Miracles, in general, produce effects that would not have happened in the ordinary course of nature. In this case, the effect that would not have happened otherwise is the believer's coming to have faith in the Christian religion. Despite the insufficiency of "mere reason", and so on, the person would find himself or herself with faith.

The idea of a divine revelation has always been a prominent element in Christianity. There is thought to be some communication from God to human beings. And that looks like a special case of a miracle. If there are genuine revelations, then, in some cases at least, those who receive that revelation come to know something, or to believe something, that they would not otherwise have known or believed. The ordinary course of nature—ordinary reason, ordinary events, and so on—would not have produced this particular effect. But a divine initiative, a divine incursion, would have the epistemic effect. And that would seem to be, according to the Humean definition, an epistemic miracle.

NOTES

1. That is not to say, of course, that Hume accepted or believed that worldview.

2. For example, the raising of Jairus's daughter, reported in Matthew 9, is sometimes classified as a resurrection. But that seems rather doubtful to me. That is not be-

cause I think that it did not happen, but because Jesus himself is reported as saying that the girl was not dead but "sleeping," that is, probably in a coma.

3. I discuss polytheism at more length in Mavrodes (1995).

4. For an example of this claim, see McKinnon (1967).

5. For some other concepts of the miraculous, see Holland (1965) and Tillich (1951).

6. For examples of appeals to the evidential value of miracles, see "Preparatory Considerations" in Paley (1794), and Swinburne (1979, ch. 12; 1992, chs. 6 and 7).

WORKS CITED

Habermas, Gary R., and Antony G. N. Flew. 1987. *Did Jesus Rise from the Dead?* San Francisco: Harper & Row.

Holland, R. F. 1965. "The Miraculous." *American Philosophical Quarterly* 2: 43–51. Reprinted in Swinburne 1989, 53–69.

Hume, David. 1777. *An Enquiry Concerning Human Understanding.* From the 1777 post-humous edition, ed. L. A. Selby-Biggs. Oxford: Clarendon Press, 1962.

Johnson, David. 1999. *Hume, Holism, and Miracles.* Ithaca N.Y.: Cornell University Press.

Mavrodes, George I. 1995. "Polytheism." In *The Rationality of Belief and the Plurality of Faith,* ed. Thomas D. Senor. Ithaca N.Y.: Cornell University Press.

———. 1998. "David Hume and the Probability of Miracles." *International Journal for Philosophy of Religion* 43: 167–82.

McKinnon, Alastair. 1967. " 'Miracle' and 'paradox.' " *American Philosophical Quarterly* 4: 308–14. Excerpt in Swinburne 1989, 49–52.

Paley, William. 1794. *Evidences of Christianity.* Excerpt in Swinburne 1989, 41–47.

Swinburne, Richard, 1979. *The Existence of God.* Oxford: Clarendon Press.

———, ed. 1989. *Miracles.* New York: Macmillan.

Tillich, Paul, 1951. *Systematic Theology.* Vol. I. Chicago: University of Chicago Press. Excerpt in Swinburne 1989, 71–74.

FOR FURTHER READING

Flew, Antony G. N. 1961. *Hume's Philosophy of Belief.* London: Routledge & Kegan Paul.

Lewis, Clive Staples. 1960. *Miracles.* London: Collins Fontana Books.

Mackie, J. L. 1982. *The Miracle of Theism.* Oxford: Clarendon Press.

Swinburne, Richard. 1992. *Revelation.* Oxford: Clarendon Press.

CHAPTER 13

FAITH AND REVELATION

C. STEPHEN EVANS

THE concepts of faith and revelation, though logically distinct, are related in a variety of ways. All of the great theistic religions, especially the Abrahamic faiths of Judaism, Christianity, and Islam, have traditionally taught that God can be known only through revelation. Because God is conceived by these traditions to be all-powerful and all-knowing, it is impossible for anyone to gain knowledge of God unless God is willing for this to occur. In some sense, all knowledge of God is made possible by God's decision to allow himself to become known.

Reflection on God's revelation in these traditions has generally distinguished between God's general revelation and what are termed special revelations. General revelation encompasses what can be known about God from the natural world, drawing on general features of that world such as its contingency and purposiveness, or general features of human experience, or specific experiences that are generally available to humans, such as experiences of moral obligation, aesthetic delight, and feelings of dependence and awe. Although some theists have claimed that faith, understood as something like a willingness to know and relate to God in a trusting fashion, is a condition for the proper reception of general revelation, the concept of faith has been more closely associated with special revelation.

Special revelations can consist of particular events, experiences, and/or teachings, often mediated through a prophet, apostle, or other exceptional religious individual. A paradigm would be the revelations associated with Moses, Elijah, and other figures of the Hebrew Bible (Christian Old Testament). For example, in Exodus, chapters 3 and 4, God catches the attention of Moses by a bush that burns but is not consumed by the fire, and then speaks a message to Moses, appointing him to deliver Israel from Egypt. While the story of such revelatory events and the content of such revelatory messages could be and presumably for some periods have been transmitted orally, the great theistic religions all possess sacred writings, which are either viewed as a record or testimony about God's revelation or as itself a form of revelation. The latter is the case, for example, for Islam, which views the Quran as a divinely authored book that was transmitted to Muhammed. The same is true, to a lesser degree, for Christianity, since many Christians claim that the Bible, though composed by human authors, is still at least partially authored by God, who inspired those human authors.

For these religions faith in God is closely linked to how humans respond to God's special revelations, since a right understanding of God is crucially dependent on such revelations. The primary object of faith is God himself, not revelation. However, because God is known only through revelation, faith in God naturally includes a believing, trusting response to what God has revealed. I first examine the nature of revelation, particularly special revelation, and the different ways this concept has been understood. I then focus on the concept of faith as a response to God and to divine revelation, focusing particularly on questions concerning the relation between faith and human reason. Though, as I have noted, the issues to be discussed arise for all of the Abrahamic religions, and even for such faiths as theistic versions of Hinduism, I mainly use debates within the Christian tradition to illustrate the issues. Also, in what follows I use the term "revelation" to mean "special revelation" unless qualified otherwise.

REVELATION AS PROPOSITIONAL

The traditional Christian view of revelation emphasizes the notion that God reveals truths, propositions that human should believe. Thomas Aquinas will serve, on this issue as on many others, as a good example. Aquinas holds that truths about God naturally fall into two types: truths that "exceed all the ability of the human reason" and those "which the natural reason also is able to reach" (1975, 63). Aquinas goes on to say that both types of truths are revealed by God and are fitting objects of human belief, since if those truths that human reason can in principle apprehend were not also revealed, they would be known by only a few people, and even for those people their grasp of these truths would come only after long inquiry and would be mixed with error (66–68). This "propositional" view of revelation is one that reformers such as Calvin and Luther unhesitatingly affirmed as well, and it can be clearly seen in early Protestant creeds, such as the Belgic Confession, the Westminster Confession, and the Augsberg Confession. The Belgic Confession is typical in affirming that "we receive all these books [of Scripture] ... believing, without any doubt, all things contained in them" (Schaff 1877, 386).

REVELATION AS NONPROPOSITIONAL

This traditional view of revelation as propositional in character was questioned by many twentieth-century theologians, especially those linked with "neo-orthodox" or "dialectical theology," who affirmed that revelation is not the proposing of propositions for belief, but the unveiling of God himself so as to establish a personal relation with humans. A follower of this movement summarizes what is often termed the "nonpropositional" view of revelation as follows: "What God reveals is not propositions or information—what God reveals is God. In revelation we do not receive a doctrine or esoteric piece of information ... In revelation we are brought into a living relationship with the person of God" (Hordern 1959, 61–62).

This nonpropositional view of revelation must be understood in part as an indirect response to historical and critical analysis of the Bible during the nineteenth and twentieth centuries. The liberal theology that developed during this period basically shared the traditional understanding of revelation as propositional in character, but as a result of critical study concluded that the Bible could not be seen as a divinely inspired, infallible book, as many theologians had thought. Rather, the Bible must be seen as a record of the evolving religious consciousness of the Jewish people, a witness to increasingly profound religious experiences, rather than a set of writings directly inspired by God. On such a view the truths of the Bible are truths that contemporary humans must verify through their own religious experiences and reflection rather than believe because they have been revealed by God. Such a view seems to undermine the authority of special revelation and erode the distinction between such revelation and general revelation.

The neo-orthodox theologians, under the influence of such giants as Karl Barth and Emil Brunner, attempted to restore the importance of special revelation by making a distinction between the revelatory historical events and the Bible itself, which is seen as a human witness to those events. Those special events are not merely part of generic human religious experience, but represent acts by which God disclosed himself to humans. The God who acted in this way in biblical history is still a God who acts and who discloses himself to the believer who reads the Bible or hears the Word of God preached. The Bible is thus both a witness to revelation, a record of revelation, and a means by which revelation continues to occur, as the Spirit of God illumines the hearts of those who read and listen with openness. In this way, the nonpropositional account of revelation attempts to maintain the primacy of special revelation while being open to the critical scholarly study of the Bible that sees it as a very human book.

The nonpropositional view of revelation is very attractive; it contains powerful insights that must be part of a viable account of revelation. However, it is open to powerful objections if it is understood as a *replacement* for the traditional view. We may note first of all that if one is prepared to accept the notion of God acting in special ways of history, there is no a priori reason to doubt the possibility of a propositional revelation, for communicating is itself a type of act that God could perform. Second, we should note that much of the Bible does not consist of history at all, but doctrinal teachings, poetry of various kinds, proverbs, and other literary forms, and much of this material is surely propositional in character. However, these are not the most serious problems.

The major difficulty with the nonpropositional view of revelation, understood as a rival to the traditional view, is that it is not possible to make a clear distinction between a God who reveals propositions and a God who reveals himself. It is true that a personal relation with God is far more than a mere knowledge of propositions, and that knowing another person cannot be reduced to knowing facts about that person. It is, however, impossible to conceive of a case of personal knowledge that does not involve propositional knowledge as well. One cannot come to know another person without coming to know some things about that person at the same time. I know a woman named Susan, but I could hardly be said to know Susan if I did not know many things about her. It is, of course, frequently the case that our knowledge of other people is not explicitly formulated and reflected on, but it is no less real for that. For example, I know that Susan is a human being, that Susan is a woman, that Susan is a person with great energy and commitment, and that Susan is a person who has shown courage in the face of a serious illness, even though I may not have explicitly formulated those thoughts before now.

The same thing would appear to be true in the case of God. Knowing God in a personal way is hardly reducible to knowing facts about God. However, I could hardly know God at all if I knew nothing about him. Traditionally, Christians (and other theists) have affirmed that God exists necessarily, is the Creator of all that exists other than himself, and is supremely good and loving. Christians have gone beyond these theistic claims to hold that God reveals himself as the Father of Jesus and as three-in-one. It is hard to see how one could come to know God in a personal way without at the same time acquiring at least some minimal knowledge about him. If we had no propositional knowledge of God at all, then it would not even be possible to affirm the nonpropositional view of revelation, for to claim that God acts in history to reveal himself we must believe that God is real and is enough like a person that we can properly conceive of him as acting, and these are beliefs with propositional content.

I conclude, then, that we cannot coherently conceive of the nonpropositional view of revelation simply as an alternative to the traditional propositional view, for if God truly reveals himself so as to make it possible for humans to know him, then he must inevitably reveal to them some truths about himself as well. We can, however, welcome the nonpropositional view as making explicit and emphasizing themes that were doubtless present in traditional accounts but perhaps not sufficiently highlighted, namely, that the *primary* object of revelation is God himself, not propositions about God, and the *primary* purpose of revelation is making possible a relationship with God. Knowing God is certainly not reducible simply to knowing truths about God, and the nonpropositional view puts this important truth in the center of the picture rather than on the periphery.

That the themes emphasized by the nonpropositional account were at least implicit in the traditional account can be seen by noticing that, according to the traditional view, the propositions revealed by God were not to be believed simply because they were true, but because God had revealed them (Aquinas 1975, 77). One of the ways trust in a person manifests itself is in a willingness to believe what the person says, and thus personal trust is at least implicit in belief in what God reveals for Aquinas. The person of faith believes the propositions she does because of her trust in God; the beliefs both stem from and contribute to a personal relationship with God.

REVELATION AS INSPIRED, INFALLIBLE, AND INERRANT

What about the critical problems with the Bible that partially inspired the nonpropositional account? If the Bible is itself revelation, then must it be seen as inspired by God? And if it is inspired, must it be seen as infallible or perhaps inerrant? Are such beliefs about the Bible compatible with contemporary Biblical scholarship?

In answering such questions much depends on the nature of the relation between God and the inspired human agent of revelation. If one thinks of God as literally the author of a revelation, which is simply dictated to the prophet or human agent, as Islam claims is the case for the Quran, then it would appear that the revelation would be completely inerrant as well as inspired, since God is incapable of error. Most Christian theologians, however, have rejected such a dictation model of inspiration, and urged that God's inspiration in some way employs the ordinary human capacities of the prophet, taking the term "prophet" here as a general term for the human agent involved in the giving of a revelation.

A number of different models seem possible. For example, God could instill an understanding of some truth in a prophet and then allow that person to express the truth in his or her own characteristic manner. Or God could, being omniscient, know that some human is going to speak the truth and then declare that this person is authorized to speak for God, that is, that this person is a prophet. Alternatively, God could simply adopt the words of some human and declare that they express what he wishes to reveal, that they have the status of prophecy, much as a human being might take the words of some other person's poem as expressing what the first person wishes to communicate. All of these possibilities and more would seem to give a large role in the process of revelation to the human author.[1] However, there is much disagreement about the nature of inspiration thus conceived and about the implications of taking seriously the role of the human author.

One view, especially associated with Protestant fundamentalism, is that inspiration logically implies that the revealed Scriptures are inerrant, without error with respect to all the truths contained, including historical and scientific truths as well as those concerning morality and religion. Such a position might appear to be an extreme one that is difficult to defend, but in reality, claims for inerrancy are always heavily qualified in a number of ways. First of all, only the original "autographs," now presumably irrecoverable, are actually alleged to be inerrant, which allows for errors to develop as the Scriptures are copied and translated.

An even more significant qualification, however, is that the Scriptures are claimed to be inerrant only when properly interpreted. As soon as the issue of interpretation emerges, matters become complicated. For example, the proper interpretation of a particular passage depends on the identification of its proper genre. If the Book of Jonah was intended as history, then if no such prophet in fact was swallowed and then regurgitated by a giant fish, the book contains falsehood. If, however, the book was composed as a parable, and was meant to be understood as such, as many scholars think is likely the case, then its truth would not depend on its historical versimilitude, but on the soundness of its ethical and theological point, which seems to be that God is willing to show mercy on all who repent, including the people of Nineveh and not just the Israelites.

Defenders of inerrancy usually accept other interpretive principles that restrict the scope of inerrancy. For example, the biblical authors use the language of appearance, rather than the precise language of science, in speaking of the sun rising and setting and going around the earth, and such phenomenal language is neither false nor intended to be scientifically informative. Richard Swinburne develops this point by making a distinction between the informative content of a revelation and what he terms the "presuppositions" or "assumptions" of whatever culture in which that revelation might occur, that are used to communicate that informative content (1992, 84). On such a view, a revelation might communicate the truth that God created the natural world but describe that natural world in terms that were culturally common to the period of the revelation but are no longer scientifically acceptable. In such a case, Swinburne argues that it is reasonable to disregard the falsity of the cultural presupposition in judging the truth of the revelatory claim. In this way, one avoids the inference that the Bible teaches that the world is flat or that the sky is a dome suspended over it, and so forth. Another common qualification is that, because the biblical authors use round numbers and assume only the standards of accuracy current in their culture, an account of a speech, for example, does not have to be "word for word" to be true, but will be counted true if it embodies the main thrust of what was said.

One can therefore see that when it is claimed that some revelation, such as the Bible, is inerrant when properly interpreted, this claim is not as extreme and hard to defend as might initially appear to be the case. A natural extension of these qualifications to inerrancy, perhaps already implicit in them, is a doctrine of limited inerrancy. Limited inerrancy is the claim that the Bible (or whatever book is claimed to be a true special revelation) is inerrant only with respect to those areas in which God intends to reveal truths. One might claim, for example, that the Bible is without error in its religious and moral teachings ("in matters of faith and practice") but deny that this inerrancy extends to scientific and historical matters.

However, it is not always easy to determine what the scope of God's intended revelation is. Some historical claims, such as the claim that Jesus was crucified and resurrected on the third day, seem to have religious and theological importance. For some Christians, even some apparently scientific claims, such as the claim that humans were created by God in a special act, have theological and even ethical import. Perhaps, for example, the special creation of humans in the image of God gives human persons a special moral status. On the other side of the ledger, some teachings that are apparently explicitly ethical in character, such as Old Testament regulations, are commonly interpreted as applicable merely to the culture in which they were promulgated and not viewed as having general moral significance. To be viable, then, a doctrine of limited inerrancy should hold that inerrancy is not absent from all matters of history and science but only those incidental or unimportant to what God intends to reveal. However, this does not seem so different from the claim that a proper interpretation is one that disregards false cultural presuppositions that are used to communicate a truth without being part of the truth being communicated. In practice, then, it is not easy to distinguish a doctrine of limited inerrancy from a doctrine of inerrancy with the usual qualifications.

Some theologians distinguish between a doctrine of inerrancy and a claim that the Scriptures are infallible (though others use the terms "inerrancy" and "infallibility" synonymously). There are various ways of making such a distinction. One is to understand by infallibility simply limited inerrancy as explained in the previous paragraph. Another is to interpret inerrancy as a characteristic of the propositions in the text itself, while viewing infallibility as a characteristic of the text in relation to its readers. An infallible text, it might be claimed, is one that will always guide its readers properly. It might be claimed that a revelation can be infallible without being inerrant, because any errors that the text contains will not affect its intended revelatory function.

Once again, it is not clear that such a claim of infallibility can be sharply distinguished from a properly qualified doctrine of inerrancy, or at least some doctrine of limited inerrancy. If one of the functions of a revelation is to convey truths about God, and if a revelation contains propositions for this purpose, then it is hard to see how the question of whether the revelation properly guides its readers can be sharply separated from the question of whether the propositions, or at least some of the propositions, in the revelation are true. The reader or hearer will not be properly guided if he or she is led to believe falsehood (unless this is God's intention in giving the revelation, a possibility that most would reject). If the proponent of infallibility responds that much of a revelation has a different function from the conveying of information and is not intended as the communication of truths, then he or she would seem to be making a claim that could also be used by a defender of inerrancy, who could rightly affirm that such points must be taken into account when arriving at the proper interpretation of a revelation. A revelatory passage that makes no truth claims contains no falsehoods either. Such an infallible revelation could be inerrant as well. A proper interpretation must certainly consider questions of genre and the intentions of an author, including a divine coauthor.

THE NATURE OF FAITH

There is a dispute over the nature of faith that corresponds to the dispute between propositional and nonpropositional accounts of revelation. If we think of faith as a human response to God's revelation, then those who think of revelation as primarily propositional in character naturally emphasize faith as consisting of belief. Those who defend a nonpropositional account of revelation, in which God reveals himself through events, naturally think of faith as consisting of something like personal trust.

If we think of these two views of revelation as complementary rather than rivals, as I argued above, then we can take the same complementary view of faith. Trust and belief are intertwined in a number of ways. Faith is primarily trust in God as a person. However, one can hardly trust a person if one does not believe that the person exists, or if one does not believe the person is good; hence, some beliefs seem necessary for trust. Furthermore, one of the ways trust manifests itself is in a willingness to believe what another person tells me, not merely in the case where I have independent reasons to believe what I have been told, but precisely because of the person's testimony. So trust in God naturally manifests itself as a willingness to believe what God has revealed because God has revealed it.

Many religious disputes about the nature and value of faith may rest on semantic unclarity. Some writers may mean by "faith" something like "mere belief" in propositions, without the personal trust in God that lies at the heart of the religious life; others have a richer conception of faith, including not only belief, but a trust that manifests itself in a disposition to actions. At the time of the Reformation, for example, there was an acrimonious dispute as to whether faith alone was sufficient for salvation, or whether works were also necessary. Richard Swinburne has argued that the disputants had different conceptions of faith, with Catholics understanding faith as mere belief and Protestants thinking of faith in a richer way that includes trust and a disposition to obedient action, even though faith itself does not consist of "works" (1981, 104–24). The Protestant conception of faith seems closer to what Aquinas termed "formed faith," which was seen by Catholics as sufficient for salvation. Though there may well be other important issues in dispute, Swinburne seems right to maintain that the disagreement rested partly on verbal confusion.

It therefore seems best to conceive of faith as a response of the whole person to God's self-revelation, with trust, belief, and a disposition to obedient action all being significant components. Such a "whole person" response is by no means purely intellectual. For example, Jonathan Edwards speaks of faith as involving the development of a new set of "affections," and Kierkegaard describes faith as a "passion" that seems to include either emotions or dispositions to have emotions of various kinds. Nevertheless, philosophical discussions of the legitimacy and reasonableness of faith have tended to focus on the aspect of belief. If the beliefs that are a component of faith are false, irrational, or defective in some other epistemological dimension, this would seem to imply that faith as a whole is an unreasonable stance. If I trust an individual because I falsely believe in the goodness of that person, then my trust is misplaced. The relation between faith and rational belief is therefore a crucial issue, and a proper treatment of this issue is linked to general questions about the relation of faith to reason and the nature of both.

RATIONALISM AND FIDEISM

Views on the relation between faith and reason can be arranged on a continuum, with *rationalism* and *fideism* occupying the opposite poles. The rationalist holds that faith must be limited or governed by reason; the fideist holds that reason is damaged or defective and must be repaired or restored by faith. The sense of the term "rationalism" here must not be confused with the sense it bears in epistemology, when it is contrasted with "empiricism." In theology, an empiricist, someone who emphasizes the role of sense experience in the acquisition of knowledge, can also be a rationalist, who affirms the primacy of human reason (taking "reason" as a term for all of our natural human faculties) over faith.

John Locke's epistemology provides a clear and historically influential example of the rationalist perspective. Locke is open to the possibility of a special revelation from God, and he sees faith in the traditional way as belief in a proposition "upon the credit of the proposer, as coming from God" (1975, 689). Through faith, human beings can come to grasp truths that they would have no access to apart from a revelation. Nevertheless, faith for Locke must always be governed by reason.

Locke accepts two common epistemological claims.[2] First, being a classical foundationalist, he holds that all of our beliefs must rest on a foundation of propositions that are known with certainty. Second, being an evidentialist, he holds that the beliefs that are held on the basis of this evidential foundation must be held with a strength that is proportionate to the evidence that the believer has for them (1975, 697). For Locke, humans have a duty to believe only what is supported by evidence that ultimately traces to foundational certitude, and they have a duty to hold those beliefs with a degree of assurance that corresponds to the evidence.

For Locke, it is certain that any proposition revealed by God is true. However, that any particular revelation is in fact from God is itself a belief for which a person must have evidence; it is not itself something that could be known with certitude. It follows that "*no Proposition can be received for Divine Revelation . . . if it be contradictory to our clear intuitive Knowledge*" (1975, 692, emphasis Locke's). So reason must certify the credentials of any alleged revelation, and no alleged revelation can overturn the foundational truths known by reason. Locke does, however, accept that a well-attested revelation might overturn a belief that is merely probable for reason (694–96). He concludes that faith is simply "natural *Reason* enlarged by a new set of Discoveries communicated by GOD immediately, which *Reason* vouches the truth of" (698).

The fideist view is more difficult to describe than the rationalist perspective, partly because the term is often used as a term of abuse, a close cousin of irrationalism. When the term is used in this way, it is understandable that few thinkers would be willing to own the label. Perhaps the clearest example of one who embraces this kind of irrationalism is the Russian expatriate Lev Shestov, who seems to affirm that there is indeed a contradiction between human reason and religious faith, and concludes that the believer must choose faith, even if this means he or she must reject the principles of logic (1966, 302). Most of the thinkers who have been labeled irrationalists because they are fideists, however, such as Kierkegaard and Tertullian, do not really seem to wish to reject reason, though particular passages quoted out of context may appear to suggest that they do.

A fideist who really does wish to reject reason in the form of the principles of logic is committed to a view that cannot be rationally defended or even discussed, since we cannot understand what someone might mean by an assertion if that assertion is compatible with its denial being true. I shall therefore ignore views such as Shestov's. However, the indefensibility of irrationalism should not blind us to the possibility that there are defensible claims made by some of the thinkers who have been described as fideists. The question as to whether a particular individual should or should not be described as a fideist is not that interesting, I believe. It is more important to look at the claims made by people who have been accused of being fideists. I suggest that the primary defensible claims center around the idea of the limits of human reason.

That human reason has limits of various kinds seems undeniable, and the recognition of such limits is hardly irrational. For example, science fiction has made commonplace the idea that there might be beings in other parts of the universe with cognitive powers that vastly exceed our own. I term forms of fideism that urge that human reason is limited in various ways and that those limits should be recognized and taken account of "responsible fideism."[3] As we shall see, the kinds of limits that fideists urge us to recognize are various. Some are linked to human finitude; others are associated with human sinfulness. We shall examine the limits of reason by looking at faith without reasons, faith that is some ways above reason, and finally, faith that is in some way "against" reason.[4]

FAITH WITHOUT EVIDENCE: THE LIMITS OF INFERENTIAL REASON

A common criticism of faith is that it involves belief without evidence or with insufficient evidence. What is often termed the "evidentialist objection" to religious belief rests on the assumption that rational religious beliefs must be based on evidence. However, it is far from clear that this requirement of evidence is itself one that can be rationally defended. Defenders of what has come to be known as Reformed epistemology have argued instead that religious beliefs can be "properly basic," not held on the basis of any inferential evidence at all.

Such an argument can be seen as rooted in a recognition of one of the ways human reason is limited. If some kind of foundationalist picture of human knowledge is accepted, it is clear that some beliefs must be accepted as basic by human beings. If all beliefs must be based on other beliefs, this would require an infinite chain of evidential beliefs, since the beliefs that function as evidence would require further beliefs as evidence for the original evidence, and so on. But clearly, finite human beings are not capable of holding beliefs on the basis of such an infinite chain.

The classical foundationalist, such as Locke, accepts that some beliefs must be basic but hold that properly basic beliefs must be highly certain. Alvin Plantinga summarizes the position as the claim that properly basic beliefs must be "self-evident, incorrigible, or . . . evident to the senses" (2000, 93). However, classical foundationalism seems problematic on several counts. First of all, as Plantinga has argued, the classical foundationalist restriction of properly basic beliefs does not pass its own test; it does not seem self-evident, incorrigible, or evident to the senses that only beliefs of this type should be held in a basic way, and no one has constructed a convincing argument for such a conclusion on the basis of beliefs that pass this test. Second, many of the beliefs that humans appear to possess as knowledge would not appear reasonable on the classical foundationalist view. We humans surely know that there is an external world, that other people have conscious minds, and that the world is more than five minutes old, but there are no generally accepted arguments for such conclusions that measure up to the classical foundationalist standard.

Philosophers such as Plantinga have argued that even if we have no general criterion of proper basicality, some of our religious beliefs can be accepted as properly basic. Plantinga proposes, for example, that humans have been given a *sensus divinitatis*, a God-given disposition to believe in God in certain circumstances (2000, 173). For example, when contemplating a flower or reflecting on an evil one has done, a person may be moved to believe "God has made this wondrous thing" or "God disapproves of this shoddy behavior." Recently, Plantinga has extended this claim that belief in God can be properly basic to the claim that the central truths of Christian faith can be held in a properly basic way, if they are held on the basis of "the instigation of the Holy Spirit" (2000, 265).

Plantinga does not claim to be able to demonstrate that these beliefs about the sensus divinitatis and the instigation of the Holy Spirit are true. He argues, rather, that *if* they are true, then it is likely that some individuals are reasonable to believe them, and may even know them. Such a position is unsatisfying to many philosophers, who wish to be able to determine what is true on the basis of some "neutral" epistemological position that provides a basis for examining all such truth claims. Plantinga is in effect arguing that such an epistemological stance may be beyond our human capacities. What we can know depends on the truth about our world and our capacities, and what we believe we can know may depend on our beliefs about the world and our capacities. There may be no "neutral" epistemological stance, for what we think we can know may depend on what we believe about our relation to the world we are trying to know, and that varies. The evidentialist objection to religious belief, insofar as it rests on the assumption that religious beliefs must be based on such "neutral evidence," may therefore rest on assumptions that are undermined by the limits of human reason. Though Plantinga himself rejects the label of fideism, his work may be seen as illustrating the view that reason has limits that it is rational to recognize.

One of the claims associated with fideism is what we might call the "no-neutrality" thesis, the claim that the amount of "common ground" available to human knowers is much smaller than many have assumed, especially with respect to religious claims. Once we see the way that Plantinga's claims about proper basicality are linked to the no-neutrality thesis, we can see a similarity to positions that do not claim that faith should be basic. William Wainwright, for example, has articulated a form of evidentialism that sees religious faith as based on reasons, but claims that it may be necessary for faith to be present in an individual for that individual to grasp those reasons or see their force as evidence (1995, 1–6). Such a view also implies that common ground as evidence that any person may grasp is limited.

FAITH ABOVE REASON

Given the finitude of human beings, it is hardly surprising that there might be truths about a God who is infinite in power, knowledge, and love that we are unable to grasp through our natural powers. Aquinas, for example, urges that "a created intellect cannot see the essence of God unless God by his grace unites Himself to the created intellect, as an object made intelligible to it," a state that would require us to be "uplifted out of this mortal life" (1945, 97).

There are other reasons than mere finitude for thinking that the powers of unaided human reason might be limited. Immanuel Kant (1965), for example, famously argued that human theoretical knowledge is always structured by the categories of human understanding, and by space and time, the "forms of human intuition." Our theoretical knowledge is therefore limited to knowledge of the phenomenal world, the world as it appears to humans, and may not correspond to noumenal reality, reality as it is in itself. God, for example, is regarded by many theologians as transcending space and time; if so, God cannot be known by humans through the exercise of their theoretical cognitive powers.

For both Aquinas and Kant, these cognitive limitations are partially remedied by faith. For Aquinas, as we have seen, faith includes believing some truths that God has revealed which we humans would be unable to grasp on our own. For Kant, who famously concluded that he had found it necessary to "limit knowledge to make room for faith," faith is not necessarily limited to belief in a historical revelation. Although Kant does not deny the possibility of such a revelation or the reasonableness of a believing response to one, such historical faith for him must be governed by what he terms "pure moral faith," a faith in God, human freedom, and life after death that is grounded in the demands of rational morality (1960, 100–105).

However, even if we grant the theoretical possibility that there are truths about God that are "above" human reason, is it possible for us humans to recognize our limits? If we encounter a limit to human reason, would reason have the capacity to recognize this limit, or would such a capacity to recognize the limit itself be beyond the limit? And even if we can recognize our limits, does faith really make it possible to transcend those limits in some way?

There might be various ways in which the limits of human reason could be recognized. Kant, for example, thought that when reason exceeded its proper boundaries it fell into antinomies or contradictions (1965, 384–483).[5] A more promising line of thought is that the limits are revealed to humans by God's self-revelation itself. Just as we might come to recognize certain human limitations if we encountered an extraterrestrial being who was vastly superior and lacked those limitations, so also an encounter with a self-revealing infinite God might help us to understand our own limitations.

How could we recognize such superiority? One might think that this would be impossible. By hypothesis, such a superior being would know things we humans cannot know. How, then, could we discern that this superior knowledge is genuine knowledge, since we cannot independently confirm it?

In the case of the extraterrestrial the answer is reasonably clear. There are a variety of considerations that might provide evidence for superiority. One factor might be sheer reliability. If the extraterrestrial communicated truths that we were able to verify independently, if the claims communicated were invariably true, this would be evidence of superior cognitive power, especially if the claims concerned issues where a human knower would typically make some errors. A second factor might be the manner in which the extraterrestrial's knowledge was obtained. I may know what I had for lunch today, but if an extraterrestrial knew this who was not present for lunch and had no apparent means of knowing such a thing, this would be evidence of superiority. Foreknowledge of events that a human could not reasonably foresee would also constitute such evidence. Finally, if an extraterrestrial were to show great technological prowess, such as being able to transport a physical body instantaneously over a long distance, this would naturally suggest superior cognitive power as well.

A theologian such as Aquinas maintains that we might have evidence that a revelation is from God, a being with vastly superior cognitive powers, that is roughly analogous to this kind of evidence. Aquinas says that we can come to see that the revelation is from such a being in a variety of ways. Some of the truths contained in the alleged revelation might be ones that we can independently confirm, and here the superiority of the revealer might be evident in the manner in which the truths were known. Fulfilled prophecies could show the existence of foreknowledge, and miracles and other signs could also be evidence that the revelation is from a source that vastly exceeds human beings in power, and therefore presumably in knowledge as well (1975, 71–73). It is worth noting in passing that Aquinas also mentions the "inward instigation of the Holy Spirit" as the source of a belief in the genuineness of a revelation, a claim that moves Plantinga to enlist Aquinas in the roster of those who hold that a belief in the genuineness of a revelation can be basic and not rooted in evidence (Plantinga 2000, 249).

Can a revelation from God enable human beings to acquire truths that human reason could not acquire on its own? I see no a priori reason why this should not be possible. There are a range of possibilities for the relation between such revealed truths and human reason. Aquinas himself seemed to hold that reason can develop arguments for such truths, but that the arguments can only reach probability and can never be conclusive (1975, 77–78). Kant seems to hold the more radical position that theoretical reason cannot investigate truths about God at all, for when it tries to do so, it falls into contradictions (antinomies).

However, for both of these thinkers (and Kierkegaard as well), whatever truths that are communicated must be in some way understandable. Aquinas deals with the general problem of how we humans can conceive of God by affirming that positive predicates can be applied to God analogically; when we say that God is good, we are not using the term "good" exactly as we would when affirming that a creature is good, but the use is not equivocal either, for there is a real relation between creaturely goodness and the divine goodness that is its foundation. This view that predicates can apply to God analogically does not apply only to revealed truths, but if it is viable it would seem relevant to those higher truths as well.

Kant deals with the problem by affirming that reason does possess a pure Idea of God. Though it is not a concept that can be put to empirical or scientific use, it is an Idea with enough content that it can be put to practical use. For Kant, we need only understand the concepts of God and life after death well enough to use them to guide our moral lives. Kierkegaard follows Kant here in thinking that religious truths are essentially practical. We do not need to understand God as a theoretical object, but we need to know how we are to worship God, thank God, and be obedient to God's commands. For Kierkegaard, the practical knowledge we need is given in and through a relationship to God incarnate in the person of Jesus the Christ. If we have faith that Jesus is God, then we have a God who can be for us the Pattern to be imitated, as well as the Redeemer (Kierkegaard 1990, 147).

Faith as Against Reason

Many of the writers classified as fideists do not, however, content themselves merely with affirming that faith may legitimately involve belief without reasons, or belief in that which is above reason's capacity. Rather, they seem to affirm that faith may require belief that is against reason. Tertullian, for example, is famous for his claim that the death and resurrection of Jesus "is by all means to be believed, because it is absurd . . . the fact is certain because it is impossible" (1951, 525).

Among modern thinkers it is Søren Kierkegaard who is best-known for such statements. Kierkegaard, or (more commonly) one of the pseudonymous characters he invented to "author" many of his works, frequently says that faith, particularly faith in the incarnation of God as a human person, involves a belief in what is "impossible" or "absurd," and that such a belief involves a "contradiction" (1992, 211, 233). Is this simply irrationalism, or is there a defensible claim in this neighborhood as well? I myself do not think that Kierkegaard holds that belief in the incarnation requires a belief in a *logical* contradiction, but a full defense of this view would require a lengthy detour into Kierkegaard interpretation.[6]

What might Kierkegaard mean by such claims if he does not intend to embrace irrationalism? To answer this question we must reflect more on the character of what might variously be termed "reason" or "the understanding."[7] The term "reason" is partly a normative term; it denotes whatever patterns or practices of thinking are likely to help us humans arrive at truth. To attack reason in this normative sense is simply to attack truth and would indeed be a form of irrationalism.

However, the term "reason" is not purely normative but has descriptive content as well, just as is the case for such ethical terms as "good" and "just." A purely normative conception would be entirely abstract and unable to give practical guidance. It is only when we have some idea as to what is to actually count as "rational" or "just" that these terms can guide our behavior. Every concrete human society holds up particular practices of thinking and belief formation as those that embody "reason," those that are thought to give us the best chance of arriving at truth. However, which practices are regarded as part of "reason" is not something that is historically and culturally invariant. Rather, we find substantial changes over time in the weight attached to such things as the testimony of authoritative texts, tradition, experimental evidence, and deductive theorizing. The question of what counts as "reason" is itself one about which reasonable people may disagree. If we distinguish between what we might call "ideal reason," those practices, whatever they might be, that are best suited to arrive at truth, and "concrete reason," those practices that are actually accepted by a given society as reasonable, then we can understand the possibility that a critique of concrete reason may be done for the sake of ideal reason.

A good example of what we might call the critique of what counts as "reason" (in the concrete sense) is provided by some contemporary feminists, who argue that many of the practices accepted as "reasonable" reflect a male bias rooted in male domination of society. A society characterized by true equality between men and women and in which women were full participants might therefore have a somewhat different conception of what is reasonable or rational. One does not have to accept the conclusions of these feminists to see that the kind of case they are making is one that a truly reasonable person must be open to considering. In effect, feminists have argued that male bias and domination of society constitute a condition that damages or limits concrete reason.

One way of construing thinkers such as Kierkegaard is to see them as making a similar claim. On this view, reason may not be limited merely by its finitude, as was mainly the case when we looked at faith as involving beliefs that are above reason, but by the character of concrete human beings. Suppose that some religious view of the world is true, but that the intellectual practices designated as "reasonable" in a given society are such that it is difficult or impossible to recognize this truth. For example, suppose the Buddhist claim that suffering is linked to desire is true, but that in a given society the idea that desire is something bad or defective just seems "self-evidently" false to most people, a view that a "rational" person would not consider seriously. Perhaps a person who is in such a condition can come to see the truth only if his or her character is transformed through some ascetic practice or through meditation.

For Kierkegaard and other Christian thinkers who have been termed fideists, the relevant damage to reason is due to human sinfulness. An integral part of classical Christian doctrine is the claim that the human race possesses a kind of "solidarity in sin," a strong orientation away from God and God's goodwill, and that it is only with divine assistance that humans are capable of reorienting themselves toward the good. This Christian claim is one way of spelling out what is involved in the no-neutrality thesis considered above, a big part of the reason why evidential common ground might be limited when it comes to the discovery of religious truth.

How might sin cause such damage to reason? Traditionally, sin has been conceived as centering on either *pride* or *selfishness* (or perhaps both). Pride might damage a human's ability to know God, because the recognition of God demands humility. I cannot see myself as the center of the universe if I know that God is the Creator of all things and that I am a completely dependent creature. Selfishness might be a barrier, if God is love, as many religions claim, and if there is truth in the ancient principle that "only like knows like." Perhaps a selfish, acquisitive creature has difficulty recognizing and accepting love. If humans are responsible to God, and if God demands loving concern for others, then we can certainly see that selfish creatures would have motivation for suppressing or denying any knowledge of God.

In this context, "faith" might be considered the name for the new condition that is made possible by God's help. Faith is not merely believing without evidence, or even believing what is above reason, though it may be both of those as well. Faith requires a reorientation of the individual so that pride and selfishness can be replaced by humility and love, thereby repairing the cognitive damage done by sin.

I believe that it is for these reasons that Kierkegaard insists that genuine faith involves belief in that which is "against" the human understanding. For him, Christian faith is faith in the incarnation, and he thinks that the idea of God becoming a human being is paradoxical to the human mind. God's supreme revelation then takes the form of the paradoxical "God-man" (1985, 23–36). Moved by pure love for the human race, God has put aside his divine powers to become one of us for our salvation. Because we humans have no experience of this kind of love and no understanding of it apart from God's self-revelation, unaided human reason can only judge this to be "the most improbable thing" or "strangest of all things" (52, 101). If human reason insists on its own self-sufficiency and refuses to admit it own limitations, it will be offended by the Christian claims.

When the "offended consciousness" asserts that the incarnation is absurd, Kierkegaard actually takes this as an indirect sign of the genuineness of the incarnation (1985, 49–54). To attempt to prove or demonstrate the truth of the incarnation to such human beings would be to ignore the effects of sin on human cognitive powers. No effort should be made to make Christianity appear attractive to its "cultured despisers." Rather, Kierkegaard says that the response of concrete human reason is exactly what we would predict would happen if Christianity is true, and he insists that the "possibility of offense" is a necessary element of true Christian proclamation.

What appears to be an attack on "reason" is therefore in this case not motivated by a lack of concern for truth. Kierkegaard is not affirming that faith may legitimately believe what we know to be false. Rather, he is claiming that the practices that constitute concrete human reason are not aimed at truth at all. Turning on its head the common charge that religious belief involves wish-fulfillment, he charges that human reason resists the truth because it is offended by the unflattering character of the truth about its own limitations. We would rather believe a pleasant illusion than face up to our need for divine assistance (1980, 42–44).

It could be argued that it is a mistake on the part of Kierkegaard to make a present of the term "reason" to the opponents of religion by identifying reason with what I have termed a damaged "concrete reason." For by doing so he invites confusion and suggests to some that religious belief is rooted in a lack of concern for truth and a resulting lack of personal integrity. Perhaps Kierkegaard would have been better off emphasizing that Christian beliefs *appear* absurd to sinful human beings, and highlighting what we might call the perspectival character of human thinking. I believe he did not do so because he was anxious to preserve the insight that the truth about the human condition is one that can be grasped only when the condition of faith is present; there is no "higher reason" that is capable of leaving faith behind, at least in this life.

Claims of the kind that Kierkegaard (and philosophers such as Plantinga as well) make can be frustrating to philosophers. Philosophers would like to be able to settle the issues once and for all, come up with arguments that show that religious belief is true or false. However, if the no-neutrality thesis is true, it may not be possible to realize such ambitions. Plantinga argues that *if* Christianity is true, then it seems probable that Christianity can be known to be true by faith, understood as a new condition of the person made possible by God's spirit, a condition that is both made possible by God's revelatory activity and that makes possible a positive response to the content of that revelation. Similar claims could obviously be made on behalf of other religions by their proponents. The philosopher can perhaps examine the internal coherence of the "models" of religious knowledge offered and see if there are any "defeaters" for religious knowledge-claims, any disproofs of religious truths. However, given the limits of human reason, a guarantee of the truth or falsity of a religious perspective may be something human philosophy cannot achieve.

NOTES

1. For a good philosophical exploration of some of the ways God might employ human authors to reveal himself, see Nicholas Wolterstorff, *Divine Discourse* (1995). Wolterstorff himself makes a distinction between God speaking and God revealing himself, and develops his analysis with respect to the former. However, as he himself admits, a God who speaks may also at the same time reveal himself, even if speaking is not a species of revealing.

2. For a clear account of Locke's epistemological positions and their implications for religious belief, see Nicolas Wolterstorff, *John Locke and the Ethics of Belief* (1996).

3. See my *Faith Beyond Reason: A Kierkegaardian Account* (1998), for an extensive development and defense of responsible fideism.

4. For a fuller account of all of these ways reason might be seen as limited, see ibid.

5. However, it is not at all clear that the arguments Kant presents for the contradictions are really convincing.

6. I provide such a defense in my *Kierkegaard's Fragments and Postscript* (1983, ch. 11) and *Passionate Reason* (1992, ch. 7).

7. It is well known that many philosophers, such as Kant and Hegel, make a sharp distinction between "reason" and the "understanding." I agree with David Swenson, however, that Kierkegaard does not regard such a distinction as important. See Swenson (1945, 218–23).

WORKS CITED

Aquinas, Thomas. 1945. *Summa Theologiae.* Selections included in *Basic Writings of Thomas Aquinas*, vol. 1, ed. Anton C. Pegis. New York: Random House. (Originally written 1265–1272.)

———. 1975. *Summa Contra Gentiles. Book I: God.* Notre Dame, Ind.: University of Notre Dame Press. (Originally written 1259–1264.)

Evans, C. Stephen. 1983. *Kierkegaard's* Fragments *and* Postscript: *The Religious Philosophy of Johannes Climacus.* Atlantic Highlands, N.J.: Humanities Press.

———. 1992. *Passionate Reason: Making Sense of Kierkegaard's* Philosophical Fragments. Bloomington: Indiana University Press.

———. 1998. *Faith Beyond Reason: A Kierkegaardian Account.* Edinburgh: Edinburgh University Press.

Hordern, William. 1959. *The Case for a New Reformation Theology.* Philadelphia: Westminster Press.

Kant, Immanuel. 1960. *Religion within the Limits of Reason Alone.* Trans. Theodore M. Greene and Hoyt H. Hudson. New York: Harper and Row. (Originally published 1793.)

———. 1965. *Critique of Pure Reason.* Trans. Norman Kemp Smith. New York: St. Martin's Press. (Originally published 1781.)

Kierkegaard, Søren. 1980. *The Sickness Unto Death.* Ed. and trans. Howard V. Hong and Edna H. Hong. Princeton: Princeton University Press. (Originally published 1849.)

———. 1985. *Philosophical Fragments.* Ed. and trans. Howard V. Hong and Edna H. Hong. Princeton: Princeton University Press. (Originally published 1844.)

———. 1990. *For Self-Examination/Judge for Yourself!* Ed. and trans. Howard V. Hong and Edna H. Hong. Princeton: Princeton University Press. (*Judge for Yourself* written in 1851–1852 and published posthumously in 1876.)

———. 1992. *Concluding Unscientific Postscript.* Ed. and trans. Howard V. Hong and Edna H. Hong. Princeton: Princeton University Press. (Originally published 1846.)

Locke, John. 1975. *An Essay Concerning Human Understanding.* Ed. Peter H. Nidditch. Oxford: Oxford University Press. (Originally published 1689.)

Plantinga, Alvin. 2000. *Warranted Christian Belief.* New York: Oxford University Press.

Schaff, Philip, ed. 1877. *The Creeds of Christendom: III.* New York: Harper and Brothers.

Shestov, Lev. 1966. *Athens and Jerusalem.* Athens: Ohio University Press.

Swenson, David. 1945. *Something about Kierkegaard.* Minneapolis: Augsburg Publishing House.

Swinburne, Richard. 1981. *Faith and Reason.* Oxford: Oxford University Press.

———. 1992. *Revelation: From Metaphor to Analogy.* Oxford: Oxford University Press.

Tertullian. 1951. *On the Flesh of Christ.* In vol. 3 of *The Ante-Nicene Fathers,* ed. Alexander Roberts and James Donaldson. Grand Rapids, Mich.: Eerdmans.

Wainwright, William J. 1995. *Reason and the Heart: A Prolegomenon to a Critique of Passional Reason.* Ithaca, N.Y.: Cornell University Press.

Wolterstorff, Nicholas. 1995. *Divine Discourse.* Cambridge, England: Cambridge University Press.

———. 1996. *John Locke and the Ethics of Belief.* Cambridge, England: Cambridge University Press.

CHAPTER 14

MORALITY AND RELIGION

LINDA ZAGZEBSKI

DOES MORALITY DEPEND UPON RELIGION?

VIRTUALLY all religions include a code of moral conduct. In fact, the only feature of religion that comes close to being universal is a practical one: to offer human beings a way to cope with the human condition, particularly suffering and death. Coping might be aided by the promise that suffering will eventually be overcome, or it might involve seeing suffering as a natural consequence of wrongdoing in a past life, or it might involve changing the way humans perceive suffering. In any case, suffering has to be faced, and it cannot be faced without first understanding it. Most religions give a diagnosis of the human condition and an explanation for the existence of suffering and death, as well as a remedy for the problem. Moral behavior as defined by the particular religion is part of the remedy, but each religion teaches that the ultimate goal of moral living is unattainable without the practice of that religion. So not only is morality an intrinsic feature of almost all religions, but most also teach that morality is incapable of standing alone. Morality needs religion. And one respect in which it is said that morality needs religion is that the goal of the moral life is unreachable without religious practice.

Some religious philosophers maintain that morality needs religion in at least two other respects: (1) to provide moral motivation, and (2) to provide morality with its foundation and justification. These three ways in which morality may depend on religion are logically independent, although we will see that there are conceptual connections among the standard arguments for these positions.

In the premodern age and even today in large portions of the world, the relation between morality and religion has been taken for granted. But for at least two reasons there is strong resistance in the modern West to the idea that morality needs religion. One is the naturalistic temper of the times. Many people lack belief in a deity or a supernatural world of any kind, and yet almost all believe that morality is important. Clearly, then, *belief* in a religion is not required for belief in either a code of moral behavior or a moral theory. Of course, that fact does not show that morality does not depend on religion any more than the fact that belief in tables does not depend on belief in quarks shows that tables do not depend on quarks. But, of course, if it is a fact that there is no God or supernatural world, then it cannot be a fact that morality depends on religion for the same reason that if it turns out quarks do not exist, tables cannot depend on quarks. Many Western philosophers either believe there is no supernatural world or are agnostic about its existence. This has led them to devote considerable attention to rethinking the relation between religion and morality in order to defend the autonomy of morality, and the history of Western ethics since the Enlightenment can be read as a series of attempts to ground morality in something other than God.[1]

The second reason for resistance to the idea that morality needs religion is political. We live in a world of many religions, so if morality depends on religion, on which religion does it depend? Religious exclusivism is the position that only one religion is completely true, and typically, religious exclusivists find no difficulty in maintaining that morality depends on God as they understand him. (Perhaps it is not surprising that religious exclusivists always think that the one true religion is their own.) But the Western world also treats religious freedom as an important civil liberty, an idea that has spread well beyond its boundaries. Persons have the right to practice their own religions without interference from other individuals or the state. If morality is intrinsic to and dependent on particular religions, it follows that individuals have the right to practice their own moralities without interference from the state. But no society can accept that. Morality is a system for getting along with everyone, and that requires a sufficiently common morality to ensure that a society can function. Differences in moral beliefs and behavior can be permitted within limits and within carefully circumscribed categories, for example, some behavior within families and close personal relationships. And it is not necessary that all members of a society agree on the metaphysical basis for morality, nor need all persons in a well-functioning society have the same motives for being moral. But they must agree on a substantial core area of moral behavior, or at the very least, there must be a core morality that is recognized as having authority over all members of the society, including the recalcitrant few who resist it. In a society with no common religious authority, moral authority must come from another source.

In a liberal, pluralistic society religion is a matter of choice; a large area of morality is not. You can opt out of religion, but you cannot opt out of morality. For this reason, even devout religious believers in liberal democracies generally support the search for a way to make morality independent of religion. Or, to make the point more carefully, they want to say that there is an important respect in which morality is autonomous even if there is another respect in which it is not. Distinguishing the different respects in which morality may depend on religion is therefore important for those who believe, as I do, that morality does not depend on religion in every respect.

This problem would be solved if morality has a two-tier grounding—one in God, the other in nature. That is the approach of the historically important theory of Natural Law, whose classic statement in Christian philosophy is found in the work of Thomas Aquinas. This theory teaches that the basic norms of morality sufficient for civil society have a foundation in human nature, and so morality is common to all human beings. The norms of behavior generated by human nature arise from the natural law, which is accessible, in principle, by ordinary human reason. The natural law, however, is not ultimate. Everything outside of God comes from God, including the natural law, which is an expression in the created order of the Eternal Law of God (see Aquinas 1992, I, ii, q. 91).[2] What is important for the problem of this chapter is the way natural law theory makes morality ultimately dependent on God, while giving it subultimate metaphysical grounding and justification in something all humans have in common. It is not necessary, although it is often advantageous, to refer to God's revealed word in order to know what morality teaches and why. The moral law therefore depends on God only at the deepest level of the metaphysics of morals. The way morality needs God in natural law theory does not threaten the functioning of societies internally nor in their relations with each other.

In natural law theory and in biblical ethics, wrongdoing is a violation of a law. If the ultimate lawgiver is God, and God is a being with whom the agent has a relationship through the practice of religion, wrongdoing is something more than merely doing what is morally wrong. It is a sin, an offense against God. Now, it is important to see that, whereas the concept of moral wrong serves the same function in secularized moral theory as sin does in the moral systems of Judaism, Christianity, and Islam, the concepts of sin and moral wrong are not the same. The former is a rich concept that makes no sense outside the context of personal and communal relationships, defined in part by narratives, and sometimes involving elaborate theological accounts. In contrast, the latter is a thin concept intended to be the common denominator in a set of concepts used by atheists, Jews, Muslims, Christians, Hindus, Buddhists, Confucians, and others.

All can understand the idea of doing what is wrong even though many believe that every act of wrongdoing is more than mere wrongdoing. We should be wary, then, of the idea that when the Christian speaks of "sin" and the nonreligious person speaks of "moral wrong," they are talking about the same thing. It is not just a matter of the Christian having distinctive beliefs about the implications and consequences of wrongful acts. I am suggesting that the concept of sin and the concept of moral wrong are different concepts, although they are not disjoint, and Christians or Jews are able to understand what is meant by moral wrong because of their ability to understand discourse outside their religious community and the extent to which it overlaps with their own. There are concepts analogous to sin in other religions, such as *avidya* (ignorance) in the nontheistic Advaita Vedanta. Avidya is a kind of ignorance that involves desiring, feeling, and choosing wrongly as well as thinking wrongly. If I am right in this conjecture, the idea of moral wrong is thinner than the parallel concepts in religious moralities, but it has the advantage of permitting discourse across religious divisions as well as with people who do not find a home in any religion.

The same point applies to concepts for the goal of morality, concepts of salvation, enlightenment, or Aristotle's *eudaimonia*. These concepts also have something in common even though they are distinct. All apply to the goal of living morally. The idea of an ultimate moral goal, like the idea of moral wrongdoing, is a common denominator among a wide range of religious moralities as well as some, like Aristotle's, that are metaphysically rich but not religious. Sometimes the idea of happiness is taken as the equivalent for the idea of the moral goal. The thinnest concept of happiness is identified by Aristotle at the beginning of the *Nicomachean Ethics* (2000; hereafter *NE*); it is simply the concept of what all humans ultimately aim at. This concept can be thickened by a description of the content of the goal, and Aristotle's concept of eudaimonia is gradually thickened in the course of book 1 of the *NE*, and throughout the rest of the work. Religious discourse almost always begins with a thick concept of the goal of human life, often called salvation. Salvation can be interpreted as a thickening of the goal identified by Aristotle on the first page of the *NE*, although in a different direction. So, just as sin adds to wrongdoing the idea of offending God, salvation adds to happiness the idea of existing in union with God, or recognizing one's identity with the Brahman, or realizing one's Buddha-nature.

Clearly, the thinning of religious concepts like sin and salvation into nonreligious moral concepts like wrongdoing and happiness is an advantage in a pluralistic society, but one of the consequences of thinning religious moral concepts is that it results in concepts that are so abstract, it is unclear that they are able to motivate an agent in her practical life. The question Why should I be moral? is not obviously a trivial question, whereas Why should I care about offending God? is foolish to anyone who understands the context in which such a question would be asked. It seems to me that the relation between morality and motivation is a serious one in modern secular ethics because the thinning process thins out the aspects of moral concepts most directly relevant to motivation.[2] This problem is perhaps most evident in the case of the concept of happiness. It is very difficult to be motivated by the mere concept of that at which all humans aim, whereas it is much easier to be motivated by the thicker concepts of salvation, enlightenment, or Aristotelian eudaimonia. The thinner the concept, the wider its conceptual applicability, but the price is a reduction of motivational strength.[3]

This leads to the issue of whether there are crucial religious moral concepts that cannot be thinned. Elizabeth Anscombe (1958) argued in a famous paper inaugurating the contemporary reemergence of virtue ethics that the concept of a moral law makes no sense without a moral lawgiver, and that the only lawgiver capable of filling the role is God. One way of interpreting Anscombe's point is that the concept of moral law as used in traditional natural law theory and in biblical ethics cannot be thinned; the idea of a lawgiver cannot be removed from the idea of moral law. Perhaps in implicit agreement with this point, some modern moral philosophers have searched for an alternative lawgiver: society or the moral agent herself. These attempts have been unsuccessful, says Anscombe, because neither society nor the agent is the right sort of thing to have the authority to be a lawgiver. To think so is to misunderstand the concept of law.[4] Of course, it is disputable whether Anscombe is right that there is such a conceptual connection between the moral law and a divine lawgiver, but the fact that the point arises at all suggests that it is not obvious that the thick moral concepts that developed within religious practice can be thinned without threat of incoherence. In any case, I believe that the relation between the moral concepts inside and outside religious discourse deserves more attention.

One of the greatest challenges of the contemporary world is to find a moral discourse that can reach all the inhabitants of the earth, but one that preferably does no violence to the conceptual frameworks of particular religions. If the concepts that are central to moral practice in the world's great religions cannot be thinned into a common set of concepts, the task is impossible. Or it may be impossible for some other reason, perhaps because it is impossible to get a common content to morality that is sufficient for the requirements for life in a pluralistic world. But it is a goal that should not be given up until its impossibility has been demonstrated. A given religion may find that some of its moral teachings are not feasible for interaction with the practitioners of other religions and it may have to revise or abandon them for interaction to be possible, but that is an issue that needs to be addressed within the framework of that religion.

The philosopher's task is different. One of the aims of philosophy is to understand the relation between morality and religion from a perspective outside that of any religion. This is not to deny that there can be a distinctively Christian philosophy, Islamic philosophy, and so on. But somebody needs to address the issue of whether morality can be independent of religion and, if so, what it would look like, and that is the distinctive task of the philosopher. There are important arguments that morality needs religion to reach its goal, to provide moral motivation, and to provide morality with its foundation and justification. Versions of these arguments are examined in the next three sections. I will briefly address their implications for the task of developing a common morality in the last section.

THE GOAL OF MORALITY

One important set of arguments that morality needs religion or that moral theory needs theology holds that there is a goal or point to morality, and that point is inexplicable within a naturalistic, autonomous moral theory. In this class of arguments are some of the best-known moral arguments for the existence of God. These arguments require the identification of a particular point to morality, for example, a system of cosmic justice in which the good are ultimately rewarded and the bad are punished, or the idea that there is an end of history, a goal at which all human life aims, that human life is pointless without such a goal, and the goal is unattainable without a supernatural power. Many of these arguments are in the class of transcendental arguments, or arguments that purport to identify the preconditions for the truth of some premise. These arguments begin with a premise giving the content or point of morality, and the argument attempts to show that the truth of such a premise requires the truth of important religious propositions such as the existence of God or an afterlife.

The classic statement of an argument of this type was given by Immanuel Kant. Kant accepted the ancient Greek and medieval Christian teaching that all human beings necessarily seek happiness. Where he differed from his predecessors was on the relation between virtue and happiness. The Greeks and medieval philosophers agreed that there is a strong connection between the virtuous life and the happy life, although the Greeks worried about the place of good fortune in happiness and the Christians maintained that the happiness we seek is not fully attainable in this life. Nonetheless, with some variations, they believed that the ultimate goal or end of the moral life is a unitary good in which happiness and virtue are integrated and virtually inseparable. Kant denied that. Virtue and happiness are neither conceptually nor probabilistically connected, according to Kant. They are two different ends. But because both virtue and happiness are goods, Kant argues, the highest good, or *summum bonum*, would be a world in which human beings combine moral virtue with happiness; in fact, it would be a world in which their happiness is proportional to their virtue.

With the idea of the highest good in place, Kant offers the following simple argument for theism. Morality obligates each of us to seek the good, and so it obligates us to seek the highest good. But morality cannot obligate us to seek the impossible. Hence, the highest good must be attainable. It is not attainable without a cause adequate to the effect, which is to say, unless there is a God with the power to proportion happiness to virtue. God's existence is therefore a necessary condition for the possibility of the highest good, and so it is a necessary condition for our obligation to be moral (1997, pt. 1, bk. 2, ch. 2, sec. 5).

The intuition behind Kant's argument is profound even though his description of the highest good is idiosyncratic. What may seem particularly bothersome about the argument is that Kant himself creates a problem for value theory and then argues that there must be a God to solve the problem. The ancient and medieval philosophers, among others, did not see the tension in the concept of the highest good in such stark terms to begin with, so the need to bring God to the rescue was not as glaring. Nonetheless, some of them did think that the highest good must be reachable and that it is not reachable without the existence of an afterlife. A comparison of Kant's notion of the highest good with that of Aquinas is illuminating. Aquinas accepted the Aristotelian position that all humans desire happiness by nature, that happiness is our natural end. But if we investigate what would truly fulfill the human longing for happiness, we see that it is something unattainable without God and the possibility of the enjoyment of seeing God. Aquinas's view of the ultimate human end is an extension and deepening of Aristotle's view in book 10 of the *NE* that happiness is contemplation of the highest things (2000, bk. 10, ch. 7). As Aquinas describes it, to seek happiness is to seek the satiation of the will; to be happy is to have nothing left to will (1992, I, ii. q. 5, art. 8). The will is satiated in the possession of reality, which, for human beings, is accomplished through an act of the intellect, an intellectual vision. The human desire for happiness is not satisfied with anything less than a total vision of reality. This vision is contained in the Beatific Vision, a vision of God in whom all things are seen.[5]

Aquinas does not construct his explanation of human happiness in the form of an argument for theism, since it appears in a part of the *Summa Theologiae* that presupposes his famous arguments for God's existence at the beginning of the work. But a transcendental argument for the existence of God is implicit in Aquinas's account of the nature of happiness. The natural end for humans requires union with an eternal being who satisfies our natural craving for happiness. Without such a being the end of human living is unattainable. Either there is a God or human beings aim at the impossible by nature. So, whereas Kant argues that morality puts an impossible demand on us if there is no God, the Thomistic argument understands nature as structured in such a way that it aims at the impossible if there is no God. The former argues that in the absence of God there is something wrong with morality, whereas the latter argues that in the absence of God there is something wrong with nature.

Aquinas, like the Greeks, assumed that nature is orderly and teleological in structure. There would be no point to the existence of natural desires unless they are capable of fulfillment (1992, I, q. 75, art. 6, corpus), and therefore the conditions for their fulfillment reveal important metaphysical truths. In contrast, modern thinkers are generally wary of drawing any conclusions from human needs and desires. If we come to believe that our natural human desires cannot be satisfied in this life, the typical response is to conclude that we should change the desires. This modern option displays a remarkable degree of confidence in the power of therapy. Perhaps a less naïve alternative is to conclude that life really is absurd. This is the position of an important strand of atheistic existentialist literature which accepts the Thomistic idea that human desires and aims are irremediably thwarted without God, but rejects the premise that human desires cannot be irremediably thwarted. Camus' essay "The Myth of Sisyphus" (1955) is a poignant portrayal of this view of human destiny. It contains the following epigram: "Oh my soul do not aspire to immortal heights but exhaust the field of the possible." Camus' kind of atheism makes an interesting contrast with the atheism of the Enlightenment, which simply rejects the soundness of arguments for theism while attempting to keep most of traditional ethics. The denial of God's existence is an intrinsic feature of Camus' view of the human condition. The absurdity of life is his price for accepting the major premise of the moral argument for the existence of God.[6]

The transcendental arguments addressed in this section focus on the conditions for the meaningfulness of human life. In the next section we look at another kind of transcendental argument that argues that God's existence is a condition for escaping motivation skepticism.

MOTIVATION SKEPTICISM

Transcendental arguments are most commonly used against skepticism about an external world. They attempt to show that the beliefs the skeptic doubts are preconditions for a skeptical hypothesis to make sense. These arguments also are inspired by Kant, who argued against Descartes that our consciousness of our own existence in time presupposes something permanent in perception on which our own existence depends. My consciousness of my own existence is simultaneously a consciousness of the existence of things outside of me. Kant says that the skeptical hypothesis that nothing exists except my own mind therefore turns against itself (1999, "Refutation of Idealism," 1781/B276).

Kant's argument against skepticism addresses the conditions for theoretical judgment, whereas his moral argument addresses the conditions for engaging in the moral life. What the arguments have in common is the attempt to identify the necessary condition for something to make sense, either a theoretical judgment or an act of will. Skepticism attacks thought; atheism attacks the obligation to act morally. But skepticism is not simply a problem for theoretical judgment. It is also a practical problem because confidence in the truth of beliefs is a condition for having the motive to act. In this section I propose a transcendental argument that combines features of both of Kant's arguments. It is a moral argument for theism that arises from motivation skepticism, or skepticism about the meaningfulness of engaging in the moral life.

Radical skepticism in epistemology is the threat of massive and undiscoverable failure in our cognitive life, particularly in the formation of beliefs. Skepticism is a threat because we have epistemic ends, one of which is to get the truth, and the function of skeptical hypotheses such as Descartes' Evil Genius is to lead us to see that there is no guarantee that we get the truth even when our epistemic behavior is impeccable. There are analogues of skepticism in ethics because we have moral as well as epistemic ends, and it is possible that we are radical failures in our moral lives and have no way to discover our failure. Of course, if moral beliefs have truth values, one way we can fail morally is to have false moral beliefs. But we can fail not only at the level of belief, but at the level of motivation.[7] There are at least two ways in which the moral analogue of epistemological skepticism arises at the level of motivation. One is skepticism about the motivational state itself; the other is skepticism about the point of the ensuing action.

First, skepticism can arise about motives, whether motives are understood as emotions or as desires. In my theory of emotion, a motive is an emotion that initiates and directs action toward an end. Emotions are not beliefs and they do not include beliefs, but they have a cognitive component because in an emotional state the intentional object of the emotion is construed a particular way (e.g., as fearful, lovable, contemptible, pitiful, etc.). In an emotion of fear, something is construed as fearful; in an emotion of love something is construed as lovable, and so on. In each case, the cognitive construal is internally connected to a feeling that accompanies it. Skepticism about emotion threatens as long as there is a sense in which the intentional object of an emotion can be construed correctly or incorrectly, appropriately or inappropriately. This follows from the above point that there is a threat of radical skepticism in some area of human life whenever there is a possibility of failure in that area of life that is in principle undiscoverable.

But it does not matter for the argument of this chapter that emotions can succeed or fail. What matters is that motives can succeed or fail, and that is widely accepted, for most philosophers think of motives as desires rather than as emotions. If motives are desires, we get an immediate analogy with epistemological skepticism. There is a gap between the desired and the desirable, just as there is a gap between justified or rational belief and the truth. Skepticism in its extreme form is the fear that the gap is never or almost never closed. So just as almost all of our beliefs may be false, so too, almost all of what we desire may be undesirable. And if that is the case, it is possible that we would be incapable of discovering it, perhaps because the human race is infected with a systematic moral blindness. Less extreme forms of skepticism about emotion or desire, like less extreme forms of skepticism about beliefs, are more persuasive but still threatening. If many of our beliefs and motives are unsuccessful, then even if there are also many that are successful, as long as we cannot tell the difference between the successful and the unsuccessful, the entire set of beliefs and the entire set of motives are in peril.

A second kind of motivation skepticism is skepticism about the point of our acts. The point of most acts is an end in the sense of a state of affairs that the act aims to bring about, but even acts without an end in this sense have a point in that they have a meaning within the context in which they occur. An act can miss its point, whether or not its point is an intended consequence. For example, an act expressing an emotion or the agent's principles may fail to express the emotion or principles in the way intended. The most straightforward way an act can fail in its point, however, is by failing to produce the state of affairs at which it aims. If an act has an end, success in that act includes success in bringing about the intended end. The world must cooperate not only with our beliefs but also with our intended ends if our acts are to be successful. Because it is possible that success in reaching our ends is systematically thwarted, a form of skepticism threatens the point of our acts. Our acts could fail, not because of evil demons or brains in vats, but because the world simply does not cooperate with our intentions. For example, if I am motivated by compassion, I desire that others be comforted in their suffering and I am motivated to bring about states of affairs in which I bring comfort to the suffering. I am then led to form intentions to act in specific ways that I judge will have that effect. But the guarantee that my acts will have such an effect is even less than the guarantee that my rational or justified beliefs are true on the epistemological skeptical hypotheses. After all, if an evil genius can systematically thwart my attempts at getting the truth, it would take a lesser genius to systematically thwart my attempts at alleviating the suffering of others. So it could happen that every time I attempt to act in a compassionate way, I increase the suffering of others rather than alleviate it. And, of course, this problem could occur not only for the motivation of compassion, but for the motivations of justice, fairness, gratitude, courage, kindness, generosity, and many others. It is possible that every time I try to act fairly, my act produces an unfair state of affairs; every time I try to show gratitude, my act conveys the opposite message; every time I try to be generous, my giving goes to the wrong persons or to nobody at all, and so on. And it is possible that I can never discover my failure.

Motivation skepticism is a worry that our desires, emotions, and purposes fail in a way that cannot be discovered. The fear that failure may be undiscoverable entails that motivation skepticism includes the worry that we have false beliefs, but the object of the skepticism in motivation skepticism is not the falsehood of beliefs. The fear that the world may systematically fail to cooperate with my choices is not a fear that certain beliefs are false. The fear that I may desire the undesirable is not a fear that my belief that what I desire is desirable is false. The fear that my emotion is inappropriate to the circumstances is not a fear that my belief that it is appropriate is false. Of course, in each case, I may also have the corresponding belief and fear that it is false, and when I fear that my failure in each case is undiscoverable, I fear a failure to know. But skepticism threatens the motive to act not only on the level of failure in belief, but also on the level of failure in desire and purpose. Belief skepticism and motivation skepticism combine to threaten the moral life—in fact, practical life in general, with possible paralysis.

Assuming that paralysis cannot be rational, there must be a rational way to avoid it or to get beyond it. The argument below is a form of the latter. It is an antiskeptical argument that argues that morality obligates only if there is a God. The argument has features of Kant's transcendental argument against belief skepticism as well as his moral transcendental argument for the existence of God.

An Antiskeptical Transcendental Argument for the Existence of God

(1) We have no option but to engage in the moral life. Morality obligates us, no matter what we think or believe and no matter what we feel or choose. Morality obligates us unconditionally.

(2) Morality requires us to be motivated to act in moral ways and to act on those motives in the appropriate circumstances. Many moral acts also aim at producing particular outcomes.

(3) No one can be required to engage in an activity if he reasonably judges that he is taking a risk that it is pointless or self-defeating and is unable to judge the degree of the risk.[8]

(4) The moral life requires some degree of confidence that the effort to be moral is not pointless or self-defeating.

(5) Trust in the general truth of our moral beliefs (or at least, our ability to

find out whether they are true), the accuracy of our motivational states (our emotions fit the circumstances, what we desire is desirable, etc.), and our probable success in reaching moral outcomes is a condition for confidence that the effort to be moral is not pointless or self-defeating.

(6) On the radical skeptical hypotheses we cannot have any confidence in the truth of our moral beliefs, the trustworthiness of our motivational states, or our probable success in reaching moral outcomes. On the radical skeptical hypotheses the effort to be moral, for all we know, may be pointless or self-defeating.

(7) Hence, morality does not obligate us unless we have reason to believe that the skeptical hypotheses are false. Moral obligation requires that there be a guarantor of our trust in our moral beliefs, motives, and success in action. As Kant puts it, we must suppose the existence of a cause adequate to the effect: a Providential God.

Notice that according to this argument, our motive for being moral is not threatened as long as we believe there is a God, but morality does not actually obligate us unless the belief is true. If that is the case, then this argument may be able to avoid a well-known objection to Kant's transcendental argument against belief skepticism. The problem sometimes raised against the latter argument is that it shows us how we have to think, not how things have to be. Even if we have to make judgments about an outer world in order to make judgments about the existence of our own minds, it does not follow that the judgments in either category must be true. As long as there is no requirement that the way we think lines up with the way things are, we have not escaped skepticism. I will not discuss the merits of this objection, although I think it is a powerful one. What I want to point out is that the objection cannot so easily be raised against the argument above because there *is* a requirement that our moral motives line up with moral reality. In fact, morality just is the demand that that be so. Morality requires the falsehood of both belief skepticism, and motivation skepticism and moral motivation requires a guarantor of that falsehood. A deity may not be the only metaphysically adequate guarantor, but in the absence of competitors, he is the most obvious choice to fit the role.

The above argument assumes a form of moral realism, the theory that there are moral facts independent of human perceptions and attitudes, since it presupposes that moral obligation has a source outside of the human mind. Moral skepticism, like skepticism about perception and belief, is most threatening within a realist metaphysics, and so idealism (antirealism) is a possible solution. I think it is no accident that the popularity of antirealism in ethics coincides with the decline in belief in a theistic foundation for morality. The metaphysical foundation of ethics has been problematic in modern ethics, whereas theism offers a number of plausible accounts of that foundation. A couple of these accounts are outlined in the next section.

THE METAPHYSICAL GROUND
OF MORALITY

Western religions maintain that morality arises from God. Natural law theory makes morality rest on God's nature. Divine Command theory makes morality rest on God's will. The theory I call Divine Motivation theory makes morality rest on the motives that are the primary constituents of God's virtues. In each case, the theory may not be committed to the idea that morality needs religion, as it is possible that even though morality in fact derives from God, morality would exist even if there were no God. But clearly, if morality derives from God, it depends on God in actuality whether or not morality would have existed in some other possible godless world. This is the view I investigate briefly in this section.

Other than natural law theory, the principal theory of a theistic foundation for morality is divine command theory. Divine command theory has a long and important history in religious ethics, although it is often misunderstood. In my opinion, the major objections to it can be answered and I will not discuss them in any detail. My own objections are ones that apply to law-based theories in general. The alternative I prefer is a theory I call divine motivation theory. This theory is Christian, but its structure permits variations both for other religions and for secular ethics.

According to divine command (DC) theory, the divine will is the source of morality. Many contemporary forms of DC theory limit the theory to an account of right and wrong acts, not an account of moral value in general.[9] A common form of DC theory, then, is the following: an act is morally required (an obligation) just in case God commands us to do it; an act is morally wrong just in case God forbids us to do it; an act is permissible just in case God neither commands nor forbids it. Because a divine command is the expression of God's will with respect to human and other creaturely acts, the divine will is the fundamental source of the moral properties of acts.

The nature of the relation between God's commands and moral requirements is an important issue for DC theorists. To say that "x is morally required" *means* "x is commanded by God" is too strong because it has the consequence that to say "x is morally required because God commands it" is just to say "x is commanded by God because x is commanded by God," which clearly tells us nothing. On the other hand, to say that God's commands and moral requirements are merely extensionally equivalent is too weak. That is compatible with the lack of any metaphysical connection whatever between the existence of moral properties and God's will, and it makes DC theory uninteresting. DC theory, then, aims at something in between identity of meaning and mere extensional equivalence. It should turn out that God's will *makes* what's right to be right. Acts are right/wrong *because* of the will of God. A plausible version of the intended relation has been proposed by Robert Adams (1993), who argues that the relation between God's commands and the rightness/wrongness of acts is akin to the relation between water and H_2O in the theory of direct reference defended by Saul Kripke, Hilary Putnam, and others in the 1970s.[10] "Water" and "H_2O" do not mean the same thing. To think so is to misunderstand the importance of the discovery that water is H_2O. This was certainly not the discovery of the meaning of a word, nor a change in meaning of a word. Nonetheless, it is not a contingent fact that water is composed of H_2O. The discovery that water is H_2O is the discovery that being H_2O is essential to water. We think now that nothing ever was or will be water that is not H_2O, even though nobody was in a position to understand that before the seventeenth century. Similarly, the moral properties of acts could be essentially connected to God's commands even though many people are not in a position to realize the connection and perhaps nobody was at some periods of history.

The theory I call divine motivation theory makes the ground of what is morally good and morally right God's motives rather than God's will. Because I think of a motive as an emotion that is operating to initiate action, the divine motives can be considered divine emotions. However, in philosophies influenced by Aristotelian psychology, such as that of Aquinas, emotions are thought to be essentially connected to the body and therefore do not apply to God. I see no reason to deny that emotions are components of the divine nature, but the theory does not require that. It requires only that there are states in God that are analogous to emotions in the same way that there are states in God analogous to what we call beliefs in human beings. Virtually all theists attribute to God states such as love and compassion. Whether or not these states are properly classified as emotions, they are motivating. God acts *out of* love, joy, compassion, and perhaps also anger and disgust. These are the states that I propose constitute the metaphysical basis for moral value. They are components of God's virtues. The shift I advocate from God's will to God's virtues results in a shift from a theological deontological theory to a theological virtue theory.

The overall structure of the theory is exemplarist. Moral properties are defined via reference to an exemplar of goodness. God is the ultimate exemplar, but there are many finitely good human exemplars. In this respect, the theory is similar to that of Aristotle, (2000, bk. 2, ch. 6, 1107a), who defines virtue as what would be determined by the person with *phronesis* (practical wisdom), and morally virtuous acts as acts that the *phronimos* would do in the circumstances in question. For Aristotle, then, the exemplar is the person with practical wisdom. In religious traditions, the exemplar is the Christian saint, the Buddhist arahant, the Jewish tzaddik, and so on.[11]

To get a more careful rendering of the way reference to an exemplar defines moral concepts, let us return to Putnam and Kripke's theory of natural kind terms

(Putnam 1975, Kripke 1980). They defined a natural kind such as *water* or *gold* or *human* as whatever is the same kind of thing or stuff as some indexically identified instance. For example, they proposed that gold is, roughly, whatever is the same element as *that*; water is whatever is the same liquid as *that*; a human is whatever is a member of the same species as *that*; and so on. In each case, the demonstrative term "that" refers to an entity to which the person doing the defining refers directly, typically by pointing. One of the main reasons for proposing definitions like this was that Kripke and Putnam believed that often we do not know the nature of the thing we are defining, and yet we know how to construct a definition that links up with its nature and continues to do so after its nature is discovered.

A person possesses moral properties in a greater or a lesser degree, but it is unlikely that something is more or less gold or more or less water. The exemplars of gold and water, reference to which is used in defining gold and water, are not paradigms in the sense of especially good instances of the kind defined. Virtually any instance of water or gold will do for defining a natural kind term. This is a respect in which moral concepts are disanalogous, for I propose that the latter are defined by reference to exemplary instances of goodness. Like the Aristotelian person of practical wisdom, some moral exemplars must be identifiable in advance of defining the concept they exemplify.

Divine motivation theory is an exemplarist virtue theory. It is exemplarist because the moral properties of persons, acts, and outcomes are defined via an indexical reference to an exemplar of a good person. It is a virtue theory because the moral properties of persons (virtues) are more basic than the moral properties of acts and outcomes. But I will say little in this chapter on the details of the theory. My purpose in this section is merely to show that God can have a foundational role in ethics as an exemplar rather than as a lawgiver. This approach has advantages for Christian ethics as well as for the task of constructing a common morality.

Here is a brief outline of divine motivation (DM) theory. The paradigmatically good person is God. Value in all forms derives from God, in particular, from God's motives. God's motives are perfectly good, and human motives are good insofar as they are like the divine motives as those motives would be expressed in finite and embodied beings. Motive-dispositions are constituents of virtues. A virtue is an enduring trait consisting of a good motive-disposition and reliable success in bringing about the aim, if any, of the good motive. God's virtues are paradigmatically good personal traits. Human virtues are those traits that imitate God's virtues as they would be expressed by human beings in human circumstances. The goodness of a state of affairs is derivative from the goodness of the divine motive. Outcomes get their moral value by their relation to good and bad motivations. For example, a state of affairs is a merciful one or a compassionate one or a just one because the divine motives that are constituents of mercy, compassion, and justice, respectively, aim at bringing them about. Acts get their moral value from the acts that would, would not, or might be done by God in the relevant circumstances.

The relation of being like an indexically identified instance of water is obviously much clearer than the relation of being like a trait of God or being like an act God would do in relevantly similar circumstances. To say that a human is or is acting like God is much different from saying that a portion of liquid is like another portion of liquid. We may have to investigate the chemical constitution of the liquids in order to determine whether one is like the other, but even before we do that we have some idea of what it means to be alike in nature. It is much harder to understand what it means for a human to be like God even though the idea of likeness to God can be found in many traditions including some that are not religious in the usual sense (e.g., Stoicism, Platonism).[12] In Christian theology, the problem is solved in part through the doctrine of the Incarnation. The God-man is both the perfect exemplar from whom all value derives and is a human person who can be imitated. The life of Christ is a narrative that illuminates a point of view from which we can see a number of exemplary acts, and especially exemplary motives and the virtues of which they are constituents. DM theory gives a theoretical foundation to Christian narrative ethics.

An important objection to DC theory goes back to Plato's *Euthyphro*, where Socrates asks, "Is what is holy holy because the gods approve it, or do they approve it because it is holy?" (10a). As applied to DC theory, this question produces a famous dilemma: if God wills the good (right) because it is good (right), then goodness (rightness) is independent of God's will and the latter does not explain the former. On the other hand, if something is good (right) because God wills it, then it looks as if the divine will is arbitrary. God is not constrained by any moral reason from willing anything whatever, and it is hard to see how any nonmoral reason could be the right sort of reason to determine God's choice of what to make good or right. The apparent consequence is that good/bad (right/wrong) are determined by an arbitrary divine will; God could have commanded cruelty or hatred, and if he had done so, cruel and hateful acts would have been right, even duties. This is an unacceptable consequence. It is contrary to our sense of the essentiality of the moral properties of acts of certain kinds, and the goodness of a God who could make cruelty good is not at all what we normally mean by good. It is therefore hard to see how it can be true that God himself is good in any important, substantive sense of good on this approach.

To solve this problem, Robert Adams (1979) modifies DC theory to say that the property of rightness is the property of being commanded by a *loving* God. This permits Adams to allow that God could command cruelty for its own sake, but if God did so he would not love us, and if that were the case, Adams argues, morality would break down. Morality *is* dependent on divine commands, but they are dependent on the commands of a deity with a certain nature. If God's nature were not loving, morality would fall apart.

Although Adams's proposal may succeed in answering the objection it is designed to address, it has the disadvantage of being ad hoc. There is no intrinsic connection between a command and the property of being loving, so to tie morality to the commands of a loving God is to tie it to two distinct properties of God. In DM theory there is no need to solve the problem of whether God could make it right that we brutalize the innocent by making any such modification to the theory, since being loving is one of God's essential motives. The right thing for humans to do is to act on motives that imitate the divine motives. Brutalizing the innocent is not an act that expresses a motive that imitates the divine motives. Hence, it is impossible for brutalizing the innocent to be right as long as (1) it is impossible for such an act to be an expression of a motive that is like the motives of God, and (2) it is impossible for God to have different motives. (2) follows from the plausible assumption that God's motives are part of his nature.[13]

The arbitariness problem also does not arise in DM theory. That is because a will needs a reason, but a motive *is* a reason. The will, according to Aquinas, always chooses "under the aspect of good," which means that reasons are not inherent in the will itself (1992, ST I, ii, q. 1, art. 5, corpus). In contrast, motives provide not only the impetus to action, but the *reason for* the action. If we know that God acts from a motive of love, there is no need to look for a further reason for the act. On the other hand, a divine command requires a reason, and if the reason is or includes fundamental divine motivational states such as love, it follows that even DC theory needs to refer to God's motives to avoid the consequence that moral properties are arbitrary and God himself is not good. This move makes divine motives more basic than the divine will even in DC theory.

DM theory also has the theoretical advantage of providing a unitary theory of all evaluative properties, divine as well as human. DC theory is most naturally interpreted as an ethics of law, a divine deontological theory, wherein the content of the law is promulgated by divine commands. God's own goodness and the rightness of God's own acts, however, are not connected to divine commands because God does not give commands to himself. In contrast, DM theory makes the features of the divine nature in virtue of which God is morally good the foundation for the moral goodness of those same features in creatures. Both divine and human goodness are explained in terms of good motives, and the goodness of human motives is derived from the goodness of the divine motives.

An advantage of DM theory for the Christian philosopher is that it shows the importance of Christology for ethics, whereas DC theory ignores the doctrines of the Trinity and the Incarnation, focusing on the will of the Creator-God as the source of moral value. For those who prefer virtue ethics to deontological ethics, the theory also has the advantage of being a form of virtue theory. The basic moral concept is not law, but the good.

There are innumerable ways that a moral theory can be structured with a theological foundation. The dominance of DC theory and natural law theory in Western religious ethics is probably due to a combination of the importance of law in Western thought and a particular way of reading the Bible that became standard. Virtue ethics can have a theological foundation also, whether or not it has the form I have proposed here. There are also forms of virtue theory that lack an explicit theological foundation but are compatible with a religious explanation for the existence of value. Whether ethical theory on its metaphysical side needs religious theory is an issue that cannot be disentangled from the general question of what is required for an acceptable metaphysics. When naturalistic ethical theories are preferred to religious ethical theories, it is not because they are thought to be superior as ethical theories, but because it is thought that naturalism is superior to religion. That, of course, is not a dispute that will be resolved within ethics.

RELIGION AND THE TASK OF DEVELOPING A COMMON MORALITY

Moral pluralism is a challenge to every kind of moral theory, whether or not it is religiously based. Apart from the issue of the justification of one moral system over others, there is the problem of developing a common morality. As I pointed out in the first section, it is not important for this purpose that everyone agree on the foundation of ethics or the substantive goal at which the moral life aims; nor is it important that everyone have the same motive to be moral. It is not even important that everyone think of wrongdoing the same way—as a sin, avidya, a violation of someone's rights, or something else—as long as they agree on what is wrong, and they only have to agree on that within a certain core area of human behavior.

What are the prospects for a common morality? One based on natural law? Divine commands? Universal reason? It is widely believed that there is virtually no hope for a common morality based on divine commands, and I think that must be true. Natural law and Kantian universal reason may both provide some help, but so far with only limited results.[14] It seems to me that one of the lessons of cross-cultural experience is that even though most people find the metaphysics and theology of another culture hard to swallow, they can usually relate to the narratives that have an important place in other cultures, even those that are radically different from their own. That includes other cultures' paradigms of good persons, those they seek to imitate. Of course, most of us would have no trouble distinguishing a Christian saint from a Stoic sage or a Buddhist arahant. My point is not that the exemplars are identical, but that for the most part, we have no trouble understanding why most of them are worthy of being imitated. Even the alleged exceptions, such as terrorist leaders, prove the rule because they get a very different reaction from those outside their own extremist groups than do the more standard moral exemplars in the major religions.[15] I believe it is likely that a wide range of virtues is represented by all or almost all of the moral paradigms in the major cultures, both religious and nonreligious, in different parts of the world, even though there are some differences in the particular acts that are thought to express the virtues. A common morality would in principle be that morality that derives from the overlapping character traits of moral exemplars in a wide range of cultures. Particular moralities distinctive of individual cultures would include the nonoverlapping traits of their exemplars. Religiously based moralities have an important function to serve in the development of a common morality because they have richly described moral exemplars. In contrast, secular ethics in the Western world differs from religious ethics, not so much in having different exemplars, but in not having exemplars at all. This is particularly true of consequentialist and deontological ethics, both of which aim for universality by constructing entire moral systems out of the thinnest of moral concepts.

My view is that if the aim is universal agreement, that is the wrong way to go about it. Full universal agreement is no doubt impossible in any case, but a workable common morality is more likely to arise from dialogue between richly developed religious moralities than between those who develop the most abstract systems and everyone else. If that is right, religious ethics has an important function in society quite apart from its importance in religious communities themselves.

NOTES

1. A very interesting and convincing alternative account of Enlightenment ethics has been given by J. B. Schneewind (1998), who argues that when conceptions of morality as obedience gave way to conceptions of morality as self-governance during the Enlightenment, the change was made primarily by religious philosophers who took for granted that God is essential to morality. One could make the same point about the rise of modern science, which was not precipitated by atheist scientists, but by religious believers who thought that God had created a natural order accessible to investigation by

the scientific method. That suggests that both the autonomy of moral reasoning and the autonomy of scientific reasoning are compatible with a deeper theistic metaphysics (see Schneewind 1998, esp. ch. 1, sec. 3).

2. In fact, the debate over the issue of whether the Why be moral? question is trivial may show that the concept of the moral is thinner for some people than for others. For many people, the concepts of being moral, doing the right thing, avoiding the wrong thing have an affective content lacking in the thinnest versions of these concepts. I propose a theory on the thinning of moral concepts of their motivational content in "Emotion and Moral Judgment" (2003).

3. It has been argued since Hume that no concept is intrinsically motivating. I argue that that is false in "Emotion and Moral Judgment."

4. The concepts of guilt and punishment are related to the concept of law. If the former cannot be thinned, it is unlikely that the latter can either.

5. For an interesting and accessible twentieth-century defense of the Thomistic idea that happiness is found in contemplation, see Pieper (1998).

6. It is interesting that Camus retains many features of traditional morality, including the traditional sense of justice, in *The Plague* and *The Rebel*. He is not a moral nihilist.

7. Thomas Nagel (1979, 218) says that the analogue of skepticism on the level of motivation is the problem of the meaning of life. This is not the problem I am addressing here, although it is an interesting one.

8. It is possible that one may reasonably judge that even a high degree of risk is outweighed by the good one hopes to gain (compare, for instance, Pascal's Wager). So when one cannot judge the degree of risk, one may reasonably judge that the good of the activity is worth the unknown risk. But it is unlikely that such a judgment is reasonable in every case in which morality obligates us to act.

9. Adams explicitly limits his version of divine command theory to a theory of obligation, not a general theory of the good. See Adams (1999) for his most recent detailed defense of such a theory.

10. The theory of direct reference originated with Saul Kripke's *Naming and Necessity* (1980) and Hilary Putnam's paper, "The Meaning of 'Meaning' " (1975).

11. See Owen Flanagan, "Saints" (1991), for a nice discussion of the many ways of sainthood and moral exemplariness.

12. Daniel Russell argues for the idea that virtue as likeness to God can be found in both Plato and the Stoics in "Plato and Seneca on Virtue as Likeness to God" (2001). Russell says that this aspect of Plato's thought has largely been ignored.

13. This is assuming, of course, that the motives of which we are speaking are suitably general. Love is essential to God, but love of Adam and Eve is not.

14. Perhaps the *Universal Declaration of Human Rights*, passed by the UN General Assembly in 1947, shows that a restricted range of moral rights without any religious basis can be recognized by many different cultures.

15. I've claimed in Zagzebski (2001) that all cultures have *phonimoi* and that they can in principle be recognized by those outside their own cultures.

WORKS CITED

Adams, Robert M. 1973. "A Modified Divine Command Theory of Ethical Wrongness." In *Religion and Morality,* ed. Gene Outka and John P. Reeder Jr., 318–47. Garden City, N.Y.: Doubleday. Reprinted as chap. 7 of Adams 1987.

———. 1979. "Divine Command Metaethics Modified Again." *Journal of Religious Ethics* 7: 66–79. Reprinted as chap. 9 of Adams 1987.

———. 1987. *The Virtue of Faith and Other Essays in Philosophical Theology.* New York: Oxford University Press.

———. 1999. *Finite and Infinite Goods.* New York: Oxford University Press.

Anscombe, G. E. M. 1958. "Modern Moral Philosophy." *Philosophy* 33: 1–19. Reprinted in R. Crisp and M. Slote, *Virtue Ethics.* New York: Oxford University Press, 1997.

Aquinas, Saint Thomas. *Summa theologiae.* 1992. Trans. Fathers of the English Domican Province. New York: Benziger Brothers.

Aristotle. 2000. *Nicomachean Ethics.* Trans. Roger Crisp. Cambridge, England: Cambridge University Press.

Camus, Albert. 1955. *The Myth of Sisyphus and Other Essays.* Trans. J. O'Brien. New York: Knopf.

Flanagan, Owen. 1991. "Saints." In *Varieties of Moral Personality.* Cambridge, Mass.: Harvard University Press.

Kant, Immanuel. 1997. *Critique of Practical Reason.* Ed. Mary Gregor. Introduction by Andrews Reath. Cambridge, England: Cambridge University Press.

———. 1999. *Critique of Pure Reason.* Ed. Paul Geyer and Allen Wood. Cambridge, England: Cambridge University Press.

Kripke, Saul. 1980. *Naming and Necessity.* Oxford: Blackwell.

Nagel, Thomas. 1979. *Mortal Questions.* Cambridge, England: Cambridge University Press.

Pieper, Josef. 1998. *Happiness and Contemplation.* Trans. Richard Winston and Clara Winston. South Bend, Ind.: St. Augustine Press.

Putnam, Hilary. 1975. "The Meaning of 'Meaning.'" In *Mind, Language, and Reality.* Vol. 2. of *Philosophical Papers.* Cambridge, England: Cambridge University Press. Originally published in *Language, Mind, and Knowledge,* ed. Keith Gunderson (Minneapolis: University of Minnesota Press, 1975).

Russell, Daniel. 2001. "Plato and Seneca on Virtue as Likeness to God." Paper presented at Philosophy Department colloquium, University of Oklahoma, September.

Schneewind, A. B. 1998. *The Invention of Autonomy.* Cambridge, England: Cambridge University Press.

Zagzebski, Linda. 2001. "Religious Diversity and Social Responsibility." *Logos* (winter): 135–155.

———. 2003. "Emotion and Moral Judgment." *Philosophy and Phenomenological Research* 46: 104–24.

FOR FURTHER READING

George, R. 1999. *In Defense of Natural Law.* Oxford: Clarendon Press.

Hauerwas, Stanley, and Alasdair MacIntyre, eds. 1983. *Revisions: Changing Perspectives in Moral Philosophy.* Notre Dame, Ind.: University of Notre Dame Press.

Helm, Paul, ed. 1981. *Divine Commands and Morality.* New York: Oxford University Press.

Idziak, Janine, ed. 1980. *Divine Command Morality: Historical and Contemporary Readings.* Toronto: Edwin Mellen Press.

Lewis, C. S. 1952. *Mere Christianity.* New York: Macmillan.

MacDonald, Scott, ed. *Being and Goodness: The Concept of the Good in Metaphysics and Philosophical Theology.* Ithaca, N.Y.: Cornell University Press.

MacIntyre, Alasdair. 1981. *After Virtue.* Notre Dame, Ind.: University of Notre Dame Press.

Mavrodes, George. 1986. "Religion and the Queerness of Morality." In *Rationality, Religious Belief and Moral Commitment,* ed. R. Audi and W. J. Wainwright. Ithaca, N.Y.: Cornell University Press.

Mitchell, Basil. 1980. *Morality: Religious and Secular.* Oxford: Clarendon Press.

Mouw, Richard. 1990. *The God Who Commands.* Notre Dame, Ind.: University of Notre Dame Press.

Quinn, Philip. 1978. *Divine Commands and Moral Requirements.* Oxford: Clarendon Press.

Swinburne, Richard. 1979. *The Existence of God.* Oxford: Clarendon Press.

Vacek, E. C., S.J. 1994. *Love, Human and Divine: The Heart of Christian Ethics.* Washington, D.C.: Georgetown University Press.

Zagzebski, Linda. 2004. *Divine Motivation Theory.* Cambridge, England: Cambridge University Press.

CHAPTER 15

DEATH AND THE AFTERLIFE

LYNNE RUDDER BAKER

1. INTRODUCTION

DEATH comes to all creatures, but human beings are unique in realizing that they will die. Hence, they are unique in being able to consider the possibility of life after death. Ideas of an afterlife of one sort or another have been promulgated by all manner of cultures and religions. For ancient peoples, the afterlife was a realm of vastly diminished existence populated by shades, ghostly counterparts of bodies. Ancient Indians and Egyptians before 2000 BCE postulated a judgment after death. The Greeks had Hades; the Hebrews had Sheol. Far from being a matter of wish fulfillment, an afterlife, as pictured by ancient cultures, was not particularly desirable, just inevitable (Hick 1994, 55–60).

There are many conceptions of an afterlife. To say that there is an afterlife (of any kind) is to say that biological death is not the permanent end of a human being's existence: At least some people continue to exist and to have experiences after death. The idea of reincarnation is shared by a number of religions, including Hindu, Jaina, and Buddhist. According to the idea of reincarnation, one is born over and over, and the circumstances of one's life, even what sort of being one is, depend on one's actions in the preceding life. Among philosophers, Plato had a view of reincarnation. Plato developed the idea of the immortality of the soul in the *Phaedo*. According to Plato, a person is an immaterial soul, temporarily imprisoned by a body. Death is liberation from the prison of the body, but after an interval of disembodied existence, the soul is again imprisoned and is born again into this world. On Plato's view, all this occurs in the natural course of things.

1a. Christian Doctrine

All the great monotheistic religions—Judaism, Christianity, and Islam—recognize doctrines of an afterlife. I focus on doctrines of resurrection of the dead, which are common to them, and in particular on Christian doctrines.

Christian doctrines have two sources. The first source is Second-Temple Judaism, which contributed the idea of resurrection of the body. (The New Testament mentions that the Pharisees believed in bodily resurrections, but that the Sadducees did not believe in an afterlife. Jesus endorsed the former, which was fixed as Christian doctrine by his own bodily resurrection.) The second source was Greek philosophy, which contributed the idea of the immortality of the soul (Cullman 1973).

To the early Church fathers, belief in the immortality of the soul was connected with belief in resurrection of the body. The belief that Jesus rose from the dead was the belief that his soul survived death of the body and was "reinvested with his risen body" (Wolfson 1956–57, 8). The belief in a general resurrection was the belief that surviving souls, at the end of time, would be "reinvested" with risen bodies. During the interval between death and the general resurrection, a soul would have a life without a body, but a person's final state would be embodied in some sense. In this general picture, belief in resurrection includes belief in immortal souls and belief in postmortem bodies (of some sort).

The Christian doctrine of an afterlife is pieced together out of hints and metaphors in Scripture. Jesus' resurrection is the paradigm case. According to Christian doctrine, Jesus was the Son of God, who was crucified, died, and was buried. On the third day he rose from the dead and ascended into Heaven. Although Jesus' resurrection is the ground of the Christian doctrine of resurrection, many questions are left open. Perhaps the most explicit, but still sketchy and metaphorical, account of an afterlife in the New Testament is in I Corinthians 15, with its "seed" metaphor. Our bodies are said to be sown in corruption and raised in incorruption; sown in dishonor, raised in glory; sown in weakness, raised in power; sown a natural body, raised a "spiritual" body. But this passage is notoriously open to several interpretations. What is a "spiritual body"? Is it made of the same flesh-and-blood particles as the premortem body? Of the same kind of particles if not exactly the same ones? Of some entirely different kind of stuff? There is no unanimity.

There are two kinds of leading metaphors to guide answers to these questions: on the one hand, the seed metaphor, just mentioned (I Corinthians 15), or the metaphor of tents or garments that we take on as a covering in incorruption (II Corinthians 5); and on the other hand, the statue metaphor that Augustine preferred. According to the seed metaphor, developed by Origen, the body is dynamic and always in flux. Just as the body is transformed in life, so too it is transformed in death. The resurrected body will be radically changed, and will not be made of the same material as the premortem body (Bynum 1995, 63ff). Augustine, by contrast, insisted on the reanimation of the same bodily material, which would be reassembled from dust and previous bones (Bynum 1995, 95). Thomas Aquinas rejected both metaphors for understanding the nature of the body that is to be resurrected. His concern was more with the integrity of the body than with the identity of material particles. The resurrected body will contain the same fragments and organs, if not the identical particles (Bynum 1995, 265). However, Aquinas sometimes suggested that there would be material continuity of the body in the resurrection.

The various Christian views of resurrection have at least these characteristics in common. First, *embodiment*: resurrection requires some kind of bodily life after death. Postmortem bodies are different from premortem bodies in that they are said to be spiritual, incorruptible, glorified. Even if there is an "intermediate state" between death and a general resurrection, in which the soul exists unembodied, those who live after death will ultimately be embodied, according to Christian doctrine. Second, *identity*: the very same person who exists on earth is to exist in an afterlife. Individuals exist after death, not in some undifferentiated state merged with the universe, or with an Eternal Mind, or anything else. Not only is there to be individual existence in the Resurrection, but the very same individuals are to exist both now and after death. "Survival" in some weaker sense of, say, psychological similarity is not enough. The relation between a person here and now and a person in an afterlife must be identity. Third, *miracle*: life after death, according to Christian doctrine, is a gift from God. Christian doctrine thus contrasts with the Greek idea of immortality as a natural property of the soul. The idea of miracle is built into the Christian doctrine of life after death from the beginning.

There are many questions to be answered about the doctrine of resurrection. For example, is there immediate resurrection at the instant of death, or is there a temporary mode of existence (an intermediate state) before a general resurrection at the end of time (Cooper 1989)? There is no general agreement. But whatever the details of the conception of an afterlife, a particular *philosophical* question arises: In virtue of what is a person in an afterlife identical to a certain person in a premortem state? A similar question arises for traditions of reincarnation: In virtue of what is a person of one generation the same person as a person who lived previously? The philosophical issue in any conception of an individual afterlife is the question of personal identity. To have life after death is to have postmortem experiences linked to each other and to premortem experiences in a way that preserves personal identity (Price 1964, 369).

1b. The Problem of Personal Identity

There are at least two philosophical problems of personal identity. The synchronic problem is solved by answering this question: In virtue of what is something a person, at some given time? The diachronic problem is solved by answering this question: In virtue of what is a person at one time identical to a person at another time? The problem of personal identity as it is raised by the idea of an afterlife is a diachronic problem: Under what conditions are persons at t_1 and at t_2 the same person? People change dramatically over time, physically and mentally. A woman of 50 is very unlike a girl of 10 physically, even if the woman of 50 is the same person who, forty years earlier, had been the girl of 10. They do not even have any matter in common. A girl of 10 has different memories, attitudes, personality from a woman of 50—even if the woman of 50 is the same person, considered forty years later, as the girl of 10. In virtue of what is the woman of 50 identical to the girl of 10 considered forty years later?

The needed criterion of personal identity is not epistemological. It does not say how an observer can tell that the woman of 50 is the girl at 10 considered forty years later. Rather, the criterion of personal identity is metaphysical. It says what makes it the case that the woman of 50 is the same person as the girl of 10, whether anyone recognizes the identity or not.

This question of a criterion of personal identity extends to the conception of an afterlife. The question How is survival of bodily death even possible? requires a theory of personal identity. In virtue of what is a person in an afterlife (in heaven, purgatory, or hell, say) the same person as a person who lived a certain life at a certain time on earth and died in bed at the age of 90, say? We can divide potential answers to this question into categories, according to what they take personal identity to depend on: an immaterial substance (such as a soul); a physical substance (such as a human body or brain); a composite of an immaterial substance and a physical substance; or some kind of mental or psychological continuity (such as memory). In addition, my own view is that personal identity depends on a mental property—an essential property in virtue of which a person is a person (having a first-person perspective) and in virtue of which a person is the person she is (having that very first-person perspective). Although to be a person is to be an entity with mental properties essentially, on my view, sameness of person does not require mental continuity over time.

2. EXPOSITION

Four traditional positions on personal identity yield four views on the resurrection. In virtue of what is a postmortem person the same premortem person who walked the earth? The four answers are that the premortem person and the postmortem person (1) have the same soul, or (2) are the same soul-body composite, or (3) have the same body, or (4) are connected by memory.

2a. Sameness of Soul

The idea of an incorporeal soul is the idea of a nonphysical part of a human being, a nonphysical part that thinks and wills. The early Christian Church considered three theories of the soul: (1) souls as custom-made: God creates especially for each new child a new soul at birth (creationalism); (2) souls as ready-made: God has a stock of souls from eternity and allocates them as needed (preexistentialism); (3) souls as second-hand: God created only one soul (the soul of Adam), which is passed down to his descendants (traducianism). All the traditional theories of the soul (custom-made, ready-made, traducian) describe the soul as being in a body as in a garment, or as in a temple, or as in a house. That is, they all allow that souls can exist apart from bodies. (Wolfson 1956–57, 21–2). Even Thomas Aquinas, who rejects these metaphors, takes the soul to be capable of the vision of God in a (temporary) disembodied state (Bynum 1995, 266).

These theories of the soul allow for a conception of an afterlife as populated with incorporeal souls. Experience without a biological organism has seemed to many to be conceivable. One might have visual, auditory, olfactory, sensual images—images of bodies, including one's own. The images would be mental images, acquired in premortem life, and the postmortem person's experiences would be like dreams. The images would be governed by peculiar causal laws—psychological, not physical. For example, a "wish to go to Oxford might be immediately followed by the occurrence of a vivid and detailed set of Oxford-like images; even though, at the moment before, one's images had resembled Piccadilly Circus or the palace of the Dalai Lama in Tibet" (Price 1964, 370). These images would constitute a world—"the next world"—where everything still had shape, color, size, and so on, but had different causal properties.

The postmortem world, although similar to a dream world, need not be solipsistic. One postmortem person could have a telepathic apparition of another person, who "announces himself" in a way that is recognizably similar on different occasions. Thus, an image-world need not be altogether private. It "would be the joint product of a group of telepathetically interacting minds and public to all of them" (Price 1964, 373, 377). There may be various postmortem image-worlds in which people communicate telepathically with each other.

The image-worlds would be constructed from a person's desires and memories and telepathic interactions. The postmortem worlds are "wish-fulfillment" worlds, but of one's genuine wishes. If repression is a biological phenomenon, then repressed desires and memories would be revealed. In that case, in the next world, one's mental conflicts would be out in the open, and the fulfillment of one's wishes may be horrifying. One's guilt feelings may produce images of punishments, which would be a kind of appropriate purgatory for each person. The kind of world one would experience after death would depend on the kind of person one was.

Where, one may wonder, is this "next world"? The question of its spatial relation to the physical world has no meaning. The images that make up the next world are in a space of their own, but, like dream images, they bear no spatial relations to our world. If you dream of a tree, its branches are spatially related to its trunk; you can ask how tall the dreamed-of tree is, but not how far it is from the mattress (Price 1964, 373). "Passing" from this world to the next is not a physical passage. It is more like passing from waking experience to dreaming.

Richard Swinburne (1997) has developed a contemporary view of the soul as the immaterial seat of mental life, or conscious experience. Mental events like believings, desirings, purposings, sensing, though not themselves brain events, interact with brain events. Although Swinburne believes in evolution in biology, and sometimes speaks of souls as having evolved (182), the evolution of souls requires God's hand. On Swinburne's view, the human soul does not develop naturally from genetic material, but each soul is created by God and linked to the body (199).

Although souls are in this world linked to brains, there is no contradiction, according to Swinburne, in the soul's continuing to exist without a body. Indeed, the soul is the necessary core of a person which must continue if a person is to continue (1997, 146). Because, on Swinburne's view, no natural laws govern what happens to souls after death, there would be no violation of natural law if God were to give to souls life after death, with or without a new body. Swinburne solves the problem of personal identity for this world and the next by appeal to immaterial souls.

Recently, scientific philosophers have suggested materialistic conceptions of the soul. For example, the soul is software to the hardware of the brain; if persons are identified with souls (software), they can be "re-embodied, perhaps in a quite different medium" (MacKay 1987, 724–25). Another materialistic view of the soul conceives of the soul as an "information-bearing pattern, carried at any instant by the matter of my animated body." At death, God will remember the pattern and "its instantiation will be recreated by him" at the resurrection (Polkinghorne 1996, 163).

2b. Sameness of Soul-Body Composite

Thomas Aquinas took over Aristotle's framework for understanding human beings, modifying it as little as possible to accommodate Christian doctrine. On Aristotle's view, all living things had souls: plants had nutritive souls, nonhuman animals had sensitive souls, and human animals ("men") had rational souls. The soul was not separable from the body. A human being was a substance: formed matter. The body supplied the matter, the soul the form. No more could a rational soul exist apart from the body whose form it was than could the shape of a particular axe exist apart from that axe. The soul is the form of the body. So, Aristotle had no place for an afterlife.

Following Aristotle, Aquinas agreed that the soul is the form of the body, but, building on Aristotle's concession that the "agent intellect" is separable (1941, *De Anima* 3.5, 430a17), Aquinas held that the soul is a substantial form that could "subsist" on its own. Aquinas assumed that there is a general resurrection at the end of time, before which those who have died are in an "intermediate state." The human being—the substance, the individual—does not exist as such during the intermediate state. What continues through the intermediate state is only the rational soul, which "subsists" until reunited with the body, at which time the human being is fully recovered. The disembodied soul can neither sense nor feel; it is only the part of the person that thinks and wills. While the soul is disembodied, the soul is *not* the person who died. It is merely a remnant of the person, awaiting reunion with the person's body. It is only when the soul is reunited with the body (the same body) that the person resumes life.

So Aquinas's view of a human person is rather of a composite of body and soul. He does not equate personal identity over time with identity of soul. However, Aquinas's conception of the afterlife does require separability of souls from bodies, albeit temporary, and continued existence of souls after death. So, it is reasonable to include Aquinas's view both with the theories of survival of souls and with the theories of bodily resurrection.

2c. Sameness of Body

The Christian doctrine of resurrection of the body suggests that personal identity, at least in part, consists of bodily identity. If personal identity consists in bodily identity, even in part, then reincarnation is ruled out, as is Price's (1964) conception of an afterlife. Reincarnation requires that the same person have different bodies, and Price's conception of an afterlife was of a disembodied consciousness.

For millennia "resurrection of the body" has been taken to mean that the very same body that died would come back to life. Although I Corinthians 15 plainly asserts that the resurrected body is an incorruptible "spiritual" (or "glorified") body, the spiritual body was to be reconstituted from the dust and bones of the original premortem body. The body may undergo radical change, but it is to persist in its postmortem state as the same body. The earliest Christians supposed the body to be the person; later Christians (such as Aquinas) took the body to be an essential part of the person, along with the soul. Either way—whether personal identity is bodily identity or personal identity just entails bodily identity—if a person is to be resurrected, the person's body, the same body, must exist in the afterlife.

There are at least two ways that this story may be filled out, depending on how the idea of "same body" is taken. The first way of understanding "same body," shared by most of the Church fathers, is in terms of same constituent particles. Suppose that Jane is to be resurrected. At the general resurrection, God finds the particles that had composed Jane's body, say, and reassembles them exactly as they had been before Jane's death, thereby restoring Jane's body. If personal identity is bodily identity, then God thereby restores Jane, that is, brings her back to life. The same body, in both its premortem and postmortem phases, has the same particles.

The second way of understanding "same body" appeals to a natural way to understand identity of human bodies over time. Unlike inanimate objects, human bodies undergo a complete change of cells every few years. Not a single one of Sam's cells today was one of his cells ten years ago; yet Sam has not changed bodies. So, perhaps identity of body should not consist of identity of constituent cells, or even of identity of some small percentage of constituent cells. The natural thing to say is that identity of body consists of spatiotemporal continuity of ever-changing constituent cells. Perhaps in the resurrection God slowly replaces the atoms that had composed Jane's organic cells by glorified and incorruptible elements, and He carries out the replacement in a way that preserves spatiotemporal continuity of the body. If that is possible, and if identity of bodies consists in spatiotemporal continuity, then a premortem body could be the same body as a postmortem body even though the premortem body is corruptible and the postmortem body is incorruptible.

2d. The Memory Criterion

The memory criterion is that sameness of person is determined by psychological continuity, not by continuity of substance, material or immaterial. The originator of the memory criterion was John Locke, who was explicitly motivated in part by a desire to make sense of the idea of resurrection. Locke took identity of a person over time to be identity of consciousness over time—regardless of identity of substance (1924, II, xxvii). Locke's idea allows for the possibility that a single consciousness could unite several substances into a single person and for the possibility that a single consciousness could even exist over temporal gaps. Such an approach is clearly congenial to the idea of resurrection.

Suppose we say that A and B are the same person if and only if A can remember what B did, or B can remember what A did. What it means to say that A can remember what B did is that what B did caused, in the right way, A's memory of what B did. What secures sameness of person are causal connections of a certain sort among mental states. It is difficult to spell out just the right kind of causal connection, but "of a certain sort" is supposed to rule out cases like the one where B cuts the grass and tells C what she had done; then B gets amnesia, and C reports back to B that B had cut the grass. C's telling B that B had cut the grass causes B to have a mental state of thinking that she had cut the grass, and B's apparent memory of cutting the grass is ultimately caused by B's having cut the grass. But B's apparent memory is not a real memory, because B's mental state of thinking that she had cut the grass was caused by her cutting the grass, but it was not caused in the right way. The causal chain between B's cutting the grass and her apparent memory went through C. B would not have had the apparent memory of cutting the grass if C had not told B that she had cut the grass.

So, it seems that we have a criterion for sameness of resurrected person and earthly person that does not require sameness of body or sameness of soul: if a resurrected person has Jones's memories (i.e., mental states of what Jones did, caused in the right way), then that resurrected person is Jones.

3. CRITICISM

All the traditional views of personal identity just canvassed have been targets of criticism. Some of the criticisms that follow are well-known; others, as far as I know, are novel.

3a. Sameness of Soul

There are familiar arguments in the secular literature from the seventeenth century on about the problem of understanding how immaterial minds can interact with material bodies. These arguments apply equally to the conception of the soul as an immaterial substance that can exist unembodied.

Another important criticism of the idea of a disembodied soul, however, concerns the question of individuating souls at a time: the synchronic problem. In virtue of what is there one soul or two? If souls are embodied, the bodies individuate. There is one soul per body. But if souls are separated from bodies— existing on their own, apart from bodies—then there is apparently no difference between there being one soul with some thoughts and two souls with half as many thoughts. If there is no difference between there being one soul and two, then there are no souls. So, it seems that the concept of a soul is incoherent.

As we saw in 2b, Aquinas has a response to this problem of distinguishing between one and two unembodied immaterial souls at a single time. Each separated soul had an affinity to the body with which it had been united in premortem life. Even when Smith's soul is disembodied, what makes Smith's soul *Smith's* soul—and not Brown's soul, say—is that Smith's soul has a tendency and potential to be reunited with Smith's body, and not with Brown's body. (But see 3b.) This reply is not available to proponents of immaterial souls, such as Plato or Descartes, who take a human person to be identical to a soul.

Even if we could individuate souls at a time, and thus at a single time distinguish one soul from two souls, there would still be a problem of individuating a soul over time: the diachronic problem. To see this, consider: either souls are subject to change or they are not. Suppose first that souls are not subject to change. In that case, they cannot be the locus of religious life. Religious life consists in part of phenomena like religious conversion and "amendment of life." If souls are immune to change, they can hardly participate in religious conversion or amendment of life. Souls must be subject to change if they are to play their roles in religious life.

So, suppose that souls are subject to change. In that case, the same difficulty that arises for the identity of a person over time also arises for the identity of a soul over time. Just as we asked, *In virtue of what is person 1 at t1 the same person as person 2 at t2?* we can ask, *In virtue of what is disembodied soul 1 at t1 the same soul as disembodied soul 2 at t2?* Consider Augustine before and after his conversion—at t1 and t2, respectively. In virtue of what was the soul at t1 the same soul as the soul at t2? The only answer that I can think of is that the soul at t1 and the soul at t2 were both Augustine's soul. But, of course, that answer is untenable inasmuch as it presupposes sameness of person over time, and sameness of person over time is what we need a criterion of sameness of soul over time to account for. So, it seems that the identity of a person over time cannot be the identity of a soul over time.

The materialistic conceptions of the soul (MacKay 1987; Polkinghorne 1996) do not seem to fare any better. They would seem to succumb to the duplication problem that afflicts the memory criterion (see 3d). But if the Matthews argument (see 3d) rehabilitates the memory criterion, an analogue of that argument could save these materialistic conceptions of the soul.

3b. Sameness of Soul-Body Composite

Aquinas's contribution was to give an account of what happens between death and resurrection in terms of the subsistence of the rational soul. Aquinas's view has the advantage over the substance dualists like Plato and Descartes in that it gives a reason why resurrection should be bodily resurrection: the body is important to make a complete substance.

On the other hand, Aquinas's account buys these advantages at a cost. His account commits him to a new ontological category of being: the rational soul as a subsisting entity that is not a substance. It is not really an individual, but a kind of individual manqué. We can say very little about this new kind of entity except that it fills the bill. It would be desirable to make sense of a Christian doctrine of resurrection without appealing to a new and strange kind of entity, and in section 4, there will be an attempt to do so.

More important, however, is a problem internal to Aquinas's thought. There is a tension in Aquinas, with respect to ontological priority, between his conception of the human being as a composite of soul (form) and body (matter), and his conception of the soul as itself a substantial form that accounts for the identity of a human being through an unembodied period. On the one hand, Aquinas says that the soul without a body is only a fragment, not a human being. So, the human being seems to have ontological priority. On the other hand, he says that the soul is a substantial form that carries our identity and can enjoy the beatific vision on its own; the body is just an expression of its glory. So, the soul alone seems to have ontological priority. The tension arises between whether the human being (the body-soul composite, either part of which is incomplete without the other) or the substantial soul has ontological priority.

The reason this tension threatens the Thomistic view is that Aquinas holds that disembodied souls are individuated by the bodies that they long for and desire reunion with. But if the soul is the substantial form that accounts for the identity of the resurrected person, and if the body is merely matter (potency) of which the soul is the form, then the body of the resurrected human being that rises—*whatever* its matter—will be that human being's body, by definition. As Bynum put it, "God can make the body of Peter out of the dust that was once the body of Paul" (1995, 260). If this is the case, souls cannot be individuated at a time by their yearning for a certain body—because the identity of the body (whose body it is) will depend on the identity of the soul. It is difficult to see how Aquinas can combine the Aristotelian view that matter individuates with his view that the soul is a substantial form that can "subsist"—and experience God—apart from a body.

3c. Sameness of Body

During much of Christian history, the idea of the resurrection of the body was of a literal, material resurrection. The resurrected body was considered to be the same body as the earthly body in the sense that it is composed of (at least some of) the same particles as the earthly body. At the resurrection, it was held, God will reassemble and reanimate the same particles that composed the person's earthly body, and in that way personal identity would be secured in the afterlife.

There are some well-known difficulties with taking the resurrection body to require reassembly of the premortem body. For example, in the early years of Christian martyrdom, there was concern about cannibalism: the problem becomes acute if, say, a hungry soldier eats a captive, who himself has eaten a civilian. So, the soldier's body is composed in part of the captive's, which in turn is composed of the civilian's. The same cells may be parts of three earthly bodies, and there seems to be no principled way for God to decide which parts belong to which postmortem bodies. In light of God's omnipotence and omniscience, however, I doubt that this objection is insurmountable.

Three further difficulties raise more serious logical concerns. Suppose that Jane's body was utterly destroyed, and the atoms that had composed it were spread throughout the universe. Gathering the atoms and reassembling them in their exact premortem positions relative to each other would *not* bring Jane's body back into existence. To see this, consider an analogy. Suppose that one of Augustine's manuscripts had been entirely burned up, and that later God miraculously reassembled the atoms in the manuscript. The reassembled atoms would be a perfect duplicate of the manuscript, but they do not compose the very manuscript that had been destroyed. The reassembled atoms have their positions as a result of God's activity, not of Augustine's. The duplicate manuscript is related to the original manuscript as a duplicate tower of blocks is related to your child's original tower that you accidentally knocked over and then put the blocks back in their original positions. The tower that you built is not the same one that your child built; the manuscript that God produced is not the same one that Augustine produced (van Inwagen 1992).

The situation with respect to God's reassembling the atoms of a body that had been totally destroyed is similar to God's reassembling the atoms in Augustine's manuscript. If a corpse had not decayed too badly, God could "start it up" again. But if the body had been cremated or had been entirely destroyed, there is no way that *it* could be reconstituted. The most that is metaphysically possible is that God could create a duplicate body out of the same atoms that had composed the original body. The same body that had been destroyed—the same person on the bodily criterion—could not exist again. Not even an omnipotent and omniscient God could bring that very body back into existence. So, the "reassembly" view cannot contribute to an account of the resurrection. But because the preceding argument depends on metaphysical intuitions about bodily identity, perhaps this second argument is not insurmountable either.

There is a third argument, also from van Inwagen (1992), that seems to be logically conclusive against the view that resurrection involves reassembly of a premortem person's atoms. None of the atoms that were part of me in 1960 are part of me now. Therefore, God could gather up all the atoms that were part of me in 1960 and put them in exactly the same relative positions they had in 1960. He could do this without destroying me now. Then, if the reassembly view were correct, God could confront me now with myself as I was in 1960. As van Inwagen points out, each of us could truly say to the other, "I am you." But that is conceptually impossible. Therefore, the reassembly view is wrong.

I should point out that these considerations do not make van Inwagen a skeptic about bodily resurrection. God could accomplish bodily resurrection in some other way, for example, by replacing a person's body with a duplicate right before death or cremation, and the duplicate is what is cremated or buried. This shows that it is logically possible that bodily resurrection, where the resurrected body is the same one as the premortem body, be accomplished by an omnipotent being—even if we lack the conceptual resources to see how. The present point, however, is that resurrected bodies are not produced by God's reassembling the atoms of premortem bodies.

Putting aside van Inwagen's arguments, the final difficulty for bodily resurrection comes from reflection on the following question: How can an earthly body that is subject to decay or destruction by fire be the same body as an incorruptible glorified body? I suggested that if identity of bodies consists of spatiotemporal continuity, and if God could replace the organic cells of a body by incorruptible and glorified cells in a way that preserved spatiotemporal continuity, then a premortem body could be the same body as a postmortem body even though the premortem body is corruptible and the postmortem body is incorruptible.

However, I doubt that one and the same body (or one and the same anything else) can be corruptible during part of its existence and incorruptible during another part of its existence. The reason for my doubt is that being corruptible and being incorruptible concern the persistence conditions of a thing, and a thing has its persistence conditions essentially. To say that a thing is corruptible is to say that there are a range of conditions under which it would go out of existence; to say that a thing is incorruptible is to say that there are no such conditions. It is logically impossible—or at least it seems so—that a single thing is such that there are conditions at one time under which it could go out of existence, and that there are no such conditions at another time under which it could go out of existence. This difficulty could be overcome by not requiring that the (incorruptible) resurrected body be the very same body as the (corruptible) earthly body; see section 4.

3d. The Memory Criterion

Many philosophers find psychological continuity an attractive criterion of personal identity, but there are well-known, and potentially devastating, problems with it. The major problem is called "the duplication problem." The problem is that, however "in the right way" is spelled out for the causal connections between mental states of Jones now and a future person, two future persons can have mental states caused by Jones's mental states now in the right way. It is logically possible that Jones's memories be transferred to two future persons in exactly the same "right way" (whatever that is). In that case, the memory criterion would hold, per impossibile, that two future persons are Jones. Whatever causal connections hold between the mental states of Jones now and person B in the future could also hold between the mental states of Jones now and a different person C in the future. But it is logically impossible that Jones be both B and C.

To put this point another way: there is an important constraint on any criterion of personal identity. Identity is a one-one relation, and no person can be identical with two distinct future persons. So, any criterion of personal identity that can be satisfied both by person A at t1 and person B at t2 and by person A at t1 and person C at t2 entails that B = C. So, if B is a different person from C, a criterion that allows that A is identical to both is logically untenable. However, if sameness of memories sufficed for sameness of person, one person could become two: A's memories could be transferred to B and C, where B ≠ C, in such a way that B's and C's memories are continuous with A's memories in exactly the same way ("the right way"). It would follow on the memory criterion that A = B and A = C. But since B ≠ C, this is a contradiction. Hence, the memory criterion does not work (Williams 1973a).

The problem of duplication seems insurmountable for the memory criterion. Philosophers have responded to the problem of duplication with rather desperate measures; for example, Jones is the same person as a future person, as long as there are no duplicates. If there are two future persons at t2 related to Jones at t1 in the same way, then Jones is neither. Jones just does not survive until t2; at t2, there are two replicas of Jones, but Jones herself is no longer there. But if only one future person at t2 is related to Jones at t1 in exactly that way, then, according to this response to the duplication problem, Jones is that person at t2. Thus, Jones can be made not to survive by duplication. This sort of move seems to many a most unsatisfying way to think of personal identity.

There may be another way, at least if we allow religious assumptions, to salvage the memory criterion. A religious philosopher may respond to the duplication argument by saying that God would not bring it about (or let it be brought about) that both B and C have A's memories. Thus, God in His goodness would prevent duplication (Locke 1924, II, xxvii, 13). But the memory criterion would still be vulnerable to the charge that, even if God would not allow both B and C to have A's memories, memory would not be a metaphysically sufficient criterion for personal identity. It would still be metaphysically possible for two people, B and C, to have all A's memories, that is, for each to have memories continuous with A's.

However, there is an argument using religious premises that rehabilitates the memory criterion by showing that it is metaphysically impossible for God to bring it about that B and C both have all A's memories. Because this way was suggested to me by Gareth B. Matthews, call it "the Matthews argument." The premises of this argument are explicitly religious. They appeal to God's necessary attributes— namely, that God is essentially just—and to the notion of a judgment after death. If God is essentially just and God judges everyone, and A is a person who deserves punishment, then it would be metaphysically impossible for B and C to have A's memories.

The reason it would be metaphysically impossible for B and C to have A's memories is this: A deserves punishment. God is essentially just and judges everyone. Suppose that B and C both had A's memories (caused in the right way). Whom does God punish? If God punished B but not C, or C but not B, then God would not be essentially just: B and C are related to A in exactly the same way; it is impossible to be just and to judge B and C differently. On the other hand, if God punished both B and C, then there would be twice the punishment that A deserved, and again God would not be essentially just. Either way, supposing that B and C both had A's memories (caused in the right way) violates God's essential justice in judgment. Because God is essentially just, if A deserves punishment, it is metaphysically impossible for God to bring it about that B and C both have A's memories.

If everyone deserves punishment except Christ, then this argument shows that it is metaphysically impossible for God to transfer A's memories to two distinct nondivine people. It is metaphysically impossible for God to transfer Christ's memories to two distinct nondivine people since Christ is divine. The Matthews argument relies on heavy theological assumptions, but it does rescue the memory criterion from the duplication problem.

4. Original Philosophical Development

There is yet another view of human persons, which is compatible with the doctrine of resurrection. Suppose that human persons are purely material substances—constituted by human bodies, but not identical to the bodies that constitute them (Baker 2000). On this view, "the constitution view," something is a person in virtue of having a first-person perspective, and a person is a *human* person in virtue of being constituted by a human body. (I do not distinguish between human organisms and human bodies; the body that constitutes me now is identical to a human organism.) The relation between a person and her body is the same relation that a statue bears to the piece of bronze (say) that makes it up: constitution. So, there are two theoretical ideas—the notion of constitution and the notion of a first-person perspective—that need explication. I'll discuss each of these ideas briefly.

4a. The First-Person Perspective

A first-person perspective is the ability to conceive of oneself as oneself. This is not just the ability to use the first-person pronoun; rather, it requires that one can *conceive of* oneself as the referent of the first-person pronoun independently of any name or description of oneself. In English, this ability is manifested in the use of a first-person pronoun embedded in a clause introduced by a psychological or linguistic verb in a first-person sentence. For example, "I wish that I were a movie star," or "I said that I would do it" or "I wonder how I'll die" all illustrate a first-person perspective. If I wonder how I will die, or I promise that I'll stick with you, then I am thinking of myself as myself; I am not thinking of myself in any third-person way (e.g., not as Lynne Baker, nor as the person who is thinking, nor as her, nor as the only person in the room) at all. Even if I had total amnesia and didn't know my name or anything at all about my past, I could still think of myself as myself. Anything that can wonder how it will die ipso facto has a first-person perspective and thus is a person. In short, any being whatever with the ability to think of itself as itself—whether a divine being, an artificially manufactured being (such as a computer), a human clone, a Martian, anything that has a first-person perspective—is a person.

A being may be conscious without having a first-person perspective. Non-human primates and other higher animals are conscious, and they have psychological states such as believing, fearing, and desiring. They have points of view (e.g., "danger in that direction"), but they cannot conceive of themselves as the subjects of such thoughts. They cannot *conceive of* themselves from the first person. (We have every reason to think that they do not wonder how they will die.) So, having psychological states such as beliefs and desires and having a point of view are necessary but not sufficient conditions for being a person. A sufficient condition for being a person—whether human, divine, ape, or silicon-based—is having a first-person perspective. What makes something a person is not the "stuff" it is made of. It does not matter whether something is made of organic material or silicon or, in the case of God, no material stuff at all. If a being has a first-person perspective, it is a person.

Person is an ontological kind whose defining characteristic is a capacity for a first-person perspective. A first-person perspective is the basis of all self-consciousness. It makes possible an inner life, a life of thoughts that one realizes are one's own. The appearance of first-person perspectives in a world makes an ontological difference in that world: a world populated with beings with inner lives is ontologically richer than a world populated with no beings with inner lives. But what is ontologically distinctive about being a person—namely, the capacity for a first-person perspective—does not have to be secured by an immaterial substance like a soul.

4b. Constitution

What distinguishes human persons from other logically possible persons (God, Martians, perhaps computers) is that human persons are constituted by human bodies (i.e., human animals), rather than, say, by Martian green-slime bodies.

Constitution is a very general relation that we are all familiar with (though probably not under that label). A river at any moment is constituted by an aggregate of water molecules. But the river is not identical to the aggregate of water molecules that constitutes it at that moment. Because one and the same river, call it R, is constituted by different aggregates of molecules at different times, the river is not identical to any of the aggregates of water molecules that make it up. So, assuming here the classical conception of identity, according to which if a = b, then necessarily, a = b, constitution is not identity.

Another way to see that constitution is not identity is to notice that even if an aggregate of molecules, A1, actually constitutes R at t1, R might have been constituted by a different aggregate of molecules, A2, at t1. So, constitution is a relation that is in some ways similar to identity, but is not actually identity. If the relation between a person and her body is constitution, then a person is not identical to her body. The relation is more like the relation between a statue and the piece of bronze that makes it up, or between the river and the aggregates of molecules.

The answer to the question What most fundamentally is x? is what I call "x's primary kind." Each thing has its primary-kind property essentially. If x constitutes y, then x and y are of different primary kinds. If x constitutes y, then what "the thing" is is determined by y's primary kind. For example, if a human body constitutes a person, then what there is is a person-constituted-by-a-human-body.

So you—a person constituted by a human body—are most fundamentally a person. Person is your primary kind. If parts of your body were replaced by bionic parts until you were no longer human, you would still be a person. You are a person as long as you exist. If you ceased to have a first-person perspective, then you would cease to exist—even if your body was still there.

Whether we are talking about rivers, statues, human persons, or any other constituted thing, the basic idea is this: when certain things of certain kinds (aggregates of water molecules, pieces of marble, human organisms) are in certain circumstances (different ones for different kinds of things), then new entities of different kinds come into existence. The circumstances in which a piece of marble comes to constitute a statue have to do with an artist's intentions, the conventions of the art world, and so on. The circumstances in which a human organism comes to constitute a human person have to do with the development of a (narrowly defined capacity for a) first-person perspective. In each case, new things of new kinds, with new sorts of causal powers, come into being. Because constitution is the vehicle, so to speak, by which things of new kinds come into existence in the natural world, it is obvious that constitution is not identity. Indeed, this conception is relentlessly antireductive.

Although not identity, constitution is a relation of real unity. If x constitutes y at a time, then x and y are not separate things. A person and her body have lots of properties in common: the property of having toenails and the property of being responsible for certain of her actions. But notice: the person has the property of having toenails only because she is constituted by something that could have had toenails even if it had constituted nothing. And her body is responsible for her actions only because it constitutes something that would have been responsible no matter what constituted it.

So, I'll say that the person has the property of having toenails derivatively, and her body has the property of being responsible for certain of her actions derivatively; the body has the property of having toenails nonderivatively, and the person has the property of being responsible for certain of her actions nonderivatively. If x constitutes y, then some of x's properties have their source (so to speak) in y, and some of y's properties have their source in x. The unity of the object x-constituted-by-y is shown by the fact that x and y borrow properties from each other. The idea of having properties derivatively accounts for the otherwise strange fact that if x constitutes y at t, x and y share so many properties even though x ≠ y.

To summarize the general discussion of the idea of constitution: constitution is a very general relation throughout the natural order. Although it is a relation of real unity, it is short of identity. (Identity is necessary; constitution is contingent. Identity is symmetrical; constitution is asymmetrical.) Constitution is a relation that accounts for the appearance of genuinely new kinds of things with new kinds of causal powers. If F and G are primary kinds and Fs constitute Gs, then an inventory of the contents of the world that includes Fs but leaves out Gs is incomplete. Gs are not reducible to Fs.

4c. Human Persons

A *human* person at time t is a person (i.e., a being with a first-person perspective) that is constituted by a human body at t and was constituted by a human body at the beginning of her existence. (I say "was constituted by a human body at the beginning of her existence" to avoid problems raised by the Incarnation. The orthodox Christian view is that the eternal Second Person of the Trinity was identical with the temporal human Jesus of Nazareth, and that that Being was both fully divine and fully human. How this could be so is ultimately a mystery that requires special treatment far beyond the scope of this chapter.)

According to the constitution view, an ordinary human person is a material object in the same way that a statue or a carburetor is a material object. A statue is constituted by, say, a piece of marble, but it is not identical to the piece of marble that constitutes it. The piece of marble could exist in a world in which it was the only occupant, but no statue could. Nothing that is a statue could exist in a world without artists or institutions of art. A human person is constituted by an organism, a member of the species *Homo sapiens*, but is not identical to the organism that constitutes her. The human organism could exist in a world in which no psychological properties whatever were exemplified, but no person could. Nothing that is a person could exist in a world without first-person perspectives. A human organism that develops a first-person perspective comes to constitute a new thing: a person.

Just as different statues are constituted by different kinds of things (pieces of marble, pieces of bronze, etc.), so too different persons are (or may be) constituted by different kinds of things (human organisms, pieces of plastic, Martian matter, or, in the case of God, nothing at all). What makes something a person (no matter what it is "made of") is a first-person perspective; what makes something a piece of sculpture (no matter what it is "made of") is its relation to an art world. A person could start out as a human person and have organic parts replaced by synthetic parts until she was no longer constituted by a *human* body. If the person whose organic parts were replaced by synthetic parts retained her first-person perspective—no matter what was doing the replacing—then she would still exist and still be a person, even with a synthetic body. If she ceased to be a person (i.e., ceased to have a first-person perspective), however, she would cease to exist altogether. To put it more technically, a person's persistence conditions are determined by the property of being a person (i.e., of having a first-person perspective): a human person could cease to be organic without ceasing to exist. (She might have a resurrected body or a bionic body.) But she could not cease to be a person without ceasing to exist.

On the constitution view, then, a human person and the animal that constitutes her differ in persistence conditions without there being any actual physical intrinsic difference between them. The persistence conditions of animals—all animals, human or not—are biological; and the persistence conditions of persons—all persons, human or not—are not biological.

4d. Resurrection on the Constitution View

The constitution view can solve some outstanding conceptual problems about the doctrine of resurrection. The two elements of the constitution view needed to show how resurrection is metaphysically possible are these: (1) human persons are essentially embodied, and (2) human persons essentially have first-person perspectives.

(1) Essential embodiment: although human persons cannot exist without some body or other (a body that can support a first-person perspective), they can exist without the bodies that they actually have. We can speak of human persons in the resurrection, where, though still embodied, they do not have human bodies with human organs and DNA. The same persons who had been constituted by earthly bodies can come to be constituted by resurrected bodies. The bodies on earth and in heaven are not the same, but the persons are.

(2) Essential first-person perspectives: if a person's first-person perspective were extinguished, the person would go out of existence. What makes a person the individual that she is is her first-person perspective. So, what must persist in the resurrection is the person's first-person perspective—not her soul (there are no souls), and not her body (she may have a new body in the resurrection).

What is needed is a criterion for sameness of first-person perspective over time. In virtue of what does a resurrected person have the same first-person perspective as a certain earthly person who was born in 1800? Although I think that the constitution view solves the synchronic problem of identity noncircularly (Baker 2000), I think that, on anyone's view, there is no informative noncircular answer to the question: In virtue of what do person P_1 at t_1 and person P_2 at t_2 have the same first-person perspective over time? It is just a primitive, unanalyzable fact that some future person is I, but there is a fact of the matter nonetheless.

The constitution view is compatible with the three features of the Christian doctrine of resurrection mentioned at the outset: embodiment, identity, miracle. In the first place, the constitution view shows why resurrection should be bodily: human persons are essentially embodied, and hence could not exist unembodied.

The first-person perspective is an essential property of a person constituted by a body of some kind. A nondivine first-person perspective cannot exist on its own, disembodied. So, the question Why is resurrection bodily? cannot arise. On the interpretation of the doctrine of resurrection according to which a human person exists in some intermediate state between her death and a general resurrection in the future, the constitution view would postulate an intermediate body. (Alternatively, the constitution view is compatible with there being a temporal gap in the person's existence). Because the constitution view does not require that there be the same body for the same person, the problems found with the traditional theories of body are avoided.

In the second place, on the constitution view, it is possible that a future person with a resurrected body is identical to Smith now, and there is a fact of the matter about which, if any, such future person is Smith. To see that there is a fact of the matter about which resurrected person is Smith, we must proceed to the third feature of the doctrine of resurrection.

In the third place, resurrection is a miracle, a gift from God. The constitution view can use this feature to show that there is a fact of the matter about which resurrected person is, say, Smith. The question is this: Which of the resurrected people is Smith? Because the constitution view holds that Smith might have had a different body from the one that he had on earth, he may be constituted by a different (glorified) body in heaven. So, "Smith is the person with body 1" is contingently true if true at all.

Now, according to the traditional doctrine of Providence, God has two kinds of knowledge: free knowledge and natural knowledge. God's free knowledge is knowledge of contingent truths, and His natural knowledge is knowledge of logical and metaphysical necessities. (I'm disregarding the possibility of middle knowledge here.) Again, according to the traditional doctrine of Providence, the obtaining of any contingent state of affairs depends on God's free decree. Whether the person with resurrected body 1, or body 2, or some other body is Smith is a contingent state of affairs. Therefore, which if any of these states of affairs obtains depends on God's free decree. No immaterial soul is needed for there to be a fact of the matter as to whether Smith is the person with resurrected body 1. All that is needed is God's free decree that brings about one contingent state of affairs rather than another. If God decrees that the person with body 1 have Smith's first-person perspective, then Smith is the person with body 1 (Davis 1993, 119–21). So, there is a fact of the matter as to which, if any, of the persons in the Resurrection is Smith, even if we creatures cannot know it. On the Christian idea of Providence, it is well within God's power to bring it about that a certain resurrected person is identical to Smith.

Notice that this use of the doctrine of God's Providence provides for the metaphysical impossibility of Smith's being identical to both the person with body 1 and the person with body 2. For it is part of God's natural knowledge that it is metaphysically impossible for one person to be identical to two persons. And according to the traditional notion of God's power, what is metaphysically impossible is not within God's power to bring about. So, the constitution view excludes the duplication problem.

4e. Advantages of the Constitution View

The constitution view can offer those who believe in immaterial souls (immaterialists) almost everything that they want—without the burden of making sense of how there can be immaterial souls in the natural world. For example, human persons can survive change of body; truths about persons are not exhausted by truths about bodies; persons have causal powers that their bodies would not have if they did not constitute persons; there is a fact of the matter about which, if any, future person is I; persons are not identical to bodies.

The constitution view also has advantages, at least for Christians, over its major materialistic competitor: animalism. (Animalism is the view that a human person is identical to a human organism.) On the constitution view, being a person is not just a contingent property of things that are fundamentally nonpersonal (animals).

On the animalist view, our having first-person perspectives (or any mental states at all) is irrelevant to the kind of being that we are. But the Christian story cannot get off the ground without presuppositions about first-person perspectives. On the human side, without first-person perspectives, there would be no sinners and no penitents. Because a person's repentance requires that she realize that she herself has offended, nothing lacking a first-person perspective could possibly repent. On the divine side: Christ's atonement required that he suffer, and an important aspect of his suffering was his anticipation of his death (e.g., the agony in the Garden of Gethsemane); and his anticipation of his death would have been impossible without a first-person perspective. This part of Christ's mission specifically required a first-person perspective. What is important about us (and Christ) according to the Christian story is that we have first-person perspectives. Given how important the first-person perspective is to the Christian story, Christians have good reason to take our having first-person perspectives to be central to the kind of being that we are.

The second reason for a Christian to endorse the constitution view over animalism is that the constitution view allows that a person's resurrection body may be nonidentical with her earthly biological body. According to the constitution view, it is logically possible that a person have different bodies at different times; whether anyone ever changes bodies or not, the logical possibility is built into the constitution view. By contrast, on the animalist view, a person just is—is identical to—an organism. Whatever happens to the organism happens to the person. On an animalist view, it is logically impossible for you to survive the destruction of your body. So, on an animalist view, if Smith, say, is resurrected, then the organism that was Smith on earth must persist in heaven. The resurrection body must be that very organism. In that case, any animalist view compatible with Christian resurrection will have implausible features about the persistence conditions for organisms.

Let me elaborate. If, as on the animalist view, a person's postmortem body were identical to her premortem body, then we would have new questions about the persistence conditions for bodies. Non-Christian animalists understand our persistence conditions in terms of continued biological functioning. But Christian animalists who believe in resurrection cannot construe our persistence conditions biologically unless they think that resurrected persons are maintained by digestion, respiration, and so on as earthly persons are. Because postmortem bodies are incorruptible, it seems unlikely that they are maintained by biological processes (like digestion, etc.) as ours are. But if biological processes are irrelevant to the persistence conditions of *resurrected* persons, and if, as animalism has it, biological processes are essential to *our* persistence conditions, then it does not even seem logically possible for a resurrected person to be identical to any of us. Something whose persistence conditions are biological cannot be identical to something whose persistence conditions are not biological.

To put it another way, a Christian animalist who believes in resurrection must hold that earthly bodies, which are corruptible, are identical to resurrection bodies, which are incorruptible. Because I think that biological organisms are essentially corruptible, I do not believe that a resurrection body, which is incorruptible, could be identical to a biological organism. Even if I'm wrong about the essential corruptibility of organisms, however, the fact remains that on Christian animalism, the persistence conditions for organisms would be beyond the purview of biology. A Christian animalist who believed in resurrection would have to allow that organisms can undergo physically impossible changes without ceasing to exist. For example, organisms would disappear at one place (on earth at the place where the death certificate says that they died) and reappear at some other place.

Moreover, death would have to be conceived of in a very unusual way by an animalist who is a Christian: on a Christian animalist view, a person/organism does not really die. For example, God snatches the body away immediately before death and replaces it with a simulacrum that dies (van Inwagen 1992). Alternatively, God makes organisms disappear at one place (on earth at the place where the death certificate says that they died) and reappear at some other place (Zimmerman 1999). In either case, Christian animalists who believed in resurrection would have to suppose that organisms routinely undergo physically impossible changes without ceasing to exist. Platonists would say that the body dies, but the soul never dies; it lives straight on through the body's death. Christian animalists would have to say something even stranger: the body of a resurrected person does not die either, if by "die" we mean cease functioning permanently. Death for human persons who will be resurrected, on this view, would just be an illusion. I do not think that that conception of death comports well with the story of the Crucifixion, which suggests that death is horrendous and not at all illusory.

So, there are several reasons why a Christian should prefer the constitution view to animalism. To make animalism compatible with the doctrine of resurrection, the Christian animalist would have to make two unpalatable moves: she would have to conceive of persistence conditions for organisms as at least partly nonbiological, and she would have to reconceive the death of a human person in a way that did not involve demise of the organism to which the person is allegedly identical.

Perhaps even more important is the fact that, according to animalism, the property of being a person or of having a first-person perspective is just a contingent and temporary property of essentially nonpersonal beings: animalism severs what is most distinctive about us from what we most fundamentally are. On the animalist view, persons qua persons have no ontological significance. I think that these are all good reasons for a Christian to prefer the constitution view to animalism.

5. CONCLUSION

The doctrine of resurrection has not received as much philosophical attention as some other aspects of Christian theology (e.g., the problem of evil and the traditional arguments for the existence of God), but views on personal identity suggest intriguing possibilities for identifying conditions under which a premortem person can be identical to a postmortem person. Only if a premortem and postmortem person can be one and the same individual is resurrection even a logical possibility.

WORKS CITED

Aquinas, Thomas. 1945. *Summa Theologica* I. Questions 75–89. New York: Random House.

Aristotle. 1941. *De Anima*. In *The Basic Works of Aristotle*, ed. Richard McKeon. New York: Random House.

Baker, Lynne Rudder. 2000. *Persons and Bodies: A Constitution View.* Cambridge, England: Cambridge University Press.

Bynum, Caroline Walker. 1995. *The Resurrection of the Body in Western Christianity.* New York: Columbia University Press.

Cooper, John W. 1989. *Body, Soul and Life Everlasting: Biblical Anthropology and the Monism-Dualism Debate.* Grand Rapids, Mich.: Eerdmans.

Cullman, Oscar. 1973. "Immortality of the Soul or Resurrection of the Dead?" In *Immortality,* ed. Terence Penelhum, 53–85. Belmont: Wadsworth.

Davis, Stephen T. 1993. *Risen Indeed: Making Sense of the Resurrection.* Grand Rapids, Mich.: Eerdmans.

Hick, John. 1994. *Death and Eternal Life.* Louisville, Ky.: Westminster/John Knox.

Locke, John. 1924. *An Essay Concerning Human Understanding.* ed. A. S. Pringle-Pattison. Oxford: Clarendon Press.

MacKay, D. M. 1987. "Brain Science and the Soul." In *The Oxford Companion to the Mind,* ed. Richard L. Gregory, 723–25. Oxford: Oxford University Press.

Polkinghorne, John. 1996. *The Faith of a Physicist: Reflections of a Bottom-up Thinker.* Minneapolis: Fortress Press.

Price, H. H. 1964. "Personal Survival and the Idea of Another World." In *Classical and Contemporary Readings in the Philosophy of Religion,* ed. John Hick, 364–386. Englewood Cliffs, N.J.: Prentice-Hall.

Swinburne, Richard. 1997. *The Evolution of the Soul.* Oxford: Oxford University Press.

van Inwagen, Peter. 1992. "The Possibility of Resurrection." In *Immortality,* ed. Paul Edwards, 242–6. New York: Macmillan. Reprinted from the *International Journal for Philosophy of Religion* 9 (1978).

———. 1995. "Dualism and Materialism: Athens and Jerusalem?" *Faith and Philosophy* 12: 475–88.

Williams, Bernard. 1973. "Bodily Continuity and Personal Identity." In *Problems of the Self,* 19–25. Cambridge, England: Cambridge University Press.

Wolfson, Harry A. 1956–57. "Immortality and Resurrection in the Philosophy of the Church Fathers." *Harvard Divinity School Bulletin* 22: 5–40.

Zimmerman, Dean. 1999. "The Compatibility of Materialism and Survival: The 'Falling Elevator' Model." *Faith and Philosophy* 16: 194–212.

FOR FURTHER READING

Baker, Lynne Rudder. 1995. "Need a Christian Be a Mind/Body Dualist?" *Faith and Philosophy* 12: 489–504.

Castañeda, Hector-Neri. 1967. "Indicators and Quasi-Indicators." *American Philosophical Quarterly* 4: 85–100.

Geach, Peter. 1969. *God and the Soul.* London: Routledge and Kegan Paul.

Neufeldt, Ronald W. 1986. *Karma and Rebirth: Post Classical Developments.* Albany: State University of New York Press.

O'Flaherty, Wendy Doniger, ed. 1980. *Karma and Rebirth in Classical Indian Traditions.* Berkeley: University of California Press.

Penelhum, Terence. 1970. *Survival and Disembodied Existence*. London: Routledge and Kegan Paul.

Reichenbach, Bruce. 1990. *The Law of Karma*. Honolulu: University of Hawaii Press.

Russell, Jeffrey Burton. 1997. *A History of Heaven*. Princeton: Princeton University Press.

Williams, Bernard. 1973. "Personal Identity and Individuation." In *Problems of the Self*, 1–18. Cambridge, England: Cambridge University Press.

CHAPTER 16

RELIGIOUS DIVERSITY

Familiar Problems, Novel Opportunities

PHILIP L. QUINN

RELIGIOUS diversity is, of course, nothing new. In the West, Greek observers long ago commented on Egyptian religious beliefs and practices, and the Hebrew Bible records information about the rival religions the Israelites encountered. Surely the early Christians, who were persecuted for refusing to acknowledge the divinity of the Roman emperors, were aware of religious diversity. It did not escape notice in medieval Christendom; Aquinas, for example, cited Maimonides frequently and with great respect. But when the Reformation shattered the unity of Christendom, religious diversity became more salient for the culture of modernity because it had become a source of violent conflict at the heart of Europe. And it appears to be a permanent feature of the pluralistic liberal democracies that have come to be typical of Western Europe and North America.

At the beginning of the third millennium of the common era, religious diversity seems to be increasing in importance to philosophical thought. Among the factors responsible for this change is the fact that educated people have become better acquainted than ever before with religions other than their own. Modern technologies of travel and communication facilitate contacts between the adherents of different religions. Modern scholarship has made texts from a variety of religious traditions available in many languages. And cultural anthropologists have provided fascinating thick descriptions of an enormous range of religious beliefs and practices. Moreover, those of us who live in religiously pluralistic democracies have ample opportunities to develop face-to-face familiarity with practitioners of religions other than own. Often enough, we discover that their religious commitments help to make them people we feel compelled to admire. The dangers of religious diversity also force themselves on our attention. Around-the-clock news broadcasts confront us with graphic illustrations of what can happen when religions clash in such places as Belfast, Beirut, and Bosnia.

Philosophy can come to grips with religious diversity in numerous ways. In this essay, I discuss four of them. Somewhat arbitrarily, I divide the topics I consider into two categories: familiar problems and novel opportunities. I count as familiar problems the epistemological challenge to the rationality of religious belief and practice posed by religious diversity and the political problem of religious intolerance. I classify as novel opportunities two questions that are often addressed by the emerging academic area of specialization that may be described as comparative philosophy of religion. One is the question of whether religion can be defined; the other is the question of how to carry out constructive comparisons of religions. In my treatment of each of these four issues, I focus mainly on discussions in the recent scholarly literature, though I also allude briefly to their roots in the philosophy of the seventeenth and eighteenth centuries.

Our epistemological challenge is difficult enough even if we restrict our attention to the so-called world religions. It only becomes worse if we add in the many African religions, Native American religions, and religions from other parts of the world. Religions differ along the doctrinal dimension, and often their doctrines conflict. For example, traditional Christians assert that the Supreme Being is a trinity of persons, while traditional Muslims deny that this is the case. Religions also differ along the practical dimension, and often the goals they set and the paths to those goals are also opposed. For instance, traditional Christians hold that the ultimate goal of religious striving is salvation, which consists of union of the individual self with God forever in the afterlife, while traditional Buddhists hold that the ultimate goal is liberation, which consists of reaching a state of nirvana that in some sense involves the ceasing to be of the individual self and thus freedom from repeated reincarnations. Morever, each of the world religions can offer evidence for its doctrinal and practical aspects from a variety of sources. They include philosophical arguments for doctrines and mystical experiences of practitioners. Each of the world religions also derives a kind of self-support from the way many people who follow its path come to enjoy the spiritual fruits it promises. But it seems that none of them is decisively superior to all the others in terms of evidential support. So it appears that each undermines the evidential support of all the others because it remains an uneliminated competitor for them. And the problem is that this undermining may be so severe that the epistemic status of all of them is lowered to a point at which it is not rational for anyone who is fully aware of the situation to belong to any of them.

Both history and current events bear witness to our political problem. Rivers of blood have been shed in the name of religion. Crusades and inquisitions are ugly blemishes on European history. The Reformation gave rise to devastating Wars of Religion. Even more recently, religiously inspired violence is to found in such places as Northern Ireland, the Balkans, northern Africa, the Middle East, and in Asia. Of course, religion is not the sole cause of violent conflict in many of these cases. Unscrupulous politicians manipulate religious animosities to serve their own purposes. Class differences and ethnic divisions also play causal roles. But religion makes a real causal contribution to violent conflict in the present as it has in the past. What is more, it seems unlikely that religious conflict will be eliminated by the withering away of religion at any time in the foreseeable future. Unless diverse religions can learn to tolerate one another, religious conflict will surely persist, and it might assume global proportions under unfavorable conditions. There is, therefore, an urgent need for good philosophical arguments for religious toleration. To be sure, philosophical arguments would not by themselves produce widespread toleration. However, they might reinforce settled habits of toleration and justify teaching toleration to the young, and they could thereby make toleration seem attractive to thoughtful people and help to stabilize the practice of toleration where it has already gotten a foothold in society.

Comparison of religions, or of parts or aspects of religions, seems to presuppose that we can classify things as religions antecedent to comparing them. How else could we be sure that we were comparing two religions rather than a religion and a science? The ability to classify seems to presuppose in turn that we have a concept of religion that might in principle be analyzed or defined. Defining religion by conceptual analysis would resemble what epistemologists do when they try to define knowledge. Starting from the proposal that knowledge is justified true belief, they note that Gettier cases in which justified true belief is not sufficient for knowledge are counterexamples to the proposal, and they then try to refine the proposal until it specifies conditions that are conceptually necessary and sufficient for knowledge. Proposals are to be tested against intuitive data consisting of cases we confidently classify as being instances of knowledge or as not being instances of knowledge. Thus understood, the task of defining religion would involve applying this familiar method of analysis to the concept of religion. Successful completion of the task would yield a set of conditions that are conceptually necessary and sufficient for being a religion. The problem is that there is disagreement not only about what the definition of religion is, assuming it can be defined, but even about whether religion can be defined in this fashion.

But even if we do not have a general definition of religion, we surely can pick out some clear and uncontroversial cases of religions. So perhaps useful comparisons can be made even in the absence of an agreed-upon definition of religion. Balanced comparisons would no doubt reveal a pattern of similarities and differences, and fine-grained comparisons might make manifest differences within the similarities and similarities within the differences. Such patterns would in their own right be of interest to some people. Comparisons might also serve more constructive purposes for the practitioners of the religions under study. One possibility is the discovery of unanticipated concord. The adherents of both religions might learn that they had, by different historical and cultural paths, arrived at similar destinations in terms of their understandings of the human condition. By eliminating sources of mutual mistrust, comparison might reduce friction. Another possibility is a challenge to one of the religions being compared. Its practitioners might come to recognize the inadequacy of their explanations of certain forms of human behavior through reflecting on the better explanations offered by the other religion. Comparison might stimulate novel theoretical developments within a religious tradition. A third possibility is the enrichment of religious practice. The adherents of one religion might find in the other a practice of prayer or meditation that could profitably be appropriated, perhaps with modifications, and contribute to their own spiritual growth. Comparison might provide a religion with practical resources it would not have developed on its own. Which of these constructive possibilities become actual, if any do, will, of course, depend on the details of particular comparisons that people make. There is no way of knowing a priori whether comparisons will yield constructive fruits. But examples of comparisons that have recently been worked out in some detail suggest that it is within our power to actualize some of the constructive possibilities.

So these four philosophical issues arise from religious diversity. Let us examine each of them more thoroughly.

A Familiar Problem: Epistemological Conflict

David Hume presents a special case of the epistemological challenge of religious diversity in the famous discussion of miracles that is contained in the second part of section 10 of *An Enquiry Concerning Human Understanding* (1748/2000). Religious believers cite miracles in support of their doctrinal claims, and they cite testimony as evidence for the occurrence of these miracles. Hume argues that the miracles cited in support of different religions must be regarded as contrary facts because the religions they support are mutually inconsistent. Testimony to the miracles supporting different religions is therefore conflicting testimony.

> Every miracle, therefore, pretended to have been wrought in any of these religions (and all of them abound in miracles), as its direct scope is to establish the particular system to which it is attributed; so has it the same force, though

more indirectly, to overthrow every other system. In destroying a rival system, it likewise destroys the credit of those miracles, on which that system was established; so that all the prodigies of different religions are to be regarded as contrary facts, and the evidences of these prodigies, whether weak or strong, as opposite to each other. (32)

However, conflicting or opposite testimonies cancel each other out, other things being equal; there is mutual destruction of evidential force. Thus, given religious diversity, the evidential force of miracle reports is, other things being equal, destroyed by contrary miracle reports.

There are, of course, objections to Hume's argument that have some force. His claim that the miracles of different religions must be regarded as contrary facts can be called into question. The miracles of different religions would not, for example, be contrary facts if there were many gods, each of whom worked miracles on behalf of his or her worshippers. Indeed, I suppose the God of the true religion might work miracles for the adherents of a religion containing a mixture of truth and error if those adherents were for some reason unprepared to receive the true religion and the miracles were needed to deter them from adopting a particularly wicked cult of human sacrifice. But even if his argument is not decisive, Hume is surely getting at something important. We can see more clearly what it is if we examine the way a similar problem arises for William P. Alston's epistemology of religious experience.

Alston works within what he describes as a doxastic practice approach to epistemology. A doxastic practice is a way of forming beliefs and subjecting them to epistemic evaluation in terms of a background system of beliefs that furnish potential defeaters or overriders. Alston argues that it is practically rational to engage in socially established doxastic practices that are not demonstrably unreliable or otherwise disqualified for rational acceptance. In the religious sphere, he views mystical perception as a kind of religious experience in which there occurs a presentation or appearance to the subject of something the subject identifies as the Ultimate. Applying the notion of doxastic practices to mystical perception, he urges us to suppose that there are different socially established mystical practices in diverse religions because there are wide divergences in their overrider systems of background beliefs. Christian mystical practice (CMP) is one such practice. Alston argues persuasively that it is not demonstrably unreliable. However, both the outputs of CMP and its overrider system appear to be massively inconsistent with their counterparts in the mystical practices of other religions. Assuming that the appearance of conflict cannot be explained away, religious diversity thus gives rise to a philosophical challenge to the rationality of engaging in CMP or any of its equally well-established rivals in other religions.

In his book *Perceiving God* (1991), Alston grants that this challenge is the most difficult problem for his position that it is rational to engage in CMP. He formulates the problem in this way. On account of the inconsistency, at most one of the rival mystical practices can be a sufficiently reliable way of forming beliefs about the Ultimate to be rationally engaged in. But why should one suppose that CMP in particular is the one that is reliable, if any is? To be sure, CMP can come up with internal reasons for supposing that it is more reliable than its competitors. But each of them can do the same. Hence, "if it is to be rational for me to take CMP to be reliable, I will have to have sufficient *independent* reasons for supposing that CMP is reliable, or more reliable or more likely to be reliable, than its alternatives" (269). A cumulative case argument for the truth of Christianity might provide such independent reasons. Alston does not try to show, however, that there is a cumulative case for the truth of Christianity that is decisively superior to the cases that can be made in support of its competitors. Instead, he elects to proceed in accord with a worst-case scenario in which it is assumed that there are no independent reasons for preferring CMP to its rivals.

How bad are things for CMP in the worst-case scenario? Alston invites us to look at the matter in this way. Suppose our sole respectable basis for a positive epistemic evaluation of CMP were the fact that it is a socially established doxastic practice that has not been shown to be unreliable. On that assumption, Alston admits, religious diversity would reduce its epistemic status to an alarming degree. Given the equal social establishment of several mutually incompatible mystical practices, none of which is demonstrably unreliable, he concedes that "it is at least arguable that the most reasonable view, even for a hitherto committed participant of one of the practices, would be that the social establishment in each case reflects a culturally generated way of reinforcing socially desirable attitudes and practices, reinforcing these by inculcating a sense of the presence of Supreme Reality and a way of thinking about it" (1991, 276). And that view in turn, he allows, would imply that the justificatory efficacy of all these mystical practices had been altogether dissipated.

According to Alston, things are not this bad for CMP because it derives self-support from the way promises it represents God as making are fulfilled in the spiritual lives of its practitioners, fulfilled in growth in sanctity, joy, love, and other fruits of the spirit. The rivals of CMP also enjoy self-support derived from spiritual fruits in the lives of their practitioners. Yet self-support does not wholly offset the negative epistemic consequences of religious diversity. Alston holds that "it can hardly be denied that the fact of religious diversity reduces the rationality of engaging in CMP (for one who is aware of the diversity) below what it would be if this problem did not exist" (1991, 275). So religious diversity reduces but does not altogether dissipate the justificatory efficacy of CMP and its similarly situated competitors. But does it reduce it to such a degree that it is not rational for one who is aware of it to engage in CMP?

Alston thinks not. His main argument proceeds by way of an analogy between the actual diversity of mystical perceptual practices and a merely hypothetical diversity of sensory perceptual practices. He asks us to imagine there being a plurality of sensory perceptual doxastic practices as diverse as the actual forms of mystical practice of which we are aware. As he fleshes out his story, "suppose that in certain cultures there were a well established 'Cartesian' practice of seeing what is visually perceived as an indefinitely extended medium that is more or less concentrated at various points, rather than, as in our 'Aristotelian' practice, as made up of more or less discrete objects scattered about in space" (1991, 273). We are also to imagine in other cultures an established "Whiteheadian" practice in which the visual field is seen as made up of momentary events growing out of each other in a continuous process. Further, suppose that all these practices were roughly equal in the fruits they produced: each served its practitioners well in their dealings with the environment and had associated with it a developed physical science. Finally, imagine that in this situation we were as firmly wedded to our Aristotelian practice as we are in fact, yet could find no independent grounds on which to argue effectively that it yields more accurate beliefs than the Cartesian or Whiteheadian alternatives. It seems to Alston that "in the absence of an external reason for supposing that one of the competing practices is more accurate than my own, *the only rational course* for me is to sit tight with the practice of which I am a master and which serves me so well in guiding my activity in the world" (274, my emphasis). But the hypothetical situation we have imagined is parallel in relevant respects to the actual situation of the practitioners of CMP. Hence, by parity of reasoning, the only rational thing for them to do is to stick with it and, more generally, to continue to accept and operate in accordance with the background system of Christian beliefs. And, again by parity of reasoning, the only rational course for practitioners of similarly situated rivals to CMP is to sit tight with their mystical practices and the associated systems of background beliefs.

A worry about testimony akin to Hume's emerges for Alston's position if we consider someone who is not a practitioner of CMP or any of its rivals. Assuming that the outputs of CMP have prima facie justification for its practitioners, the question then arises whether such justification can be transferred to those who are not among its practitioners by means of testimony. Alston accepts the following sufficient condition for justification by testimony: I believe that p justifiably if (1) someone else, X, is justified in believing that p; (2) X tells me that p; and (3) I am justified in supposing that X is justified in believing that p. He argues that there is no good reason to deny that this sufficient condition for justification via testimony can be satisfied in the case of someone whose only basis for belief in the outputs of CMP is the testimony of its practitioners. However, William J. Wainwright (2000) has proposed a serious objection to this conclusion. He points out that my reasons for thinking that the beliefs to which the practitioners of CMP testify are justified will be very similar to reasons I have for thinking that the beliefs to which the practitioners of some rivals, for instance, Buddhist mystical practice (BMP), testify are justified. But, by hypothesis, the outputs and associated background beliefs of CMP and BMP are massively incompatible.

Wainwright draws the following conclusion: "Hence, whatever reasons I have for assenting to the products of BMP are reasons *against* assenting to the products of CMP (and vice versa). And this seems to be a good reason for withholding assent altogether. The existence of incompatible mystical practices seems to provide the religiously uncommitted with a rather decisive reason for suspending judgment" (220). In cases of this sort, conflicting testimonies really do seem to cancel one another out.

I also think Alston's analogical argument only warrants a conclusion that is weaker than the one he actually draws from it. Let us return briefly to the hypothetical example of competing Aristotelian, Cartesian, and Whiteheadian sensory perceptual practices. I do not deny that it would be rational for me to sit tight with my Aristotelian practice in the imagined situation. But it seems to me that there is also another rational course open to me because I think it would be rational for me to revise my Aristotelian practice from within and work toward the social establishment of the revised practice. There is, after all, a precedent for making revisions in sensory perceptual practice to be found in the way people have responded to learning from modern science that such things as phenomenal colors, odors, tastes, and sounds are not mind-independent features of physical reality. At least when they are being careful, people who have learned this lesson regard the outputs of sensory perceptual practice as beliefs about how the physical environment appears to them rather than beliefs about how it is in itself, independent of them. So I have the option of revising my Aristotelian practice in a Kantian direction.

Suppose it occurs to me that a plausible explanation of the success of the diverse sensory practices in the imagined situation is the hypothesis that each of the socially established practices is reliable with respect to the appearances physical reality presents to its practitioners, but none is reliable with respect to how physical reality is in itself. Motivated by this thought and the desire to improve the reliability of my sensory practice, I modify it so that it maps sensory inputs onto doxastic outputs about the appearances physical reality presents to me but not about how it really is independent of me. And I do my best to get my revised practice socially established. If I transformed my Aristotelian practice into a Kantian practice in this way, I would not, as I see it, be worse off in terms of fruits as a result of doing so. I would not lose the ability to deal well with my physical environment. Nor would I lose access to a developed physical science, though some reinterpretation of its metaphysical import might be required. I suppose I would not have independent grounds on which to argue that the revised practice yields more accurate beliefs than its Aristotelian ancestor or the Cartesian and Whiteheadian alternatives to it. Even in that respect, however, I would not be worse off after the transformation than I was before it. So I conclude that sitting tight with my Aristotelian practice would not be the only rational course in our hypothetical situation. It would also be rational for me to transform that practice into a Kantian practice. Each of these courses of action would be rationally permissible; neither would be rationally required.

And, of course, our hypothetical situation remains, in the relevant respects, parallel to the actual situation in regard to competing mystical practices. Hence, again by parity of reasoning, though it is rational for practitioners of CMP to continue to engage in it, this is not *the only rational course* for them to follow, there being more than one thing it is rational to do in the face of competing mystical practices. Another thing it is rational for them to do is to revise CMP in a Kantian direction. Thus, I am convinced that Alston's analogy actually supports this conclusion: "Each of these courses of action is rationally permissible in the light of religious diversity. Neither of them is irrational, but neither is rationally required" (Quinn 2000, 242). Moreover, absent any relevant dissimilarities, the same goes for BMP and other socially established mystical practices that are not demonstrably unreliable and enjoy significant self-support.

The situation would obviously be rather different if we were not in Alston's worst-case scenario. If I had independent grounds on which to base an argument that my Aristotelian practice yields more accurate beliefs than either its Cartesian and Whiteheadian competitors or the proposed Kantian revision, then the only rational course would indeed be to sit tight with it. Similarly, if a cumulative case argument for the truth of Christianity provided them with independent grounds on which to base an argument that CMP yields more reliable beliefs than either rivals such as BMP or the revisionary Kantian practice, then the only rational course for its practitioners would be to sit tight with CMP. But I doubt that sitting tight with CMP will be the only rational course for them unless they come up with such a cumulative case argument. So I concur with Wainwright's verdict: "Alston's defense of CMP is impressive and, on the whole, convincing. To be fully successful, however, I believe it must form part of a persuasive cumulative case argument for the Christian world-view" (2000, 224). But Alston does not provide such an argument, and, as far as I can tell, no one else has done so either. So, though I regard Alston's response to the epistemological challenge of religious diversity as the best recent attempt to address it, I judge that it falls short of being fully successful in its own terms. The force of the challenge, though reduced, has not been altogether dissipated as a result of his efforts.

Another Familiar Problem:
Religious Intolerance

John Locke presents a classic argument for the toleration of diverse religious beliefs in "A Letter Concerning Toleration." It is summarized in the following passage:

> The care of souls cannot belong to the civil magistrate, because his power consists only in outward force: but true and saving religion consists in the inward persuasion of the mind, without which nothing can be acceptable to God. And such is the nature of the understanding, that it cannot be compelled to the belief of anything by outward force. Confiscation of estate, imprisonment, torments, nothing of that nature can have any such efficacy as to make men change the inward judgment that they have framed of things. (1689/1824, 11)

Suppose the state, personified in the quotation as the civil magistrate, has as a goal bringing all its citizens into the true and saving religion. To do so, it must ensure that they are all inwardly persuaded of the correct religious doctrines. Given diversity of doctrinal beliefs among the citizens, what is the state to do? The only means at its disposal is the application or threat of outward force against those citizens who are inwardly persuaded of incorrect doctrines. But even if the state is willing to persecute such citizens, such a policy of coercive action cannot succeed in reaching the state's goal, because outward force cannot compel change in belief. So, as it is bound to fail, persecution in order to bring citizens into the true and saving religion is instrumentally irrational.

Locke holds that outward force cannot compel change of belief because he thinks that belief is not subject to voluntary control. He insists that "speculative opinions, therefore, and articles of faith, as they are called, cannot be imposed on any church by the law of the land; for it is absurd that things should be enjoined by laws, which are not in men's power to perform; and to believe this or that to be true, does not depend upon our will" (1689/1824, 39–40). The law might enjoin me to recite the words of a certain creed every day; the words I utter are under my voluntary control, and so this daily recitation is within my power to perform. What would be absurd, according to Locke, is a law enjoining belief in the creed thus recited. The state can coerce lip service; it cannot coerce genuine faith.

Two powerful objections to this Lockean argument have been raised by Jeremy Waldron (1988). The first attacks its assumption that belief is not subject to voluntary control. Waldron grants that belief is not normally subject to direct voluntary control. If, looking directly at it, I now believe there is a green tree before me, there is no act of will I can perform that will make me believe there is a red fire engine before me. Waldron points out, however, that belief is often subject to indirect voluntary control because we can control, within limits, the sources of belief we attend to or take notice of. Suppose it is highly likely that we will believe the doctrines of the true and saving religion if we read its sacred books and attend its holy rituals frequently enough. The state could then increase the number of citizens who eventually accept the true and saving faith by coercing everyone to read those books and attend those rituals. Thus, religious intolerance can, under some conditions, be an effective means to religious ends. As Waldron puts the point, "Since coercion may therefore be applied to religious ends by this indirect means, it can no longer be condemned as in all circumstances irrational" (81). His conclusion applies to preserving citizens from falling into heresy as well as to converting them to orthodoxy. If an alluring heresy is quite likely to seduce citizens who read its scriptures and celebrate its rites away from the true and saving religion, banning those scriptures and rites will also be a rational means to the state's religious end. Hence, this Lockean argument for the irrationality of religious intolerance fails.

Waldron's other objection is moral. Even if the Lockean argument were successful, it would, he thinks, recommend toleration for the wrong reason. Its complaint is that intolerance is irrational for the persecutors to engage in, not that it wrongs the victims. Waldron objects that "what one misses above all in Locke's argument is a sense that there is anything *morally* wrong with intolerance, or a sense of any deep concern for the *victims* of persecution or the moral insult that is involved in the attempt to manipulate their faith" (1988, 85). Opposition to religious intolerance should focus, not on the frustrations of those who practice it, but on the injuries of those who suffer from it.

An argument that directly addresses Waldron's moral concern may be found in a work that was published shortly before Locke's "Letter." It is Pierre Bayle's *Philosophical Commentary on These Words of Jesus Christ "Compel Them to Come In"* (1686/1987). The words of Jesus quoted in Bayle's title come from the Parable of the Great Dinner in Luke's Gospel. According to this story, when the invited guests make excuses for not coming to the dinner party and even poor folk from the neighborhood do not fill all the places, the angry host says to his servant: "Go out into the roads and lanes, and compel people to come in, so that my house may be filled" (Luke 14:23). Starting at least as far back as Augustine, Christians used this verse as a proof-text to provide biblical warrant for forced conversions. Bayle's book contains a battery of arguments against a literal interpretation of the words "Compel them to come in" that could be used to support this kind of religious persecution.

One of Bayle's arguments anticipates the Lockean argument we have already examined. He thinks we know that the worship we owe the supreme being consists chiefly of inner acts of the mind that depend on the will and cannot be compelled.

It is evident then that the only legitimate way of inspiring religion is by producing in the soul certain judgments and certain movements of the will in relation to God. Now since threats, prisons, fines, exile, beatings, torture, and
generally whatever is comprehended under the literal signification of compelling, are incapable of forming in the soul those judgments of the will in respect
to God which constitute the essence of religion, it is evident that this is a mistaken way of establishing a religion and, consequently, that Jesus Christ has not
commanded it. (1686/1987, 36)

However, this argument confronts a difficulty that resembles the first objection
to Locke's argument. It may be that people threatened with or subjected to religious persecution cannot become converts simply by deciding to do so because
the judgments and movements of the will that constitute the essence of religion
are not under their direct voluntary control. But even if this is the case, compelling
outward practice may in the long run be an effective means to the end of inducing
those inner acts of the mind. Compulsion may after all be indirectly capable of
forming in the soul the judgments and motions of the will essential to religion.
Like Locke, Bayle is vulnerable to empirical refutation on this point. And what
we know about brainwashing counts as evidence against their views on the pow-
erlessness of compulsion to produce mental acts.

However, Bayle has the resources to bypass the question of whether compulsion is an effective means to establishing a religion. He can appeal directly to
moral considerations. Early in the book he announces that he is "relying upon
this single principle of natural light, *that any literal interpretation which carries an
obligation to commit iniquity is false*" (1686/1987, 28). As the allusion to natural
light indicates, he is working within a Cartesian epistemology in which the epistemic status of deliverances of the natural light is high enough to guarantee their
truth. Though he grants that the literal interpretation of the words "Compel them
to come in" supports the practice of forced conversion, it is open to him to hold
that it is morally wrong to use compulsion to produce the inner acts that are
essential to religion. So the following argument, which would be responsive to
Waldron's second objection, is available to Bayle. According to the literal interpretation of Luke 14:23, Jesus has commanded the use of compulsion to produce
the inner acts essential to religion. This command carries with it an obligation to
use compulsion for that purpose, because commands of Jesus are divine commands. But the obligation to make such a use of compulsion is an obligation to
commit an iniquity, because it is morally wrong to use compulsion for this purpose. Hence, by Bayle's principle, the literal interpretation of Luke 14:23 is false,
and so Jesus has not commanded the use of compulsion to produce the inner
acts essential to religion.

But what is the epistemic status of the moral principle that it is wrong to use
compulsion to produce the inner acts essential to religion? Is it a deliverance of

the natural light? Probably not. I think even Bayle himself could not consistently hold that it is true unless it is subject to an important qualification. This is because he allows for special dispensations from divine moral laws. Indeed, he believes that God can and sometimes does dispense people from the Decalogue's prohibition on homicide. There are, he affirms, circumstances that "change the nature of homicide from a bad action into a good action, a secret command of God, for example" (1686/1987, 171). The cases he has in mind are, of course, the biblical stories in which God commands homicide, the most famous of them being the *akedah*, the binding of Isaac, recounted in Genesis 22. So Bayle has left a loophole open to the advocates of religious persecution. He cannot consistently deny that they may be correct if they claim they have been dispensed by God from the principle that it is morally wrong to use compulsion to make converts or claim they have received a secret divine command to employ compulsion for this purpose. One might think that the possibility of such individual dispensations or secret commands is enough to preclude the principle that it is always wrong to use compulsion to make converts from being a deliverance of the natural light.

In my opinion, though here I go beyond anything I find explicitly stated in his text, Bayle's best strategy at this point would be to conduct the argument without making any dubious appeals to the Cartesian natural light. The epistemic credentials of two conflicting claims are to be assessed and then compared. One is a moral principle to the effect that intolerant behavior of a certain kind is wrong; the other is a conflicting religious claim. The epistemic principle called on to adjudicate the conflict is that, when two conflicting claims differ in epistemic status, the claim with the lower status is to be rejected. In the case of special interest to Bayle, the moral principle is that using compulsion to produce the inner acts essential to religion is wrong. This is an intuitively plausible principle, even if, because of the possibility of a few divinely ordained exceptions, it falls short of being evident by the natural light. So the epistemic status of the moral principle is fairly high. The conflicting religious claim is that employing compulsion to produce those inner acts is obligatory because Jesus commanded it. Considerations Bayle dwells on in the *Philosophical Commentary* can be mobilized in assessing the epistemic status of the religious claim. For instance, after arguing that Luke 14:23 should be interpreted in the light of its context, Bayle contends that reading this verse in a way that supports forced conversion "is contrary to the whole tenor and general spirit of the Gospel" (1686/1987, 39). Considerations of this sort show that the epistemic status of the religious claim is lower than that of the moral principle. The religious claim is, therefore, to be rejected. The Baylean strategy succeeds in this particular case.

Of course, this successful application of my Baylean strategy eliminates only one ground for the use of compulsion by the religiously intolerant. Many successful applications would be needed to eliminate all the grounds of all forms of religious intolerance. And it cannot be guaranteed in advance that enough applications will succeed to justify the extensive regime of religious toleration favored by contemporary liberals. Perhaps the strategy will work well enough against the inquisitors who would like to kill, torture, or imprison heretics. But consider exile, which Bayle cites as a form of compulsion, or, more generally, exclusion from a community. Does the principle that it is morally wrong to exclude people from a political community because of their religious faith have a very high epistemic status? I doubt it. Is it highly plausible that the magistrates of Calvin's Geneva would have done wrong if they had expelled Catholics from the city under conditions in which the exiles were compensated for forfeited property? Is it highly plausible that the elders of a contemporary Amish farming community would do wrong if they excluded those of other faiths from their community? I tend to think not. Living in a religiously homogeneous community can realize some very important values. It does not seem highly plausible to me that it is always wrong to endeavor to defend or preserve such values by means such as exclusion.

A serious difficulty becomes urgent if we envisage making use of my Baylean strategy with principles of moral wrongness that do not have a fairly high epistemic status. As traditionally conceived, God is omnipotent or, at least, very powerful. It would thus seem to be within God's power to communicate to us through experience a sign that transmits to the claim that God commands some intolerant behavior, such as excluding heretics from our community, a fairly high epistemic status. It hence seems possible for experience to bestow on the claim that an intolerant act is obligatory because it is divinely commanded an epistemic status greater than that of a conflicting principle of moral wrongness that does not have a fairly high epistemic status. In that case, according to my Baylean argumentative strategy, it is the moral principle that is to be rejected. The strategy seems to yield a good argument for intolerance in this particular case.

It is at this point, I believe, that the negative epistemic consequences of religious diversity do something to advance the cause of religious toleration. The existence of religious diversity will (for those who are aware of it) reduce the epistemic status of claims that God has commanded and thereby made morally obligatory intolerant conduct to levels below those that they would occupy were there no negative epistemic consequences of religious diversity. So when my Baylean strategy is applied using moral principles that are less than certain or evident by the natural light, it is likely to succeed more often, given the negative epistemic consequences of religious diversity, than it would otherwise. Religious diversity thus both creates the need for toleration and contributes to the epistemic grounds for it. It is probably impossible to say with quantitative precision how many cases of success will result from this factor. And there is no guarantee that, even with its assistance, the strategy will succeed in all the cases in which liberal champions of religious toleration would like to have strong arguments against intolerant actions or social practices (see Quinn 2001).

Of course, contemporary liberal political theories typically have strong doctrines of religious toleration built into them. Thus, for example, the liberal political conception of justice constructed by John Rawls (1993, 58–62) can provide internal reasons for extensive regimes of religious toleration. But opposed political conceptions can no doubt offer internal reasons for various sorts of religious intolerance. The results of our examination of some classical arguments for religious toleration will surely seem disappointing to those in search of independent reasons for the tolerant habits now widespread in liberal democracies. There are powerful objections to Locke's argument, and my Baylean strategy may well lack the power to support the full array of tolerant practices dear to the hearts of contemporary liberals. I therefore judge that the arguments we have inherited from the early modern champions of religious toleration leave some of its practices resting on rather shaky philosophical grounds.

A NOVEL OPPORTUNITY: DEFINITIONS OF RELIGION

Immanuel Kant presents a famous definition of religion in *Religion within the Boundaries of Mere Reason* (1793/1996). According to Kant, "*Religion* is (subjectively considered) the recognition of all our duties as divine commands" (177). This simple formulation illustrates one sort of problem that arises when a philosopher attempts to define religion. It is generally acknowledged that Theravada Buddhism is a religion. However, its doctrines do not include belief in a personal divinity capable of issuing commands. So it seems that recognition of duties as divine commands on the part of its adherents is not a necessary condition for being a religion. It thus appears that Kant's formulation does not specify the correct extension for the concept of religion; it seems to fail to provide conceptually necessary and sufficient conditions for being a religion. If we agree that this is a failure, we may wish to excuse Kant on the grounds that he knew much less about the full extent of religious diversity outside the West than we do. And we may think that the increased knowledge of religious diversity we have acquired since Kant's time provides us with a novel opportunity to work out an adequate definition of religion. As a result of this expanded knowledge, we have many more examples than Kant did that can serve as data against which to test a proposed definition of religion. Framing definitional proposals and testing them against such data might be regarded as one of the main tasks of a comparative philosophy of religion. In an essay that proposes an agenda for this kind of philosophical work, Paul J. Griffiths counts the strategy of definition and classification as one of "three kinds of intellectual enterprise that have title of some kind to be called comparative philosophy of religion" (1997, 616).

We owe much of our increased knowledge of religious diversity to the work of anthropologists in the field. There is something important at stake for anthropology in the enterprise of defining religion; a definition will circumscribe the data that must be covered by proposed empirical generalizations. So we would expect anthropologists with a theoretical cast of mind to have a keen interest in defining religion. Rival definitions of religion have been proposed by Clifford Geertz and Melford E. Spiro. Comparing their definitions will enable us to explore some of the problems that confront the project of formulating a definition of religion.

According to Geertz, "A *religion* is: (1) a system of symbols which acts to (2) establish powerful, pervasive, and long-lasting moods and motivations in men by (3) formulating conceptions of a general order of existence and (4) clothing these conceptions with such an aura of factuality that (5) the moods and motivations seem uniquely realistic" (1966, 4). To facilitate understanding of his definition, Geertz offers some commentary on each of its five parts. A symbol, on his view, is anything that serves as a vehicle for a conception. Moods and motivations are dispositions to perform certain sorts of actions and experience certain sorts of feelings in certain sorts of situations. Conceptions of a general order of existence provide a framework of cosmic order to help deal with threats of chaos at the limits of human analytical abilities, the limits of human endurance, and the limits of human moral insight. Ritual is the chief instrument by which the conviction that these conceptions are veridical is generated. And they alter the landscape presented to common sense in such a way that the moods and motivations seem supremely practical, the only sensible ones to have, given the way things really are.

An obvious objection to this definition is that it is too broad. Systems of symbols that characterize secular ideologies such as Nazism satisfy the defining conditions it proposes but are not religions. Hence, it does not provide a sufficient condition for being a religion. One might respond to the objection by biting the bullet at this point and granting that Nazism is a religion. Thus, for example, John Rawls claims that "Hitler's demonic conception of the world was, in some perverse sense, religious" (1999, 20). Citing the work of Saul Friedländer, Rawls attributes to Hitler a redemptive anti-Semitism, "born from the fear of racial degeneration and the religious belief in redemption" (Friedländer 1997, 87). But many people will insist that Nazi symbols belong to a secular political ideology, not a religion, while acknowledging that Nazism resembles a religion in several respects. There have been similar controversies about whether Soviet Marxism is a religion or is only analogous to a religion in some ways.

Spiro's proposal goes as follows: "I shall define 'religion' as 'an institution consisting of culturally patterned interaction with culturally postulated superhuman beings' " (1966, 96). On his view, interactions include both "activities which are believed to carry out, embody, or to be consistent with the will or desire of superhuman beings or powers" and "activities which are believed to influence superhuman beings to satisfy the needs of the actors" (97). Because interaction thus understood requires only belief in superhuman beings and not their reality, religious actors can, odd though it sounds, interact with superhuman beings that do not exist. Assuming that the Wagnerian gods are for Nazism window dressing rather than objects of serious belief, Spiro's definition will not count Nazism as a religion. Nor will it classify atheistic and wholly naturalistic varieties of Marxism as religions.

The obvious objection to Spiro's definition is that it is too narrow. Like Kant's definition, it proposes defining conditions that religions without superhuman beings in their ontologies, such as Theravada Buddhism, fail to satisfy. Hence, it does not provide a necessary condition for being a religion. Spiro is aware of this objection and has a good deal to say in response to it. According to one line of defense he offers, we must distinguish between the teachings of atheistic philosophical schools and the beliefs of a religious community. Even though the pure philosophical Theravada of the Pali canon is atheistic, we always find it in traditional societies coupled with a belief system that is committed to superhuman beings, such as the *nats* of Burma and the *phi* of Laos and Thailand. Hence, "it cannot be denied that Theravada Buddhists adhere to another belief system which is theistic to its core" (1966, 94). But not all Theravada Buddhists do adhere to such a theistic belief system. So this line of defense has the awkward consequence that Theravada Buddhism is, for some people, part of their religion but is not a religion when it is found in its purest form.

However, Spiro seems to rest more weight on another line of argument. He insists that a definition of religion must satisfy a criterion of intuitiveness. For him, at least, "any definition of 'religion' which does not include, as a key variable, the belief in superhuman—I won't muddy the metaphysical waters with 'supernatural'—beings who have power to help or harm man is counter-intuitive" (1966, 91). Belief in superhuman beings will, therefore, be a defining condition of religion according to any definition that is intuitively adequate for Spiro. His appeal to a criterion of intuitiveness indicates that he takes the task of defining religion to involve more than merely framing a definition that will prove useful in anthropological research. In addition to satisfying this pragmatic constraint, which will require cross-cultural applicability of a definition, an adequate definition must also analyze or reflect the concept of religion the anthropologist brings to the study of religious phenomena.

A comparison of the definitions proposed by Geertz and Spiro reveals two significant kinds of disagreement between them. The two definitions are not even coextensive. Pure Theravada Buddhism and Nazism satisfy the defining conditions proposed by Geertz but not those proposed by Spiro, if we assume that neither of them postulates superhuman beings. This disagreement could be accounted for on the supposition that the two definitions serve to analyze the concepts of religion the two anthropologists bring to their research. For they might well have slightly different concepts of religion. Of course, we would expect their concepts to overlap to a large extent, differing only in their applicability to a minority of cases. But it is possible that each definition satisfies a criterion of intuitiveness with respect to the intuitions of its framer. The two definitions also disagree about the kind of entity a religion is. For Geertz, a religion consists of symbols; for Spiro, a religion is an institution. It seems that a perspicuous social ontology would treat symbols and institutions as belonging to rather different metaphysical kinds. The difference in kind between the American flag (a symbol) and the American League (an institution) is at least as large as the difference between chalk and cheese. This disagreement could be accounted for by the supposition that the two anthropologists favor somewhat different approaches to their discipline. If one has been trained in cultural anthropology and it provides useful methods for studying symbols, then defining religions in terms of symbols will portray them us proper objects of investigation for cultural anthropology. Similarly, if one has been trained in social anthropology and it provides useful methods for studying institutions, then defining religions as institutions will portray them as proper objects of investigation for social anthropology. So this disagreement could be rooted in pragmatic considerations. However, these two disagreements are not trivial even if they turn out to have rather simple explanations.

It should not be thought that the problem Theravada Buddhism raises for certain attempts to define religion is without parallels to other cases. Chad Hansen (1997) has argued that, though we usually classify Confucianism and Daoism among the world's major religions, we will doubt that they are religions if we compare them with our conceptual stereotype religions. This is because "classical Chinese philosophy shows signs neither of creation myths, of attempts to explain 'why we are here,' of a mind/body (or spirit/body) dichotomy, nor of supernaturalism" (25). So we might expect otherwise attractive definitions of religion to disagree about whether classical Confucianism and Daoism count as religions.

Such disagreements have given rise to skepticism about the possibility of analyzing or defining the concept of religion in terms of conceptually necessary and sufficient conditions. An alternative view, derived from Wittgenstein, who uses the example of games to illustrate his point, is that the concept of religion is a family-resemblance concept. John Hick, an advocate of this view, argues that it is "illuminating to see the different traditions, movements and ideologies whose religious character is either generally agreed or responsibly debated, not as exemplifying a common essence, but as forming a complex continuum of resemblances and differences analogous to those found within a family" (1989, 4). Thus, for example, "the bloodthirsty worship of Moloch in the ancient Near East had nothing directly in common with Theravada Buddhism; but on the other hand, although in most other ways in startling contrast to Christianity, the cult of Moloch overlaps with it in involving the worship of a personal deity; and Christianity in turn overlaps with the Theravada in the quite different respect that it offers a comprehensive interpretation of life" (5). If the concept of religion is a family-resemblance concept, such resemblances allow us to classify the cult of Moloch, Christianity, and Theravada Buddhism as religions without supposing that all three of them satisfy a single set of necessary and sufficient conditions for being a religion. According to Hick, once we understand the concept of religion in this way, we have resolved or, perhaps, dissolved the problem of defining religion.

Cognitive psychologists have developed more refined versions of the family-resemblance view. According to one version, some concepts are organized around an example that serves as a prototype (see Rosch and Mervis 1975). As a result of complex patterns of resemblances to and differences from the prototype, other cases lie at various distances from the prototype in a similarity space. Cases near enough to the prototype clearly fall under the concept; cases far enough away from the prototype clearly do not fall under the concept. And there may be a gray area in between where borderline or contested cases are to be found. Applying this general idea to my own concept of religion, we may imagine that the prototype is the religion I was brought up in, which is Christianity. Judaism and Islam are near enough to my prototype to be clear cases of religion, but soccer is far enough away that it clearly does not fall under my concept of religion, though I understand what is meant when it is said that some people make a religion of soccer. Confucianism, Daoism, and Thervada Buddhism are near enough to my prototype to count as religions, and Nazism and Soviet Marxism are far enough away to lie in the gray area for me.

It seems to me this refinement of the family-resemblance view does some real work in explaining the classificatory practices I engage in using my concept of religion. So I do not find it surprising that the family-resemblance view is currently the dominant or received view of the concept of religion. However, it does not command unanimous agreement. Jim Stone (2001) has recently proposed and defended against putative counterexamples a new theory of religion that provides its own definition of religion. According to Stone, "A religion is a system of practices meant to place us in a relation-of-value to a supermundane reality so grand that it can figure centrally in the satisfaction of substantial human needs" (188). He advertises his achievement with the bold claim that "religion has an essence, I will maintain, which the new theory reveals" (177). It may be that Stone's definition will prove to be immune from clear counterexamples. But even if this turns out to be the case, I doubt that he will convince many philosophers that it reveals the essence of religion. Structural theories in the natural sciences provide definitions of natural kinds that are plausibly construed as revealing their essences. Familiar examples are the claim that water is H_2O and the claim that gold is the element with atomic number 79. However, there is no good reason to suppose that religion is a natural kind, for religions are social products rather than things we discover in nature. So even if Stone's definition cannot be shown by means of counterexamples to be mistaken about the extension of the concept of religion, there is no good reason to conclude that it will, on that account, be what is sometimes described as a real definition, which is to say a definition that captures the essential nature of some entity.

I therefore doubt that the problem of defining religion has been either solved or dissolved. There is no consensus among students of religion about whether the concept of religion can be analyzed or defined in terms of conceptually necessary and sufficient conditions. There is more to be said on the topic of defining religion or, more generally, understanding the concept of religion. Hence, this topic should remain on the agenda of comparative philosophy of religion.

ANOTHER NOVEL OPPORTUNITY: CONSTRUCTIVE COMPARISONS

Christian Wolff paints a sympathetic picture of classical Chinese ethics in his 1721 *Discourse on the Practical Philosophy of the Chinese* (1992). According to Mark Larrimore, "China's being perceived as outside of (Western) history made it a resource specifically for the antivoluntarist ethics and moral anthropology which, in Wolff's time, were struggling against the voluntarism of a Christian ethics premised on original sin" (2000, 213). But Wolff did not appeal to Chinese ethics to support the view that ethics is independent of religion; his own ethical theory is religious but antivoluntarist. According to a theory that is religious but anti-voluntarist, ethics is independent of God's will but depends on something else about God, for example, the goodness of the divine nature, whereas for voluntarism, ethics depends specifically on God's will or the divine commands that express it. However, the *Discourse* set off a controversy with the pietist theologians at the University of Halle. It resulted in the royal banishment of Wolff from Halle in 1723, an exile that lasted until his return in 1740 under the newly crowned Frederick II.

According to Griffiths, for whom constructive work is another of the items on the agenda of comparative philosophy of religion, "The main interests of those doing comparative philosophy of religion constructively are in making a contribution of a normative kind to some question that belongs to or arises out of one or more particular religions" (1997, 619). Judged in the light of this characterization, Wolff's engagement with Chinese ethics is constructive because it speaks to the issue, which arises out of Christianity, of whether an antivoluntarist religious ethics can be developed and defended. We, of course, have opportunities to make constructive comparisons that were not available to Wolff. In at least two respects, they are novel. We bring to the task scholarly resources, for instance, editions and interpretations of texts, that Wolff did not have. And, not an insignificant point, those of us fortunate enough to be housed in the Western academy are unlikely to suffer from the wrath of religious zealots in the way that Wolff did. Constructive comparisons, however, constitute a relatively unexplored territory within philosophy of religion. What they are capable of yielding by way of fruits must be gathered from examples. I shall discuss two cases I regard as exemplary. Both of them involve Chinese ethics and so can be thought of as continuing a tradition that goes back at least as far as Wolff and Leibniz.

Bryan W. Van Norden (2001) compares Mencius and Augustine on the explanation of human moral evil or wrongdoing. His aim is "to show that in his *Confessions* Augustine's narrative of his adolescent theft of some pears cannot be accounted for by Mencius's philosophical psychology" (314). If this conclusion is correct, Augustine's philosophical psychology, which can account for the theft of the pears, is superior to that of Mencius with respect to explanatory power. Augustinian psychology would then serve as a challenge to Mencian psychology in virtue of its greater explanatory power. The result of the comparison would be constructive because it taught a lesson about the conditions an adequate explanation of the full range of human wrongdoing must satisfy.

Augustine dwells on the theft of the pears in his *Confessions* because he finds it very puzzling. He cannot easily identify a good that attracted him to the theft. He did not steal the pears on account of their beauty or taste or because he was hungry; he already had plenty of pears of his own, he tells us, better than those. Was he seeking to do evil for evil's sake? But according to Augustine, evil does not exist; it is the mere absence or lack of good. How could he be drawn to something that does not exist? Van Norden spells out the crucial part of the response he attributes to Augustine as follows:

> The free exercise of human will is a good. Indeed, to freely exercise the will is to act like God. Even without the Grace of God, humans recognize this, at least inchoately. Humans also recognize that, at least in some sense, freedom involves acting without any constraint that is alien to them. Consequently, acting in violation of moral law *appears* to be an expression of perfect freedom, since it shows contempt for a standard that *seems* to be external to oneself. (2001, 332)

So rebellion against the moral law appears to be good because the exercise of free will is godlike and appears to be at its most perfect in acting contrary to what seems to be an alien constraint. Of course, the appearances are deceptive. Because humans were created to love and obey God, the moral law is not an alien constraint. But rebellion is rendered intelligible and thereby explained by showing that it is action for the sake of an apparent good rather than action for evil's sake.

Van Norden argues that an explanation of this kind is not available to Mencius. This is not because there is nothing in Mencius's psychology analogous to the Augustinian will. He thinks that Mencius supposes humans possess a capacity to cultivate or neglect the inclinations to or sprouts of virtue that are innate in them. It is a capacity to orient desires and perceptions in ways that help or hinder the growth of the sprouts of virtue. So Van Norden's conclusion about Mencius is that he believes "humans have something internal to their psychology that chooses (at least partially) the content and strength of their desires, beliefs, and the focus of their concentration" (2001, 328). But the exercise of this capacity does not have for Mencius the importance that the exercise of free will has for Augustine. The exercise of free will is extremely valuable for Augustine because it is godlike. There is no hint in Mencius that the exercise of the capacity to choose whether or not to cultivate the sprouts of virtue is itself a great good. For him, the valuable part of human nature is the inclinations to virtue themselves, not the capacity to choose whether to cultivate them or its exercise. There is no hint that exercising that capacity without constraint is, for Mencius, even a great apparent good. "Consequently," according to Van Norden, "there seems to be no obvious place in Mencius's world view for a desire to exercise one's will (per se) without constraint" (2001, 334). Absent such an apparent good and a desire for it, Mencius's psychology will not be able to make sense of or explain cases of rebellion against the moral law such as the theft of the pears.

One might, of course, doubt that human beings can rebel against the moral law in the way envisaged in this interpretation of the theft of the pears. If they cannot, then the explanatory advantage Van Norden attributes to Augustine's psychology would turn out to be illusory. I think rebellion against morality's constraints is a type of moral evil that has quite a few real instances, and so I am prepared to grant that Augustine's psychology has the explanatory power Van Norden ascribes to it. I therefore accept his conclusion that "Augustine's narrative of his youthful theft of some pears presents a serious, and direct, challenge to Mencius's explanation of human evil" (2001, 335). However, I see nothing in his discussion that precludes a neo-Mencian psychology that would successfully meet this challenge. Van Norden does not claim that Mencius denies value to the capacity to choose whether to cultivate or to neglect the sprouts of virtue or to its exercise. Hence, it seems to me that a neo-Mencian psychology in which great value is attributed to that capacity and to its exercise would be a consistent extension of Mencius's psychology. Such a psychology could then attribute apparent goodness to the exercise of the capacity unconstrained by morality and postulate a desire for that apparent good to help explain the evil of rebellion against morality. In this way, the challenge could at least provoke debate and might even stimulate progressive theoretical developments within the Confucian tradition.

Lee H. Yearley's *Mencius and Aquinas: Theories of Virtue and Conceptions of Courage* (1990) is perhaps the most impressive specimen of constructive comparison so far published. He describes his work as a contribution to the comparative philosophy of religious flourishings. The book develops a large array of comparisons between the accounts of the virtues offered by Mencius and Aquinas. I focus on just one of them: the comparison of their understandings of human failures to be virtuous. My selection is motivated by the obvious connection between Yearley's discussion of Mencius on ethical failure and Van Norden's reflections on Mencius on wrongdoing.

It might be thought that Mencius and Aquinas are worlds apart on the topic of human failure because Mencius thinks human nature is good and Aquinas thinks it is sinful. According to Yearley, however, this sharp contrast is too simple to capture what is interesting about these two subtle thinkers. Aquinas holds that human nature contains an inclination to virtue which is diminished but not destroyed by original sin. And though Mencius holds that the inclinations to or sprouts of virtue present in human nature are good, he recognizes that many people do not cultivate them and so often do bad things. So Mencius and Aquinas actually agree that "fundamental inclinations toward the good remain, even if the force of those inclinations is diminished in almost all people" (Yearley 1990, 88). More important to Yearley are three more specific differences in their views on people's propensities toward virtue and vice: "The first concerns their views on *the role of more subtle deformations* or sins. The second concerns their position on the principle that *to know the good is to do the good*. The third concerns their notion of what is involved in *changing acquired inclinations*" (90). Let us briefly examine each of these topics.

On the issue of subtle deformations, Aquinas is particularly attentive to subtle sins such as envy and vanity because they distort the higher human capacities and so are likely to corrupt the whole personality. Mencius, by contrast, tends to focus on tendencies to vice that arise largely from bodily appetites, that is, matters that Aquinas would regard as instances of lust or gluttony. When Mencius does treat more subtle deformations, he is apt to regard them as if they resembled those found in the cruder cases that are his paradigms.

The principle that to know the good is to do the good is endorsed by both Mencius and Aquinas. However, Aquinas differs from Mencius because he often discusses cases from his own tradition that challenge or cast doubt on the principle. Yearley calls attention to three such cases:

> One especially powerful example is St. Paul's statement in Romans that he cannot do the good he would do or avoid the bad he would avoid. Another is Augustine's depiction in the second book of the *Confessions* of an action, his theft of pears, that seems explainable to him only as an attempt to act against all possible goods. A third is the general phenomenon that spiritual apathy

(*acedia*) describes, a state first identified by the desert fathers and a familiar
feature of the monastic life. (1990, 92)

Mencius, on the other hand, considers fewer examples in tension with the principle, and he repeatedly insists that knowledge of the good will always issue in
good action and character. It is striking that both Yearley and Van Norden emphasize the importance of the example of Augustine's theft of the pears in reflections on moral evil within the Christian tradition and make use of that example
in their comparisons with Mencius.

On the topic of changing acquired inclinations, Aquinas holds the pessimistic
view that humans are oriented toward vicious rather than virtuous states or, at
best, turned toward a mixture of vicious and virtuous states, and cannot reorient
themselves under their own power. He therefore invokes a transcendent power
to reorient us and insists that only divine grace can save us from sin. Mencius
usually adopts the more optimistic position that people are always capable of
becoming good under their own power, though he sometimes mentions aids to
improvement such as forms of virtuous leadership (*te*), psychophysical energy
(*ch'i*), and being raised in a good society. Yearley summarizes the difference as
follows:

> When Mencius speaks in his most voluntaristic fashion and claims we can re-
> orient ourselves just by refocusing our attention, he differs fundamentally from
> Aquinas. When Mencius speaks in a less voluntaristic vein, however, he moves
> closer to Aquinas's position that only a separate power can rescue individuals
> from the destructive circle they inhabit. But even when Mencius speaks this
> way he usually asserts that human forces (if ones that draw on other powers)
> can affect the needed changes. Aquinas, in contrast, believes all human efforts
> are too corrupt to produce all the changes needed. (1990, 95)

Mencius and Aquinas thus disagree significantly about whether humans can flourish if they rely solely on their own resources.

Yearley's constructive interests become clear when he remarks that, on the
issue of moral reorientation, "Mencius and Aquinas present the general outlines
of what, to my mind, are the two most viable positions" (1990, 223). He does not,
however, try to decide between their views. It seems to me that Aquinas has a
better appreciation of the human moral predicament than does Mencius, though
of course my view of the matter may be biased because I was brought up in the
same tradition as Augustine and Aquinas. I have already recorded my conviction
that examples of the sort represented by Augustine's story of the theft of the pears
must be accounted for by an adequate moral psychology. Aquinas is on the right
track in trying to grapple with them. I also think Aquinas's understanding of what
John E. Hare (1996) describes as the moral gap between what morality demands
of us and what we are capable of achieving by our own efforts hits the mark. So

I am persuaded that Aquinas has a more realistic grasp of the problems of human moral failure than Mencius does.

The two examples of constructive comparisons I have discussed are obviously only a tiny fraction of the comparisons that could be made and might serve constructive purposes. The possibility for further contributions to the enterprise of constructive comparison in philosophy of religion are almost limitless.

To conclude: my discussion of the philosophical problems to which religious diversity gives rise has not been exhaustive. I have not considered the third item on the agenda Griffiths proposes for comparative philosophy of religion, which is structural analysis of the kind carried out in books by William A. Christian Sr. (1972, 1987). Nor have I discussed the way John Rawls (2001) transformed his justice as fairness from a comprehensive doctrine, which extends beyond the political to include values and virtues that are in the limit to inform the whole of human life, to a more modest political conception, whose scope is restricted to political values and virtues, in large measure because he came to recognize the importance of the fact of reasonable pluralism of religious and nonreligious comprehensive doctrines in free and democratic societies. And I have not brought to closure debate on any of the four topics I have considered. There remains more to be said about the epistemological challenge of religious diversity, about the justification of religious toleration and about how to understand the concept of religion. The enterprise of constructive comparison also offers some new directions for work in philosophy of religion. So religious diversity bestows on philosophers of religion a large bouquet of exciting issues to ponder.

WORKS CITED

Alston, William P. 1991. *Perceiving God: The Epistemology of Religious Experience.* Ithaca, N.Y.: Cornell University Press.

Bayle, Pierre. [1686] 1987. *Pierre Bayle's Philosophical Commentary: A Modern Translation and Critical Interpretation.* Trans. Amie G. Tannenbaum. New York: Peter Lang.

Christian, William A., Sr. 1972. *Oppositions of Religious Doctrines: A Study in the Logic of Dialogue among Religions.* New York: Herder and Herder.

———. 1987. *Doctrines of Religious Communities: A Philosophical Study.* New Haven: Yale University Press.

Friedländer, Saul. 1997. *Nazi Germany and the Jews.* Vol. 1. New York: HarperCollins.

Geertz, Clifford. 1966. "Religion as a Cultural System." In *Anthropological Approaches to the Study of Religion,* ed. Michael Banton, 1–46. New York: Praeger.

Griffiths, Paul J. 1997. "Comparative Philosophy of Religion." In *A Companion to Philosophy of Religion,* ed. Philip L. Quinn and Charles Taliaferro, 615–20. Oxford: Blackwell.

Hansen, Chad. 1997. "Chinese Confucianism and Daoism." In *A Companion to Philosophy of Religion,* ed. Philip L. Quinn and Charles Taliaferro, 25–33. Oxford: Blackwell.

Hare, John E. 1996. *The Moral Gap: Kantian Ethics, Human Limits, and God's Assistance.* Oxford: Clarendon Press.

Hick, John. 1989. *An Interpretation of Religion: Human Responses to the Transcendent.* New Haven: Yale University Press.

Hume, David. [1748] 2000. "Of Miracles." In *The Philosophical Challenge of Religious Diversity,* ed. Philip L. Quinn and Kevin Meeker, 29–37. New York: Oxford University Press.

Kant, Immanuel. [1793] 1996. *Religion within the Boundaries of Mere Reason.* In Immanuel Kant, *Religion and Rational Theology,* ed. Allen W. Wood and George di Giovanni, 39–216. Cambridge, England: Cambridge University Press.

Larrimore, Mark. 2000. "Orientalism and Antivoluntarism in the History of Ethics: On Christian Wolff's *Oratio de sinarum philosophia practica.*" *Journal of Religious Ethics* 28.2: 189–220.

Locke, John. [1689] 1824. "A Letter Concerning Toleration." In John Locke, *Works.* Vol. 5. London: G. and J. Rivington.

Quinn, Philip L. 2000. "Toward Thinner Theologies: Hick and Alston on Religious Diversity." In *The Philosophical Challenge of Religious Diversity,* ed. Philip L. Quinn and Kevin Meeker, 226–43. New York: Oxford University Press.

———. 2001. "Religious Diversity and Religious Toleration." *International Journal for Philosophy of Religion* 50: 57–80.

Rawls, John. 1993. *Political Liberalism.* New York: Columbia University Press.

———. 1999. *The Law of Peoples.* Cambridge, Mass.: Harvard University Press.

———. 2001. *Justice as Fairness: A Restatement.* Cambridge, Mass.: Belknap Press.

Rosch, E., and C. Mervis. 1975. "Family Resemblances: Studies in the Internal Structure of Categories." *Cognitive Psychology* 8: 382–489.

Spiro, Melford E. 1966. "Religion: Problems of Definition and Explanation." In *Anthropological Approaches to the Study of Religion,* ed. Michael Banton, 85–126. New York: Praeger.

Stone, Jim. 2001. "A Theory of Religion Revised." *Religious Studies* 37: 177–89.

Van Norden, Bryan W. 2001. "Mencius and Augustine on Evil: A Test Case for Comparative Philosophy." In *Two Roads to Wisdom,* ed. Bo Mou, 313–36. Chicago: Open Court.

Wainwright, William J. 2000. "Religious Experience and Religious Pluralism." In *The Philosophical Challenge of Religious Diversity,* ed. Philip L. Quinn and Kevin Meeker, 218–25. New York: Oxford University Press.

Waldron, Jeremy. 1988. "Locke: Toleration and the Rationality of Persecution." In *Justifying Toleration: Conceptual and Historical Perspectives,* ed. Susan Mendus, 61–86. Cambridge, England: Cambridge University Press.

Wolff, Christian. [1721] 1992. *Discourse on the Practical Philosophy of the Chinese.* In *Moral Enlightenment: Leibniz and Wolff on China* (Monumenta Serica Monograph Series). Ed. and trans. Julia Ching and Willard G. Oxtoby. Nettelal, Germany: Steyler Verlag.

Yearley, Lee H. 1990. *Mencius and Aquinas: Theories of Virtue and Conceptions of Courage.* Albany: State University of New York Press.

PART II

APPROACHES

CHAPTER 17

....

ANALYTIC PHILOSOPHY
OF RELIGION

....

WILLIAM HASKER

ANALYTIC philosophy of religion was gestated in the 1940s, born in the early 1950s, spent its childhood in the 1960s and its adolescence in the 1970s and early 1980s. Since then it has grown into adulthood, and it reached the turn of the millennium in a state of vigorous maturity, with decline and senile degeneration nowhere in sight.

Like all metaphors, this one has its limitations. One could hardly describe the philosophical writings of the earlier stages as childish, let alone infantile. But the field of study itself was discernibly immature, and since then there has been notable progress both in the topics addressed and in the manner of treating them. This essay divides the history into three phases, characterized by differences in the subject matter most actively discussed. In the first phase, lasting until about 1965, the overwhelming preoccupation was with religious language, especially with the cognitive meaningfulness of such language. In the second phase, lasting through the early 1980s, much effort was focused on what may be termed the "philosophy of theism." In the most recent period there has been a notable diversification, and the field now embraces a greater variety of topics than at any previous time.

THE EARLY YEARS: RELIGIOUS LANGUAGE

During the early decades of the twentieth century, the place of the philosophy of religion in analytic philosophy was less than marginal. G. E. Moore, after a fervently evangelical childhood, was content, in "A Defense of Common Sense," to remark that he differed from philosophers "who have held that there is good reason to suppose that there is a God . . . [or] that we, human beings, shall continue to exist and to be conscious after the death of our bodies" (1925, 127). Bertrand Russell's fulminations against religion were considerably more demonstrative but were remote from his serious philosophical work. And Ludwig Wittgenstein's invocation of the Mystical in the concluding section of the *Tractatus*, striking and provocative though it was, fell far short of any systematic articulation of the philosophical issues concerning religion. During these years religious thought ran in other channels, and insofar as it was philosophically engaged the philosophy of choice was often some variety of post-Hegelian idealism.

What changed all this was the advent of logical positivism, especially its introduction to the English-speaking world by means of A. J. Ayer's *Language, Truth, and Logic* (1936). Ayer's work was not particularly original in comparison with that of the continental positivists, but it had the effect of challenging the foundations of religious thought in a way that was hard to ignore. Not merely the *truth* of theological assertions was in question, but even their very *meaningfulness*: what was denied was that these utterances possessed cognitive significance sufficient to allow them to be evaluated as *either* true or false. Furthermore, the varieties of philosophy that in the past had been used to articulate religious belief were themselves equally under challenge, and thus offered no effective defense.

The 1940s saw the beginnings of efforts by religious thinkers to come to terms with this new challenge. The controversy came to a head in the "theology and falsification" debate that took place in 1950–51 in the pages of *University* and was reprinted in part in the 1955 volume, *New Essays in Philosophical Theology* (Flew and MacIntyre, eds.). The stage was set for the debate by Antony Flew, who adapted a parable originally composed by John Wisdom:

> Once upon a time two explorers came upon a clearing in the jungle. In the
> clearing were growing many flowers and many weeds. One explorer says,
> "Some gardener must tend this plot." The other disagrees, "There is no gardener." So they pitch their tents and set a watch. No gardener is ever seen.
> "But perhaps he is an invisible gardener." So they set up a barbed-wire fence.
> They electrify it. They patrol it with bloodhounds . . . But no shrieks ever suggest that some intruder has received a shock. No movements of the wire ever
> betray an invisible climber. The bloodhounds never give cry. Yet still the Believer is not convinced. "But there is a gardener, invisible, intangible, insensible

to electric shocks, a gardener who has no scent and makes no sound, a gardener who comes secretly to look after the garden which he loves." At last the Sceptic despairs, "But what remains of your original assertion? Just how does what you call an invisible, intangible, eternally elusive gardener differ from an imaginary gardener or even from no gardener at all?" (Flew et al. 1955, 96)

Flew explains his point by saying, "In this parable we can see how what starts as an assertion, that something exists or that there is some analogy between certain complexes of phenomena, may be reduced step by step to an altogether different status, to an expression perhaps of a 'picture preference.'" And this, according to Flew, is what typically happens to theological assertions: starting out as (apparently) "vast cosmological assertions," they are progressively qualified in the face of objections until there is nothing left; they die the "death of a thousand qualifications" (97). They are incapable of being falsified, and for that reason meaningless.

There are logical difficulties in the way Flew presents his challenge, but his central point has struck many readers as compelling: "Someone tells us that God loves us as a father loves his children. We are reassured. But then we see a child dying of inoperable cancer of the throat. His earthly father is driven frantic in his efforts to help, but his Heavenly Father reveals no obvious sign of concern" (Flew et al. 1955, 98–99). We may ask, Is the assertion about God's love really *saying anything*, as opposed to providing some vague emotional reassurance? Flew challenges his fellow symposiasts with the question, "What would have to occur or to have occurred to constitute for you a disproof of the love of, or of the existence of, God?" (99).

In his response, R. M. Hare concedes that "on the ground marked out by Flew, he seems to me to be completely victorious." So he counters with a parable of his own, about a "lunatic who is convinced that all dons want to murder him" (Flew et al. 1955, 99). Introduced by his friends to an assortment of dons, all of whom manifest kindliness, goodwill, and a complete absence of murderous intentions, the man remains convinced that they are secretly plotting against his life. Hare describes this situation by saying that the man "has an insane *blik* about dons" (100), whereas we have a sane blik about them. A blik, then, is a sort of attitude toward, or way of looking at, the world that is not based on reasons (for the lunatic has all the reasons the rest of us have to believe in the harmlessness of dons), but that determines in a profound way our feelings about and responses to various situations. And religious belief should not be treated (as Flew has done) as though it were a sort of explanatory hypothesis; rather, religious assertions express a blik, a fundamental attitude, in which a religious person differs from an unbeliever. Flew's rebuttal is terse: "If Hare's religion really is a *blik*, involving no cosmological assertions about the nature and activities of a supposed personal creator, then surely he is not a Christian at all?" (108). Hare's theory of bliks is representative of a number of similar proposals, for instance, by R. B. Braithwaite (1955), in which the cognitive content of religious belief is surrendered in the interest of defending its personal and ethical significance in the life of the believer.

Basil Mitchell's contribution to the debate offered yet another entry in the contest of dueling parables:

> In time of war in an occupied country, a member of the resistance meets one night a stranger who deeply impresses him. They spend that night together in conversation. The Stranger tells the partisan that he himself is on the side of the resistance—indeed that he is in command of it, and urges the partisan to have faith in him no matter what happens. The partisan is utterly convinced at that meeting of the Stranger's sincerity and constancy and undertakes to trust him. (Flew et al. 1955, 103)

As time passes, the Stranger is sometimes seen to be helping the resistance, but at other times he fails to help when asked, and at yet other times he appears to be helping the enemy. But even in the face of this, the partisan continues to insist, "He is on our side." When his friends ask him, "Well, what *would* he have to do for you to admit that you were wrong and that he is not on our side?" the partisan refuses to answer: "He will not consent to put the Stranger to the test" (104).

In commenting on this parable, Mitchell makes three points about religious faith. First, unexplained evil *does count* as evidence against the existence and goodness of God, just as the Stranger's ambiguous behavior counts against his being a supporter of the resistance. Second, both the partisan and the religious believer are *committed* to the objects of their respective faiths, so neither will allow that the negative evidence counts *decisively* against that faith. But third, at some point it might become "just silly" for the partisan, or the believer, to maintain faith in the face of contrary evidence, though it is impossible to say in advance exactly when that point would be reached. (Yet a fourth point lies just below the surface of the parable: the source of the faith in the first place lies in an actual encounter that has occurred; for Mitchell, this encounter surely is the one recounted in the Christian Story.)

In replying to Mitchell, Flew admits that his response is actually more typical of theologians than the one Flew attributed to them in his original article. But this is not, he claims, a response that can be successfully maintained in the face of the actual evidence. The Stranger is only another human being, and so there can be plausible excuses for his ambiguous behavior. But Mitchell "has given God attributes which rule out all possible saving explanations . . . We cannot say that he would like to help but cannot: God is omnipotent. We cannot say that he would help if he only knew: God is omniscient. We cannot say that he is not responsible for the wickedness of others: God creates those others" (Flew et al. 1955, 107).

What should not be overlooked in this response is that, in giving it, Flew has shifted the terms of the debate—and shifted them in a very traditional direction.

No longer is it being said that theological assertions are meaningless because unfalsifiable; rather, the claim is that, in the light of the evidence, they must be judged to be *false*. And the reason behind this claim is also very traditional, namely, the problem of evil. If this shift in the debate had been clearly recognized at the time, we might have been spared some of the subsequent protracted discussion of the "problem of religious language."

I. M. Crombie (1955), in commenting on the falsification debate, elaborates views that are generally consistent with Mitchell's. In accounting for religious language he develops, in effect, a doctrine of analogy, though one less burdened with metaphysical baggage than traditional Thomism. Like Mitchell, he admits that unfavorable evidence counts against faith, but (being a believer himself) he does not allow that the evidence counts decisively against faith, because that faith is in fact true. But what would it take to decisively refute Christian faith? According to Crombie, the Christian

> has his prepared positions on to which he retreats; and he knows that if these
> positions are taken, then he must surrender . . . There are three main fortresses
> behind which he goes. For, *first*, he looks for the resurrection of the dead, and
> the life of the world to come; he believes, that is, that we do not see all of the
> picture, and that the parts which we do not see are precisely the parts which
> determine the design of the whole . . . *Second*, he claims that he sees in Christ
> the verification, and to some extent also the specification, of the divine love . . .
> *Third*, he claims that in the religious life, of others, if not as yet in his own,
> the divine love may be encountered, that the promise "I will not fail thee nor
> forsake thee" is, if rightly understood, confirmed there. (129)

Crombie's reference to "the resurrection of the dead, and the life of the world to come," is taken up and elaborated by John Hick (1957) in his doctrine of "eschatological verification." The idea here is that Christian faith is after all verifiable (though perhaps not falsifiable): all we have to do is die! Naturally, Hick was faced with various challenges to this proposal. Some have questioned whether the doctrine of life after death is itself meaningful. Another question is whether whatever it is after death that decisively confirms the truth of Christianity could not in principle confirm it in this life. And of course, the notion of eschatological verification does not, by itself, cast light on the way language can be used to describe a transcendent reality such as God. Nevertheless, Hick's proposal does underscore the fact that, in certain respects, religious believers entertain quite concrete expectations that are different from the expectations of nonbelievers. This is a far cry from Hare's blik and Flew's "picture preference."

Any discussion of the problem of religious language that did not mention the later philosophy of Wittgenstein would be seriously incomplete. The most striking thing about Wittgenstein's philosophy, when the *Philosophical Investigations* first appeared, was its proposal to take the various forms of discourse—the different "language-games"—on their own terms. Rather than having to fit into what many perceived as the straitjacket of verificationism, religious language (among other forms) was to be understood as it is actually used by religious persons. Furthermore, believers are not asked to justify their use of such language; rather, the demand for justification "bottoms out" in the "form of life" of which it is a part. *Within* the language-game and *within* the form of life, there are demands for justification and standards for what counts as justification. But if the language-game and the form of life are questioned from the outside, the only possible response is, "This language-game is played."

This approach to language, then, promised to liberate religious language from the oppressive requirements of verificationism and to permit it to be studied in a way that is more congenial to the actual intentions of the language users. This liberation, however, comes at a price. "This language-game is played"—true enough, but so are other, competing religious language-games, and so are secular language-games that altogether reject talk about God. So if the project of justification bottoms out at the form of life, it appears that, at best, we will arrive at some form of pluralism or relativism—and this, whatever its intrinsic merits, is far removed from the intentions of many of the actual participants in religious language-games. Internally, within the religious language-game and form of life, universal claims and pronouncements can still be made. But the philosopher, for whom justification terminates on the form of life, cannot allow the validity of such claims and pronouncements outside of the language-game in which they originate.

This can be connected with yet another feature of Wittgenstein's philosophy. In general, Wittgenstein's later philosophy (unlike the *Tractatus*) abandons the search for the truth-conditions of propositions in favor of assertibility-conditions. He asks, not "What would make this true?" but rather, "Under what circumstances would it be appropriate to say this?" But whereas truth-conditions—for instance, for assertions about a transcendent God—can be as remote from experience as one pleases, assertibility-conditions have to be accessible to the users of language. Because of this, metaphysics is ruled out just as much as it was for the positivists. And religious assertions, while ostensibly about a transcendent being beyond the world, must be judged correct or incorrect solely in terms of the conditions of life, and attitudes toward life, of the believers themselves. The upshot, arguably, is that Wittgensteinian philosophy of religion does not, in the end, allow religious language to mean what its ordinary users take it to mean. It is understandable, then, that a separation has grown up between the Wittgensteinians and mainstream analytic philosophy of religion, which has increasingly taken a metaphysical realist turn.

In surveying the overall contours of this debate, several conclusions emerge. First of all, the claim that language referring to God is meaningless has become virtually a dead issue. No criterion of meaning that has been proposed to support this conclusion has withstood criticism, and the objection has simply lost its power to intimidate. This does not mean, however, that the use of language to speak about God is unproblematic. Given the transcendence and infinity of God as traditionally understood, it is evident that many attributes cannot possibly be ascribed to God in precisely the same sense as they are to human beings and other creatures. Some form of the doctrine of analogical predication seems inevitable. (A particularly careful development of such a doctrine is due to James Ross [1969].) On the other hand, it is plausible that there must be some univocal core of meaning, some respect in which we are saying *the same things* about God and about other beings; otherwise, our speech about God threatens to collapse into sheer equivocation. One philosopher who has argued for some degree of literalism in our language concerning God is William Alston (1989). Alston's literalism, however, is far from naïve; for instance, he employs a functionalist analysis of psychological terms to arrive at a limited univocal meaning for these terms as applied both to human persons and to God.

The Middle Period: Attacking and Defending Theism

Sometime in the late 1960s the claim that speech about God is devoid of cognitive import died a quiet death. There was no quick, decisive refutation of this claim, but many of the arguments supporting it had been answered, and the claim simply ceased to be convincing. The philosophical establishment did not, however, greet the newly rediscovered cognitive claims of theology with marked enthusiasm. Many critics moved easily, and with no apparent discomfort, from their earlier complaint that assertions about God were meaningless to the logically incompatible claim that these assertions are false. (The ease with which this transition was made might cause some to wonder whether the earlier claims of incomprehension were entirely genuine.) The objections raised against theism set up a budget of problems that were addressed in subsequent decades. It was necessary for theists to define the main theistic attributes as rigorously as possible and to defend the definitions as logically coherent. The problem of evil emerged as by far the most important objection to theistic belief and has required intensive scrutiny. The arguments for the existence of God, which at the beginning of the period tended to be written off as a lost cause, have inspired continued interest and not a few defenders. And lurking over all of this were epistemological questions about the kind of justification required, and the kind that might be available, for religious belief—traditionally, the problem of faith and reason.

The attributes of God most commonly held to be essential for theism are omnipotence, omniscience, and perfect goodness. Both omnipotence and omniscience have been intensively discussed, and though nothing like complete consensus has been reached, it does not seem that insuperable problems remain concerning either attribute. Omnipotence seems to imply God's ability to "intervene" supernaturally in the world in performing miracles, and analytic theists have defended this possibility against the objections of Hume and his modern successors. With regard to omniscience, it would be generally acknowledged that this attribute entails God's knowing everything it is possible for a perfect being to know. There remain, however, intense disagreements as to whether it is logically possible for God to foreknow the actions of creatures who are free in the libertarian (incompatibilist) sense. An extension of this controversy concerns divine "middle knowledge": whether it is possible for God to know the (libertarian) free choices that *would be made* by actual and possible free creatures in situations that never in fact arise. The divine goodness, on the other hand, has been comparatively neglected—an unfortunate omission because (among other reasons) the conception of divine goodness plays a crucial role in considering the problem of evil. The prevailing view, however, seems to have been that divine goodness is sufficiently understood without a detailed or painstaking investigation.

Other traditional divine attributes remain deeply contentious. The trend has been against the traditional conception of divine timeless eternity derived from Augustine and Boethius. Analytic philosophers are inclined to think that "mysteries are not to be multiplied beyond necessity," and divine timelessness has seemed to many of them one mystery too many. Still, the doctrine has found a few energetic defenders, first in Eleonore Stump and Norman Kretzmann (1981, 1992), and more recently in Brian Leftow (1989). The doctrine of divine simplicity has been even more embattled, and many (though not all) analytic theists would subscribe to the view that this doctrine has not yet received a formulation that is sufficiently perspicuous to make it a serious candidate for acceptance. Finally, there is the doctrine of necessary divine existence—that God is a Necessary Being. Early on, the prevailing assumption was that Kant has shown that existence is not a predicate and that the existence of no being can be logically necessary. Most analytic theists, however, have come to reject this position, and to hold that God's existence is indeed logically necessary, though this view is by no means unanimous. Overall, considerable progress has been made in the philosophical accounting for the divine attributes and the divine nature.

Even after the positivist embargo had been lifted, the theistic arguments suffered from formidable difficulties, stemming historically from Hume and Kant. There was the ban on necessary existence, which immediately invalidated the ontological argument and (if Kant was to be believed) the cosmological argument as well. Arguably even more important was the doctrine, common to Hume and Kant, that causation requires an observable relation between phenomenal entities.

This not only excludes the possibility of a causal argument for divine existence, but it rules out the very possibility of a causal relationship between God and the world, such as is implied in the doctrine of creation. Finally, there was the assumption that a successful theistic argument (or "proof," as they used to be called) must be one that is compelling for any rational person who contemplates it—that it must proceed from premises known (or readily knowable) to all, by means of inferences whose validity is evident to all. Because arguments of this strength are seldom available for any philosophically interesting conclusion, this assumption does a lot to make life easy for critics of the theistic arguments.

All of these assumptions have been forcefully challenged in recent years. After providing, early in his career, a refutation for the argument of Anselm's *Proslogion* 2, Alvin Plantinga (1974) astonished himself by discovering an ontological argument, loosely based on *Proslogion 3*, that is unquestionably valid. (Similar arguments were devised by the Norman Malcolm [1960], a Wittgensteinian, and by the process philosopher Charles Hartshorne [1962].) Plantinga himself admits, however, that his argument is "not a successful piece of natural theology" (1974, 219), since its premise—that divine necessary existence is logically possible—is itself in question and cannot be supported by compelling arguments. Still, the ontological argument is back in play, which is a most unexpected development in view of the situation just a few decades ago.

The Hume-Kant ban on causation by unobservables not only puts a crimp on theological discourse; it also rules out the postulation of unobservable causes in science, and even (as both Hume and Kant recognized) casts a shadow over realism concerning ordinary physical objects. Once their arguments had been overturned (too long a story to be told here), the way was open for a reexamination of the cosmological argument. An impressive contribution along this line came from William Rowe's *The Cosmological Argument* (1975, 1998), a study of Samuel Clarke's version of the argument based on the principle of sufficient reason. Rowe is a nontheist and does not fully endorse the argument, but he considers that "this old argument for the existence of God is far better than most philosophers of the modern period have thought it to be" (1998, xi). A version of the argument that does not appeal to the principle of sufficient reason is given by Richard Swinburne in *The Existence of God* (1979). Swinburne's claim is that the existence of a complex physical universe is more comprehensible if it is taken to be created by God than if it is an unexplained, brute fact. William Lane Craig (1979) has been active in promoting the Kalam cosmological argument, which contends on both logical and scientific grounds that the universe cannot always have existed and points to an intelligent personal cause as the source of its coming into existence.

The design argument has been under a cloud, not only because of Hume's rhetorically masterful critique, but because Darwinian evolution has undermined the most popular version of the argument, based on the adaptedness of living creatures. Hume's objections have been effectively challenged, but the task of refuting Darwin as a prologue to constructing a design argument has not appealed to philosophers. Richard Swinburne (1979), however, has put forth a version of the argument based on the existence of natural regularities, contending that these are better explained through the operation of an intelligent cause than accepted as mere brute facts. More recently, John Leslie (1989), along with others, has promoted a design argument based on the "fine-tuning" of the fundamental physical constants of the universe. The values of these constants are held to stand in need of explanation, because if they were even very slightly different (as they well might be), our cosmos would be such as to make intelligent life impossible.

What standards should these arguments be expected to meet? The claim that has traditionally been made for them is that they are, or should be, convincing to any rational person: the premises are propositions that are (or can become) evident to anyone who examines the matter, and the conclusions follow from the premises by reasoning whose validity is likewise evident to any competent reasoner. Unfortunately, by this standard there are virtually no successful arguments in all of philosophy (none, at least, that establish interesting positive conclusions; some refutations may meet the test). George Mavrodes (1970), however, has pointed out that the success of arguments is in many cases "person-relative": that there are arguments that are convincing for some person, and actually enable that person to know the truth about some matter, and yet those same arguments fail for other, equally intelligent persons. This may be so because of differences in background knowledge, training, and experience, or because of personal experiences that cannot be fully communicated to someone who has not had them. Furthermore, predispositions and value orientations greatly affect the plausibility of beliefs and arguments for a person (see Wainwright 1995), and such factors are not readily altered by reasoning.

All of this may come as a disappointment to those who still cherish the Enlightenment ideal of a single, neutral philosophical reason that will place us securely in possession of the truth about all important matters. But it is as clear as anything can be that this ideal is unattainable in human life, and recognizing this fact enables us to consider philosophical arguments, such as the arguments for the existence of God, without setting impossibly high standards for their success. An interesting stance on these matters has been defended by Richard Swinburne. Swinburne accepts, in principle, the idea of a neutral philosophical reason. He does not, however, consider that the employment of this reason leads to rational certainty, but only to a degree of probability for this or that proposition. The intrinsic probability of a proposition is an a priori matter, depending primarily on simplicity; this probability is then modified in the light of evidence, according to the principles of the probability calculus. In *The Existence of God* (1979), Swinburne uses this framework to construct a cumulative case argument; he concludes that on the evidence he has adduced (comprising versions of all of the traditional theistic arguments), the existence of God is more probable than not.

A sharply contrasting position is found in the "Reformed epistemology"[1] developed in the 1980s by Alvin Plantinga and Nicholas Wolterstorff (1983). The central contention of Reformed epistemology is that belief in the existence of God (along, perhaps, with some other crucial religious beliefs) is "properly basic"; it is a belief that a person can be *justified* in accepting without basing it on other beliefs she accepts. This claim is of course highly controversial; the Reformed epistemologists' defense of it has in effect two phases, an "external" phase directed to other philosophers regardless of their own beliefs, and an "internal" phase directed specifically to other Christian thinkers. The external defense trades heavily on what Wolterstorff has termed "perspectival particularism"[2] (1996, 19; 2000, 154–55). In brief, perspectival particularism recognizes that there is an irreducible plurality of fundamental perspectives on reality, with a particular person's acceptance of one of them strongly influenced by her prephilosophical beliefs and commitments. Furthermore, it is not in general possible to show, by neutral philosophical argument, that some one of these perspectives is correct and all the rest mistaken. In view of this, it is perfectly appropriate and in no way irrational for a person to philosophize on the basis of her own perspective, even if she has not been able to demonstrate the correctness of that perspective in a way that is convincing to others. In particular, the Christian philosopher is entitled to her own perspective, and to her own "set of examples" (Plantinga's term) by which she determines the criteria for properly basic beliefs.

So much for the external defense of the claim that belief in God can be a properly basic belief. The internal defense goes beyond this, by providing an explanation for how it is that one can be justified in believing in God, even in the absence of evidence in support of this belief. The answer is found in the claim that God has implanted in each human being a natural inclination to form such a belief (Calvin called this inclination the *sensus divinitatis*) under appropriate circumstances. Such circumstances might include being impressed by the wonder of nature and spontaneously recognizing it as God's creation, or reading the Bible and finding God speaking to one through it. In view of this divinely implanted disposition, one is justified in believing in God, in the appropriate circumstances, just as a person who sees a horse is justified in believing that there is a horse in the vicinity. Now of course, nontheists cannot be expected to accept the assertion that God has implanted in us the sensus divinitatis. They may, however, come to recognize that belief in the sensus is a legitimate, integral part of the Christian worldview (or at least, of some Christian worldviews). And in recognizing this, they may also be brought to concede that the person who believes in God in a basic way violates no epistemic duties in doing so.

The problem of evil is not the only objection to theism in contemporary philosophy, but it has been by far the most prominent. Discussion of this problem has passed through at least two distinct phases. In the earlier period, represented by J. L. Mackie's "Evil and Omnipotence" (1955) the claim commonly made was that the existence of evil is *logically inconsistent* with the existence of God; this, then, is the "logical problem of evil." According to Mackie, the propositions that generate the logical inconsistency are:

1.   God is omnipotent.
2.   God is wholly good.
3.   Evil exists.

According to Mackie, this contradiction shows, "not [merely] that religious beliefs lack rational support, but that they are positively irrational, that the several parts of the essential theological doctrine are inconsistent with one another" (200).

The classic response to Mackie's argument came in Alvin Plantinga's (1974) "free will defense." Plantinga's strategy is to prove that propositions (1) through (3) are consistent with each other, by providing a fourth proposition that is consistent with (1) and (2) and which, when conjoined with them, has (3) as a logical consequence. (Plantinga is relying on a theorem of modal logic: $\{\Diamond(p \ \& \ q) \ \& \ [(p \ \& \ q) \to r]\} \to \Diamond(p \ \& \ r)$.) The proposition Plantinga comes up with is in effect the following:[3]

4.   God actualizes a world containing moral good, and it was not in God's power to actualize a world containing moral good but no moral evil.

And from this, together with (1) and (2), it does indeed follow that

3.   Evil exists.

The crucial claim here is that it is possible that it was not in God's power to actualize a world containing moral good but no moral evil. The idea behind this is that moral good (which is taken to be an especially valuable and important form of good) is possible only for creatures possessing libertarian free will, but if God creates such creatures it is the creature, and not God, who determines whether it does evil or good. So it may be that whatever creatures of this sort God might have chosen to create, at least some moral evil would result. An omnipotent God can control whatever he chooses to control, but even he cannot both control and refrain from controlling at the same time.

As one might expect, Plantinga's argument resulted in prolonged and intensive discussion. The upshot of this discussion is that it is now widely conceded, by atheists as well as theists, that Plantinga's answer is successful, and that the existence of evil is not, as such, logically inconsistent with theism. It is important, however, to recognize the limitations of Plantinga's success. He has by no means shown by this argument (nor did he claim to show) that the evil in the world cannot support an objection to belief in God. Nor does he claim by his argument to have *explained* the existence of the evil that we see in the world. His argument is a *defense*, which shows that a particular version of the problem of evil does not succeed; it is not a *theodicy*, which would vindicate God by showing that God does indeed have good reasons for permitting evil to occur. It is especially important to note that Plantinga's defense does not depend on our assuming that (4) is *true*, or even that it is something that is *reasonable to believe* based on the evidence we have. All Plantinga needs is that (4) is *logically possible*, and that it is consistent with (1) and (2). If that much is true, Mackie's logical problem of evil fails.

In the aftermath of the collapse of the logical problem, discussion of the problem of evil has taken a different turn. Most commonly, it is not evil as such, but *gratuitous evil*, evil that is not the occasion for any greater, outweighing good, that is held to be inconsistent with theism. It is claimed that our experience strongly indicates that such gratuitous evil does indeed exist, and therefore that God does not exist. A classic statement of this "evidential problem of evil" is due to William Rowe:

1. There exist instances of intense suffering which an omnipotent, omniscient being could have prevented without thereby losing some greater good or permitting some evil equally bad or worse.
2. An omniscient, wholly good being would prevent the occurrence of any intense suffering it could, unless it could not do so without thereby losing some greater good or permitting some evil equally bad or worse. *Therefore,*
3. There does not exist an omnipotent, omniscient, wholly good being.
    (Howard-Snyder 1996, 2)

The argument is undeniably valid, so the question that must be considered is whether we have good reason to accept the premises. Most of the discussion has centered on premise (1). The theist, presumably, wants to reject this premise, but what are the possibilities for doing so reasonably? One possibility is to reject (1) on the basis that God does in fact exist and that, since God exists, (1) cannot be true. One who takes this line would hold that even if our experience suggests to us that (1) is true, the fact that God does exist means that our experience must be misleading us in this respect, and that there is in fact some greater good that results from each instance of evil that God allows.

Such a response comes at a price. If this line is taken, then the weight of our experience that suggests the existence of gratuitous evils *counts against* the existence of God and must be subtracted from whatever degree of rational support one's belief in God derives from other sources. If that support is strong enough, the counterevidence from evil may not seriously undermine it. But if the support we have for belief in God is less robust, it may be overwhelmed by the evidence of evil, resulting in a belief that, if it persists at all, is no longer rational.

The answer of traditional theodicy is that (1) is false because we can see that there very likely are in fact outweighing goods for all the evils that exist. To be sure, no one could sensibly claim to be able to identify the outweighing good in each particular case. But we can see enough of the general types of good that result from God's permission of various sorts of evils to make it plausible that our inability to discern these good consequences in some particular instances is merely a result of our limited knowledge. Unsurprisingly, this sort of theodicy has not been a popular pursuit during the later part of the twentieth century. Given the two World Wars, the numerous smaller wars and other calamities, and—not least important—our much greater awareness of disasters and human suffering occurring all over the globe, the optimism of a Leibniz-type theodicy is neither plausible nor especially appealing.

Perhaps the most popular response during the past two decades has been what can be termed the skeptical solution for the problem of evil. This solution, pioneered by Stephen Wykstra (1984), admits that we are unable to construct a credible theodicy of the sort discussed above. However, it denies that the evils by which we are surrounded, and for which we can see no justifying reasons, provide even prima facie evidence that there is genuinely gratuitous evil. The reason they do not is that we are simply not in an epistemic position to detect such outweighing goods were they to exist; therefore, our failure to detect them gives us no reason to suppose that they do not exist. Our impression that there is unjustified evil results from our failure to recognize our severe epistemic limitations in these matters.

This line of defense has been powerfully criticized by Richard Swinburne (1998, 25–29). Swinburne does not deny that we suffer from epistemic limitations, affecting both our ability to trace the causal connections between various situations and our ability to recognize and weigh properly the goods and evils that occur. However, the skeptical solution makes a further, completely unwarranted assumption. It assumes that these epistemic limitations bias our judgment in one direction only: that of failing to identify, and to weigh properly, the goods that result from particular evils. But why assume this? Why may it not be that our limitations lead us to overlook or minimize some of the world's evils and to overestimate the likelihood that good comes out of evil? (Arguably, some traditional theodicies have been guilty of precisely this fault.) There is no basis in reason or experience for assuming that our epistemic limitations cut in one direction only—but without this assumption, the skeptical solution collapses.[4]

There remains yet another strategy for replying to Rowe's argument, namely, to accept the first premise of the argument but to reject the second (Peterson 1982; Hasker 1992). This entails the affirmation that *the goodness of God is consistent with the existence of gratuitous evils*—evils that God could prevent, without losing any greater good or permitting any equal or greater evil. A possible key to making this plausible is to ask what the consequences would be if God were, in fact, known to prevent all genuinely gratuitous evils. If we knew this to be the case, we would also know that any evil that we ourselves fail to prevent will be allowed by God to occur only if it is the necessary condition for some greater good that could not be achieved without permitting the evil in question. Arguably, however, knowing this would seriously undermine our own motivation and sense of responsibility to prevent serious evils. So it may reasonably be held, instead, that God creates a world that makes possible a great many diverse forms of good as well as evil, and to a very large extent leaves it to us to be responsible for preventing or alleviating particular instances of evil. The "greater good" on account of which evils are permitted would then be found, not (or not always) in particular goods resulting from particular instances of evil, but rather in the "overall structure of the world order and the values that are generally able to emerge from it" (Peterson et al. 1998, 141). This, in turn, opens the way for a more modest type of theodicy. Such a theodicy will not claim that "every evil leads to a greater good," but rather that the nature and structure of the world as a whole make possible many and great goods and that the evils the world contains, however tragic they may be, do not negate the goodness of God's creation taken as a whole. The most famous example of such a theodicy is John Hick's (1978) "soul-making theodicy," but there are other examples, and much more work along these lines remains to be done.[5]

TOWARD MATURITY: MULTIPLE CHALLENGES

All of the topics mentioned in the previous section continue to be actively discussed, but the past two decades have seen a notable broadening of the field of analytic philosophy of religion, with many new, or previously underexplored, topics becoming important subjects for research. These topics include philosophical studies of particular religious (especially Christian) doctrines, divine command theories of ethics, the relation between religion and science, the philosophical analysis of non-Western religions, the problem of religious pluralism, religious realism and antirealism, and the implications of religious beliefs for general epistemology, along with still others. It is out of the question for all of these to be discussed here even briefly, so this section is limited to two main topics. First, we will survey recent philosophical work on the doctrine of divine providence. Then

I will propose a topic that has not recently been a major part of the agenda but that, I suggest, needs to become so in the near future: the nature of necessary truth.

That God exercises providential control and guidance over earthly events is a common tenet of the monotheistic religions. According to the Talmud, for example, "The Holy One sits and nourishes both the horns of the wild ox and the ova of lice" (Shabbat 107b), and "He is occupied in making ladders, casting down the one and elevating the other" (Genesis Rabbah 68.4). Recent philosophical discussions concerning this doctrine have been carried out in a Christian context, but are in principle applicable as well to Judaism and Islam.

From a philosophical standpoint, the crucial variables for a doctrine of providence are divine power, divine knowledge, and human free will. However, the nature and extent of divine power are not in question among the major candidate views on the topic: they would agree that the exercise of God's power is limited only by what is logically possible and by what is "morally possible" for God in view of God's essential moral perfection. The one exception to this generalization is the process theism based on the thought of A. N. Whitehead (see Griffin 1976), which holds that God's power is "always persuasive, never coercive." On this view God can and does "lure" finite beings toward the direction that will best fulfill their potential. But having done this, God has no control whatever over the choices actually made by the creatures. It is often claimed that this view is much less troubled by the problem of evil than is traditional theism, but this has recently been disputed (Hasker 2000). What is clear, however, is that the degree of divine control is far less than seems to be required by the monotheistic faiths, at least in anything like their traditional forms. Analytic philosophers of religion, with a few exceptions, tend to shun process theism. Even those who are atheists usually disbelieve in the God of traditional theism rather than in the process deity!

Perhaps the most crucial divide for theories of providence is the presence or absence of libertarian free will on the part of human beings. Theists who opt for compatibilism (i.e., for the view that free will and moral responsibility are compatible with causal determinism) become theological determinists, a view associated historically with Augustine, Calvin, Luther, and probably Thomas Aquinas (for a recent exposition, see Helm 1994). On this view, God alone sovereignly determines each and every event that occurs. In view of his infallible foreordination, God is able to know with certainty exactly what will happen. This view, however, has extreme difficulty with the problem of evil; in fact, it is likely that no rationally comprehensible explanation for evil, especially moral evil, is possible. (Calvinists themselves often say that the relationship between God and evil is an impenetrable mystery.) How is it intelligible that God has decreed the existence of moral evil, and has then assumed toward what he has deliberately chosen to bring about an attitude of utter, implacable hostility?

If libertarian free will is accepted, the question arises as to how, and whether, it is possible for God to know genuinely undetermined events before they take place (see Hasker 1989; Fischer, 1989). Especially crucial is the doctrine of divine "middle knowledge," termed "Molinism," for the sixteenth-century Jesuit theologian Luis de Molina (1988). On this view, God knows, not only the *actual* free choices made by creatures, but also the choices that *would be made* by actual *and possible* free creatures under circumstances that never in fact arise. (These truths are commonly referred to as "counterfactuals of freedom.") Opponents of Molinism claim that there are no such truths to be known. Truths about actual future decisions correspond to the actual making of the decisions, but in the case of decisions that are never made, nothing exists in reality to "ground" the truth of assertions about the free decisions that *would be* made. Discussions of these matters have become both intense and extremely technical (see Flint 1998; Hasker et al., 2000).

Divine middle knowledge, if its existence is granted, makes possible an extremely strong doctrine of providence—probably the strongest doctrine available short of complete theological determinism. God, by consulting his middle knowledge, knows precisely the outcomes that would result from any decisions he might make concerning his own creative actions. Thus, God is able to select the best among the available options and to know with absolute certainty what the outcome will be; any need for divine risk-taking is eliminated entirely. There may, however, be a price to pay for these advantages: it has been argued that in such a scenario, God would be a manipulator of human beings rather than engaging in a genuinely personal relationship with them. Furthermore, on this view, it will arguably be the case that God specifically plans and intends each instance of evil that occurs, resulting in a problem of evil second only to that which faces theological determinism.

The remaining view of providence is variously entitled "free will theism," "open theism," or the "openness of God" (see Sanders 1998). One significant, and quite controversial, tenet of this view is that it is logically impossible for God to know with certainty the future choices to be made by free persons. This should not be seen as a denial of omniscience, any more than it is a denial of omnipotence to say that God cannot perform actions that are logically impossible. Somewhat surprisingly, the assertion that God lacks comprehensive knowledge of the future *has no effect* on our understanding of God's providential governance of the world. The reason for this is that, absent middle knowledge, divine knowledge of the actual future would add *nothing whatever* to God's ability to govern the world, over and above what God would have with comprehensive knowledge of the past and present (for argument, see Hasker 1989, 53–63; Sanders 1998, 200–206). Furthermore, the same is true of the knowledge of the future that might be possessed by a timeless God.

The two themes most characteristic of open theism are, first, the assertion that God is genuinely and personally interactive with free human persons and, second, the recognition that, in governing the world, God is a risk-taker. In choosing to create free persons and to respect their freedom, God allows for the very real possibility that such persons will choose their own ways in contradiction to his loving and gracious will for them. Because God does not have a complete "blueprint" of the future, divine governance of the world can be seen in part in terms of general policies or strategies rather than as divine ordination of each particular event that occurs. (Thus, open theism is highly congruent with the last of the four responses detailed above to the problem of gratuitous evil.) God's omnipotence is shown, not in unilaterally decreeing how things shall be, but in working together with his creatures to achieve the best possible future. Molinists and Calvinists, on the other hand, claim that open theism unacceptably compromises God's sovereign control over worldly happenings.

Necessary truth has not been ignored in analytic philosophy of religion. The developments in modal logic during the 1970s were seized on and exploited by analytic theists in discussing topics such as essential divine attributes and necessary divine existence. Alvin Plantinga's *The Nature of Necessity* (1974) developed an account of modality and defended it against the modal nihilism of W. V. Quine, who first reduced necessary truth to analytic truth and then undermined the idea of analyticity. In this book, Plantinga crafted a structure of modal concepts including essences, essential and accidental properties, and possible worlds that has served many philosophers ever since. Ironically, Plantinga never tells us what the nature of necessity *is*; instead, he says, "The distinction between necessary and contingent truth is as easy to recognize as it is difficult to explain to the sceptic's satisfaction . . . We must give examples and hope for the best" (1974, 1).

But suppose we do want to know what necessary truth is? Two options are set forth by Richard Swinburne:

> Logical necessities, claims the Platonist, make it inevitable that the world is one sort of place rather than another—by a hard, inexorable necessity than which there is none harder. The Platonist's opponent is the logical nominalist, who believes that the only truths at stake concern *nomina*, words. There is, claims the nominalist, no timeless realm of statements and logical necessity, just facts about how humans use language . . . I shall argue that the nominalist is basically correct. (1994, 105–6)

Though Plantinga is not fully explicit, it is clear that he comes down on the Platonist side of this argument. A more explicitly Platonist affirmation comes from Robert Adams:

> Many philosophers believe that absolute necessity is "logical" or "conceptual" in such a way as to be confined to a mental or abstract realm and that it cannot escape from this playground of the logicians to determine the real world in any way . . . If, on the other hand, it is a necessary truth that God exists, this must be a necessary truth that explains a real existence (God's); indeed it provides the ultimate explanation of all real existence . . . Thus, if God's existence

follows from his essence in such a way as to be necessary, his essence is no mere logicians' plaything but a supremely powerful cause. (1987, 213–14)

Like Swinburne, I regard Platonism (or modal realism) as unsatisfactory. The main reason is that it leaves us in the dark about the nature of necessity; we simply have no idea, on this account, what makes a proposition necessary or why a proposition's necessity should have the importance it apparently does have. That an essence should be a "supremely powerful cause" is no doubt an exciting idea, but this combination of excitement and obscurity is a dubious recommendation for a philosophical theory. The obscurity lends itself to an unbridled faith in "modal intuition," and to an excessive reliance on thought experiments that is inherently anti-empirical. The obscurity is not relieved if possible worlds are taken as primitive; doing this simply refuses to address the question as to what makes possible worlds possible.

On the other hand, Swinburne's nominalism does not seem to be a satisfactory alternative. When he says that the laws of logic "are simply generalizations about language" (1994, 108), he arguably leaves himself unable to account for the necessity that is characteristic of logical truth. As a third option, I propose *modal conceptualism*, a view that, like nominalism, denies that logical necessity and possibility pertain to the mind-independent world, but that does not, like nominalism, make them merely properties of linguistic expressions. Instead, necessity and possibility pertain to *concepts*, understood as ways it is possible for a mind to grasp and classify the world and its contents. Conceived thus as *possibilia*, concepts are necessary entities, existing even in worlds where there are no minds to think them. Logical impossibility is then a matter of contradiction in concepts and propositions, and from impossibility possibility and necessity can be defined in the usual way. A possible world is one that is free from contradiction; a necessary truth is one whose denial is explicitly or implicitly self-contradictory.

The most formidable challenge to this conceptualist account is found in the "synthetic necessary truths" championed by Saul Kripke. Kripke (1980) convinced many philosophers that "Hesperus = Phosphorus" and "Water is H_2O" are necessary truths, in spite of the fact that the negations of these propositions do not appear to be contradictory. The right way of dealing with these examples is the one proposed by Alan Sidelle. According to Sidelle (1989, 34), the key to such situations lies in "analytic general principles of individuation" of the form

(x)(If x belongs to kind K, then if p is x's P-property, then it is necessary that x is p).

The particular principle that applies to chemical kinds such as water is

(x)(If x is a chemical kind, then if p is x's chemical formula, then it is necessary that x is p).

This is an analytic or conceptual truth, because it is part of our concept of a chemical kind that the chemical formula of a substance is definitive of its chemical kind. Instantiating, this yields:

> If water is a chemical kind, then if water's chemical formula is H_2O, it is necessary that water is H_2O.

When combined with the empirical information that the formula for water is indeed H_2O, this yields the desired modal conclusion: necessarily, water is H_2O. Clearly, much more needs to be done to fully develop this modal conceptualist proposal and to defend its viability. I believe, however, that it can account for all clear cases of necessary truth without embracing the profound obscurity and the dubious rationalism that attend modal realism.

If modal conceptualism is accepted, what will be the impact on philosophy of religion? It is always a gain for any branch of philosophy when fundamental concepts that are clear and well understood replace those that are obscure and confused. In view of the prevalence of modal and essentialist reasoning in philosophy of religion, the implications of the proposed replacement are bound to be far-reaching. Almost certainly, the ontological argument will be recognized as being unsound, and not merely dialectically ineffective. *Pace* Anselm, no one has come close to showing that possible worlds lacking God are thereby rendered self-contradictory. Some, to be sure, will see the denial of logically necessary existence as a diminution of the divine majesty. But for God to exist necessarily means merely that worlds (nonactual states of affairs) lacking God contain a contradiction, and it is difficult to see how the greatness of the Creator of all things hinges on the presence or absence of such a contradiction.

The abandonment of logically necessary divine existence should spur a more thorough exploration of alternative (nonlogical) senses in which God's existence may be said to be necessary. It should also encourage study of versions of the cosmological argument that do not depend on the notion of logically necessary divine existence. The doctrine of divine simplicity, already on shaky ground, will not be able to survive the abandonment of necessary divine existence, since *what* God is and *that* God is will turn out to be, after all, distinct facts. And the disappearance of simplicity removes what, in the minds of many supporters, is the main bulwark of divine timelessness. On the whole, the recognition that God's existence is logically contingent should be highly favorable toward the conception of God promoted by the open or free will theism discussed in the first part of this section. The stakes in the question about the nature of necessity are not low.

The Analyst among the Philosophers of Religion

What can be said about analytic philosophy of religion in the broader context of philosophical studies of religion? A good starting point is to compare the analytic approach with other approaches. Some of the differences between the approaches merely represent varied interests, and the results achieved by one approach can in principle be accepted and incorporated by others. But there are also differences of principle that cannot easily be reconciled.

There is no reason why analytic philosophy should not be open to the concerns and emphases of feminism, and a number of analytic philosophers consider themselves feminists or friends of feminism. However, analytic philosophers will tend to reject the idea that one's philosophical work as a whole ought to be dominated by a particular ideological agenda such as feminism. Postmodernism is a large and varied category, and responses to it from analytic philosophers will vary accordingly. To the extent that postmodernism is antirealist and considers the meaning of texts to be systematically indeterminate, it will be rejected by analytic philosophers, including philosophers of religion. On the other hand, understanding of the social location of particular philosophies and movements of thought can be extremely valuable, and there is sometimes need for a "hermeneutic of suspicion." But a hermeneutic of suspicion must be preceded and enveloped by a hermeneutic of trust, which takes the utterances and writings of others at face value and assesses them on their merits. Few things are so destructive of dialogue as to disqualify the statements of one's potential partners in advance of any serious consideration of their merits.

One would think that Wittgensteinian and analytic philosophies of religion should have much in common, and to some extent this is so. But insofar as prominent Wittgensteinians reject metaphysical realism, most analytic philosophers will demur. The Wittgensteinians do not, to be sure, think metaphysical realism is false, but rather that it is hopelessly confused and lacking in definite meaning. This question should in principle be amenable to argument, but hopes for an early resolution do not run high. Nothing, however, prevents analytic philosophers from appropriating Wittgensteinian insights and techniques. William Alston's *Perceiving God* (1991), to take a single example, makes extensive use of Wittgenstein in defending the claim that God is perceived in religious experience.

The comparison of analytic philosophy of religion with Thomism is particularly interesting. Clearly, there is a great deal of overlap between the two, both in the topics addressed and in the general style of treatment. The response of analytic philosophers to Thomism, however, depends on how Thomism is understood. The mainstream of modern Thomism, stemming from the encyclical

Aeterni Patris issued in 1879 by Pope Leo XIII, tended to take Thomas's achievements as the foundation for all philosophical reflection. Thomistic categories were adapted and applied to modern circumstances, but both the fundamental assumptions and the technical philosophical apparatus remained conspicuously medieval. More recent philosophy was regarded largely as an aberration that needed to be put aside or refuted in order to recover the sanity, balance, and wisdom of the Angelic Doctor. To the extent that these attitudes persist, analytic philosophers find discussion with Thomists frustrating and unprofitable. But there is another way Thomism can be understood, and on this reading it is perfectly feasible to be both an analytic philosopher and a Thomist. Thomists of this stripe think Aquinas was mostly right about a great many things, but they are willing to translate his insights into a more contemporary idiom. They also criticize, modify, and even on occasion reject Thomistic views in a way that more traditional Thomists were unwilling to do. By doing this they are in effect mining Aquinas, and other medieval philosophers, for ideas that can challenge and enrich contemporary philosophical theology.

Like other successful philosophical enterprises, analytic philosophy of religion has been subjected to criticisms, only a few of which can be addressed here. One criticism is that it tends to be ahistorical, and no doubt this has sometimes been true. But it is much less the case now than previously, as analytic philosophers of religion engage seriously with a wide range of historical exemplars in both philosophy and theology. Another criticism is directed at the emphasis on formalized arguments, which is said to mimic mathematics and natural science and to concede to the latter an undeserved, and harmful, position of hegemony. Clearly, formalization can be overdone and can lead to obfuscation rather than clarity. Nevertheless, there is an old tradition in philosophy (long antedating the rise of modern natural science) that recognizes the need for technical precision, and just plain hard philosophical work, in trying to get clear about fundamental issues. (Think of Aristotle, or the later dialogues of Plato.) There is also a long tradition of at least partly successful attempts to integrate the philosophical/scientific study of nature into a fuller conception of "the way things are." It is rather the postmodernists, with their denigration of science and their scorn for comprehensive worldviews, who are the innovators. Whether good can come from these innovations remains to be seen.

Perhaps the most interesting criticism of analytic philosophy of religion is that it is guilty of an inordinate preoccupation with theism. This criticism is complex and can be interpreted in a number of different ways. If it is meant as a reminder that other, nontheistic religious traditions are worthy of philosophical exploration, then the point is well taken—and work on those other traditions is beginning to be done, though not as yet fully developed. Another relevant observation is that theism as discussed by philosophers is but a pale, skeletal abstraction, far removed from the rich complex of beliefs and practices of a living religion. This also is correct, but it is less than a devastating criticism. The truth of theism is far from sufficient, but is certainly a necessary condition for the general truthfulness of either Christianity, or Judaism, or Islam, or theistic forms of Hinduism. Furthermore, the field has broadened to address particular religious doctrines and a much wider range of concerns than previously; it is by no means limited to "mere theism."

Other versions of the criticism are harder to classify. When we are told that by the word "God" "something of unutterable significance is intended, but for that very reason any literal and unmediated reference to God is conceptually vacuous" (Crites 1996, 44), what are we to make of this? If arguments were offered for this conclusion they could be discussed. But what we are actually given is often no more than a few hand-waving references to Kant, made without any recognition of the rebuttals to Kantianism in recent analytic philosophy. Some of this postmodern critique gives every impression of being about a quarter-century out of date.

The merits of analytic philosophy of religion can be rather simply stated. This approach to philosophizing offers the best means yet available for clarifying the meaning of religious claims and for assessing the reasons for and against the truth of those claims. Those who are uninterested in clarity and truth as applied to religious assertions will naturally find this style of philosophizing uncongenial. Those who do care about such matters may well find it indispensable.

NOTES

1. So called because of certain affinities with the Reformed, or Calvinistic, branch of Protestantism. One need not, however, be a Calvinist, or even a Christian, to be a Reformed epistemologist.

2. The use of this term is relatively new, but the idea has been in place since the beginning of Reformed epistemology.

3. I have greatly simplified Plantinga's argument; in particular, I have omitted his incorporation into the argument of divine middle knowledge, which permits God to know, prior to his own decision about what sort of world to create, exactly what any possible free creature would freely do in any situation in which it might be placed. Plantinga, however, agrees that the free will defense does not depend on the assumption of middle knowledge.

4. Swinburne's argument presupposes the principle of credulity, which states that "other things being equal, it is proper and rational to believe that things are as they seem to be (and the stronger the inclination, the more rational the belief)" (1998, 20). If Wykstra means to deny this (I doubt that he does), he may succeed thereby in defeating

Rowe's argument—but only at the cost of landing himself in a skeptical bog from which there is no escape.

5. For a clear statement by Hick that his theodicy is of this kind, see (1991, 127–31); for other theodicies of this type, see Farrer (1962), Peterson (1982), and Reichenbach (1982).

WORKS CITED

Adams, Robert M. 1987. "Divine Necessity." In *The Virtue of Faith and Other Essays in Philosophical Theology*, 209–20. New York: Oxford University Press. Originally published in *The Journal of Philosophy* 80 (1983): 741–52.

Alston, William. 1989. *Divine Nature and Human Language: Essays in Philosophical Theology*. Ithaca, N.Y.: Cornell University Press.

———. 1991. *Perceiving God: The Epistemology of Religious Experience*. Ithaca, N.Y.: Cornell University Press.

Ayer, A. J. 1936. *Language, Truth, and Logic*. London: Gollancz.

Braithwaite, R. B. 1955. *An Empiricist's View of the Nature of Religious Belief*. Cambridge, England: Cambridge University Press.

Craig, William Lane. 1979. *The Kalam Cosmological Argument*. London: Macmillan.

Crites, Stephen. 1996. "The Pros and Cons of Theism: Whether They Constitute the Fundamental Issue of the Philosophy of Religion." In Wainwright 1996, 39–45.

Crombie, I. M. 1955. "Theology and Falsification: Arising from the *University* Discussion." In Flew and MacIntyre 1955, 109–30.

Farrer, Austin. 1962. *Love Almighty and Ills Unlimited*. London: Collins.

Fischer, John Martin, ed. 1989. *God, Foreknowledge, and Freedom*. Stanford: Stanford University Press.

Flew, Antony, et al. 1955. "Theology and Falsification: From the *University* Discussion." In Flew and MacIntyre 1955, 96–108.

Flew, Antony, and Alasdair MacIntyre, eds. 1955. *New Essays in Philosophical Theology*. New York: Macmillan.

Flint, Thomas P. 1998. *Divine Providence: The Molinist Account*. Ithaca, N.Y.: Cornell University Press.

Griffin, David Ray. 1976. *God, Power, and Evil: A Process Theodicy*. Philadelphia: Westminster Press.

Hartshorne, Charles. 1962. "What Did Anselm Discover?" *Union Seminary Quarterly Review* 17: 213–222.

Hasker, William. 1989. *God, Time, and Knowledge*, Ithaca, N.Y.: Cornell University Press.

———. 1992. "The Necessity of Gratuitous Evil." *Faith and Philosophy* 9: 23–44.

———. 2000. "The Problem of Evil in Process Theism and Classical Free Will Theism." *Process Studies* 29: 194–208.

Hasker, William, David Basinger, and Eef Dekker, eds. 2000. *Middle Knowledge: Theory and Applications*. Frankfurt: Peter Lang.

Helm, Paul. 1994. *The Providence of God*. Downers Grove, Ill.: InterVarsity Press.

Hick, John. 1957. *Faith and Knowledge*. Ithaca, N.Y.: Cornell University Press.

————. 1978. *Evil and the God of Love,* 2nd edition. New York: Harper and Row.

————. 1991. "Response to Mesle." In C. Robert Mesle, *John Hick's Theodicy: A Process Humanist Critique.* New York: St. Martin's Press, 115–34.

Howard-Snyder, Daniel, ed. 1996. *The Evidential Argument from Evil.* Bloomington: Indiana University Press.

Kripke, Saul. 1980. *Naming and Necessity.* Oxford: Blackwell.

Leftow, Brian. 1989. *Time and Eternity.* Ithaca, N.Y.: Cornell University Press.

Leslie, John. 1989. *Universes.* London: Routledge.

Mackie, J. L. 1955. "Evil and Omnipotence." *Mind* 64: 200–12.

Malcolm, Norman. 1960. "Anselm's Ontological Arguments." *Philosophical Review* 69: 41–62.

Mavrodes, George. 1970. *Belief in God: A Study in the Epistemology of Religion.* New York: Random House.

Molina, Luis de. 1988. *On Divine Foreknowledge: Part IV of the Concordia.* Trans. Alfred J. Freddoso. Ithaca, N.Y.: Cornell University Press.

Moore, G. E. 1925. "A Defense of Common Sense." In *Contemporary British Philosophy* (second series), ed. J. H. Muirhead. London: Allen and Unwin. Reprinted in Thomas Baldwin, ed., *G. E. Moore: Selected Writings.* London: Routledge, 1993, 106–33.

Peterson, Michael. 1982. *Evil and the Christian God.* Grand Rapids, Mich.: Baker.

Peterson, Michael, William Hasker, Bruce Reichenbach, and David Basinger. 1998. *Reason and Religious Belief,* 2nd edition. New York: Oxford University Press.

Plantinga, Alvin. 1974. *The Nature of Necessity.* Oxford: Clarendon Press.

Plantinga, Alvin, and Nicholas Wolterstorff, eds. 1983. *Faith and Rationality: Reason and Belief in God.* Notre Dame, Ind.: University of Notre Dame Press.

Reichenbach, Bruce. 1982. *Evil and a Good God.* New York: Fordham University Press.

Ross, James. 1969. *Philosophical Theology.* Indianapolis: Bobbs-Merrill.

Rowe, William. 1975. *The Cosmological Argument.* Princeton: Princeton University Press. Reprinted with a new preface by Fordham University Press, 1998.

————. 1979. "The Problem of Evil and Some Varieties of Atheism." *American Philosophical Quarterly* 16: 335–41. Reprinted in Howard-Snyder 1996, 1–11.

Sanders, John. 1998. *The God Who Risks: A Theology of Providence.* Downers Grove, Ill.: InterVarsity Press.

Sidelle, Alan. 1989. *Necessity, Essence, and Individuation: A Defense of Conventionalism.* Ithaca, N.Y.: Cornell University Press.

Stump, Eleonore, and Norman Kretzmann. 1981. "Eternity." *Journal of Philosophy* 79: 429–58.

————. 1992. "Eternity, Awareness, and Action." *Faith and Philosophy* 9: 463–82.

Swinburne, Richard. 1979. *The Existence of God.* Oxford: Clarendon Press.

————. 1994. *The Christian God.* Oxford: Clarendon Press.

————. 1998. *Providence and the Problem of Evil.* Oxford: Clarendon Press.

Wainwright, William J. 1995. *Reason and the Heart: A Prolegomenon to a Critique of Passional Reason.* Ithaca, N.Y.: Cornell University Press.

————. ed. 1996. *God, Philosophy, and Academic Culture: A Discussion between Scholars in the AAR and the APA.* Atlanta: Scholars Press.

Wolterstorff, Nicholas. 1996. "Between the Pincers of Increased Diversity and Supposed Irrationality." In Wainwright 1996, 13–20.

———. 2000. "Analytic Philosophy of Religion: Retrospect and Prospect." In Lehtonen and Koistinen 2000, 152–70.

Wykstra, Stephen J. 1984. "The Humean Obstacle to Evidential Arguments from Suffering: On Avoiding the Evils of 'Appearance.'" *International Journal for Philosophy of Religion* 16: 73–94.

FOR FURTHER READING

Gale, Richard. 1991. *On the Nature and Existence of God.* New York: Cambridge University Press.

Harris, James F. 2002. *Analytic Philosophy of Religion.* Dordrecht: Kluwer.

Koistinen, Timo. 2000. *Philosophy of Religion or Religious Philosophy: A Critical Study of Contemporary Anglo-American Approaches.* Helsinki: Luther-Agricola Society.

Lehtonen, Tommi, and Timo Koistinen, eds. 2000. *Perspectives in Contemporary Philosophy of Religion.* Helsinki: Luther-Agricola Society.

Martin, Michael. 1990. *Atheism: A Philosophical Justification.* Philadelphia: Temple University Press.

Quinn, Philip L., and Charles Taliaferro, eds. 1997. *A Companion to Philosophy of Religion.* Cambridge, Mass.: Blackwell.

CHAPTER 18

....

WITTGENSTEINIANISM

Logic, Reality, and God

....

D. Z. PHILLIPS

THE twentieth century saw a revolution in philosophy. The philosophical giant in that revolution was Ludwig Wittgenstein. P. M. S. Hacker writes: "Wittgenstein's influence dominated philosophy from the 1920s until the mid 1970s. He was the prime figure behind both the Vienna Circle and the Cambridge school of analysis, and the major influence upon Oxford analytic philosophy in the quarter of a century after the Second World War" (2001, 124). Yet, the influence of Wittgenstein on the philosophy of religion, even during this period, was never dominant. Neither is it dominant today, although Wittgensteinianism is one of the main movements in the subject. How is one to account for this? There are at least five reasons that come to mind.

First, there was the influence of logical positivism, which held that all religious and theological propositions are meaningless (see Ayer 1936). People wrongly associated Wittgenstein with this view. He, by contrast, respected religious belief as a deep tendency in human beings, but, in his early views, struggled with the issue of how its sense is to be understood. Wittgenstein reacted angrily to the positivists' misunderstanding of his *Tractatus*. Second, the Cambridge and Oxford movements Wittgenstein influenced were analytical and antimetaphysical. Most philosophers who adhered to them simply assumed that religion shares the fate of metaphysics. Third, even among philosophers influenced by Wittgenstein, many came to the same conclusion with respect to religion. Fourth, there were and are philosophers sympathetic to religion, who were influenced by Wittgenstein but who parted company with him when it came to his remarks on religion. The most important reason is the fifth, namely, that the twentieth-century revolution in philosophy had little effect on mainstream philosophy of religion, whose concerns remained rooted in the epistemology of the seventeenth and eighteenth centuries.

Wittgensteinianism's relation to contemporary philosophy of religion is complex, especially its relation to analytic philosophy of religion. The use of "analytic," in this context, is very different from its use as a description of the Cambridge and Oxford movements Wittgenstein influenced. Whereas those movements were antimetaphysical, contemporary analytic philosophers of religion take metaphysical realism for granted (see Wolterstorff 2000).[1] Further, the earlier analytic debates about the meaning of religious belief involved the leading philosophers of the day, believers and atheists alike (see Flew and MacIntyre 1955). Reformed epistemologists, on the other hand, such as Nicholas Wolterstorff, hold that one's personal perspective and commitments shape one's philosophy. Different philosophies, each in its intellectual ghetto, live in a noninterference pact with their neighbors, all claiming an epistemic right to their basic presuppositions. For Wittgensteinians, this is a sad surrender of philosophy's age-old contemplative tasks in the academy (see Phillips 1993b, 2000d).

In the wider context of contemporary analytic philosophy, especially in the United States, it seems to me that atheism has given way to indifference, one expressed in suspicion of the very practice of philosophy of religion.[2] Wittgenstein's philosophical methods are certainly not central in contemporary philosophical practice. His methods have to do with giving a proper conceptual attention to the world in all its variety. To appreciate these methods, we need to go beyond the "perspectival particularism" of Reformed epistemology and the Enlightenment conception of philosophy as the rational assessor of all our beliefs and practices. These are not the exclusive choices facing us. To see why, we need to ask the following question: What is the difference between the reality philosophy investigates and that notion of a divine reality in which believers say that they live and move and have their being?

DESCARTES' LEGACY

Descartes' epistemological legacy opens up a gap between consciousness and reality. This can be illustrated by a familiar incident that occurred while he was writing his *Second Meditation*. Descartes looked out of his window and saw people crossing the square. Had there been someone else with him in the room to ask what he was seeing, Descartes would have replied, quite naturally, "People crossing the square." But there was no one in the room as he posed a philosophical question to himself. "Yet do I see more than hats and coats which could conceal automatons? I *judge* that they are men" (1990, 21).

Descartes wants to know how that judgment can be justified. If we take his worry to be epistemological, it seems to call for a practical resolution: off with those hats and coats! We can imagine exclaiming, as a result, in a particular case, "My God! It's an automaton." Perhaps we are on a film set where advanced robots are being used. As figures cross the square, we say, "Aren't they good! With those hats and coats, you can't tell which ones are the human beings."

These practical responses do not do justice to Descartes' concern, since they take for granted the very category "human being" that Descartes is questioning. He wants a judgment about *that*. Although Descartes' legacy is epistemological, his own deepest concerns are logical. In the case of epistemological concerns, the emphasis is on whether we have the right to say that we know, let us say, that a particular figure is a human being. The *sense* of what we may or may not know is not questioned. In a logical concern, it is the very possibility of that sense that is being questioned. It is this latter concern that makes Descartes a great philosopher.

In his dream argument, any feature of waking life we choose to distinguish it from dreaming is promptly imagined to be in a dream. So how do we know that we are not dreaming all the time? Alternatively, how do we know that we are not in the hands of a malignant demon who deceives us even about the ways we distinguish between being and not being deceived? So how do we know that we are not being deceived all the time? As Barry Stroud (1991) has said, if we cannot answer Descartes' questions, we lose the whole world; we lose the sense of things.[3]

Descartes' questions led him to the one thing he could not doubt: his consciousness. The window through which, or in which, Descartes "sees" human beings is not the familiar window that looked out on the square, but the window of his own consciousness. He is asking a question in logic: How can it *mean* anything to say that my consciousness is in contact with reality?

Is there a feature of consciousness that guarantees that contact? It cannot be any of his bodily characteristics, since Descartes thinks these may be simply part of a dream he is having. Neither can it be his conviction of mathematical certitude, since this may turn out to be a devil's ploy. It seems to Descartes that he needs nothing less than proof of the existence of a God who is no deceiver: "For if I do not know this, it seems that I can never be certain of anything else" (1990, 25). Suddenly, Descartes realizes that he has, in his consciousness, an idea of such a God. And what an idea it is! It is an idea than which no greater can be conceived, since it entails the existence of the God it is an idea of. Descartes can exclaim, "O happy day! When all my doubts have gone away." Descartes logical perplexity is put to rest by the conviction that he has found an Archimedean point, a realm beyond his familiar world, which provides a *logical* foundation for our categories of thought.

Descartes' dilemma is: How, from *inside* my consciousness, can I make contact with a reality *outside* it? Note the spatial metaphors for meaning which contribute to the idea that we need a bridge from consciousness to reality. Wittgenstein attacked the terms of reference of this dilemma: the Cartesian concepts of consciousness and reality.

Does this mean that Wittgenstein has no interest in the nature of reality? On the contrary, he thinks it is philosophy's primary concern. He argues, however, that metaphysical conceptions of reality obscure actual realities, including what is meant by the reality of God. My aim in this essay is to put flesh on the bones of this assertion.

PHILOSOPHY OF RELIGION'S
EPISTEMOLOGICAL INHERITANCE

For the most part, contemporary philosophers of religion do not complain about the accuracy of the accounts of their views given by Wittgensteinians, whereas this is a common complaint by Wittgensteinians about accounts given of their views. Why should this be so? Most philosophers are content to say that theories they disagree with are intelligible but false. Wittgenstein, on the other hand, says that the theories are the product of confusion. It follows that someone in the grip of that confusion will not appreciate the character of a critique of it. Wittgensteinians claim that in contemporary philosophy of religion, that confusion is found in its epistemological inheritance. It is that confusion which leads to many philosophers giving an epistemological caricature of Wittgenstein's thought. Let us see how this comes about.

Most contemporary philosophers do not think that Descartes, even on his own terms, managed to break out of the circle of his own consciousness. The proof of God's existence, which is supposed to guarantee even our clear and distinct ideas, depends on our idea of God being clear and distinct. Nevertheless, *the form* of Descartes' dilemma has remained unchanged for the majority of philosophers of religion: How, from my consciousness, can I make contact with a reality outside it?

First, consider those contemporary philosophers of religion influenced by *empiricism*. On this view, we are immediately acquainted only with our ideas. But the ideas come between us and the world. I cannot step outside my ideas to compare them with the world. Why should I think that there is a world there at all? Empiricism's traditional reply is that we infer the existence of such a world from the quality of our ideas. Ideas of perception are said to have a greater consistency or vivacity than our imaginings. The logical objection to this view is that no matter how consistent or lively is our idea of, say, an apple, this is quite consistent with the apple's not being there (Austin 1962, Warnock 1969). Again, a memory cannot be established from the quality of an idea. There must be a relation between a memory and the actual occurrence of what is remembered (Holland 1954).

There are deeper incoherencies in empiricism. What makes the ideas of consciousness the ideas that they are? They cannot be self-identifying. There must be a distinction between "thinking something is so" and its being so. To sever so-called ideas from any wider reference than themselves reduces them, in the end, to a meaningless concatenation of sensory data (Holland 1954). In this way, empiricism loses the whole world.

These logical objections to empiricism are often forgotten. But even when they are, the best empiricism can offer is a probable contact with reality. Its problematic inference gives us no more than a probable world, probable human beings, and a probable God.[4]

Second, consider Reformed epistemologists and others informed by the epistemological naturalism of Thomas Reid (1843). Understandably, they are anxious to avoid the problematic inference from ideas to the world found in empiricism. What if there is a more direct way of moving from one to the other? Reid argues that we do so by way of suggestion: certain sensations suggest certain beliefs to us. He distinguished between our original perceptions and our acquired perceptions, saying that the former suggest the latter. Thus, a sound may suggest immediately a friend's voice. Reid thought he was simply analyzing everyday experience when, in fact, he robs us of its sureness. Where there is uncertainty, as there may be when I hear people speaking in another room, I may *think* a sound suggests the voice of my friend. But when I hear his voice in the next room, that is what I hear, not a sound that *suggests* the voice of my friend. The point is even more obvious when my friend is talking to me face to face, although Reid's analysis is meant to apply to this case, too.

What of the original perception, the sound itself? According to Reid, this, too, is suggested by a different sensation perceived by a distinct faculty. The problem is that there is no such faculty, and Reid had difficulty in locating what he called his "fugitive sensation" perceived by it, resorting, in the end, to the desperate measure of claiming that a sensation suggests a sound with such immediacy that we are unaware of having it.[5]

Reformed epistemologists, too, claim that our beliefs about the external world are formed by certain psychological processes that occur immediately without inference or any kind of argument. Thus, I believe that I am seeing a tree when I am appeared to treely. I have a memory of what I had for breakfast in response to a question asked of me. But the logical objection that haunted empiricism returns. One can be appeared to as often as one likes, and find alleged memories forming in response to questions, but the fact remains that this is compatible with not seeing the tree, or not having had what one thinks one had for breakfast. This is admitted by Reformed epistemologists (Plantinga 2000).

Why, then, should we trust the mental phenomena called beliefs? The answer given is that it is rational to do so if we have no good reason not to (Alston 1991). We trust the faculties that provide the beliefs. Further, religious believers think that the harmony thus brought to our experiences is best explained by a further assumption that they are designed by God. It is not difficult to see why critics of these views have accused them of heaping assumption upon assumption. A critic of Reid talks of finding ourselves in "a maze of first principles" (O. M. Jones 1927). Hume's Cleanthes in the *Dialogues* would call this a matter of building in the air.

We can see how in Reid, and in Reformed epistemologists, our epistemic relation to "being in the world" is one of *belief*. The belief in the existence of such a world is one we cannot help having, whatever skeptics may say. Some suggest that belief in God is also a natural belief, formed in us by certain experiences. Others argue, with Reid, that it is an assumption we make to account for the order our natural beliefs bring to experience. But whether we say belief in God is a natural belief or that the assumption of God's existence is a natural propensity of the mind, the fact that the belief and the propensity are not universal has led to disputes over whether either should be called "natural" in Hume's sense of "natural instinctive beliefs."[6]

Third, consider the influence of neo-Kantianism in nonanalytic contemporary philosophy of religion. There are continuities between the naturalist claim that we have natural, instinctive beliefs, and Kant's claim that the categories of consciousness are presupposed in everything we experience. H. O. Mounce (1999) argues that there is little difference between Hume's distinction between what is manifest and what is ultimate, and Kant's distinction between the phenomenal and noumenal realms. In each case, we are acquainted with how reality appears to us, rather than with reality as it is in itself, which is forever beyond the reach of our finite faculties. If God is ultimate reality, isn't this what we should expect?

Some neo-Kantians have argued that in the appearances of reality presented to us, what we have are *interpretations* of reality. It has been argued, notably by John Hick (1989), that the world religions are interpretations of ultimate reality. This has led some to be skeptical about the possibility of certitudes or absolutes in religion (Katz 1978).[7]

We have now looked at the epistemological legacy of three schools of thought in contemporary philosophy of religion. It will be recalled that my purpose in doing so was, first, to show that they accept *the form* of Descartes' dilemma: How, from my consciousness, can I have contact with a reality independent of it? In a discussion between American analytic and nonanalytic philosophers of religion, the former claimed to possess a robust conception of truth (Wainwright 1996).[8] Wolterstorff (1996) criticized neo-Kantians for their "interpretation-universalism," but with what right? Do not all these schools suffer the same epistemological fate? Reidians have *suggestions* that we are in contact with reality. Reformed episte-mologists offer us *beliefs* that we have such contact. Both schools say that we must *trust* the faculties that produce these beliefs. Neo-Kantians offer us *interpretations* of reality. None offers us certitude about our everyday world. Given their own epistemological inheritance, it is little wonder that we find many adherents of these movements offering an epistemologised caricature of Wittgenstein's thought, in which he, too, is seen as denying that we can come into contact with how things really are. Here is the caricature which has been accepted all too readily by many nonreaders of Wittgenstein:

> Wittgenstein turned from a concern with reality to a concern with language. As language users we are locked in our language games. We cannot get outside them to see how things really are. Of course, within the games we can talk of "facts" and "truths," but these turn out to be facts and truths about language, not about a reality that is independent of anything we do or say. In fact, what is said in one language game has no implications for what is said in any other. Religious language games, like all others, can be understood only by those who participate in them. They are immune to external criticism. Such immunity, however, is bought at a high price. It leads to a radical perspectivism and rela-tivism, where things can be true or false only from some point of view. Given these views, it is impossible to believe in a God who exists prior to language. This is but one example of the way in which Wittgensteinians, who claim to be describing religious belief, distort what believers actually say.

So much for the caricature. Even if it were true, all the others should say is, "Welcome to the Cartesian epistemological club." To see through the caricature we need to appreciate that Wittgenstein's deepest questions, like Descartes', are questions in logic rather than in epistemology.

THE RETURN FROM
METAPHYSICAL REALITY

Talk of a revolution in twentieth-century philosophy can be misleading. Wittgenstein insisted, again and again, that his problems were the same as Plato's. In fact, these problems begin when the Presocratics ask, "What is the nature of all things?"[9] According to Aristotle, they sought a first philosophy, a science of being qua being. This suggests that the difference between philosophy and science is one of generality. Whereas the sciences investigate aspects of reality, philosophy investigates reality as such. But what is "reality as such"?

Can we say that reality exists? If we say that something exists, we can speak of the conditions of its existence, which are independent of it. But how can we say this of reality? What is independent of it? According to most of the Presocratics, all one can say of reality is that "it is." We cannot think of it as any kind of substance, since we can ask further questions about the reality of any substance we specify. Thales said, "All things are water," but what about the reality of the water?

Reality, it seems, is what all real things have: they all have "being." In this way, the verb "to be" is reified into a realm in which all real things inhere. But to speak of "Being being," is as senseless as to speak of "Running running." Walt Disney can show us the Eiffel Tower running, but not even he could show us "Running running" or "Being being" (Sprague 1962).

Because of these logical confusions, many philosophers in the wider Anglo-American analytic tradition have concluded, perhaps under Frege's influence, that it is incoherent to say that "what is" is. The preoccupation of continental philosophers with the notion of "being" is often dismissed as an instance of the reification of the verb "to be" (Williams 1997). Premature though that dismissal certainly is, the problem of talking of "being as such" that begins with the Presocratics runs through the history of philosophy. Can Plato's Forms be said to exist? Can this be said of Locke's substratum? Can Hegel's Absolute Spirit be said to exist? Can Heidegger's "Being" be said to be?

How does the notion of "being as such" become connected with Wittgenstein's thought and lead to a caricature of it? It is easy to miss if we simply concentrate on certain aspects of Wittgenstein's analogy between language and games, those that stress the various forms language takes. Of course, a great deal of confusion is caused by confusing the grammars of these forms, for example, the grammar of physical object language with the grammar of "God." This was an aspect of philosophy emphasized in Oxford linguistic philosophy. To remain here, however, would be to miss the deepest aspect of Wittgenstein's thought, which has to do, not with confusions *between* different forms of language, but with *confusions about language itself.* These confusions cannot be treated in the same way. We bring out the confusion between different forms of language by giving perspicuous representations of the different grammars. But confusions about language as such, those that lead to postulating a metaphysical realm, cannot be treated in the same way, for how could one give a perspicuous representation of the whole language? That means nothing.

How do confusions about language lead to the claim that, according to Wittgenstein, the only reality we have contact with is the reality of language, not contact with reality as such? Let us consider a simple case of a disagreement over whether a tablecloth is red in the absence of the tablecloth. The two persons who disagree agree, of course, about the meaning of "red"; they agree in their reaction to colors.[10] But this does not mean that when I say "The tablecloth is red" I am saying anything about language, about the meaning of "red." I am saying something *about the color of the tablecloth.* What is more, if I am standing in front of the tablecloth, that is something I may be certain of. I do not say, in those circumstances, as the other epistemologies argued I ought to say, that the tablecloth is *probably* red, that I *believe* that the tablecloth is red, that it is *suggested* to me that the tablecloth is red, or that I interpret that the color of the tablecloth is red. When I say that the tablecloth is red, I am referring to what Reformed epistemologists call a sober truth about the world, the fact of the matter. How, then, can it be said that the notions of "fact" and "truth" in Wittgensteinianism refer only to facts and truths about language?

According to Wittgenstein's critics, "truths about language" come between us and contact with "reality as such." How does language give rise to the latter notion? The answer is that propositions articulating the grammar of concepts are confused with propositions that describe reality (Hacker 2001). As we have said, when one person says "The tablecloth is red" and another says "The tablecloth is not red," the meaning of "red" does not change. Even when the tablecloth is not red, it might be said, the meaning remains. But where does it remain? It is tempting to think of "the meaning" as an independent realm, existing in its own right, a realm that appears to transcend the affirmative and negative judgments about the color of the tablecloth. Here is the transcendent reality of metaphysics, one that our concepts are said to describe, or that determines the forms our concepts take. It is in this metaphysical space that the epistemologists we have considered place "God." Our task, with respect to "God," is the same as with any other word, namely, to bring it back from its metaphysical to its everyday use.

GOD AS METAPHYSICAL REALITY

If "Being" is thought as the inclusive, metaphysical category that includes all things, do those things include God? It may be said that there are degrees of being, as though being were a property of things (Rhees 1997d). But if the difference between God and other beings is one of degree, and one says, for example, that God is *more* powerful than the devil, what measure of comparison would one be using (Rhees 1997b)? Such a comparison leads to the anthropomorphic God of Cleanthes in Hume's *Dialogues*, a conception all too common in contemporary philosophy of religion. Advocates of Radical Orthodoxy argue that the confusion of treating "God" as a being among beings can be traced to Duns Scotus, who departed from Aquinas's insight that God is not a substance, not a member of any species or genus (Blond 1998).[11]

To avoid the difficulty of talking about God as a being among beings, some have sought to identity God with the metaphysical notion of "ultimate reality." Mounce (1999, 105) argues that in Reid's epistemological naturalism, "the order of the world . . . points to a source which is transcendent and therefore cannot be comprehended in human categories." According to Radical Orthodoxy, "If one wishes to avoid idolatry it must be understood that God's reality has to be seen as the source of any created object's reality. Which is to say that insofar as any object or thing has reality it only does so because all reality owes its origin not to itself but to God" (Blond 1998, 7).

We have already seen how this idea of "the source of all things" can arise from confusions about language. But in Reid and Radical Orthodoxy, if "God" is meant to fulfill the same role as the metaphysical "ultimates" of the Presocratics, familiar difficulties arise. If God is thought of as a quasi-empirical substance, the problem of measuring the measure reappears. We cannot simply say that God "is," any more than we can say this of any other ultimate substance.

In response, it will be said that God is an *incorporeal* substance. Is it not the sine qua non of supernaturalism, as opposed to naturalism, the acknowledgment that in addition to all human consciousnesses, there is an additional consciousness called God? Swinburne (1979) and Plantinga (2000) call it "a person without a body," a notion that fails to do justice to biblical language concerning God (Sherry 1982). The notion of pure consciousness has to face at least four logical objections.

First, God as a pure consciousness, preexisting all things, is said to have ideas and to entertain thoughts. But what makes these ideas and thoughts what they are? The logical difficulties inherent in the empiricist notion of "ideas" reemerge, difficulties encapsulated in Wittgenstein's arguments against a logically private language. Nor will it do to say that God's thoughts and ideas need be only potentially shareable, not actually shared, since this will not secure the essential distinction between "following a rule" and "thinking one is following a rule," between "getting it right" and "thinking one has got it right" (Malcolm 1995). For the idea that the rule is intelligible prior to its having a common use, would require the rule to provide, without such mediation, its own application. To postulate a rule for the use of the rule would leave us with the same problem, plus the prospect of an infinite regress. To know whether an individual is following a rule correctly, there must be a context other than the individual user in which a distinction between correct and incorrect has a purchase.

Second, "consciousness" cannot yield the identity of its possessor. Consciousness cannot tell me who I am. If it is supposed to pick me out, I'd need to experience a number of consciousnesses, which is absurd (J. R. Jones 1967). If, on the other hand, consciousness is taken to mean my awareness of the world, or "there being a world for me," others are in that world just as much as I am. It is a world in which I may see others in pain, or cry out in pain myself, for example. The "I" has no privileged status here, as solipsism would require. Hence, the claim that, faced by this ordinary use of awareness, solipsism collapses into realism (Phillips 2000c). I am who I am in a human neighborhood, as *this* person, not *that* one. But God has no neighbors. It may be thought that he could identity himself for himself with a self-authenticating definition: "I am *this*." But this reverts to the initial difficulty. It falls foul of Wittgenstein's critique of a magical conception of signs, the view that the meaning of a word or sound is a power inherent in them, rather than something that is found in their application. The divine "This!" is meant to operate as a supersign, a sign that guarantees its own idea, a transcendental signified, to use Derrida's (1998) term.

Third, the divine consciousness is supposed to be the source of the reality of all things, but we have seen that this metaphysical space is an intellectual aberration. Consider such a space in the Pythagorean claim that numbers entail the existence of ultimate units, which are supposed to account for our actual arithmetical configurations. Granting that the units are mathematical, they cannot fulfill this metaphysical role, since arithmetic does not spring from the units like shoots from a bulb (Rhees 1970). It is not the units that give sense to the arithmetic, but the arithmetic that gives sense to the units. It is only in that context that they are mathematical units at all. Similarly, it is not "consciousness," metaphysically conceived, that shows us what is meant by "the mind of God," but the religious practice in which that notion has its application. But do not be drawn into the old confusion: if one finds out what is meant by "the mind of God" and gives heed to it, *that* is what one is heeding, not the practice!

Fourth, God's consciousness is often associated with the notion of a divine plan which is supposed to explain all things, but no actual explanation is advanced. If I say that something has happened in accordance with a plan, I can check to see whether what happened deviates from the plan. But if *whatever* happens is said to be in accordance with a plan, reference to a plan becomes superfluous, an idle wheel (Phillips 1993a).

These four logical objections cannot be evaded by saying that God is beyond human categories. The word "God" is in our midst and awaits analysis like any other word. What the objections show is that the metaphysical realm in which God is said to dwell is an intellectual aberration.

CERTITUDES

According to the philosophical schools of thought we have considered, from Descartes to Reformed epistemology, we are said to stand in various epistemological relations to "our being in the world." We are said to be *knowers, believers, trusters,* or *interpreters* of that fact. In Wittgenstein's last work, *On Certainty* (1969), he shows that the search for such an epistemological relation is confused. He considers the roles of certain empirical certitudes in our thinking: that the earth has existed for a long time, that we were born, that this door in my house leads to a familiar corridor, and so on. These are matters we do not question.

Why not? Is it because we *know* these things are true? If we say this, we will be asked *how* we know, but any answer given will be less certain than the certainties they are meant to justify. As Peter Winch says, "Much of Wittgenstein's discussion seems to take the form of trying to substitute some other word for 'know' in these contexts, such as 'believe,' 'assume,' 'presuppose,' 'take for granted.' The outcome of these attempts is that none of these suggestions is satisfactory. But the conclusion is not meant to be that we must look harder till we have found the right word, but that we are looking in the wrong direction altogether" (1998, 192). Mounce, on the other hand, thinks that we have found the right word in the natural *beliefs* of epistemological naturalism. He argues that when William Hamilton says "Belief is the primary condition of reason and not reason the ultimate ground of belief," this "might have served as a motto for Wittgenstein's *On Certainty*" (Mounce 1999, 139, n. 2). So far from searching for "belief," or something else, as a substitute to describe our epistemological relation to the world, Wittgenstein regards all the substitutes offered as eggshells of older material still sticking to the new things he wants to say (Winch 1998).

What are these new things? Wittgenstein is saying that we misunderstand our being in the world if we search for an external, epistemological relation in which we are alleged to stand to it. Wittgenstein is not asking whether reason or trust, knowledge or belief, are the primary relations. His concern is with what goes deep *in* our thinking, with issues of logic, not of epistemology. So far from downgrading reason, Wittgenstein is bringing out that what counts as reasonable or unreasonable is shown *in* the ways we think and act and, notably, in what we do not question.

Wittgenstein thinks that to seek a metaphysical underpinning for our practices, which will show why what we regard as reasonable *is* reasonable, is to have thought chasing its own tail. He does not give the same account of every certainty in our thinking and acting. Some of them, for example, our certainty that every skull contains a brain, result, initially, from a discovery, whereas our certainty that we live in a human neighborhood does not.

Wittgenstein is saying, not that we *cannot* question certain things, but that we *do not*. To say we *cannot* is to invoke some kind of metaphysical necessity that determines our modes of thought and action. To wean us away from *that* thought, Wittgenstein asks us to imagine certain fundamental changes taking place. Again, he does not treat them as forming a class or give the same account of them all.

What if water froze when heated? No doubt we would be absolutely astonished. But some explanation would be sought, and science would go on. More radically, what if the same seeds led to the growth of different plants? Despite the most diligent research over many years, no difference in the seeds is found. We could imagine that, gradually, interest shifts from the seeds to the plants. Seeds would be identified by the plants that grow from them. Biology would be revolutionized, but we can imagine inquiry of some kind going on. But what if I could not be sure of my name, of the friends I have known for many years, or of my familiar surroundings? What would "going on" mean? All my yardsticks would be breaking up. I would think I was going insane. I would certainty not say that I had made a mistake, albeit a rather large one! I would not be in a position to say what is or what is not a mistake. The philosophical importance of the distinction between "mistake" and "insanity" is missed by those who say that it is logically possible that we are wrong, or mistaken, in *any* situation (Plantinga 2000, 334).

Wittgenstein's purpose, in these imaginings, is not *prophecy*. He is not asking, What would happen if? In asking us to imagine fundamental changes, Wittgenstein is underlining, not undermining our ways of thinking and acting. He is certainly not saying that these ways are open to a postmodern conception of choice. On the contrary, he is calling attention to what goes deep *in* our thinking, to what is not questioned in our thinking, to what holds fast there, and does so by asking us to imagine these certainties withdrawn.[12]

RELIGION AND REALITY

A fundamental worry may keep recurring. If Wittgenstein's emphasis is on the rootedness of our concepts and certitudes *in* our practices, how can we believe in a God who is *other than* the world? Does not that appeal to "otherness" show, after all, that religious belief entails the very notion of a metaphysical foundation that Wittgenstein attacks throughout his work?

Peter Winch (2001) has asked us to compare our puzzlement about God's place beyond the world with a comparable puzzlement one may have about the claim, in geometry, that parallel lines meet at infinity. If we leave out the geometry and think of "meeting" in terms of the lines converging, we will conclude that, in fact, the parallel lines do not meet, and that infinity is no place at all. We may be tempted to reject the claim that parallel lines meet at infinity as nonsense. Yet, the notion does have an application. To appreciate it, however, we must look to geometry to see what it comes to; we must look to the proofs and demonstrations it enters into and makes possible.

Similarly, when we hear that God is other than the world, we may wonder where that can be. Leaving religion out of consideration, we may think the belief entails locating God in a quasi-empirical place outside all things, as though the world were itself a thing, or bounded place, one can get outside of, or that the belief leads one to think of a pure consciousness that, somehow, is the source of all things. Such thoughts may lead one to conclude that the belief in a God who is other than the world is senseless. Nevertheless, the belief has application, but one must look to religion to appreciate it. This can be done in more ways than one. I want to do so by considering a religious reaction to that very aspect of Wittgenstein's thought that is said to be the main obstacle to the intelligibility of belief in a God who is other than the world.

As we have seen, Wittgenstein argues against any notion of a transcendent, metaphysical order that determines the form our language games take. On the contrary, he says that the language games are "the given" which we must accept— they are there, like our lives (Wittgenstein 1953, 226; 1969, par. 559). We know by a favor of nature (Wittgenstein 1969, par. 505). It is a confusion to try to get behind the language games to some underlying form.

On the other hand, although we cannot get behind "the given," people react to it in different ways. Among them are religious reactions. Believers not only know (like everyone else) by a favor or grace of nature (a remark in logic), but also see nature as a gift of grace (a spiritual reaction) and feel grateful for it. This is the radical sense of being a creature, one who has nothing by right but is a recipient of grace.

The sense of creaturehood I am referring to is closely related to the sense of life as a mystery. They are not identical, since this sense of mystery may not lead to a sense of grace. Nevertheless, the big divide in contemporary philosophy of religion is not between religious and secular reactions to mystery, but between those who recognize mystery on the one hand, and those who seek religious or secular explanations of life's contingencies on the other (Phillips 1993a).

The mystery I refer to is connected with our being creatures in space and time. There are radical contingencies in human life. Relationships one trusted break down, things get worse just when one thought the worst was over, lives end when there was so much to live for, even modest hopes are dashed because of malice, weakness, or accident. These things seem to happen without rhyme or reason. They can lead to a sense of bewilderment at life, or to a view that we are victims of a cruel or mindless caprice. But it can also lead to the view that we are in the hands of God, creatures in need of grace. Both reactions, however, recognize mystery, that the limits of human life are beyond our understanding. I am exploring the religious reaction to mystery.

At this point, many philosophers will say that I have not yet earned the reference I have made to God. I have talked of human beings who see themselves as recipients of grace, but that presupposes, it will be said, a giver of the grace, about whom I have said nothing. But so far from omitting the notion of divine reality, I am endeavoring to elucidate its grammar. It is a misunderstanding to try to get "behind" grace to God, since "grace" is a synonym for "God." As with "generosity is good," so with "the grace of God" we are not attributing a predicate to an indefinable subject. We are being given a rule for one use of "good" and "God," respectively. God's reality and God's divinity, that is, his grace and love, come to the same thing. God is not "real" in any other sense.

Rush Rhees has expressed the point I am trying to make as follows: "Winston Churchill may be Prime Minister and also a company director, but I might come to know him without knowing this. But I could not know God without knowing that he was the Creator and Father of all things. That would be like saying that I might come to know Churchill without knowing that he had face, hands, body, voice or any of the attributes of a human being" (1997c, 61). It is easy to express Rhees's point in a way that does not get to the heart of the matter.[13] One might say that in the case of Churchill, there is a way I can refer to him independently of his being prime minister or a company director; there is a further "it" involved: that human being. Whereas having spoken of the grace and love of God, there is no further "it" to which they refer. This way of putting the matter gives the impression that a subject is missing, and it leads, naturally, to the puzzle of how grace or love can be spoken of without that love or grace being predicated of something. The force of Rhees's point is different. He is saying that unlike "prime minister" and "company director," which are predicated of a human being, we do not predicate "face," "hands," "feet," and so on of a human being. These are internally related to what we *mean* by a human being. Rhees's point is that "grace" and "love" stand to "God" as "face, hands, feet" stand to human being. In *neither* case does it make sense to postulate a further bearer of what we are talking of. God *is* love. God *is* grace. To know this love and grace *is* to know God.

When I have argued in this way, some philosophers have responded by saying that, like Feuerbach, I have reduced religious belief to a matter of human attitudes. To which I reply that Feuerbach was right in his rejection of "the metaphysical subject," but crucially wrong in his conclusion that, as a result, the divine predicates must become human predicates, that divine love and grace must become human love and grace. From what has been said it should be obvious that human attitudes could not occupy the conceptual space said to be filled by divine love and grace. This can be emphasized further by bringing out what Feuerbach is at pains to deny, namely, that divine grace is *other than the world* (Phillips 2001a).[14] There are at least four reasons for this "otherness."

First, the spiritual reality called grace is other than the world in that it is other than the ways of the world, other than worldliness. Second, the spiritual reality is other than the world in that it makes no sense to speak of any human being possessing this reality in its fullness. Third, the spiritual reality is other than the world in the sense that believers are answerable to this reality they can never fully possess and measure themselves with respect to it. Fourth, the spiritual reality is other than the world insofar as we can be mistaken about it in being guilty of idolatry. Hence, as Rhees says, "It would be ridiculous to suggest that religious language was concerned with calling forth certain attitudes. Religious language is concerned with God, with thanking God, praying to God and praising God. It will not do at all to say that it is directed towards attitudes" (1997a, 61). And at the end of life, what one is answerable to is not one's attitudes, but to God. Here is one impressive expression of such answerability:

> I know only that when I see my life for what it is—see myself for what I am: when I see how *incapable* I am of directing my *life* to anything holy—then the contemplation of death is the greatest *hope*. (And I do not mean this in a negative sense: that here at last will be an end of my own adding to my degradation.) . . . I know that with death I shall reach something not myself. That— saving possible nonsense in this—even my damnation will have something divine about it . . .
>
>   . . . My tendency to write melius fuerit non vivere ("It would have been better not to live") is an expression of . . . *unwillingness to know*—which—if it masters me—will keep me from seeing death as the sole beauty and majesty; as the centre of "Thy will be done." To look on death if this means looking away from the world—is again a form of deception: a *failure* to see death as the word of God . . . (Is this the tendency which finds its most vulgar expression in "That will be glory for me"?). (Rhees 1997e, 235–37; see also Phillips 1970, 2001a)

What we have seen is that to believe in the things of the spirit is to believe in God. The use of "belief" in this context refers to a conviction or confession, not to the epistemological use of "belief" which is a second-best to knowledge and which turns religious belief into a matter of probability or epistemic trust. What is acknowledged when God is acknowledged is the spirit, the light, the element in which the believer sees all things. If I come to acknowledge the existence of Snowdon, having denied it for some reason previously, I do so within a logical space I already possess, my knowledge of other mountains, valleys, and so on, but if I come to acknowledge the reality of divine grace for the first time, no prior logical space awaited it. I come to acknowledge a spiritual reality, a *kind* of reality (Winch 1996). This is why to see one's life as a gift of grace, or to lose this perception, is to have one's life wax or wane as a whole. To acquire or to lose faith is not to change one's opinion within a perspective, but to acquire or to lose a whole mode of illumination, the illumination of grace.

Given what has been said about the acknowledgment of a divine reality, it is not difficult to see why it is important not to make a mistake about it. This is "Why people wish to say that 'there is some reality corresponding' to our religious beliefs. I can see no objection to saying that, provided it is not thought to be the sort of 'correspondence' (and the sort of 'reality') that we have in physics" (Rhees 1997a, 61). It is not like thinking that there is a person in the room when it is empty, or thinking that something is gold when it is not. What is involved, rather, is "The dangers of doing something that claims to be worship of God, but is not really worship of God at all" (Rhees 1997a, 58). This would be giving oneself to something unworthy of worship, something unworthy to be God. "Mistake" and "idolatry" come to much the same thing in this context.

At the end of this section, I can do no more than indicate one example of what I take to be the kind of mistake I have in mind. It is to be found in religious apologetics, in the ways explanatory answers are given to the problem of evil, either in theodicies that claim to show why God has allowed so much suffering in the world, or in defenses that claim that God could have a good reason for allowing the suffering, although we mortals cannot know what that reason is. It is claimed that there is a distinction between intellectual arguments in this context, ones said to meet a logical problem, and the actual problems people have to face in their lives. The distinction is a spurious one, since the trouble comes from *the way* God and suffering are spoken of in these intellectual arguments, ways that, for some philosophers, many theologians, and a vast number of people, believers and unbelievers alike, make theodicies one of the saddest features of contemporary philosophy of religion. They are appalled at the way human life is talked of as a moral experiment for character building by God, how suffering is talked of as a means to a greater good, and how a God, looking back at the huge tracks of human lives laid waste, from the vantage point of the eschaton, is said to feel no remorse for what he has allowed nor admit that he has blood on his hands. I want to say with Rhees: "If I could put my questions more strongly, I should do so. For I think that religious apologists have generally been irresponsible and frivolous in writing about this matter. They have deceived both themselves and others by such phrases as 'suffering for Christ,' 'joyful sacrifice,' etc." (1997f, 304). This is a serious charge, but, then, these are serious matters. It is what an accusation of a mistake looks like where worship of God is concerned.

Probably no way of talking of human suffering is without its difficulties, but there are other religious responses to it far away from the inevitable consequentialism of theodicies. I do no more than indicate one of these responses here. We have talked of "grace" and "love" as synonyms for "God." To see life as a grace is to be grateful for it. Such gratitude, in relation to other human beings and the natural world, involves seeing them as graces, not to be exploited for our own purposes. This is to see others as the children of God, and the natural world as God's creation. But God's creation is a *human* world, one that inevitably involves suffering of various kinds. The recognition of suffering is involved in recognizing life as a grace, and this means that compassion for the human condition is involved, from the outset, in the notion of human life as a grace. Sometimes, compassion enables one to relieve suffering, but there is also the compassion toward affliction of a kind for which nothing can be done. This is a compassion that does not purchase the sufferer, and that, when received in that spirit, may rescue the afflicted one from despair. But such a view entails facing the greatest difficulty of all, namely, the fact that men, women, and children have been crushed by affliction without receiving any compassion. It is important to have real words here, ones that recognize that it cannot be said that these deaths are sustained or informed by a sense of God's presence. It seems that all we have is their story, a story of how human beings are crushed by the world. When theodicies rely, in the end, on massive compensations in the eschaton, they half-recognize the emptiness of the general claim that suffering leads to improved character. Would that they wondered more at the terrible lack of economy in such a conception of the divine plan.

At the heart of Christianity is a crucified one who is said to be both man and God. He dies abandoned with spittle on his face. In Gethsemane's garden, when he prays that this should not be, the heavens are silent. Yet, the story of the Passion, in laying bare human affliction, is suffused with compassion in the recognition of what is happening. Do we not need to acknowledge that the divine simply suffers? The compassion that suffuses the story of the Passion shows what can happen to innocence and love, and that "showing" intercedes for us simply in revealing what it does. But once we say that this was done *in order* that we are shown these things, a horrible mockery is made of human affliction. As against a consequentialist eschaton, when Christ is exalted, raised on high, it is not with healed wounds.[15]

Religion and Philosophical Investigation

At the close of my introductory remarks to this chapter, I asked what the difference is between acknowledging a divine reality and the philosophical investigation of reality. As we have seen, religious belief is a confession, the expression of a conviction. The philosophical investigation, on the other hand, is the struggle to do conceptual justice to the world in all its variety. It is born of wonder at the world and a readiness to combat our confusions concerning it. This is philosophy's contemplative task in the academy.

There are philosophical objections to this conception of philosophy. Some have thought that it leads to an evasion of questions of truth (Wainwright 1995). Others have said that one's philosophy is always determined by one's personal perspectives and commitments, and that philosophers seek in vain for a perch above the fray (Wolterstorff 2000, 155). Still others have thought, absurdly, that a contemplative conception of philosophy expresses the following desire: "Attachment to ideals is fine for common men; as philosophers, however, we should set aside all ends and aims. We should strive to be past caring" (Denham 2000).

A contemplative conception of philosophy has none of these consequences. The perch above the fray is not, as some have thought, one from which the philosopher arbitrates between our beliefs in the name of rationality. Neither is it a view from nowhere. It is a contemplation of the world from the vantage point of disinterested inquiry. Nor does it mean that the person engaged in such inquiry does not have, or ceases to have, personal values and perspectives. On the contrary, as Winch says, doing conceptual justice to the world "is a task of enormous difficulty, both at the technical level and also because of the moral demands it makes on the writer, who will of course him or herself have strong moral or religious commitments and will also be hostile to certain other possibilities" (1996, 173).

Philosophers who resist a contemplative conception of philosophy will have to meet its challenge in any discussion of the place of philosophy in the academy. No talk of different, basic presuppositions will be able to evade it. If it is claimed that the way we see things is determined by our perspectives, not personally, but in philosophy, one will have to refute in detail the countless examples of Wittgenstein's descriptive conceptual success in showing us *different* perspectives; the way he teaches us to give attention to perspectives and voices that are not our own, and to do conceptual justice to them *in their own terms*. It would have to be shown that Wittgenstein does not teach us differences, that he does not show us the city with no main road. For Wittgenstein, there is a fundamental vocational difference between a philosopher who is not a citizen of any community of ideas, and a philosopher whose use of philosophy subserves such a community.[16] The difference is shown in *the kind* of sensibility we find in Wittgenstein's work, particularly in doing justice to perspectives that are not his own.[17] Such a sensibility is precisely what is needed if philosophy, in the academy, is to get beyond apologetics, either for or against, religion.

In this chapter, I have tried to do two things. First, I have tried to relate Wittgensteinianism in the philosophy of religion to some central issues in the history of philosophy that Wittgenstein discussed. Second, I have tried to relate those connections to a wide range of other movements in contemporary philosophy of religion.

Given contemporary philosophical practice, I have also been mindful of the fact that I am probably writing for nonreaders of Wittgenstein. In *that* context, my main concern is with anti-Wittgensteinians who are nonreaders of his work, but whose views of it have been shaped by accusations of nonrealism, relativism, expressivism and fideism,[18] and so on. My closing remarks, adapted from Schleiermacher, are for them: "Let us deal honestly with one another. You do not like [Wittgenstein], we started from that assumption. But in conducting an honest battle against [him] which is not completely without effort, you do not want to have fought against a shadow like the one with which we have struggled" (1996, 21).

NOTES

1. Wolterstorff claims that as a result of Moore's and Russell's interventions against idealism, *metaphysical* realism reasserted itself. But they intervened in the name of *realism*. Wolterstorff uses the terms interchangeably. For my critique of his reading of twentieth-century philosophy, see Phillips (2001a).

2. As a reaction, we have the amusing, and not so amusing, advice against doing philosophy of religion in one's doctoral dissertation, even if it is one's main interest.

3. For a fuller discussion, see Phillips (2000a).

4. For this tradition, see Swinburne (1977, 1979, 1981).

5. For these and other criticisms of Reid, see Winch (1953) and his Oxford B. Phil thesis on Reid (Winch 1951). I made great use of these criticisms in Phillips (2001a). See also Phillips (2004a).

6. For this dispute in relation to Hume, see Gaskin (1988); Butler (1960); Penelhum (1983); Ferreira (1999); Harvey (1999); and Phillips (1999b).

7. For my critique, see Phillips (2000b).

8. For my critique, see Phillips (1998).

9. In what follows I am indebted to Rhees (unpublished ms.). I was equally indebted to Rhees's insights in Phillips (1999a), where there is a parallel discussion.

10. Our primitive reactions, in this case our color reactions, are not the *foundations*

of language. Wittgenstein is not advancing anything like a genetic theory of meaning. For a discussion of this issue, see Malcolm (1982) and Rhees (1997g) incorporated into Rhees (1998) in a wider setting.

11. Aquinas says in *Summa Contra Gentiles*: "Unde relinquitur quod nullo modo est in genere substantiae."

12. In my discussion of *On Certainty* I am indebted to Rhees (2002).

13. I am grateful to Richard Amesbury for pointing this out.

14. See my chapter on Feuerbach (Phillips, 2001b).

15. A proper discussion of the problem of evil needs a book to itself. See Phillips (2004b). For my earlier criticism of contemporary theodicies, see Phillips (1981, 1977), the later essays in Phillips (1991, 1986b), and Phillips (2002a, 2002b). See also Rhees (1997f). But for the profoundest discussion, see Weil (1959).

16. For my discussion of Kierkegaard and Wittgenstein in this context, see Phillips (1999a).

17. For a discussion of this sensibility, see Winch's response in Malcolm (1994).

18. I have relegated the unscholarly term "Wittgensteinian fideism" to a footnote in this context. It is ironic that Wittgenstein, who was not a believer, has had his name used for a view which holds that only religious believers understand religious belief! The original charge of fideism was made in Nielsen (1967). I provided detailed textual refutations in Phillips (1986a). The term disappeared for a while thereafter, but is now back in circulation. I have therefore repeated part of my critique in Phillips (2001b). Some philosophers think that the only consequence of the critique is to arrive at a different definition of "Wittgensteinian fideism," whereas the real task is to overcome an obstacle of the will, not an obstacle of the intellect, and admit that the use of the term was confused from the outset. Will this happen? Of course not.

WORKS CITED

Alston, William. 1991. *Perceiving God.* Ithaca, N.Y.: Cornell University Press.

Austin, J. L. 1962. *Sense and Sensibilia.* Ed G. J. Warnock. Oxford: Clarendon Press.

Ayer, A. J. 1936. *Language, Truth and Logic.* London: Gollancz.

Blond, Philip, ed. 1998. *Post Secular Philosophy: Introduction.* London: Routledge.

Butler, R. J. 1960. "Natural Belief and the Enigma of Hume." *Archiv für Geschichte der Philosophie* 42: 73–100.

Denham, Alison. 2000. "How Long Can You Stay Cool at the Dance?" *Times Literary Supplement,* June 23.

Derrida, Jacques. 1998. *Of Grammatology.* Corrected ed., trans. Gayatri Chakravorty Spivak. Baltimore: Johns Hopkins University Press.

Descartes, René. 1990. *Meditations.* In *The Philosophical Works of Descartes.* Cambridge, England: Cambridge University Press.

Ferreira, M. Jamie. 1999. "Hume's Mitigated Scepticism." In *Religion and Hume's Legacy,* ed. D. Z. Phillips and Timothy Tessin. Basingstoke, England: Macmillan.

Flew, A. G. N., and Alasdair MacIntyre. 1955. *New Essays in Philosophical Theology.* London: S.C.M. Press

Gaskin, J. L. 1988. *Hume's Philosophy of Religion,* 2nd edition. London: Macmillan.

Hacker, P. M. S. 2001. "On Wittgenstein." *Philosophical Investigations* 24: 121–30.

Harvey, Van H. 1999. "Is There Anything Religious about Philo's 'True Religion.' " In *Religion and Hume's Legacy,* ed. D. Z. Phillips and Timothy Tessin. Basingstoke, England: Macmillan.

Hick, John. 1989. *An Interpretation of Religion.* Basingstoke, England: Macmillan.

Holland, R. F. 1954. "The Empiricist Theory of Memory." *Mind* 62: 464–86.

Jones, J. R. 1967. "How Do I Know Who I Am?" *Proceedings of the Aristotelian Society,* supp. 41: 1–18

Jones, O. M. 1927. *Empiricism and Intuitionism in Reid's Common Sense Philosophy.* Princeton: Princeton University Press.

Katz, Steven T. 1978. "Language, Epistemology and Mysticism." In *Mysticism and Philosophical Analysis,* ed. Steven T. Katz. New York: Oxford University Press.

Malcolm, Norman. 1982. "The Relation of Language to Instinctive Behaviour."*Philosophical Investigations* 5: 3–22.

———. 1994. *Wittgenstein: A Religious Point of View.* Ed. with a response by Peter Winch. Ithaca, N.Y.: Cornell University Press.

———. 1995. "Wittgenstein on Language and Rules." In *Wittgensteinian Themes.* Ed. G. H. von Wright. Ithaca, N.Y.: Cornell University Press.

Mounce, H. O. 1999. *Hume's Naturalism.* London: Routledge.

Nielsen, Kai. 1967. "Wittgensteinian Fideism." *Philosophy* 42: 191–201.

Penelhum, Terence. 1983. "Natural Belief and Religious Belief in Hume's Philosophy." *Philosophical Quarterly* 33: 166–81.

Phillips, D. Z. 1970. *Death and Immortality.* London: Macmillan.

———. 1977. "The Problem of Evil." A symposium with Richard Swinburne. In *Reason and Religion,* ed. S. Brown. Ithaca, N.Y.: Cornell University Press.

———. 1981. *The Concept of Prayer.* Oxford: Blackwell. (First published London: Routledge, 1965.)

———. 1986a. *Belief, Change and Forms of Life.* Basingstoke, England: Macmillan.

———. 1986b. *R. S. Thomas: Poet of the Hidden God.* Basingstoke, England: Macmillan.

———. 1991. *From Fantasy to Faith.* Basingstoke, England: Macmillan.

———. 1993a. "On Not Understanding God." In *Wittgenstein and Religion,* ed. D. Z. Phillips. Basingstoke, England: Macmillan.

———. 1993b. "Advice to Philosophers Who Are Christians." In *Wittgenstein and Religion,* ed. D. Z. Phillips. Basingstoke, England: Macmillan.

———. 1998. "Religion, Philosophy and the Academy." *International Journal for Philosophy of Religion* 44: 129–44.

———. 1999a. *Philosophy's Cool Place.* Ithaca, N.Y.: Cornell University Press.

———. 1999b. "Is Hume's 'True Religion' a Religious Belief." In *Religion and Hume's Legacy,* ed. D. Z. Phillips and Timothy Tessin. Basingstoke, England: Macmillan.

———. 2000a. "Epistemic Practices: The Retreat from Reality." In *Recovering Religious Concepts,* ed. D. Z. Phillips. Basingstoke, England: Macmillan.

———. 2000b. "Turning God into One Devil of a Problem." In *Recovering Religious Concepts,* ed. D. Z. Phillips. Basingstoke, England: Macmillan.

———. 2000c. "The World and 'I.' " In *Recovering Religious Concepts,* ed. D. Z. Phillips. Basingstoke, England: Macmillan.

———. 2000d. "Anglo-American Philosophical Culture: Religion and the Reception of

Wittgenstein." In *Recovering Religious Concepts,* ed. D. Z. Phillips. Basingstoke, England: Macmillan.

———. 2001a. " 'What God Himself Cannot Tell Us': Realism versus Metaphysical Realism." *Faith and Philosophy* 18: 483–500.

———. 2001b. *Religion and the Hermeneutics of Contemplation.* Cambridge, England: Cambridge University Press

———. 2002a. "Theism without Theodicy." In *Encountering Evil,* ed. Stephen T. Davis. Louisville, Ky.: Westminster John Knox Press.

———. 2002b. "Reply to My Critics." In *Encountering Evil,* ed. Stephen T. Davis. Louisville, Ky.: Westminster John Knox Press.

———. 2004a. *Religion and Friendly Fire.* Aldershot, England: Ashgate.

———. 2004b. *The Problem of Evil and the Problem of God.* London: SCM Press.

Plantinga, Alvin. 2000. *Warranted Christian Belief.* Oxford: Oxford University Press.

Reid, Thomas. 1843. *An Inquiry into the Human Mind on the Principles of Common Sense.* In *Essays on the Active Powers of the Human Mind.* London: Printed for Thomas Tegg, Cheapside.

Rhees, Rush. 1970. "On Continuity: Wittgenstein's Ideas 1938." In *Discussions of Wittgenstein.* London: Routledge.

———. 1997a. "Belief in God." In *On Religion and Philosophy.* Ed. D. Z. Phillips. Cambridge, England: Cambridge University Press.

———. 1997b. "Natural Theology." In *On Religion and Philosophy.* Ed. D. Z. Phillips. Cambridge, England: Cambridge University Press.

———. 1997c. "Religion and Language." In *On Religion and Philosophy.* Ed. D. Z. Phillips. Cambridge, England: Cambridge University Press.

———. 1997d. "The Ontological Argument and Proof." In *On Religion and Philosophy.* Ed. D. Z. Phillips. Cambridge, England: Cambridge University Press.

———. 1997e. "Death and Immortality." In *On Religion and Philosophy.* Ed. D. Z. Phillips. Cambridge, England: Cambridge University Press.

———. 1997f. "Suffering." In *On Religion and Philosophy.* Ed. D. Z. Phillips. Cambridge, England: Cambridge University Press.

———. 1997g. "Language as Emerging from Instinctive Behaviour." Ed. D. Z. Phillips. *Philosophical Investigations* 20: 1–14.

———. 1998. *Wittgenstein and the Possibility of Discourse.* Ed. D. Z. Phillips. Cambridge, England: Cambridge University Press.

———. 2002. *Wittgenstein's "On Certainty": There Like Our Life.* Ed. D. Z. Phillips. Oxford: Blackwell.

———. 2004. *In Dialogue with the Greeks, Vol. I: The Presocratics and Reality.* Ed. D. Z. Phillips. Aldershot, England: Ashgate.

Schleiermacher, Friedrich. 1996. *On Religion: Speeches to its Cultured Despisers.* Ed. Richard Crouter. Cambridge, England: Cambridge University Press.

Sherry, Patrick. 1982. "Are Spirits Bodiless Persons?" *Neue Zeitschrift für Systematische Theologie und Religionsphilosophie* 24: 35–52.

Sprague, Elmer. 1962. "On Professor Tillich's Ontological Question." *International Philosophical Quarterly* 2: 81–91.

Stroud, Barry. 1991. *The Significance of Philosophical Scepticism.* Oxford: Clarendon Press.

Swinburne, Richard. 1977. *The Coherence of Theism.* Oxford: Clarendon Press.

———. 1979. *The Existence of God.* Oxford: Clarendon Press.

———. 1981. *Faith and Reason*. Oxford: Clarendon Press.

Wainwright, William J. 1995. "Theism, Metaphysics and D. Z. Phillips." *Topoi* 14: 87–93.

———, ed. 1996. *God, Philosophy, and Academic Culture*. Atlanta: Scholars Press.

Warnock, G. J. 1969. *Berkeley*. London: Penguin Books.

Weil, Simone. 1959. "The Love of God and Affliction." In *Waiting on God*. London: Fontana Books.

Williams, C. J. F. 1997. "Being." In *Companion to Philosophy of Religion*, ed. Philip Quinn and Charles Taliaferro. Oxford: Blackwell.

Winch, Peter. 1951. "Thomas Reid." B. Phil thesis, University of Oxford.

———. 1953. "The Notion of 'Suggestion' in Thomas Reid's Theory of Perception." *Philosophical Quarterly* 3: 327–41.

———. 1994. Response in Norman Malcolm, *Wittgenstein: A Religious Point of View?*, ed. Peter Winch, Ithaca, N.Y.: Cornell University Press.

———. 1996. "Doing Justice or Giving the Devil His Due." In *Can Religion Be Explained Away?*, ed. D. Z. Phillips. Basingstoke, England: Macmillan.

———. 1998. "Judgements, Propositions and Practices." *Philosophical Investigations* 21: 189–202.

———. 2001. "What Can Philosophy Say to Religion?" *Faith and Philosophy* 18: 416–30.

Wittgenstein, Ludwig. 1953. *Philosophical Investigations*. Oxford: Blackwell.

———. 1969. *On Certainty*. Oxford: Blackwell.

Wolterstorff, Nicholas. 1996. "Between the Pincers of Increased Diversity and Supposed Irrationality." In *God, Philosophy, and Academic Culture*, ed. William J. Wainwright. Atlanta: Scholars Press.

———. 2000. "Analytic Philosophy of Religion: Retrospect and Prospect." In *Perspectives in Contemporary Philosophy of Religion*, ed. Tommi Lehtonen and Timo Koistinen. Helsinki: Luther-Agricola Society.

FOR FURTHER READING

Bouwsma, O. K. 1984, *Without Proof or Evidence*. Ed. R. Hustwit. Lincoln: University of Nebraska Press.

Cavell, Stanley. 1976. "Kierkegaard's *On Authority*." In *Must We Mean What We Say?* Cambridge, England: Cambridge University Press.

Malcolm, Norman. 1960. "Anselm's Ontological Arguments." *Philosophical Review* 69: 41–62.

——— 1964. "Is It a Religious Belief That God Exists?" In *Faith and the Philosophers*, ed. J. Hick. London: Macmillan.

Moore, Gareth. 1998. *Believing in God*. (Edinburgh: T & T Clark.

Phillips, D. Z. 1995. *Faith after Foundationalism*. Boulder, Colo.: Westview Press.

Poteat, W. H. 1959a. "Birth, Suicide and the Doctrine of Creation: An Exploration of Analogies." *Mind* 68: 309–21.

——— 1959b. "I Will Die." *Philosophical Quarterly* 9: 46–58.

Rhees, Rush. 1998. *Wittgenstein and the Possibility of Discourse.* Ed. D. Z. Phillips. Cambridge, England: Cambridge University Press.

———— 1999a. *Moral Questions.* Ed. D. Z. Phillips. Basingstoke, England: Macmillan.

———— 1999b. *Discussions of Simone Weil.* Ed. D. Z. Phillips. New York: State University of New York Press.

Winch, Peter. 1972. "Understanding a Primitive Society." In *Ethics and Action.* London: Routledge and Kegan Paul.

———— "Can a Good Man Be Harmed?" In Winch 1972.

———— "Ethical Reward and Punishment." In Winch 1972.

———— 1987. "Meaning and Religious Language." In *Trying to Make Sense.* Oxford: Blackwell.

———— "Who Is My Neighbour?" In Winch 1987.

———— "Ceasing to Exist." In Winch 1987.

Wittgenstein, Ludwig. 1966. *Lectures and Conversations on Aesthetics, Psychology and Religious Belief.* Ed. Cyril Barrett. Oxford: Blackwell.

———— 1993. "A Lecture in Ethics." In *Ludwig Wittgenstein: Philosophical Occasions,* ed. James Klagge and Alfred Nordmann. Indianapolis: Hackett.

CHAPTER 19

CONTINENTAL PHILOSOPHY OF RELIGION

MEROLD WESTPHAL

THE term *continental philosophy* is not much used on the European continent. In the English-speaking world it is used to signify (1) thinkers, texts, and traditions from the European continent, especially France and Germany, from German idealism to the present, and (2) the work of Anglophone thinkers primarily engaged in the critical analysis and creative development of those thinkers, texts, and traditions. The term regularly implies a contrast with "analytic philosophy," a widely used if not very precise name for the dominant form(s) of Anglo-American philosophy, whose provenance is, for the most part and not surprisingly, Anglo-American.

There is no continental equivalent to the analytic philosophy of religion industry, with a large number of practitioners and a standard list of topics to be discussed. One will look in vain for much discussion of the proofs for the existence of God, the problem of evil as a counterproof, the divine attributes, the evidential value of religious experience, and so forth. But if "continental philosophy of religion" does not signify a well-defined subdiscipline, richly articulated in standard subdivisions, it does point to the interesting and important things continental philosophers have to say about religion and theology.

It is not possible to do justice to this dimension of continental philosophy in a single essay. The nineteenth century alone gives us, among others, the work of Hegel, Feuerbach, Marx, Kierkegaard, and Nietzsche, which continues to inspire and provoke contemporary discussion and debate. To reduce the task from impossible to merely daunting, this essay will limit itself (with one major exception, Heidegger) to the latter half of the twentieth century and to the work of thinkers from the European continent. Even with these restrictions selection means substantial omission, and the reader will get but a sampling of a richer and more complex domain.

PHENOMENOLOGY AND RELIGION: HEIDEGGER

During the twentieth century no tradition has been more widely pervasive in continental philosophy than phenomenology. So it is not surprising that the question of the relation of philosophy to religion should be asked in terms of phenomenology. Husserl, the founder of the phenomenological movement (though not without precedent; see Spiegelberg 1971), had little to say about God and religion, and it is just as well. For the Cartesianism of his most influential works, namely, the demand for utter clarity and absolute certainty, might well be seen as a methodological bias against any religious subject matter. Because of (1) Heidegger's hermeneutical critique of Husserl's Cartesianism, (2) his own religious journey, and (3) the important role of religious texts in his early philosophical formation (Kisiel 1993; Van Buren 1994), it is appropriate that he should be the one to pose the question. In 1927, the year he published *Being and Time* (1962), he gave a lecture at Tübingen entitled "Phenomenology and Theology." Rejecting the "popular" view that they represent two competing worldviews, addressing the same subject matter from the standpoints of reason and faith, respectively, Heidegger distinguishes them as two radically different sciences. Phenomenology is the ontological science, whereas theology is one of the ontic, positive sciences of what is given and, as such, more like chemistry and mathematics than philosophy (1998, 40–41)!

As a positive science, Christian theology (the only theology Heidegger discusses) has its own distinctive content, its *positum*. This is (1) "a mode of human existence," (2) given by revelation to faith, and (3) centered in "Christ, the crucified God." It turns out that the "popular" view, according to which theology has a link to faith and revelation not found in philosophy as such, is on target after all. Because theology arises from faith and intends to give rise to faith, and because faith is "not some more or less modified type of knowing" but, as Luther said, is "permitting ourselves to be seized by the things we do not see," it follows that theology "is not speculative knowledge of God." Precisely because of this relation to revelation and the faith to which it gives rise, theology is "a fully autonomous ontic science" (Heidegger 1998, 43–50).

But no sooner has Heidegger said this than he seems to take it back. Even if faith does not need philosophy, theology as the science of faith does. Not, to be sure, to establish or disclose its content, but to clarify its conceptual articulation. Husserl had hoped that phenomenology could be the foundational queen of the sciences, not by dictating their methods or results but by developing regional ontologies that would clarify the meaning of their domains. Heidegger still thinks in these terms. The ontic sciences interpret their distinctive regions under the guidance of an implicit ontology. As the ontological science, phenomenology's task is both to make the ontological dimension explicit and to subject it to phenomenological critique by asking whether our (pre)understanding of the being of a certain kind of beings corresponds to the way they are actually given to us. Theology is no exception. Its concepts have "as their *ontological* determinants meanings which are pre-Christian and which can thus be grasped purely rationally," in other words, apart from revelation and faith. This is because "All theological concepts necessarily contain that understanding of being which is constitutive of human Dasein [Heidegger's name for the beings we are, meaning being-there], insofar as it exists at all." Thus, for example, the theological concept of sin needs to turn to the phenomenological interpretation of guilt, entirely apart from revelation and faith as a "pre-Christian" and "purely rational" concept, so the latter can "function as a guide for the theological explication of sin" (1998, 50–52).

Almost immediately Heidegger replaces this notion of guidance with the stronger notion of correction and no fewer than nine times describes the relation of theology to philosophy as one of receiving correction (1998, 52–53). Both in terms of Heidegger's example and in terms of the general principle involved, this must appear to theology to be an unfriendly takeover. According to Heidegger's phenomenological/ontological analysis of guilt as the call of conscience, the call is Dasein's call to itself and it says nothing, has no specific content (1962, 319–26). It "formally points out the ontological character of *the* region of Being to which the concept of sin as a *concept of existence* must necessarily adhere" (1998, 52). But how can a concept this formal, devoid of any reference to God and to any behavioral or attitudinal content, serve to "correct" the theological understanding of sin? Why *must* theology necessarily adhere to a conceptuality that is at once purely formal and pre-Christian?

More generally speaking, does not the claim of philosophy to preside over ideas that are not merely "pre-Christian" but "purely rational" betray that Heidegger, for all the postmodern hype surrounding his work, is an unrepentant child of the Enlightenment, disavowing out of one side of his mouth its illegitimate claim to intellectual hegemony over anything bearing the marks of tradition, particularity, and historical contingency, while out of the other side insisting on maintaining monopoly rights for philosophy as pure reason? No wonder Jean-Luc Marion (1991) complains so bitterly. Heidegger would free theology from the clutches of metaphysics (read: Cartesian modernity) only to impose on it a thralldom just as pagan and idolatrous (25–107).

Without questioning the force of Marion's critique, two points can be made in Heidegger's defense. First, he says that although it belongs to the essence of philosophy to serve as this ontological corrective for all the other ontic, positive sciences, this is not true in the case of theology. Heidegger does not say why, but perhaps the reason is the relation of theology to revelation and faith, which distinguishes it from the other sciences and makes its autonomy vis-à-vis philosophy unique. In any case, the demand that philosophy *must* serve as a corrective to theology "is not made by philosophy as such but rather by theology" (1998, 53). In other words, it is for theological reasons that theology turns to philosophy for "correction."

But what might these reasons be? This second point is crucial. Ontology *"functions only as a corrective to the ontic, and in particular pre-Christian, meanings of basic theological concepts"* (1998, 52–53). According to Heidegger's hermeneutics, every interpretation is guided by preunderstanding. Thus, the Christian theologian, who hasn't dropped straight down from heaven, brings to the task of interpreting the Christian faith presuppositions from "pre-Christian" sources, some of which may be quite pagan or secular. Examples might include the impact of Greek philosophy or scientific rationalism or materialistic consumerism on the culture in which the theologian has been socialized. In focusing especially on the way these pre-Christian (if not purely rational) ideas have found their way into theological thinking, Heidegger suggests that theologians might want all the help they can get in weeding out the ways secular presuppositions may have distorted their interpretations. Read this way, Heideggerian ontology does not dictate the language theologians must use but offers a tool they can use when and insofar as they find it useful by their own criteria.

But Heidegger himself keeps us from becoming too irenic about the relationship. The theologian is inspired by faith and in the service of faith, which is "the mortal enemy of the *form of existence* which is an essential part of *philosophy*" insofar as there is a fundamental opposition "between faithfulness and a human's free appropriation of his whole Dasein" (1998, 53). Once again Heidegger identifies with the Enlightenment and its aspiration toward the autonomy of human thought. Theology should be aware of the danger of turning to Heidegger for help. It is like going to the Philistines to sharpen one's tools (1 Samuel 13:19–22) or, to use an example more popular with spiritual writers, like plundering the Egyptians (Exodus 12:33–36). Some of the jewelry given to the Israelites doubtless ended up adorning the tabernacle, but some if it ended up as the golden calf (Exodus 32)!

Phenomenology and Religion: Ricoeur

Since Paul Ricoeur does not simply identify phenomenology with philosophy, he poses a somewhat different question: What is the relation of "purely descriptive phenomenology that permits the believing soul to speak" to the religious experience that it "is no longer" and to the philosophy that it "is not yet" (1967, 19, 4). The question about philosophy's relation to religion now involves a triadic rather than a dyadic relation.

In its relation to religion, this descriptive phenomenology involves a hermeneutical distanciation from the "primitive naïveté" or "immediacy of belief" that marks the believing soul (1967, 351). "The philosopher adopts provisionally the motivations and intentions of the believing soul. He does not 'feel' them in their first naïveté; he 're-feels' them in a neutralized mode, in the mode of 'as if.' It is in this sense that phenomenology is a re-enactment in sympathetic imagination" (19). Happily, for purposes of comparison with Heidegger, Ricoeur is also interested in sin and guilt and seeks, in *The Symbolism of Evil*, to reenact the believing soul's confession of fault. More interested in faithfulness than in the science of faith, to use Heidegger's language, he turns not to the theologian but to the believing soul as such and thus to the language of symbol and myth in which confession takes place prior to second-order theological reflection.

But what is the relation of this project to philosophy, which it "is not yet"? Ricoeur understands philosophy as reflection in a double sense: pausing to think things over, and thinking about oneself in the search for self-understanding. But he believes the Cartesian cogito has been shattered in a variety of ways. For example, the Husserlian transcendental ego has been deconstructed by Heidegger's analysis of Dasein as always already constituted by preunderstandings within the hermeneutical circle. We never stand at the origin of meaning but always in medias res, and this has an important methodological consequence. "In contrast to the tradition of the *cogito* and to the pretension of the subject to know itself by immediate intuition, it must be said that we understand ourselves only by the long detour of the signs of humanity posited in cultural works" (Ricoeur 1981, 143; compare 158 and 1970, 42). Descriptive phenomenology is this detour.

But it is only a detour and not the destination. We must pass "from a simple 're-enactment' without belief to autonomous 'thought.'" This involves the need to pose the question of truth (Do I believe that?) that is "unceasingly eluded" in the comparative phenomenology of which Éliade (and, to be sure, Ricoeur himself) is such a good example (1967, 353). But philosophy is not content merely to pose the question of truth. It seeks to be "pure reflection" that "makes no appeal to any myth or symbol; in this sense it is a direct exercise of rationality" (347). But, given the shattering of the cogito and the necessity of the hermeneutical detour, are these notions of "autonomous thought," "pure reflection," and "direct rationality" anything more than pipe dreams? Are they even legitimate as regulative ideals?

Surprisingly, Ricoeur thinks the question is a difficult one. He has abundantly made it impossible to answer, Yes, reflection can be autonomous, pure, and direct, but he is reluctant to give up on these traditional ideals. So his slogan, "The symbol gives rise to thought," is a highly nuanced negative reply. Beyond the detour, he wants reflection to be "a creative interpretation of meaning, faithful . . . to the gift of meaning from the symbol, and faithful also to the philosopher's oath to seek understanding." Reflection needs what the symbol gives. "There is no philosophy without presuppositions . . . But what the symbol gives rise to is thinking. After the gift, positing . . . It is this articulation of thought given to itself in the realm of symbols and of thought positing and thinking that constitutes the critical point of our whole enterprise" (1967, 348–49).

Ricoeur seeks "a revivification of philosophy through contact with the fundamental symbols of consciousness . . . In short, it is by *interpreting* that we can *hear* again." But we do so in a hermeneutical circle in which "we must believe in order to understand." But the philosopher as such is not the believing soul, and the reflection of which Ricoeur speaks is not theology. So just what is the nature of this necessarily presupposed "belief"? We have just heard it described as "contact" and as "hearing again." Ricoeur gives several other accounts. For example, "The interpreter does not get near to what his text says unless he lives in the *aura* of the meaning he is inquiring after." Or again, quoting Bultmann, "The presupposition of all understanding is the vital relation of the interpreter to the things about which the text speaks directly or indirectly." What is required is "a kinship of thought with what the life [embodied in the work being interpreted] aims at— in short, of thought with the thing which is in question" (1967, 351–52).

None of this language signifies the belief of the believing soul. But even this very weak "belief" that enables the phenomenologist to understand signifies a hermeneutical circle that must be transcended by reflection. Awareness of the need for the detour and of the circle it involves "is to instigate [the philosopher] to think with the symbols as a *starting-point*, and no longer *in* the symbols." I get beyond this starting point and the hermeneutical circle it involves by making a wager. "I wager that I shall have a better understanding of man and of the bond between the being of man and the being of all beings if I follow the *indication* of symbolic thought." The task, then, is to verify that wager as follows: "The symbol, used as a means of detecting and deciphering human reality, will have been verified by its power to raise up, to illuminate, to give order to that region of human experience [in this case, the confession of fault] . . . beginning from this contingency and restrictedness of a culture that has hit upon these symbols rather than others, philosophy endeavors, through reflection and speculation, to disclose the rationality of its foundation" (1967, 355, 357).

But we must ask: Power to illuminate whom, disclosure of rationality to whom? If it is to the believing souls already within the contingent and restricted community that defines itself in terms of the symbols in question, reflection would seem to be theology pure and simple. If it is to believing souls from other religious communities as well, so that Christians receive illumination from Muslim symbols and Jews perceive the rationality embodied in Buddhist symbols, it would seem that reflection is still theological, though of a more ecumenical sort. If what one writes is persuasive only to those within the circle of certain presuppositions, it is not clear that reflection has transcended the hermeneutical circle in which it began. But can one assume that the rationality of one's foundation or starting point will be perceivable independently of the reader's own starting point without an overdose of wishful thinking and self-deception?

Ricoeur acknowledges that the question of how to get from descriptive phenomenology to "reflection in the full sense" is not fully answered in *The Symbolism of Evil* and the work that precedes it, *Fallible Man* (1965). He promises a solution in "the third part of this work" (1967, 19). But when he turns in *Freud and Philosophy* to "take up again the problem left unresolved at the end of my *Symbolism and Evil*, namely the relation between a hermeneutics of symbols and a philosophy of concrete reflection" (1970, xii), he does not so much clarify the unresolved tensions of the earlier work as introduce another necessary detour for reflection: suspicion. What the phenomenology of religion learns from the masters of suspicion, Marx, Nietzsche, and Freud, is that the believing soul must not only be allowed to speak but also subjected to hostile cross-examination as well. Symbols do not disappear, since for Freud both dreams and obsessive neurosis, his models for religious belief and practice, respectively, are highly symbolic. But now one interprets symbols not as traces of the truth that sets us free but as disguises of the self-deceptions that keep us in bondage. Because Freudian theory is an especially dramatic shattering of the Cartesian/Kantian/Husserlian cogito, Ricoeur speaks of it as an antiphenomenology that is an essential corrective to any phenomenology that clings to the rationalism or idealism of those projects (1970, 117–22, 424–28). Behind the back of the cogito and keeping it from being a pure origin of meaning are not only its embeddedness in cultural contingency but also its internally generated self-deceptions.

Beyond a simple reading of *The Future of an Illusion* (1958), Ricoeur shows how the entire Freudian corpus presents a hermeneutics of suspicion that is of major importance for the phenomenology of religion. Moreover, he clearly recognizes that Freud (and, by implication, Marx and Nietzsche) overreach themselves when they claim that the story they tell us is the whole story of religion, that it is nothing but wish fulfillment, ideology, or the will to power. His hypothesis is "that psychoanalysis is necessarily iconoclastic, regardless of the faith or nonfaith of the psychoanalyst, and that this 'destruction' of religion can be the counterpart of a faith purified of all idolatry. Psychoanalysis as such cannot go beyond the necessity of iconoclasm. This necessity is open to a double possibility, that of faith and that of nonfaith, but the decision about these two possibilities does not rest with psychoanalysis . . . The question remains open for every man whether the destruction of idols is without remainder; this question no longer falls within the competency of psychoanalysis" (1970, 230, 235).

Ricoeur does not develop the link between suspicion and "a faith purified of all idolatry." Implicit in this latter notion is the idea that the believing soul, and not just the modern atheist, as in Marx, Nietzsche, and Freud, has powerful motives for engaging in the hermeneutics of suspicion, not just of "them," whether "they" are the irreligious or the differently religious, but of oneself and one's own religious community. Moreover, this notion reminds us of important historical antecedents to the suspicion that has played such a key role in modern atheism. The prophetic dimension of biblical religion, both in the Hebrew scriptures and in the New Testament, is the true birthplace of the hermeneutics of suspicion. The prophets know that "the heart is devious above all else" (Jeremiah 17:9) and that this is no less true of the covenant people of God than of their neighbors; and the gospels present the disciples of Jesus as driven by devious desires (Westphal 1998).

But it would be shameless ingratitude to complain about this lacuna without recognizing our enormous debt to Ricoeur for showing us the importance of the hermeneutics of suspicion for the phenomenology of religion or to complain about the unresolved question about transcending the hermeneutical circle in pure reflection without acknowledging the methodological and substantive gift he has given us in a descriptive phenomenology of the images and narratives that shape the self-understanding of the believing soul. If Husserl's ideal of phenomenology as rigorous science looks like a methodological bias against the whole region of religious experience and belief, Ricoeur's hermeneutical phenomenology represents a double openness. The hermeneutical turn itself, which we can call the hermeneutics of finitude, with its emphasis on the embeddedness of human understanding in contingent cultural constructions, is open to a theology of human createdness, and the expansion of this to incorporate a hermeneutics of suspicion is open to a theology of human fallenness. But Ricoeur develops the double detour through the texts and subtexts of the religious life without appeal to religious belief or theological principle as norms.

PHENOMENOLOGY AND RELIGION:
JANICAUD AND MARION

For Heidegger the question concerned the relation of (philosophy as) phenomenology to (religion as) theology. For Ricoeur it was a question of a phenomenology of religion that was no longer religious belief and not yet philosophical reflection. Like Ricoeur, Jean-Luc Marion turns phenomenology in the direction of religion prior to theological reflection, but the relation of this phenomenology to theology is made an issue by those who accuse it of being theology in disguise. The loudest such complaint comes from Dominique Janicaud in a 1991 book entitled *The Theological Turn in French Phenomenology* (2000). He argues that Emmanuel Levinas is the new Socrates, who corrupts the youth—in particular, Marion, Jean-Louis Chrétien, and Michel Henry—by allowing what is presented as phenomenology to be contaminated by theological commitment. In the work of Levinas, "phenomenology has been taken hostage by a theology that does not want to say its name . . . The dice are loaded and choices made; faith rises majestically in the background. The reader, confronted by the blade of the absolute, finds him- or herself in the position of a catechumen who has no other choice than to penetrate the holy words and lofty dogmas . . . the only response [to the reader's questions] could be a reference to the initial presuppositions: 'Take it or leave it' " (43, 27–28).

Levinas' work is of special importance to ethics but not clearly to philosophy of religion. He talks, to be sure, about God, but when all the constraints he places on God-talk are taken seriously it is no longer clear that God is anything more than the depth dimension of the human Other in terms of which I am responsible to and for my neighbor as the widow, the orphan, and the stranger. But Janicaud clearly intends this critique to apply to the corrupted sons as well as to the corrupting father, and, since Marion's phenomenology of religion has had a broader impact than that of his brothers, Chrétien and Henry, and since his God-talk is not ambiguous in the manner of Levinas', it is his work we can look at in the light of Janicaud's critique. If there is any excuse for seeing his phenomenology as theology in disguise, it is that Marion is also a theologian, who admits "the insurpassable primacy of Christian revelation" (2001, 20). But if one is willing, it is not too difficult to distinguish his phenomenology from his theology.

Perhaps this is clearest in relation to Janicaud's complaint that in the theological turn French phenomenology abandons Husserl's ideal of rigorous science and the complementary idea of the philosopher as a neutral observer. But this ideal is radically compromised by the hermeneutical turn in which intuition is supplanted by interpretation and seeing is recognized always to be a seeing-as not dictated by the object "out there." In the give and take of experience, the given is constituted by the mode in which it is taken. This turn takes place in the later writings of Husserl, in spite of his desperate attempt to sustain his earlier ideal. It also occurs, as Janicaud recognizes, in Heidegger, Merleau-Ponty, and Ricoeur, none of whom are accused of a hidden theological agenda. Janicaud acknowledges that fruitful work can be done by such phenomenological heretics, but wishes to restrict the term phenomenology to projects that retain the original ideal of rigorous science and philosophical neutrality. But apart from the fact that this appears to be little more than a nostalgic, personal preference, it is not clear that this ideal can be affirmed from a neutral standpoint rather than from within a hermeneutical circle laden with the presuppositions of a tradition we might call Enlightenment objectivism. The idea of philosophy without presuppositions is, unfortunately, not without its own presuppositions.

This, however, is not Marion's own defense. He does not overtly espouse the hermeneutical turn, and though he does not explicitly fly the flag of rigorous science, he is more nearly Husserlian than either Heidegger or Ricoeur on this point. He presents his phenomenological analyses of the distinction between idol and icon, of the saturated phenomenon, and of the pure form of the call (about which more shortly) in the full anticipation that their persuasiveness will not depend on the theological position of the reader. He expects any careful observer to be able to see what he is pointing to.

There is another way in which the "neutrality" of Marion's phenomenology can be seen. Janicaud thinks that the theological turn means that the dice are loaded and the outcome predetermined. Correspondingly, he thinks certain possibilities are precluded at the outset. Thus, in contrasting Levinas unfavorably with Merleau-Ponty, he claims that the latter "excludes nothing, but opens our regard to the depth of the world." For phenomenology "the open field is that of the entire human experience" (2000, 27, 94–95). But this is Marion's norm as well. For him "it is an essential of phenomenology that the a posteriori makes it possible and therefore that no forbidden a priori predetermines it," to which he adds his own slogan, "It is forbidden to forbid!" (1997, 289). As we shall see, precisely this principle is the reason he finds it necessary to go beyond the phenomenologies of Husserl and Heidegger to what he calls the "third reduction" and the "pure form of the call."

On another, closely related, point Marion gives Janicaud nothing to complain about methodologically. In the "theological turn" the latter sees "strict treason of the reduction" and thus the abandonment of the idea that phenomenology should be "a space of possible truths" (2000, 27, 94, emphasis added). He has in mind the phenomenological reduction, the epochē, in which the natural standpoint is bracketed or suspended and with it the question of the empirical actuality of what is given to consciousness. Once again, Marion is in full agreement: "Between phenomenology and theology the frontier passes between revelation as possibility and revelation as historicity. Between these two domains there is no possible danger of confusion" (1997, 293; compare 280). Speaking of the phenomenon that is central to mystical theology, he sees the task of phenomenology as conceiving "the formal possibility of the phenomenon which seems to demand an 'absence of divine names' and our entering into the Name. Let this be noted: We have said 'to conceive its formal possibility' and nothing more than this possibility, since phenomenology cannot, and therefore must not, venture to make any decision about the actuality of such a phenomenon—this question is entirely beyond its scope. Phenomenology is to make decisions only about the type of phenomenality which would render this phenomenon thinkable" (1999, 39).

Beyond these methodological considerations, Marion's phenomenology is substantive. It involves a revision of the subject-object relation as portrayed by Husserl in terms of the correlation of noesis (intentional act) and noema (intentional object). In two of his theological works (1991 and 2001), Marion presents a phenomenological distinction between the idol and the icon. The distinction is theologically neutral since it does not concern the content of the intentional object but rather the mode in which it is intended. It follows, of course, that the same content could be an idol in one situation and an icon in another. An object of presumptive religious significance is an idol when the gaze comes to rest on it, assuming that it is fully present to the gaze and that there is no need to think about that which has surpassed and escaped the gaze. The (re)presentation is fully adequate to what is given. In this way, the object becomes a mirror of the gaze, which in turn becomes the measure of the object. Whatever my net doesn't catch isn't a fish. The icon is just the opposite. It is apprehended as that which cannot be fully grasped by the gaze but always exceeds its constituting activity. This does not make the icon a sign, for what is given in the icon does not point beyond itself to something other than itself, but rather to itself as exceeding its givenness. Marion argues that the distinction between idol and icon applies to our concepts just as much as to our images.

The notion of an icon is elaborated by the notion of the saturated phenomenon. Because physical objects are given to vision in perspectives or aspects (*Abschattungen*), it might seem that every visible is an icon. But, drawing on Kant and Husserl, Marion draws a distinction. On Husserl's analysis of ordinary perception, the idea or intention of the object always exceeds what is given in intuition, since I can never observe an object from every possible perspective, though I intend it as having those aspects not yet given to me. Similarly, in the case of what Kant calls the rational idea, no experience (read: intuition) can be given that is adequate to the concept (for example, "God"). In both cases, adequation fails because intuition is lacking. Marion asks, "To the phenomenon that is supposed to be poor in intuition can we not oppose a phenomenon that is saturated with intuition . . . a phenomenon in which intuition would give *more, indeed unmeasurably more*, than intention ever would have intended or foreseen?

... but it is no longer a matter of the non-adequation of the (lacking) intuition that leaves a (given) concept empty; it is a matter, conversely, of a failure of the (lacking) concept that leaves the (overabundantly given) intuition blind" (2000, 195–96). In ordinary perception and the rational idea, adequation fails because intuition can never catch up with the concept; with the saturated phenomenon, it fails because the concept can never catch up with intuition. (N.B. Marion speaks the Husserlian language of intuition rather than the hermeneutical language of interpretation.) One might say that the saturated phenomenon is one that gives itself as an icon.

Perhaps it would be better to say "in the iconic mode," since the saturated phenomenon is not necessarily of religious import. Marion draws heavily on Kant's *Critique of Judgement* in developing this notion, and in a certain sense it is Kant's aesthetic idea, the representation of the beautiful or sublime, in contrast to the rational idea of the *Critique of Pure Reason*, that is the paradigmatic saturated phenomenon. But other examples include historical events, the face of the beloved, and theophany. This last, of course, is what makes the saturated phenomenon important for the phenomenology of religion.

The icon and saturated phenomenon are not Husserlian noemata, intentional objects constituted by the intentional acts of the I or ego, whether transcendental or not. We have, rather, a reversed intentionality in which the I is constituted by that at which it looks. For it discovers itself to be more seen than seer. Thus, "the icon opens in a face that gazes at our gazes ... here our gaze becomes the optical mirror of that at which it looks only by finding itself more radically looked at" (Marion 1991, 19–22). Similarly, the theophanic saturated phenomenon involves "the paradox that an invisible gaze visibly envisages me and loves me" (2000, 215; compare 208–11).

This reversal of intentionality is more fully developed in the third dimension of Marion's phenomenology of religion. In his analysis of the pure form of the call, he reinterprets the "subject" of religious experience so as to accord with the revised understanding of the "object." Developing the notion that phenomenology ought to be open to the whole range of human experience ("It is forbidden to forbid"), Marion asks what gets excluded in Husserlian and Heideggerian phenomenology. For Husserl, the phenomenological reduction reduces experience to the transcendental ego as constituting intentionality and the objects constituted within its horizon. "It thus excludes from givenness everything that does not let itself be led back to objectity [*sic*]" (1998, 204). Heidegger reduces experience to Dasein as concretely engaged being-in-the-world and its encounter with the phenomenon of being through its involvement with beings as a whole within the horizon of time. This means, as Heidegger explicitly makes clear, that the question of being has priority over the question of God. But this excludes the possibility that our understanding of being should be derived from our understanding of

God. The God who must conform to Dasein's prior understanding of being is an idol (1991, 37–43). Dasein is the measure and God is the mirror image of Dasein's understanding.

Marion's goal is simple enough, at least to state: "To think God without any conditions, not even that of Being" (1991, 45). To that end he seeks a third reduction that allows for a subject more open than the transcendental ego or Dasein and thus not restricted to the horizons of objectivity or being. The subject is now the *interloqué*, the one addressed, "an auditor preceded and instituted by the call which is still absolute because indeterminate" (1998, 204). Because he develops this notion in dialogue with the later Heidegger's notion of the call of Being (*Anspruch des Seins*), Marion also speaks of the interloqué as *der Angesprochene* (the one claimed, appealed to). But for this subject, the "object" is a another subject, the as yet unspecified caller. What is no longer excluded is the possibility of being claimed, or, in Levinasian terms, of responsibility.

But this is not theology. While describing a possible experience excluded by other phenomenologies, this analysis does not make the theological move of naming the caller. That which lays claim to me might be God, but it also might be Being, or the Other, or the Tribe (ethnic nationalism), or the Family, or the Party, or the Environment, or Whatever. Marion rejects "the illusory presupposition that it is necessary to name the instance that claims in order to suffer its convocation. Now, following the order of a strict phenomenological description, the reverse happens: I recognize myself as *interloqué* well *before* having consciousness or knowledge . . . especially of what leaves me *interloqué*" (1998, 202).

Marion's phenomenology of the icon and the saturated phenomenon are about the gaze, and his "third reduction" is about the call. As in Augustine's *Confessions* and in Levinas' *Totality and Infinity*, vision is trumped by the voice. This means that transcendence, including the transcendence of God, is not so much to be understood in terms of an "object" that I can locate within my field of "vision," but in terms of a "subject" within the sound of whose "voice" I find myself.

THE CRITIQUE OF ONTOTHEOLOGY: OVERCOMING METAPHYSICS

Marion regularly contrasts phenomenology with metaphysics. It is phenomenology that can both keep the philosophy of religion from lapsing into *metaphysica specialis* under the domination of the principle of sufficient reason and keep theology from playing the same game with the help of revelation. We hear here an echo of a central theme in the later work of Heidegger: overcoming metaphysics or, more specifically, overcoming metaphysics in its ontotheological constitution.

In the 1949 introduction to *What Is Metaphysics?* entitled "The Way Back into the Ground of Metaphysics" (1998), Heidegger argues that metaphysics needs to be overcome because in its interpretation of beings it forgets being. Aristotle sets out to think being as such, but to do so finds it necessary to think the Highest Being, God. In this way, ontology becomes theology, or rather, ontotheology. Reminding us that many different beings can play the role of Highest Being, Heidegger sees ontotheologically constituted metaphysics as a tradition stretching from Anaxagoras to Nietzsche, with Aristotle, Leibniz, and Hegel as high points. As the Highest Being becomes the key to the whole of being, philosophy remains fixated on beings and forgets being, and this is bad for philosophy, whose task, according to Heidegger, is to think being.

But it is also bad for theology, and this for two reasons. First, there is the Heideggerian reason, expressed most emphatically in the "Letter on Humanism": "Only from the truth of being can the essence of the holy be thought. Only from the essence of the holy is the essence of divinity to be thought. Only in the light of the essence of divinity can it be thought or said what the word 'God' is to signify" (1998, 267). Here again the question arises as to why theology should accept this hegemony of philosophy and whether the "God" who is understood in terms of a prior understanding of "being," "the holy," and "divinity" will not be an idol.

But Heidegger gives a second Pauline reason why ontotheology is bad for theology. He says he leaves it to the theologians to decide whether it was for better or worse that Christian theology wedded itself so tightly to Greek philosophy. But he reminds them of the Pauline question, "Has not God let the wisdom of this world become foolishness?" (1 Corinthians 1:20) and asks his own question. "Will Christian theology one day resolve to take seriously the word of the apostle and thus also the conception of philosophy as foolishness?" (1998, 288).

These two objections are far from identical. Paul speaks of the foolishness of the cross and of preaching, and it is anything but self-evident that the wisdom of the world was foolishness in his eyes because it focused on beings and forgot being. Given his earlier portrayal of philosophy and the faith that is theology's arche and telos as "mortal enemies," we can assume that Heidegger realizes this. Theology has its own reasons for vigilance in the face of philosophy's seductive charms, whether philosophy appears as metaphysics or as the overcoming of metaphysics for the sake of thinking being.

In 1957 Heidegger published "The Onto-theo-logical Constitution of Metaphysics" as part of *Identity and Difference* (1969). Here he adds a series of different but closely related objections to ontotheology. First, he poses the question, "How does the deity enter into philosophy?" He answers that "the deity can come into philosophy only insofar as philosophy, of its own accord and by its own nature, requires and determines that and how the deity enters into it" (55–56). As we have just seen, there are times when Heidegger himself seems guilty of this arrogance. To think God, theology must first come to philosophy to learn how to think being. But here he has a different mode of philosophy in mind, namely, metaphysics as ontotheology. It allows God into its discourse only in the service of its project, and it is important to be clear just what that project is. It begins with the claim that there is a Highest Being who is the key to the meaning of the whole of being. But beyond that, it is the project of rendering the whole of being intelligible to human understanding with the help of this Highest Being, whether it be Nous, or the Unmoved Mover, or the Triune God, or Spirit, or the Will to Power, or Whatever. For this reason God must function as causa prima, ultima ratio, and causa sui. Under the rule of the principle of sufficient reason, and in modes of thought Heidegger calls representational and calculative reason, God's raison d'être is to enable us to explain everything. "Taken to its extreme, this means that God exists only insofar as the principle of reason holds" (1991, 28). Although Nietzsche still belongs to metaphysics insofar as his Will to Power is itself such a Highest Being, his death of God announces the death of the gods of ontotheology and calls for an overcoming of metaphysics he is unable himself to achieve (Heidegger 1997).

Three further points of critique can be taken as corollaries to this notion that in metaphysics God is reduced to being a means to philosophy's end. First, Heidegger argues that in ontotheology the sense of mystery and awe is lost as the dialectic of concealment in unconcealment is forgotten (1969, 64–67; compare 1998, 233–37). Second, ontotheology plays into the hands of modern technology, "the metaphysics of the atomic age" (1969, 51–52). Presumably, both theology and the faith that is its ground and goal have as good reasons as philosophy (in the mode of trying to think being) to take these two critiques seriously. But Heidegger adds a third, this one relating directly to faith (and thus, indirectly, to theology, but not to philosophy). As we have seen, causa sui "is the right name for the god of philosophy. Man can neither pray nor sacrifice to this god. Before the *causa sui*, man can neither fall to his knees in awe nor can he play music and dance before this god." By becoming useful to philosophy, the God of ontotheology has become religiously useless. Doubtless with Nietzsche in mind, as well as himself, he adds that to abandon such a god "is thus perhaps closer to the divine God. Here this means only: god-less thinking is more open to Him than onto-theo-logic would like to admit" (1969, 72).

Heidegger's critique of ontotheology is often taken to be a critique of theistic discourse as such. After all, does it not posit a Highest Being who is the key to the meaning of the whole of being? But the matter is not that simple. To be sure, the affirmation of a personal Creator, Lawgiver, Judge, and Redeemer who is Love Itself is meant to focus our attention on a being and not on being as such. So theistic God-talk, whether the first-order discourse of the plain believer or the second-order discourse of the theologian, is like metaphysics in failing to be philosophy in Heidegger's sense: it fails to give priority to the question of being. But in spite of his hankering for hegemony over theology, Heidegger gives us, both early and late, compelling reasons for theology (and a fortiori first-order God-talk) to resist this hegemony. Even if we grant that the question of being as such is *the* philosophical question, Heidegger gives us no reason why faith and theology should not make God not only the key to the meaning of the whole of being but also the key to the meaning of being as such.

The second point is, if anything, more important. If faith and theology, like metaphysics, focus attention on a Highest Being, they do not do so metaphysically or ontotheologically. Because they know, at least implicitly, that the wisdom of the world is foolishness so far as God is concerned, whether it be ontotheologically constituted metaphysics or the thinking of being that seeks to overcome metaphysics, and because they want the God of whom they speak to be one before whom we fall to our knees in awe and to whom we can pray and sacrifice and sing and dance, they repel the seductions of ontotheology. They recognize that God remains a mystery to human understanding and resist the temptation to reduce God to a First Explainer in terms of which we can render both the Highest Being and the whole of being fully intelligible to human understanding.

In other words, overcoming ontotheology does not mean the abandonment of theistic discourse (Westphal 2001, especially ch. 1). Heidegger's prime targets are not Augustine and Aquinas but Aristotle and Hegel. The heart of his critique is not directed to the *what* of our God-talk but its *how*. He offers no reasons to discredit belief in a personal Creator, Lawgiver, Judge, and Redeemer who is Love Itself. He only points out that when we allow that God into our discourse only in the service of our project, whatever that project may be, we transubstantiate God. So far as appearances are concerned, it may seem that we are speaking about the same God, perhaps the biblical God, but the substance is totally changed. In this case, however, instead of the second substance having a religious significance not to be found in the first, it is just the opposite. The second substance, the "god" of ontotheology, is without religious import. We might call this "god" an idol, for once we see it for the human construction it is, we are no longer tempted to worship at its temple.

THE RETURN OF THE REPRESSED:
NEGATIVE THEOLOGY AFTER METAPHYSICS

Taking Marion's distinction between phenomenology and metaphysics as a cue, we might notice (1) that the phenomenologies of Heidegger, Ricoeur, and Marion are not ontotheological discourses, (2) that they all have a significant relation to matters religious, but (3) that none is theology. So what about theology after metaphysics? We might take this "after" historically to mean after modernity, the heyday of metaphysics. Or we might take it psychologically to mean after theology has seen the blandishments of ontotheology for what they are and is consciously determined not to be seduced. Our three phenomenologies seem to point theology in the same general direction. Heidegger's emphasizes the importance of mystery and the inseparability of concealing from unconcealment. Ricoeur's emphasizes the shattering of the cogito and the correspondingly necessary detour through the contingencies of the text that reflection must take in the search for self-understanding, including self-understanding before God. Marion's emphasizes the way the sacred appears as always exceeding our cognitive grasp of it and, beyond being an "object" to which we can never quite catch up conceptually, is experienced in reversed intentionality as a subject who calls, thereby decentering the wounded cogito even further. All protest the repression of divine ineffability. A theology that finds it has its own reasons for taking these themes seriously will be epistemically modest, not necessarily in the claims it makes about God but in the metaclaims it makes about those claims. It will remember that just as we do not become purple by talking about violets, our discourse does not become absolute by being about a God we take to be absolute. It will know that even with the help of revelation it does not see God face to face but "in a mirror, dimly" (1 Corinthians 13:12).

In contemporary continental philosophy of religion, a renewed discussion of negative or apophatic theology is the scene of reflection on these matters (see, e.g., Caputo 1997; Carlson 1999; Bulhof and ten Kate 2000; Hart 2000; and Kosky 2001). The primary stimulus has been Jacques Derrida's attempt to distinguish deconstruction from negative theology and Marion's response.

Derrida says that very early on he was "accused . . . of negative theology" (1992a, 74; compare 88–89). His 1968 (1982) response points to two important differences he sees between the negative, if you like skeptical dimension of deconstruction and negative theologies. The latter "are always concerned with disengaging a superessentiality beyond the finite categories of essence and existence, that is, of presence, and always hastening to recall that God is refused the predicate of existence, only in order to acknowledge his superior, inconceivable, and ineffable mode of being. Such a development is not in question here" (6; compare

26). Corresponding to this is the absence of nostalgia or hope for "a lost native country of thought" in which language could express pure presence without difference and thus without absence (27). In other words, unlike negative theologies, which conjoin mysticism with their conceptual skepticism, deconstruction is in the service of no mysticism.

In 1987 (1992a) Derrida repeats these two points. Deconstruction does not rest on the "ontological wager of hyperessentiality that one finds at work both in Dionysius and in Meister Eckhart" (78). Nor does it aspire to "a silent intuition of God . . . the promise of that presence given to intuition or vision. The promise of such a presence often accompanies the apophatic voyage. It is doubtless the vision of a dark light . . . but still it is the immediacy of a presence. Leading to union with God . . . a truth that is not an adequation but an unveiling . . . contact or vision, that pure intuition of the ineffable, that silent union with that which remains inaccessible to speech" (74, 79–80). But now Derrida presents a corollary to his first two points. If deconstruction does not posit a hyperessential God with whom it seeks union, then a fortiori it does not address such a deity in prayer and praise, as does Pseudo-Dionysius.

When Derrida returns to the question of negative theology in 1993 (1995), he points to a further corollary to his first two points. Absent the wager of hyperessentiality, the negativity of deconstruction is not directed toward a particular, transcendent "object" but is about the nature of language as such: "As soon as there are words . . . direct intuition no longer has any chance" (30). Deconstruction could well be identified as nothing but an explication of this thesis.

But within the limits of its special concern, negative theology has long since anticipated this insight. It is "what questions and casts suspicion on the very essence or possibility of language." It is a " 'critique' (for the moment let's not say a 'deconstruction')" of language, the very "Kenōsis of discourse." It is a "sweet rage against language, this jealous anger of language within itself and against itself." For this reason, "I trust no text that is not in some way contaminated with negative theology" (1995, 48–50, 59, 69). By shifting focus from God-talk to language as such, Derrida offers what John Caputo calls a "generalized apophatics" (1997, 41). The claim is quite simply that language is never able to be adequate to what it refers to beyond itself. It may be that for Kant there is an important difference between God and objects of ordinary sense experience. But the absence of adequation is not limited to the theological case, and in this respect deconstruction's "generalized apophatics" is simply a linguistic Kantianism.

This negative semantics, which echoes and extends the apophatic traditions, is a kind of skepticism (neither Pyrrhonian nor Humean). We have seen that it is not in the service of mysticism. If it were in the service of nothing but the deconstructor's desire to be free from all constraints, it would be the cynical nihilism its critics are so eager to assure us it is. But like Hegelian dialectic, deconstruction is not so much something we do as observe. Moreover, as presented by Derrida, it is in the service of the good, at once political and religious. When first distinguishing deconstruction from negative theology, Derrida tells us the former is "the death of the tyrant" (1982, 4). In his later writings three political motifs emerge as especially central: justice, hospitality, and the democracy to come (e.g., 1992b, 1994).

But there is a future dimension to all of these, gathered around the word "Come" (1989). This has two important implications. First, deconstruction is a philosophy of hope that is not yet sight. Not only do we not see justice, hospitality, and genuine democracy as realities, but we do not see clearly just what it would mean for them to be fully actual. In this sense they differ from Kantian regulative ideals, to which they are otherwise akin. Second, Derrida gives a messianic coloring to this futurity (especially in 1994). Deconstruction is the experience of a messianic hope untied to any messianism, the historically specific interpretations of a messianic future grounded in some bible, including the Marxist bible. This "religion without religion" is the attempt to preserve hope for and commitment to a better world outside the framework of established, institutional religion. It is a revival of the Enlightenment ideal of religion within the limits of reason alone, remembering that it appeals to a postmodern rather than a modern conception of reason (1998; see Caputo 1997, ch. 3). For that reason it is a religion of faith rather than knowledge because what it hopes for is not present to it either in actual fact or in conceptual clarity.

In response to the "accusation" that deconstruction is a form of negative theology, Derrida says (1) that its skepticism is more encompassing than that of the apophatic traditions, and (2) that although it is in the service of political ideals that have a religious, that is, messianic, dimension to them, it is not in the service of any mystical union with a hyperessential divinity. Marion takes this latter claim to be the countercharge that negative theology claims "to put us in the presence of God in the very degree to which it denies all presence . . . to deconstruct God and nevertheless to reach him." In this sense, it "remains in submission to the privilege of presence" (1999, 22).

As we have seen, Derrida sees apophatic theology as in the service of an intuitional immediacy which is sheer presence without absence, unconcealment without concealment. But while Derrida, unlike Dionysius, does not aspire to this presence, deconstruction has nothing to say against it. To be sure, Derrida says, "As soon as there are words . . . direct intuition no longer has any chance." But apophaticism agrees and insists that mystical union with the hyperessential is ineffable. Moreover, Derrida is fully aware, as we have seen, that what it aspires to is "that silent union with that which remains inaccessible to speech." Derrida, personally, may doubt the value of mystical experience, but deconstruction provides no arguments against the mystic. It denies immediacy, sheer presence, unconcealment free of all concealment within the boundaries of linguistic meaning and propositional truth. The mystic agrees.

It would seem, then, that Derrida is not accusing apophaticism of being the metaphysics of presence he regularly resists, a "metaphysics" that is more nearly the epistemic claim that our concepts can be adequate to their intended objects, so that neither in terms of meaning nor in terms of fact does the intentional relation of subject to object refer beyond itself. Marion's response is important nevertheless. He reminds us that for Dionysius both affirmation and negation are surpassed by a third way, the *via eminentiae,* and he interprets this third way in terms of his earlier claim that "predication must yield to praise" (1991, 106). This could have two meanings. It could mean that predication must be teleologically suspended in praise, that speech acts of assertion are not ends in themselves but serve to make possible acts of adoration. (It is by forgetting this that ontotheology becomes religiously otiose.) Predication is not abandoned but relativized; it is recontextualized as ancillary to a higher purpose. Or it could mean that predication is abolished to make way for praise, as if the two were somehow mutually exclusive.

For Aquinas, to speak of eminence is to speak of analogical predication. Since it does not give us quidditative knowledge of God it is not "true" in the classical sense of being the *adaequatio intellectus et res.* But it is the right way to talk about God. This would seem to be the view of Dionysius as well, for he does not abandon predication. After reminding us in *The Mystical Theology* that none of our images or ideas is adequate to the reality of the hyperessential Trinity, he spends a great deal more time in *The Divine Names* telling us how to name God (outside of mystical experience) with names given to us in scripture. As with Aquinas, these names signify perfections that God possesses more perfectly than creatures. We attribute them to God analogically on the basis of the imperfect participation in them by creatures. If one asks the point of this predication that does not yield truth as adequation, Dionysius will answer, "Praise." But so far from abandoning predication, he devotes great attention to how to do it properly.

So it is surprising that Marion's interpretation of "predication must yield to praise" is the second one given above. The third way is not only beyond affirmation and negation but beyond true and false as well, so that "one can no longer claim that it means to affirm a predicate of a subject . . . It is no longer a question of naming [the God who is praised] . . . It concerns a form of speech which no longer says something about something . . . but which denies all relevance to predication, rejects the nominative function of names, and suspends the rule of truth's two values" (1999, 26–27).

Beyond the fact that this is hard to reconcile with what Dionysius does in *The Divine Names,* it is highly questionable in its own right. Consider the following words of praise from the *Gloria* of the Mass:

> *tu solus Sanctus*
> *tu solus Dominus*
> *tu solus Altissimus*

Do not all acts of praise, these included, presuppose acts of predication? One need not claim that these predicates, as we understand them, are adequate to the God who is addressed in this praise. But suppose there is no sense in which they are appropriate to God, no sense in which they point us, however imperfectly, in the right direction, no sense in which they are "true" (even if inadequate in the technical sense, though not inadequate to call forth praise). Is not praise then undermined? Is not the speech act inappropriate through futility?

The critique of ontotheology reminds us of the dangers of granting autonomy to assertoric speech acts when it comes to talking about God. Too easily our God-talk can become the attempt to capture God in our conceptual nets rather than a way of offering ourselves to God in adoration, in gratitude, and in obedient service. But the insights of apophaticism do not require the abolition of assertion. Predication must yield to praise not by disappearing but by placing itself humbly at the service of a love that goes beyond knowing.

WORKS CITED

Bulhof, Ilse N., and Laurens ten Kate, eds. 2000. *Flight of the Gods: Philosophical Perspectives on Negative Theology.* New York: Fordham University Press.

Caputo, John D. 1997. *The Prayers and Tears of Jacques Derrida: Religion without Religion.* Bloomington: Indiana University Press.

Carlson, Thomas A. 1999. *Indiscretion: Finitude and the Naming of God.* Chicago: University of Chicago Press.

Derrida, Jacques. 1982. "Différance." In *Margins of Philosophy.* Trans. Alan Bass. Chicago: University of Chicago Press.

———. 1989. "Psyche: Inventions of the Other." In *Reading de Man Reading,* ed. Lindsay Waters and Wlad Godzich. Minneapolis: University of Minnesota Press.

———. 1992a. "How to Avoid Speaking: Denials." In *Derrida and Negative Theology,* ed. Howard Coward and Toby Foshay. Albany: State University of New York Press.

———. 1992b. "Force of Law: The 'Mystical Foundation of Authority.' " In *Deconstruction and the Possibility of Justice,* ed. Drucilla Cornell, et al. New York: Routledge.

———. 1994. *Specters of Marx: The State of the Debt, the Work of Mourning, and the New International.* Trans. Peggy Kamuf. New York: Routledge.

———. 1995. *On the Name.* Ed. Thomas Dutoit. Stanford: Stanford University Press.

———. 1998. "Faith and Knowledge: The Two Sources of 'Religion' at the Limits of Reason Alone." In *Religion,* ed. Jacques Derrida and Gianni Vattimo. Stanford: Stanford University Press.

Freud, Sigmund. 1958. *Civilization and its Discontents.* Trans. Joan Riviere. Garden City, N.Y.: Doubleday.

Hart, Kevin. 2000. *The Trespass of the Sign: Deconstruction, Theology and Philosophy.* New York: Fordham University Press.

Heidegger, Martin. 1962. *Being and Time*. Trans. John Macquarrie and Edward Robinson. New York: Harper & Row.

———. 1969. *Identity and Difference*. Trans. Joan Stambaugh. New York: Harper & Row.

———. 1991. *The Principle of Reason*. Trans. Reginald Lilly. Bloomington: Indiana University Press.

———. 1997. "The Word of Nietzsche: 'God Is Dead.' " In *The Question Concerning Technology and Other Essays*. Trans. William Lovitt. New York: Harper & Row.

———. 1998. *Pathmarks*. Ed. William McNeill. New York: Cambridge University Press.

Janicaud, Dominique. 2000. *The Theological Turn in French Phenomenology*. Trans. Bernard G. Prusak. In *Phenomenology and the "Theological Turn": The French Debate*. New York: Fordham University Press.

Kisiel, Theodore. 1993. *The Genesis of Heidegger's "Being and Time."* Berkeley: University of California Press.

Kosky, Jeffrey L. 2001. *Levinas and the Philosophy of Religion*. Bloomington: Indiana University Press.

Marion, Jean-Luc. 1991. *God Without Being*. Trans. Thomas A. Carlson. Chicago: University of Chicago Press.

———. 1997. "Metaphysics and Phenomenology: A Summary for Theologians." In *The Postmodern God: A Theological Reader*, ed. Graham Ward. Oxford: Blackwell.

———. 1998. *Reduction and Givenness: Investigations of Husserl, Heidegger, and Phenomenology*. Trans. Thomas A Carlson. Evanston: Northwestern University Press.

———. 1999. "In the Name: How to Avoid Speaking of 'Negative Theology.' " In *God, the Gift, and Postmodernism*, ed. John D. Caputo and Michael J. Scanlon. Bloomington: Indiana University Press.

———. 2000. "The Saturated Phenomenon." Trans. Thomas A. Carlson. In *Phenomenology and the "Theological Turn": The French Debate*. New York: Fordham University Press.

———. 2001. *Idol and Distance*. Trans. Thomas A. Carlson. New York: Fordham University Press.

Ricoeur, Paul. 1965. *Fallible Man*. Trans. Charles Kelbley. Chicago: Henry Regnery.

———. 1967. *The Symbolism of Evil*. Trans. Emerson Buchanan. New York: Harper & Row.

———. 1970. *Freud and Philosophy*. Trans. Denis Savage. New Haven: Yale University Press.

———. 1981. *Hermeneutics and the Human Sciences*. Trans. John B. Thompson. New York: Cambridge University Press.

Spiegelberg, Herbert. 1971. *The Phenomenological Movement: A Historical Introduction*. 2 vols. The Hague: Martinus Nijhoff.

Van Buren, John. 1994. *The Young Heidegger: Rumor of the Hidden King*. Bloomington: Indiana University Press.

Westphal, Merold. 1998. *Suspicion and Faith: The Religious Uses of Modern Atheism*. New York: Fordham University Press.

———. 2001. *Overcoming Onto-Theology: Towards a Postmodern Christian Faith*. New York: Fordham University Press.

....

CHAPTER 20

FEMINISM AND ANALYTIC PHILOSOPHY OF RELIGION

....

SARAH COAKLEY

THE relation between analytic philosophy of religion and feminist thought has to date been a strained one. To the extent that most analytic philosophers of religion have attended to feminist theory or feminist theology at all, their acknowledgment has generally gone no further than a belated concession to the use of gender-inclusive language. More substantial issues raised by feminist philosophy or theology have in large part been ignored in the standard literature. Although there have been certain notable exceptions to this "rule," it is undeniable that analytic philosophy of religion remains predominantly "gender blind" in its thinking, and thus, no doubt unsurprisingly, when feminist thinkers have troubled to comment on the discipline, their criticisms have tended to be severe.

The primary purpose of this chapter, then, is to probe the reasons for the mutual incomprehension between the disciplines of analytic philosophy of religion and feminist thought, and to chart—and assess—the feminist criticisms leveled against analytic philosophy of religion for what is claimed to be its covert "masculinist" bias.[1] Although there is now a burgeoning literature in the genre of "feminist philosophy of religion,"[2] most of the woman scholars involved have no truck with analytic philosophy of religion at all, and are primarily engaged with French feminist thought, or American pragmatism, or both. But as the focus of this chapter is the potential interchange between feminist thought and analytic philosophy of religion, I shall concentrate on the two feminist thinkers who have recently devoted book-length accounts to a critique of analytic philosophy of religion: Pamela Sue Anderson (1998) and Grace Jantzen (1998). Some of their criticisms overlap, but they are by no means in agreement about what, if anything, can be salvaged from the project of analytic philosophy of religion as far as future feminist work is concerned. A critical comparison of their views will thus prove instructive in highlighting what the prospects are for a rapprochement between feminist thought and analytic philosophy of religion. As we shall see, much depends here on whether analytic philosophers of religion are already prejudiced from the outset against post-Kantian continental traditions of philosophy, psycholinguistics, and social theory. A complete refusal to learn from these traditions will certainly also prevent fruitful interaction with feminist thought.

The second, and much shorter, purpose of this chapter is more speculative. It is to suggest some ways in which future philosophy of religion in the analytic tradition might usefully—and indeed, creatively—take up the task of responding to the challenges of such feminist critique *without* altogether abandoning its own most cherished goals. Because such qualities as clarity, logical incisiveness, generalizable philosophical persuasiveness, and a commitment to a realist theory of truth are commonly deemed prime desiderata by analytic philosophers of religion, it will be clear following our discussion below that feminists who are *unreservedly* committed to French psycholinguistic feminist theory are unlikely to be persuaded of a possible accord between the disciplines. For Jantzen, especially, such highly vaunted characteristics of analytic philosophy of religion as clarity and rational persuasiveness are themselves prime manifestations of "phallocentric" thought (of the "male," "symbolic" realm, in Jacques Lacan's terms), and hence intrinsically demeaning to the project of feminist revision. That there is nonetheless a remaining possibility of mutual enrichment between feminist thought and analytic philosophy of religion, on rather different theoretical presumptions, it will be the purpose of the final part of this chapter to suggest. Anderson also suggests some possibility of positive mediation, which we shall duly note; my own suggestions will probe a little further. In short, I show that imprecise judgments on the possible positive interactions between analytic philosophy of religion and feminism are to be avoided: it is the *particular* form of feminist theoretical or theological commitment that is the crucial variable, along with the willingness of analytic philosophy of religion to broaden its consideration about what could "count" as relevant to its task.

Let us now turn, first, to an analysis and comparative critique of the work of Jantzen and Anderson.

Although Jantzen's book appeared a few months after Anderson's, it will be more illuminating pedagogically to treat it first in this comparison of the two. As will quickly emerge, Jantzen's book is the more radical of the two in its sweepingly critical account of the practices and goals of analytic philosophy of religion, and because Anderson's position is decidedly more eirenic in comparison, it will be useful to clarify how she softens the divide. Anderson's book fell into Jantzen's hands only as she was writing the final version of her introduction, and she (perhaps slightly defensively) describes Anderson as having a "quite different" "approach" (1998, 2). My own judgment is that Anderson's *initial* "approach" (especially her use of French feminist materials) is remarkably similar to Jantzen's, but her chosen form of feminist epistemology, and thus her practical conclusions and proposals, are markedly different. Let us now explain why this is so.

JANTZEN'S CRITIQUE OF ANALYTIC PHILOSOPHY OF RELIGION

A simple account of Jantzen's book is not easy, since she discusses a great deal of diverse literature and her central themes only emerge, cumulatively, throughout the book. Nonetheless, a brief résumé of her core thesis might go as follows. At the outset she claims to be writing her book to "find [her] own [sc. feminist] voice in the philosophy of religion" (Jantzen 1998, 1), and simultaneously to build a "bridge" between analytic and continental traditions in philosophy of religion (4). But the reader rapidly begins to wonder whether the "bridge" metaphor is somewhat disingenuous. Once the key categories of French psycholinguistics have been introduced, it becomes clear that Jantzen sees modern Western thought in general, and analytic philosophy of religion in particular, as hopelessly in thrall to a "masculinist imaginary"—a "symbolic" order (to use the terminology of Lacan) that is obsessed with death and incapable of delivering the liberative vision of God that would allow women to "flourish." This large-scale thesis undergirds Jantzen's whole book and imparts to it a deep pessimism about the cramping restrictions of the existing status quo in Anglo-American philosophy. Right from the start, it is hard to see how Jantzen actually *could* build a "bridge" between her position and that of analytic philosophy of religion, for the latter, according to her, hides under its "cool, guarded, ostensibly neutral" approach a "modern," "Protestant," and "scientific" obsession with "truth" and "belief" that can lead only to "patriarchal necrophilia" (18, 20–23). The only solution to this state of affairs is for women to construct for themselves (with explicit debt to Feuerbach and to the French feminist Luce Irigaray) a new so-called feminine imaginary. This must be a vision of the divine that will sustain women's interests and *release* them from the "masculine symbolic," which, from the moment of their very entry into language, has enslaved them in "masculinist" modes of thinking.

Why exactly is the interest in "truth" in analytic philosophy of religion associated with "masculinism," and especially with death? And why is any language system thought of as intrinsically tainted by such "masculinism"? The answer lies in the theoretical underpinnings provided by French post-Freudian psycholinguistics, especially in Luce Irigaray's feminist adjustment of Lacan's contrast of the so-called symbolic and semiotic realms. As Jantzen explains (1998, ch. 1), Lacan's understanding of the "symbolic" realm explains the child's entry into language (and thence into civilization and culture), and the achievement thereby of a conscious "subjectivity"; in the case of the male child, this is associated, according to Lacan, with a crucial repression of his desire for the mother and a more or less unconscious identification with "phallocentric" goals: order, control, "system," and "truth." The "semiotic" realm, in contrast, is that which disturbingly *interrupts* the "male" or "phallocentric" thought-forms of the "symbolic" and brings a disruptive reminiscence of identification with the maternal. (It is often expressed in poetry, art, or music that defies "order," or it may be theorized in psychoanalytic or cultural theory.)

Once this basic psycholinguistic gender binary between symbolic and semiotic is taken as given, it takes a feminist critique, provided most notably by Irigaray (1985a, 1985b), to point out that "feminine subjectivity" is fatally occluded by the dominance of the "symbolic" in this theory. For as in Freud, so also in Lacan, woman is fundamentally defined as "lack" (of the penis in Freud, of "phallocentric" consciousness in Lacan). And if the *normative* entry into independent personhood is conceived of as "male," and the repression of the maternal presumed to be a necessity of such growth, how could the theory possibly accommodate an adequate account of "feminine" personhood? If a young woman follows the directives of the "symbolic," she can at best achieve a false "equality" with men on their own terms; her own distinctive subjectivity will remain undeveloped and unacknowledged. For Irigaray, Lacan's "Law (or Name) of the Father" is assumed to be so deeply inscribed into Western culture that, despite pervasive secularism, it still summons the authoritative power of a *male* "God." Jantzen adds to this insight her insistence that the "Law of the Father" is also death-obsessed: "necrophilia" is intrinsically bound in with the "Law of the Father," since it ceaselessly seeks to conquer, master and subdue the "other". The same goes, mutatis mutandis, for the quest for "truth," which, for Jantzen, equally assumes this competitive and destructive attitude. Only a different, "feminine imaginary" can provide a God who does not repress, but sustains, women's "flourishing."

It is Jantzen's claim from early on in her book that analytic philosophy of religion, specifically, is incapable of acknowledging the existence of the "Rule of the Father" to which it is nonetheless enslaved (1998, 24). Even when an analytic philosopher of religion occasionally mentions the significance of the "unconscious" (a rare enough event in itself),[3] there is a "deafening silence," she says, about the relation of this realm to questions of gender and the problem of women's subjectivity. Jantzen applies at this point the pragmatist criterion of what is "helpful" to further women's goals. Women must rejoice in their "natality" rather than becoming absorbed in questions of death, judgment, and afterlife. They must develop what Irigaray has called a "sensible transcendental," that is, a new vision of the divine which does not abstract from the earthly and physical but rejoices in them. Indeed, the ultimate solution for Jantzen is for women to see *themselves* as "becoming divine," a projective and imaginative task that she links (at the end of her book) with process thought and a pantheistic metaphysics (ch. 11).

These are the central themes in Jantzen's work, and together form what we might call the "bookends" of *Becoming Divine* (1998, chs. 1 and 11). As Jantzen herself recapitulates the core thesis of the book in chapter 11 (254): "The central contention . . . has been that it is urgently necessary for feminists to work towards a new religious symbolic focused on natality and flourishing rather than death, a symbolic which will lovingly enable natals, women and men, to become subjects, and the earth on which we live to bloom." But the intervening chapters of the book greatly complexify the picture and allow Jantzen to draw on a wide range of continental heroes and heroines from post-Kantian philosophy, social theory, and feminist thought. Interestingly, Jantzen has little time for the work of the pioneering feminist theologians (Rosemary Radford Ruether, Elisabeth Schüssler Fiorenza, Daphne Hampson, for instance), whom she regards as making philosophically naïve appeals to "women's experience" as privatized and generically female, and as failing to acknowledge the "irreducibly diverse" nature of the many variables in women's lives (race, class, sexual orientation, and so on; see Jantzen 1998, ch. 5). Indeed, besides the French feminists Luce Irigaray and Julia Kristeva, and the German American ethicist Hannah Arendt, it is noteworthy that Jantzen's main intellectual heroes are all *male*: Martin Heidegger, Jacques Derrida, Emmanuel Levinas, and Michel Foucault, while the "enemy" is represented repeatedly as analytic philosophy of religion and its major male exponents (Richard Swinburne, Paul Helm, Alvin Plantinga, Brian Davies, Vincent Brümmer, D. Z. Phillips, and John Hick are all singled out for trenchant criticism, despite their own many differences of opinion). Because much of the force of Jantzen's book depends on how one reads *this* further disjunctive binary (between male continental social theory/philosophy and male analytic philosophy of religion), we need to examine it in a little more detail in order to assess the success and consistency of Jantzen's proposal. What we shall find here is that the occasional calls made by Jantzen—in the spirit of Derrida—to overcome *all* disjunctive binaries (Jantzen 1998 62, chs. 3 and 11), are seemingly rendered merely rhetorical by the relentless force of her dismissal of the analytic school. Likewise, the more eirenic moments when Jantzen calls for some kind of "fusion or healing of the rift between semiotic and symbolic" (203) ring rather hollow given the repetitive fury commonly manifested by her against the "symbolic" realm tout court. Let us now scrutinize these paradoxical dimensions of the book a little further, and in so doing relate a number of important subthemes in Jantzen that have bearing on our assessment of the possibility of any future fruitful interaction between feminism and analytic philosophy of religion.

It is important, first, to explicate in greater detail why Jantzen associates analytic philosophy of religion specifically with "necrophilic" imagination. As we have seen, the very commitment to truth and clarity tars the discipline with the "male," "symbolic" brush at the outset, as far as Jantzen is concerned; the first thing we need to examine is why she presumes that analytic philosophers of religion necessarily fall into male idolatry by claiming "the God's-eye view." But Jantzen has other objections to the concerns and thought-forms of analytic philosophy of religion, which are related to the charge of necrophilia. Five (other) such objections appear paramount in *Becoming Divine*, according to my reading: Jantzen's profound distrust of evidentialism (including her analysis of what she sees as question-begging appeals to "religious experience"); her identification of a recurrent mind-body split in analytic philosophy of religion (which she thinks involves a fatal occlusion of "desire"); her charge of a covert identification of the male subject with God (which leads on, rather oddly, to a radical critique of "analogy"); her claim of an unhealthy obsession with "salvation" and life after death; and finally, her accusation of an equally morbid interest in theodicy and the problem of evil. Many of these charges are entwined with one another in a way that makes them difficult to disentangle, but a brief examination of each in turn will draw out the further subthemes of the book before we attempt an assessment.

First, Jantzen's appeal (1998, 205) to Thomas Nagel's (1986) celebrated dictum about the "God's-eye view" being nothing but the "view from nowhere"[4] indicates her strong commitment to dissolving the realism-antirealism binary and replacing it with criteria of "justice" and "trustworthiness" (Jantzen 1998, ch. 9). Likewise (ch. 10), "ontotheology," as critiqued by Heidegger, must be replaced by primary ethical concerns for the "other"; yet Levinas' ethical "first philosophy" also must be adjusted—with the help of Arendt's stress on action and community—to acknowledge how *gendered* "otherness" can easily be forgotten. This pragmatist and ethical "turn" supposedly rebuts the epistemological realism of most analytic philosophy of religion by a quick rejoinder of false consciousness: *any* claim to such privileged access to the "real" must be playing "God" from the platform of the "male symbolic"—"the phallus as universal signifier" (Jantzen 1998, 204). It would appear, then, that "Any claim to objective (let alone universal) truth . . . would have to be abandoned in favour of a respectful pluralism" (214). But here Jantzen wavers; she has to acknowledge that not all epistemological "standpoints" are equally valid (else we would have to be "respectful," likewise, to the perspectives "that slavery is acceptable" or "that lesbians should be killed"). Yet Jantzen refuses—and here is an important contrast with Anderson, which we shall explore later—to adopt the well-known feminist "standpoint epistemology" of Nancy Hartsock (1983) and Sandra Harding (1993), and claim a *greater* "objectivity" for the perspectives of the oppressed (Jantzen 1998, 121–27; 215). Because, for Jantzen, *any* claim to "truth" or "objectivity" is tainted by "phallocentrism," it can thus only serve the deathly agonistics of "male" power. This leaves her in a sticky position epistemologically, which she seeks to alleviate by appeal to the intrinsic pragmatic worth of "struggle" (215), the admission of an irreducible plurality of "perspectives," and the need for discernment on the basis of the criteria of "justice" and communal "trustworthiness." Whether Jantzen can ultimately avoid *all* appeals to "truth," metaphysical or otherwise, is a question to which we shall return. But certainly, it is her avowal, in the spirit of Foucault, that such claims invariably hide devious attempts at power-mastery.

Notable, too, is Jantzen's complete disdain for the strategies of apophatic discourse, which one might have expected her to employ as a feminist riposte to "literal" truth claims about the divine from some analytic philosophers. But as she has discussed more extensively in previous work (Jantzen 1995), so here again: she denounces "darkness mysticism" in the tradition of Pseudo-Dionysius as yet another elitist "male" ploy to establish the hegemony of the intellect and to prevent women's voices being heard at the apex of the "ecclesiastical hierarchy" (1998, 174–75).

The remaining cluster of objections to analytic philosophy of religion, identified above, are wielded by Jantzen as other parts of her argument unfold. The penchant among some philosophers of religion (but by no means all) toward "evidentialism" is discussed by Jantzen (1998, ch. 4) as a foil to her thesis that "desire" is repressed in the discourses of analytic philosophy. To seek to "justify" religious beliefs by "evidences," she argues, is ostensibly a quest for objective "rationality" but actually hides a *desire* to project one's own image into the divine: "A deconstructive reading of this . . . discourse . . . reveals that although the insistence on evidence is meant as a denial or repression of desire and projection, these elements are always already operative" (77). Richard Swinburne (1979) and Paul Helm (1994), especially, receive harsh criticism for failing to note the lessons of Nietzsche and Feuerbach on power and projection; Swinburne's and Helm's concern about the weighing of "evidences" ignores their *own* projective desire for divine power and fatally "constructs desire as rationality's other" (Jantzen 1998, 81). Jantzen, in contrast, marshalls the aid of Feuerbach and Irigaray to insist that the "path of desire" is a necessary means to women "becoming divine" and to ousting the "male symbolic" in favor of a new "feminine imaginary." As we have already seen, however, a naïve appeal to (female) "religious experience" is to be avoided here, according to Jantzen, since it can already be part of a false objectification and privatization of religious piety, which merely plays back into the hands of the "male symbolic."[5]

Unsurprisingly, we find Jantzen also launching an attack on analytic philosophy of religion's presumed tendency to a mind-body dualism, and its failure to acknowledge gendered difference, as part of her theory about the discipline's occlusion of "desire" (1998, 31–34). Once again, as elsewhere in this book, Jantzen does not stop to comment on the great variety of views within analytic philosophy of religion on the mind-body issue and other matters, and her wide sweeps of judgment about the Christian tradition's views of the "self" (from Augustine to Descartes) also do not recount the internal complexity of this history. She admits (31) that "The intensity with which embodiment, gender and the unconscious are wilfully ignored and repressed in much Anglo-American philosophy of religion, and the anxiety such repression bespeaks, would be a significant study in itself," which she cannot here explore in detail. Her discussion (in the same chapter) of the purported identification of the "male" philosophical subject with God in analytic philosophy of religion is equally brief: three very different scholars (Richard Swinburne, Keith Ward, and Vincent Brümmer) are taken to task for an "unproblematic" assumption that "God is . . . a relatively straightforward analogate of a human person" (29). The criticism has a point, especially in the case of Swinburne's earlier work,[6] but, as we shall see, Jantzen will not have recourse to a sliding scale of "analogy" to help either her or those whom she accuses off the hook of the "literal" identification between the human and the divine.

It is in fact somewhat later in Jantzen's book, in connection with her critique of the apophatic, that she launches her attack on "analogical" speech for God (1998, 173–77). Again, one cannot help wondering whether this ploy is in her own best feminist interests; for might one not think that a nuanced account of how God profoundly *differs* from humans—ontologically, and thus also in our mode of linguistic apprehension—would help the deconstruction of "male" idolatry? But in fact, for Jantzen, the appeal to "analogical" speech can only be subject to the same hermeneutic of suspicion that attended her dismissal of "negative theology." Her (frankly, eccentric) reading of "analogy" in Thomas Aquinas and his various modern followers starts with the assertion that "the doctrine of analogy . . . [shows] how the masculinist imaginary . . . [forecloses] the divine horizon by trying to *pin down* the sense and reference of words about God" (175, my emphasis). She goes on to assert, even more oddly, that "philosophers of religion who appeal to analogy" fail to notice Thomas's "debt to Pseudo-Dionysius." Whether or not this is true, it would not help them, according to Jantzen, if they did notice the debt, since she has already claimed to reveal the fatal "masculinism" in Dionysius's own valorization of "men's minds" (177).[7]

Jantzen's final criticisms of analytic philosophers of religion circle back, more explicitly, to the question of necrophilia. In her discussion of "salvation" in philosophy of religion, Jantzen claims that the doctrine is central to Christian, especially Protestant, thought, precisely because it is "embedded in an imaginary of death" (1998, 159). "Patriarchal" interests in "salvific" individual rewards and punishments repress the material and the maternal, she claims, and should be contrasted with a feminist focus on natality. Her attack here on John Hick (1973, 1976) for his well-known interests in "salvation" in the context of world religions seems a little strained granted Hick's own "liberal" reduction of metaphysical belief structures to ethical or pragmatist alternatives, a ploy that Jantzen herself endorses (see 1998, 168–69). More predictable, doubtless, are Jantzen's objections to the way that the problem of evil has classically been handled in analytic philosophy of religion. As we might expect, she finds the emphasis on the "free will defence," and especially the "higher order goods theory," morally repugnant as strategies of theodicy; the "conundrum" of the problem of evil "does not arise," she avers, "unless the attributes of omnipotence, omniscience, and goodness are explicitly accepted as those of the God of the western onto-theological tradition" (260). Only, in other words, if "God" looks suspiciously like the male moral agent of the "symbolic" consciousness will the arguments fall out as they do: "By making [the problem of evil] an intellectual problem to be solved, concentration on the adequacy . . . of the preferred solution can take up all the time and energy that could otherwise be devoted to doing something about the suffering itself" (260).

Once again denouncing such purportedly "masculinist" presumptions, Jantzen feels free to move on at the end of her book to enunciate her own explicitly "pantheistic" projection of the "feminine divine." Although she has drawn heavily on the thought of Feuerbach, Heidegger, Derrida, and Levinas in the course of her book, she finally finds all these—her male "pantheon" of continental heroes—inadequate when it comes to the "Western" masculinist "dread of death" (Jantzen 1998, 129), in which, she claims, even these scholars share. Some help, however, is provided by the French feminist Julia Kristeva, whose analysis of the transgressive potential of the "semiotic"—expressed in poetry, music, childbirth, or Mariology—suggests ways of escaping the dominating power of the "male imaginary" and the "change of *Gestalt* to an imaginary of natality" (Jantzen 1998, 200).[8] Finally, Jantzen hangs her hope on the possibility of such a redefinition of the divine.

This detailed account of Jantzen's argument has indicated how complex and rich is her network of appeals to continental philosophy and feminist theory, but also how deep is her resistance to the discourses of analytic philosophy of religion. Can that discipline represent anything but a whipping boy for Jantzen? That is the question we must face as we now attempt a brief assessment of her book. In doing this, we shall point forward to those themes that Pamela Sue Anderson will treat rather differently, themes that will have crucial implications for our interest in a possible future rapprochement between analytic philosophy of religion and feminist theory.

Perhaps the most puzzling aspect of Jantzen's book, first, is the ambivalence one detects in her adherence to the Lacanian theory of the male symbolic and to Irigaray's and Kristeva's critical enunciation of the same theme. There are times when Jantzen announces the Rule of the Father as if there were no hope of shifting its influence, at one point (1998, 217) declaring it impossible even for good-hearted feminist women to escape its power and linguistic constraints altogether: "We speak in our fathers' tongue." Because the pessimistic theory of language as intrinsically phallocentric is so general as to fall foul of the Popperian principle of empirical nonfalsifiability, Jantzen rests her whole case on a dangerously fragile fundament. Yet her own blanket dismissal of "empiricism" would presumably disallow any investigation of this matter according to *evidences*. But what if we were to *challenge* the theory of the repressive masculinism of all systems of language? Would we not merely underline or reinscribe the mutual incomprehension of discourses that currently exists between analytic philosophy of religion and French feminist psycholinguistics? But it is precisely that incomprehension that we seek to overcome, and Jantzen, ironically, does little to help us here. Indeed, she herself shows considerable indecision about the extent to which even the tactics of French feminism can indicate a liberating escape route from Lacan's binaries of the regnant symbolic and the marginalized semiotic. At times, as we noted above, she speaks of a hope for a "fusion"—some sort of sublation of the linguistic (and gender) binary that so exercises and afflicts Western culture; when following Kristeva's leads on the creativity of semiotic expression, she will voice a hope that "women can and do become speaking subjects" (Jantzen 1998, 203). At other times, she writes as if the heavy hand of masculinism is a cultural given that is simply immovable.

The same indecision affects Jantzen's attitudes to binaries in general. Following Derrida (Jantzen 1998, ch. 11), she would ostensibly seek to up-end and subvert the binaries of symbolic/semiotic, male/female, or death/life. Yet her own argument is curiously ambiguous on this front, at times generalizing incautiously about the male symbolic, while simultaneously insisting on a *deconstruction* of generalizing claims about women; at times accusing the entire Western religious tradition of an obsession with death, while also refusing the possibility that life and death might need to be considered *together* in a religion committed to the doctrines of incarnation and resurrection (life through death). If only natality is acceptable for Jantzen, and death suppressed, has she not precisely recapitulated the binary she is seeking to overcome?

In sum, if the Lacanian view of language is as repressive as Jantzen would have it, and Irigaray's and Kristeva's solutions for adjustment are inadequate, then a more confident, mediating, and robust strategy for cultural escape from the symbolic is needed than Jantzen appears to provide. This, indeed, is the final irony of her poststructuralist commitment: if the symbolic is as pervasive and as powerful as she avers, there is seemingly little hope for feminism except to withdraw into an alternative sectarian world. Jantzen's last chapter on process thought, and the world as "God's body," represents views she came to hold long ago (see Jantzen 1984), before her interest in deconstruction and French feminism developed; it is somewhat hard to see how these older interests cohere with the new theoretical perspective: how exactly does process thought relate to the semiotic, or indeed escape the taint of making realist claims? Jantzen brushes this objection away by claiming that the realism/nonrealism debate is a stale and unproductive one. Yet her new commitment (with Irigaray) to a Feuerbacherian form of "projectionism," in which women themselves "become divine," *disposes* of a transcendent divinity and of realist truth-claims in a way that is unlikely to satisfy many Christian believers spiritually and may cause them to worry about new forms of "feminine" idolatry. Her answer to such critics can only be that they are suffering from the delusions of masculinism—and so the circularity of the argument repeats itself.

Jantzen's further claim that *all* appeals to truth or rationality smack of feminist false consciousness and necrophilic obsession seems self-defeating granted that she herself makes many "truth" claims, en passant, in her book. For instance, as we have already noted, her commitment to pantheistic process thought is definitely recommendatory and "realist" in tone, and her view that women are universally marginalized and repressed is not, surely, expressed as a mere relativistic "perspective." Further, her insistence that there *is no* God's-eye view (even for "God"?) has all the paradoxicality of a passionate conviction voiced by one who has ostensibly disclaimed all truths. But even Jantzen admits at one point that the claims of truth cannot be evaded altogether (1998, 127); it is to be doubted whether her substitution of "justice" can altogether escape continuing (if somewhat covert) "truth" claims as well.[9] Similarly, it is hard to see how her ethical commitments to natality and flourishing can ultimately evade the taint of some sort of *belief*; Jantzen's attempt to overcome "intellect" with ethics thus looks suspiciously like another unsublated binary. This is why, finally, her position on feminist "standpoint epistemology," already discussed, also seems open to question: if *all* perspectives are "partial" (126–27), how can one appropriately reckon one more partial than another? Does not the Foucauldian charge of self-interest merely boomerang back on the feminist critic? To this crucial point we shall return in our discussion of Anderson's work, whose position on standpoint epistemology is importantly different from Jantzen's.

Finally, we must mention the awkwardness of the part played by the "enemy"—analytic philosophy of religion—in Jantzen's work. As we mentioned at the outset, Jantzen is ostensibly set on a mediating exercise to bring analytic philosophy of religion to its senses, as it were, and to instruct it in the insights of continental and feminist philosophy. But in fact, for the most part, the discipline does indeed play the part of whipping boy in Jantzen's text, and, being larded with blame, is therefore hardly able to contribute anything to the future way forward in philosophy of religion that Jantzen announces.

One of the effects of this scapegoating ploy is that Jantzen finds it difficult to acknowledge that "analytic philosophy of religion" is by now itself a highly diverse discourse; her "identikit" caricature of the disembodied "man of reason," repressive of feeling, anxiety, and gender consciousness, may well fit *some* authors in the field, but really cannot any longer be applied to all. Indeed, there is an increasing consciousness of post-Kantian continental philosophy in the guild of Anglo-American analytic philosophy of religion, which one would expect Jantzen to applaud. Moreover, her vehemence against Protestant thought, more generally, only occasionally stops to acknowledge that "Reformed epistemology" has of late disavowed itself of many of the features of evidentialism and foundationalism that Jantzen particularly abhors. And as for the varieties of Thomism that are now represented in the field, Jantzen has little to say of them at all. Her own rejection of analogy and apophaticism tends to make her read Thomists, negatively, as covert evidentialists or honorary Protestants, and her irritation at the discipline of philosophy of religion as a whole allows only grudging acknowledgment that Wittgensteinians like D. Z. Phillips, liberals like John Hick, or scholars like William Wainwright, who have investigated the significance of "affectivity" for rational judgment, might occasionally be saying something rather akin to her own pronouncements.[10] In sum, Jantzen's rhetorical strategy of "castigation by lumping" where analytic philosophy of religion is concerned makes her occasional suggestions that the way forward lies in an *expansion* of rationality, rather than its rejection (1998, 69), look half-hearted and undeveloped. More commonly, one senses that Jantzen wants no more truck with the "male" discipline at all, and may thereby have permanently relegated herself to the semiotic margins of the currently constituted academic discussion.

However, it is precisely at this point of strategic, political decision vis-à-vis the academic status quo that Pamela Sue Anderson's work is of relevance and interest. Sharing, as we shall see, many of the same feminist interests and bibliographical sources as Jantzen, she nonetheless sketches a more hopeful path of possible interchange between the disciplines than Jantzen is able to envisage. To Anderson's alternative proposals we shall now turn, before moving to our own final assessments and positive suggestions.

ANDERSON'S VISION OF FEMINIST PHILOSOPHY OF RELIGION

It may be most illuminating in this context to discuss Anderson's work in contrapuntal relation to Jantzen's by drawing out the chief contrasts between their ideas. For in many respects, their books witness to the same interests and concerns, and these can be quite briefly mentioned at the outset, without requiring lengthy repetition. All these central themes are already laid out in the first chapter of Anderson's *A Feminist Philosophy of Religion* (1998, 3–27).

Like Jantzen, Anderson draws deeply, first, on the resources of contemporary continental philosophy, especially on the insights of the post-Lacanian French feminists Luce Irigaray and Julia Kristeva. Likewise, "desire" is also a key category for Anderson, and a theme that she sees largely repressed in current analytic philosophy of religion. Like Jantzen, she traces that repression to a latent mind-body split in the thought of many in the guild, as well as to an unacknowledged epistemological normativity given to the male self (as falsely "male-neutral," in her terms), and to an accompanying modeling of "God" on the same idolatrous male self. Like Jantzen, Anderson is particularly scathing of the discipline's classic investment in *empirical* and probabilistic demonstrations of God's existence—a Lockean endeavor which Anderson takes in any case to be defunct since Kant's first *Critique*, but especially tinged with "masculinist" repression of feminist interests. Why she makes this charge of *empiricism*, in particular, we shall have reason to probe and query later. She is scathing, too, of the metaphysical "realism" that commonly accompanies such an endeavor, since she assumes (again summoning Nagel),[11] that such claims can arise only from blinkered male attempts at epistemological privilege. A moral disgust, similar to Jantzen's, with the way that the problem of evil has been discussed in the discipline again appears in Anderson's book, though here with more attention to distinctive recent contributions by female analytic scholars.[12] The Foucauldian question of whose *interests* are served by the discourses of analytic philosophy of religion attends Anderson's whole exercise, as it does Jantzen's, and the commitment to reconceive the divine, and along with it the entire enterprise of philosophy of religion, drives the whole project. The goal of this undertaking, finally, again as in Jantzen, is to allow women, and themes stereotypically associated with them (desire, birth, death, excess, the unconscious, any despised or subordinated "other"), to be fully accommodated into the discussion.

Such central commonalities of theme justify, I believe, my earlier contention that Anderson and Jantzen at least *start* with a shared set of concerns, interests, and bibliographical influences. But the way Anderson's analysis and proposals then develop are markedly different from Jantzen's, for reasons that we shall now explore.[13]

Probably the most decisive difference between the two women's projects arises in the area of their fundamental *epistemological* commitments. Early on in her book (1998, 42–47, and ch. 2) Anderson helpfully spells out three broad epistemological options that feminist philosophers have at their disposal.[14] The first, and least radical, is an extension of the empiricist project for feminist ends: on this view, what is needed to liberate women in the sphere of philosophy is simply the *taking into account* of empirical factors (about women, their lives, their concerns, etc.) which have been falsely occluded in traditional "male-neutral" philosophy. Anderson declares herself less than fully satisfied with this first option, on the grounds that it cannot take sufficiently critical account of the all-encompassing epistemological *perspective* of male privilege from which women's issues have classically been marginalized. And she has, in any case, as we have seen, already expressed her reservation about covert sexisms in empiricist approaches. Hence, the second, and somewhat more radical, epistemological option appeals to her more: that of so-called standpoint epistemology. We have already mentioned Jantzen's (rather hasty) dismissal of this approach, above; Anderson spends much more time and trouble (ch. 2), explicating its possibilities. Following Sandra Harding's (1993) important development of this option, Anderson takes the view that differing epistemological "standpoints" are capable of revealing *perspectives* on truth, and indeed that perspectives from the "margins" (whether from women, or blacks, or other oppressed people) are intrinsically *more* likely to be revelatory of truth than those that are bolstered by the prejudice and delusions of male privilege (Anderson 1998, 73). Thus, as Harding suggests, this approach can ironically claim a *stronger* "objectivity," epistemologically speaking, than standard "male-neutral" theories of knowledge, whose blindnesses ironically "weaken" their presumed objectivity, and whose implicit claim to occupy the God's-eye view actually results in an epistemic *disadvantage*. (This argument, as Harding explains, has its origins in Hegel's master/slave parable and in Marxist interpretation of it.) But what primarily commends the standpoint approach to Anderson is that, like the empiricist option, it does not give up on a shared domain of "truth" seeking alongside the male-neutral. But, unlike the straightforward empiricist alternative, it attends to the specificity of the standpoint of feminism(s), not simply to an additional collection of *facts* to be accounted for. The crucial point is that objectivity and perspective can thereby be seen as *coincident*: purported "perspective-lessness" (the "view from nowhere") is, by contrast, a chimera (78).

Anderson, however, is not entirely confident about the success of Harding's argument for "strong objectivity," chiding her at one point with a slippage into relativism that would undermine that possibility (1998, 77); yet she also seeks, as we shall see, to set her own standpoint epistemology in a more strongly Kantian framework than does Harding, thereby appearing to *weaken* the possibility of an achieved "realism" from any one particular standpoint (even a "marginalized" one). Frankly, these two divergent strands in Anderson's thesis on standpoint do not find a satisfactory resolution in her book. The first causes her to announce that her ultimate epistemological aim is to learn to "think from the lives of *others*" (78, my emphasis) in order to offset the necessary restrictions even of her own, feminist perspective; at this juncture the notion of standpoint seems to start to dissolve in the cause of a more universal perspective. The second strand, however, presses Anderson in the opposite direction, even to the point of admitting that standpoint epistemology must embrace "incoherence," given the apparent incommensurability to be found between widely differing perspectives (86). To this core problem of coherence in Anderson's position we shall return shortly, but what she nonetheless helpfully clarifies, in detailing her remaining commitment to standpoint epistemology, is its important *difference* from the poststructuralist, psycholinguistic epistemology of the French feminists and of Jantzen. For whereas this *third* feminist epistemological option, as we have described at length above, invites one into the magic epistemological circle of those who *see* the repressive power of the male symbolic realm, it appears to provide no clear way of persuading the skeptical male-neutral philosopher that he is suffering from its baleful influence in the first place. But nor, equally worryingly, does it present the post-Lacanian feminist with any obvious mode of epistemological reform for *all*; she is seemingly consigned to the margins, fated to resort to minor, destabilizing semiotic interruptions, or at best, as Jantzen espouses, called to reimagine a feminine divine to which only some, liberated natals will be drawn.

Having opted for standpoint epistemology as the most promising way to revitalize the scope of philosophy of religion, and having retained thereby a specifically feminist commitment to truth and objectivity (duly redefined), Anderson also spells out other reasons why she is unwilling to abandon the modern Western project of "rationality" (which is for Jantzen, of course, intrinsically and hopelessly tainted by sexism). For a start, Kant figures largely in Anderson's appreciative feminist reappraisal of certain Enlightenment strands of thought. Not only, as we have already mentioned, does Anderson consider Kant's critique of the traditional arguments for the existence of God to be definitive and successful (thus undermining, she believes, the attempts to revive them in analytic philosophy of religion), but, along with many post-Kantians, she also interprets Kant's epistemology as demonstrating a "*lack of correspondence* between rationality and reality for any individual embodiment of reason" (1998, 11, my emphasis), and she happily embraces this view as an aid to her critique of what see dubs the "naïve realism" endemic to analytic philosophy of religion. In other words, Anderson reads Kant's epistemology as one that first and foremost *distances* the knower from the known, even though it also allows, as she proposes later, a form of "perspectival" realism (76–94). Anderson is equally insistent that some of the classical Enlightenment enunciations of personal and political goals—justice, universal love, liberty, rights—are abandoned at the contemporary feminist's peril; so, although each of these key terms is necessarily subject to feminist rethinking, she conceives of her project as a feminist *renegotiation* of rationality, not as a tolling of its death knell.

That this defense of rationality is held (contra Jantzen's more extreme pessimism about the phallocentric taint of all claims to rationality and truth), is in large part explained by Anderson's different mixture of philosophical and feminist influences. As we now see, it is a form of Kantianism that undergirds her standpoint epistemology (no one has privileged or complete access to reality, but we all have *some* access), and she conjoins that view with an important appeal to W. V. Quine's (1953) famous image of the Neurathian ship, on which marinerepistemologists—now to be joined by their feisty feminist counterparts!—continuously pull up planks and renegotiate the seaworthiness of the epistemological ship as it ploughs on its continuing way through the watery darkness of the unknown. As Anderson puts it, "Once recognized as philosophers, women could seek to rebuild the ship's planks of mistaken belief" (1998, 12). It is with the aid of this adjusted Quinean image that Anderson is willing to enunciate the possibility of a future creative accord between feminist epistemology and analytic philosophy of religion.[15] For if the standpoint approach is promising for the claims to incorporate feminist insights into the human world, why not also apply it to divine states of affairs?

But a final, and crucial, feminist influence on Anderson also impinges on her chosen epistemology, and here we note the distinctiveness of a French feminist voice not discussed by Jantzen. Unlike Irigaray and Kristeva (whom Anderson will also utilize, but rather differently from Jantzen), Michèle Le Doeuff (1989, 1990, 1991) argues convincingly, on rather different grounds, for an *expanded* feminist notion of rationality, rather than for its displacement. Her analysis of what she calls the "Héloise complex" (1991) is particularly telling in this regard. Taking the famous medieval love story of Abelard and Héloise as her paradigm, Le Doeuff suggests that even the few women philosophers of the modern era who have achieved eminence have tended to shelter under the guardianship of their male mentors (Beauvoir's relation to Sartre is a notable instance). As Anderson puts it (1998, 50), citing Le Doeuff, "A woman's admiration for her male mentor, which as a philosopher he genuinely needs, prevents her from seeing the value of her own thinking. This prevents the faithful woman from scrutinizing the rationality of her own beliefs, emotions or feelings, and desires." Once freed from this vicious circle of male narcissism, however, the woman philosopher is intellectually fully equipped to develop her own authentic insights and intuitions. The rationality she took for granted in her mentor she now sees to be narrow and deficient, but the male "philosophical imaginary," she also sees, was all along feeding off the unacknowledged power of her "feminine" contribution—the "other of reason," as Le Doeuff calls it.

However, there is a crucial difference in Le Doeuff's understanding of the philosophical imaginary from the Lacanian parsing of the male symbolic that we have seen in both Irigaray and Jantzen. In Le Doeuff's distinctive usage, as Anderson explains (1998, 25 n. 26), the category of the imaginary is not primarily psychoanalytic, and thus not *intrinsically* male, as in Lacan's usage; rather, it bespeaks the mythological and imagistic subtext that laps at the base of the philosophical discourse and actually sustains the power of its argument (Le Doeuff 1989, 4–20). As such, this material is not inexorably destined to remain as the marginalized feminine/semiotic, but in principle is capable of transformation and conscious integration into an expanded feminist rationality. However, as we shall shortly chart, this task of integration involves the subtle unearthing and recasting of moods of "desire" and "mimesis" latent in the texts of philosophy. As such, an element of psychoanalytic assessment, it would seem, still hangs over the enterprise; we are dealing here with materials more latent in the text than overt (the "often unrecognized use of figures and imagery"; Anderson 1998, 25), and thus presumably always subject to a response of blanket denial by the male-neutral author. To this issue we must return, when we examine Anderson's revealingly "suspicious" reading of some of the influential texts of analytic philosophy of religion.

By now we have spelled out in some detail the first, and central, *epistemological* divergence of Anderson's views from those of Jantzen. Anderson is a standpoint epistemologist rather than a poststructuralist; thus, we are not surprised that, en passant, she can remark that her views clearly diverge "from the extremes of postmodernism" and that she does not "give up completely the modern, Enlightenment project of epistemology and its claims concerning the autonomous reason" (1998, 53). In the same breath she forecasts the *second* way her project differs most obviously from Jantzen's; this lies in the fact that she does not "assume that an essential *female desire* exists which should be valued more highly than an essential male reason" (53, my emphasis). In other words, more clearly and consistently than Jantzen, Anderson seeks to find a way of integrating desire and reason. It is to Anderson's particular construal of desire, then, that we now turn, for in it is encapsulated much of what she proposes in the latter part of her book for a renewed, feminist philosophy of religion. Anderson's understanding of the category is different not only in substance from Jantzen's, but also in range of application. While Anderson, too, draws extensively on Irigaray and Kristeva at this point in her book, she not only reads them rather differently from Jantzen, but supplements and adjusts their views by superimposing insights from Le Doeuff's concept of the philosophical imaginary.

The arguments in this second major portion of Anderson's book (1998, chs. 3–5) are somewhat diffuse and unfinished, by Anderson's own admission, but perhaps the central theses can be summed up in the following way. First, Anderson utilizes her own reading of Irigaray and Kristeva to argue that "feminist poststructuralism does not *necessarily* privilege desire over reason, irrationality over rationality" (246, my emphasis). Anderson realizes that she is apparently backtracking here on what she has said critically about feminist poststructuralism in her previous chapter on standpoint. But her point now is that we can still learn from the psycholinguistics of the poststructuralist school, without subscribing to its apparently fatal epistemological binary; for "it offers feminist epistemologists the psycholinguistic tools to begin to unearth what has been buried by patriarchal structures of belief and myth" (246). Accordingly, she uses Irigaray's work, first, to illustrate how male "scientific" rationality may draw on the erotic power of female desire while also repressing it out of sight: "In [the male's] quest for God," as Irigaray puts it, "he takes her light to illuminate his path . . . He [has] stolen her gaze" (1993, 209–10; see Anderson 1998, 99). Anderson's use of Kristeva's writing is rather different (and indeed, she is more careful than Jantzen not to elide the views of the two thinkers, or to subsume one in the other). Thus, whereas Anderson reads Irigaray as conjoining the quest for God with repressed *female desire* in the unconscious motivation of the male subject, Kristeva, in contrast, is seen as focusing more on the "repressed maternal" in patriarchal culture, and its link back to the divine through the figure of Mary, the "mother of God." And whereas Irigaray hypothesizes the absolute need for a projected "feminine divine" in order for women to claim their full ("feminine") identity, Kristeva looks more subtly to the saving irruptions of the semiotic for the location of divine power. Here, according to Kristeva, the evocations of the "maternal" break through the gaps of male, symbolic discourse and return us to the unspeakable sense of original union with the mother. Anderson thinks we can draw richly on these poststructuralist and psychoanalytic insights to demonstrate that the discourses of analytic philosophy of religion, too, occlude female desire and the maternal in their quest for God; but she does not thereby recommend a straightforward acceptance of Irigaray's or Kristeva's thought as "theology" (Anderson 1998, 117); nor, as we have seen, does she embrace the problematic, dualistic epistemology that accompanies their insights.

Hence, what remains for Anderson to indicate in the final sections of her book (1998, chs. 4–5) is that desire and reason are capable of some new alignment, which in turn could transform the shape of philosophy of religion in creative and liberating ways. To demonstrate this possibility, Anderson argues that only "mythology" has the power to be the medium of this realignment, and that "mimesis" (understood by Irigaray as a creative reconfiguration of the hierarchy of gender) must be the means by which that power is enacted to disrupt male-neutral distortions and to bring forth the impassioned "woman of reason" (135–47). We note in this exposition of mythology and mimesis that Anderson's (1993) earlier work on the philosophy of Paul Ricoeur strongly influences her view that radical changes in philosophical thinking cannot be effected without the mediation of these (apparently more subliminal) forms of expression and practice. For it is also Le Doeuff's philosophical imaginary that is at stake here, with all its previously unacknowledged cargo from the male unconscious; the mere taking of thought is insufficient to shift the key of the discourse. For similar reasons, another category that becomes important for Anderson's exposition of the transformation of female desire at this point is bell hooks's (1990) notion of "yearning." Anderson adopts this term as a means of rethinking the notion of female desire as a desire precisely to *transform* rationality through passion. Later she can speak of the "substantive form" of reason as *consisting in* yearning (1998, 213).

A final twist in Anderson's argument at the end of her book links to this attempt to mediate between passion and intellect, and presents a fascinating contrast with Jantzen's attack on necrophilia and the patriarchal culture of death.

Rather than avoiding the subject of death, or simply identifying it with male obsession, Anderson sees the acknowledgment of death as a sign of embodiment accepted, of "death's intimate connection with yearning for love between fully embodied men and women" (1998, 247). Perhaps this may stand as the final, and most revealing, contrast between Anderson's and Jantzen's construal of the philosophical significance of the French feminists. For Jantzen, the feminine imaginary should flee from death and embrace natality, whereas for Anderson, the presence of death in the philosophic discourse is, at worst, a reminder that embodiment cannot be denied and, at best, a signal of the necessary presence of desire in the discourses of reason.

As we have seen from the start of this exposition of *A Feminist Philosophy of Religion*, Anderson, unlike Jantzen, does not reject analytic philosophy of religion tout court; instead, she seeks to build feminist bridges toward it, and so to transform its thought-forms, goals, and interests. But it must be said that her final proposals for change in the subject, drawing as they do on ancient Greek and Hindu materials (the "myths of dissent" of Antigone and Mirabai), seem hardly likely to catch the (admittedly narrow!) imaginations of the existing guild of analytic philosophy of religion. Further, although it is Anderson's explicit aim (1998, 155–56) to *avoid* promoting a "new religion on the basis of an ideal and essential Woman" while ignoring "actual social problems," there is also a certain difficulty in making the leap at the end of her book from Antigone and Mirabai to the downtrodden members of our own industrialized society in the contemporary West. But Anderson herself modestly admits, in closing, that her arguments and lines of thought represent only a beginning for new forms of feminist philosophy of religion, and that "the categories presented here are not meant to be definitive" (245). For this reason she would clearly welcome criticism and extension of her feminist philosophical proposals, which will duly be attempted below.

But before we deliver some judgments on Anderson's project as a whole, and relate those to some further thoughts of our own on the future relation between feminist thought and analytic philosophy of religion, we must return briefly to the specific criticisms levied against the discipline by Anderson at the opening of her book. These turn out to be revealing, precisely in their *difference* of nuance from those of Jantzen. Although, as we mentioned above, they share the presumption that analytic philosophy of religion is predicated on the dominance of a "disembodied" male subject, in whose image its patriarchal God is idolatrously constructed, Anderson has some more specific criticisms that bear scrutiny. Her main ire is reserved for the empiricist basis of many of the justificatory arguments for theism (1998, 13), which she regards as a front for a discriminatory, male-neutral posture of privilege, covertly erasing the concerns and interests of women. But she also charges the discipline of analytic philosophy of religion with a widespread "naïve realism" (37, 68–69), which not only favors "literal" speech about God over other modes of expression, but also makes spurious claims to "unmediated experience" of the divine, purportedly escaping the Kantian epistemological grid. Indeed, Anderson's *chief* criticism of analytic philosophy of religion, it seems, is not one that is intrinsically tied to feminist concerns; rather, it is that there is a vicious circularity at the heart of analytic philosophy of religion's claims to "justify" belief in God at all. Whether through evidentialism (Swinburne, par excellence), through examination of "doxastic practices" (Alston), or through the "proper basicality" of Reformed epistemology (Wolterstorff, Plantinga), all these philosophers, claims Anderson, are really appealing to an "experience" into which their Christian belief has already been smuggled (ch. 1). The resultant "scandal of circular reasoning" simultaneously occludes what has been pushed to the margins by privileged, white male philosophers: the concerns of women, blacks, the poor, and the non-western world disappear in a miasma of talk of "justification" and "warrant" (58). Further, the whole enterprise is sustained by a barely perceptible philosophical imaginary, which assumes female desire while also repressing it; when women *do* appear in the texts of analytic philosophers of religion, it is often as "passive items for . . . men's seduction" (43). Anderson additionally charges that when women philosophers occasionally manage, *per impossibile*, to succeed professionally in this particular guild, they are often notable examples of Le Doeuff's Héloise complex: strongly devoted to male mentors or protectors, whose intellectual hegemony and institutional privilege they obligingly do not question (50–52).

Anderson's argument seems to be at its strongest when she is *explicitly* charting the presence of a "myth" of female subordination in the texts of analytic philosophy of religion. In her analysis of Richard Swinburne's earlier work, in particular, she is able to give bountiful, even embarrassing, evidence of a philosophical imaginary of male privilege and female subordination, which is shot through many of his illustrative examples. When women do appear in his text (which is rarely), they feature as potentially seductive sirens or as mutely submissive spouses. Only the hardened could dismiss *this* "evidence" as mere psychological projection on the part of the critic; indeed, it is a sign of the partial success of such criticism that Swinburne has in a number of ways modified his position and mode of expression in recent revisions of his work.[16] But Anderson's more sweeping criticisms of analytic philosophy of religion for its *empiricist* bias (especially its appeals to "religious experience"), its purportedly *naïve realism*, and its *epistemic circularity* seem more problematic, and do not accord well with the position she herself takes up later in the book on standpoint theory. This matter needs some spelling out, but it will lead on naturally to the final, constructive, section of this chapter. Let us then turn a critical eye on Anderson's standpoint theory, which, as I hope to have demonstrated, is the epistemological lynchpin in her whole feminist project and that which most clearly distinguishes her project from that of Jantzen.

There are three main areas of difficulty in the standpoint position of Anderson in *A Feminist Philosophy of Religion*, as I see it. The first relates to her use of

Kant's work in support of her view that "perspectival" knowledge can achieve "strong objectivity" and hence preserve a commitment to realism. As we have seen, Anderson also believes that Kant shows us that the knower is irretrievably *distanced* from the object of knowledge, and that there is no available God's-eye view from which this distancing could be overcome. Quite apart from the question of whether this is a proper reading of Kant's intentions in the first *Critique* (which is at the very least a moot point),[17] Anderson's dogmatism on this matter of epistemic distancing leaves her in a paradoxical position as far as her equally strong commitment to realism is concerned. If we are *all* distanced, impenetrably, from that which we seek to "know," how can we *also* know that our "perspectives" all participate in some way in that reality? And why would we seek to enter empathetically into the perspective of another (especially a male-neutral other) unless we did know this? Despite Anderson's stated endeavor to cut through the binary between God-like epistemic "privilege" and epistemological relativism, there are times, as we have seen, when she aligns herself, confusingly, with first one and then the other. She wavers, in fact, on whether true epistemological relativism is implied by the perspectivalism she is proposing; this leaves her position in the book puzzlingly inconsistent. Her more recent work on feminist standpoint theory clears up some of the confusion, but in a more consistently realist way: now we are abjured to enter imaginatively into others' standpoints in order to achieve ever-widening perspectives on the truth, and "less biased knowledge" (2001, 131). (The perspective of the margins is no longer granted compensatory epistemic privilege, as it was, in Marxist mode, in the book.) However, it is hard to see how we can engage in this ongoing empathetic task without reliance on *evidences*, and without a fundamentally *realist* commitment to universal "truth" as at least a teleological ideal. If so, then much of Anderson's initial animus against analytic philosophy of religion's empiricism and realism must surely fall away.[18]

This first and central epistemological puzzle relates directly to another problem on standpoint that is also not successfully tackled in the book. When Anderson first lays out the three epistemological options open to feminism (see discussion above), she does not sufficiently explain how the adoption of a standpoint epistemology would differ qualitatively from an expanded feminist empiricism that simply takes more *facts* into account. Such a line is in fact notoriously hard to draw, as was demonstrated long ago in Donald Davidson's famous article "On the Very Idea of a 'Conceptual Scheme'" (1984): the bounded edges, so to speak, of a standpoint (or conceptual scheme) are often so difficult to delineate that one is caused to query whether it exists at all as an *identifiable* epistemological filter. But if Anderson cannot say what a feminist standpoint (as opposed to a set of long-neglected facts about women's issues) finally *is*, then she is in a worryingly weakened position philosophically. Her whole project of the distinctiveness of feminist insight is at stake. She would seemingly do better to withdraw to her first feminist epistemological option (feminist empiricism), which would still be fully compatible with the Quinean form of epistemological revisability suggested by the image of the Neurathian ship. However, Anderson's more recent work has clarified the notion of standpoint and thus blocked the reduction to a mere feminist empiricism. Here, Anderson not only helpfully distinguishes a confusing range of possible meanings of standpoint in previous feminist standpoint epistemology (2001, 137–38), but herself now opts for an idea of standpoint as ethical *achievement* rather than as epistemological filter. This signals a considerable shift; no longer is there the hovering suggestion that women possess, qua marginalized, a distinctive epistemological apparatus (a view that tends towards gender essentialism), but rather, "*A standpoint signifies a particular point of view, or . . . epistemically informed perspective, that is achieved—but not without struggle—as a result of gaining awareness of particular positionings within relations of power*" (145). Anderson notes that this definition no longer suggests that "a standpoint necessarily claims any epistemic privilege" (145)—a significant new admission. But it does allow men to share such a standpoint with women, given goodwill and commitment. Presumably, then, the difference from mere feminist empiricism in this new view resides in the *ethical* dimensions of attempting to take empathetic account of others' perspectives; as such, one might dub it a "virtue ethics" more than a strictly feminist one. But therein lies the puzzling surd: has this shift of Anderson's actually taken the teeth out of an epistemological project that originally claimed *special* insight from the feminist camp? The original goal was to release female desire into an explicit acknowledgment in the discourses of philosophy of religion; whereas Anderson's more recent project seems to flatten or sideline gender difference and aim instead for a greater self-"reflexivity" and recognition of "partiality" in all our epistemic negotiations (146–47).

The third critical issue that arises with Anderson's standpoint epistemology is a pragmatic one of how to *convert* the luminaries of analytic philosophy of religion to a perspective cognizant of female desire. If this is now more a matter of ethical commitment than the embracing of a mysterious feminist *blik*, then the burden rests on Anderson to convince her readership, first, that the writings of analytic philosophy of religion have indeed been the products of repressed female desire, and second, that there is a creative, indeed *virtuous*, way forward in terms of a renegotiated standpoint. My hesitations about the success of Anderson's existing strategies in this third area have already been voiced: not only is it lamentably easy for the analytic philosopher of religion to express blanket denial of collusion in sexism (perhaps especially once his pronouns have been tidied up!), but the loose sort of appeal that Anderson makes to myth and mimesis in the area of desire is arguably too far removed from the existing discourses of analytic philosophy of religion to attract attention, regrettable as this may be.

What, then, are the alternatives? After this exacting analysis and critique of

Jantzen's and Anderson's projects, it is time to sketch some of my own proposals in closing. At the same time I shall gather up a number of the loose ends and questions that I have left along the way.

FEMINISM AND ANALYTIC PHILOSOPHY OF RELIGION: PROSPECTS FOR RAPPROCHEMENT?

To ask whether there are prospects of rapprochement between analytic philosophy of religion and feminist theory and philosophy is of course in one sense to beg the whole question with which this chapter has been concerned. The more one's commitments in feminist theory veer toward the post-Lacanian end of the spectrum (in which male phallocentrism is deemed a deep and irremovable feature of Western intellectual life), the less will one be inclined to seek out opportunities for such rapprochement or expect the prospects to be fruitful for women— whether spiritually or professionally. Because my critique of the epistemological sectarianism of this particular school of feminist theory will by now be evident, however, what is offered in this last section is a discernibly different feminist strategy. It relies neither on the apparently immovable gender binaries of French psycholinguistic feminist theory (for, contra Jantzen, I urge a more *fluid* understanding of the negotiations of gender),[19] nor does it appeal to the brand of feminist standpoint epistemology that presumes an inexorable *distancing* of the knower from the known (for, contra Anderson, feminist epistemology may arguably afford claims to intensified *intimacy* with the known, rather than the opposite).[20] However, *with* Jantzen and Anderson, I take it as read that feminist critiques of analytic philosophy of religion have, at the very least, established the existence of a suspicious gender "subtext" in much writing in the discipline: the making of "God" in the image of the autonomous, Enlightenment "generic male," and, as I have argued elsewhere,[21] the positing of an unconditioned "incompatibilistic" view of freedom as a supposedly necessary adjunct to the solution of the problem of evil are just two signs of the inherent elevation of a certain form of masculinism over the concerns of relationship, closeness, desire, or dependence, which have rightly exercised feminist theorists and ethicists. Yet it would, I believe, be a caricature to suggest that *all* (and especially all recent) analytic philosophy of religion is subject to these same failings, as seems to be Jantzen's and Anderson's view. On the contrary, there are signs of such masculinist traits already starting to crack under their own weight: the notable recent turn to the discussion of

God-as-Trinity, for instance, or of the relationship between the human and the divine in Christ, while also subject potentially to the distortions of the masculinist imaginary, are nonetheless at least telling first signs of an increasing interest in *communion* and *relationship* as philosophical categories.[22]

Thus, I shall be making here some rather different suggestions from those of Jantzen and Anderson for further feminist interrogation of, and interaction with, analytic philosophy of religion. I believe these have greater prospects for pragmatic success in persuading the guild that gender is *already* intrinsic to its operations, and thus urgently in need of the sort of attention and clarification for which its discipline is justly famed. Gender theory cannot then be safely left to angry women who have denounced and left the analytic guild, or to exponents of Eastern myth and mimesis who appear to have departed from the central concerns of the current analytic discussion. Rather, gender *is,* already, at the heart of this discussion. If it be objected that this strategy is objectionably taking up the master's tools, I can only reply that these tools are so powerful and significant already that the demands of Realpolitik drive me to handle, redirect, and imaginatively renegotiate their usage. This indeed is a vital first part of the task of developing a *transformed* rationality. As I suggested at the start of this chapter, clarity, incisiveness, coherence, and philosophical persuasiveness are not in themselves the feminist problem: their valorization should not be the central cause of feminist anguish;[23] rather, it is precisely the attempt to clarify and convict that fuels the feminist attempt to identify the sexisms that lurk in the regnant philosophical discourse in the first place.

Let me then highlight programmatically in closing just three related areas in which a feminist perspective nuanced rather differently from that of Jantzen's and Anderson's might suggest a fruitful future interchange between analytic philosophy of religion and feminist theory.

The first area concerns the notable and sophisticated developments in recent analytic philosophy of religion in the epistemology of "religious experience," developments that, one might argue, already herald a disturbance or destabilization of masculinist thought patterns. One thinks here of such diverse, but influential, approaches as (1) the appeal to the evidence of religious experience as both the most subjective and yet also the most definitively significant component in a "cumulative case" approach to the existence of God (Swinburne 1979); (2) the development of nonfoundationalist appeals to "proper basicality" in so-called Reformed epistemology, and of the significance granted there to direct intimacy with the Holy Spirit (Plantinga and Wolterstorff 1983; Plantinga 2000); (3) the rehabiliation of the Reidian notion of "credulity" or "trust" (in contradistinction to a fundamental Humean skepticism) as a starting point in reflection on the cultivation of religious affections, and the implicit acknowledgment of the importance of child development in this epistemological move (Wolterstorff 2001); (4) the assessment of "affectivity" as a vital factor in religious epistemology and cognitive regulation (Wainwright 1995); and (5) the attempt to show that *direct* intimacy with, or "perception" of, the divine is a defensible epistemological possibility (contra Kant), and that appeals to the narratives of female mystics (especially Teresa of Avila) can provide significant support for such a position (Alston 1991).

We have already seen how Anderson attacks such epistemological developments as these as signs of a fatal circularity in the guild's thinking, and of its unhealthy obsession with evidences; and how Jantzen is even more dismissive of naïve *feminist* appeals to experience. But my own reading of these highly sophisticated developments in analytic philosophy of religion is a different one. I want to argue, contrariwise, that once some gender sensibility is developed theoretically, this explosion of interest and creativity in recent analytic philosophy of religion in religious epistemology is actually already a sign of the discourse covertly "feminizing" itself.[24] By this I mean that we see philosophers of religion already turning away here, in their different ways, from classic Enlightenment epistemological concerns with foundationalism, public evidentialism, and universalizability, and making appeals instead to the more subtle and contestable categories of experience, trust, affectivity, subjectivity, interiority, and mystical theology. Such categories are often, either implicitly or explicitly, founded in *women's* narratives of transformation; but even if they are not, they bear much of the freight of stereotypical femininity. Put thus, we may suggest that these developments constitute not only a "postmodern" disposition, but more pointedly, a sign of the male philosopher of religion now attempting to "tak[e] *her* light to illuminate his path," as Irigaray has charged.

But are these developments then necessarily negative? Must we dismiss them as another suspicious assimilation by the male philosopher of the occluded power of the feminine?[25] Is this just one more way in which male philosophy obliterates the feminist voice by stealing and controlling the insights of women? Much will depend here on our fundamental gender-theoretical perspective; if we presume a fixed, Lacanian binary (which I have progressively critiqued in this chapter), we may remain deeply pessimistic about the sublation of it. But if we have a more fluid and negotiable view of gender, then the way the argument proceeds in each philosophical case, and how much consciousness is evidenced of an implicit gender subtext in the discussion, will become crucial. Even then, there is a great difference between welcoming, and even pedestalizing, the power of femininity to transform the male psyche or religious dilemma (a recurrent theme in Romanticism), and allowing the *woman* to speak for herself and enunciate her particular concerns and interests. As we have demonstrated above, the subtext of gender often laps at the edges of the philosophical argument in the form of tellingly sexist examples that include women in subordinate or stereotypical roles. But once this is demonstrated, it is at least *possible*, I submit, to imagine a transformed discourse in which these dangers could be consciously named and averted. The problem of gender denial remains a deep one, but the strategy of demonstrating lively current philosophical debates precisely *as* gender-laden holds better prospects of success, I believe, than that of diverting the discourse to completely other fields (as in Anderson).

The second area for possible future rapprochement between analytic philosophy of religion and feminist theory seems to me to reside precisely where Jantzen, for one, finds least hope. This is in the area of apophatic discourse, on which analytic philosophy of religion has made notably little contribution to date, for reasons that might also have connection to its purported masculinism and literalism. It might seem odd that a topic that Jantzen derides as supremely masculinist and elitist (negative theology in the Dionysian tradition) could become a fruitful source of feminist critique of the discourse of analytic philosophy of religion, which, until recently, has been so notably resistant to feminist concerns. But Jantzen's over-hasty dismissal of the negative theology tradition fails to acknowledge the purgative potential of this tradition in confronting sexist idolatry in the naming and desciding of God. It is unfortunate in this regard that a whole generation of "liberal" feminist *theologians* have adopted what William Alston (1989) has called the "pan-metaphorist" strategy where God-talk is concerned; that is, they have declared in a neo-Kantian vein that *all* talk of God is "metaphorical" and (necessarily, for them) "nonliteral," and so subject to revision simply according to the imaginative "construction" of the feminist theologian. Deep issues are of course at stake here concerning the apparent rejection of dominical and biblical authority, the skepticism about the possibility of divine revelation, and a certain cavalier attitude toward the complex nature of religious language. But it should simply be noted that the more it is declared that the Kantian heritage demands an epistemological *distancing* from reality (especially from divine reality)—a trait we have repeatedly commented on in Anderson's work—the more an anthropomorphic or explicitly Feuerbachian projectionism becomes the norm for religious utterance, whether in masculinist or feminist forms. What the Dionysian tradition of apophaticism holds out as an *alternative*, then, is a form of religious speech that rigorously denies not only its positive but its negative statements about God, and simultaneously points to a transformative contemplative *encounter* with God that transcends even this playful language-game of negations. As such, it claims to participate in a consistent exposure of human projectionism and submits itself to an ongoing purgation of human idolatry (whether in masculinist or feminist form). The Thomistic variant of negative theology in contrast, makes an adjustment to Dionysius's own position by allowing, on the basis of revelatory authority, an important distinction between analogical and metaphorical speech for God, the former being "literal" but, at the Godward end, humanly unknowable in its full semantic *richesse*, the latter being "creaturely," and thus technically inappropriate to God. The parody of Thomas's theory of analogy presented by Jantzen (and briefly discussed above) thus fails altogether to consider the feminist *potential* that this theory, too, holds, especially in its apophatic dimensions. That analytic philosophy of religion has attended rather sparingly to the Dionysian tradition of negative theology—whether directly, or as mediated through Thomas's work—seems, among other things, to be an indication of its lack of appreciation of the pervasive problem of idolatry, and hence a sign of its concomitant lack of concern about sexism. That feminist critiques of such a resistance could develop a rigorous and nuanced account of the potential of a Dionysian perspective seems an urgent priority.[26]

The third arena for possible mediation between feminist concerns and analytic philosophy of religion lies in the related area of claims to an immediate contact with the divine. It is here that Jantzen's and Anderson's rightful interests in the category of desire seem to me to come into relation with an important existing epistemological discussion in analytic philosophy of religion about the possibility of direct "perception" of God. If God is to be "perceivable" in some sense analogous to (but not identical with) the direct perception of objects (so Alston, seeking to evade Kant's objections), then certain "doxastic practices" may, according to Alston (1991), be the crucial means and mediation of such perception. Desire, as a core factor in the quest for God, *cannot* be ignored—indeed, is projected into center-stage—if women mystical theologians such as Teresa of Avila are utilized as key examples of epistemic intimacy with God, as in Alston's work; but nor can the transforming practices of "contemplation" (that are the *means* of that erotic desire being propelled toward God) be pushed to one side epistemically. Here we have a nexus of entangled themes—desire, intimacy, relationship, transformative practice, knowledge of God, and *gender*—which urgently require further analytic explication. Why is it that the woman stars so often as the site of highest intimacy with the divine in the discourses of analytic philosophy of religion? And what can we conclude from this about the necessary *transformation* of existing epistemic categories in the light of gender analysis, reflection on "practice," and an acknowledgment of the centrality of desire for an adequate account of the perception of God?[27] My approach here, unlike Anderson's, again suggests that analytic philosophy of religion is already signaling its *need* of gender analysis if it is even to further its own current projects and disputed issues. But that is a continuing task, and challenge, for the future.

I have attempted in this chapter to give a detailed account of the two most developed feminist critiques of analytic philosophy of religion (to date), and to show how their *particular* understandings of gender theory and of feminist epistemology fuel the accounts they give. As we have seen, both their philosophical presumptions and their pragmatic conclusions are very different from one another, even though they share a number of central themes and influences, and both *claim* to be seeking some sort of bridge between the disciplines of feminism and analytic philosophy. After providing an appreciative, but critical, account of these first two options, I have suggested a third alternative set of ploys to effect a transformation of gender consciousness in the discourses of analytic philosophy of religion. In so doing, I have urged—on rather different gender-theoretical and epistemological grounds—that analytic philosophy of religion may already be well on the way to undoing its own, and deeply rooted, masculinism. And it is notable that this undoing is closely related to a critique of foundationalism (in all its forms), and also, perhaps more surprising, of the neo-Kantian "recession from reality" stance. As the discipline continues to engage the insights of contemporary continental philosophy and social theory, and to begin to interact more deeply with current feminist theory, we may indeed hope for some significant signs of rapprochement and mutual learning. Perhaps only humility is needed.

NOTES

1. Jantzen (1998) uses the term "masculinist" to denote that which covertly privileges men's position of privilege; I follow her in this usage throughout this chapter. Other cognate terms used by both Jantzen and Anderson (1998) are "sexist," "patriarchal," "phallocentric" (with specifically Lacanian psychoanalytic overtones, discussed intra), and (in Anderson) "male-neutral": a view or philosophical position posing as universal in its validity, but actually assuming male privilege. My own term for the latter is "the generic male."

2. Here one might cite, to indicate the variety of current approaches, the special issue of *Hypatia: A Journal of Feminist Philosophy* 9: 4 (1994), devoted to feminist philosophy of religion in all its guises, and writers such as Frankenberry (1987), Armour (1999), or Hollywood (2002), who have no connections with analytic philosophy of religion.

3. See Jantzen (1998, 23–24; compare 32–40); and compare my brief discussion of this theme in relation to analytic philosophy of religion's treatment of "two-nature" christology, in Coakley (1997, 604–5).

4. This oft-cited view of Nagel is frequently misunderstood, as I suspect it is also by Jantzen. Nagel's point (as I read him: see Nagel 1986, 27, 84–85) is *not* that there cannot be a "God's-eye view" for *God* (a matter with which Nagel scarcely concerns himself), but rather that Descartes used a sleight of hand to posit "God" as "the personification of the fit between ourselves and the world for which there is no explanation but which is necessary for thought to yield knowledge" (85). What readers often forget to mention is that Nagel then goes on precisely to insist that we give some *other* account of the possibility of "objective" knowledge.

5. One odd feature of Jantzen's argument against the appeal to "experience" is, in effect, to read Schleiermacher through the lens of William James, and then to blame this "Schleiermacherian" tradition for a philosophically naïve, but also "imperialist," use of "religious experience" as an epistemic category (Jantzen 1998, 116–19).

6. The usual butt is Swinburne's definition of God at the beginning of his first edition of *The Coherence of Theism* (1977, 2); see also the discussion in Anderson (1998, 15).

7. Jantzen's reading of Denys as supremely "masculinist" fails to account *either* for

the Dionysian insistence on the negation even of *negations* in proper speech about God, *or* for his theory of "contemplation" as taking one "beyond the mind." For a brilliant recent discussion of the important difference between Denys's thought and postmodern "deferral," see Rubenstein (2003).

8. Here, in her discussion of Kristeva's essay "Stabat Mater," Jantzen comes closest to seeing a point of rapprochement between "reason" and the "semiotic" (Jantzen 1998, 200–203).

9. On this point (of the inextricability of "truth" claims and appeals to "justice"), see Fricker (1994).

10. See, e.g., Phillips (1970, 1993); Hick (1973, 1976); Wainwright (1995).

11. See Anderson (1998, 61, n. 12), who is aware that "It is worth considering whether Nagel's original account has been misconstrued by both value theorists and feminists." Compare n. 5, above.

12. Anderson briefly discusses the work of Marilyn McCord Adams (1986) and Eleonore Stump (1993) in this regard (see Anderson 1998, 41–42).

13. It should be mentioned here that, since the appearance of their 1998 books, Jantzen and Anderson have engaged in a number of published critical interactions on each other's work: see, e.g., Anderson (2000) and Jantzen (2001).

14. Here she seemingly follows Lorraine Code's (1992) analysis; also see Coakley (1997, 605–6).

15. The adjustment of Quine's ship image (see Anderson 1998, x–xii, 12–13) actually makes for some metaphorical strain when it is brought into relation with Kant's idea of "the territory of pure understanding" as an island surrounded by a "wide and stormy ocean" (11). Anderson reads the sea in Kant as stereotypically feminine, containing fluid and tempestuous elements that cannot be constrained into masculinist reason. But she also wants there to be *feminist* mariners on the new Neurathian epistemological ship.

16. Anderson's citations from Swinburne here are deeply telling: see Anderson (1998, 43–44). Also, compare my similar points of criticism in Coakley (1997, 602). In Swinburne's most recent work he has finally acceded to an inclusive use of pronouns; it is not clear to what extent this indicates any substantial responsiveness to feminist critique.

17. On this point, see especially McDowell (1994) and Plantinga (2000, ch. 1).

18. See Anderson (1998, 81): "Ultimately objectivity is to be made strong by weighing all evidence for or against a hypothesis including the systematic examination of background beliefs."

19. I develop this argument about gender "fluidity" (a view that owes much to the patristic author Gregory of Nyssa) in Coakley (2002, ch. 9), and more fully in a forthcoming first volume of "systematics": *God, Sexuality and the Self: An Essay "On the Trinity."*

20. The feminist epistemological essays in Alcoff and Potter (1993) note, among other matters, the significance for initial cognitive competence of a child's intimate *relationship* with a primary caregiver (32–39) and the importance of relational *communities* for epistemic negotiations (121–29).

21. See Coakley (1997, 601–3).

22. See ibid., 603–5.

23. Harriet Harris (2001) has recently argued this broad point in more detail.

24. This point is argued in more detail in my 1999 Riddell Lectures, in preparation

as *Diotima and the Dispossessed: An Essay "On the Contemplative Life."* Anderson gives a critical account of this aspect of my manuscript in her recent article, "Feminist Theology as Philosophy of Religion" (2002, esp. 43–50).

25. See Coakley (1997, 606), where I suggest that "Bringing 'religious experience' to the bar of rational 'justification' may . . . appear as the modern counterpart of the male confessor's hold over the medieval female saint's theological status and credibility."

26. This issue is discussed at some length in my forthcoming *God, Sexuality and the Self: An Essay "On the Trinity."*

27. These themes are given a preliminary treatment in Coakley (2002, ch. 8), but are more thoroughly treated in *Diotima and the Dispossessed* (see n. 24).

WORKS CITED

Adams, Marilyn McCord. 1986. "Redemptive Suffering: A Christian Solution to the Problem of Evil." In *Rationality, Religious Belief and Moral Commitment,* ed. Robert Audi and William J. Wainwright, 248–67. Ithaca, N.Y.: Cornell University Press.

Alcoff, Linda, and Elizabeth Potter, eds. 1993. *Feminist Epistemologies.* New York: Routledge.

Alston, William P. 1989. *Divine Nature and Human Language: Essays in Philosophical Theology.* Ithaca, NY: Cornell University Press.

———. 1991. *Perceiving God: The Epistemology of Religious Experience.* Ithaca, N.Y.: Cornell University Press.

Anderson, Pamela Sue. 1993. *Ricoeur and Kant: Philosophy of the Will.* Atlanta: Scholars Press.

———. 1998. *A Feminist Philosophy of Religion.* Oxford: Blackwell.

———. 2000. "Correspondence with Grace Jantzen." *Feminist Theology* 25 (Sept.): 112–19.

———. 2001. " 'Standpoint': Its Rightful Place in a Realist Epistemology." *Journal of Philosophical Research* 26: 131–53.

———. 2002. "Feminist Theology as Philosophy of Religion." In *The Cambridge Companion to Feminist Theology,* ed. Susan Frank Parsons, 40–59. Cambridge, England: Cambridge University Press.

Armour, Ellen T. 1999. *Deconstruction, Feminist Theology, and the Problem of Difference: Subverting the Race/Gender Divide.* Chicago: University of Chicago Press.

Coakley, Sarah. 1997. "Feminism." In *A Companion to Philosophy of Religion,* ed. Charles Taliaferro and Philip Quinn, 601–6. Oxford: Blackwell.

———. 2002. *Powers and Submissions: Spirituality, Philosophy and Gender.* Oxford: Blackwell.

Code, Lorraine. 1992. "Feminist Epistemology." In *A Companion to Epistemology,* ed. Jonathan Dancy and E. Sosa, 138–42. Oxford: Blackwell.

Davidson, Donald. 1984. "On the Very Idea of a 'Conceptual Scheme.' " In *Inquiries into Truth and Interpretation,* 183–98. Oxford: Clarendon Press.

Frankenberry, Nancy. 1987. *Religion and Radical Empiricism.* Albany: State University of New York Press.

Fricker, Miranda. 1994. "Knowledge as Construct: Theorizing the Role of Gender in Knowledge." In *Knowing the Difference: Feminist Perspectives in Epistemology,* ed. Kathleen Lennon and Margaret Whitford, 95–109. London: Routledge.

Harding, Sandra. 1993. "Rethinking Standpoint Epistemology: What Is 'Strong Objectivity'?" In *Feminist Epistemologies,* ed. Linda Alcoff and Elizabeth Potter, 49–82. London: Routledge.

Harris, Harriet A. 2001. "Struggling for Truth." *Feminist Theology* 28 (Sept.): 40–56.

Hartsock, Nancy. 1983. "The Feminist Standpoint: Developing the Ground for Specifically Feminist Historical Materialism." In *Discovering Reality: Feminist Perspectives on Epistemology, Metaphysics, Methodology and Philosophy of Science,* ed. Sandra Harding and Merrill Hintikka, 283–310. Dordrecht: Reidel.

Helm, Paul. 1994. *Belief Policies.* Cambridge, England: Cambridge University Press.

Hick, John. 1973. *God and the Universe of Faiths.* Basingstoke, England: Macmillan.

———. 1976. *Death and Eternal Life.* Basingstoke, England: Macmillan.

Hollywood, Amy. 2002. *Sensible Ecstasy.* Chicago: University of Chicago Press.

hooks, bell. 1990. *Yearning: Race, Gender, Cultural Politics.* Boston: South End Press.

Irigaray, Luce. 1985a. *Speculum of the Other Woman.* Trans. Gillian C. Gill. Ithaca, N.Y.: Cornell University Press.

———. 1985b. *This Sex Which Is Not One.* Trans. Catherine Porter. Ithaca, N.Y.: Cornell University Press.

———. 1993. *An Ethics of Sexual Difference.* Trans. Carolyn Burke and Gillian C. Gill. Ithaca, N.Y.: Cornell University Press.

Jantzen, Grace. 1984. *God's World, God's Body.* London: Darton, Longman and Todd.

———. 1995. *Power, Gender and Christian Mysticism.* Cambridge, England: Cambridge University Press.

———. 1998. *Becoming Divine: Towards a Feminist Philosophy of Religion.* Manchester, England: Manchester University Press.

———. 2001. "Feminist Philosopher of Religion: Open Discussion with Pamela Anderson." *Feminist Theology* 26 (Jan.): 102–9.

Kristeva, Julia. 1986. *The Kristeva Reader.* Ed. Toril Moi. Oxford: Blackwell.

Le Doeuff, Michèle. 1989. *The Philosophical Imaginary.* Trans. Colin Gordon. London: Athlone Press.

———. 1990. "Women, Reason, Etc." *Differences* 2: 3, 1–13.

———. 1991. *Hipparchia's Choice: An Essay Concerning Women, Philosophy, Etc.* Trans. Trista Selous. Oxford: Blackwell.

McDowell, John. 1994. *Mind and World.* Cambridge, Mass.: Harvard University Press.

Nagel, Thomas. 1986. *The View from Nowhere.* New York: Oxford University Press.

Phillips, D. Z. 1970. *Death and Immortality.* Basingstoke, England: Macmillan.

———. 1993. *Wittgenstein and Religion.* Swansea Studies in Philosophy. London: Macmillan.

Plantinga, Alvin. 2000. *Warranted Christian Belief.* New York: Oxford University Press.

Plantinga, Alvin, and Nicholas Wolterstorff, eds. 1983. *Faith and Rationality: Reason and Belief in God.* Notre Dame, Ind.: University of Notre Dame Press.

Quine, W. V. 1953. *From a Logical Point of View: Logico-Philosophical Essays.* New York: Harper and Row.

Rubenstein, Mary-Jane. 2003. "Unknow Thyself: Apophaticism, Deconstruction, and Theology after Ontotheology." *Modern Theology* 19: 387–417.

Stump, Eleonore. 1993. "Aquinas on the Sufferings of Job." In *Reasoned Faith: Essays in Philosophical Theology in Honor of Norman Kretzmann,* ed. Eleanore Stump, 328–57. Ithaca, N.Y.: Cornell University Press.

Swinburne, Richard. 1977. *The Coherence of Theism.* Oxford: Clarendon Press.

———. 1979. *The Existence of God.* Oxford: Clarendon Press.

Wainwright, William J. 1995. *Reason and the Heart: A Prolegomenon to a Critique of Passional Reason.* Ithaca, N.Y.: Cornell University Press.

Wolterstorff, Nicholas. 2001. *Thomas Reid and the Story of Epistemology.* Cambridge, England: Cambridge University Press.

INDEX

....

epistemology of religious experience, 517–19

Jantzen, 496, 499, 504–5

realism

Anderson, 506, 508, 512, 513, 514

Jantzen, 499, 504

reason and rationality, 339, 500, 505, 508–12

salvation, 501–2

semiotic/symbolic binary split, rejection of, 496–97, 498, 503, 508, 516

standpoint epistemology, 499–500, 504, 507–8, 514–15

truth, analytic obsession with, 496–97, 499–500, 504

women philosophers' subjection to male mentors, 509, 513, 518

Fenwick, P., 160

Feuerbach, Ludwig

continental philosophy, 473

feminist critiques of analytic philosophy, 496, 500, 502, 504, 519

Wittgensteinianism, 462

fideism, 332–33, 335, 338–41, 466

Findlay, J. N., 82

Fiorenza, Elisabeth Schüssler, 498

Fischer, John Martin, 437

Flew, Antony G. N., 157, 306–7, 422–25, 448

Flint, Thomas P., 20, 437

Fodor, Jerry A., 49

Forgie, William, 152

Forman, Robert K. C., 145, 147, 149

Forms, Platonic concept of, 45, 46–47, 454

Foucault, Michel, 498, 500, 506

foundationalism, 264, 521

Frazer, James (The Golden Bough), 259

Freddoso, A., 20

free will, human

Augustine and Mencius compared, 412–13

contingent propositions, 43

evil, free-will response to, see evil, problem of

knowledge of God (omniscience) and, 29–32

power of God (omnipotence) and, 19

providence, divine, 436, 437–38

sovereignty of God and, 36

free will theism, 437–38

freedom, divine, 36–37, 54–56

Frege, Friedrich Ludwig Gottlob, 454

Freud, Sigmund, 8, 9, 478–79, 497

Friedländer, Saul, 407

Fulmer, Gilbert, 131

fundamentalism, Protestant, 328

Gale, Richard M.

biographical information, ix

cosmological and design arguments, 116–37

James, William, and "The Will to Believe," 183

mystical and religious experience, 143, 155, 156

Galileo, 274

Game Theory, 168, 409

Gassendi, Pierre, 102–3, 106

Gaunilo of Marmoutiers and ontological argument

Anselm, Reply to Gaunilo, 89–91

parody of Proslogion 2, 92–96

Gautama Sakyamuni, see also Buddhism

body of, 74

life of, 72–73

Geach, Peter, 20

Geertz, Clifford, 407–9

Gellman, Jerome I., ix, 138–67

gender issues, see feminist critiques of analytic philosophy

Gesteland, R. F., 130

al-Ghazali, 3, 15

Gilson, Etienne, 5

Glasenapp, Helmuth von, 73

Gödel, Kurt, 108–11

"God's-eye view," 499–500

Goldenberg, Naomi, 163

good and evil, human, see evil, problem of; morality and religion

goodness of God, 21–27

acquisition of perfect goodness by nature vs. by free will, 23

actions of divine in world, 286–88

analytic philosophy of religion, 428

best of all possible worlds conundrum, 24–27

deviations from perfect goodness in concept of God, 15–16

evil as problem for, 191–92, see also evil, problem of

existence of morality and goodness apart from God, 22–23

grace, Judeo-Christian concept of, 25–27

metaphysical goodness, 23, 32–33

moral vs. nonmoral goodness, 21–23, 32–33

power of God restricted by, 19–20, 21, 24–25

praising and thanking God for good acts, consistency with, 23–27

providence, divine, 436